DA   Lockyer, Roger.
390.1
.B82   Buckingham, the life
L6   and political
1981   career of George
              Villiers, first
              Duke of Buckingham,
              1592-1628

DATE			

BUCKINGHAM

A chalk drawing of Buckingham by Rubens, *c.* 1625

Buckingham

The Life and Political Career
of George Villiers,
First Duke of Buckingham
1592–1628

ROGER LOCKYER

LONGMAN
London and New York

Longman Group Limited

Longman House
Burnt Mill, Harlow, Essex, UK
Published in the United States of America
by Longman Inc., New York

First published 1981

British Library Cataloguing in Publication Data

Lockyer, Roger
  Buckingham.
  1. Buckingham, George Villiers, *1st Duke of*
  2. Statesmen – England – Biography
  3. Great Britain – History – James I, 1603–1625
  4. Great Britain – History – Charles I, 1625–1649
  942.06'1'0924   DA391.1.B9   80-40578

ISBN 0-582-50296-9

Set in 11/12pt Linotron 202 Garamond No. 3.
Printed in Singapore by
Kyodo Shing Loong Printing Industries Pte. Ltd.

For Percy

Contents

PART TWO
Buckingham in Power

CONTENTS

List of illustrations

Between pages 364 and 365

The Constant Reformation. (*National Maritime Museum, London*)

Gateway to the Citadel of St Martin, which Buckingham besieged but was unable to capture during his expedition to the Ile de Ré in 1627. (*Roger Viollet*)

The English fleet and army besieging the Citadel of St Martin in the Ile de Ré, 1627. (*Roger Viollet*)

The Villiers family, artist unknown, 1628. (*British Royal Collection, Copyright reserved*)

'Ecce Homo', Titian, formerly in Buckingham's collection. (*Mansell Collection*)

Felton's declaration. (*British Library*)

The house in Portsmouth High Street, formerly called the Greyhound Inn, in which Buckingham was assassinated. (*Photograph in the author's possession*)

The memorial to Buckingham in Portsmouth Cathedral, put up by his sister, Susan Feilding, Countess of Denbigh. (*Portsmouth City Records Office*)

Buckingham on his deathbed, Van Dyck. (*National Portrait Gallery*)

Buckingham's tomb in Westminster Abbey. (*National Monuments Record, London*)

MAPS

GENEALOGICAL TABLES

Preface

Anyone foolhardy enough to embark on a historical biography is confronted with the problem of striking a balance between exposition and analysis. I originally thought in terms of a number of narrative chapters alongside a number of thematic ones, but it rapidly became apparent that such a treatment would necessitate an intolerable degree of cross-referencing and would also result in a very odd distribution of the space available: Buckingham as patron of the arts, for instance, would take up a mere twenty or so pages; Buckingham as Lord Admiral would require a quarter of the entire book; while Buckingham as the formulator of foreign policy would need virtually a book to itself. Rather than produce a number of overlapping and ill-fitting chapters, I therefore decided to adopt a basically narrative approach, but to concentrate on certain themes at those places where they seemed to be most relevant. I apologise to readers whose concern is with specific aspects of Buckingham's career rather than his life as a whole, but would refer them to the index, which, under the general heading of Villiers, George, 1st Duke of Buckingham, includes a number of sub-headings designed to facilitate their quest.

A biography is, of course, chronological by its very nature, since it begins with birth and ends with death. And in the case of Buckingham, who was often described by his contemporaries as a comet or shooting star, there is considerable fascination in tracing his speedy transit across the heavens. Such an approach also has the merit of demonstrating how, at any given moment, Buckingham was subject to a wide variety of pressures. In 1626, for instance, at the crisis of his career, when he was facing a Parliamentary impeachment, he was also deeply involved in trying to maintain an adequate defence of the coasts despite a crippling shortage of money; in making preparations for long-range offensive operations; and in conducting a sophisticated and complex foreign policy. The rush of events in which he was caught up did not distinguish between separate themes because in practice they were not separate: problems overlapped and interacted to such an extent that none was capable of solution by itself, and to treat them in isolation is to make Buckingham's task seem much simpler than it really was.

However, I have not been content merely to establish what Buckingham did. I have also tried, within the limits of the evidence, to suggest why he did it. Inevitably I have found myself on occasion at variance with both traditional and more recent interpretations of Buckingham's motives. In the bibliographical note at the end of this book I have listed those publications which give a somewhat different picture of Buckingham as a politician, but I would like to call particular attention to Conrad Russell's work on early Stuart Parliaments which has done so much to change the accepted view of the period. In many instances I have modified my original interpretation in order to bring it into line with his. In others – such as the reasons for the dissolution of the 1621 Parliament and the possibility of divergence between the political aims of Buckingham and Charles I – I have preferred my own version. There are a number of issues on which the evidence is so fragmentary and elusive that it can legitimately be interpreted in markedly different ways, and rather than footnote every divergence between my own views and those of other writers, I would refer the interested reader to the books mentioned in the bibliographical note. But I should like to emphasise that where I have put forward interpretations of Buckingham's policies that differ from those of other scholars working in this field, I have done so only after careful consideration. In other words, I should not like it to be assumed that where I have strayed, historically speaking, into the paths of heresy, I have done so either out of arrogance or ignorance. Indeed, one of my aims in looking at the early Stuart political scene from the point of view of the Court and through the eyes of Buckingham, was to indicate a different, and in some respects a novel, perspective, and thereby contribute to the reinterpretation of this most exciting of periods which is now taking place.

Throughout this book I have modernised quotations, both in spelling and punctuation, and have extended abbreviations. For dates I have used the Old Style, current in England in the early seventeenth century, but have taken the year as beginning on 1 January and not 25 March.

Acknowledgements

In the many years spent in working on this biography I have received a great deal of help from the staffs of libraries and record offiices both here and abroad, and should like to express my thanks to them. As far as England and Scotland are concerned, this applies to the Berkshire County Record Office, Reading; the Bodleian Library, Oxford; the British Library, London; Cambridge University Library; the Codrington Library of All Souls College, Oxford; the Kent County Archive Office, Maidstone; the London Library; the National Library of Scotland, Edinburgh; the Public Record Office, London; the library of Royal Holloway College, Egham; Sheffield Central Library; and the Warwickshire County Record Office, Warwick.

For French documents I was dependent upon the good services of Mlle Battez, the librarian of the city of Angers; and on the officials of the library of the Ministère des Affaires etrangères, Paris. For Spanish ones, my thanks are due to the staffs of the Archivo General, Simancas, and the library of the Palacio Real, Madrid.

I owe a particular debt of gratitude to Lady Fairfax of Cameron and Sir Richard Graham for permission to consult the documents in their possession. I also acknowledge with thanks the cooperation of the Earl of Jersey. The references to the Trumbull manuscripts are from the papers of the Marquess of Downshire in the custody of the Berkshire Record Office, by permission of the County Archivist; while those to the Wentworth manuscripts are from the Wentworth Woodhouse Muniments in the Sheffield City Libraries, by permission of Earl Fitzwilliam and Earl Fitzwilliam's Wentworth Estates Company, and the City Librarian.

I am most grateful to the principal and governors of Royal Holloway College for the grant of a sabbatical year, which made it possible for me to consult documents in foreign archives.

If I were to record the names of all those friends and colleagues who have helped me in one way or another, I should have to add yet more pages to what is already a long book, so I hope they will accept this general but most sincere expression of my thanks. However, there are three friends whose assistance has been of such major importance that I should be doing an injustice if I did not thank them by name. The first is the Reverend Henry Thorold, whose knowledge of English country houses is only equalled by his capacity for gaining entry to them. I have spent many hours in his company, pursuing Buckingham through the Midland counties of England, and recall them with the greatest pleasure. The second is Didier Coupaye, whose aid was invaluable when it came to dealing with French archives, who answered innumerable difficult questions with uncomplaining accuracy, and who made it possible for me to retrace Buckingham's steps in the Ile de Ré. The third is Percy Steven, whose unfailing encouragement over many years and readiness to shoulder additional burdens at moments of great stress contributed more to the writing of this book than perhaps he realises. The dedication is intended as an acknowledgment, however inadequate, of my gratitude for all that he has done.

London, February 1980

Table 1. The House of Stuart

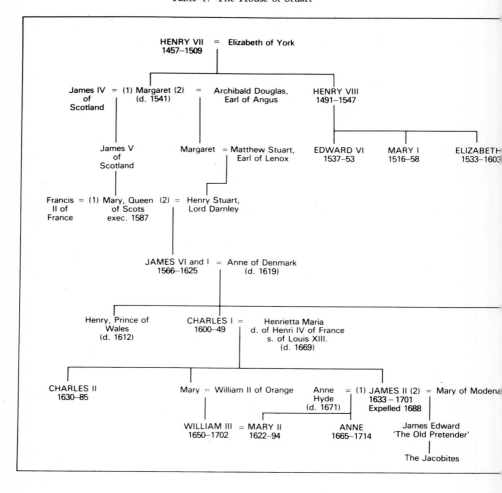

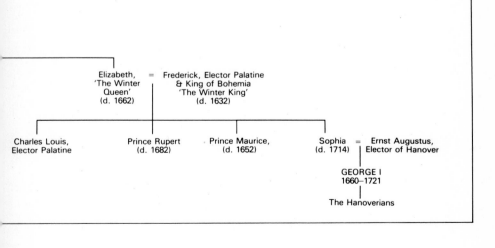

Elizabeth, = Frederick, Elector Palatine
'The Winter & King of Bohemia
Queen' 'The Winter King'
(d. 1662) (d. 1632)

Charles Louis,   Prince Rupert   Prince Maurice,   Sophia   =   Ernst Augustus,
Elector Palatine   (d. 1682)   (d. 1652)   (d. 1714) | Elector of Hanover

                                                                            GEORGE I
                                                                            1660–1721

                                                                            The Hanoverians

PART ONE

The Apprentice Years

MENDOZA: Now good Elizium, what a delicious heaven is it for a man to be in a Prince's favour. O sweet God! O pleasure! O fortune! O thou best of life! What should I think? What say? What do? To be a favourite! A minion! To have a general timorous respect observe a man; a stateful silence in his presence; solitariness in his absence; a confused hum and busy murmur of obsequious suitors training [conducting] him; the cloth held up and way proclaimed before him; petitionary vassals licking the pavement with their slavish knees; whilst some odd palace lampreels [lampreys] that ingender with snakes and are full of eyes on both sides, with a kind of insinuated humbleness fix all their delights upon his brow. O blessed state! What a ravishing prospect doth the Olympus of favour yield.

John Marston, The Favourite, Act I, Scene v

CHAPTER ONE

1592–1616:
'The Gracing of young Villiers'

I

George Villiers, future Duke of Buckingham, was born at Brooksby Hall in Leicestershire on 28 August, 1592. The house, though much altered and extended, still stands on rising ground in the Wreake valley, just off the main road that runs from Leicester to Melton Mowbray. The back of the house looks across gently rolling, open country, but from the front there is not much to catch the eye except the medieval church, with its fine tower and crenellated parapet. John Leland, the sixteenth-century antiquary, who visited Brooksby in the course of his peregrinations, would find that little has changed over the past four hundred years. 'There lie buried in the church', he recorded, 'divers of the Villars', and many of their monuments are still there.[1] On the northeast wall of the chancel, however, is a memorial that Leland could not have seen, for it is sacred to the memory of Sir William Villiers, who died in 1712. With him, as the inscription records, 'determined the male line of the eldest house of that honourable name', for he was the last representative of 'a race of worthy ancestors, upwards of five hundred years happily enjoying a great revenue in this county in a right noble and hospitable use thereof'.

The Villiers were indeed an ancient family, although Buckingham's enemies were only too eager to pour scorn upon his descent and to comment, sourly, that there was 'nothing more proud than basest blood when it doth rise aloft'. The name is, of course, French in origin, and it may be that the family was a branch of the Villiers who were Seigneurs de l'Isle Adam in Normandy. But whether or not they came over with the Conqueror they were certainly settled at Kinoulton, in Nottinghamshire, by the early thirteenth century. There they might have remained, but for the fact that Alexander de Villiers married the heiress to Brooksby, some nine miles due south, and is recorded in 1235 as holding land there – the first Villiers to be seated in Leicestershire.[2]

From then on Brooksby was handed down in the male line, and the Villiers lived – as Sir Henry Wotton, Buckingham's first biographer, delicately put it – 'rather without obscurity than with any great lustre', following the pattern

3

of life common to gentry families all over England. They entertained friends and neighbours and arranged marriages with them; they added to their estates; they hawked and hunted; and they carried out the unpaid public duties with which they were entrusted by the reigning monarch. John Villiers, for example, served as sheriff for Leicestershire under Henry VII and was knighted for his pains. His son, another John Villiers, also served as sheriff and received the honour of knighthood, this time from the hands of Henry VIII. The second Sir John had no male heirs, and was succeeded by his brothers, the third of whom, William Villiers, married Collett, the widow of another Leicestershire gentleman, Richard Beaumont of Cole Orton. Collett presented her husband with the longed-for male heir, who was christened George. In due course he succeeded to the lands and lordships of Brooksby and Hoby, served as sheriff of Leicestershire in 1591, and was knighted by Queen Elizabeth two years later.[3]

When Leland visited Brooksby in Henry VIII's reign he observed that 'this Villars at this time is a man but of a 200 marks [£133 6s. 8d.] of land by the year'. Yet by the time Sir George inherited the property it was worth a good deal more. This was because his immediate predecessors had improved their estates by enclosing the arable lands and turning them over to sheep. The well-watered, open countryside was ideally suited to pasture farming, and with the demand for English wool reviving in Elizabeth's reign there was a great deal of money to be made out of this. But the profits were confined to the owners of land. The poor tenants – apart from the handful who found

Table 2. The Villiers family

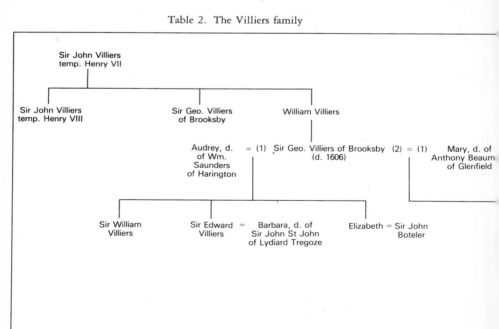

employment as shepherds – had no work and no way of keeping body and soul together now that the fields and commons which had previously afforded them a livelihood had been enclosed. Sheep, as Sir Thomas More observed, 'eat up and swallow down the very men themselves', and as the number of inhabitants decreased so their houses crumbled into dust. Brooksby was no exception. By 1584 the village had virtually disappeared; only the church and manor-house remained, as they do to this day, looking out over the peaceful pastures.[4]

Among Sir George's other properties in Leicestershire was Goadby Marwood. This had earlier belonged to the Beaumont family, but in 1575 the Beaumonts sold it to Sir George, and it remained in the possession of the Villiers for the next hundred years. The Beaumonts and the Villiers, being near neighbours, had long been connected by ties of friendship and marriage, and these were drawn even closer after the death of Sir George's first wife, Audrey Villiers, in 1587. He was still a relatively young man, not much above forty, and widowhood held out no obvious attractions to him. It was probably while he was visiting his Beaumont cousins at Cole Orton that he met Mary Beaumont, who came from a younger, and poorer, branch of that family and was serving as companion and waiting-woman to her richer relatives. Mary Beaumont had no fortune, but by all accounts she was a beautiful and attractive woman, and it was not long before she became Sir George's second wife. Many years later, when she was the mother of the most powerful man in England, and a wealthy, influential countess in her own right, the enemies of Buckingham took delight in exaggerating her lowly origins.

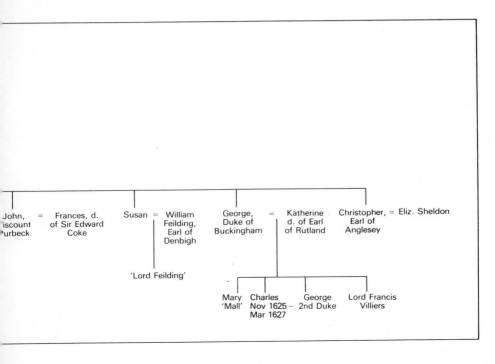

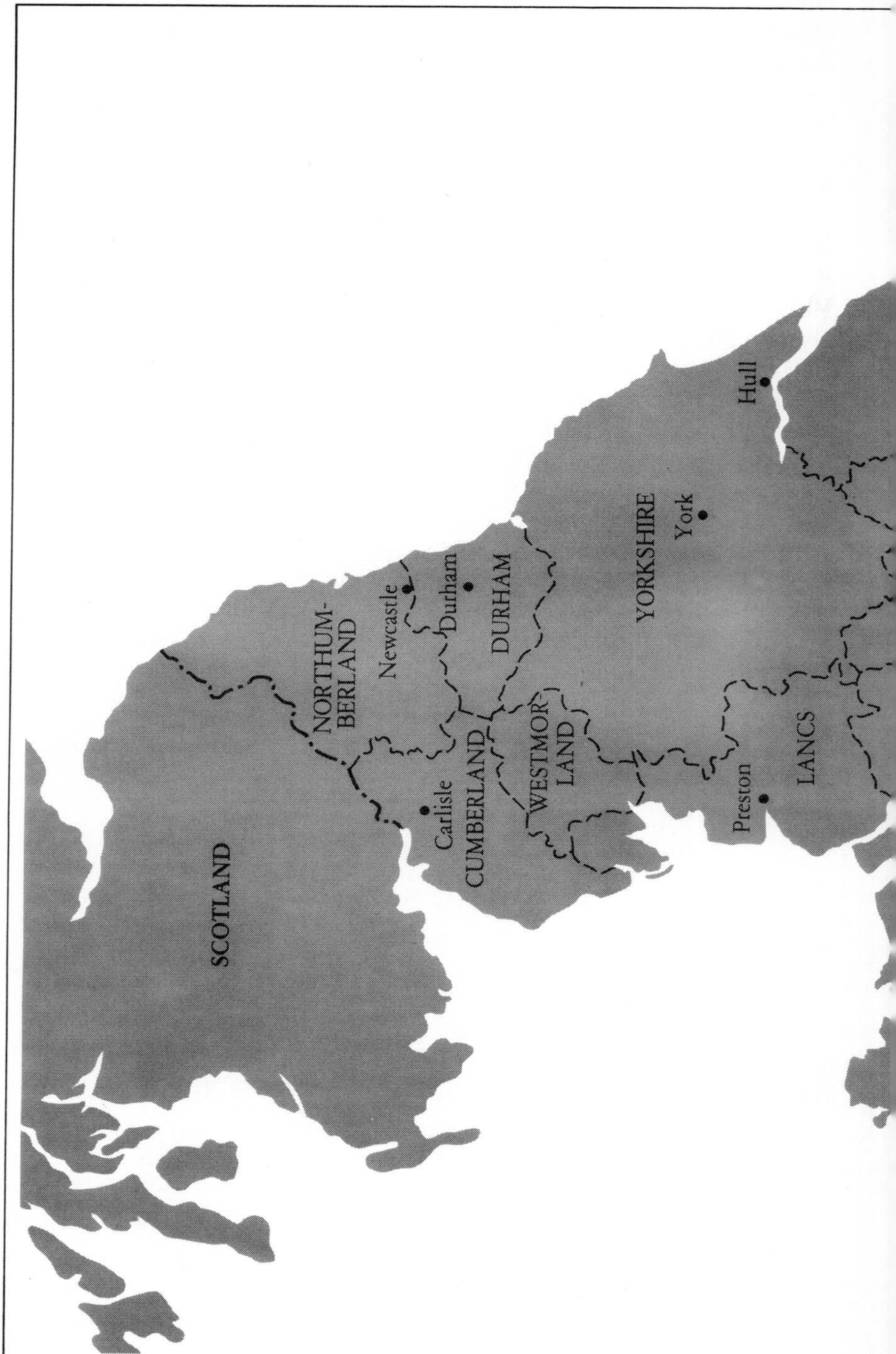

Map 1. England, showing places of significance in Buckingham's life

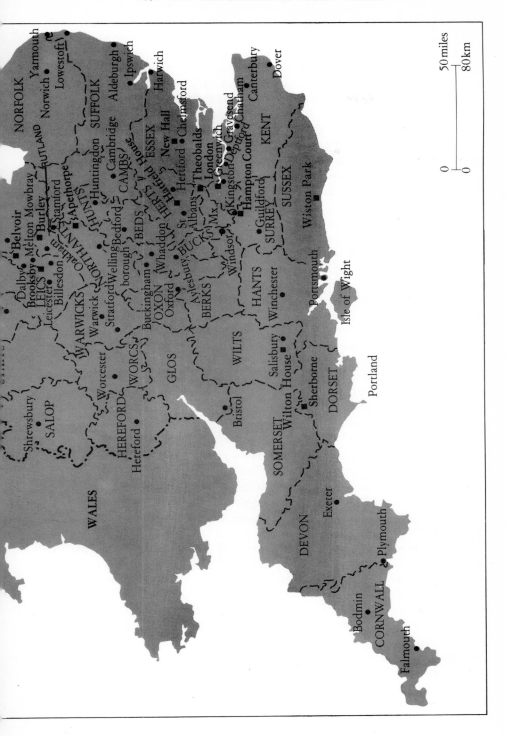

Anthony Weldon declared that she came from a mean family, while Roger
Coke (grandson of Sir Edward, the great lawyer) reported a rumour that she
had been 'entertained in Sir George Villiers's family in a mean office'. Coke
adds that 'her ragged habit could not shade the beautiful and excellent frame
of her person', and that Sir George was so struck by Mary's looks that he
persuaded his wife 'to remove her out of the kitchen into her chamber, which
with some importunity on Sir George's part, and unwillingness of my lady, at
last was done'. Soon after this, if Coke's account is to be believed, Audrey
Villiers died, and Sir George was now dependent upon Mary for solace and
companionship. Coke relates how he soon 'became very sweet upon' her, and
gave her £20 with which to buy a dress that would display her fine figure.
This she did, and the result obviously fulfilled all Sir George's expectations,
for his 'affections became so fired that to allay them he married her'.[5]

Coke's account of the development of the relationship between Sir George
Villiers and Mary Beaumont may be well founded, but there is no basis for
Weldon's slur about her lowly origins. As far as descent was concerned, she
could match, if not excel, Sir George's own, for although her father, Anthony
Beaumont of Glenfield, was simply a Leicestershire gentleman, he was a direct
descendant in the male line of the Barons Beaumont, and, in the female, of
Henry III, King of England. Sir George, of course, married Mary primarily
for her beauty and not her family connexions, but he must also have felt the
need of someone to look after his family of two sons and three daughters.
Whether the children welcomed Mary as a stepmother is not recorded, but the
fact that Buckingham maintained close and friendly relations with his half-
brothers and sisters suggests that Sir George's two families got on well
together, and this would hardly have been possible if Mary had been treated as
an interloper. She brought little with her apart from her beauty, but there was
one valuable addition to the household in the shape of Thomas Vautor, who
had been retained as a musician in her father's house, and now followed Mary
to Brooksby. When, many years later, Vautor published a collection of songs,
he dedicated it to Buckingham, since, as he recalled, 'some were composed in
your tender years and in your most worthy father's house (from whom, and
your most honourable mother, for many years I received part of my means and
livelihood)'.[6]

The date of Mary Beaumont's marriage to Sir George is unknown, but can
hardly have been later than 1590 (at which time, of course, he was still plain
Mr Villiers). Her first child by him was a boy, John Villiers; her second a
daughter, Susan. Buckingham, named after his father, was the third child,
and he was followed by another son, Christopher. Brooksby, which was not a
large house, must by now have been bulging at the seams. There was, however, a second house, at Goadby, and the fact that a number of Sir George's
children were baptised or buried there suggests that it was used as a home. In
any case the male members of the family were probably sent away to school as
soon as they reached an appropriate age. This was certainly the case with
Buckingham, and there is no reason to assume that he was treated any differently from his brothers and half-brothers. Local schools were increasing in

number in the sixteenth century, and were at first patronised mainly by yeomen, artisans, and small shopkeepers. But during Elizabeth's reign the sons of gentlemen and even peers began attending local schools, and among these was Buckingham. Leicester and Melton Mowbray were both good centres and reasonably near to Brooksby, but Sir George sent his ten-year-old son across country to Billesdon. This was because the local vicar, Anthony Cade, had already made a reputation for himself as a man of learning and integrity. The vicarage at Billesdon served as a school, and Cade, as he recorded himself, 'was thought worthy to be employed in the training up of some nobles and many other young gentlemen of the best sort . . . in the learned tongues, mathematical arts, music, and other, both divine and human, learning'.[7]

Buckingham was not a natural scholar. He preferred the active life to the contemplative, and subsequently blamed his lack of scholarship for his inability 'to manage those moral and natural parts which God had blessed him withal'. According to Wotton he was taught the principles of music and 'other slight literature' at Billesdon. No doubt he also struggled with the rudiments of Latin, though in later years he was to disclaim any ability in the language. But Cade would have made it his first task to instil in his pupils the principles of the Christian religion as exemplified in the doctrines of the Church of England, and his success in this particular instance may be indicated by the fact that while Buckingham was to develop close connexions with a number of catholic families during his years in power, he never abandoned the protestant faith in which he had been brought up.[8]

Although Buckingham probably learnt little at Billesdon he developed an abiding affection for Anthony Cade. When he became favourite he introduced Cade to James I, and some years later was instrumental in procuring for him the offer of what Cade described as 'a right famous and noble place, to raise my fortunes and exercise my ministry in (the like whereof many have sought with great suit, cost and labour, and have not found)'. Whatever this place was, Cade – who practised humility as well as preaching it – declined the offer, but he showed his gratitude by dedicating his published sermon on 'St Paul's Agony' to his former pupil. Some years later Buckingham arranged for him to be presented with the living of Grafton Underwood, which he held along with Billesdon. Cade was already a pluralist, and – contrary to what one might assume from his religious leanings – seems to have had no qualms about holding more than one living. The benefits to a scholar were only too apparent, for, as he told the Lord Keeper, this increase of means would enable him 'both to live in better sort without want (and thereby without contempt), and especially to furnish me with many useful books of all kinds and sides: in perusing, examining and extracting the quintessence whereof is my daily labour and my greatest worldly contentment'.[9]

Buckingham had been under Anthony Cade's tuition at Billesdon for three years, and was by now thirteen, when, in January 1606, his father died. Sir George Villiers, at the time of his death, was a man of wealth and property, but the greater part of this went to his eldest son by his first marriage. Mary Villiers now had to move out to the dower house at Goadby Marwood. She took George, and possibly her other children, with her, and from then on Goadby, rather than Brooksby, was Buckingham's home. Mary had a life interest in the house at Goadby Marwood, with three hundred and sixty acres attached to it, and also a jointure of £200 a year, so she was far from destitute. Furthermore, in June 1606, less than six months after the death of her first husband, she married Sir William Reyner. This marriage was of brief duration, since Reyner died in November of that year, but she was presumably entitled to her dower out of his lands, and this must further have improved her financial position. But money can hardly have been plentiful, and Wotton's reference to Buckingham's 'beautiful and provident mother' suggests that she counted her pennies carefully. Mary Villiers can have had no easy task in bringing up her family at Goadby, for in later years Buckingham was to recall his childhood as a time 'when I did nothing else but unreasonably and frowardly wrangle'. Even when Buckingham was a grown man he was still, in his mother's eyes, 'the same naughty boy, George Villiers', but she loved him deeply and he returned her affection in full measure. He never ceased to be thankful for the 'more than ordinary natural love of a mother, which you have ever borne me', and could not be happy until she had given him 'as many blessings and pardons as I shall make faults'. [10]

As Buckingham grew up it became apparent that he had inherited both his mother's beauty and his father's dignified bearing. Mary Villiers, recognising that her son was no scholar, 'chose rather to endue him with conversative qualities and ornaments of youth, as dancing, fencing, and the like . . . to which lessons he had such a dextrous proclivity as his teachers were fain to restrain his forwardness'. It could well be that even at this early stage Mary Villiers was thinking in terms of an opening at Court for her favourite son, for she would quickly have perceived that he had many of the qualities of a courtier, not least charm and good looks, and her ambition for his advancement would have prompted her to aim high. Mary, although she lived quietly, was not so cut off from the stream of public life as the remoteness of Goadby Marwood would suggest. She was already on close terms with Sir Thomas Compton, son of a peer and brother to the future Earl of Northampton, who moved in a more elevated social circle than that to which she was accustomed. A knight's widow could hardly have commanded the influence, let alone the money, to open the way to a career at Court for her favourite son, but as the wife of Sir Thomas Compton – which she shortly became – her opportunities would be far greater. The date of her marriage to Sir Thomas is unknown, but by May 1609 he was already sufficiently interested in the future of Mary's children to procure a pass from the Privy Council for 'John and George Villars, gentlemen, to repair unto the parts beyond the seas, to gain experience'. [11]

At the age of sixteen, then, Buckingham set off for France, the centre of the civilised world, with four servants to attend upon him and his elder brother. The two boys spent some three years abroad, passing part of that time at Blois, where Buckingham was taught French by the future bishop of the diocese. He learnt to understand the language well, but was later to declare that he spoke it only with difficulty and could hardly write it at all. At the time when he made this announcement he had good reasons for exaggerating his imperfections in this respect, but even if he did return from France with little skill in speaking or writing the language, he would not have been the first Englishman to do so. In any case he had other things to learn there, among them how to ride the 'great horse' — the big-boned animal used for tournaments (and war). In Italy and France the techniques of *manège* had been brought to a high pitch of perfection, and they made it possible for the rider who acquired them to manoeuvre the ponderous 'great horse' as if it were a much lighter animal. It was probably the desire to master these techniques that led Buckingham and his brother to Angers, where they were resident in 1611, along with a number of well-born students from England and Germany. But the informal academy at Angers provided lessons in other subjects as well as equitation. The classical languages were taught, and so, it may be assumed, were such skills as fencing and dancing, which would be very useful to a young man thinking of a career at Court. [12]

Buckingham returned to England sometime in 1612 or 1613, and went back to Goadby to stay with his mother. As the second son of a second marriage, he had little but his looks to commend him, and it was already a truth universally acknowledged that a single man who was not in possession of a good fortune must be in want of a wife — preferably a rich one. The woman whom Buckingham picked on was Ann, the youngest daughter of the late Sir Roger Aston, Gentleman of the Bedchamber and Master of the Wardrobe to James I. Buckingham had no difficulty in winning Ann's affections, for she was said to have loved him so deeply that she would have married him on the spot. But her trustees were more cautious, for fear that she might be committing herself to a penniless adventurer. They insisted that Buckingham should produce evidence of his ability to maintain a wife by raising the sum of a hundred marks, and when the young man professed his inability to do so, they broke off all negotiations. Since it was they rather than Ann herself who had the last word, the marriage never took place. [13]

There is no way of discovering how Buckingham felt about this rebuff — if that, indeed, is what it was, for the story as it has come down to us has a number of weak links. It is extremely unlikely, for instance, that Buckingham would have found it impossible to lay his hands on a relatively small sum like one hundred marks (£66 6s. 8d.). Sir Thomas Compton, who was by now his stepfather, could easily have provided it, had he wished to do so. But Sir Thomas — whose brother, the future Earl of Northampton, had recently become, through the death of his father-in-law, one of the richest men in England — may well have decided that his handsome protégé should set his sights much higher than Sir Roger Aston's daughter. This was certainly the view of Buckingham's close friend, Sir James Graham, one of the Gentlemen of the King's Privy Chamber. Graham advised Buckingham to give up all thought of marriage at this stage, and to seek his fortune at Court. If Buckingham loved Ann as much as she loved him, he would no doubt have been inclined to reject this advice; but in that case Sir Thomas Compton's refusal to lend him

11

the essential one hundred marks would have forced him to think again. Whatever the circumstances, the decision was made. Ann Aston was not to become Buckingham's wife. He turned his ambitions, instead, towards the Court.[14]

II

It was probably sometime in 1614 that King James first set eyes on Buckingham. Wotton says that it was during the summer progress, when James was staying at Apethorpe, the great Northamptonshire house belonging to Sir Anthony Mildmay. James started his progress in mid-July, but was almost immediately summoned back to London by the news that his brother-in-law, Christian IV, King of Denmark, had arrived unexpectedly. James, who had little liking for London in high summer, was compelled to entertain his royal visitor, but no sooner had Christian boarded his ship at Gravesend on 1 August than James left town post-haste to resume his progress. Two days later he was at Apethorpe, where his hunting dogs and the pleasures of the chase were awaiting him. Among the unexpected pleasures was the company of a young man of twenty-one, endowed by nature with exceptional grace, charm and good looks. He must have made an immediate impression upon the susceptible king, for a mere four weeks later Lord Fenton, writing to his cousin to give him the news from Court, said 'I think your lordship has heard before this time of a youth, his name is Villiers, a Northamptonshire man; he begins to be in favour with His Majesty'.[15]

Buckingham was by no means the first young man to attract the King's interest. James had become King of Scotland when he was only thirteen months old, following the enforced abdication of his mother, Mary, Queen of Scots. As he grew up, he was submitted to a regime of intensive study that made him one of the most learned kings in Europe, but while books could satisfy his intellectual curiosity they could not fill the gap left in his life by the absence of a mother, brother, or family of any sort. Not until the arrival of one of his French relatives, Esmé Stuart, Seigneur d'Aubigny, in 1579, did James find someone whom he could love. D'Aubigny (whom James created Duke of Lenox) had the handsome presence, the self-assurance, and the exquisite manners that the King so conspicuously lacked, and James was captivated by him. 'His greatness is greatly increased,' wrote one observer, 'and the King so much affected to him that he delights only in his company.' D'Aubigny set the pattern that was to be repeated in the King's relations with all his male favourites. James showed his affection by giving, and since kings have more to give than other men, his bounty was prodigal: titles, honours, pensions, and grants of land and money flowed out of him, as if of their own volition, towards those he loved.[16]

D'Aubigny aroused such hatred among the Scottish nobles that in 1582 he was forced to leave the country, and James never saw him again. But his influence was ineradicable, for he had brought to the surface in the young king something that had always been latent, and from then on James was rarely without a favourite. The reigning one in 1614 was Robert Carr, a Scot by birth, who had accompanied James to England as a page and had then spent some time in France before returning to Court. Good looks and fine French manners were, after D'Aubigny, sure keys to James's favour, and by 1612 Carr was Viscount Rochester, a Privy Councillor and a Knight of the Garter. Carr's rapid rise to wealth and influence aroused envy among those who had not been so lucky, but his enemies also included a number of people who detested him not so much for his person as for the company he kept and the causes he espoused. Like all political centres the Jacobean Court was a hotbed of intrigue, where conflicting factions struggled for ascendancy. Sometimes these factions were little more than family groups, out for office and the riches that flowed therefrom. Sometimes the bond was a religious or political one, with members of a faction sharing the same objective aims. But more often than not personal ambitions, family interests, religious beliefs and political ideals were all mixed up in a kaleidoscopic pattern that was perpetually changing its shape.

The object of all factions was to gain the confidence of the King, for only he could give them the offices, the riches, or whatever else it was they wanted. Such groups were not treacherous or even disloyal, for they never challenged the accepted convention that ultimate authority was vested in the King, by divine appointment. Nor were they seeking to arrogate to themselves functions that belonged only to the sovereign. They operated in that ill-defined area which lay between the abstract concept of royal rule and the practical implementation of it, and they were prompted as much by fear as by ambition, for beneath its polished surface the Jacobean Court was a jungle in which the strong preyed on the weak and hunted them down. They took only what the King was prepared to let them have, but in this respect James was weaker, or at any rate more circumscribed, than his predecessor. Elizabeth had balanced one faction against another, and thereby retained control in her own hands – until, that is, the last decade of her reign, when the factions had been narrowed down to two, and she was forced, much against her natural inclination, to make a clear choice between them. One of these factions revolved around her young favourite, the Earl of Essex. The other had at its head Robert Cecil, the son of Elizabeth's greatest servant, William Cecil, Lord Burghley. Robert Cecil was a far less glamorous figure than his ambitious and impatient rival, but he had inherited all his father's political skill and used it, often unscrupulously, to win the Queen's confidence and thereby strengthen his position. In 1596 he was made Secretary of State, and three years later, after the death of Burghley, the Queen appointed him to the lucrative office of Master of the Court of Wards. Essex, sensing that the tide was running against him, broke the rules of the game by appealing to force. In February 1601 he rode into the City of London at the head of a body of armed men, crying out 'For the Queen! For the Queen!'. He hoped that a great popular rising in his favour would sweep him to power at the same time as it carried Robert Cecil into oblivion, but he had miscalculated. The populace held aloof, and

13

his rebellion – for such it was, despite his claim that he had intended only to serve the Queen by freeing her from the grip of the Cecils – collapsed before it had even started. Essex met his end on the scaffold, and his faction collapsed in ruins. Robert Cecil was left in unchallenged control of public affairs, subject only to the authority of an ageing and disillusioned Queen. Knowing that Elizabeth's reign must be nearing its end, Cecil decided to mend his bridges with James VI of Scotland, the heir presumptive to the English throne. James had been a partisan of Essex, and regarded Cecil as an enemy, but as it became clear to him that the minister was in fact prepared to smoothe the path to his accession his attitude underwent a dramatic change. 'My dearest and trusty Cecil,' he wrote, 'my pen is not able to express how happy I think myself for having chanced upon so worthy, so wise, and so provident a friend.'[17]

As a result of these secret exchanges Cecil confounded the general expectation by surviving, unharmed and unshaken, the transition from Tudor to Stuart rule which took place after Elizabeth's death in March 1603. James not only kept him in power but demonstrated his approval by raising him to the peerage, and subsequently, in 1605, conferring upon him the earldom of Salisbury. A few years later, in 1608, he appointed him to the key office of Lord Treasurer. But although Salisbury had the confidence of the new King he was aware that his enemies were continually intriguing against him and that he could never take his power for granted. Yet while he lived he had sufficient skill (born of long practice) to hold the competing factions in check, and he thereby gave the opening decades of James's reign in England a deceptive appearance of calm, which perhaps misled the King into underrating the difficulty of ruling his new subjects. After his death in 1612, however, 'Cecil's Commonwealth' fell apart and the factional struggle became intense. James was aware of the threat which this situation presented to his freedom of manoeuvre, and in order to avoid becoming the prisoner or unwilling accomplice of any single faction he decided to do much of the work of government himself. He acted as his own Secretary, using Robert Carr as his assistant, and instead of naming a Treasurer, and thereby indicating a preference for a particular group, he left that office in commission. But however determined James may have been to retain his freedom, he did not have sufficient experience of the factional struggle, from which Salisbury had shielded him; nor did he have the inclination or the capacity for regular, routine work which administration entailed. Gradually, and perhaps insensibly, James allowed himself to be drawn into the embrace of the Howards. One member of this clan was Henry Howard, Earl of Northampton and Lord Privy Seal, who became, in fact though not in name, James's chief minister. Another was his cousin, Charles Howard, who as Lord Howard of Effingham had commanded the English fleet against the Armada in 1588 and now, as Earl of Nottingham, held the appropriate office of Lord Admiral. The third leading member of this faction was Northampton's nephew, Thomas Howard, Earl of Suffolk, whom James appointed Lord Chamberlain and one of the commissioners of the Treasury.

The Howards, although they did not form a solid political bloc, were inclined to be sympathetic to the English catholics, favoured an alliance with the catholic monarchy of Spain, and were anxious to prevent the summoning of Parliament, since this body was certain to be opposed to everything they stood for – not least their own continuance in power. Against the Howards was ranged a more loose-knit faction in which religious beliefs and political aims played a larger part than family interests. Its leading members were George Abbot, Archbishop of Canterbury, and William Herbert, Earl of Pembroke, and it advocated a popular, anti-Spanish policy and uncompromising defence of protestantism. Carr belonged to neither group. His dependence upon royal favour might have inclined him to the Howards, but he resented their growing influence, which was often used to check his own, and through the agency of his friend and adviser, Sir Thomas Overbury, he made overtures to the 'protestant' lords. Overbury's aim was to increase Carr's power by playing off one faction against another. But this was a dangerous strategy, for it did not take account of the narrow limits within which a favourite could operate effectively. Nor did Overbury allow for the possibility that Carr himself might betray him.[18]

Yet this is what happened, for Carr fell in love with Suffolk's daughter, Frances Howard, and Northampton and Suffolk saw in the furtherance of such a union the welcome prospect of attaching Carr to their interest. The situation was complicated by the fact that Frances was already married, to the Earl of Essex (the son of Elizabeth's favourite); but she detested her husband and had been considering bringing an action for annulment against him on the grounds of impotence. This proposal was now taken up by the Howards and also won the support of the King, who saw the advantages of reconciling his favourite with Northampton and Suffolk. In May 1613, therefore, the King issued a commission to a mixed body of bishops and lawyers, under the presidency of Archbishop Abbot, to examine the whole question and pronounce judgment. Despite the reservations of a number of members, including Abbot himself, the majority of the commissioners decided in favour of annulling the marriage. By the end of 1613, then, Frances Howard was free to take a new husband, and in December of that year she married Robert Carr, who had just been created Earl of Somerset.

After the death of Northampton in June 1614, Suffolk and Carr formed a duumvirate. The King wound up the Treasury commission and appointed Suffolk as Lord Treasurer, while Carr took Suffolk's place as Lord Chamberlain. Suffolk had no easy task, for James was already short of money, and the failure of the Addled Parliament – which met for a few weeks in the spring of 1614 and accomplished nothing – meant that there was no obvious remedy. James, however, had for some time been considering a marriage alliance between his son, Prince Charles, and the Infanta Maria of Spain, and one of the conditions of this would be a substantial Spanish dowry, which would go a long way towards solving his financial problems. A Spanish marriage also had other advantages to offer. The House of Commons, in its recent meetings, had been so critical of the King's policies, and some of its members had been so extreme in their language, that James – who was by nature timorous – feared that at some time in the future there might be a violent outburst against him. In such circumstances the support of the most powerful ruler in Christendom would be a great comfort. And even if he never needed to call on such support, the knowledge that the King of Spain stood behind him would – in James's opinion – restrain his critics and reinforce his royal authority. When James broached the question of opening formal negotiations for a Spanish marriage, the Count of Gondomar – who was Philip III's ambassador in London – advised him to go ahead. In late 1614, therefore, James decided to send an embassy to Spain to negotiate the marriage terms, and he chose as his envoy John Digby, who was experienced in dealing with the Spaniards, and had only recently returned from Madrid.[19]

The Carr-Suffolk alliance and the pro-Spanish policy were anathema to the Abbot-Pembroke faction, which detested Spain and preferred reliance on Parliament to subservience to a foreign, catholic power. Its members could do little while Carr was so firmly seated in the King's affections, but they were on the lookout for some way in which to unseat the favourite. The most obvious method was to put forward a counter-favourite, in the hope that he would capture James's attention and gradually draw him away from Carr; but tampering with the King's affections was a hazardous undertaking which could, if badly handled, do more harm than good. For the time being they had no choice but to accept Carr's supremacy, for as Fenton reported in September 1614, 'all things are absolutely done by one man, and he [is] more absolute than ever he was'.[20]

III

Buckingham probably knew little about the tensions between the two factions in the late summer of 1614, but he could not have timed his appearance upon the public stage to better advantage if he had written the play himself. The Court was soon buzzing with rumours of a change of favourite, but Lord Fenton – who had been brought up with James and knew him as well as anybody – probably read the King's mind correctly when he commented, in December 1614, that the effect of Buckingham's appearance would be 'rather to kindle a new fire than to extinguish the old one'. Somerset, nevertheless, was alarmed about the reports that reached him of James's growing infatuation with George Villiers, and when, in November 1614, there was some talk of the young man being sworn of the King's Bedchamber, he blocked this by securing the post for one of his own kinsmen. Yet James constantly assured Somerset that Villiers, far from being a threat to him, was in fact a safeguard. Carr was unpopular, not least because he was one of the Scots who had come south of the border with James and made his fortune at the expense of the English. James now argued that by pushing Villiers forward as a showpiece English favourite, he would shield Carr and turn the stream of public hatred away from him. Somerset may have chosen to accept this argument, in the hope that the King's obsession with Villiers would be of short duration. But he feared that his enemies, particularly the Abbot-Pembroke faction, were planning to use Buckingham to overthrow and destroy him.[21]

Somerset had always been moody and hot-tempered, but now he took to railing at James, upbraiding him in bitter terms at all hours of the day and night. He also used his physical strength to overawe the king and subdue him to his will. By so doing, however, he provoked the very reaction he was trying to avoid, for he destroyed the love that James still felt for him. Early in 1615 James, stung beyond endurance by Somerset's behaviour, wrote him an extraordinarily frank letter, warning him of the consequences of the course he was following. He acknowledged Carr's many merits, but pointed out that they had become 'especially of late, since the strange frenzy took you, so powdered and mixed with strange streams of unquietness, passion, fury, and insolent pride, and (which is worst of all) with a settled kind of induced obstinacy, as it chokes and obscures all these excellent and good parts that God hath bestowed upon you'. He assured Somerset yet again that he had nothing to fear and that no other person should ever 'come to the twentieth degree of *your* favour'. All he needed to do to retain his hold on the King's affections was to 'be kind'. But James warned Somerset that 'if ever I find that you think to retain me by one sparkle of fear, all the violence of my love will in that instant be changed into as violent a hatred . . . . It lies in your hands to make of me what you please: either the best master and truest friend; or, if you force me once to call you ingrate – which the God of heaven forbid – no so great earthly plague can light upon you.'[22]

Although Somerset had managed to prevent Buckingham from being sworn of the Bedchamber, he could not keep him out of the royal presence. The King gave secret directions to Sir James Graham about how the young man should behave, and Graham – who had been something of a favourite himself and knew what favour could lead to – invested in Villiers and acted as his manager. Money was a problem, since Villiers only had £50 a year of his own, and such a sum, even in the early seventeenth century, would not go far at Court. Indeed it may have been at about this time that Villiers was seen 'at a horse-race in Cambridgeshire in an old black suit, broken out in divers places; and at night . . . he could not get a room in the inn to lodge in, and was therefore glad to lie in a trundle-bed in a gentleman's chamber'. But Graham, like any good promoter, knew how to interest other backers. Sir Arthur Ingram, a canny Yorkshire businessman, was one of these, and Graham persuaded him to put up £100. Among the others were the Earl of Pembroke and Sir Thomas Compton, Buckingham's step-father, who between them secured the place of Cupbearer for their protégé. This gave Buckingham the duty, every alternate month, of waiting on the King at table, and courtiers were quick to observe that James, who loved to talk while he was eating, found Buckingham well informed about affairs and publicly commended him for the quality of his conversation.[23]

In these early weeks of his attendance at Court Buckingham was, in a sense, on trial, for although there were many people only waiting for a suitable opportunity to overthrow the reigning favourite, they had to be sure that his rival was no mere will o' the wisp. James's public commendation of his Cup-bearer was a sign of the way in which things were moving, but since every-thing depended, in the last resort, upon the King's inclinations, there could be no short cuts. All the conspirators could do at this stage was to keep Buckingham in the King's eye and show him off to best advantage. James was, to some extent, a willing accomplice. In December 1614 John Chamber-lain – a London resident, whose full and witty letters to his friend Sir Dudley Carleton, the English ambassador at the Hague, contain all the current gossip – reported that despite the prevailing lack of money the King had given £1,500 towards the preparing of a Twelfth Night masque, 'the principal mo-tive whereof is thought to be the gracing of young Villiers and to bring him on the stage'.[24]

The King was delighted with the masque and ordered it to be repeated a day or two later. This was further encouragement to Villiers's backers, and it was probably they who arranged for him to appear at Cambridge in March 1615, when the King visited the university to watch a student play. 'At this play,' according to one account, 'it was so contrived that George Villiers should appear with all the advantages his mother could set him forth: and the King, so soon as he had seen him, fell into admiration of him, so as he became confounded between his admiration of Villiers and the pleasure of the play . . . . This set the heads of the courtiers at work, how to get Somerset out of favour, and to bring Villiers in.'[25]

The details of this new plot were hatched in April 1615, and Archbishop Abbot played a key role. In the account which he wrote many years later, Abbot does not mention the other conspirators by name, but it may safely be assumed that William Herbert, Earl of Pembroke, was among them, for the Herberts and their allies were said to have held a supper party at which they concerted plans for Somerset's overthrow. Pembroke had a personal grudge against Somerset, for he had earlier been promised the office of Lord Chamber-lain, but had seen Carr step in before him. Pembroke's opposition, however, was prompted by more than wounded pride. He and Archbishop Abbot be-lieved that the interests of the King and country would be best served by a committedly protestant, anti-catholic policy, and that if James followed their advice his difficulties with Parliament would diminish, if not altogether disappear.[26]

There could be no doubt that James was a convinced protestant, for he made this clear in his writings as well as his conversation. But there could also be no doubt that something, or someone, stood between him and wholehearted adherence to the cause of protestantism. Abbot, Pembroke, and many others believed that Somerset was the major obstacle, and that with his removal the direction of the King's policy would be altered. In this they were wrong, for James was his own policy-maker, and perhaps had a wider vision than they did. For him the proposed Spanish marriage was not simply a source of much-needed capital and a guarantee of his own security in case his subjects gave trouble; it was also a way of healing the tragic rift in Christendom that had opened with the Reformation in the sixteenth century. James had already married his daughter, Elizabeth, to the Elector Frederick of the Palatinate, one of the leading protestant princes of Germany. If he could now match his son with the Spanish Infanta he would be, in his own person, the link between catholics and protestants, able to speak to both on equal terms and thereby help to bring about the reconciliation that had so far eluded human endeavour. James was no mean theologian, and his relatively unfanatical attitude towards the Pope and Roman Catholicism in general came from his conviction that his opinions were soundly based. But James's subjects did not share the King's confidence in his own judgement. They feared that he was being duped by unscrupulous advisers who were taking advantage of his good nature and love of peace to lead him and his people into dishonourable and perilous courses for the sake of their own private concerns. Hence the determination of the 'protestant interest' to get rid of Carr and then, in due course, of the Howards as well.

Abbot and his fellow conspirators planned, as a first step towards this objective, to obtain for Villiers the post of Gentleman of the Bedchamber which Carr had so far denied him. For this they needed the support of the Queen. James and his wife, Anne of Denmark, had a certain fondness for each other, but were not on intimate terms, and in most matters the King would not have dreamed of asking her advice. But when it came to appointments to his household, particularly those which entailed personal attendance upon him, he liked the request to come from his wife, so that if, at a later stage, she should, in Abbot's words, 'complain of this *Dear one*, he might make his answer, "It is long of yourself, for you were the party that commended him unto me" '.[27]

Since Anne was a catholic – though a discreet one – and had been among those who first mooted the idea of a Spanish marriage for her son, it might seem unlikely that she would consent to give her support to the anti-catholic, anti-Spanish interest. But Anne had very considerable respect for the Archbishop, whose advice she was inclined to follow, and she may well have relished the prospect of getting rid of Somerset, who treated her with marked lack of consideration. But she had no illusions about a new favourite. 'My lord,' she told Abbot, 'you and the rest of your friends know not what you do. I know your master better than you all, for if this young man be once brought in, the first persons that he will plague must be you that labour for him. Yea, I shall have my part also. The King will teach him to despise and hardly entreat us all, that he may seem to be beholden to none but himself.' However, the Archbishop assured her that Villiers was far better natured than Carr, and that even if he did turn out badly it would be a long time before he could do as much harm as the present favourite.[28]

Anne may or may not have been convinced, but she agreed to support the plan, and during the course of the next few days she won the King over to it. James delighted in plays, and loved, as Bacon observed, 'to do things unexpected', so it may have been he who suggested the scenario for the performance that took place on the evening of 23 April 1615, St George's Day. The King and his son, Prince Charles, went to call on the Queen, who had warned

Buckingham to be within easy distance. At the appropriate moment she had him brought in, and then asked the Prince to lend her his rapier. Thereupon, with the drawn sword in her hand, she knelt before the King 'and humbly beseeched His Majesty to do her that special favour as to knight this noble gentleman, whose name was George, for the honour of St George, whose feast he now kept. The King at first seemed to be afeard that the Queen should come to him with a naked sword, but then he did it very joyfully.'[29]

The Queen also asked James to swear Buckingham as a Gentleman of the Bedchamber. But at this point Somerset, who was standing at the door amid a throng of onlookers, sent a message to the King, asking him to appoint the new knight to the lesser position of Groom. Abbot and his friends were in readiness for this, however, and sent a counter-message to the Queen, urging her to stand firm and persuade James to grant the greater honour. James, no doubt in high good humour, agreed to his wife's request, and Sir George Villiers was duly sworn Gentleman of the King's Bedchamber.[30]

No sooner was the brief ceremony over than the young knight came bounding out of the Queen's apartments and flung himself at Abbot's feet, protesting 'that he was so infinitely bound unto me that all his life long he must honour me as his father'. Buckingham had good cause for exaltation, for with the King's love, the Queen's favour, and the Archbishop's blessing, his career at Court was well and truly launched. His financial situation was also dramatically improved, for the King awarded him a pension of £1,000 a year.[31]

Buckingham made a very favourable impression upon everyone he met, for his attractive appearance and ease of manner were combined with a genuine humility (as though he was awed by his own good fortune) and a desire to please. A portrait of Buckingham, painted in 1616, shows a tall, slender young man, delicate-featured, with long tapering fingers and finely shaped legs. This impression is confirmed by the account of the antiquarian Simonds D'Ewes, who watched Buckingham talking to a group of French lords in 1621, and found 'everything in him full of delicacy and handsome features; yea, his hands and face seemed to me especially effeminate and curious'. Another eye-witness, Bishop Goodman, described Buckingham as 'the handsomest-bodied man of England; his limbs so well compacted and his conversation so pleasing and of so sweet a disposition'.[32]

Those who had backed Buckingham, for whatever motive, had every reason to be pleased with the outcome of their manoeuvres, and factionalism at Court increased in bitterness as the challenge to Somerset and the Howards moved out into the open. Both sides mounted a show of strength in May 1615, when Lord Fenton and Lord Knollys, whom James had appointed to the Order of the Garter, were due to ride in state to Windsor for their investiture. Fenton had the support of Abbot and the 'protestant interest', since, like many Scots, he favoured an alliance with France, not with Spain. Knollys, on the other hand, was Suffolk's son-in-law, and therefore represented the Somerset-Howard alliance. At first it was reported that Villiers would ride in Fenton's entourage, but when it came to the point the King forbade him to go at all, and kept him by his side, at Somerset House, to watch the procession set out.[33]

IV

The rise of Buckingham, even though it threatened Somerset, did not result in his immediate fall. On the face of it, Somerset was so firmly ensconced in power, particularly with the Howards to back him, that he would not easily be dislodged, and Sir John Holles, who was one of Somerset's clients, expressed his belief that Villiers would not be able to 'raze a Chamberlain and a Treasurer (both rooted by long service and many offices of great latitude in our state) out of the book of life, and turn the stream down another channel'.[34] Yet Holles, like all those who were in any way connected with the Court, watched carefully for any signs that the established power pattern was breaking up. The fall of a favourite was not just a personal matter. Simply because he was favourite, Somerset held the key to grants of money, offices and titles, and many men had attached themselves to him, become his 'clients' or 'creatures', and thereby linked their fortunes to his own. If he were to fall, they would go with him, unless they switched their allegiance. Timing was the problem. If they deserted Somerset at too early a stage, they might well find out, to their cost, that he was successful in retaining the King's favour; yet if they left it too late they would not be able to lay claim to any reward from the new dispenser of patronage. For major courtiers, like Pembroke and Archbishop Abbot, the choice was not a matter of life and death. Pembroke could count on the King's friendship, and had great estates, as well as a considerable clientage of his own, to buttress him. Abbot, as Archbishop of Canterbury, was among the most important of the King's Councillors, and his great office shielded him from all but the most violent storms. Lesser men, on the other hand, had to make a choice upon which their entire future could depend, and the moment of greatest danger for any favourite came when their rate of desertion turned from a slow trickle into a flood.

Despite James's earlier warning to him, Somerset was still behaving in a manner calculated to anger rather than conciliate the King. Driven by suspicions, many of which were justified, Carr sought constant reassurance as he struggled to break the hold of Villiers upon the King's heart. But James, whose love for his old favourite was now clearly fading, insisted that Somerset must acknowledge his faults and return to a more respectful manner of behaviour. 'Heaven and earth shall bear me witness that if you do but the half your duty unto me, you may be with me in the old manner; only by expressing that love to my person and respect to your master that God and man crave of you, with a hearty and feeling penitence of your by-past errors.' As far as James was concerned the situation was quite clear. He would not abandon Villiers, and if Somerset wished to retain his influence he must accept this fact. If Somerset could not, or would not, do so, the fault would lie with him, not with the King. It was to give Somerset the opportunity of a reconciliation that James arranged another piece of play-acting. He let Somerset know that Villiers would call on him with offers of devotion and loyal service. All that Somerset need do was to make a generous response, and the rift between him and the King would be healed. But Somerset was not prepared to play the role he had been assigned. Villiers came to call on him, as arranged, and made a formal declaration that 'I desire to be your servant and your creature and shall desire to take my Court preferment under your favour, and your lordship shall find me as faithful a servant unto you as ever did serve you.' But Somerset returned a 'quick and short answer'. 'I will none of your service and you shall have none of my favour. I will, if I can, break your neck, and of that be confident.' It was, in effect, a declaration of war.[35]

By now the King was on his summer progress, visiting one great country house after another – and not only great houses, for among the places he honoured with his presence was Goadby Marwood, Buckingham's boyhood home, where he was magnificently entertained. On its return to London the royal procession passed through Hampshire, and at the end of August 1615 the King paused for a few days at Farnham Castle. It was there that Buckingham played the trump card which ensured his victory over Somerset. The King – who celebrated his forty-ninth birthday in June 1615 – had long been starved of physical affection. His relations with his wife were those of a friend, not a lover; and as for Somerset, one of the faults which the King laid to his charge was 'your long creeping back and withdrawing yourself from lying in my chamber, notwithstanding my many hundred times earnestly soliciting you to the contrary'. The King's desires now centred on the young man who had everything to gain from gratifying him, and as Sir Anthony Weldon recorded in the gossipy memoirs that he left to posterity, 'in his passion of love to his new favourite . . . the King was more impatient than any woman to enjoy her love'. Where the details of private relationships are concerned, nothing, of course, can be known for certain, but Buckingham himself provides the evidence that at Farnham he at last gave in to the King's importunity: writing to James many years later to thank him for a particularly enjoyable visit to Court he told him how he had spent the return journey pondering the question 'whether you loved me now . . . better than at the time which I shall never forget at Farnham, where the bed's head could not be found between the master and his dog'.[36]

By giving himself to James, Buckingham confirmed his supremacy, for what he had to offer was a combination of qualities which the King could find nowhere else – youth, beauty, high spirits, sensuality, sweetness of character, and devotion. Perhaps it was the awareness on the part of observant courtiers that the relationship between James and Buckingham had entered a much deeper, and probably more enduring, stage that prompted the Secretary of State, Sir Ralph Winwood, to reveal to the King an important piece of information concerning Somerset.

Somerset's marriage to Frances Howard had been opposed by his intimate friend, Sir Thomas Overbury, who feared, rightly, that it would mark the end of his influence with the favourite. But Somerset was besotted with Frances, who was already his mistress, and was determined to make her his wife. In order to get Overbury out of the way, the King, in the spring of 1613, offered him a diplomatic post abroad. Overbury, however, was too proud to accept defeat, and may not have given up hope of changing Somerset's mind. He therefore rejected the offer and was promptly imprisoned in the Tower for disobeying the King's commands. It was intended that he should stay there only for some months, until the marriage was a *fait accompli*, but in fact he never came out alive. Frances Howard arranged for him to be poisoned, and long before the marriage took place Overbury was dead.

Foul play was not at first suspected, but in July 1615 Sir Ralph Winwood received reports that Overbury had been murdered, and it was this information which he passed on to the King, as the summer progress drew to its close. James promptly ordered Sir Edward Coke, the Lord Chief Justice, to conduct an investigation into the whole affair and to find out the truth regardless of who might be involved. By the end of the month Coke had evidence implicating both the Countess of Somerset and her husband, and at his request James enlarged the commission to include a number of the great figures at Court, who would reinforce Coke's own authority. Somerset was with the King at Royston when he first heard reports that he was under suspicion. He determined to go up to London to face his accusers, assuring the King that he was completely innocent. According to Weldon, who claims to have witnessed the leave-taking, 'the King hung about his neck, slabbering his cheeks, saying, "For God's sake, when shall I see thee again? On my soul I shall neither eat nor sleep until you come again."' No sooner was Somerset in his coach, however, than the King was heard to say 'I shall never see his face more'.[37]

Whether the King was relieved, gloating, or merely prophetic, is not clear, but this was indeed his last meeting with Somerset. Early in 1616 formal charges of murder were laid against the Earl and his wife, and Somerset was imprisoned in the Tower. Frances, who was pregnant, was allowed to stay at liberty until the birth of their daughter, which took place in March. In May they were brought to trial before their peers, in Westminster Hall. There could be little doubt about the Countess's responsibility for murdering Overbury, and although Somerset may have been kept in the dark, the Lords found them both guilty. Neither, however, was to die. James issued a pardon for Frances almost immediately, and stayed the execution of her husband. But they mouldered in prison for some six years, and it was only at the end of 1624, not long before James's death, that the King finally sealed Somerset's pardon.

With Somerset effectively removed from the scene, Buckingham was the undisputed favourite. Now the crowds of suitors who had previously flocked to Somerset thronged round him, and as the dispenser of the King's bounty he was courted and flattered by all those who sought money, office or titles. It was a dazzling prospect for a young man, and a dramatic change of fortune for the second son of old Sir George Villiers's second marriage. But the position was not without its dangers, as Saint Simon — whose father rose by the same means — was latter to observe: '*Mon père devint tout à fait favori, sans autre protection que la bonté seule du Roi.*'[38] As long as Buckingham had the King's goodwill, he had nothing to fear. But kings are mortal, and their affections — as the fall of Somerset had demonstrated — are liable to change. When, during the course of his career, Buckingham struck hard at anyone who dared promote a rival favourite, this was because he understood the precarious nature of his own tenure of favour. And if he used language to the King that to modern ears (though not necessarily to his contemporaries) sounds over-fulsome and obsequious, that shows how well he appreciated the terms of the contract between him and his master.

NOTES

(Abbreviations are explained in the Bibliography, pp. 477–86)
1. *Leland*. IV, 120.
2. *Eglish*. 65; *Farnham*. VI, 247; *Leics*. III, Part I, 189.
3. *Wot*. 208; *Leics*. III, Part I, 189; *Shaw*. II, 155.
4. *Leland*. IV, 120; *Parker*. 239–40; Sir Thomas More, *Utopia*, Book I; *Leics*. III, Part I, 189.
5. *Farnham*. II, 61; VI, 263; *Notes*. 469–70; *Wel*. 89; *Detection*. 80–81.
6. *Russ*. 434–45; *Vautor*, Dedication.
7. *Cum*. 39–56.
8. *Eg. MSS*. 2533, 62v; *Wot*. 208; *Bac*. XIV, 437.
9. Anthony Cade, *Saint Paul's Agony* (1618), Dedication; *Fort*. 168; *Cum*. 44.
10. *Notes*. 470; *Detection*. 81; *Wot*. 208–9; *H.M.C.*(4), 256.
11. *Wot*. 209; *Add. MSS*. 11,402. 147v.
12. *H.M.C.*(10), 116; *Bas.MSS*. 60.221v.; Bibliothèque de la Ville d'Angers, MS 994 (870), 653; *Joubert*.
13. *Wot*. 209; *Wel*. 89; *Frank*. 29–30.
14. *Wot*. 209.
15. *Wot*. 209; *H.M.C.Supp*. 56.
16. *Jas*. 33.
17. *Jas*. 154.
18. *Carr*. passim.
19. S.R. Gardiner, 'On Certain Letters of Sarmiento de Acuña, Count of Gondomar', *Arch*. XLI (1867).
20. *H.M.C. Supp*. 56.
21. *H.M.C.Supp*. 58; *Ch*. I, 559; *Till*. 14.
22. *Hall*. II, 126–33.
23. *Wil*. 698; *D'Ewes*. 86; *Upton*. 78; *Carte*. Book XXI.
24. *Ch*. I, 561.
25. *Detection*. 82.
26. *Aulus*. 261; *Birch*, I, 336.
27. *Rush*. 456.
28. *Rush*. 456.
29. *Bac*. XIV, 345; *Goodman*. I, 224.
30. *Rush*. 457.
31. *Ch*.I, 602; *Wot*. 210.
32. *Piper*. No. 3840; *D'Ewes*. 166–7; *Goodman*. I, 225–6.
33. *Ch*. I, 597, 599.
34. *Holl*. I, 66–7.
35. *Hall*. II, 133; *Wel*. 98.
36. *Progresses*. III, 99; *Hall*. II, 129; *Wel*. 94; *H.M.C. Bath*. 71.
37. *Wel*. 102–3.
38. *Simon*. I, 81.

CHAPTER TWO

1616–18:
'Marks of extraordinary Affection'

I

On 4 January 1616, James I appointed Buckingham Master of the Horse. This was a post which carried great prestige, and had frequently been held by favourites of the reigning monarch. Leicester and Essex, for instance, had been successive Masters of the Horse to Elizabeth I, and in 1612 Somerset was angling to get the same post himself. However, the existing holder, the Earl of Worcester, wanted too high a price for relinquishing it, and Somerset abandoned the idea. It was a sign of Buckingham's hold on royal favour that he achieved what Somerset had been unable to do. Worcester was persuaded to hand over his office in return for a pension of £1,500 a year and appointment as Lord Privy Seal.[1]

As Master of the Horse, Buckingham was responsible for the running of the King's stables and the provision of horses and coaches for all the King's occasions. To assist him in this task he had a staff of about two hundred, but he received for his pains the far from princely sum of one hundred marks a year (£66 13s. 4d.). However, he was also entitled to a 'Diet' of sixteen dishes, which meant that twice a day he could feed himself, his servants and his friends at two tables in the King's household, at the King's expense. 'Diets' were the normal accompaniment of royal office, and helped to compensate for the absurdly low official salaries. They could be commuted for money payments, and a sixteen-dish diet was worth about £1,500 a year. The Master of the Horse also had the right to take for his own use horses, saddles, liveries and provisions that were no longer suitable or necessary for the King's service, and since the decision on whether they were or not was left to the Master he could reckon to run his own stables far more cheaply than would otherwise have been the case. There was nothing illegal or immoral about this, or course. Perquisites were built in to the governmental system, and the real value of office was for this reason far in excess of the nominal stipend.[2]

Buckingham, as befitted the son of a Leicestershire squire, was keenly interested in horses. Generally speaking English bloodstock was inferior to that of the Continent, and when Buckingham was appointed Master he immediately set about remedying this situation. He sent his agents to Spain and Italy to purchase the finest horses that money could buy, and in December 1616 he spent the considerable sum of £154 on purchasing a pure-bred Arab stallion for the King's use. Some years later he persuaded Count Gondomar, the Spanish ambassador, to arrange for the despatch to England of four Spanish mares and four Barbary ones. Through these and similar measures Buckingham enormously improved the quality not only of the royal studs but of English breeds in general, and he displayed a capacity for rapidly acquiring information, as well as a refusal to be disheartened by difficulties, that were to prove characteristic of him. James was delighted, and called on God to 'thank the Master of the Horse for providing me such a number of fair, useful horses, fit for my hand. In a word, I protest I never was master of such horses.'[3]

So evident was the King's favour to Buckingham that it was widely assumed that further honours would shortly be heaped upon him. The Venetian ambassador reported that he had been created Viscount Leicester as well as Master of the Horse, and Holles noted rumours that he 'shall be (as the town babbles) a viscount, an earl, *quid non?*'. In fact Buckingham received no further advancement until April 1616, when he and the Earl of Rutland were both appointed to the Order of the Garter. The Manners Earls of Rutland were the leading family in the part of the world from which Buckingham came, and when he was out riding or hunting he must often have looked up to the hill from which their great house, Belvoir Castle, dominated the surrounding country. The Manners were related by marriage to the Comptons and the Bretts, both connexions of Buckingham on his mother's side, and were obviously on close terms with the Villiers as well, as is indicated by the fact that when the fifth earl drew up his will in 1612 he bequeathed 'to Mr Villiers all my hounds for the hare'. It was the sixth earl, Francis Manners, who received the Garter, along with Buckingham, in April 1616. It may be that even at this early stage Buckingham was thinking in terms of a closer relationship between himself and his neighbours at Belvoir, for as Holles shrewdly observed 'when the times shall be proper for marriage [the Earl] hath a daughter for him'.[4]

The new knights were installed at Windsor in July 1616, and in the following month the rumour-mongers were proved true prophets when the King elevated his favourite to the peerage. Earlier reports had suggested that he would take the title of Beaumont, after his mother's family, or Leicester, after the county of his birth. But following his appointment to the Garter the King presented Villiers with the lands of Lord Grey of Wilton, who had been convicted of treason earlier in the reign and had died in the Tower in 1614. These lands, which were said to be worth £1,500 a year, were centred round Whaddon (in Buckinghamshire) and this was the title eventually chosen for Buckingham's barony. But James was not content with making his favourite Baron Whaddon. He simultaneously created him Viscount Villiers – which, as Bacon observed, 'is a well-sounding and noble name, both here and abroad; and being your proper name I will take it for a good sign that you shall give honour to your dignity, and not your dignity to you'.[5]

The ceremony took place at Woodstock, outside Oxford, in the late afternoon on 27 August 1616. First of all Buckingham was brought in to the King's presence as Baron Whaddon, and then, after a brief withdrawal, he came in again as Viscount Villiers, clad in a 'surcoat of crimson velvet, girt with his sword'. The King, watched by the Queen and Prince, 'performed the ceremonies of that action with the greatest alacrity and princely cheerfulness'. The new Viscount and his supporters then retired to supper, but later 'came all joyfully up in their robes with glasses of wine in their hands, kneeled all round about the King before he was risen from supper, and drank to His Majesty's health; which he very graciously and cheerfully pledged'.[6]

The Grey lands might have been enough to maintain the dignity of a Knight of the Garter, but they were hardly sufficient for a viscount. The King proposed to give Buckingham the estate at Sherborne which had previously belonged to Somerset, but Buckingham declined this 'in a most noble fashion, praying the King that the building of his fortunes may not be founded upon the ruins of another'. Sherborne therefore went to Sir John Digby, but the King insisted that his favourite should accept lands of equal value. During the next few months the title deeds of royal properties from various parts of England were gradually brought together to form a grant or 'book' to Buckingham. Chamberlain reported that they would be worth £80,000, but the true figure was nearer £30,000. Even so it was an extraordinary act of bounty on the King's part, and one that was not relished by all his subjects. Fenton had already observed, in September 1616, that although the King loved Buckingham beyond measure the young man had 'lost much affection of his particular friends and generally of all men', and in the following month Lionel Cranfield, the canny merchant-financier who was already acting as Buckingham's agent and adviser, warned him that 'the favours of princes are looked on with many envious eyes'. There was some doubt about the King's right to part with the royal inheritance in this way, since earlier in his reign a substantial portion of the crown estates had been entailed and thereby made inalienable. But Bacon pointed out that Sherborne had not been among the crown lands at the time the entail was drawn up and that if it was made clear that Buckingham's land-book was in exchange for Sherborne, then it could not be said that he was deriving benefit through a breach of the law. For this reason Bacon 'carved it in the declaration as that this was not gift to your lordship, but rather a purchase and exchange (as indeed it was) for Sherborne', and Buckingham himself wrote to the commissioners who were dealing with the matter, making the position plain: 'It pleased His Majesty to bestow upon me the manor of Sherborne, and afterwards, upon my dislike thereof, to condescend to an exchange of it for other lands . . . . My desire is that by this exchange the King have no disadvantage nor I any benefit . . . for I desire not to gain but by His Majesty's free gift.'[7]

The King's infatuation with his new favourite was shown by the nickname he gave him of 'Steenie' – a diminutive of Stephen – because, as the Bible records, all those who looked on St Stephen saw 'his face as it had been the face of an angel'. It seemed hardly possible that such intensity of emotion could endure, and no sooner did another good-looking young man make his appearance at Court than rumour ran riot. In early December 1616 it was reported that Buckingham 'doth much decline in the King's favour', and there were said to be at least two rivals to him for the King's affections. Chamberlain duly informed Sir Dudley Carleton of 'a *sourd bruit* as if the blazing star at Court were toward an eclipse' and added that Buckingham was unwell. If this was the case there may have been something in these rumours, for it was to become apparent later on that Buckingham was highly strung and liable to physical collapse at moments of great tension. He had been unwell in the spring, perhaps as a consequence of the death of his friend and promoter, Sir John Graham, and his critics were already commenting on the possible connexion between these bouts of illness and the periodic attacks of insanity which afflicted his elder brother, John Villiers.[8]

If the King's affections did waver it was only for an instant. In September 1616 he appointed Villiers Lord Lieutenant of Buckinghamshire, and some months later, according to one observer, he sent him, as a New Year's gift, a miniature of himself with his heart in his hand. This symbolic declaration of love was swiftly followed by something more substantial, for on 6 January 1617 the same observer recorded that the Court held 'a day of oblation and sacrifice [on which] the Viscount Villiers was adored, with the title of Earl of Buckingham'. The ceremony of creation took place in the royal palace at Whitehall, where the King was seated in state with the Queen and Prince Charles at his side. It was soon over, but as the new Earl left the presence chamber he can hardly have failed to reflect that a mere twenty months had elapsed since he had taken his first major step along the road to advancement when he received the accolade of knighthood. With so auspicious a beginning, what limits could there be to his hopes and ambitions?[9]

On 4 February 1617, one month after his creation as Earl, Buckingham 'was by His Majesty's special commandment sworn one of His Highness's Privy Council, sat at the Board, and signed letters as a Councillor'. In theory the Privy Council was the ruling body of early Stuart England and by attending meetings Buckingham would gain an insight into the functioning of government. This was no doubt James's intention, for, as he said himself, 'I daily take care to better your understanding, to enable you the more for my service in wordly affairs' – and in James, as Bacon noted, Buckingham had 'the best tutor in Europe'. In practice, however, Buckingham was not a frequent attender at Council meetings, for his place was by the King's side, and James was always on the move. This was not a serious handicap, for James kept policy-making largely in his own hands and received regular reports both from his ministers at home and his ambassadors abroad. As Buckingham established himself at Court he became the filter through which such reports were passed to the King, and he was also used by James to carry messages to foreign ambassadors resident in England – it was during the course of 1617, for instance, that Buckingham became friendly with the Spanish envoy, Count Gondomar. A great deal of Buckingham's time was spent in hunting, feasting and gambling, but the Court was a political as well as a social and ceremonial institution, and the royal favourite – particularly when, like Buckingham, he was alert and intelligent – would swiftly become intimate with the details as well as the broad scope of English policy. This is the significance of Wotton's observation that James 'hardened and polished' Buckingham in 'the school of observance (for so a Court is) and in the furnace of trial about himself (for he was a King could peruse men as well as books)'.[10]

II

Although the King was Buckingham's chief tutor, he was not the only one. Buckingham realised that, as a young man unversed in politics or statecraft, he needed advice, and he turned to Francis Bacon, who at this time was Attorney-General. Bacon, now in his middle fifties, had been involved in politics, as a member of Parliament and minister, for the greater part of his adult life. He was intensely ambitious and had hoped that with his family connexions and intellectual powers he would swiftly rise to high office. But his hopes had been dashed, partly – or so at least he believed – through the jealousy of Robert Cecil, Earl of Salisbury. Yet even after Salisbury's death, and despite the fact that he attached himself to Somerset and became his 'creature and most intimate friend', Bacon was still denied high office of the sort that he held to be commensurate with his talents.[11]

When a new star appeared in the political firmament, Bacon quickly hitched himself to it. Soon he and Buckingham were exchanging frequent letters, and Bacon, with the King's encouragement, acted as the favourite's mentor. He wrote him, at a later stage, a long letter of advice on how he should conduct himself. This was presumably in response to Buckingham's expressed desire to be of real use to the King and not simply a plaything. Bacon commended this ambition, 'for favour so bottomed is like to be lasting, whereas if it be built but upon the sandy foundation of personal respects only, it cannot be long-lived'. He went on to instruct Buckingham on how to deal with suitors and their petitions, how to conduct negotiations, and how to carry himself at Court. A great deal of this was, inevitably, couched in general terms, but it was designed as a theoretical background to the detailed advice on particular matters which Bacon was always willing – indeed anxious – to proffer.[12]

Bacon's motives were not, of course, entirely altruistic. No doubt he enjoyed offering the fruit of his long experience to a young aspirant to fame, especially one as attractive as Buckingham – for Bacon, like James, was susceptible to masculine charm and beauty. But he was also aware of the fact that by serving Buckingham he would ingratiate himself with the King, and by this means he might be able, at long last, to fulfil his high ambitions. Already in February 1616, when Lord Chancellor Ellesmere was said to be dying, Bacon had pressed his claim to succeed him; and when Ellesmere unexpectedly recovered he renewed his suit to Buckingham to be made a Privy Councillor, 'not for my own strength . . . but for the strength of my service'. He left the timing to Buckingham, declaring that 'now I have no greater ambition than this, that as the King showeth himself to you the best master, so I might be found your best servant'.[13]

In June 1616 Bacon was duly appointed to the Privy Council, having been offered either this or the reversion of the Lord Chancellorship upon Ellesmere's death. He was swift to express his thanks. 'Sir,' he wrote to Buckingham, 'the King giveth me a noble choice, and you are the man my heart ever told me you were.' Bacon must have appreciated almost as much as the recipient himself the honours that were heaped on Buckingham, for as the favourite became more influential he could more effectively promote the interests of those who, like Bacon, had vowed themselves to his service. Bacon never let slip an opportunity to remind the favourite of the way in which he should exercise his increasing power. In August 1616, for instance, when he sent Buckingham his patent of creation as baron and viscount, he gave him a piece of general advice which clearly had a particular application. It was that Buckingham should 'countenance and encourage and advance able men and virtuous men and meriting men in all kinds, degrees and professions. For in the time of the Cecils, the father and the son, able men were by design and of purpose suppressed.'[14]

The great prize for which Bacon was aiming was the Lord Chancellorship. Birth, as well as talent, had given him a claim to this, for his father, Sir Nicholas Bacon, had held the office, though with the lesser title of Lord Keeper of the Great Seal. But Bacon's ambition went beyond the mere holding of office. Just as he urged, in the sphere of philosophy, the reorientation of human knowledge, so, in matters of state, he advocated the sweeping away of all obstacles which impeded the efficient functioning of royal government. Bacon's reverence for monarchical rule went far beyond sycophancy. Brought up in what many people were coming to regard as the golden days of Queen Elizabeth, Bacon saw the crown as the only institution strong enough to break down the barriers erected by localism, sectional loyalties, private interests, corruption and lethargy. He was not an advocate of tyranny but of efficiency. Representative institutions, for instance, had their due place in the scheme of government as he envisaged it, but their role was essentially informative; if they encroached on the field of policymaking they would hinder the working of government rather than facilitate it.

Bacon applied the same logic to the common law, which, he insisted, must serve the King at the same time as it safeguarded the subject's rights, since essentially there was no conflict of interests between the two. The judges, as guardians of the law, must be lions, 'but yet lions under the throne, being circumspect that they do not check or oppose any points of sovereignty'. Such a view brought Bacon into conflict with the Lord Chief Justice, Sir Edward Coke, who had so great a veneration for the common law that he seemed to regard it as an autonomous system of arbitration between King and people, with the judges as independent umpires. Bacon, who was himself a common lawyer of distinction, admired Coke's learning but had little respect for his judgement when it came to constitutional matters. Nor had the King, and James's patience, strained to breaking-point by repeated clashes with his Chief Justice, finally gave way in November 1616, when he removed Coke from the judicial bench. Bacon was now in the ascendent, and in March 1617 he was appointed Lord Keeper. Buckingham had been sent by the King to collect the Great Seal from Ellesmere – who was now really dying – and Bacon had no doubt about the favourite's part in securing his promotion. 'In this day's work,' he told him, 'you are the truest and perfectest mirror and example of firm and generous friendship that ever was in Court. And I shall count every day lost wherein I shall not either study your well doing in thought, or do your name honour in speech, or perform your service in deed.'[15]

Bacon was useful to Buckingham in a number of ways, apart from giving him advice. As Attorney-General he was involved in the transactions concerning the land-grant in lieu of Sherborne, and Cranfield told the favourite that Bacon was taking his time over this in order to ensure that the estates should be of the highest quality. Bacon also managed to persuade the Lord Treasurer to agree to value Sherborne at £32,000 rather than the accepted figure of £26,000, thereby increasing the amount of property that the favourite could take in its place.[16] There was another transaction, also involving a former possession of the Earl of Somerset, in which Bacon smoothed Buckingham's path. Somerset had held reversionary rights to the office of Protonothary or Chief Clerk for the enrolment of pleas in the Court of King's Bench, which was reckoned to be worth some £4,000 a year. With his conviction this interest passed to the King, who determined to give it to Buckingham. But certain difficulties had first to be overcome. For one thing there were doubts about the King's legal right to dispose of the reversion of an office which came within the purview of the Lord Chief Justice. And, for another, the Chief Clerkship was in the actual possession of Sir John Roper, who was determined to hold on to it. Buckingham wanted the office itself, not simply the reversion, and he eventually persuaded Roper to agree to surrender it in return for a peerage. But the King – who was, as usual, short of money, and urgently needed £10,000 to finance a mission to France – gratefully accepted this amount from Roper, and made him a baron by way of thanks. Roper now felt he had done all that was required and need not sacrifice himself further by abandoning the lucrative Chief Clerkship.

By this time Bacon was already acting on Buckingham's behalf. Early in 1616 he had ascertained from Sir Edward Coke that the judges would raise no objection to the transfer of the reversionary rights, and now he brought pressure to bear on Roper. The outcome was a compromise, in which the office was formally transferred to two nominees who were to hold it on Buckingham's behalf but pay the profits to Roper as long as he lived. There was some difficulty over the choice of nominees, since Roper had already picked James Whitelocke, a well-known lawyer and future judge. Whitelocke was not in good odour at Court at this time, being thought to stand too near Coke in his attitude towards the prerogative, and in any case Buckingham wanted the place for Robert Shute, whom Whitelocke described, not unjustly, as a 'hangby and pettifogger' of the Villiers family. Bacon tried to persuade Whitelocke to withdraw, and, when he refused to do so, called for the surrender of both his patent and that of Robert Heath, the other nominee. All this was taking place in November 1616, and therefore coincided with, though it was not responsible for, the dismissal of Coke from the judicial bench. The new Chief Justice, Sir Henry Montagu, was far more amenable than his predecessor, and since he was still nominally responsible for making the appointment he agreed that Shute should replace Whitelocke. Montagu was rewarded for his cooperation by being granted £500 a year out of the profits of the office. He had good reason, therefore, to be happy with the transaction, as did Bacon, who had demonstrated not only his willingness but his ability to serve the favourite. Roper was presumably content to have the profits of the office and a peerage into the bargain. Only Whitelocke had cause to complain, but he took comfort in the reflection that Heath and Shute would be 'but bankers or cashmen at the Earl of Buckingham's command, and I am a freeman and hope so to continue'. Whitelocke's comments clearly have the flavour of sour grapes, but his summary of the situation was accurate enough. As the formal contract makes clear, the nominees were, after Roper's death, to 'dispose of the profits of the said office . . . in such sort as the said Earl of Buckingham should declare and appoint'. Buckingham did not have long to wait for the useful addition of some £4,000 to his yearly income, for in October 1618 it was reported that 'by the death of the Lord Roper the Marquis Buckingham is come to the possession of that great and wealthy office of Prothonotary or Chief Clerk in the Court of King's Bench'.[17]

The use of the title 'Marquis' was no slip of the pen, for Buckingham had less than a year in which to enjoy his earldom before being once more elevated in status. The marquisate was conferred after the King had returned from a state visit to Scotland — the only time he re-visited the land of his birth. Buckingham, who accompanied James, conducted himself 'with singular sweetness and temper' and made a number of good friends among the Scottish lords. In May the King appointed him to the Scottish Privy Council — a rare honour for an Englishman — and in July, when the King rode in state to open the Scottish Parliament, Buckingham was once again the only English peer in the procession. Perhaps it was as a reward for the favourite's conscientious performance of his duties while in Scotland that the King decided, suddenly and secretly, to raise him yet higher in the peerage. Buckingham became a marquis on 1 January 1618. There was no ceremony;

not so much as a trumpet sounded. The patent of creation was read out, and then delivered by the King into the hands of the favourite. The transaction was witnessed by a number of courtiers, including Hamilton, Pembroke, and Arundel, as well as by Bacon, now Lord Keeper of the Great Seal. The news, of course, was swiftly reported. Chamberlain called it 'the greatest novelty' and said the King had bestowed this rare honour upon Buckingham 'for the affection he bare him, more than ever he did to any man, and for the like affection, faith, and modesty that he had found in him'. There was some surprise that the marquisate, like the earldom, was of Buckingham, but Carleton was told by another informant that 'the King would have it so, because he so much affects the name of Buck'. The reference, of course, is to the hunting field, where Buckingham and his master spent much of their time together, but the sexual implications should not, perhaps, be overlooked.[18]

Buckingham's physical charms, and his capacity to soften the King's ill-humour, were demonstrated a week or so later at the Prince of Wales's Twelfth Night masque. The King became bored with the spectacle, and burst out 'Why don't they dance? What did they make me come here for? Devil take you all! Dance!' Buckingham immediately sprang forward and gave a brilliant display of cutting capers – much in vogue at the time – in which his long, slender legs were displayed to full advantage. This spurred on the other masquers, but in the opinion of the Venetian ambassador 'none came up to the exquisite manner of the Marquis', who 'rendered himself the admiration and delight of everybody'. The King's ill-humour vanished, and he patted Buckingham's face, kissed him and embraced him 'with marks of extraordinary affection'.[19]

The King was never ashamed about giving public expression to his love for his favourite. On the day after his creation as marquis, Buckingham held a great feast in the Cockpit at Whitehall for the King, the Prince and the leading members of the Court. The food was rich and abundant, and the wine plentiful. James was in a warm good humour, and half way through supper rose from his place, took the Prince by the hand, and walking to the table where the other guests were seated, publicly toasted Buckingham. 'My lords,' he told them, 'I drink to you all and I know we are all welcome to my George. And he that doth not pledge it with all his heart, I would the Devil had him for my part.' Having delivered himself of this resounding declaration he returned to his seat.[20]

Later that same year, in June 1618, Buckingham again feasted the King and Prince. This time he acted the part of mediator, bringing together James and his son who had been involved in a family quarrel. Buckingham's relations with the Prince had at first been stormy. Charles was a quiet, re-served boy, and lived very much in the shadow of his father, whom he feared as well as loved. He can hardly have been indifferent to the rise of Villiers, for the favourite rapidly became a second son to James and was far more in the King's company than Charles himself. In March 1616 the two young men quarrelled over a ring which had been given to Buckingham, quite possibly by the King. Charles saw this on Buckingham's hand, admired it, and transferred it to one of his own smaller fingers. Next day, when Buckingham asked for it back, the Prince could not find it. Buckingham flew into a passion and poured out the whole story to James, who promptly sent for the Prince and 'used such bitter language to him as forced His Highness to shed tears'. Some months later there was another scene between Charles and Buckingham, this time in the park at Greenwich. The Prince, 'being merrily disposed', turned a tap in a fountain and spurted water into Buckingham's face. The favourite was not amused, and the King, seeing this, was so angry that he boxed Charles's ears.[21]

Such incidents were not necessarily of profound importance. Charles, who was born in 1600, was young for his age, and the gap between a sixteen-year-old and a young man of twenty-four is a big one, even when there is not the additional complication of an uncertain triangular relationship. But observers were quick to comment upon Buckingham's lack of judgement in making an enemy of a boy who, if death chose to remove his father from the scene, would at once become King. And when there were signs that the bond between father and son was strengthening, the implications of this were noted with interest. In late 1617, for instance, the Prince was on holiday with his father in the country, and a foreign observer, commenting on the way in which Charles was steadily rising in James's favour and affections, added that this was 'a danger for some other great person'.[22]

As the Prince grew older, however, he and Buckingham became good friends. Charles accepted Buckingham as a member of the royal family, and found in him not only the company he had hitherto lacked but also a replacement for his lost elder brother. It was to Buckingham, therefore, that the Prince turned, in the summer of 1618, with a request to restore relations between him and his father. He addressed him affectionately as 'Steenie', assured him that 'there is none that knows me so well as yourself ', and signed himself 'your true, constant, loving friend'. Buckingham's response was equally forthright, and the great feast which he made for the King in June 1618 was highly successful in its purpose of bringing together father and son. The Prince was so pleased that he christened the occasion 'the friends' feast'. As for James, he was in excellent spirits, and drank to the members of the Villiers family who were present, publicly declaring that he desired to advance them above all others. 'I live to that end', he added, in case there should be any doubt about his sincerity, and he promised them that his heirs and successors would be instructed to elevate the house of Villiers above all other houses whatsoever.[23]

The King was as good as his word, for in 1619 Buckingham's elder brother, John, was raised to the peerage as Viscount Purbeck, and four years later his younger brother, Christopher, was made Earl of Anglesey. His mother was also honoured, in 1618, by being created Countess of Buckingham in her own right. The royal bounty did not fall only on Buckingham's immediate kindred. Half-brothers and sisters, cousins, aunts, and connexions by marriage could all count upon some mark of favour – a title perhaps, or an office or pension. The initiative in many cases came from the King, but Buckingham never felt guilty about advancing his relatives. His attitude was that since a man owed so much to his family he was bound to reward its members if ever the opportunity came his way. It would have been dishonourable not to do so. It would also have been foolish, since a wide circle of kindred, tied together with bonds of obligation as well as blood, could be a source of strength and comfort in times of uncertainty. Elizabeth's chief minister, the great Lord Burghley, had recognised this when he advised his son to 'let thy kindred and allies be welcome to thy table, grace them with thy countenance, and ever further them in all honest actions', for by so doing he would 'double the bond of nature'. The same sentiment was expressed, at a less exalted level, by John Chamberlain in 1617, when he commended Buckingham's 'good disposition in doing good to his kindred and friends'.[24]

III

The first serious challenge to Buckingham's hold on royal favour came early in 1618, when a new contender emerged. He was William Monson, son of an Elizabethan seadog who had subsequently become a client of the Howards. It is the Howard link that explains young Monson's significance. He was not simply a good-looking boy on the make, but the tool of the pro-Spanish Howard faction, in much the same way that Buckingham had been the instrument of the 'protestant interest'. There was one important difference, however. Buckingham had been pushed forward for political reasons, but the Howards' main concern was to preserve their dominant position at Court and in the administration. They had no quarrel with Buckingham on grounds of policy, for his rise to favour had not caused James to swerve from the path of friendship with Spain. What the Howards feared was that the rapid growth of Buckingham's influence and the continual extension of his patronage network would all too soon leave them isolated and exposed. They planned, therefore, to remove him from the scene before he became too powerful, and they pinned their hopes on William Monson. They 'took great pains in tricking and prancking him up, besides washing his face every day with posset-curd', and they urged their protégé to seize every opportunity to catch the King's eye. Monson was so assiduous that he became something of a laughing-stock, but by that time James had realised what was happening, and he ordered Monson to absent himself from Court. This was not, however, the end of the matter. In late March 1618 one of Carleton's correspondents informed him that 'at Court, the faction among the greatest increaseth strangely' and was likely to burst into 'an infinite flame . . . . There is hope conceived that His Majesty will connive at the return of young Monson, by the mediation of his greatest friends.' And as late as May another observer commented that the 'hopes of a new favourite are still alive, while the strife between factions is as strong as ever'.[25]

Buckingham was not by nature vindictive, nor did he ever try to monopolise influence. He recognised the existence of power groups other than his own, and was fully prepared to come to terms with them, but only on condition that they accepted the principle of co-existence. The Howards, however, were not interested in co-existence. They were determined to destroy Buckingham and he therefore had no choice but to defend himself by striking back. If he was to be successful he would need all the strength he could muster, and it was fortunate for Buckingham that during the course of 1617 he had drawn closer to Hamilton and Pembroke, two of the major figures at Court. In August 1617 Hamilton was appointed to the English Privy Council 'by my Lord of Buckingham's means'. A few months later Benjamin Rudyerd, a client of Pembroke, referred to 'the strict correspondence [that] is now between him [Pembroke] and my Lord of Buckingham'. This 'correspondence' was put to the test early in 1618, when a general shuffle of minor administrative posts took place as a result of Secretary Winwood's death and his replacement by Sir Robert Naunton, a dependant of Buckingham. Naunton's post of Surveyor of the Court of Wards had been offered to Sir Humphrey May, but Pembroke wanted it for Rudyerd, and proposed that May should be given the Chancellorship of the Duchy of Lancaster instead. Buckingham, however, had already promised to procure the Chancellorship of the Duchy for another of his dependants, Lionel Cranfield. His honour was at stake, for as Cranfield reminded him, he had been 'pleased with a noble freeness to engage your honourable word, upon which I do wholly rely'. So also was his reputation, for patrons were judged by their success in obtaining offices for their clients, and failure to do so would diminish the number and significance of their following.[26]

The first essential, however, was self-preservation, and for this Buckingham needed allies. He therefore abandoned his advocacy of Cranfield's claim to the Chancellorship of the Duchy and eventually, in March 1618, agreed to May's appointment – though only, as he made plain, 'for my Lord Hamilton's and the Lord Chamberlain's sake'. At about the same time he drew his bonds with the Herberts still closer by consenting to act as godfather to the child of Pembroke's brother, the Earl of Montgomery. This new alliance – or rather the revival of the old alliance which had first brought Buckingham into favour – showed its strength in a light-hearted manner in April, when the Court divided over which of two footmen to back in a race from St Albans to London. One of the footmen, Ralph, had come to Buckingham's service from the household of Lady Bedford, Pembroke's cousin and a close friend of Hamilton. Buckingham backed him to the tune of £1,000 and Pembroke and Montgomery also ventured 'great sums'. 'All the Howards', as one observer noted, 'laid on the other'. Significantly enough, Ralph won.[27]

Buckingham was now strong enough to counterattack the Howards, and the King was soon made aware of rumours that Suffolk, or at any rate his wife, was demanding 'rewards' for all payments made out of the Treasury.

There was no doubt that Suffolk had acquired a great fortune through serving the Crown – the vast palace which he built at Audley End still bears witness to this. There is also no doubt that his lack of scruple in the matter of perquisites and 'rewards' was widely shared. Yet it was only when political and factional considerations made his removal necessary that the charge of corruption was laid against him; moral indignation was in this case, as in so many others, the language of political conspiracy. But whatever the motives, the charges were valid enough, and in July 1618 the King dismissed Suffolk from his post as Lord Treasurer. Sir Thomas Lake, an associate of the Howards, was also in danger, since, in the words of the Florentine resident, 'no security can be found for the Secretary's continued loyalty sufficient for the Marquis, who has refused the offer of 60,000 crowns'. Another Howard casualty was Suffolk's son-in-law, William, Lord Knollys, who had recently been created Viscount Wallingford; he was forced to give up his lucrative office of Master of the Wards in December 1618.[28]

With the fall of the Howards the bitter faction struggle at Court died down, at least for a time. There was now no predominant faction. James had apparently learnt the lesson that Bacon was later to put into words. 'When factions are carried too high and too violently it is a sign of weakness in princes and much to the prejudice both of their authority and business. The motions of factions under kings ought to be like . . . inferior orbs, which may have their proper motions, but yet still are quietly carried by the higher motion of *primum mobile*.' The King continued to make policy, as he had done all along, but now he relied increasingly on his favourite for assistance, and Lord Fenton recorded in August 1618 that 'I think he imparts to nobody but to [the] Marquis of Buckingham'. The favourite had been acting as James's secretary since at least October 1617, when Winwood died, and it was noted at the time that he was playing much the same role as that previously filled by Somerset. There was this difference, however. Somerset, although he enjoyed the exercise of power, lacked energy and consistency when it came to pursuing his objectives. This was not the case with Buckingham. He kept in close touch with a wide range of people, and never relaxed his grasp. One example among many which illustrates this is a letter written to him in December 1618 by Sir John Ogle, one of the English officers serving with the Dutch. 'I understand', Ogle wrote, '(and am grieved at it) that you are offended with me, for that I have neither followed your counsel nor answered your letter.' He offered profuse apologies and begged Buckingham 'to discharge me of all burdens of dislike and displeasure, and both hold me up in His Majesty's good opinion and your own'.[29]

Buckingham had one major advantage, denied his predecessor, in that much of the routine work of administration was carried out by the two Secretaries of State, Sir Thomas Lake and Sir Robert Naunton. Lake had survived the fall of the Howards by loudly proclaiming his loyalty to the favourite, but he was not in Buckingham's confidence. Naunton, on the other hand, was one of Buckingham's men. His bid for the vacant Secretaryship had been supported by the anti-Spanish faction, which wanted another 'protestant' to replace the dead Winwood, and he was said to have ensured Buckingham's approval by making Christopher Villiers heir to estates worth some £500 a year. Financial transactions of this sort were not uncommon at a time when offices were regarded as pieces of property, to be bought and sold, but while Buckingham welcomed the proposed arrangement it was not his principal motive in pressing for Naunton's appointment. He had, if rumour spoke true, turned down much larger offers, including one of £10,000 from Holles. What he saw in Naunton was a man who would, in the words of one of his correspondents, 'be so free from other dependency as that you may reasonably presume to have him absolutely and immediately enough your own'.[30]

Buckingham's official – or, rather, quasi-official – duties remained much as they had been before Naunton's appointment. He exchanged letters and visits with foreign ambassadors. He kept in touch with English representatives abroad and did his best to make sure that their salaries were paid. He also acted, in the words of John Hoskins – a member of the Addled Parliament who had been imprisoned for his outspokenness – as a 'sweet conduit of the King's mercy'. Amongst those who appealed to him to soften James's anger was Sir Walter Raleigh, awaiting execution in the Tower in the autumn of 1618. Raleigh, who described Buckingham as 'remarkable in the world for the nobleness of your disposition', begged him to 'vouchsafe to become my intercessor', and made the significant promise that if he did so he would 'bind an hundred gentlemen of my kindred to honour your memory'. The Queen also wrote to him on Raleigh's behalf, and the tone of the letter, which begins 'My kind dog', shows that Buckingham, unlike Somerset, went out of his way to maintain the Queen's goodwill. In this particular instance, however, there was little that Buckingham could do. The King had made up his mind that Raleigh should die, and although James, as Fenton perceptively remarked, 'will in any indifferent matter yield to his affections, yet . . . in matters of that weight he trusts to himself and to nobody else'.[31]

IV

As Buckingham's favour increased so did the range of his patronage. His relatives were among the first to obtain office through his influence. In 1616 his brother John was made Groom of the Bedchamber and Master of the Robes to the Prince, while in 1617 his other brother, Christopher, was appointed to similar positions in the King's household. Buckingham's half-brother, Edward Villiers, who was knighted in 1616, became Master of the Mint in the following year and Comptroller of the Wards twelve months later. Through marriage connexions the 'kindred' expanded enormously. Sir Edward Villiers married Barbara, niece of Sir Oliver St John, who was given the major office of Lord Deputy of Ireland in April 1616 through the favourite's intercession. In the following February St John wrote to Buckingham thanking him for securing the reversion of the Chancellorship of the Irish Exchequer for his son-in-law; and so the net spread.[32] Those ambitious for advancement who did not have the advantage of a Villiers connexion often hastened to secure one. Sir Christopher Perkins, for instance, who in 1617 was well over seventy and could not afford to wait much longer for promotion, married Buckingham's aunt, and thereby made sure of being appointed Master of Requests. Another Mastership of Requests went to Ralph Freeman, who had married a member of the Countess of Buckingham's household, while the Lieutenancy of the Tower of London was conferred upon Sir Allen Apsley, whose third wife was another of the nieces of Sir Oliver St John. It soon became common knowledge that, just as the favourite had young cousins ready to be married off to rich heirs, so also 'he might have some old aunts for old men', and while entry into the kindred was not necessarily a passport to office and riches, it seldom acted as a hindrance.[33]

There was considerable comment, much of it unfavourable, about the rapid expansion of the patronage empire which Buckingham created; though criticism was directed not so much at the system itself as at the ruthless and cynical manner in which aspirants to office were encouraged to link their destinies (and their fortunes, if any) to the Villiers clan. Yet the system was perhaps not as pernicious as it seems. For one thing, there was no reason to suppose that Buckingham's relations and clients were *ipso facto* less qualified than other candidates for office. And, for another, the absence of any system of competitive examination meant that patronage and money always played a major part in appointments. In any case, the King had publicly declared his determination to raise not simply the favourite but his entire family, and just as Buckingham acted as a conduit along which royal favour flowed to his relatives, so, in the other direction, he transmitted to the King the assurance of loyal service and devotion from those who were connected to him.

Buckingham never confined his patronage to members of his kindred. His range of activity was too great for that, and his decision on whether to use or withhold his influence depended upon a wide spectrum of considerations of which family connexion was only one. Where nobles were concerned he had to weigh the advantages of their friendship against the danger of their enmity. When it was a question of appointing officers of state he had to take into account their suitability for the position. With lesser men the main consideration was whether or not they would serve him faithfully and be committed to him alone. Sir Humphrey May, for example, had incurred Buckingham's anger at the time of the negotiations over the Chancellorship of the Duchy by applying simultaneously both to him and Pembroke. Buckingham regarded this as double-dealing and withheld his consent to May's appointment until Sir Humphrey had confessed that the loss of his favour had been 'matter of extreme grief and discontentment' and had assured him that 'nothing could be more pleasing unto me than the recovery thereof '.[34] Buckingham's insistence that his clients should be totally and exclusively devoted to him was not a sign of neurosis, nor did it derive simply from vanity. The great figures of Jacobean England were all poised, more or less uneasily, on pyramids of patronage. The higher the pyramid the more important the patron, but the base and sides had to be soundly constructed. Any movement among the lower layers could bring the whole edifice tumbling down.

Patronage became, when it reached a certain degree of magnitude, an end in itself. Sir Henry Wotton once observed, with respect to the bounty of princes, that 'albeit at first they give only upon choice and love of the person, yet within a while themselves likewise begin to love their givings and to foment their deeds'. The same could have been said of great patrons: the act of retaining men to their service became the objective rather than the means, and this is why it is so often difficult to perceive any pattern or meaning in the operation of patronage. Buckingham, it was noted in 1618, 'doth use his favour very much to oblige men to him', and this included all levels of the political nation. He was instrumental in procuring the Lord Treasurership of Scotland for the Earl of Mar, and he was approached by no less a person than the Queen herself when she wished to obtain a wardship for one of her followers. But he also took an interest in those who were much further down the social scale. He procured an appointment as English agent in France for Sir William Beecher, and he assured Sir William Trumbull, the English ambassador in Brussels, 'that he would spend his blood in my service . . . that he were an ungrateful man if he employed not himself to the uttermost of his power for my good'. He cultivated relations with members of Parliament, even when, like John Hoskins, they had been imprisoned for making remarks that James held to be derogatory. Hoskins, who was released through Buckingham's mediation, declared that 'this merit of his becomes as visible to the world as if it had been conferred upon a more eminent man; nay more, and is of greater account . . . more conspicuous and beneficial than a torch upon the top of Paul's'. Sir Dudley Digges, who had also suffered a brief spell of imprisonment for his speeches in the Lower House, thought it worth while to write to Buckingham from Archangel, asking him to 'continue your noble favour in doing me good offices'; while Sir Edward Montagu, who had offended the King earlier in the reign by championing the puritan cause in the county of Northampton which he represented in Parliament, 'received so many favours [from Buckingham] that I bestowed a fine horse on him; which he took very kindly; and I think him very well bestowed'.[35]

Buckingham's influence extended into the judicial as well as the administrative sphere — though the two were not then as separate as they are today. Bacon's promotion to the Lord Keepership led to a general post of legal offices. The new Attorney-General was Sir Henry Yelverton, who had formerly been Solicitor-General. His place was taken by Sir Thomas Coventry, the Recorder of London, who was in turn replaced by Anthony Ben. Buckingham was said to have been responsible for the appointment of both Coventry and Ben, and according to one source the two men had to pay the favourite for their advancement. In Yelverton's case no money was involved – though after the appointment was confirmed Yelverton made the King a gift of £4,000. Buckingham's candidate for the office of Attorney-General had been Sir James Ley, who offered £10,000 for it. But the King had already made known his wish that Yelverton should be promoted, and all Buckingham could do was to delay the final outcome. This led to a quarrel between him and some of Yelverton's patrons – particularly the Scottish Duke of Lenox, one of James's oldest friends and counsellors, with whom he exchanged hot words. The deadlock was eventually broken by Buckingham himself. He sent for Yelverton, whom he treated with great courtesy, explaining that he would not have stood in his way if only Yelverton had approached him in the first instance. By neglecting to do so, he added, Yelverton was causing people to believe that his favour was waning 'and he not thought to be of that power he had been'. Despite these friendly advances Yelverton still refused to hand over his warrant of appointment for Buckingham to present to the King, on the grounds that this was not the usual practice. Buckingham insisted, however, and pointed out that the position of Attorney-General was of considerable importance and 'that the greatest men in the realm might have hurt or good by it'. Yelverton, apparently impressed by this argument, thereupon agreed to receive his warrant through the favourite's intercession, and departed on good terms with him. The whole incident is very revealing, for it shows Buckingham's concern that men in key posts should be well disposed towards him, if not actually his dependants. Where all other things were equal, financial considerations might well be decisive; but security came first.[36]

Although Buckingham spent the greater part of his life at Court, this did not mean that his influence was confined to the area around London. The Court itself was rarely stationary, for the King loved to switch from one residence to another, particularly in the summer months, when he went on progress through the southern counties. Most courtiers had estates of their own, which linked them to local communities, and in any case the range of the royal authority was so extensive that a man's standing in his own shire often depended upon evidence of the King's goodwill. As the disposer of that goodwill, Buckingham was brought into direct contact with the localities. When a Welsh country gentleman, Sir John Wynn of Gwydir, heard that his enemies were trying to get the better of him by insinuating one of their connexions into Buckingham's service, he immediately used all the influence he could bring to bear to win the favourite to his side. In much the same way Buckingham was dragged into the quarrel between Sir Thomas Wentworth and Sir John Savile over who should hold the post of Custos Rotulorum in the county of Yorkshire. Both sides plied him with letters, and Wentworth reminded him that 'I fully rely upon your lordship's indifferent favour in a matter of this nature that so deeply concerns my credit in the country where I live'.[37]

From early on in his career Buckingham linked himself with a number of important landed families. The Manners of Belvoir in Leicestershire were one of these, and the Montagus of Boughton, Northamptonshire, another. In both these cases Buckingham's preference was probably guided by the fact that they had been neighbours or friends of the Villiers, but there seems no obvious reason for his cultivation of the Cecils of Hatfield – unless, as rumour had it, he was in love with the Countess of Salisbury. Her husband, the second Earl, was almost an exact contemporary of Buckingham, and the favourite was obviously on good terms with him as early as 1617, when he encouraged him to apply for the post of Captain of the Guard. The King was just about to leave for Scotland, and Buckingham persuaded him to invite Salisbury to join the train of courtiers who were to accompany him. But Salisbury, whose wife was pregnant, preferred the comforts of Hatfield to the rigours of a northern journey, and decided to stay behind. The Captaincy of the Guard, in consequence, went to the Queen's candidate, the handsome Sir Henry Rich. Salisbury apparently blamed Buckingham for this outcome, though the fault was clearly his own. Relations between the two men were cool for some years, but meanwhile Buckingham's links with the Cecils were drawn tighter, though in a different direction, through the marriage of his elder brother, John. Buckingham had a great affection for this brother, and had arranged for his own honours to be entailed upon John and his issue. Buckingham apparently assumed, at this stage, that his position as the King's favourite ruled out any prospect of marriage, but the desire to see his name and titles passed down in perpetuity made him all the more determined to find a suitable bride for his brother. One possibility was Frances Coke, the younger daughter of Sir Edward Coke by his second wife, Elizabeth Cecil, the widow of Sir William Hatton. Frances was a beautiful and attractive girl, not yet fifteen, while her prospective husband was more than ten years older, but her inclinations were not taken into account. The decision rested with Sir Edward, who hoped that an alliance with the Villiers family might open the way to his restoration to favour, following his dismissal from the judicial bench at the end of 1616. In February 1617, therefore, Coke gave his formal consent to the marriage.[38]

Unfortunately for Coke's hopes he could not secure the agreement of his wife. Lady Hatton, as she was always known, was a high-spirited and hot-tempered woman whose relations with her husband were stormy. She was, at this very moment, engaged in a bitter dispute with him about the ownership of some property, and the mere fact that he was in favour of the marriage made her determined to resist it. Her resistance could not simply be brushed aside, for she had inherited from her first husband the considerable estates of Elizabeth's favourite, Sir Christopher Hatton. This property would go to Frances, and without it the match would be, from a financial point of view, far less desirable. Sir Edward, who was not a man to be trifled with, declared that the marriage would go ahead despite his wife's objections, but Lady Hatton spirited Frances away to her cousin's house at Oatlands, near Hampton Court, and announced that the girl could not possibly marry Sir John Villiers since she was already engaged to somebody else. Coke, now in his sixties but with all the fire of a much younger man, refused to listen to such specious pleading. He obtained a search warrant from Secretary Winwood, rode post-haste to Oatlands with a posse of retainers, and ordered his wife to hand over Frances. When she refused, he battered down the door and carried off his daughter by force.

Even former Lord Chief Justices were not allowed to practise forcible entry without being called to account, and when Lady Hatton appealed for justice to the Privy Council its members were at first inclined to uphold her. There was talk of bringing a Star Chamber action against Coke, and Winwood was criticised for issuing a warrant in the first place – unlike Bacon, who had declined to do so. But Winwood had a trump card in the form of a letter from the King authorising him to support Sir Edward, and when he played it the Councillors changed their tune. They seem to have been unaware that Buckingham and the King were not only strongly in favour of the match but had also been kept in touch with events by Coke and Winwood during their return journey from Scotland. In fact, when the King heard of the Council's initial reaction, he was furious and determined to make an example of the errant members. He was dissuaded from this by Buckingham, but nevertheless the Councillors were summoned to Hampton Court, where James made plain his displeasure at the way in which they had apparently disregarded the interests of one who stood so close to him. He was, he informed them,

a man like other men, who did what other men did, and confessed to loving those he loved . . . . And they should be quite clear that he loved the Earl of Buckingham more than any other man, and more than all those who were here present. They should not think of this as a defect in him, for Jesus Christ had done just what he was doing. There could therefore be nothing reprehensible about it, and just as Christ had his John, so he, James, had his George.[39]

The combination of Coke and Buckingham was too much for Lady Hatton, and as she refused to change her attitude she was confined to the house of a London alderman and told to stay there during the King's pleasure. There was now no obstacle to the marriage, particularly since Frances had been persuaded by Sir Edward to give her formal consent. 'I think it will be a means of the King's favour to my father', she said, and she added that as far as her future husband was concerned he was 'not to be misliked; his fortune is very good; a gentleman well born'. The marriage took place at Hampton Court on Michaelmas Day 1617, and the King himself gave the bride away. Coke was now restored to favour, though not to the judicial bench, and once again took his seat at the Council table.[40]

Lady Hatton was not present at the ceremony since she was still under house arrest. But when she was confronted with the *fait accompli* and realised that further resistance would merely exclude her from the Court circles and the high living which she so much enjoyed, she decided to give in. On the first day of November, Buckingham, with a host of courtiers and members of the Cecil and Villiers families, went to fetch her from her comfortable prison. Within a few days she was received at Court and made her peace with Buckingham's mother, Lady Compton, who may well have proposed the match in the first place and therefore regarded her opposition to it as a personal affront. Buckingham, his mother and his brothers were entertained at Cecil House 'where a great supper was made for reuniting them with the Lady Hatton', and a few days later Lady Hatton herself feasted the Villiers family at her house in Holborn. It was, said Chamberlain, a 'very magnifical' occasion, 'and the King graced her every way, and made four of her creatures knights . . . . But the principal graces and favours lighted on the Lady Compton and her children; whom the King praised and kissed, and blessed all those that wished them well.'[41]

All that remained was for Lady Hatton to endow the newly married couple with some of the property she had inherited from her first husband. This included the Isle of Purbeck in Dorset, and it was understood that as soon as the transaction had been completed, Sir John would be raised to the peerage and given the title of Viscount Purbeck. But Lady Hatton could not bring herself to part with her possessions, and as late as 1619 she was still blowing hot and cold, one day declaring her readiness to endow her son-in-law with lands worth £7,000 a year, and the next announcing that she must have power to revoke her grant if and when she wished. The King eventually lost patience, and in June 1619 bestowed the long-promised viscountcy on Sir John. It is not clear how much, if any, of Lady Hatton's wealth eventually went to her son-in-law, but some years later Buckingham had to entangle his own finances in order to provide for his brother, and at the time of his death he seems to have been Purbeck's chief support.[42]

The Coke-Villiers marriage negotiations cast a cloud over the burgeoning friendship between Buckingham and Bacon. This was not entirely Bacon's fault, for Winwood, who was deeply involved in the business, had little love for the proud Lord Keeper and kept him as much as possible in the dark. Bacon seems to have thought that the initiative in the affair had come from Lady Compton without her son's knowledge, and he therefore wrote to Buckingham, who was with the King in Scotland, to advise him against supporting the match. It would, he pointed out, link John Villiers with a man who had recently been disgraced, and it might well deprive Buckingham himself of 'all such your friends as are adverse to Sir Edward Coke — myself only except, who, out of a pure love and thankfulness shall ever be firm to you'. Bacon, of course, detested Coke, whom he regarded as a dangerous rival, but he also believed, with good reason, that Coke's return to favour would revive 'ruffling humours' and might well obscure the royal prerogative just as it was rising 'some first degrees above the horizon'.[43]

Bacon received no reply to his letter, and therefore wrote again in late July, 1617. This time he did receive a reply, but not one that he welcomed. 'My lord,' wrote Buckingham, 'in this business of my brother's that you overtrouble yourself with, I understand from London by some of my friends that you have carried yourself with much scorn and neglect, both toward myself and friends; which, if it prove true, I blame not you but myself, who was ever your lordship's assured friend.' The tone of this letter was markedly different from the earlier requests for advice and assurances of goodwill, and showed the 'choleric' side of Buckingham's nature. There is something distasteful about the idea of the young favourite rebuking a man who was not simply old enough to be his father, but also one of the principal officers of state. Yet Buckingham had good reason, as he saw it, to be offended. He had given Bacon his full support and he had been instrumental in securing the Lord Keepership for him, yet when it came to a little matter like assisting his brother to make a good marriage, Bacon, despite his vows of devotion, had led the opposition. Buckingham had not heard Bacon's version of events, and no doubt ought to have waited for it before sending such a stinging rebuke. But he had heard from Coke and Winwood, and he was also under pressure from his mother and brother, who spoke of Bacon 'with some bitterness and neglect'. He was also aware that Bacon had a reputation for treachery, having turned against former favourites, such as Essex and Somerset, to whom he had been attached.[44]

In attempting to defend his conduct to the King, Bacon incautiously suggested that 'the height of his [Buckingham's] fortune might make him too secure'. James rejected such a suggestion. 'We know not how to interpret this in plain English otherwise than that you were afraid that the height of his fortune might make him misknow himself.... We find him furthest from that vice of any courtier that ever we had so near about us.' Bacon hastened to assure the King that he had never meant to imply that Buckingham had 'turned proud or unknowing of himself.... My meaning was plain and simple: that his lordship might, through his great fortune, be the less apt to cast and foresee the unfaithfulness of friends and malignity of enviers and accidents of times.'[45]

If this was indeed Bacon's meaning, he had misread the favourite, for Buckingham had an instinctive understanding of the weaknesses as well as the strengths of his own position, and was always on the lookout for indications of unfaithfulness. Political friendships were, as he saw it, a form of contract in which the benefits and obligations were reciprocal. If one party broke the contract, then the friendship was dissolved, and Buckingham was at pains to make clear that those who were not his friends would have to risk his enmity. For this reason he made no attempt to conceal his anger, protesting that 'he would not secretly bite, but whosoever had had any interest or tasted of the opposition to his brother's marriage, he would as openly oppose them to their faces, and they should discern what favour he had by the power he would use'.[46]

Buckingham's anger was rarely long-lasting. It was a form of threat, the reverse side of the coin of favour, and as long as due submission was made and assurances given of future dutiful behaviour, the contract would usually be renewed. This was the case with Bacon. Some time in September 1617 he had an interview with Buckingham at which he was able, at last, to explain the reasons for his actions and to clear away any misunderstandings about his motives. The effect was immediate. 'I do freely confess', wrote Buckingham, 'that your offer of submission unto me, and in writing (if so I would have it), battered . . . the unkindness that I had conceived in my heart for your behaviour towards me in my absence.' It had been, he added, 'no small grief unto me to hear the mouth of so many upon this occasion open to load you with innumerable malicious and detracting speeches . . . which made me rather regret the ill nature of mankind, that, like dogs, love to set upon him that they see once snatched at'. Now, however, the slate could be wiped clean, and Buckingham was happy in the knowledge that Bacon would have 'a fair occasion so to make good hereafter your reputation by your sincere service to His Majesty, as also by your firm and constant kindness to your friends, as I may (your lordship's old friend) participate of the comfort and honour that will thereby come to you'.[47]

Bacon's offer to make a written submission to Buckingham suggests a very unequal relationship, in which the client's role was that of unquestioning obedience. In such matters a great deal depended upon the office and rank of the client in question, but generally speaking Buckingham welcomed advice and even criticism as long as it was inspired by goodwill and not by malice. In his own very revealing phrase, 'I know well the difference between naked obedience and that where affection is joined to it.' This was fully understood by Bacon, who told Buckingham that he would be 'ever ready to further anything your lordship recommendeth; but where the matter will not bear it, your lordship, I know, will not think the worse but the better of me if I signify the true state of things to your lordship'.[48]

One of the most delicate areas in the relationship between Buckingham and Bacon was that which concerned the working of the Court of Chancery, over which the Lord Keeper presided. As Buckingham's influence increased, so did the number of suitors who thronged around him pressing for his assistance in despatching their business. Bacon, in his letter of advice to the favourite, had warned him that 'what time can be well spared from your attendance on your master will be taken up by suitors, whom you cannot avoid nor decline without reproach . . . . There is nothing will bring you more honour and more ease than to do them what right in justice you may, and with as much speed as you may.' A number of these suits concerned cases in Chancery, and following the reconciliation between Bacon and Buckingham, there was a marked increase in the number of letters sent by Buckingham asking for favourable treatment for one or other of his clients. Even so, the total was not large: there were seven such letters in 1617, fourteen in 1618, and a mere nine in the following three years. The wording varies from case to case, but usually includes some such phrase as 'out of my love and respect toward him [the client in question] I have thought fit to recommend him unto your favour so far only as may stand with justice and equity'.[49]

The effect of such letters was obviously to speed up proceedings, and this in itself could be of great benefit to a plaintiff or defendant. They would also prompt Bacon to enquire closely into the case, and even if he did not decide in favour of Buckingham's client, the latter might feel satisfied that he had received equitable treatment. This applied, for instance, to Sir Rowland Cotton, who had judgment given against him but acknowledged the 'noble and patient hearing he did then receive.' In one case, however – that of Dr Steward in December 1618 – Buckingham seems to have gone beyond his usual request for Bacon to come to a speedy decision or do 'what lawful favour you may'. The Lord Keeper had already issued a decree against Steward, but Buckingham, while acknowledging that 'it is unusual to your lordship to make any alterations when things are so far past', asked if there was any possibility of mitigation, 'in regard I owe him a good turn, which I know not how to perform but this way'. So far Buckingham's request seemed reasonable, but in another letter on the following day he used language that sounded more threatening. After describing Steward as 'a man of very good reputation' he added that 'I should be sorry he should make any complaint against you. And therefore if you can advise of any course how you may be eased of that burden and freed from his complaint without show of any fear of him or anything he can say, I will be ready to join with you for the accomplishment thereof.' On the face of it, Buckingham was giving friendly notice to Bacon that Steward was spreading complaints against him, but there was clearly an implied invitation to the Lord Keeper to reopen the case and see if he could arrive at a judgement more favourable to the doctor. This is, in effect, what happened, and it may well be that a miscarriage of justice took place. But it is equally possible that Bacon had been in the wrong and that Buckingham was warning him to cover his position. As events were to show only a few years later, the Lord Keeper had many enemies, and complaints against the equity of his judgements might well be the first signs of a major attempt to unseat him.[50]

In August 1617, when Bacon was struggling to regain Buckingham's favour, he wrote him a letter in which he assured him that he would 'rely upon your constancy and nature, and my own deserving, and the firm tie we have in respect of the King's service'.[51] The reference to the King's service was no mere form of words, for Buckingham, conscious of all that he had received from James, was determined to advance the work of reforming the royal administration. This was one of the reasons why he had given his support to Bacon in the first instance, and although it seemed for a time in 1617 that he had abandoned him in favour of Sir Edward Coke, this was not the case. There was, on the face of it, no reason why Buckingham should not have acted as Coke's patron, perhaps at the same time as he supported Bacon. In view of the widespread (albeit unjustified) fears that the King wished to expand the scope of his prerogative and override the common law, it would have been of great advantage to have a man like Coke closely identified with the royal government. Coke was, in his own way, a reformer. His vast learning, retentive memory, and constant citation of precedents made him appear a reactionary figure – as indeed in some ways he was – but in practice he often used precedents in a creative manner, to bring the law into closer relationship with the needs of a changing society. Coke's view of the role of the common law was visionary rather than historical, and he may well have underestimated the need for stronger and more efficient government. But his emphasis on the rights of the subject made a strong appeal to his contemporaries, and his belief in reformation under the guise of restoration might have been more acceptable to them in the long run.

There is no indication, however, that Buckingham ever understood Coke or penetrated beneath his formidable exterior. He probably assumed that at the age of sixty-five Coke's career was all but over, and despite the marriage link that was supposed to have bound them together the two men regarded each other with mutual suspicion and antagonism. Bacon was ten years younger and much more approachable. He was also full of ideas about ways in which to reform the royal government and only too eager to put them into effect. At this time he was working very closely with Lionel Cranfield, another of the great servants of the early Stuart state whom Buckingham took under his protection. Cranfield, a self-made London merchant, had first been brought to the King's attention by Henry Howard, Earl of Northampton, who had himself been something of a reformer, though not a very effective one. Cranfield, as King James later explained, 'made so many projects for my profit that Buckingham fell in liking with him . . . and brought him to my service . . . I never saw a young courtier that was so careful for the King's profit, without any respect, as Buckingham was. He found this man so studious for my profit that he backed him against great personages and mean, without sparing of any man.'[52]

V

Cranfield must have made Buckingham's acquaintance soon after the young favourite first appeared at Court, for as early as 1615 he was acting as his adviser on financial matters. In October of that year the King granted Buckingham the profits from a tax on the trade of alien merchants, but the grant was made out in the name of Cranfield, who was to account to Buckingham for the proceeds. Cranfield was also a partner in the syndicate which farmed the Irish Customs, and it was presumably at his suggestion that Buckingham made a bid for them. Buckingham apparently intended at first only to buy his way into the syndicate, but in 1618 the farmers were persuaded to surrender their lease, and the King then granted a new one to the favourite. The Irish Customs were eventually to be worth more than £3,500 a year to Buckingham, so he had good reason to be grateful to Cranfield, whom he rewarded with a percentage of the profits. There were many other ways in which Cranfield built up his credit with the favourite. He cooperated with Bacon in the negotiations which secured for Buckingham the Clerkship of King's Bench; he helped choose the royal lands which James granted to the favourite in 1616, doing his best to pick out under-exploited properties which might be 'improvable by fair means, without any strain of power or just clause of clamour and discontent to any of His Majesty's subjects'; and he also advanced Buckingham money to purchase the lease of Whaddon Chase.[53]

At the same time as he was helping Buckingham in these private transactions, Cranfield was also embarking, with the favourite's support, on a reform programme intended to eliminate waste and corruption in government. In January 1618 he informed Buckingham that he and his fellow-commissioners were labouring from morning till evening in 'that great business of the [royal] household wherein it hath pleased your lordship, for His Majesty's service, to engage me'. Such was the commissioners' success in this first operation that they were soon instructed to enquire into other departments as well, and one apprehensive government servant reported in September 1618 that the 'scourging and dreadful commission that hath done such wonders in the Lord Treasurer's office is now in hand with the office of the Ordnance, from which it is said they will post to examine the secrets of the Navy'.[54]

Cranfield's ruthless probing brought him into conflict with powerful vested interests, and his humble background meant that he lacked support in high places. When he was appointed Master of Requests extraordinary in November 1616 one minor official expressed his amazement 'that so base a fellow, who hath no manner of learning nor experience, should be admitted to such a place of justice' and there were many others who shared his opinion. Cranfield was safe as long as he had the King's support, but he knew from the failure of Northampton's reform attempts that the King's interest in such matters would be at best sporadic. Cranfield poured out his fears to Buckingham, who gave him an unequivocal reply: 'I would not have you disquiet yourself, but to refer all to me, who am very careful of you, and as I have been, will be still ready to do you all good offices I can.' This was Buckingham's self-appointed task, to make sure that the reform programme was pressed ahead and to cast his protection over all those who, like Cranfield, were engaged in it. James was speaking no more than the truth when he later declared that 'Buckingham laid the ground and bare the envy. [Cranfield] took the laborious and ministerial part upon him . . . . He was an instrument, under Buckingham, for reformation of the Household, the Navy and the Exchequer, Buckingham setting him on and taking upon himself the envy of all the officers; and he himself many a time protested unto me that he had not been able to do me any service in the ministerial part if Buckingham had not backed him in it.'[55]

The Navy was certainly in need of reform by 1617. Its nominal head was the Lord Admiral, Charles Howard, Earl of Nottingham, but he was now over eighty and no longer exercised effective control. Corruption was rife, large sums of money were either wasted or embezzled, and the few ships that were built proved all too often to be unseaworthy. While Nottingham was merely inefficient, the principal officers of the Navy, who were responsible for day-to-day administration, were actively corrupt. Sir Robert Mansell, the Treasurer, has been described as Nottingham's evil genius, a man 'who stands without a rival in our naval history for malversation in his office'.[56] Sir John Trevor, the Surveyor, was only slightly better, if at all, and the rot had spread down to every level. The Navy was not simply incapable of defending England if the need should arise; it could not even mount an operation against pirates in 1617, despite James's plans to unite his ships with those of Spain to sweep the seas clean.

Bacon, in his letter of advice to Buckingham, recommended to him 'the care of our outwork, the Navy Royal and shipping of the kingdom, which are the walls thereof ', and towards the end of 1617 rumours began to circulate that the favourite was about to be appointed Lord Admiral. It seems likely that Buckingham was actually offered the post by James, but declined it on the grounds of lack of experience. Nevertheless his interest had been aroused, and he became even more involved when, in the summer of 1618, his protégé, Cranfield, began to enquire into the state of the Navy. With Cranfield in charge there was a good chance that the commission of 1618 would be more effective than that of 1608, and in September he wrote to inform Buckingham that 'we spend our time wholly about the Navy, and now take comfort in our work, finding it falls out far beyond our hopes for the service of His Majesty and his kingdoms; and do rest in assurances, by the continuance of your lordship's favour towards us to the King, to effect that work which hath been so often attempted in vain'. He summarised some of the flagrant abuses they had already exposed, and sketched out a plan to repair two ships and build a further two every year. 'I hope your lordship will be pleased to be of my opinion,' he added, 'that God reserved this great work for His Majesty's time, and hath raised your lordship to be the honourable mean and instrument to His Highness in it.'[57]

This was the sort of appeal that Buckingham found irresistible, particularly since he had been searching for an opportunity to prove that he was worthy of the trust the King reposed in him. His lack of experience was not as crippling as it seemed, for most previous Lord Admirals had been courtiers with little sea time to their credit. What an Admiral needed above all was commitment to his work and good men to act as his subordinates. Buckingham had the necessary degree of commitment, and already had ideas about the men he would use. All that now stood in the way of a radical reformation of the Navy was the old Lord Admiral, but it seems to have been Nottingham himself who suggested that he should resign in favour of Buckingham. In October 1618 it was agreed that Nottingham and Buckingham should hold office jointly, with the younger man doing the work while the old sailor enjoyed the honour to which his long service had entitled him. But this arrangement never had time to take effect, for as the commissioners sent in their reports it became clear that the Navy was in a desperate state and that only a new broom could sweep away the accumulated abuses. On 28 January 1619, therefore, King James issued the requisite patent, and from then on until the day of his death Buckingham was Lord Admiral of England.[58]

NOTES

(Abbreviations are explained in the Bibliography, pp. 477–86)

1. *Cam.* II; *Slo.MSS.* 826.1v.
2. *Aylmer.* Table 60.
3. *Devon.* 326; *Sp.Tr.MSS.* 23.92; *Prior.* 74.
4. *C.S.P.V.* XIV, 104; *Holl.* I, 102, 128; Will of Roger Manners, Earl of Rutland, 8 May 1612, P.R.O. PCC 64 Fenner.
5. *Dom.MSS 14.* 88.57; *C.S.P.V.* XIV, 104; *Holl.* I, 126; *Bac.* XIII, 5.
6. *Harl.MSS.* 5176.221 v.; *Dom.MSS 14.* 88.61.
7. *Birch.* I, 431; *Ch.* II, 25; *H.M.C.Supp.* 64–5; *Tann.MSS.* 74.79; *Bac.* XIII, 116; *H.M.C.(10).* 119.
8. Acts vi. 15; *Dom.MSS 14.* 89.68; *Ch.* II, 41.
9. *Sainty.* 12; *Trum.MSS.* 18.5.
10. *A.P.C. 1616–17*, 135; *Meditation.* Dedication; *Bac.* XIII, 239; *Wot.* 163.
11. *Arch.* XLI, Appendix 4.
12. *Bac.* XIII, 27.
13. *Bac.* XII, 260.
14. *Bac.* XII, 348; XIII, 6–7.
15. *Bac.* VI, 510; XIII, 152.
16. *Tann.MSS.* 74.79; *Bac.* XIII, 116.
17. *Lib.* 58, 59; *Dom.MSS 14.* 90.59; *Trum.MSS.* 18.28.
18. *Wot.* 211; *Dom.MSS 14.* 95.3, 6; *Cam.* 1 Jan. 1618; *Ch.* II, 125.
19. *C.S.P.V.* XV, 113–14.
20. *Dom.MSS 14.* 95.6.
21. *Dom.MSS 14.* 86.95; 87.40.
22. *Sal.* 14 Nov. 1617. A[rchivio] M[ediceo] 4192. For this and other Salvetti references in 1617–21 I am most grateful to Caterina Maddalena for allowing me to use her translations of the original despatches in the Archivio di Stato at the Uffizi in Florence.
23. *Harl.MSS.* 6986.196; *Birch.* II, 78.
24. *Wright.* 11; *Ch.* II, 52.
25. *Ch.* II, 144; *Dom.MSS 14.* 96.94; *Sal.* 7 May 1618, A.M. 4193.
26. *Dom.MSS 14.* 93.20, 149; *Harl.MSS.* 1581.89.
27. *Dom.MSS 14.* 96.48; 97.10.
28. *Sal.* 11 June 1618, A.M. 4193.
29. *Bac.* VI, 500; *H.M.C.Supp.* 86; *Bod.MSS.* D.110.215.
30. *Sal.* 14 Jan. 1618, A.M. 4193; *Dom.MSS 14.* 94.11; *Bod.MSS.* D.110.183.
31. *Sack.MSS.* EN.M.990; *Cab.* 327; *Tann.MSS.* 74.138; *H.M.C.Supp.* 83.
32. *Bod.MSS.* D.109 139.
33. *Goodman.* I, 334.
34. *Fort.* 46.
35. *Wot.* 211; *Dom.MSS 14.* 96.74; *H.M.C.Supp.* 66–7; *Harl.MSS.* 6986.194; 1581. 154; *Ch.* II, 97–8; *Sack.MSS.* EN.M.990; *Tann.MSS.* 74.121; *H.M.C. Bucc.* I, 249.
36. *H.M.C.Hast.* IV, 16; *Lib.* 54, 56–7.
37. *Wynn.* Nos 791, 802, 831; *Str.P.MSS.* 21/11.
38. *Sal.* 6 Mar. 1617, A.M. 4192; *H.M.C.Sal.* 47; *Dom.MSS 14.* 92.15; *Trum.MSS.* 18.11.

39. *Docs.* I, 101–2.
40. *Bowen.* 352; *Ch.* II, 100.
41. *Ch.* II, 113, 117; *Trum.MSS.* 18.20.
42. *Birch.* II, 166–9; *H.M.C.(4).* 256.
43. *Bac.* XIII, 224, 233.
44. *Bac.* XIII, 236–7, 243.
45. *Bac.* XIII, 239, 244, 246.
46. *Bac.* XIII, 247.
47. *Bac.* XIII, 251–2.
48. *H.M.C.Coke.* 142; *Bac.* XIII, 269.
49. *Bac.* XIII, 28; *Harl.MSS.* 7006.15.
50. *Harl.MSS.* 7006.93, 98, 110, 112.
51. *Bac.* XIII, 242.
52. *L.J.* 343–4.
53. Indenture between Buckingham and Cranfield, 7 Nov. 1615, referring to grant of 10 Oct. 1615; another indenture, of 30 May 1618, *Fair.MSS.* The details of the Irish Customs Farm are given in V.W.Treadwell, *Irish Financial Administrative Reform under James I: the Customs and State Regulation of Irish Trade* (Ph.D. Thesis, Queen's University of Belfast, 1960). I am grateful to Hans Pawlisch for bringing this to my attention. *Tann.MSS.* 74.79; *Sack.MSS.* EN.M, 810.
54. *Fort.* 41; *Trum.MSS.* 18.26.
55. *Dom.MSS 14.* 89.33; *Sack.MSS.* EN.M, 820; *L.J.* 344.
56. *Corbett.* 70.
57. *Bac.* XIII, 44; *Ch.* II, 118; *Trum.MSS.* 18.21; *Dom.MSS 14.* 95.8; *Goodman.* II, 164–7.
58. *Aulus.* 264; *Rush.* 378; *Dom.MSS 14.* 103.14; *Birch.* II, 92; *Ch.* II, 173; *Pat.MSS.* C.66, 2181.

CHAPTER THREE

1618–20: 'Happy Entrance' and 'Constant Reformation'

I

The system of primogeniture which prevailed in Stuart England meant that a man's estate passed to his eldest son. Only if he was very rich, or if his wife had property of her own, was it possible for him to endow other members of the family. Generally speaking the heir got everything, and the other children had to be content – in the words of Thomas Wilson, himself a younger son – with 'that which the cat left on the malt-heap'.[1] Buckingham was typical in this respect, for Brooksby, where he had been born, passed to Sir George's eldest son, while Goadby Marwood became the property, for her lifetime, of Buckingham's mother. There was no reason to doubt that he would always be welcome at Goadby, but it was natural that as he became more established he should look for somewhere of his own. He was not without a house, for as Master of the Horse had had official lodgings in the royal palace of Whitehall. These were in a handsome timber-framed house, standing on four great pillars, which overlooked the Privy Garden. They formed part of major additions to the old palace carried out by Inigo Jones, who also designed, in 1619–20, a rich painted ceiling for Buckingham's dining-room. But apartments, however resplendent, were not a permanent asset. If James were to die, for instance, or if he were to transfer his affections, Buckingham might well be left homeless. He would also have very little to live on, unless he had managed, during his years in favour – and who knew how long they would last? – to accumulate capital. The best possible investment was land, and for this reason, therefore, as well as his desire for a place of his own, Buckingham was looking out for somewhere to buy.

He had already been granted estates in Buckinghamshire, but these were of limited value in the short run, for they were all leased out. Furthermore, Buckingham had an understandable desire to acquire property in that part of England where he had been born and spent his childhood. His opportunity came in March 1617 when a former neighbour, Sir Edward Noel, decided to sell his estate at Dalby and move his seat to Rutland. Buckingham negotiated to buy Dalby, and eventually acquired it for £29,000. Where the money came from is something of a mystery, for in this very month of March 1617 Buckingham asked Cranfield for a loan of £2,500, giving as his reason the fact that he had spent all his ready cash on the purchase of Whaddon Chase. Buckingham was well placed to make money by gifts and bribes, of course, but he can hardly have raised £29,000 by these methods alone. What seems more likely is that he resorted to large-scale borrowing. There were a number of rich men only too willing to gain credit with the royal favourite by lending him money, and Cranfield, with his City connexions, would have known whom to approach.[2]

Noel had good reason to be pleased with his bargain, for he not only obtained a very fair price for his property but was also elevated to the peerage as Baron Noel. Buckingham's effectiveness as a title-monger was demonstrated even more clearly in the following year, 1618, when Mountjoy Blount was given an Irish baronage in return for handing over to Buckingham his great house at Wanstead in Essex. Buckingham became something of a specialist in selling Irish titles, and between 1618 and 1622 he and his agents made nearly £25,000 from this source. In 1619 a new order of Irish baronets was created, and a recent historian of the aristocracy has suggested that 'it was devised and operated on behalf of Buckingham and his dependants'.[3]

Buckingham was also active in the sale of Scottish and English titles, and it was no mere coincidence that the eighty-one peerages extant in December 1615, at the time of his rise to power, had increased to one hundred and twenty-six by the time of his death in 1628. The sale of honours was not as indiscriminate as it appears to be at first sight. Elizabeth had been very parsimonious when it came to bestowing titles, and there were many men of wealth and standing in their local communities who felt aggrieved at the fact that their social status had not been confirmed by an appropriate honour. Most of the peers, baronets and knights created by James I and Charles I came from this group of well-established county families, and although there were exceptions they were not always unworthy. Among the honours that Buckingham procured was the earldom of Middlesex for his protégé, Lionel Cranfield. Cranfield, it is true, was of low birth and had made his money in trade, but these inherent disadvantages were more than outweighed by the exceptional services he rendered to the crown. Buckingham clearly profited, and on a considerable scale, from the sale of honours, but he did not initiate the practice, which began in 1611 with the creation of a new order of baronets. Throughout Europe the costs of administration, in an age of inflation and conspicuous consumption, were outstripping royal revenues, and among the devices that governments resorted to were monopoly grants of trade in specified articles, the sale of offices and the sale of honours. Such expedients caused friction and ill-will, often out of all proportion to the limited financial benefits they provided, but from the Crown's point of view they were the only alternative to bankruptcy.

One of the criticisms made of newly-created Irish and Scottish peers was that they had no connexion with the land from which they derived their title. This was not the case with Lord Mountjoy, however, for his father had been Lord Deputy of Ireland in the closing years of Elizabeth's reign. As for Mountjoy's house at Wanstead, this had earlier belonged to Elizabeth's favourite, the Earl of Leicester, and had the advantage of being accessible to London while providing excellent hunting. In June 1618 Buckingham held a great feast at Wanstead, at which the King was the guest of honour. Dinner was served 'in an extremely well-devised artificial wood, which was planted like a palace, having its hall and presence chamber, bedroom, drawing-room, cabinet and so forth, formed by drawing the hangings from one tree to another'. The King was obviously delighted with his entertainment, and even more so when Buckingham presented him with the house. According to one account James gave him one of his own properties in return, but in fact Buckingham's gesture was only symbolic, a formal acknowledgment that all that he had was the King's. In practice he held on to Wanstead until June 1619, when he sold it for £7,300.[4]

It was in January 1619 that rumours began to circulate that James wished Buckingham to marry, and by June his name was being linked with that of Katherine Manners, daughter of the sixth Earl of Rutland. These reports prompted the inevitable speculation about Buckingham's future, and the Florentine agent gave his opinion that it would be 'very dangerous for such a powerful courtier to marry at all; in fact a marriage will be taken as evidence of approaching disgrace'. Such speculation was groundless, for the King's favour towards Buckingham showed no sign of diminishing. In February 1619 he published his *Meditation upon the Lord's Prayer* which he dedicated to Buckingham, 'for divers times before I meddled with it, I told you, and only you, of some of my conceptions upon the Lord's Prayer, and you often solicited me to put pen to paper'. The *Meditation* is a short work, but as James pointed out, that made it particularly suitable to Buckingham who, 'because . . . of your continual attendance upon my service, your daily employments in the same, and the uncessant swarm of suitors importunately hanging upon you without discretion or distinction of times', had little opportunity for meditation of his own. James also acknowledged, with joy, that Buckingham deserved this dedication 'in not only giving so good example to the rest of the Court, in frequent hearing the word of God, but in special in so often receiving the sacrament'.[5]

In April 1619 the King fell seriously ill, and at one stage thought he was dying. In the presence of his Councillors, who had hastened to Royston when the news reached them, the King recommended his chief servants and courtiers to the Prince's care, 'but specially the Marquis Buckingham and Hamilton'. This was a time of great strain for Buckingham. He was in constant attendance upon his master at all times of the day and night, and he knew that if James were to die the outlook for himself would be gloomy. He had made many enemies through his rapid rise to power, and he could not, as yet, rely on the friendship of the Prince. It must therefore have been with enormous relief that Buckingham watched the King recover his

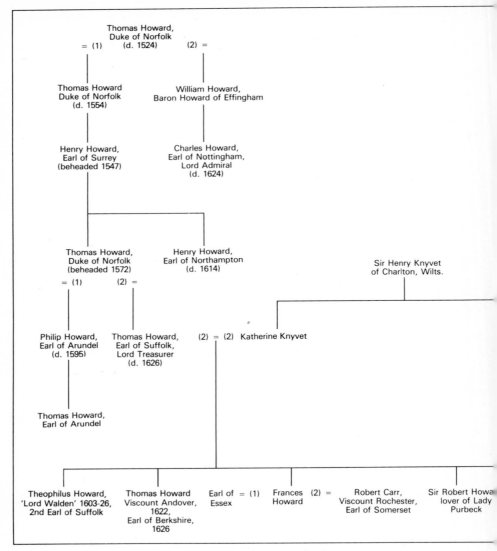

Table 3. The Howard and Manners families

strength. By the end of April James was said to have completely shaken off the effects of his illness, while Buckingham was 'no less happy than heretofore'. Yet the strain of watching and worrying had taken toll of the young man, and in June he fell ill and had to keep to his bed. Now it was the turn of the King to be an anxious watcher, and he and the Prince made repeated visits to the sick favourite. Fortunately Buckingham's illness was of brief duration and by the end of the month he felt fit enough to go running with his brother Kit and some of the gentlemen of his household, 'to try his activity'. But he overtaxed his still enfeebled body and succumbed to a suc-

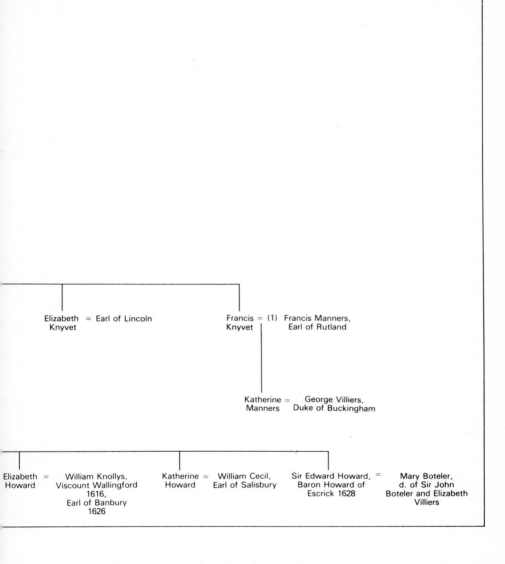

cession of fainting fits. These alarmed the King, and when Buckingham recovered he 'gave him a sharp, kind chiding for adventuring himself so
much'.[6]

James had been deeply moved by Buckingham's care of him during his
illness, and told a special envoy from France – to whom he had despatched
his favourite with a message of welcome – that 'short of sending his heart he
could not send him more than Buckingham'. He also demonstrated his gratitude in a more tangible form. Queen Anne had died in March 1619, and
after her funeral in May the King disposed of her possessions. The greater

part went, of course, to the Prince, but Buckingham was rewarded with jewels and a gift of land worth £1,200 a year. A further sign of the King's desire to please his favourite was the pressure put upon the Lord Mayor of London to permit the marriage of his daughter to Christopher (Kit) Villiers. When James was in town in July he sent for the Mayor and personally recommended the young man as a suitable husband. Chamberlain thought this would do the trick, for Kit Villiers's suit surely 'must speed when the King pleads and works so openly for him'. But the Lord Mayor had other plans for his daughter, and Kit had to do without his rich bride.[7]

Meanwhile Buckingham was negotiating for his own marriage to Katherine Manners. The Manners family had risen to prominence under ·the Tudors, when they acquired the earldom of Rutland and made some very profitable speculations in the lands of dissolved monasteries. The fifth Earl, Roger, had nearly destroyed the family fortunes by becoming involved in the Essex rising at the end of Elizabeth's reign. He was imprisoned in the Tower and sentenced to pay an enormous fine, but the accession of James I, Essex's former patron, led to his release before a penny of the fine had been paid. He was succeeded by his brother, Francis, who took as his first wife the daughter and heiress of a rich Wiltshire gentleman, Sir Francis Knyvet of Charlton. She died of smallpox in 1605, leaving behind her a daughter, Katherine. Some years later Francis married again, and had two sons, but both of these 'died in infancy by wicked practice and sorcery'.[8] Katherine Manners was therefore heir not only to the Knyvet property which had gone to her mother, but also to the unentailed portions of the extensive Manners' estates in Northamptonshire and Yorkshire.

No doubt Buckingham was alive to the advantages of marrying a rich and well-connected woman, but these were not in short supply at Court, and some would have brought with them not simply money and looks but valuable political connexions as well: the Earl of Exeter's granddaughter, Lady Diana Cecil, was one such, and in early 1619 Chamberlain reported that her aunt, Lady Hatton, was doing her utmost to persuade Buckingham 'to cast an eye' towards her.[9] There was certainly no political advantage for Buckingham to gain from a Manners marriage, for Francis had become a convert to Roman Catholicism, and had thereby put an end to all hopes of advancing his career at Court. Nor was Buckingham winning a great beauty, for portraits of Katherine show her to have been rather a plain woman. Why then was Buckingham determined to marry her? One possibility is that he already knew her, from his Leicestershire days, and either loved her or else recognised in her the qualities he wanted in a wife. Another is that marriage with the greatest family in the part of the world where he had been born and bred would confirm his standing in provincial society and establish the Villiers, beyond challenge, as the equal of any other family in the midland region of England.

By August 1619 negotiations between Buckingham and Rutland were said to be far advanced, but they foundered on the rock of religion.[10] Katherine was, like her father, a Roman Catholic, and would not abandon her faith even for the most handsome man in England. This might not have deterred Buckingham, for he was tolerant in matters of religion, and his mother was on the verge of becoming a catholic herself. But James, as head of the protestant Church of England, would never consent to an alliance between his favourite and a papist. Either Katherine must renounce her faith, or she must give up all hope of marrying Buckingham.

Religion was not the only problem, for Rutland was said to have found the financial terms proposed by Buckingham and his mother unacceptable. According to Chamberlain the Marquis was demanding a dowry of £20,000 in cash as well as land worth £4,000 a year, and his pressure on Rutland apparently offended the Earl and made him even more reluctant to part with his daughter. Mediators had to be called in to try and effect an agreement. Among them was Cranfield, who worked in conjunction with another of Buckingham's friends, Sir Thomas Savage, and was later to claim that they alone made the marriage possible. But John Williams, one of the King's chaplains, also claimed the credit. He had been virtually ordered by the King to become Buckingham's client, and since he already had some acquaintance with the Earl of Rutland he was well placed to bring the two sides together. According to his biographer, John Hacket, Williams 'brought the Earl about so dextrously with his art and pleasant wit, that his lordship put it into his hands to draw up all contracts and conditions for portion and jointure; which he did to the fair satisfaction of both sides'. Williams was also commanded by the King to use his best endeavours to show Katherine the error of her Romish beliefs and bring her into the bosom of the Church of England. He had no easy task, for as late as March 1620 the Spanish ambassador, Gondomar, was telling his government that Katherine was determined to hold fast to her faith, and that Buckingham's mother had agreed that no attempt should be made to shake her.[11]

Matters might have dragged on indefinitely but for a *coup de théâtre* by the Countess of Buckingham. One day in early March 1620 she went to call on Katherine and brought her back to supper at her own house, where Buckingham was also present. Katherine spent the night at the Countess's, but when she was taken back to her father the next day, he refused to receive her, and the poor girl had to take refuge with her uncle. Rutland felt cheated and betrayed. His last surviving son was near death – struck down, so Rutland believed, by witchcraft – and now his daughter, whom he had instructed 'to avoid the occasion of ill', had compromised herself by sleeping under the same roof as her suitor. Whether she was still a virgin he did not know, but he was determined not to allow her back into his house until Buckingham had committed himself to marry her.[12]

Buckingham was far too proud and hot-tempered to be blackmailed into marriage, even with the woman he wanted. His immediate reaction was to break off all negotiations, and he informed Rutland that

since you esteem so little both of my friendship and her honour, I must now, contrary to my former resolution, leave off the pursuit of that alliance any more, putting it in her free choice to bestow her[self] elsewhere to your best comfort; for whose fortune it shall ever be to have her, I will constantly profess that she never received any blemish in her honour but that which came by your own tongue.

Buckingham's anger was understandable, but so also was Rutland's, for the favourite's morals were not above reproach when it came to sexual liaisons, and his relations with a number of Court beauties – particularly Lucy Percy, the wife of Lord Doncaster – were rumoured to have passed well beyond the stage of friendship.[13]

Buckingham now turned to James for help, and begged the King to order Rutland 'to call home his daughter again', so that, if he did eventually marry Katherine, he might have 'so much respite of time given me as I may see some one act of wisdom in the foresaid lord as may put me in hope that of his stock I may sometime beget one able to serve you at least in some mean employment'. But there was no longer any need for the King to put pressure on Rutland, for the Earl had at last reconciled himself to the idea of the marriage. As for Katherine's religion, this was not strong enough to hold out against her emotions. In Hacket's words 'she easily perceived that conjugal love would be firmest and sweetest when man and wife served God with one heart'; but Buckingham was later to put the matter more pithily when he attributed his wife's alteration of her religion to lechery.[14]

Buckingham and Katherine were married with the minimum of ostentation in a private ceremony on 16 May, 1620. It took place at Lumley House, near Tower Hill, where Rutland was staying, and the officiating minister was, appropriately enough, John Williams, who thereby secured his place among the favourite's friends and began his ascent to high office. Under the terms of the agreement between Buckingham and Rutland, Katherine was to bring with her a dowry of £10,000 in cash and lands worth some £4,000 or £5,000 a year. These financial advantages, as well as the prestige which he gained from so close an alliance with an old landed family, were obviously important considerations to Buckingham; but he had also set his heart on Katherine, and in the event the marriage turned out to be an exceptionally happy one. Katherine was no doormat. She had a temper to match her husband's, and there were occasions when relations between them were, in Buckingham's words, 'something stormy'. Katherine could be jealous – she particularly detested Lucy Percy who remained on terms of intimacy with Buckingham despite his marriage – and she often bemoaned the fate that had tied her to a husband who had to spend so much time away from her, at Court or on state business abroad. Yet she could also be remarkably generous and understanding, as in forgiving him his 'one sin [of] loving women so well', and when Buckingham was absent she poured out her feelings to him in language that came straight from the heart. 'Never woman was so happy as I am,' she wrote to him in 1623, 'for never was there so kind a husband as you are, and God make me thankful to Him for you . . . . I am sure God will bless us both for your sake, and I cannot express the infinite affection I bear you; but for God's sake believe me that there was never woman loved man as I do you.'[15]

By the time of his marriage, Buckingham was already — thanks to the King's generosity — among the wealthier members of early Stuart society, and in February 1619 he had appointed Cranfield and Sir John Coke 'to take a view of his own private estate and to give our advice how to settle and order his affairs'. The two men started by drawing up a statement of Buckingham's financial position, which shows how rapidly a fortune could be acquired through royal favour and the influence that flowed therefrom. At that time Buckingham had possession of Whaddon and other properties in Buckinghamshire which brought him in nearly £1,500 a year. Dalby and other Leicestershire lands yielded £1,200 and Wanstead in Essex added a further £360. In other words, Buckingham was receiving not far short of £3,000 a year in rents, and he also had the reversion of leases in various parts of the country that were estimated to be worth £1,850. In addition to this landed revenue, Buckingham had the profits of office and favour. The salaries for the official posts he held were relatively insignificant. As Master of the Horse he received £66 13s. 4d.; as Lord Admiral £133 6s. 8d.; as Justice in Eyre of all the King's Forests beyond the River Trent £166 13s. 4d.; and as Keeper of Hampton Court £64 6s. 8d.. The actual rewards of office-holding were many times the nominal value, however, and in any case Buckingham had other sources of income. He was in receipt of a royal pension of £1,000 a year; the grant of threepence in the pound on the trade of alien merchants brought him in some £1,300 annually; the Irish Customs at least £1,500; and the Clerkship of the King's Bench £4,000.[16]

Buckingham, then, was enjoying an 'open' income of some £14,000 a year by 1620, quite apart from the sums he received through gifts and the general workings of the patronage system. This 'concealed' income must have been considerable, as is indicated by his agent's accounts of the sales of honours and offices in Ireland. On the assumption that only fifty per cent of the money paid out in these transactions actually reached Buckingham's hands, he would still have been getting £3,000 a year from this source alone, and similar operations in England may have brought him in half as much again. In other words his real income was, at a conservative estimate, about £18,500 a year, and quite possibly a good deal higher. Buckingham's expenditure, however, was also high. He had a number of members of his family to support, not least his mother, to whom he contracted to pay £1,300 a year in July 1620. Then, as the King's favourite, he was obliged to dress richly and spend lavishly, for such a lifestyle was not only a symbol of his success but also an assurance to all those who had tied their lives and their fortunes to his. The Court was a highly competitive society of very wealthy men, each trying to outshine the others, and Buckingham simply could not afford to be eclipsed. On St George's Day 1618, for instance, the courtiers and their followers were, according to Chamberlain, 'very gay and gallant', but, he added, this was specially the case with Buckingham, 'who was very bountiful to forty of his gentlemen, in giving them £50

61

a piece to provide themselves and £20 a man to ten yeomen . . . besides an hundred pound he gave to make them a supper and a play the next night at the Mitre in Fleet Street'. In other words, this day's entertainment alone cost the Marquis £2,000. [17]

He had also to spend a good deal of money on hospitality, and if his guests included the King and Prince the bill was likely to amount to several hundred pounds. Gambling was another major item of expenditure, for hunting by day and gambling by night were traditional ways of passing the time at Court, and the sums involved could be sizeable – such as the £1,000 which, as already mentioned, Buckingham bet on his servant in a foot-race. Even sporting activities were costly, particularly ball games, for in two successive sets of tennis which he played with the Prince, Buckingham managed to lose a total of thirty-two dozen balls, which cost him £3 4s. 0d. [18]

While several thousand pounds a year could literally 'disappear' in the course of life at Court, Buckingham also had to pay for all the services that were rendered him. The sums involved were not large in themselves, but they added up. When Buckingham sent his footman from Royston to Goadby, he gave him ten shillings. When he drove from London to Theobalds in May 1619, he had to pay 4s. for torches to light his way, 2s. 6d. for having the gates on the road opened and £1 2s. for drinks for his thirsty servants. Crossing the river to Lambeth could cost him 2s. 6d., while the bargemen who rowed him to Greenwich (presumably against the tide) received £3 6s. for their pains. Nothing was free. Even the stool cost him 6d. a time and paper for it 3d. [19]

It seems likely that Buckingham's income, enormous as it was, did little more than cover his expenditure, and the purchase of Dalby must have strained his finances heavily – hence the appointment of Cranfield and Coke as his advisers. It was probably on their recommendation that he sold off many of his Yorkshire properties in 1619, and also parted with Wanstead. In 1620, however, following his marriage, he was looking for a new house, and needed all the money he could lay hands on. At this juncture Cranfield and the King came to his assistance. Cranfield, as a member of the Treasury commission which was looking into ways of increasing the royal revenue, suggested the imposition of a tax on the export of coal, with alien merchants paying twice as much as English ones. But alien merchants were already subjected to a levy of threepence in the pound on their trade, and this tax was farmed by Buckingham, who was allowed to keep any profits above the £3,000 which he had contracted to pay annually to the King. There was some doubt about whether the new imposition would be an infringement of his grant, and it was probably Cranfield who suggested that the King should 'buy out' the coals from Buckingham's patent by offering him half of the £16,000 which the farmers of the new coal tax were willing to pay for their lease. James was delighted with this suggestion, but it was some time before Buckingham heard about it officially, for the King, who loved springing surprises, ordered that the plan should be kept secret, so that 'it might take my lord upon the sudden, to be the more acceptable unto him'. [20]

Buckingham used this windfall to help finance the purchase of Burley-on-the-Hill, a great estate in Rutland which he doubtless knew from his boyhood, since it was only thirteen miles from Brooksby as the crow flies. The property, which carried with it 'the castle, manor and lordship of Oakham', had passed by inheritance to Lucy, Countess of Bedford, but she was said to be £50,000 in debt by the end of 1619 (despite the grant of 'an imposition of twopence a chaldron upon sea-coal') and was therefore 'selling all the land that descended to her from her father or her brother'. According to the official contract, Buckingham paid her £14,000 for Burley, but his private accounts show that in addition to this amount — which was made up of the £8,000 from the farmers of the coal duty and £6,000 from Kate's dowry— Buckingham also transferred to the Countess of Bedford one of his Warwickshire properties, making a total purchase price of £28,000.[21]

When Buckingham acquired Burley there was an old house still standing there on the hill, and it was into this that he moved, during the early summer of 1621. By July he and Kate were sufficiently settled to plan a lavish housewarming, at which the King was to be the guest of honour. Nicholas Lanier, one of the most fashionable composers and performers of his day, was called on to superintend the music, for which he was paid £200, while Ben Jonson was commissioned to provide 'The Masque of the Gipsies' for a fee of £100.[22] Festivities began at the moment of the King's arrival at Burley on 3 August 1621, for Jonson had provided the porter with rhyming couplets with which to greet the distinguished visitor:

> Welcome, O welcome then, and enter here
> The house your bounty hath built, and still doth rear
> With those high favours and those heaped increases
> As shows a hand not grieved but when it ceases.
> The master is your creature, as the place,
> And every good about him is your grace.

On entering the house, James found a great company assembled to salute him. The Prince was there, as were numerous members of the Villiers and Manners families and their friends. In the masque itself, Buckingham took the role of the first gipsy; the three others were played by Lord Denbigh (husband of his much-loved sister Susan); Endymion Porter, his servant and kinsman; and Lord Purbeck, his elder brother. The masque was full of topical references which delighted the audience not only at Burley but at subsequent performances at Belvoir and in London. Jonson had also provided appropriate verses in which the first gipsy could express his gratitude to his royal benefactor:

> Myself a gipsy here do shine
> Yet are you maker, sir, of mine
>
> . . .
>
> And may your goodness ever find
> In me, whom you have made, a mind
> As thankful as your own is large.

63

James's brief visit to Burley was clearly a resounding success, and the King, as always, showed his pleasure openly. After a magnificent banquet on the day of his departure, he rose from the table where he had been dining apart with the Prince and went over to the rest of the company. Standing bareheaded, he drank to the health of his host, the Lord Admiral, and debated the topic of who loved him best — his wife, his family or his sovereign.[23] Finally he read some verses which he had been inspired to compose in honour of the occasion, and declared that they should be engraved in marble and set up at Burley as a perpetual remembrance of his visit. In these verses James began by expressing his delight in the way that all nature — the stags, the bucks, even the weather — had seemed to smile, which gave good hope of 'a smiling boy within a while'. He concluded, in classical vein, by praying the gods to pour their blessings on the newly-married couple:

> Thou by whose heat the trees in fruit abound,
> Bless them with fruit delicious, sweet and fair,
> That may succeed them in their virtues rare.
> Firm plant them in their native soil and ground.
> Thou Jove, that art the only god indeed,
> My prayer hear. Sweet Jesus, intercede![24]

II

Buckingham's marriage, even while it was only at the negotiating stage, began to affect his relationships with a number of other families, particularly the Howards. Katherine's aunt, after whom she had been named, was the wife of Thomas Howard, Earl of Suffolk, the disgraced Lord Treasurer, and since relations between the Manners and the Howards were apparently close and friendly, Buckingham came under increasing pressure to moderate the King's wrath against Suffolk. Another influence tending in the same direction was that of the Earl of Salisbury, Buckingham's friend, who was Suffolk's son-in-law. The Lord Treasurer had been brought to trial before the Court of Star Chamber in October 1619, and sentenced to a fine of £30,000 and restitution of the money he had embezzled. He and his wife were also imprisoned in the Tower, but through Buckingham's intercession they were released before the end of the year. The Earl wrote to the favourite to thank him, 'for what I have received, both in abatement of my fine and speedy liberty, I must confess to come from your noble mediation to His Majesty'. In January 1620 it was reported that Suffolk and his sons — Lord Howard de Walden and Sir Thomas Howard — had been partially restored to the King's favour and in that same month Buckingham stood as godparent to Lord Howard de Walden's newborn child. In February Suffolk was granted an audience with the King and allowed to kiss his hands, and in the following month the cloud of royal disfavour was lifted completely. Buckingham, who had demonstrated his power to hurt when he brought about the fall of the Howards, had now given clear evidence of his power to heal. No wonder Suffolk assured him of 'the hearty acknowledgement of a whole family, and all theirs, that shall as faithfully serve and honour you as the best of those that would succeed them'. In acknowledging his dependence, Suffolk was recognising the undoubted fact that Buckingham had become the major single political influence at Court. It had taken the favourite five years to destroy the Howard empire, but now that he had done it there was no apparent challenge to his supremacy.[25]

It would be a mistake, however, to assume that Buckingham had a monopoly of power, or, indeed, that he was aiming at it. There were other influential figures, both in the Court and outside it, with whom he had to come to terms, and he was engaged in a perpetual balancing act, now asserting himself, now giving way, seizing the opportunities of advancing his own concerns but acting in such a way as not to provoke a coalition of interests against him. How far this was conscious and how far unconscious it is impossible to say, but in Buckingham the instincts of the gambler and the 'trimmer' existed side by side. The King's illness in April 1619 brought out the balancing instinct in Buckingham, for if James had died he would have found himself beset with enemies. Among these might well have been numbered the Earl of Southampton, Shakespeare's patron, who felt that he had never achieved the high offices for which his talents fitted him, particularly the post of Lord Admiral, which had gone, instead, to Buckingham. It was no coincidence, then, that in that same month of April one of Buckingham's footmen was sent with a message to Southampton, and that in early May the Earl was appointed to the Privy Council. This, as the Florentine resident acutely observed, was not because the King 'has any liking for this man, who has long been trying to obtain this appointment, as because he wanted to please Buckingham, who had intervened on Southampton's behalf. And in fact, had the Marquis not been forced to seek supporters during the King's illness – the Earl is a very powerful man – Southampton would not have obtained it even now, because the King does not like his restless and forceful character and is somewhat suspicious of his popularity.'[26]

Another incident, which took place in the autumn of 1619 and was much commented on at the time, indicates the limits on Buckingham's freedom of action. In August of that year the place of Groom Porter to the King fell vacant, and Buckingham secured the grant of it for one of his household officers, Clement Cotterell. But the Earl of Pembroke claimed that this office fell within his sphere as Lord Chamberlain, and therefore appointed his own nominee. When the King heard of this he made it clear that he had no intention of infringing the Lord Chamberlain's rights, but he asked Pembroke to produce precedents to prove that his claim was well founded. Buckingham had probably acted in good faith, not knowing that Pembroke had any interest in the appointment, and there is no reason to suppose that the Lord Chamberlain disapproved of Cotterell as a person. He had chosen to take a stand on this issue simply to check the growth of Buckingham's power and to make it clear that while he was willing to accept the favourite's supremacy in general — because it derived from the King's will, which Pembroke respected — it must not be at the cost of his own position.[27]

Buckingham refused to abandon Cotterell, but he did not take his stand on principle. His argument was that he had already given way to Pembroke over the question of the Chancellorship of the Duchy — in which he had originally supported Cranfield's claim — and that now it was Pembroke's turn to make a concession. Both parties appealed to the King, but James took his time before intervening. Not until November did he summon Buckingham and Pembroke to a private audience at which the Prince was the only other person present. At this meeting the King 'spake much of his affection to both and of both their noble dispositions' and asked Pembroke whether he was prepared to accept his decision. Pembroke replied that he would 'freely submit all to His Majesty, which the King taking with a most gracious acknowledgement, my Lord Marquis made a large and free profession of his respects to my Lord Chamberlain'. James in fact allowed Cotterell to retain the place of Groom Porter, but Pembroke had achieved what was probably his main purpose in reminding Buckingham that, while his position as favourite made him undoubtedly *primus*, he was *primus inter pares* and must respect the rights of others as jealously as he asserted his own. This was a principle on which, as it happened, Buckingham and Pembroke were in agreement — though lines of demarcation were never easy to draw — and the quarrel gave way to an uneasy blend of friendliness and suspicion, typical of relations between men of influence and ambition. By September of the following year the Earl of Leicester was able to tell his wife that 'all things at the Court are in the wonted course, and very great shows of love between my Lord Admiral and my Lord of Pembroke'.[28]

While ambition and differing attitudes on major political matters would from time to time throw Buckingham and Pembroke into opposition, there were other forces tending to draw them together. Among these were the friendship between Buckingham and the Earl of Montgomery — himself a former favourite — Pembroke's younger brother and heir. In April 1618 Montgomery had invited Buckingham to be one of the godfathers of his new-born child, and although this invitation came to nothing because the baby died before he could be christened, it was repeated in September 1619, when Montgomery's wife gave birth to a boy. Montgomery was not a major figure at Court. His main interests were hunting and gambling — tastes which he shared with Buckingham — and he had no political ambitions. But as Pembroke's brother and a man much favoured by the King he was an essential part of the network of connexions which Buckingham took pains to cultivate. He was also linked, through his wife, to the Cecil family, with which Buckingham was careful to keep his friendship in good repair, acting as godfather to Lady Salisbury's child in June 1619, and inviting the Countess of Exeter and Lady Hatton to his housewarming at Burley in August 1621.[29]

Another relation of the Herberts was Thomas Howard, Earl of Arundel, who, like Pembroke, had married a daughter of the Earl of Shrewsbury.

Arundel had been a close friend of Prince Henry, with whom he shared a discerning passion for works of art, and the premature death of the Prince had been a blow to his hopes of a political career. Arundel was conscious of his dignity, as grandson of the fourth Duke of Norfolk, and wished not only to recover the office of Earl Marshal, which had become attached to his family, but to play the major part in affairs which he believed his descent and his own abilities entitled him to. In November 1619 Chamberlain commented on 'his perpetual plying the Marquis Buckingham with all manner of observance, and likewise his lady to the mother Countess', in hopes of obtaining the office of Lord Treasurer. If this was Arundel's objective he was unsuccessful, but Buckingham was obviously anxious to keep his goodwill, for when the Earl was imprisoned in the Tower in May 1621 after insulting a fellow peer in the House of Lords, he was 'very much visited and courted by the Lord of Buckingham'. It may also have been through Buckingham's mediation that Arundel was appointed Earl Marshal in August 1621. The relationship between the two men was never close, any more than it was between Buckingham and Pembroke. As contenders for power they regarded each other with a certain wariness, but there was no fundamental opposition between them at this stage.[30]

Among the lesser luminaries at Court, Buckingham was on friendly terms with James Hay, one of the King's Scottish favourites, who had been created Viscount Doncaster. The King had despatched him to the continent in 1619 on a diplomatic mission, but Doncaster kept in touch with the favourite and assured him, in the conventional language of the time, that 'this poor servant of yours doth respect you with the best wishes of his soul'. Buckingham returned the compliment. 'There is none living more your faithful and humble servant', he assured him, in a letter in which he reported on James's reactions to Doncaster's negotiations and passed on the King's instructions. Beneath the formality, however, there was a genuine warmth and friendliness. On one occasion Buckingham used a secretary to write his letter, pleading, by way of excuse, that he was off to inspect the ships of the Royal Navy; but he added, in a postscript, 'Either forgive me for not writing with mine own hand, or else go hang yourself!'[31]

III

Beyond the immediate circle of the Court Buckingham maintained and extended his range of influence, and as it became apparent that his favour was likely to be lasting, more and more aspirants to office turned to him. In January 1619, for instance, Sir Henry Montagu, who had succeeded Sir Edward Coke as Lord Chief Justice, wrote to Buckingham about a rumour that the King was thinking of appointing him to the Lord Treasurer's place, left unfilled since the dismissal of Suffolk. 'For my obligation to you', he assured Buckingham, 'I would leave the earnest of ten thousand pounds, to bestow where and when you shall appoint.' In case this should seem like a straight bribe, he added 'this proceeds not of baseness, to buy that which otherwise I were not worthy of, nor of pride to be made better than I am, but sincerely to show how much I zeal my master's good'. Buckingham accordingly opened negotiations – using his half-brother, Sir Edward Villiers, as intermediary – and by the end of 1620 terms had been agreed. Sir Henry was to pay £20,000 for the Treasurer's office (and comforted himself with the reflection that 'my estate, God be thanked, is worth that and twenty thousand more'). But the money was to go to the King, not to the favourite. At his impeachment in 1626 Buckingham claimed that James made Montagu Lord Treasurer without any conditions, and that Sir Henry then offered to lend the King £20,000 for a year, to meet his immediate necessities. 'And according to the King's direction, that very money was fully paid out to others, and the Duke [Buckingham] neither had, nor disposed of a penny thereof to his own use.'[32]

Buckingham's explanation of the circumstances surrounding Montagu's appointment as Lord Treasurer was given at a time when he was under violent attack, and cannot therefore be accepted at face value. But it could well be that the decision to appoint Sir Henry, and to create him Viscount Mandeville, came from James, who had a liking for the Montagus, 'whom he thought loved him and were faithful to him', and needed their support in the forthcoming Parliament. Furthermore, when Mandeville was persuaded to relinquish the Treasurership in September 1621, after holding office for little more than a year, he asked for his money back. Buckingham acknowledged the justice of Mandeville's demand, and, since neither he nor the King had ready cash available, transferred to Mandeville a number of his own manors in Herefordshire. Those remained with Mandeville as security until June 1625, when the crown at last repaid the £20,000 and the lands were restored to Buckingham.[33]

Mandeville's successor as Lord Chief Justice was Sir James Ley, and current gossip was quick to attribute his appointment to the machinations of the Countess of Buckingham. But although the Countess obviously exerted a certain influence upon appointments – particularly in those cases where her son had no marked preference – she had nothing like as much as she was credited with. In this particular instance Chamberlain reported that Ley had been chosen because he was going to 'marry in the kindred of the Countess of Buckingham', but in fact Jane Boteler, the future Lady Ley, was not related to the Countess at all.[34] She was the granddaughter of Sir George Villiers through his first wife, and her mother, Elizabeth Villiers (wife of Sir John Boteler), was Buckingham's half-sister. It was well known that Buckingham held Elizabeth in high regard and promoted marriages for all her children with friends and supporters of his own. Jane was a case in point, for her first husband was, as predicted, the seventy-year-old Sir James Ley – whom she married in June 1621, when she was only seventeen – and her second was William Ashburnham, brother to John Ashburnham, who was a member of Buckingham's household. Jane had many sisters, and they were all similarly provided for. Audrey Boteler married Francis Leigh, who was given a peerage; Helen became the wife of Sir John Drake of Ash, who was one of Buckingham's Admiralty officials in Devonshire; while Olive took as her husband Endymion Porter, another of Buckingham's household officers. Mary Boteler was used to cement Buckingham's new-found friendship with the Howards, by marrying Sir Edward Howard, who was also given a peerage; while Anne became the wife of Mountjoy Blount, the former owner of Wanstead, who was made a baron in 1627 and in the same year commanded the cavalry in the expeditionary force which Buckingham led to the Ile de Ré. It is clear from the history of this branch of the Villiers family that the gossips were wrong in attributing the advancement of Buckingham's nieces mainly to the Countess. It was Buckingham himself who cheerfully accepted the obligation to promote the interests of all his kindred, no matter how distant the relationship.

Membership of the Villiers connexion, either by marriage or clientage, was rarely, however, the sole cause of a man's rise to power; nor did it guarantee his hold on office (as Cranfield was to discover). For one thing, Buckingham was never, in James's reign, the sole dispenser of patronage; nor was James himself a mere cipher. In early 1621, for example, Sir Robert Naunton, who had been promoted to the office of Secretary of State because of his favour with Buckingham (as well as his own capabilities), was threatened with dismissal because he had engaged in unauthorised negotiations with the French ambassador. The fact that he was a client both of Buckingham and the Countess could not shield him from James's wrath. Because of the favourite's intercession he was granted a stay of execution, but at the beginning of 1623 he had to resign his office. Buckingham ensured that he did not suffer financially, by procuring for him the lucrative post of Master of the Wards, but Naunton's political career was effectively over. The King, as always, had the last word.

Because of Buckingham's influence with James it was frequently assumed that he was responsible for an appointment even when this was not the case. In February 1619, to take one example, the King decided to appoint a new Secretary of State, and Buckingham pushed the claims of his own secretary, John Packer, and also those of Dudley Carleton, the ambassador at the Hague. The King, however, wanted Sir George Calvert, and when this became clear, Buckingham abandoned his own candidates and backed Calvert instead. One of Carleton's correspondents reported how Buckingham 'pretended he had no interest in it, but that it was only the King's own work'. The writer's disbelief is apparent, but in fact Buckingham was telling the truth.[35]

An even more striking example of the limitations upon Buckingham's freedom of action came in 1621, when a new Lord Keeper was needed to replace the fallen Bacon. Buckingham put forward Cranfield, and, when it became apparent that he was unacceptable, Sir James Ley. The Prince, meanwhile, was pushing his own candidate, the Chief Justice of the Common Pleas. In July, however, the King delivered the great seal into the keeping of John Williams, now Dean of Westminster, having declared that he thought lawyers to 'be all knaves'. D'Ewes, who reports this, adds that the choice of a cleric was 'as the Marquis of Buckingham had intended', and the Venetian ambassador also attributed Williams's elevation to pressure from the favourite and his mother (to whom Williams was at this time chaplain). But it seems that James alone was responsible for the appointment. He had decided on Williams as early as June 1621, and all that the Prince and Buckingham could achieve was a delay of a few weeks. Buckingham, of course, made the best of the situation, and immediately set about attaching Williams more firmly to his interest, but the new Lord Keeper owed his appointment to the King and not the favourite.[36]

Buckingham's influence with the King in matters of patronage was most effective in one of two ways. Where the King had no very strong opinion on whom to appoint to an office or elevate to a dignity – and there must, in the nature of things, have been many such cases – Buckingham's recommendation would usually be accepted. If other leading courtiers expressed a strong preference for someone else, they might have to be bought off, and they might even succeed in holding up the appointment, but they were not likely to prevail if it came to an open test of strength. Where, on the other hand, the King had already made his own choice, Buckingham could only exert a negative influence. By taking a determined stand against a proposed appointment, he could delay it, as he did with Yelverton, until the beneficiary had come to terms with him and agreed to be his client. It was a game in which there were no clear rules, and everything depended upon the balance of forces at any given moment. A great deal of Buckingham's success was due to the way in which he instinctively adjusted his course to the prevailing winds.

Whatever the practical limitations upon Buckingham's freedom of action, it remained true that no man could hope to prosper without his goodwill, and those lucky enough to be his protégés were lavish in their expressions of devotion. In May 1619 Bacon, who had just received a royal grant of £1,200 a year, wrote to Buckingham to thank him and assure him that 'my affection may and doth daily receive addition, but cannot, nor never could, receive alteration'. A few months later he wrote again to express his pleasure in the fact that 'as I find every day more and more occasions whereby you bind me to you, so this morning the King of himself did tell me some testimony that your lordship gave of me to His Majesty . . . . I can be but yours, and desire to better myself, that I may be of more worth to such an owner.' The tone of Bacon's letters to his patron is distasteful to modern ears, since it suggests fawning servility. But such was the convention of the day, and it should no more be taken at face value than current usages like 'Yours sincerely', or 'Your most humble and obedient servant'. Bacon was simply acknowledging the facts of life when he professed his total reliance upon his patron and his thanks for favours received, but it was understood on both sides that clientage depended upon the receipt of benefits; the patron as well as the client had his obligations, and failure to fulfil them would invalidate the contract.[37]

When Buckingham had cause to disagree with Bacon he used the same courteous language and assurances of continued care – except on the occasion already noted when he suspected that Bacon had broken the contract by going directly against his declared intention. Sometime in 1620 Bacon asked the favourite to obtain for him the King's permission to put somebody forward for a peerage – a not uncommon way of making a profit. Buckingham, however, judged the moment inopportune, and told him so, but in such a way as to cause the minimum offence. 'I know that to a man of so much nobleness nothing will be so acceptable as sincerity and plainness. And therefore before I move His Majesty in your suit I will take the liberty of a friend to deliver unto you mine opinion of it.' The King, he explained, was opposed to the idea of selling honours, and although such a grant might have been given to previous Chancellors in recognition of their work during a Parliamentary session, it would be unwise to ask for it now, before the session had even begun. Nevertheless Buckingham made it clear that he was willing to forward Bacon's request if this was what he wanted. 'Having thus freely delivered to your lordship my opinion,' he told him, 'I now leave it to yourself whether I shall move His Majesty in your suit or no; wherein I will be ready so to carry myself as I shall be further directed by your lordship.' Bacon, of course, took the hint, and no more was heard of the matter.[38]

Bacon was a married man, so there was no question of attaching him more firmly to the Villiers interest by finding one of Buckingham's relatives for him. This was not the case, however, with Cranfield, who was a widower, and some time in 1619 it was suggested to him that he might care to take, as his second wife, Anne Brett, the Countess of Buckingham's niece. Cranfield was not thrilled at the prospect. Anne was a large, plain woman, with no fortune, and in any case Cranfield was hoping to conclude a more attractive match. He therefore, in the words of one commentator, 'dared to contest with him [Buckingham] and against him for endeavouring to put upon him by way of wedlock one of his kinswomen that had little to value her save the blood of Villiers'. If this account is correct Cranfield went even further and reported the whole matter to James. Now it was Buckingham's turn to defend himself, which he did by asserting 'that he never intended to thrust his kinswoman upon him, but only commended the match unto him, from no other ground but upon the great desire he had to have him for his friend and ally'.[39]

Buckingham finally prevailed, and Anne Brett became Lady Cranfield. She was, in fact, quite a good bargain for her husband, since the King, who liked the whole idea of a marriage bond between his good servant and his favourite, appointed Cranfield to the Privy Council and also allowed him to keep all the profits he made as Master of the Wardrobe, which ran into several thousand pounds a year.[40] Buckingham's action in forcing a wife upon his adviser and client may seem heartless, but wives at this time were rarely chosen for romantic reasons, and a marriage alliance was one way of directing Cranfield's formidable (and potentially dangerous) egoism into friendly rather than hostile channels.

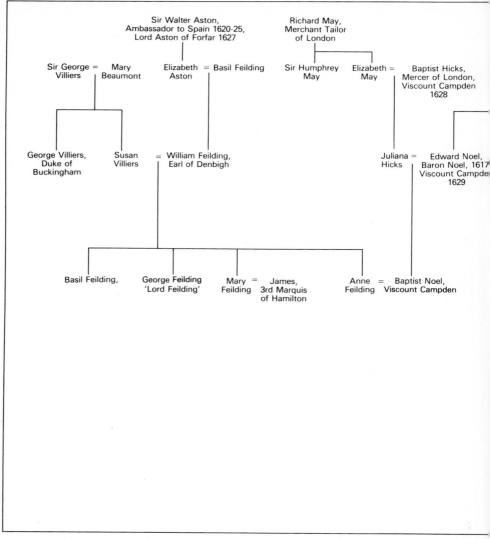

Table 4. The Feilding, Noel, Harington, Brett and Cranfield families

Whatever reservations Buckingham may have had about the range of Cranfield's ambitions, he continued to support him because Cranfield was the only man with sufficient expertise and reforming zeal to make the King solvent. Even Buckingham, who was by nature optimistic, occasionally lost hope, but Cranfield urged him 'not to despair, no, not so much as be discouraged, for the more desperate the King's estate is presented, the more honour will be to rectify it, and the more shall your lordship merit of his Majesty, to be that happy instrument to do it'. This insistence on the favourite's role in fostering the reform of the royal administration throws

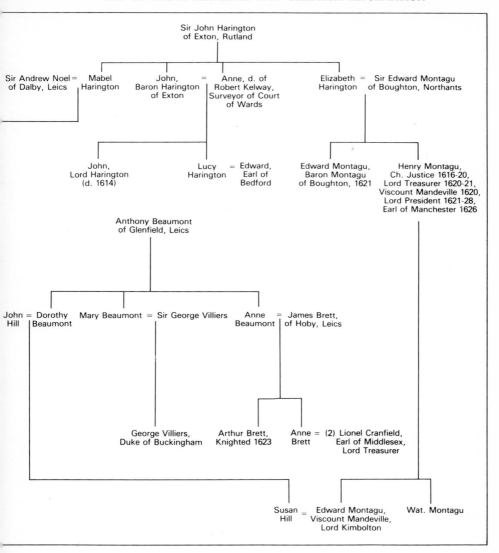

light on Buckingham's own view of himself, for Cranfield, Bacon, and others who knew him well, would not have made repeated references to his zeal for the King's service unless they had known that such appeals would call forth a favourable response. Buckingham's frequent expressions of thanks to James for the bounty showered upon him were not hypocritical, and he hoped to make some repayment by improving the royal administration and freeing the King from the burden of perpetual indebtedness. More than this, by showing his aptitude for the unique position he held, he intended to demonstrate that whatever the means by which he had risen to power, he had,

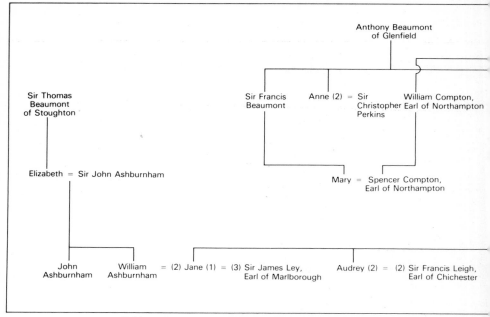

Table 5. The Compton and Boteler families

in James's own words, 'a brain capable to receive and a bosom trusty to lay up and a person active to execute any great design of a King'.[41]

The need to protect his clients and promote their work did not lessen with the years. In 1621 Cranfield was still appealing to him to hold fast to the course he had chosen and assuring him that, if he did so, 'I will perfect the work, and the King shall live with honour upon his own, in despite of all the world.' By this time, Cranfield's reforming activity had reached the point at which it began to impinge upon the King's own freedom of action, particularly his open-handedness, and Cranfield had already called on Buckingham to restrain James's generosity as well as his own. 'Good my lord,' he urged him,

be constant yourself, and be the happy means to hold the King so. . . . I have called some men to account who have not accounted these seven years. I doubt some will make their addresses to His Majesty or your lordship. I pray let their answer be, His Majesty hath referred the trust of ordering his estate to me . . . . The pains and envy shall be mine; the honour and thanks your lordship's.

Buckingham was not offended by such pleas and gave assurances that he was doing all he could 'to hold the King in that way to the uttermost of his power'. Buckingham did not dare make a total denial of his favour for fear of weakening his own position, but one of Cranfield's correspondents told how he heard the favourite 'answer divers . . . that the King hath command-ed him not to move him in any businesses of revenue for a year'. In one sense, of course, Buckingham was the worst enemy of the reformers, since

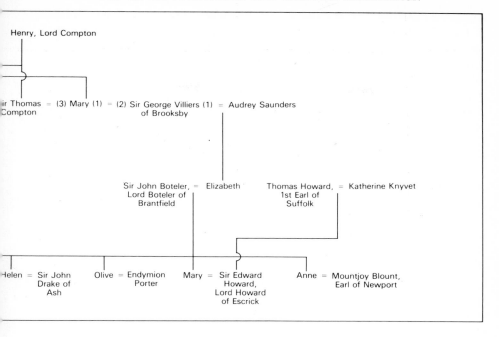

he was himself the major beneficiary of the King's generosity. But given James's natural extravagance, and the fact that seventeenth-century courts throughout Europe were centres of conspicuous consumption, there was much to be said for a favourite who was aware of the need for reform and, within the limits dictated by his own position, laboured to bring this about. Certainly Cranfield, without Buckingham to support him, would have accomplished far less than he did.[42]

The relationship between Buckingham and Cranfield was one of reciprocal benefits. Cranfield began the Herculean task of putting the favourite's finances into some semblance of order; and he also gratified Buckingham's desire to advance members of his own family by resigning his office of Master of the King's Wardrobe to Buckingham's brother-in-law, William Feilding. Buckingham, likewise, had more to offer than merely the protection of his name and influence for the reform programme. It was through Buckingham's patronage that Cranfield became a baron in July 1621. Later that year he replaced Mandeville as Lord Treasurer, and in 1622 he was created Earl of Middlesex. And all the time, through royal favour (mediated by Buckingham) as well as through the ruthless pursuit of his own interests, Cranfield was building up his fortune. In 1620 he estimated that his lands and possessions were worth £90,000, and a few years later, just before his fall from power, this figure had risen to £130,000. As for Cranfield's annual income, this was probably between £25,000 and £28,000 – considerably more than that of the favourite himself.[43]

Of all Cranfield's reforms, none had meant more to Buckingham than the attack on corruption in the Navy, for Buckingham took his responsibilities as Lord Admiral seriously and was eager to learn his new trade. He showed his customary flair for picking the right men to serve him, by choosing Sir John Coke as his mentor. Coke had been Deputy-Treasurer of the Navy in the closing years of Elizabeth's reign and was at this time the leading figure in the reform Commission. He was a very hard-working, conscientious and devout man – the Samuel Pepys of his day, although lacking the diarist's zest for life. He cared deeply for the King's honour, and had felt something like despair as the Navy, under the increasingly feeble administration of Nottingham, sank into decay. Now Buckingham's youthful vigour and enthusiasm raised his hopes, and he began his lessons by reminding the new Lord Admiral that the greatness of his office was 'not to have a market under him of base and unworthy people that betray the King's honour and his by the sales of places, havoc of provisions and ruins of the ships; but his true and real greatness is the power and greatness of the King, the confidence of his favour, the trust of his service, and the reputation and flourishing estate of the Navy'.[44]

These sentiments were shared by Buckingham, who was an Elizabethan in spirit, and in the formal instructions which he issued soon after his appointment he called on all the officers and men of the Navy to 'do their best endeavours' to 'advance the same to a greater strength than it had in former times'. As for himself,

being obliged far above others by His Majesty's most gracious favour and trust in this principal charge... I thought it the best account I could give of the first fruits of my labour, out of former ill manners to beget some good laws by which the government of the ships may hereafter be settled and the governors and others contained in their duties.[45]

The administration of the Navy, under the Lord Admiral, was left in the hands of the Commissioners, who were gradually fulfilling their promise to halve costs and at the same time build two new ships a year. In July 1619 Buckingham made his first official visit to the fleet at Chatham, where he singled out Phineas Pett, the leading English ship designer of his day, for special commendation. In the following November he accompanied the King to Deptford to see the launching of two new ships. The King was delighted with this visible evidence of improvement in naval affairs, and named the vessels 'Happy Entrance' in honour of Buckingham's inauguration as Lord Admiral, and 'Constant Reformation' as a symbol and reminder of the high purpose to which he had committed himself.[46]

IV

One of Buckingham's first tasks was to assemble a fleet for the Mediterranean, where it was to join with the Spaniards in suppressing the pirates who threatened the trade of all nations. For the details of preparing and fitting out the ships, Buckingham relied on Coke, assuring him that he had· made good use of his recommendations 'and followed that way which you chalked out'. As for the command of the expedition, he gave this to Sir Robert Mansell, who, despite his poor record as an administrator, was an experienced seaman. Mansell's fleet was to consist of six royal ships, ten merchantmen and two pinnaces, and was to be ready to sail by midsummer 1620. Preparations went ahead very slowly, however. One reason was the shortage of money, and Sir Allen Apsley, the Victualler of the Navy, had to advance nearly £5,000 out of his own pocket to provision the ships. Another was the worsening international situations, and the increasing hostility shown in England towards Spain. The Spanish ambassador, Count Gondomar, seems to have feared that the expedition might be used to attack Spain rather than defend her, and in a remarkable outburst he warned Buckingham against listening to those among his fellow-countrymen who were trying to persuade him 'that with war, all the ships which he sends against Spain, will return loaded with gold and silver'. Buckingham reassured Gondomar. The orders given to Mansell were, he told the ambassador, 'to run along the coasts of Spain and to pursue such pirates as he shall find, and so to enter into the Straits of Gibraltar and the Mediterranean Sea, and to attend upon the coast of Algiers, watching their going-in and coming-out'. There was no reason for the Spaniards to be alarmed about Mansell's intentions, for he had 'special order from the King my master to serve his majesty of Spain and in all things to observe his will and service, as if it were for the King my master'. In case any lingering doubt should remain in the ambassador's mind, he added that the 'resolution here is to conserve the good correspondency we have with Spain, and more and more to increase it every day in all things'.[47]

Not until early October 1620 did Mansell at last set course for Spain. During the winter months he could accomplish little, but in May 1621 he anchored his fleet off Algiers and sent in his men with orders to fire the pirate ships in harbour there. The sailors, 'fearless of danger (even in the mouth of the cannon and small shot which showered like hail upon them) . . . fired the ships in many places', and then withdrew. At this point, however, the defenders, who had retreated behind their walls, sallied out and with the aid of a sudden downpour extinguished the flames, so that only two of their ships were destroyed. This setback need not have meant the abandonment of Mansell's expedition, for with fresh ships and supplies he could have maintained his presence and held the pirates in check. The Spaniards themselves recognised this and offered to provision Mansell's fleet at their own cost, but James had already decided on its recall.[48]

The reason for the King's change of plan was not the failure of the attempt on Algiers but the news of repeated attacks on English men and ships by the Dutch in the East Indies, where a bitter struggle was taking place for control of the rich spice islands. The relationship between England and the republican state of the United Provinces was an uneasy one. The English approved of the Dutch as fellow protestants, and had not only helped them to gain their independence from Spain but also allowed them to retain a number of English regiments in their service. Yet at the same time they envied and hated the Dutch for their conspicuous success as traders and their domination of the commerce not only of Europe but of the orient as well. James, in particular had a kingly dislike of republicans, and the news of the outrages committed against his subjects made him so angry that the Dutch hastened to send commissioners to England to arrange a peaceful settlement. They arrived in early 1621, but the gap between the two sides was so big that it could not easily be bridged, and in April of that year they returned home. James was now considering taking action in the Channel against Dutch ships returning from the east, and he decided that Mansell's fleet would be of more use to him in home waters: hence his decision to recall it. Buckingham, as Lord Admiral, was closely involved in these developments. He shared James's anger, and regarded the Dutch attacks on English vessels as a personal affront. But it was James who made policy, and in this, as in so many other matters, Buckingham was merely the executant of the King's orders.[49]

Much the same is true of Buckingham's attitude towards 'the Spanish match', the proposed marriage between Prince Charles and the Infanta Maria of Spain, for although he had been thrust into the limelight by the anti-Spanish 'protestant interest', he was content to follow where the King led. After all, James was, in his own words, 'an old and experienced King'; he was also a political thinker of some originality, convinced of the correctness of his own opinions. Why should an inexperienced favourite question the judgement of a monarch who himself had no doubts? If James was, in Bacon's phrase, 'the best tutor in Europe', all Buckingham could hope to be was the best pupil. As far as the Spanish match was concerned he echoed the King's sentiments, and in July 1616 he assured Gondomar 'that he wished the beginning and end of his good fortune might be established upon the true friendship of the crown of England with his majesty [of Spain]'. Over the course of the next two years Buckingham made repeated visits to Gondomar – usually to carry messages from the King assuring the ambassador of his unshakable determination to maintain friendship and unity with Spain – and he would take these opportunities to emphasise his own commitment to the Spanish marriage and alliance. Gondomar, on his first arrival in England, had been somewhat suspicious of the favourite, assuming that he was a member of the anti-Spanish faction, but as he came to realise that Buckingham had no wishes other than those of the King he spoke to him with greater freedom. He also offered to put him on the Spanish pension list, but Buckingham – perhaps aware of the scandal which had erupted some years before over the revelation that certain English ministers were in receipt of Spanish annuities – declined receiving any money until such time as he had done something to deserve it; a time, which, in practice, never came.[50]

James was obviously very pleased at the good relations which Buckingham had established with Gondomar, since the favourite was his main channel of communication. Sometimes, of course, James dealt directly with the ambassador, but Buckingham was never far away and was kept informed of every-thing that passed between them. On one of these occasions, in May 1618, the King sent for his favourite after the audience was over and asked the ambassador whether he trusted Buckingham. 'Yes,' replied Gondomar. 'You do well to do so', said the King, 'for he is as Spanish as you are!'[51]

Gondomar left for Spain in the summer of 1618, shortly after John Digby had returned to England, bringing with him the articles on religion which the Spaniards had put forward as a basis for negotiations. The leisurely pace at which the whole marriage business was going forward was due to a num-ber of reasons, quite apart from the length of time required to convey mes-sages between London and Madrid. There was, firstly, the comparative youth of the parties involved. Charles was eighteen in 1618; the Infanta Maria six years younger; and although child marriages were not uncommon, particu-larly between members of ruling houses, there seemed at this stage to be no obvious reasons for haste. Secondly there was the considerable distrust that existed between England and Spain, which all James's protestations of friendship could not remove. James is often portrayed as a puppet of Gondo-mar, dancing to the Spanish tune, but this is certainly not how Gondomar saw the situation. He regarded James as an incorrigible heretic and a slip-pery negotiator whose word could not be trusted. It was for this reason that he advised the Spanish government to insist on watertight guarantees about concessions to English catholics, rather than rely upon James's promises, and this, of course, meant further delay.[52]

Negotiations might have dragged on indefinitely had it not been for the dramatic changes in the international situation in the years 1618-21. In May 1618 the Bohemian nobles renounced their allegiance to their elective king, Ferdinand, and in the following year offered the vacant throne to Frederick, the Elector Palatine. Frederick, who was the leading Calvinist ruler in Germany and head of the Protestant Union, could not resist this invitation to extend his faith and his authority into the heart of Europe, and therefore accepted. In the winter of 1619 he set out for his new kingdom and before the end of the year had been formally crowned King of Bohemia in Prague. Meanwhile the deposed Ferdinand, a pupil of the Jesuits who was determined to restore the Roman Catholic religion to those areas from which the protestants had expelled it, was elected Holy Roman Emperor in August 1619. Although his authority as Emperor was more apparent than real, he had a strong power base in the Habsburg hereditary lands in Austria, and he could count on the support of the catholic church. He could also hope for assistance from his cousins, the Spanish Habsburgs, who were preparing to renew their war against the rebel Dutch provinces in 1621 and would need to be assured of a safe passage through Germany.

Frederick's assumption of the throne of Bohemia was greeted with enor-mous enthusiasm in England. Not only was he the protestant David going forth to attack the catholic Goliath; he was also the King's son-in-law, and carried with him to Prague James's daughter, Elizabeth – named after the great Gloriana – who now became Queen of Bohemia. James did not share this enthusiasm. As a man of peace he dreaded the inflaming of religious passions, and as a divinely ordained ruler he could not approve of the deposition of sovereigns, even catholic ones. He had advised Frederick not to accept the offer of the Bohemian throne, but Frederick and his advisers assumed that once the die had been cast, family feeling, religious sentiment,

Map 2. Germany and the Netherlands at the time of Buckingham

and the pressure of public opinion would compel James to support him. Frederick's triumph, however, was short-lived. In November 1620 his army was destroyed in the battle of the White Mountain, outside Prague, and Frederick and Elizabeth became refugees. They could not even flee to their hereditary palatinate on the Rhine, for this had been partly occupied by

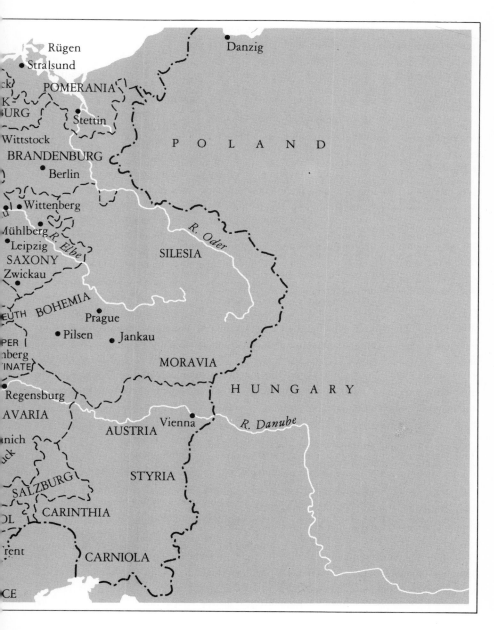

Spanish troops, acting in the name of the Emperor, in August of that year. The 'Winter King' and his wife had therefore to take refuge at the Hague, while they waited for protestant Europe to come to their aid.

If ever an arbitrator was wanted to settle the affairs of Europe it was now, and James determined to strengthen his ties with Spain as speedily as possible, so that he could act this part. The need for speed was emphasised by James's dangerous illness in 1619. He had been sharply reminded of his own mortality and of the urgency of seeing his only surviving son and heir married, with children of his own, to assure the continued rule of the House of Stuart. Otherwise, if Charles were to die unexpectedly as his elder brother had done, the throne of England would pass to Elizabeth, the Winter Queen. Such a prospect filled James with alarm, since it would mean the involvement of England in a bloody religious war whose outcome no one could foresee.

James's doubts, fears and hesitations, however wisely grounded, were not shared by the majority of his subjects. They saw the situation in much starker terms of black and white, and believed, along with Archbishop Abbot, that

God had set up this prince, His Majesty's son-in-law, as a mark of honour throughout all Christendom, to propagate the gospel and to protect the oppressed . . . . Therefore let not a noble son be forsaken for their sakes who regard nothing but their own ends. Our striking in will comfort the Bohemians, honour the Palsgrave [the Elector Palatine], strengthen the Princes of the Union, draw on the United Provinces, [and] stir up the King of Denmark . . . to cast in their shares . . . . Therefore let all our spirits be gathered up to animate this business, that the world may take notice that we are awake when God calls.

The popularity of such sentiments was shown by one of the correspondents of William Trumbull, the English ambassador at Brussels, who told him, in September 1619, of a report that Buckingham had lately declared 'that as he had received all he had from His Majesty's most gracious favour and bounty, so he was ready to spend it all in the cause of the King of Bohemia, wherein this kingdom had so great an interest'. If these really were Buckingham's sentiments, added the correspondent, 'I know not how these realms or the people can honour and love him sufficiently.'[53]

V

England's response to the call for help depended upon James, and since it was known that Buckingham carried great influence with his master, he became the focus of attention from all quarters. Elizabeth wrote to him when she sent her ambassador, Baron Dohna, to England in 1619, asking him 'to use your best means in persuading His Majesty to show himself now, in his helping of the prince here, a true loving father to us both', and referred to the 'many testimonies of your affection' which both she and her husband had received. And in the summer of the following year a certain Thomas Alured called on Buckingham, in a letter which was widely circulated and aroused much comment, to throw the weight of his influence against the Spanish match with all that it implied. 'The many talents you have cannot be better employed,' he assured him, 'for if you would lay in wait for an opportunity . . . for advancing God's glory and your honour, you cannot find or invent an occasion more pleasing to God and more plausible to the best and most men than in dissuading privately by humble entreaties, and opposing publicly by your solid reasons, this Spanish match.'[54]

These two examples – and there are many others – show how the European crisis which marked the opening of the Thirty Years War turned Buckingham, willy-nilly, into a political figure. Up to 1618 he had simply been the King's favourite, a man upon whom fortune had smiled and who used his new-found favour to advance his friends and family. But from 1618 onwards he was seen in an altogether different light. With passions running high, James's flexible and ambiguous approach was increasingly unacceptable to his subjects, and the widespread frustration that his policy of non-commitment engendered vented itself on Buckingham. People persuaded themselves that their King *must* be on the side of righteousness, and that his hesitations were caused by the influence of evil counsellors. The most apparent of these was Buckingham, and the conviction spread that he was a crypto-papist or Spanish agent, standing between the King and his loyal subjects. Buckingham thereby became a victim of the clash between appearances and reality, for, as an early historian of James's reign perceptively observed, the King made him 'his instrument and the only bossom counsellor in those affairs, which afterwards brought the hatred of the people with the more violence upon him. For they look not upon the King in any miscarriage with an eye of anger . . . but upon such intimate ministers as he makes active in those things which are contrary to their affection.'[55]

Indications of Buckingham's own opinions in the opening months of 1620 may be gleaned from the courteous way in which he received Baron Dohna. A number of observers commented on this, and there would have been general agreement with Naunton's view that 'all the best sort of His Majesty's people applaud and honour your noble forwardness and furtherance in gracing the Bohemian ambassador with your visits and introducing him to conferences and audiences with His Majesty'. The Prince and Buckingham were said to be very zealous on behalf of Frederick, and to be urging James to send support to the states of the Protestant Union so that they could intervene on the Palatine's behalf. The Spaniards, who were aware of the mounting anger in England and the pressures on the King, decided to send Gondomar back, and he arrived in London in March 1620. By this time James had agreed that a volunteer force should be allowed to go to the Palatinate, solely to aid in its defence, and among the first sounds that Gondomar heard in the City was that of the drums beating in the streets to summon men to the colours. With his customary vigour, Gondomar immediately set about redressing the balance in favour of Spain, working mainly through Digby, who was high in the King's favour at this time, and Buckingham. Once again Buckingham acted as the King's secretary, and Gondomar reported that James 'shows him everything and gives him account of everything, desiring to keep him informed and make him capable of handling negotiations; and so the Marquis gives him all the letters he receives, and the King gives him the minutes of the replies he has to make in matters of importance'. Buckingham, who received reports from English ambassadors as well as other correspondents in various parts of the world, must have been among the best-informed men in England, even though he was as yet a passive observer of events. His later intervention in state affairs was based not upon ignorance, as has frequently been assumed, but upon knowledge.[56]

Buckingham's enthusiasm for the Bohemian cause was cooled by a quarrel with Baron Dohna over the appointment of an English officer to command the volunteer force of some four thousand men that was being prepared for the Palatinate. This post was coveted by Sir Edward Cecil, a grandson of Elizabeth's chief minister, Lord Burghley, and a member of a family with which Buckingham had formed close ties. Cecil was a professional soldier with a record of distinguished service in the Low Countries. He was also on good personal terms with Frederick, and Buckingham therefore encouraged him to press his claim. But the final decision rested with Dohna, as Frederick's representative, and Dohna chose Sir Horace Vere, commander of the English regular forces serving with the Dutch. Buckingham was furious at what he regarded, with some justification, as an affront, and according to the French envoy he told Dohna that if it had not been for his privileged status he would have thrown him out of the window. He sent a message to Elizabeth, complaining of her apparent lack of confidence in his judgement, and he also confided to Gondomar that Frederick was becoming too haughty and needed taking down a peg or two before he would be persuaded to accept the advice offered him by his father-in-law.[57]

No doubt Buckingham was here echoing James's opinion, but events in Europe in the autumn of 1620 led to a change of heart on the part of both King and favourite. The Spaniards had never given up their claim to sovereignty over all the Low Countries, including the United Provinces, and although they had been forced by sheer exhaustion to accept a truce with the Dutch, this was due to expire in 1621, and both sides were preparing for a renewal of war. Because the Dutch controlled the sea routes from Spain to the Netherlands, Spanish armies and the materials and money to maintain them had to be first shipped to Italy, from where they made their way across the Alps and down to the Rhine. They then followed the river all the way through Germany until they reached their destination. The Lower Palatinate, which was the principal part of the Elector Frederick's hereditary possessions, straddled the Rhine route as it neared the Netherlands, and was therefore of critical importance to the Spaniards. They could not risk allowing this section of their lifeline to be closed to them now that war with the Dutch was imminent, and for some time they had been assembling a large force in Germany under one of their best commanders, the Marquis Spinola. They gáve out that this army was for use in Bohemia, but in September 1620 Spinola led his troops into the Palatinate and started occupying the southern half of it. Even James was shocked by this unwarranted invasion of his son-in-law's territory, and he publicly announced his intention of intervening, by force if necessary, to restore the *status quo*. Such a declaration was just what James's subjects were longing to hear, and it was received with general rejoicing. Elizabeth wrote to Buckingham from Prague, entreating him 'to use your best means with the King that he would now assist us, for he hath ever professed that he would not suffer the Palatinate to be taken from us. I do most confidently rely upon your affection to me', she added, 'and you can show it in nothing more than in this matter, which I earnestly recommend to you.'[58]

Buckingham needed little prompting to follow this course, especially now that the King seemed ready to commit himself. He quickly patched up his quarrel with Dohna and contributed the enormous sum of £5,000 to the voluntary 'benevolence' which James ordered to be raised for the defence of the Palatinate. He was not, however, a free agent, and when Gondomar complained to the King of reports that he had deliberately deceived James about Spinola's intentions, it was Buckingham who had to write to the ambassador and confirm that the King had never been given any assurance that Spinola's armies would not enter the Palatinate. Gondomar made this letter public, hoping thereby, in the words of one observer, 'to put away from himself the odiousness of the imputation laid here commonly to his proceedings'. It is doubtful whether the letter had any effect on the general belief in Spanish perfidy, but to many people it would have seemed like confirmation that Buckingham was on the side of the devil.[59]

Among the persons with whom Buckingham kept in touch were experienced soldiers like Sir Edward Cecil, Sir John Ogle and Sir Edward Conway – men whose age and experience filled the gaps in his own knowledge of affairs. They were, without exception, anti-Spanish, strong supporters of Frederick and Elizabeth, and advocates of a closer alliance with the Dutch. Among other things, they made him aware that, as Conway told him in December 1620, failure to unite with the protestants in Germany would lead to the domination of the Habsburg House of Austria over the whole of Europe, and would ultimately threaten England itself. All Buckingham could do at this stage, however, was to send messages of encouragement to his friends – among them Elizabeth, who wrote to him in January 1621 thanking him for his good wishes and assuring him that he had no need to 'mistrust that I did doubt of your affection to the King's [Frederick's] service and mine, for you have given, both by your letters and by the effects which we both daily see, so much testimony' of your affection as the King and I should be the most ungrateful creatures in the world if we should so much as have thought to doubt of your love to us'.[60]

By the time Elizabeth wrote her letter she and her husband were refugees. The battle of the White Mountain, had put an end for ever to their reign in Bohemia, while the Rhine Palatinate was being overrun by Spanish and Imperial forces. From James's point of view the loss of Bohemia clarified the situation. He had never approved of Frederick's action in accepting the crown of that country, and had held back from aiding him partly because he feared that to do so would be to condone an illegal transfer of power. But there could be no question, in James's eyes, that the Palatinate belonged to Frederick, and he decided to send a messenger to him, with an assurance that he would aid him, if necessary by force, on condition that Frederick formally renounced the Bohemian throne. The person chosen to convey this message was Buckingham's half-brother, Sir Edward Villiers, and it may be assumed that Buckingham had not merely recommended Sir Edward for this important mission but had taken the opportunity to send with him his own assurances to the unfortunate Winter King and Queen. He also strongly supported Frederick's suggestion that James should maintain the army of the Protestant Union (which was on the brink of breaking up) while he was negotiating with the Emperor and other powers, in order to give more weight to his recommendations. Buckingham pointed out that it would require no great sum of money to keep the army in being for some two or three months, 'and that possibly His Majesty might by this occasion obtain such a supply of his people as that himself might be a gainer by it'. James was momentarily convinced, but later changed his mind. Nevertheless Carleton, writing to Buckingham from the Hague in May, told him how much pleasure his advocacy of their cause had given Frederick and Elizabeth.[61]

Buckingham's reference to the aid that James might expect from his subjects was no idle fancy, for by May 1621 Parliament was in session. Seven years had passed since the last meeting of Parliament – the one known as 'Addled' because it produced nothing – and James would probably not have summoned another had it not been for the need to find money to finance a possible war. The benevolence had produced about £30,000, which he planned to send to his son-in-law, but much more substantial sums would be needed if England was to enter the war. In November 1620, therefore, James took the decision to summon a Parliament for the new year, and on 30 January 1621 he made his way in solemn procession to the House of Lords to declare the session open.[62]

NOTES

(Abbreviations are explained in the Bibliography, pp. 477–86)
1. *State.* 24.
2. *Bac.* XIII, 118; *Ch.* II, 66; *Sack.MSS.* EN.M, 810.
3. *Mayes; Crisis.* 96.
4. *C.S.P.V.* XV, 251; *Cam.* 26 June 1618; *Clo.MSS.* C.54 2397, Part 4.
5. *Ch.* II, 200, 247; *Sal.* 16 July 1619, A.M. 4193; *Meditation.* Dedication.
6. *Ch.* II, 227; *Dom.MSS 14.* 108.82; 109.112.

7. *C.S.P.V.* XV, 548; *Ch.* II, 253.
8. From the inscription on the tomb of Francis Manners, 6th Earl of Rutland, in Bottesford church, Leicestershire.
9. *Ch.* II, 200.
10. *Dom.MSS 14.* 110.22.
11. *Ch.* II, 293; *H.M.C. (4).* 290; *Hack.* I, 41–2; *Docs.* II, 274.
12. *Ch.* II, 297; *Trum.MSS.* 6. 128; *Goodman.* II, 189–91.
13. *Harl. MSS.* 1581. 134; *Bas.MSS.* 53.52.
14. *Harl.MSS.* 6986. 198; *Hack.* I, 42; *Goodman.* II, 314–19.
15. *Cam.* 16 May 1620; *Hack.* I, 43; *Family.* 198–9; *Dom.MSS 16.* 8.10; 101.43; *Goodman.* II, 309–14.
16. *H.M.C.Coke.* 104; The figure for the Irish Customs is taken from Treadwell (see Ch. 2, n.53).
17. *Clo.MSS.* C.54, 2616; *Ch.* II, 159.
18. *Dom.MSS 14.* 119. 56.
19. *Dom.MSS 14.* 104.11; 109.37; Accounts of Gabriel Marsh, *Fair.MSS.*
20. *Clo.MSS.* C.54, 2420, 2397; Deed dated 12 Jan. 1621, *Fair.MSS.*; *Sack.MSS.* ON. 2448.
21. *Clo.MSS.* C. 54, 2479; *Ch.* II, 275; Deed dated 12 Jan. 1621, *Fair.MSS.*
22. *Dom.MSS 14.* 121.32.
23. *Jonson.* 539, 576; *C.S.P.V.* XVII. 117; *Bas.MSS.* 55.192.
24. *Ch.* II. 397; *H.M.C. (5).* 409
25. *Cab.* 333–4; *Cam.* Jan. 1620; *Ch.* II, 284; *Trum.MSS.* 6.122, 143.
26. *Dom.MSS 14.* 109.37, 16; *Sal.* 13 May 1619, A.M. 4193.
27. *Dom.MSS 14.* 110.19; *Ch.* II, 263.
28. *H.M.C.Sal.* 104; *H.M.C.Sid.* 421.
29. *Dom.MSS 14.* 97.10; 110.83; *Ch.* II, 249.
30. *Ch.* II, 272, 375.
31. *Tann.MSS.* 74.225; *Eg.MSS.*2592.55, 235.
32. *Tann.MSS.* 74.178; 290.31; *Rush.* 387.
33. *H.M.C.Bucc.* I, 255; *Clo.MSS.* C.54, 2487.
34. *Ch.* II, 338.
35. *Dom.MSS 14.* 105.112.
36. *Thom.*; *D'Ewes.* 188; *C.S.P.V.* XVII, 88.
37. *Bac.* XIV, 13, 37.
38. *Bac.* XIV, 158–9.
39. *Dom.MSS 14.* 109.59; *Trum.MSS.* 18.48.
40. *Ch.* II, 281; *Prestwich.* 261–2.
41. *Tann.MSS.* 74.239; *Eg.MSS.* 2533.63–63v.
42. *Goodman.* II, 210–18, 207–9; *Sack.MSS.* ON.2415.
43. *Sack.MSS.ON.*6844; *Prestwich.* 420.
44. *H.M.C.Coke.* 99.
45. *Slo.MSS.* 3232.139–139v.
46. *Cam.* 19 July 1619; *Pett.* 120; *Ch.* II. 271; *C.S.P.V.* XVI, 53–4.
47. *H.M.C.Coke* 106; *Sack.MSS.ON.*182; *Sp.Tr.MSS.*21.133v.; *Add.MSS.*36, 444.165–165v.
48. *Cab.* 298.
49. *Reade MSS.* 1/2.38.
50. *Tanner.* 284; *Bac.*XIII, 239; *Hecho.*130; *Docs.*I, 108, 130; *Sp.Tr.MSS.* 26. unpag.

51. *Docs.* I, 329–30.
52. *Gond.*
53. *Rush.* 12; *Trum.MSS.* 18.43.
54. *Tann.MSS.* 74.219; *Gutch.* 170–80.
55. *Wil.* 726.
56. *Fort.* 119; *Dom.MSS 14.* 112.93; *Bas.MSS.* 53.79; *Ch.* II, 294; *Docs.* II, 274.
57. *Dalton.* I, 325–26; *Holl.MSS. 96.32; 97.173; Bas.MSS.* 54.127; *Sp.Tr.MSS.* 23.73v.
58. *Fort.* 138.
59. *Trum.MSS.* 6.153; *Tann.MSS.* 290.9.
60. *Harl.MSS.* 1580.285; 6987.3.
61. *Holl.MSS.* 101.9, 79.
62. *Dissolving.* 294.

CHAPTER FOUR

1621–22: 'The only Author of all Grievances and Oppressions'

I

The King had summoned Parliament in the hope that it would demonstrate the unity between him and his people, and thereby strengthen his hand when it came to dealing with foreign rulers. But members of Parliament, and in particular members of the House of Commons, did not necessarily share the King's order of priorities. As representatives of the local communities they were only too conscious of the many evils that cried out to be remedied, and the fact that Parliament met so rarely made the redress of grievances all the more urgent. In theory the King, as guardian of his people, should have been the person to whom they looked to sweep away abuses, but in practice many of the most resented burdens came from the royal government itself. Principal among these were monopolies – grants made to one or more individuals, giving them the sole right to manufacture or trade in a specified commodity. Linked with monopolies were the letters patent which authorised the grantees to enforce some particular branch of the royal authority, in return for payment. Monopolies, patents and the like were not new subjects for complaint. The last Parliaments of Elizabeth had been soured by the resentment which members felt at the increasing range and number of such grants, and the Queen had only defended her prerogative by promising to take action herself. Yet neither Elizabeth nor James could afford to dispense with monopolies altogether, for by so doing they would have lost the revenue which such grants brought in. Even worse from their point of view, they would have had to find some other way in which to reward the courtiers and servants who were the main beneficiaries, and this would have meant a further depletion of their already inadequate resources. Fundamentally it was the financial weakness of the crown, resulting from the impact of inflation upon inadequate endowments, which drove the royal government into actions that alienated the affections of the King's subjects and made them look to Parliament rather than the Crown for redress.

Monopolies and the like were unacceptable at the best of times, but particularly so in the early 1620s, when the economy was depressed. John Chamberlain, commenting in the autumn of 1620 upon reports that the King had decided to summon Parliament, declared that 'impositions and patents are grown so grievous that of necessity they must be spoken of'. 'Many new patents come forth,' he added, 'and more daily expected.' He listed some of these – including that for saltpetre (an essential ingredient of gunpowder) which the Earl of Worcester had been more or less compelled to give up 'by reason of the continual complaints' but which was 'not like to be lighter or less burdenous in the Lord of Buckingham's hands'. Buckingham was not, in fact, a major monopolist in his own right, but he had been responsible for procuring a number of monopoly grants, particularly to his relatives. Indeed, among the new devices that Chamberlain mentioned was one for an office for the probate of wills, the profits from which were to go to Buckingham's brother, Kit Villiers. Kit was also involved, along with his half-brother Sir Edward Villiers, in Sir Giles Mompesson's patent for regulating inns. This was a function which belonged in law to the assize judges, but they were usually too busy to deal with it, and complaints about the large numbers of inns, and the poor management of them, were frequent. Justices of the Peace, who had the requisite local knowledge, were only empowered to deal with ale-houses, not inns, and on the face of it there was much to be said for the idea of setting up a separate office for licensing inns and supervising their management. In practice, however, the patent was a device to make money, for Mompesson cared little who ran the inns, or how many there were, so long as his profits increased. This particular patent became notorious for the abuses with which it was associated, and in November 1620, after a Parliament had definitely been decided on, Bacon wrote to Buckingham suggesting that he should encourage the King to cancel it, along with other patents which were likely to be attacked in the Commons. 'I thought it appertained to the singular love and affection which I bear you,' he told the favourite, 'that your lordship . . . would put off the envy of these things (which I think in themselves bear no great fruit) and rather take the thanks for ceasing them than the note for maintaining them.'[1]

Buckingham would have been well advised to follow this suggestion, but he did nothing. He may not have realised how unpopular these patents were, or he may simply have assumed that as the King's favourite he would be able to ride out any storm. Buckingham had not yet experienced a Parliament, and he had no reason to suspect, at this early stage, that the anger of the Commons would be focussed directly on his family and indirectly upon himself. Simply because of his power and influence, Buckingham had come to be identified with the corruption which characterised early Stuart government, and while he thought of himself – with some reason – as a champion of reform, the majority of people regarded him as the principal obstacle in the way of its achievement. It is doubtful if Buckingham realised just how unpopular he had become. In the circles in which he habitually moved, the King's favour – as well as his own charm and good looks – guaranteed him adulation, and the suitors and sycophants who thronged around him outvied each other in singing his praises. Bacon, who was not insulated from public

90

opinion to the same extent, was clearly more aware of the pressures building up against the favourite – hence his advice to the Marquis. It may have been at Bacon's suggestion that the King, in his opening speech to Parliament, took up the subject of reform. He related how he had cut the cost of the royal household, and reduced the amount of money eaten up by the Navy, without any reduction in the number or quality of the ships; 'wherein he did acknowledge the good service of the Lord Admiral; that albeit he was young and unexperienced, yet with a great deal of pains he had informed himself in such sort that, taking upon him the obloquy and displeasure of many, he had effected it with so much profit to the King and safety to the state'.[2]

James hoped that by emphasising his own and his servants' commitment to reform he would encourage the Commons to be generous when it came to voting supply. But only a handful of members could confirm from their experience how effective Cranfield's reform programme had been. For the majority, the royal administration was associated with waste and corruption on a massive scale, and as Bacon had foreseen, they were determined to deal first with those grievances of which their constituents had complained. On 19 February 1621 Sir Edward Coke proposed that the House should take into consideration the patent of inns, since Mompesson was a member of the Commons. On the following day Mompesson delivered in his patent for examination, declaring that if it was 'contrary to law, let it die'. He also asserted that he had taken on the task of licensing inns not out of any desire for filthy lucre but in order to further the work of reform. When attacked by Sir Robert Phelips, who pointed out that 'every patent hath a specious show of good to the King or subject', he roundly insisted that he had not himself been guilty of any abuses and had, on the contrary, put down all those that had been called to his attention. There the matter might have ended, had it not been for the intervention of one of Buckingham's relatives, John Drake of Ash. Drake, as a Devonshire Justice of the Peace, had turned out a certain alehouse keeper, by name William Quick, on the grounds that he had been involved in a murder plot. Quick appealed to Mompesson, who promptly licensed him as an innkeeper; and when Drake protested that Quick was unfit to hold such a position, Mompesson wrote him a letter couched in haughty terms, which Drake produced to the Commons. In this letter Mompesson announced that he could not possibly 'give way to the will of every Justice of Peace, in derogation of His Majesty's so just and great benefit', and made it plain that if he and Drake had not been kinsmen he would have taken quite a different course with him, 'as he had done with others'.[3]

The production of this letter aroused intense indignation in the Lower House, in which Justices of the Peace were very well represented. Mompesson himself was taken aback by the irrefutable evidence of his own complicity, and after confessing that the letter did indeed appear to be in his hand, he left the whole matter to the judgement of the House. Not surprisingly the House voted 'that it is a grievance in Sir Giles Mompesson to the commonwealth', and later ordered that he should be kept in custody until such time as he could be presented to the Lords for trial.[4]

Mompesson, who was Sir Edward Villiers's brother-in-law and could therefore claim kinship with the favourite, now wrote to Buckingham appealing for his help. He complained that general charges were being made against him but nothing specific which he could rebut and thereby clear himself. As for his actions, he had, he declared, done nothing that would not be fitting for 'an honest man and a faithful servant', and if it should be proved that he had erred he was willing to 'endure as great a punishment as ever delinquent did'. This was not the first occasion on which Mompesson had protested his innocence to the favourite. Even before Parliament opened, Buckingham had sent for Mompesson and asked him if there was any truth in the rumours circulating about his conduct. Mompesson 'boldly and with much confidence assured him that his carriage had been so just and so honest as he would never [ask] . . . to be protected under his lordship's favour, the King's, or anybody's else'. After the opening of the session, Buckingham again questioned Mompesson, warned him that Parliament was likely to call him to account, and advised him, if he had done anything wrong, to confess it. 'Yet still he did answer with that confidence and boldness that he desired no favour but to justify himself.'[5]

Buckingham was at Court when he received Mompesson's appeal for help, but he immediately left for town. Whatever doubts he had about Mompesson's conduct he was not prepared to abandon him at this critical juncture: in his own words, 'he did never love to lose a friend or leave him for his adversity, except there were good cause', for 'he thought that whosoever did so would never have friend'. But when Buckingham reached London he learnt that Mompesson had escaped from custody and gone into hiding, thereby implicitly acknowledging his guilt. The Commons asked the Lords for a conference, to discuss what steps should be taken to recapture Mompesson, and the Lords appointed a committee – which included the Prince and Buckingham – to join with them. It was at this meeting that Buckingham gave an account of his involvement with Mompesson, and assured his hearers that 'truly I thought the projects had been good for the King and commonwealth, as was pretended'. He added that now that he had been convinced of Mompesson's guilt he would be 'the chiefest and forwardest against him'.[6]

Buckingham seems to have been relaxed and confident at this conference. He even permitted himself a wry joke at Coke's expense, for when Sir Edward, fulminating against the misdeeds of Mompesson, declared that 'Empson and Dudley were [but] fools to this projector', Buckingham commented that this was indeed the case, 'for they stood to it and were hanged, but Sir Giles hath taken his heels'. There is no reason to doubt Buckingham's account of his dealings with Mompesson. A man who could assure an angry House of Commons that he had been engaged in the project solely for the King's honour and not for any considerations of profit would have had no qualms about deceiving the Lord Admiral: indeed, Mompesson may have convinced himself of his own innocence, for his actions – and those of his subordinates – had been unwise rather than illegal. His patent had, as was usual in such cases, been submitted to referees, to see whether it was both lawful and beneficial, and only after the referees had given their formal approval did the King confirm the grant. Mompesson could reasonably complain, as he did in his letter to Buckingham, that if anyone was to blame it was the referees. No doubt he also thought that his conduct was no worse than that of many other patentees and monopolists, and that he had been picked on because of his connexion with the unpopular favourite.[7]

II

No sooner had Buckingham weathered this storm than another one broke over his head, for the Commons went on to consider the patent for a monopoly of the manufacture of gold and silver thread, in which Buckingham's half-brother, Sir Edward Villiers, was involved. This particular monopoly had a long history behind it, for the first grant had been made in 1605, and the patentees committed themselves to enrich not only the King but also the country through the import of bullion. The monopoly would not be effective, however, unless all makers of silver and gold thread agreed to be licensed by the patentees and pay the fees involved. A number refused to do this, and the Attorney-General, Sir Henry Yelverton – who was also one of the commissioners appointed by the crown for enforcing the monopoly – was called on to take appropriate action. Among those who pressed him was Sir Edward Villiers, who had invested £4,000 in the business and was eager to secure an adequate return on his capital. When Sir Edward informed Yelverton that 'the cause now lay a-bleeding, therefore he must either now imprison them or all was lost', Yelverton reluctantly agreed, but only on condition that his action was ratified by the Lord Chancellor. Bacon duly gave his approval, and a number of small manufacturers were thereupon imprisoned. This caused a scandal in the City of London, where most of them lived, particularly since rich and important companies such as the Goldsmiths felt that the patent infringed their own privileges. The City complained to the King, who immediately ordered the release of the offenders, declaring that he would not govern his people by bonds. When this story was revealed to the House of Commons it caused an uproar. Cranfield, who was a member, hastened to divert the storm from the favourite by assuring members 'that Sir Edward Villiers had no encouragement or comfort from the Marquis [and] that Sir Henry Yelverton confessed my lord of Buckingham never did write, speak or send to him about it'. But the temper of the House was more accurately reflected by Sir Edward Giles, who declared that monopolists and projectors were 'bloodsuckers of the kingdom and vipers of the commonwealth'. 'Let no man's greatness daunt us,' he added. 'The more we do to great men, the more we prevent in future these mischiefs.'[8]

It looked as though the Commons' anger might drive Parliament in dangerous directions, so the King decided to intervene. On 10 March, therefore, he went to the House of Lords and made a long speech in which he reviewed the patents under attack and defended his own action – or rather inaction – with regard to them. He was clearly also concerned to defend his favourite from the criticisms that had been made of him. 'Buckingham hath moved me many times in things of this kind,' he said, 'being informed that they were not prejudicial to my people and would redound much to my profit. But always with this protestation, saying, "If they be good, it is fit for Your Majesty. But for myself, I will have none of them".' He went on to give a picture of Buckingham besieged by suitors and projectors clamouring for his support. 'For Buckingham, since he came to me, being so near to me, hath been more troubled than ever any that served me, that I may say his time hath been a purgatory to him; and that he hath had more ease this Parliament than he hath had of a long time before, for now he is not pestered and troubled at his chamber with projects or projectors.'[9]

The King had made it clear that he did not hold Buckingham guilty of any offence – except, perhaps, a lack of discrimination. This was an implied warning to the favourite's critics and enemies not to press home their attack, but the King had, at the same time, to make clear his concern for justice and impartiality. He therefore desired the Lords to look on the favourite not 'as adorned with these honours, as Marquis of Buckingham, Admiral of England, Master of my Horse, Gentleman of my Bedchamber, a Privy Councillor and a Knight of the Garter, but as he was when he came to me, as poor George Villiers; and if he prove not himself a white crow, he shall be called a black crow'. Buckingham's response was to fall to his knees and declare 'Sir, if I cannot clear myself of any aspersion or imputation cast upon me, I am contented to abide Your Majesty's censure and be called the Black Crow.' Some time later, after the Lord Chancellor and Lord Treasurer had also made statements exculpating themselves, Buckingham again declared his desire 'to be purged by Your Majesty's gracious declaration whether, since I had the honour to serve you, I have solicited you in anything that is hurtful to your people. If I have not, I beseech Your Majesty I may still live in your gracious opinion.'[10]

Bearing in mind the close relationship between the King and his favourite, and the love of plays and acting which they shared, it is probable that this little scene had been previously rehearsed. Yet the element of play-acting should not be allowed to conceal the very real dangers of the situation, for both parties. The King had suffered public humiliation, and could have won credit by disowning Buckingham and leaving him to his fate. But James chose not to sacrifice his favourite. His affection for the young man was still too great, and had he abandoned him he would have been tacitly confessing that his own judgement had been at fault in trusting him so much. Yet his reference to 'poor George Villiers' was a reminder, if one were needed, that the King who had made Buckingham could as easily unmake him. His titles and offices were as nothing. In the last resort only the King could save him, and if Buckingham brought the King into disrepute by continually stepping over the invisible line that divided what was acceptable from what was not, he would bring about his own fall. Coming from James, who had encouraged his favourite to enrich himself and his family at the public expense, such a warning might seem unfair and hypocritical. But James, like his subjects, took it for granted that kings could do no wrong: it was their counsellors who must bear the blame. Buckingham, who was a realist, would have seen nothing strange in this assumption.

Buckingham must by now have been apprehensive about the way in which events were shaping. According to Hacket he lost all peace of mind and feared if not for his own safety then at least for his reputation. It was John Williams – at that time Dean of Westminster – who (again according to Hacket) advised him to swim with the tide.

If you assist to break up this Parliament, being now in pursuit of justice, only to save some cormorants who have devoured that which must be regorged, you will pluck up a sluice which will overwhelm yourself.... My sentence is, cast all monopolies and patents of griping projections into the Dead Sea ... and your lordship must needs partake in the applause. For though it is known that these vermin haunted your chamber, and is much whispered that they set up trade with some little licence from your honour, yet when none shall appear more forward than yourself to crush them, the discourse will come about that these devices, which take ill, were stolen from you by misrepresentation when you were but new blossomed in Court; whose deformities being discovered, you love not your own mistakings but are the most forward to recall them. [11]

There is some reason to doubt whether Buckingham was quite so alarmed, or so dependent upon Williams, as Hacket asserts. A letter from Bacon to the favourite written on 9 March shows that Buckingham had already decided to speak out, if necessary, against his brothers, and indeed it needed no great perception to see that this would probably be the best course. Williams may well have been thinking along the same lines, but in his letter – if it was ever sent – he advised Buckingham to 'give your brother, Sir Edward, a commission for an embassage to some of the princes of Germany . . . and despatch him over the seas before he be missed': sound advice, indeed, but not very appropriate in March 1621, by which time Sir Edward Villiers had already been abroad some months. As for Buckingham's state of mind, there is the perhaps significant absence of any mention of the sort of physical collapse that often indicated emotional strain on the favourite. His continued good health in the early months of 1621 suggests that, while no doubt alarmed, he was far from panic-stricken. He was, as always, seeking and taking advice from all quarters, learning fast, and rapidly adjusting his position to changed circumstances. In short, he was doing on the larger stage of Parliament what he had already learnt to do so skilfully at Court. [12]

By 13 March Buckingham had clearly recovered his balance, for on that day he took the opportunity, at a conference of the two houses, to make his own attitude clear. Buckingham began with a message from the King – a deliberate reminder of whose servant he was and how useful he could be to his hearers – announcing James's 'gracious acceptance of the proceedings in Parliament' and his wish that the Commons would 'insist upon great matters and not upon points of law and form'. He then spoke on his own behalf, thanking the Commons 'for clearing those imputations which were laid upon himself' and declaring his determination to use his best endeavours 'to further the good of the King and kingdom, which could not be severed'. He had had no experience of Parliaments, as he reminded members, but now that he knew what they were he 'would be a scholar and learn to do my King and country service'. As for his two brothers, 'if it should appear they were faulty he would not protect them; but we should see that the same father who begot them that were the offenders begot a third that would get them to be punished'.[13]

Buckingham had to face critics in the Upper as well as the Lower House. Early in the session a number of peers met at the homes of Lord Salisbury and Lord Dorset to draft a petition against the holders of new titles in the Irish and Scottish peerage who claimed the precedence of their rank in England. Some thirty-three English lords put their names to the petition, about a third of them holders of pre-Stuart titles. James was furious at this criticism of his undoubted right to confer honours, and Buckingham, who saw the petition – rightly – as a criticism of his own role in procuring them, told Salisbury and Dorset that he was astonished at their attitude. He had previously thought them his friends, but now knew them for what they were worth and would act accordingly.[14]

While this petition undoubtedly reflected the discontent created among English peers by the inflation of honours, and in particular the sale of new titles, it did not, as has sometimes been suggested, signal a closing of the Lords' ranks against Buckingham or a split between the 'old' nobility and the 'new'. There was certainly opposition to the favourite in the Lords, but it was led by the Earl of Southampton and Lord Sheffield, whose motives were a mixture of political and personal and who were both, as it happened, only the third holders of titles granted as recently as 1547. Politically they stood for the 'protestant interest' and opposed Buckingham because they regarded him as a crypto-catholic and tool of Spain. But they also opposed him because of his quasi-monopoly of power. Southampton, in particular, wanted to topple the favourite so that he could take his place, and the nakedness of his ambition made him unacceptable to men such as Pembroke who were otherwise in sympathy with his aims. This accounts for the fact that there was no fusion between the Southampton faction and that led by Pembroke and Archbishop Abbot.

Another of Buckingham's critics in the Upper House was William Fiennes, Baron Saye and Sele, described by Clarendon as 'a man of a close and reserved nature . . . of great parts and of the highest ambition, but whose ambition would not be satisfied with offices and preferment without some condescensions and alterations in ecclesiastical matters'. Saye's title dated back to the fifteenth century, but his opposition to Buckingham – to whom he was distantly related – sprang from religious rather than genealogical considerations. Saye was a low churchman, of the sort sometimes described as puritan, and he feared the growing influence of the high church or Arminian party. Buckingham was not yet identified with this – though he was becoming friendly with the Arminian cleric William Laud, and in 1622 one of his chaplains preached what was described as an Arminian sermon at Cambridge. Saye probably distrusted Buckingham because he held him responsible for the King's pro-Spanish policy and consequent mildness towards the Roman Catholics. Politically speaking, Saye seems to have inclined to the view later associated with the Whigs, that the King should rule in close association with the representatives of the people gathered in Parliament, and should listen, in particular, to the peers and other landowners who had the greatest stake in the country. He would therefore have distrusted James's absolutist tendencies and blamed Buckingham for encouraging them.[15]

Yet in fact Buckingham's views on the role of the aristocracy were not all that far removed from Saye's. Buckingham believed that nobles had a duty, in return for the privileges they enjoyed, to serve the Crown and state. On 5 March, therefore, he made a formal proposal in the House of Lords that 'forasmuch as the education of youth, especially of quality and worth, is a matter of high consequence . . . some fit and good course might be taken for erection and maintenance of an academy for the breeding and bringing-up of the nobility and gentry of this kingdom in their younger and tender age'. This speech was well received and a committee was appointed – of which the Prince and Buckingham were members – to frame proposals. No record survives of the committee's meetings, if indeed they ever took place, and little or nothing more was done at this stage. Buckingham, however, continued to press the matter. He was himself distinguished, in Conway's words, by 'a nobleness born with him, increased with practice and breeding', and recognised the need for some institution in England similar to the academy for nobles established in France. He persuaded James to agree to the erection of an establishment to be called 'King James's Academy, Society Heroic, or College of Honour', but the shortage of money which frustrated so many of James's plans stifled this one also.[16]

III

It may be that Buckingham timed his speech about an academy in order to rally opinion around him in the Lords while he was under attack in the Commons. In fact the attack was shifting – for the time being, at any rate – away from Buckingham towards his protégé, the Lord Chancellor, Francis Bacon, who had been created Viscount St Alban in January 1621. On 6 February Sir Edward Sackville had explained to the House of Commons that before the King approved of any patent he referred it to 'those of place and trust about him who, by reason of their places, in all presumption should best understand the business'. Only after the referees had certified that the patent was both lawful and of sound benefit did the King allow it to go ahead. Sackville was not concerned simply to explain the workings of government. He called for an enquiry into the names and motives of the referees who had approved the patents now under question, 'so the faults might be taken from His Majesty and lie upon the referees, who misled His Maje ⁻y and are worthy to bear the shame of their own work'.[17]

Sackville's attack on the referees is in some ways surprising, for he was on close terms with Bacon, who, both as Attorney-General and Lord Chancellor, had been frequently used as a referee. Sackville was also concerned to keep in Buckingham's favour. Could it be that even at this early stage he was acting at Buckingham's direction to switch the Commons' investigation away from the King and favourite towards the less politically sensitive area of the referees? If there was any collusion it might explain why it was another of Buckingham's dependants, Lionel Cranfield, who kept Sackville's proposal alive. On 24 February he urged 'that the referees of all patents of grievances may be considered of and examined, for His Majesty's honour, who by them hath been abused', and three days later he again called to 'have the referees examined and known, who presumed to certify the lawfulness or conveniency of any patent that is a grievance'.[18]

Whether Cranfield and Sackville acted on their own initiative or by direction, they can hardly have assumed that the assault on Bacon would have such a dramatic outcome. It was a century and a half since the Commons had succeeded in removing a major officer of state without direction from the sovereign, and Cranfield probably assumed that the members would expend their fury in vain expostulations against the referees. It seems unlikely that he ever wanted the case against Bacon to reach the Lords, for as Bacon told Buckingham on 7 March, 'Sir Lionel Cranfield, who hath been formerly the trumpet, said yesterday that he did now incline . . . not to have the referees meddled with, otherwise than to discount it from the King; and so not to look back, but to the future.' Unfortunately for both Bacon and Cranfield, Sir Edward Coke was also engaged in the hunt against the referees, and his vision of Parliament as the grand inquisitor was one far removed from theirs. It was also one which he, with his vast legal learning and knowledge of precedents, was uniquely well qualified to carry into effect.[19]

On 20 March the Lord Treasurer, Viscount Mandeville, gave the House of Lords an account of a conference held the previous day with representatives of the Commons, at which they had accused Bacon of taking bribes. After the Treasurer had finished speaking, Buckingham rose and told how

he had been twice with the Lord Chancellor to visit him, being sent to him by the King. The first time he found his lordship very sick and heavy. The second time he found him better and much comforted, for that he heard that the complaint of the grievances of the Commons against him were come into this House, where he assured himself to find honourable justice.

Buckingham then handed over a letter which Bacon had written to the House, asking for time to prepare his defence to the charges made against him.[20]

Bacon, who was genuinely ill, wrote to the favourite, reminding him that he was 'my anchor in these floods', but it looks as though James had already decided to sacrifice the Lord Chancellor. If he were to go, the Commons would presumably be satisfied and drop their investigation into the role of other referees. Also the King, by concurring in the overthrow of Bacon, would be able to demonstrate that he was on the side of reform. This was probably the motive behind his speech to the Lords on 26 March, in which he assured them that 'so precious unto me is the public good that no private person whatsoever, were he never so dear unto me, shall be so respected by me . . . as the public good'. The reference could have been taken to apply to Buckingham also, and this is presumably what the King intended. He had declared his readiness to punish even his favourite if this would be for the benefit of his kingdom, but he clearly did not believe that Buckingham was guilty of anything more than lack of discernment, for he went on to make specific mention of the good offices he performed on all occasions 'both for the House in general, and every member thereof in particular'. In a remark that was clearly meant to heal the breach which had opened at the beginning of the session between Buckingham and the lords who had signed the petition against 'foreign' titles, he described 'how earnestly [Buckingham] spake to me in that matter'. And on the following day he appointed the favourite to communicate to the Lords his thanks for their sentence against Mompesson, to which he added perpetual banishment. With harmony apparently restored, Parliament then adjourned for Easter.[21]

During the recess there was a great deal of speculation about Buckingham's future. The Florentine agent reported the widespread opinion that the King had now authorised Parliament to investigate Buckingham's actions, and that members would start on this as soon as they returned. The French ambassador also referred to reports that the King would sacrifice Buckingham just as he had done Somerset, and described the favourite and his followers as being in the grip of 'une grande mélancholie'. Meanwhile an English observer noted that 'on Easter Day . . . the King sent no meat from his table to the Marquis, which is the strangest news of all'. Buckingham, he added for good measure, had taken himself off to a horse-race.[22]

All these rumours were little more than speculation, but the reassembling of Parliament in mid-April was awaited with excitement because of the great events that were pending. The Lords' first task was a formal trial of the Lord Chancellor, but Bacon had decided to give in without a fight. He was probably advised to do this by Buckingham, who had paid him repeated visits and presumably promised him that whatever sentence was passed on him would be, at least in part, remitted. Bacon wanted Buckingham to use his influence in the Upper House to save him from any punishment, on the grounds that his dismissal from the Lord Chancellorship was penalty enough, but the evidence against Bacon was too great merely to be swept aside. He clearly had been guilty of taking bribes, and further investigation, which a trial would entail, might reveal many more skeletons that the King and his favourite preferred to leave uncovered. On 3 May, therefore, the

Lords passed judgement on Bacon, sentencing him to be fined £40,000, imprisoned in the Tower during the King's pleasure, to be barred forever from the holding of office, and to be forbidden to sit in Parliament or go to Court. Buckingham's sole contribution to the debate was the comment that the Lord Chancellor was so sick that he was not likely to live long, but when it came to the vote, he, alone in the House, registered his dissent. It was a brave action, even if it showed his own impotence, and it suggests that whatever Buckingham's feelings were at this stage, he was not scared.[23]

The King had warned Parliament on 20 April that they 'should do all for love of justice, not for private purposes or spleen'. He had consented to the overthrow of Bacon because the Lord Chancellor had confessed his guilt, but he was not willing to have his other servants called to account merely for doing their duty. The Commons were beginning to direct their fire at Lord Treasurer Mandeville, another of Buckingham's protégés, who had been one of the referees for the patent of alehouses in which Kit Villiers had a share, but the King made it clear that he would resent any further movement in this direction. He told Cranfield that while he thanked the Lower House for their care for his honour, he 'wished that we should not be so careful for his honour as to destroy his service'. To make his meaning perfectly plain, he added that the Commons should not question 'those who certify on a reference from His Majesty, either for matter of law or conveniency, touching any patent or grant; for if their opinion be not right which they certify, yet if there be no corruption proved against them, then he would not have them troubled for it'. In other words, the attack upon the referees was now over. If the Commons persisted in their investigations, then they would risk dissolution.[24]

IV

The majority of members of the Commons were probably genuinely concerned about the harmful effects of patents and monopolies, and wished to see the projectors called to account. A smaller group saw the need to take action against the referees who had provided the cover under which the projectors had been able to operate. And a much smaller group – which included Sir Edward Coke, Sir Robert Phelips, Sir Francis Seymour, and William Mallory – not only believed that effective action must be taken against Buckingham, as the protector of the referees, but also had the daring (as well as, in Coke's case, the skill) to deploy their forces against him. It was this group which combined with the dissident peers in the Lords to concert the attack against the favourite. Buckingham had a good idea of what was going on, for one of his informants wrote to tell him, on 12 May, 'that your adversaries continue their meetings and conferences here in Holborn, how to give His Majesty some foul distaste of you, as making you the only author of all grievances and oppressions whatsoever, for your private ends'. Southampton was obviously involved, and after his arrest in June he was questioned not only about his own conduct in the Lords but also about the activities of his associates in the Commons. The cause of his discontent is indicated by the question 'whether he had not said that there would never be a good reformation while one did so wholly govern the King', and that he 'liked not to come to the Council Board because there were so many boys and base fellows'.[25]

The King had warned the Commons not to press new charges against the referees, but there were still some outstanding charges against Sir Henry Yelverton, who, as former Attorney-General, had been one of the commissioners for the execution of the gold and silver thread patent, and had been responsible for imprisoning offenders. Yelverton was already in disgrace, for in 1620, when he drew up a new grant to the City of London of certain crown lands used for charitable purposes, he had far exceeded the limits laid down for him in the King's instructions. He was accordingly summoned before Star Chamber, sentenced to pay a fine of £4,000 and dismissed from his office. Yelverton was convinced that the action against him was inspired by Buckingham, who was said to have boasted that 'he would make me the poorest Attorney that ever was', and Chamberlain reported the current opinion in April 1620 that Yelverton's 'greatest fault is that he is not, nor seeks to be, in favour with the favourite'.[26]

Yelverton, during the period in which he had been Attorney-General, had been well placed to acquire a great deal of information about patents and projectors, and about the various interests involved – including, of course, Buckingham's kindred. It looks as though Buckingham's enemies now hoped to use him for a further attempt to topple the favourite, and the opportunity came when he was brought before the Lords in April 1621 to answer charges concerning his conduct in the enforcement of the gold and silver thread patent. Yelverton's speech was indeed sensational. He threw all the blame on Sir Edward and Kit Villiers, and declared that he had only consented to the imprisonment of unlicensed manufacturers because he knew 'that my Lord of Buckingham was ever at His Majesty's hand, ready upon every occasion to hew me down'. Going on to discuss his role in the patent of inns, which was another of the charges against him, Yelverton declared that he had received a message from Mompesson to the effect that Buckingham would bring about his dismissal if he did not cooperate. This, said Yelverton, was a startling message, 'for I saw here was a great assuming of power to himself to place and displace an officer . . . for now it was come to this: whether I would obey His Majesty or my Lord'. He resolved, he said, to be as stubborn as Mordecai and not exceed the limits laid down by his position, but he found that nearly all the fees associated with his office were diverted from him and whatever suit he put forward was certain of rejection. 'Howbeit,' he added, 'I dare say if my Lord of Buckingham had but read the articles exhibited in this place against Hugh Spencer, and had known the danger of placing and displacing officers about a King, he would not have pursued me with such bitterness.'[27]

This reference to the Despensers, the hated favourites of Edward II – not, from James's point of view, the most flattering of comparisons – caused uproar in the House. The Prince declared that he could not sit there and hear 'his father's government to be so paralleled and scandalised'; if Yelverton had anything to say against Buckingham, let him leave it till later. Lord Treasurer Mandeville was of the same opinion: 'let Yelverton stick to the point'. But Buckingham would not hear of it. 'Let him proceed', he said. 'He that will seek to stop him [is] more my enemy than his.' Yelverton, in fact, had little more to say. Indeed, he had already said more than enough. The Lords could not possibly let his remarks go unpunished, and while Buckingham declared that for the slander against himself he was prepared to leave the penalty to the Lords, he proposed that Yelverton should be sent to the Tower for impugning the King's honour. He was immediately challenged by Sheffield, who asserted that the King's honour had not been touched. Arundel countered this. What about Yelverton's assertion that Buckingham had assumed the regal power to place and displace officers, he asked? Was not this a reflection upon the King? Yes, added the Lord Treasurer, 'particularly since he referred to [the] example of Hugh Spencer'. But Southampton would have none of it. 'Those words', he asserted, 'were not applied to that example.' Saye was of the same opinion: 'Yelverton by those words wronged the lord he spake of, not the King.'[28]

James himself had no doubts about the implications of Yelverton's words. 'If Yelverton be Mordecai,' he protested, 'Buckingham must be Haman and be hanged. If he Spencer, I Edward II . . . . To reckon me with such a prince is to esteem me a weak man, and I had rather be no king than such a one as King Edward II.' He ordered Yelverton to be imprisoned, and announced that he would take whatever action he thought fit to redeem his honour. As for the offence against his favourite, he was content, at Buckingham's insistence, to leave that to the Lords. When Buckingham made this announcement on 2 May, he unleashed further bitter argument. Southampton suggested that the King had been misinformed by those who had told him that Yelverton had impugned his honour, and argued that the House should therefore assert its right to complete the case on which it had embarked. Buckingham declared that such a procedure would be a direct violation of the King's orders, and was supported by the Lord Chamberlain, Pembroke, and the Duke of Lenox. He was opposed, as usual, by Sheffield and Saye, as well as the Bishop of Bangor, who went so far as to say that 'a hard construction' had been made of certain phrases used by Yelverton, and that they should not squeeze blood out of words. Buckingham immediately demanded an explanation of the Bishop's meaning, and would not rest until the unfortunate prelate had 'excused and explained himself'. Sheffield then raised the point that the House's privileges were infringed by the fact that they had been deprived of their prisoner before completing their proceedings against him. His remarks were echoed by Southampton, and, surprisingly, by Buckingham, who agreed that 'this is a scruple that may very well be touched upon'.[29]

Buckingham, by accepting his critics' views on this issue, had in fact gained a tactical victory, for when James, at his suggestion, offered to remit Yelverton to the House for judgement, he left the Lords with little choice but to find him guilty and impose a severe penalty. When, on 8 May, the dissident peers pressed for further delay, in order to consider the exact meaning of Yelverton's words, they provoked an outburst from Arundel, who declared that this was no time for splitting hairs. Once again tempers rose, and when Spencer reminded Arundel of the fate of two earlier Howards who had been condemned unjustly because they were denied a hearing, Arundel retorted that Spencer could know nothing of such matters because his ancestors – unlike Arundel's – had never done anything but keep sheep. The House was shocked by this breach of good manners, and sent Arundel to the Tower for insulting a fellow peer. There he was frequently visited by Buckingham – a graceful acknowledgement from a new noble of the invaluable assistance given him by the holder of one of the oldest titles in the House.[30]

Yelverton was finally brought to judgement on 14 May, and in delivering the formal charge against him the Attorney-General, Thomas Coventry, made a speech in which he showed his understanding of the position of favourite. 'The abuses of Hugh Spencer', he argued, 'are fastened upon the Lord of Buckingham. They reflect upon the King because Lord Buckingham is so near the King. He could not do this without the King.' On the next day the House sentenced Yelverton to a heavy fine and imprisonment for impugning the King's honour, and on the 16th took into consideration his offence in using words which 'did directly tend to the scandal of the Marquis of Buckingham, Lord High Admiral of England'. Buckingham withdrew while his fellow peers debated what sentence to pass upon Yelverton, and the length of the debate shows that his opponents were still full of fight. Eventually Buckingham and Yelverton were both called into the House to hear the Lord Chief Justice – acting in place of the disgraced Bacon – pronounce judgement. Yelverton was to pay a fine of five thousand marks [£3,333 6s.8d.] to the Lord Admiral, suffer imprisonment for his behaviour, and make formal submission. Buckingham immediately remitted the fine, and Yelverton 'humbly thanked his lordship'. The campaign to topple Buckingham had received an abrupt check, partly because of the skill with which Buckingham – supported by the King and Prince – had defended himself, partly because the plan of attack had not been sufficiently well thought out. Chamberlain saw the significance of what had happened. 'Great men weakly opposed,' he commented, 'thereby become the stronger; and it is no small comfort to him [Buckingham] . . . (as he professes) that he is found Parliament-proof.'[31]

By this time opposition to the anti-Buckingham faction was also showing itself in the Commons. On 2 May Sir Edward Villiers took his seat at last in the Lower House. Some weeks earlier Buckingham had protested against the generally held opinion that he had sent Sir Edward abroad 'of purpose to avoid his trial touching some grievances complained of by the Commons'.

On the contrary, declared the favourite, he had hastened his brother's return and 'desired that the said Sir Edward Villiers might come to his accusation; for so he should have the greatest honour, his lordship not doubting but he would clear himself'. When Sir Edward appeared in the Commons, he was immediately challenged by Mallory on the grounds that no man who had been a beneficiary from a patent condemned by the House should have the right to sit there. Mallory was supported by Sir Edward Coke and Sir Robert Phelips, among others, but Samuel Sandys protested that the House was being diverted 'by motions rather springing from passion than judgement', and Sir Thomas Wentworth advised members to press ahead with bills for the reformation of the commonwealth rather than spend their time and energy on 'muskets and shot'. Since opinions were clearly divided, the House took no decision on how to treat Sir Edward, but he decided to absent himself until after the Lords had given judgement on the charges against him. This they did on 1 June, when they notified the Commons that they 'do find Sir Edward Villiers clear of those matters mentioned by them'. Sir Edward was now free to resume his seat, but only a few days later the King adjourned Parliament.[32]

There were many people who attributed the adjournment to the evil influence of Spain and the pleadings of the frightened favourite, but the Venetian ambassador observed that 'in the opinion of those of the best judgement, it is due to the King'. From James's point of view Parliament had done all that it was likely to do for the time being. The Commons had voted him two subsidies which brought in £145,000, and while this sum was not enough to fit out and maintain an army for the relief of the Palatinate, it was better than nothing. They had also shown their desire for an active commitment by the King to the defence of his son-in-law, and had thereby perhaps strengthened the bargaining position of Digby, who had been despatched to the Emperor in May 1621 to try and negotiate a peaceful settlement of the question of the Palatinate. If anything more was needed it came in the shape of a declaration made by the Commons before they adjourned. In this they promised

that if His Majesty's pious endeavours by treaty to procure their peace and safety shall not take that good effect which is desired . . . they shall be ready, to the utmost of their powers, both with their lives and fortunes, to assist him, so as, by the divine help of Almighty God . . . he may be able to do that with his sword which by a peaceable course shall not be effected.

The declaration was passed by general acclamation, while the excited members flung their hats in the air. One of the members for London gave his word that the City would not be backward. 'If ten subsidies will not serve,' he promised, 'twenty shall. If twenty will not, thirty shall.' On this happy, brave and patriotic note, the Commons adjourned.[33]

The King was thinking in terms of another session in the autumn, but in order to ensure that it should not be so unruly as that which had just ended he took action against the leading dissidents. The Earl of Southampton was arrested, on suspicion that he was 'party to a practice . . . to hinder the King's ends at the next meeting', and so was Sir Edwin Sandys, who was thought to be the principal link between the Earl and the Commons. Southampton was fortunate in having the friendship of John Williams, to whose custody he was committed. Williams used all his influence with Buckingham to secure the Earl's release, and by the middle of July was successful. Southampton was given permission to retire to his country estate, and the threat of a Star Chamber prosecution against him was· allowed to lapse. The news of his release was well received. One letter-writer described how in London 'we keep here a kind of jubilee for the enlargement of that noble lord, the Earl of Southampton, who is accounted the darling of the people and the chief able man for the leading of any great action, if His Majesty should have cause for employment'. Williams congratulated Buckingham and hoped that he also was enjoying 'the general applause of your goodness to the Earl'. Williams added that he found Southampton 'more cordially affected to the service of the King, and your lordship's love and friendship, than ever he was'. Later, in a letter to Southampton himself, Williams took up the theme of the necessity to win Buckingham's goodwill and urged Southampton to 'make good your professions to this noble lord, of whose extraordinary goodness your lordship and myself are remarkable reflections – the one of his sweetness in forgetting of wrongs; the other of his forwardness in conferring of courtesies'. Southampton was too proud to follow this course immediately, but he could not afford to hold out indefinitely, for a key item in his shaky finances was the £3,000 he received in royal pensions. In the summer of 1622 James announced his intention of cancelling these pensions, whereupon Southampton quickly made his submission. As Chamberlain noted, 'he hath taken the best way and addressed himself to the Lord of Buckingham, from whom he hath fair promises'. A few weeks later it was rumoured that Southampton had agreed to a marriage between his son and Buckingham's niece. But the report was apparently false and Southampton remained outside the Villiers circle and kept his distance from the favourite even though he never again openly challenged him.[34]

V

Southampton took no part in the second session of Parliament, which opened on 20 November 1621, and Buckingham was rarely present. He had been an assiduous attender in the first session, but James liked to pass the autumn in the country, and Buckingham spent much of his time at Newmarket, keeping the King company in the hunting-field. In fact the second session would have been postponed until the new year but for the return of Digby at the end of October, bringing with him the news that the Emperor was not prepared to negotiate a peaceful settlement of the

Palatinate question. England, insisted Digby, must now intervene by force to redress the situation, and he urged James to take action. James, as always, was reluctant to commit himself, but he had considerable trust in Digby's judgement, and also recognised that aggressive gestures on his part might produce more fruitful results. Buckingham was reported as saying that the King would 'be compelled at length to make up his mind to war', but this did not mean that James was prepared to undertake hostilities immediately. He recalled Parliament in hopes of getting further supply in case he had to fight, and in order to make plain to the outside world the popular pressure for war, which he might be unable to resist. Of one thing James was certain, because Digby had told him so in the clearest possible terms: Spain alone held the key to peace. The Emperor was too heavily dependent upon allies such as Maximilian, Duke of Bavaria – who wanted both Frederick's lands and the electoral title – to be able to reach a peaceful settlement. He would only do so if he were put under very great pressure, and such pressure could come from nowhere except Spain. It was Spain, after all, which provided a good deal of financial, as well as moral, support for the imperial Habsburgs, and it was Spanish armies which were in occupation of half of the Lower Palatinate. James by himself could do nothing, as Digby realised when he was at Vienna, for – as he told Aston, the English ambassador at Madrid – 'the interest of state is so little betwixt the Emperor and His Majesty that all that I can say to them here will little move them'. Spain must be called in to redress the balance, and 'what is to be done must be by reflection upon Spain and Flanders and by the authority of the two kings'.[35]

There was nothing new about the idea of using Parliament as an instrument in foreign policy. Digby himself, when he had been ambassador in Spain towards the end of 1617, had suggested that Parliament should be summoned in order to spur on the Spaniards, who were being dilatory in producing their terms for the proposed marriage. This strategy was apparently successful, for Digby was subsequently able to report that the Spaniards had now agreed to 'directly and freely declare their demands' and that therefore 'the calling of a Parliament will be in no kind useful in as much as it may have relation to the businesses'.[36] The danger of using Parliament in this way was that it might get out of control. Good management and close supervision were essential, and James made a big mistake in staying away from London and leaving the conduct of Parliamentary business in the hands of Privy Councillors who appear to have been given little guidance. He may have assumed that the issues were clearcut, and that the Commons, in the light of the declaration which they had made on the eve of their adjournment, would be only too glad to respond to his appeal for aid. He therefore authorised Digby to make a full report on his negotiations, and he told Lord Keeper Williams to press the Commons to make a speedy vote of supply and to leave the question of grievances until after Christmas.

The Commons were unenthusiastic in their response. There was the continuing problem of the economic depression, which had hit some parts of the country particularly badly: one west country member affirmed that poverty was so widespread that it was proving almost impossible to levy the subsidies already voted. There was also the fear that once the King had been given a further grant he would not recall the Houses for a discussion of grievances. Even more important, however, was the difference of approach to the whole question of war. The Commons tended to think in terms of a religious crusade by means of a profitable sea war against Spain on the Elizabethan model. They felt the dishonour of the humiliation inflicted on Frederick and Elizabeth, and they were genuinely anxious to see the Elector restored to his territories and dignities; but they were convinced that the best way to do this was by attacking Spain. In a sense they shared Digby's view that the Emperor must be influenced 'by reflection' from Brussels and Madrid, but they wanted to force Philip IV's hand rather than rely upon persuasion. They also felt that military operations in the Palatinate might well cost more than they were worth. They would have agreed with John Chamberlain that 'a war of diversion' was best 'and not to stand pottering and pelting in the Palatinate only to consume both our men and means'.[37]

James's attitude was different, even though he, like the Commons, believed that the key to the European situation was to be found in Spain. He could not understand why Spanish assurances of a desire for a peaceful settlement were not reflected in a softer line in Vienna, and suspected that he was being double-crossed. He therefore wanted to increase the pressure on Spain by showing her, through Parliament, that even though he might be prepared to wait a little longer, his subjects were not. Yet he knew that while the threat of hostilities might push the Spaniards into a more conciliatory and constructive attitude, open war would drive them in the opposite direction. This did not mean that James proposed to remain inactive. If Parliament provided sufficient money he was prepared to consider armed intervention in Germany, not simply to save what was left of the Palatinate but also to spur on the German princes, the King of Denmark, the Dutch and other potential allies. It was true that operations in the Palatinate might lead to confrontation with Spanish forces, but this need not be a cause of war between the two crowns, for Philip's troops were acting in the name of the Emperor, while James's would be under the nominal command of Frederick.

As for religion, the less said about this, in James's view, the better. The King realised what most members of the Commons did not, that the increasing power of the Habsburg Emperor was as much of a threat to German catholic princes as it was to protestant ones, and he hoped to create an anti-Habsburg, not an anti-catholic, league. If he could do this he might be able to secure the open or covert adhesion to it of France — a major catholic state but one that felt herself increasingly menaced by the tightening ring of Habsburg power around her. James, in short, wanted to play down the religious element which the Commons wished to emphasise, and he was determined to keep all his options as wide open as possible. In particular he did not intend to respond to the demand of certain members of the Commons that he should name the enemy against whom they were to fight. In practice it would probably be the Emperor, but if Spain thought herself threatened, so much the better: the essence of his approach lay in blurring the details, but this made it difficult for his Councillors in the Commons to rally support.

At one stage it looked as though the House, carried away by its desire for a war of diversion against Spain, might go beyond the limits that were implicit in the King's policy, but on 27 November Sir George Goring — who kept his patron, Buckingham, closely informed of proceedings in the Commons (of which he was a member) — reported that they had decided to go into committee to consider voting further supply, and that in general 'the House is now in much better order and temper than yesterday it was . . . His Majesty might know the stream of their affections . . . is as great as ever was to any king, and no way to cross upon his prerogative or direct him in his counsels'. This message probably reached Newmarket late that night, and on the next day Buckingham drafted a letter in which he gave Goring detailed instructions about a proposal he was to make in the House at the first opportunity. This came on the morning of Thursday, 29 November, when the Commons had temporarily put the great business of foreign affairs behind them and were considering the implications of a legal action brought against Sir Edward Coke, with, it was believed, the encouragement of Buckingham. Goring first of all outlined the course taken by the King to bring about the restoration of the Palatinate, and referred to a letter lately written by James to Philip IV in which he called on the Spanish king either to bring about a cessation of arms in Germany or to withdraw all aid and comfort from the Emperor. Goring then proposed that the Commons should petition James that

in case the King of Spain shall not condescend to either of these so just and reasonable demands, His Majesty will be pleased to declare unto them that he will not spare to denounce war as well against the King of Spain and any other prince or state that shall oppose or assist against his children, as against the Emperor or any other that shall go about to dispossess them of their ancient inheritance.[38]

Goring's proposal seems, on the face of it, a mystery. Why should Buckingham stir up aggressive feelings and focus them on Spain when the fundamental intention of the King's policy was to avoid naming an enemy? Was this Buckingham's own initiative, carried through without the King's knowledge? Was it, perhaps, a skilful, if dastardly, move to bring about the break between King and Parliament that in fact occurred? Was Gondomar behind this move? No certain answers can be given to any of these questions, and much depends upon how the relationship between Buckingham and the King is seen at this particular moment. Buckingham's contemporaries, like later historians, were often inclined to the view that James was clay in his favourite's hands, content to leave policy matters to Buckingham as long as he could enjoy the pleasures of the chase. But such a view has no basis in reality. Buckingham was still, in effect, the King's secretary, and it may be taken for granted that the instructions to Goring were written with the King's full knowledge and approval. Indeed Goring, when he wrote his account to Buckingham, assured him that 'His Majesty's end is not known to any (flesh)'. It is, of course, possible that Buckingham had referred to the King's intentions merely to give colouring to what was in fact his own device. This would have been a suicidal move, however, for the King had many sources of information other than Buckingham, and his anger would know no bounds if he discovered that the favourite had used his name for private ends.

Buckingham, in any case, had no compelling reason for wanting a sudden end to the Parliamentary session. The King apparently knew of his involvement in the proceedings against Sir Edward Coke, and is likely to have approved of them; and with James firmly behind him, Buckingham could safely ignore the bluster of the Commons. The simplest solution, therefore, to the problem of Goring's intervention is that it was prompted by James himself, who hoped thereby to step up the pressure on Spain which this session of Parliament had all along been intended to provide. This strategy had already been sketched out by Sir Edward Sackville – another of Buckingham's intimates – who on 27 November called on his fellow members to vote further supply in order to save what was left of the Palatinate, and assured them that 'it will not be long before we discover plainly whether the King of Spain be our enemy or no; which, if he be, then will the King without question, understanding of our affections and inclinations, proclaim a general war against him, and then we shall have our desires'.[39] Goring's motion, which he made two days later, was along much the same lines. What he proposed, in accordance with the instructions he had received from Court, was that James should be asked to express his readiness to declare war against any state, including Spain, which opposed the restitution of the Palatinate. Such a petition would not have infringed James's sole right to decide what policy his country should pursue, nor would it have bound his hands. It would, on the contrary, have enabled him to demonstrate to Gondomar – and through him to Philip IV of Spain – that only he, James, stood between his people and their desire for war. It would then be up to Spain to choose which course to follow.

The petition which the House of Commons eventually presented to James went far beyond the proposal made by Goring. Admittedly it contained the request that 'seeing this inevitable necessity is fallen upon Your Majesty, which no wisdom or providence of a peaceable and pious king can avoid, Your Majesty would not omit this just occasion speedily and effectually to take your sword into your hand', which was more or less what Goring had asked for. But it also called on James to enforce the penal laws against catholic recusants; it advised him to undertake a war of diversion and not to rest content with operations in the Palatinate; and it proposed that in order to frustrate the hopes of the English catholics 'our most noble Prince may be timely and happily married to one of our own religion'. It was this last request which, more than any other, was calculated to offend James. It was a clear invasion of his sole right to decide whom his children should or should not marry; and it would enfeeble rather than strengthen his hand when it came to dealing with Spain. The marriage, although James set great store by it, was really his weakest card. If he said to Spain, in effect, 'Restore the Palatinate or I may be forced to regain it by war' he could hope to obtain a helpful and conciliatory response. But he could hardly say 'Restore the Palatinate or there will be no marriage' for this would have been to play into the hands of those elements in the Spanish and Roman courts which did not want such a marriage and had only been forced to consider it by the King's constant pressure and assurances of goodwill over many years. It is therefore hardly surprising that when the Commons were debating the insertion of the marriage clause on 3 December Sir Edward Sackville warned them not to include it, 'for it is the privilege of princes to marry where they list; and since we are so careful of our own privileges he would not have us seek to limit our Prince'. He added that if they did so they were likely to cause a great confusion.[40]

Neither Buckingham nor James could reasonably have anticipated the insertion of the marriage clause, and speculation about their Machiavellian purposes is therefore unfounded. It is not clear who was responsible for proposing this clause, but Goring's speech was followed by one from the influential but impulsive Sir Robert Phelips, and this gave such offence to James that the King subsequently imprisoned him. In a letter defending his conduct, Phelips referred to 'those words of the Spanish match, which I hear are . . . much strained to my disadvantage', and added that he had spoken them 'not positively, but with qualification'. If it was indeed Phelips who persuaded the Commons to insert the marriage clause into their petition, the King's anger against him is hardly to be wondered at. The art of bringing pressure to bear on Spain by alternately encouraging and restraining the House of Commons was at all times a difficult one, and, as it happened, James had just received a forcible reminder of the extent to which he was dependent upon Spanish goodwill. In November 1621 a number of Dutch envoys arrived in England, to try and negotiate a settlement of the differences between the two countries, and they brought with them some intercepted letters from the Emperor to the King of Spain. In these letters the Emperor Ferdinand announced his intention to transfer the electoral title and dignity from Frederick to Maximilian of Bavaria, and he made a number of disparaging references to the heretic King of England.[41]

The envoys reached London on 28 November, and it seems reasonable to assume that the intercepted letters were in James's hands by the 29th – the very day on which Goring made his proposal to the Commons. They revealed not simply the duplicity and intransigence of the Emperor, which James deeply resented, but also 'the real, good proceeding of the King of Spain . . . wherewith His Majesty is very much satisfied'. James therefore instructed Sir Walter Aston, his ambassador at Madrid, to assure Philip of his 'real and sincere intention in all things, and how willing and ready he will be to requite and deserve his kindness and amity in all good occasions that shall be offered him'. Goring's motion was part of the strategy of threatening Spain, which James had adopted because of his belief that Philip IV was not dealing honestly with him. Such an assumption had now been shown to be unjustified, and although it was too late to alert Goring and change his instructions, the policy of which he was the instrument no longer had any validity. The time for threats was past, for as one reporter commented when the news of the transfer of the electoral title was made public 'there will be no other refuge for us than by the speedy consumming of the marriage'. The timing as well as the wording of the Commons' petition was therefore singularly inappropriate, and far from uniting the King with the representatives of his people, the petition led to a series of bitter exchanges which culminated in the adjournment of Parliament shortly before Christmas, and its subsequent dissolution.[42]

VI

Buckingham's 'connexion' suffered some hard blows during the 1621 Parliament. Quite apart from the attacks upon the favourite himself, which revealed to him just how unpopular he was, there had been the overthrow of Lord Chancellor Bacon, Buckingham's friend and mentor, and the resignation, under pressure, of another of the favourite's protégés, Lord Treasurer Mandeville. Buckingham could take comfort, however, from the thought that the new office-holders were as much his men as their predecessors. Lionel Cranfield, who became not simply Lord Treasurer but also Earl of Middlesex, owed his rise to Buckingham and was now a member of the Villiers family. The Countess of Buckingham wrote to him in November 1621, to congratulate him on the birth of his child, and later that year she was at Cranfield's great house at Chelsea for the christening. Buckingham and the King were also there, since they had agreed to be godparents to the baby boy. The two families of Cranfield and Villiers were obviously on close terms, for in August 1622 Buckingham, his wife and a number of relatives and dependants were invited 'to be very merry' at Wiston House, just outside Steyning in Sussex, which the Lord Treasurer had recently purchased.[43]

As for the new Lord Keeper, John Williams, he had already built up his credit with Kate Buckingham by providing the theological arguments which buttressed her resolve to abandon the Roman Catholic faith and accept the doctrines of the Church of England. And although he had not been her husband's choice for the Lord Keepership, he lost no opportunity to profess his devotion to the favourite. 'Let God suffer me no longer to be,' he wrote to Buckingham on one occasion, 'than I shall be true, plain, faithful and affectionately respectful of your lordship, as being most bounden unto your lordship for these so many fruits, but far far more for the tree that bare them – your love and affection.' Later in the same letter, after seconding

Cranfield's request to retain his position as Master of the Wards, Williams added 'Let him hold it but by your lordship's favour, not his own power or wilfulness; and this must be apparent and visible. Let all our greatness depend, as it ought, upon yours, the true original. Let the King be Pharaoh, yourself Joseph, and let us come after as your half-brethren.'[44]

One of the major difficulties with which Cranfield and Williams had to contend was that of restraining the generosity of both the King and the favourite where the granting of suits was concerned. As Hacket noted, 'the Lord Marquis was of a kind nature . . . not willing to deny a suit, but prone to gratify all strangers, chiefly if any of his kindred brought them in their hand, and was far more apt to believe them that asked him a favour than those that would persuade him it was not to be granted'. Cranfield wanted a general restraint upon the granting of suits, but such embargoes were, from their very nature, unselective and could cause hardship in individual cases. In March 1622, for example, Buckingham wrote to Cranfield on behalf of Lord Cromwell (an old friend of his from their days together at Angers) requesting the Treasurer 'for my sake, setting all excuses aside, [to] afford him this favour'. The tone is untypically peremptory and the demand might seem unreasonable, but in fact Cromwell was a poverty-stricken peer who held a military command in Ireland and was only asking for part of his two years' arrears of pay to be given him. His was not the only case in which considerations of public policy ran counter to those of justice for individuals, and not all Buckingham's requests for favour to his clients can be dismissed as examples of undiscriminating extravagance. Cranfield could always appeal to Buckingham's care for the public good and did not hesitate to remind him that 'I am engaged in this miserable condition by your means and upon your word'. On more than one occasion he called on the favourite to bear in mind the appalling difficulties of his position as Lord Treasurer, 'that must either suffer our most gracious master to be made a prey and his service to be overthrown – to the ruin of yourself and me – or to do that I do, which is to oppose all propositions of this nature with which I am too well acquainted, the pretence being His Majesty's service and profit, but are indeed against both'.[45]

Cranfield's protestations were not entirely fruitless. Buckingham's letters nearly always contained a qualifying phrase, to the effect that Cranfield should give a certain cause 'all the expedition you can, according to the justice thereof' or should show a certain suitor 'what favour you may'. All that Buckingham wanted, in order to satisfy the throng of suitors who pressed continually upon him, was evidence that Cranfield had tried to give him satisfaction, and, if he had not been able to do so, had been moved by good reasons. After all, Buckingham, no less than Cranfield, was subject to pressures. In October 1622, at a time when Cranfield was again calling on him to stand firm in 'the way of reformation under His Majesty's royal commandment and your lordship's noble mediation', Buckingham, in conjunction with the King and Prince, concocted a very revealing letter. In this he informed Cranfield that being importuned by many, from which I see I cannot free myself, to write to your lordship in their favour – and some will not be content with a letter without a postscript of mine own hand – that whatsoever this unavoidable importunity shall force me unto, you will do no more than you shall think fit in your own judgement, knowing that nothing is more dear to me than what may best stand with His Majesty's service.

'Unavoidable importunity' was no empty phrase, for Buckingham's position, and his reputation for getting things done, made him the prey of all those who sought favour, advancement, redress of real or imagined wrongs, and any other benefit which it was thought he might be able to confer. From the point of view of a suitor there was not much point in going to anyone else. As one of Trumbull's correspondents advised him 'you absurdly stray in your means if your *Ora Pro Nobis* be not directed to the right saint. I have no conceit of those petty ones, who for their own selves can obtain no grace except they bow and beseech at the shrine of the great one. Direct your suit to His Majesty by his hand, if you will think to prosper. . . . He will glory in your dependence on him, and will, I doubt, be an enemy unto you if you seek to carry it without him.'[46]

In his choice of clients Buckingham was not always or necessarily motivated by considerations of profit. In 1622, for instance, he secured the appointment of Francis Cottington, the English agent in Spain, as Secretary to the Prince, provoking the grateful Cottington to reflect 'how mere a stranger I am unto you; how unable I have ever been to do your lordship any service; and what little hope I have ever to merit anything from you'. In the following year he extended his favour by persuading James to make Cottington a baronet, without paying the customary fees, in regard of his long and faithful service. Buckingham also continued his care for the well-being of Sir John Coke – 'a plain homely man, but one that hath been a useful organ to communicate the mysteries of the Navy to the Lord Admiral' – by obtaining for him the office of Master of Requests. This took some time, since the claims of other suitors had to be satisfied, but the Lord Admiral assured Coke that he should not think 'I am forgetful of you'. The delay had been caused only through his desire 'so to contrive your satisfaction that it may be without the prejudice of others'.[47]

One further example, out of many that show Buckingham putting public considerations first, was the appointment of Sir Edward Conway as Secretary of State. The reasons for this were tied up with foreign policy and will be considered later, but Conway had nothing to offer apart from his long experience as a soldier, his sense of duty and his patriotism. There was general satisfaction, as well as astonishment, that Buckingham had chosen a man 'who is neither rich, nor Spanish, nor easy to be held within his tether'. Rumours of Conway's appointment began circulating in the summer of 1622, but his formal confirmation in office did not come until early the following year. This was because of Buckingham's consideration for Sir Robert Naunton, who, despite his recent disgrace, was still the nominal holder of the office. Naunton reminded Buckingham that when his wife had last been with child she miscarried of a son because of apprehensions brought on by rumours that Naunton was about to lose his office. Now she was again pregnant, and this might be the last chance for him to obtain the son he longed for. Would the favourite therefore consider postponing Naunton's dismissal until after the birth of his child? Buckingham, who had only recently become a father himself, accepted the request immediately, and made the necessary arrangements with both the King and Conway. Shortly before the end of 1622 'the Lady Naunton' as Chamberlain reported, 'was delivered of a son . . . that is to be christened . . . by the Lord Marquis Buckingham'. Only after this happy event did Conway receive his seals as Secretary. It was a not untypical instance of Buckingham's consideration for those who claimed his friendship, and it helps to explain the nature of his hold not merely on the King and the Prince but on many lesser men and women who experienced his overflowing courtesy. He was, in the words of one of his chaplains, 'of a most sweet disposition and conversation, disrespective to none, and affable and courteous to the most'.[48]

VII

There were, of course, many people who remained impervious to Buckingham's charm, and they were to be found in considerable numbers among those elements within the Church of England which, on account of their detestation of popery, Arminianism and ritualism of all sorts, were sometimes referred to as puritan — although they remained within the mainstream of the life of the church and had no wish to separate themselves from it. Buckingham was not without friends among the puritans — John Coke, for instance, and also John Packer, who was one of the favourite's secretaries. But the 1621 Parliament had shown that the puritans in general were deeply distrustful of Buckingham on account of his supposedly lukewarm commitment to the protestant faith, and one of his kinsmen, Sir Ralph Freeman, reminded him that 'those they called puritans were growing, and in the Parliament were thought considerable . . . [and] that the King's affection might cool, and he [Buckingham] need friends'. Freeman suggested that the best way in which Buckingham could win over the puritans and demonstrate his steadfastness in religion would be by advancing the interests of a distinguished preacher, John Preston, who was much admired by them. This suggestion, which was strongly supported by Packer, appealed to Buckingham, who sent for Preston, asked him for a copy of one of his recent sermons, and assured him 'that he would be ready to the best and utmost of his power to serve him'. Shortly afterwards Preston was appointed chaplain to the Prince, presumably at Buckingham's intercession, and, some time later, Buckingham intervened to secure the mastership of Emmanuel College, Cambridge, for his new client. Emmanuel was a notoriously puritan foundation, and the master was Laurence Chaderton, a leading puritan divine, now very advanced in years. Chaderton was in favour of Preston succeeding him, but feared that if he resigned he would have no means left to him to subsist on. It was Buckingham who put these fears at rest by securing a promise of maintenance for him from the King. He was then able to write to Chaderton, in September 1622, to tell him that 'I have moved His Majesty concerning Master Preston's succeeding of you in the mastership of Emmanuel College; who is not only willing but also graciously pleased to recommend him to the place in special manner before any other.'[49]

While Buckingham was stretching out one hand to the puritans, he was also drawing closer to the high church Arminians whom they detested. This came about through the friendship that developed between him and William Laud during the course of 1622. It was prompted by the religious doubts which assailed Buckingham's mother, the Countess, after 'those dangerous and busy flies which the Roman seminaries send abroad had buzzed about . . . and infected her'. Williams advised Buckingham that for the sake of his own reputation he should seek to persuade his mother not to abandon the Church of England, and he suggested that she might be invited to listen to some debates between the champions of the opposed faiths on those points which troubled her. The King had already spoken to Laud about the problem and invited him to do what he could, and in May Laud acquitted himself with honour at a disputation with the Jesuit who had undermined the Countess's beliefs. He did not achieve his principal object, since the Countess eventually decided to become a Roman Catholic, but he had been brought into close touch with the favourite. Buckingham was obviously impressed by Laud, and found his religious teachings helpful, for on Whitsunday, 1622, he was pleased, as Laud records in his diary, 'to enter upon a near respect to me'. Later that month Laud 'became C[onfessor?] to my Lord of Buckingham' who on the following day received the sacrament from him at Greenwich.[50]

There had been little indication before that date that Buckingham was particularly interested in religion. He was on good terms with George Montaigne, Bishop of London – himself a high churchman – and in January 1622 went with his wife, his mother and other relatives to be confirmed by him in St Paul's Cathedral. He also took an active interest in ecclesiastical promotions, securing the Deanery of St Paul's for John Donne, for instance. But his recommendations show no preference for any particular theological attitude, and it looks as though, in his ecclesiastical as in his secular patronage, his main concern was to satisfy the importunity of his relatives and friends.[51]

VIII

The Villiers connexion continued to expand and flourish, not only in England. Oliver St John, the Lord Deputy of Ireland, who had come under heavy criticism partly because he owed his appointment to the favourite, was recalled in the spring of 1622, but was almost immediately appointed a Privy Councillor and in the following year was raised to the Irish peerage as Viscount Grandison. His replacement, Sir Henry Cary, Viscount Falkland, was just as much a client of Buckingham, and had undertaken the farming of the Irish Customs for him. Buckingham had many useful contacts with members of the Irish administration, among them Sir William Parsons – whom he persuaded the King to appoint as Master of the newly formed Irish Court of Wards in September 1622 – and Sir Francis Blundell, who handled the sale of Irish honours for him. Buckingham always took a close interest in Ireland, even though he never went there and had not, at this stage, become involved in the plantation of Ulster. This interest extended to his family, for Grandison's letters patent as viscount provided that his title was to pass to the heirs of his brother-in-law, Sir Edward Villiers. Another Irish viscountcy was conferred in 1622 upon Buckingham's nephew, George Feilding, who married the Earl of Desmond's daughter and later succeeded to his title.[52]

Buckingham himself was appointed Lord-Lieutenant of Middlesex in June 1622, which created some surprise, since the county had never before had a permanent Lieutenant. This proof – if proof were needed – of his continuing favour with the King was confirmed a few weeks later when James, accompanied by the Prince, came to see the new Lieutenant review the trained bands of the county. Favour extended, as always, to Buckingham's family. In September 1622 his brother-in-law William Feilding, husband of his much-loved sister Susan, was created Earl of Denbigh. Earlier in the year, in a flurry of marriage alliances, Feilding's daughter had been married to the son and heir of the Marquis of Hamilton, the head of one of the oldest aristocratic houses in Scotland and a leading courtier. Buckingham's half-brother, Sir Edward Villiers, who had suffered financial loss through the cancellation of the gold and silver thread patent as a result of its condemnation by Parliament in 1621, was compensated in the following year by a lease of the duties which the King had decided to impose on all imports of this thread. The nominal reason for the King's grant was that Sir Edward had given up the lucrative office of Master·of the Mint, but in fact he was restored to this a year or two later.[53]

Buckingham's full brothers were not enjoying the benefits which his favour had procured for them. John Villiers, Viscount Purbeck, was increasingly subject to fits of madness which became a cause of public comment. In June 1622, for instance, Chamberlain recorded how Purbeck 'getting into a room next the street in Wallingford House . . . beat down the glass windows with his bare fists and, all bloodied, cried out to the people that passed by that he was a catholic and would spend his blood in the cause'. Various remedies were tried, including the drinking of spa waters and rest in the country, but none had any long-term effect. Purbeck remained the victim of sudden outbursts of unstable behaviour which lasted two or three days, when a 'dull fit' would come over him and he could be calmed down. The strain was too great for Lady Purbeck, particularly as she had been forced into the marriage and had no great love for her husband. She began living apart from him, and Buckingham undertook to provide for her maintenance.[54]

Kit Villiers was not afflicted by madness, but had no luck in the marriage stakes. After failing to win the Lord Mayor's daughter, he paid court, in the spring of 1622, to Lady Elizabeth Norris, daughter of the Earl of Berkshire. She regarded Kit as 'a gentleman of high worth and quality'; but her heart was set on one of Buckingham's bosom friends, Edward Wray, a Groom of the Bedchamber, and rather than have Kit forced on her she eloped with her lover and secretly married him. By this time, however, Kit had committed himself to his cousin, Elizabeth Sheldon, who became his wife shortly afterwards. The marriage was apparently not approved of, for when a number of earldoms were conferred in September 1622, among them those of Kit's relatives, Feilding and Cranfield, his name was conspicuous by its absence. In a letter to his mother he expressed his feelings at being passed over. 'I am but what I was', he commented sadly, and added that his wife would find it very difficult 'to digest my Lady Cranfield's going before her'. Yet, if he spoke truly, he had no cause to complain, for his wife declared that 'she cares not for all their honours so she may but truly enjoy my love'.[55]

While Elizabeth Sheldon married Kit Villiers and in due course became Countess of Anglesey, her sister Philippa was married off to Sir Anthony Ashley, an ambitious old time-server, then well into his seventies, whose interests, if current gossip was to be believed, had hitherto centred on boys rather than girls. Early in the following year, 1623, Buckingham provided a handsome dowry for another of his cousins, Susan Hill, who married Edward Montagu, the eldest son of Viscount Mandeville, the former Lord Treasurer. The ceremony, which was carried out by Lord Keeper Williams, was performed 'in the King's bedchamber, who took great joy in it and blessed the bride with one of his shoes'. There is, of course, something distasteful about these arranged marriages, but they were the custom of the day and could often turn out to be love matches. This seems to have been the case with Edward and Susan Montagu, who were parted shortly after their marriage, since Edward went to Spain to attend upon Buckingham and the Prince. He left his young wife pregnant, and she wrote a letter to him full of tenderness, in which she told him how she was about to go 'into the little bed which I find less than ever it was, and never have no mind to go into it because I cannot find my sweeting there'.[56]

IX

Among those who had benefited from their connexion with Buckingham few had received more than Bacon, who owed his peerage and his Lord Chancellorship to the favourite's advocacy. Bacon seems to have believed that he could never fall while he had Buckingham to support him, but nobody could have foreseen the violence of the Parliamentary tempest that swept him away in 1621. Buckingham did all he could to soften the blow. He saved Bacon from degradation, and in June 1621 he secured his release from the Tower. He also persuaded the King to consider issuing a pardon to Bacon under the great seal, and provoked a warning from Lord Keeper Williams that he should 'meddle with no pardon for the Lord of St Albans' for this might lead to 'mistakings . . . between the Parliament and His Majesty' and open the way for Buckingham's enemies to attack him again.[57]

Bacon had been forbidden to approach the Court, and his political career was almost certainly over – although he himself was probably the last person to accept this. He was also in desperate financial straits, having always lived above his income even in the times of his prosperity, and he made frequent appeals to Buckingham to secure a pension for him. Buckingham persuaded James to refer this matter to Lord Treasurer Cranfield, on the understanding that it would be given favourable consideration, but Cranfield was not likely to act speedily, if at all. Buckingham therefore proposed, as a measure of short-term relief, that he should purchase from Bacon his lease of York House. This ancient property, which stood between the river and Charing Cross, belonged to the Archbishops of York, but was customarily leased out to the Lord Chancellor or Keeper of the day. Bacon's father, Lord Keeper Nicholas Bacon, had occupied the house, and Bacon himself had been born there. When he was given custody of the great seal in 1617 he took a twenty-one-year lease on the house, and in 1621, on the day when he made his formal confession of guilt to the crimes alleged against him by the Commons, he assigned the lease to trustees to hold for him, on condition that he should have the use of the property. Buckingham's attitude was that York House was, in effect, an official residence, and now that Bacon was no longer Lord Chancellor and could not even come to town he would doubtless be glad to be relieved of it. Bacon, however, thought differently. As he told the Duke of Lenox, who also expressed an interest in acquiring the property, York House was 'where my father died and where I first breathed, and there will I yield my last breath, if it so please God and the King will give me leave'.[58]

Buckingham was not impressed by Bacon's reasons for wishing to retain York House. He had done a great deal for the Lord Chancellor, both before and after his fall, and Bacon had made repeated protestations of goodwill and devotion. Yet now that he was asked to give proof of his goodwill by parting with a property that could no longer be of any use to him, he was unwilling to do so. There was consequently a marked cooling off in the tone of Buckingham's letters to the fallen Chancellor, but matters improved early in 1622, after Sir Edward Sackville brought about an interview between the Marquis and Lady Bacon. Buckingham wrote to his old friend to assure him that 'I shall be very far from taking it ill if you part with it [York House] to any else; judging it alike unreasonableness to desire that which is another man's.' He also promised to press the King for permission for Bacon to come to London, not simply for Bacon's advantage but so that he himself might 'be sometimes happy in visiting and conversing with your lordship, whose company I am much desirous to enjoy, as being tied by ancient acquaintance'. Bacon responded to these indications of a return of the former friendly relations, and protested that as far as the house was concerned 'I was ever resolved your lordship should have had it, or no man.' Buckingham, in fact, had not much longer to wait, for early in 1622 Bacon at last agreed to sell the remainder of the lease to him for £1,300, and York House passed into the possession of the favourite.[59]

Bacon seems to have been pleased with the bargain, for Buckingham's goodwill was likely to be far more useful to him than an old, dank building which needed endless and expensive maintenance. To show his gratitude for all that Buckingham had done (and, he hoped, would continue to do) Bacon presented him with a copy of his latest work, the *History of King Henry VII*, and promised to dedicate his next book to him. This promise was fulfilled in 1625, when Bacon's *Essays* appeared with a dedication to the favourite, in which the author expressed the hope that Buckingham's name, like the essays themselves, would be remembered with honour by succeeding generations, 'for your fortune and merit both have been eminent, and you have planted things that are like to last'.[60]

While Buckingham was negotiating with Bacon he was also completing arrangements to purchase another property, Wallingford House, at a cost of £3,000. This was a good deal less than the house would have fetched on the open market, because it stood in a prime position, next to the royal palace of Whitehall and overlooking St James's Park. The owner of the house was William Knollys, Viscount Wallingford, whose career had been blighted by the fall of his relatives, the Howards, in 1618, and he only agreed to part with it at this price as part of a bargain involving his sister-in-law, the Countess of Somerset. She and her husband had been prisoners in the Tower ever since their conviction for the murder of Sir Thomas Overbury. Now they were allowed to go free on condition that they lived at Wallingford's country house. Buckingham's action in securing the release of the man he had superseded in the King's favour was a remarkable demonstration of his confidence that he had nothing more to fear. It also marks the final stage of the reconciliation between Buckingham and the Howards, for at the same time Thomas Howard, Suffolk's second son, was created Viscount Andover and married into the Cecil family. In these circumstances it was hardly surprising that Suffolk himself later wrote to the Marquis from Audley End to assure him 'that no man is prouder of your favour, neither shall any man be more desirous to hold it than I am and will be'.[61]

Wallingford House now became Buckingham's London home, and by early 1622 he and his wife had taken up residence there. The move came none too soon from Kate's point of view, for as the Countess of Buckingham had told Cranfield in late 1621, when she wrote to congratulate him on the birth of a boy, Kate 'hopes to bring a kinsman to your son ere it be long, for we feel him kick, thanks be to God'. Buckingham longed for a male heir to inherit his name and titles, but on 28 March Kate gave birth to a daughter, who was christened Mary, after the Countess, but was always known affectionately as Mall. The King, as soon as he heard the news, went in person to offer his congratulations, but rejoicing gave way to alarm when Kate, who had had a difficult labour, fell dangerously ill with smallpox. The christening – in which the King, the Countess, and the Duchess of Lenox took part – was held without ceremony a few days later, for fear that the baby, which was weak and sickly, might also be struck down. Fortunately Kate made a quick recovery, due in part to devoted care and attention by the Duchess of Lenox, to whom the King sent a miniature of himself, set in a diamond chain, as a token of gratitude. He had been daily at Wallingford House during Kate's sickness, and watched over her and her child as if they had been his own. Tillières, the French ambassador, reported that the King was enchanted by little Mall, whom he constantly fondled and embraced, and one of James's early biographers commented on the irony of the fact that 'the King, that never much cared for women, had his Court swarming with the Marquis's kindred, so that little ones would dance up and down the privy lodgings like fairies'.[62]

Buckingham's finances were severely strained by the move to Wallingford House, since, as the King forced him to reveal, 'he must pay £20,000 for his land at Burley, and these provisions for her [Kate's] lying-in, and meubling [furnishing] are like to cost £10,000, besides £3,000 for his new house, and all this he must borrow'. James had already discussed the problem repeatedly with Lord Treasurer Cranfield and urged him to 'do quickly therefore what ye are to do for him', since 'if he once run in arrear he will ever go backward'. It is not at all clear what Cranfield had in mind, since at this very moment he was trying to commit the King and favourite to a programme of retrenchment, but he obviously found means to prevent Buckingham sinking even further into debt. The requisite sums of money probably came from the royal exchequer, though not necessarily by way of direct grant, for in September 1622 Buckingham surrendered to the crown a number of properties which he had formerly been given, and obtained in return 'a discharge and release of all moneys by him received from His Majesty's own hands or from others by His Majesty's order'.[63]

Buckingham now had a London residence – Wallingford House – with another, and much larger one, York House, being made ready for him. He also had a substantial estate at Burley in Rutland. All he now needed was a country property nearer town, which he could use to escape from the press of suitors, and for entertaining. In June, Buckingham and his mother went to look at New Hall, north of Chelmsford in Essex, a palatial mansion built for Henry VIII early in the sixteenth century, and modernised some fifty years later by the Earl of Sussex, to whom it was presented by Queen Elizabeth. Buckingham was obviously taken with the house, for in July 1622 he agreed to buy it for £20,000. He paid £12,500 down in cash, and the other £7,500 within a year. Chamberlain reported that Inigo Jones, the King's Surveyor, had been ordered to alter it 'according to the modern fashion', and in September Buckingham displayed his new acquisition to

James and the Prince, who spent two days there as his guests. Where the money came from to pay for New Hall is far from clear. As Lord Admiral, Buckingham had £3,000 prize money due to him from captures made by Mansell's expedition. He was also owed substantial sums, including £3,000 by the Duchess of Lenox which the King ordered to be paid to him out of the Exchequer. There may have been something left still from Kate's dowry, but it seems likely that Buckingham had to resort to substantial borrowing. It is hardly surprising, therefore, that Sir Robert Pye, on whom he relied for financial advice, sought him out at Hampton Court in October 1622, to discuss 'putting your house in order and settling some things in your estate'. As it happened, Pye was unable to achieve his purpose, for 'the multitude of your great affairs and the importunity of greedy suitors did so perplex your nobleness as it did prevent my intent', but he subsequently committed his thoughts to paper. He recommended Buckingham to set aside £3,000 a year for household expenses and other charges of his wife, and £2,000 for his mother. The favourite should also decide what needed to be sold, to pay his debts, for as Pye reminded him 'a great man is first judged by his own government in his estate, and accordingly the world will censure. If you stand firm in your own estate, you will be the abler to do His Majesty service.'[64]

At the end of his letter of advice, Pye urged Buckingham not to delay putting his affairs in order. 'Protraction', he pointed out, 'is dangerous, and your lordship's family want good guiding in this unsettled time.' This last phrase probably referred to the international situation, for it looked as though war might break out between England and Spain. But Pye must also have been aware of rumours that were circulating about a new favourite. Such rumours would have carried no weight in the early part of 1622, when Buckingham and the King seemed as close as ever, and Tillières, the French ambassador, reported that Buckingham's favour was increasing to such an extent that people believed he had bewitched the King. James, apparently, could not do enough for his favourite, and even in small matters, like getting fir seeds sent from Scotland for planting at Burley, he showed his concern. When the Earl of Oxford was imprisoned in the spring of 1622 – allegedly for saying, in a drunken moment, that he wished the King were dead – it was widely believed that his real offence was crossing the favourite. It was in his house that Elizabeth Norris had taken refuge after escaping from the attentions of Kit Villiers, and Oxford refused to hand her over. Worse than this, he was also reported to have told Buckingham that he 'hoped there would come a time when justice should be free and not pass through his hands only'. The imprisonment of Oxford suggested that the King regarded opposition to his favourite as opposition to himself.[65]

There were, however, straws in the wind, which pointed in a different direction. In March it was reported that the King had excluded Buckingham from an audience with the Dutch ambassadors, and left him biting his lip in anger. Some weeks later the King bestowed the place of Groom of the Bedchamber on Arthur Brett, who was Lady Cranfield's brother and Buckingham's cousin. The appointment did not cause much comment at the time, nor did the grant of a £300 Star Chamber fine to Brett in July. No doubt it was assumed that such rewards were only to be, expected for one who had the good fortune to be related not merely to the favourite but to the Lord Treasurer as well. Early in September, however, the Earl of Kellie, in one of his letters to the Earl of Mar, mentioned the opinion held by some people about Court 'that His Majesty should begin to love and favour one young man called Brett'. He added that he himself did not believe the story, but in a later letter he admitted that there was something in it.[66]

By the end of 1622 the rumours had become current. According to Tillières, Buckingham was so alarmed at the glances which James was casting at Brett that he heaped reproaches on the King and menaced the young man. There was clearly more than idle gossip behind these rumours. Kellie was well informed about what was going on at Court, and although he was still professing scepticism as late as December, he made the revealing comment that 'the Marquis does not well to resist, but [should] willingly applaud to His Majesty's pleasure. I think the experience he had of the last business may teach him so much that if His Majesty have a mind to it there is no resisting of it.' Yet if there was a crisis in the relationship between the King and Buckingham, it was apparently over by the end of the year, for one observer referred to Brett in December as 'a new star ... suddenly down', and the Venetian ambassador reported that 'matters have quieted down, and the Marquis seems more in favour than ever, and now has under seal a fresh gift from the King'. Only a month or two later Buckingham felt sufficiently secure in the King's affections to take the enormous risk of accompanying the Prince of Wales to Spain — leaving his enemies free to intrigue against him. But it was noted that shortly before he left 'young Monson, who stood once to be a favourite, was knighted ... by the Lord of Buckingham's means, and sent to travel. The same order is taken for Brett.'[67]

NOTES

(Abbreviations are explained in the Bibliography, pp. 477–86)
1. *Ch.* II, 323; *Bac.* XIV, 148–9.
2. *C.D.* V, 428.
3. *C.D.* VI, 254–5.
4. *P.D.* I, 71–2; *C.D.* VI, 257.
5. *L.D.* 150; *C.D.* VI, 303.
6. *C.D.* II, 161; VI, 303–4.
7. *C.D.* II, 161.
8. *C.J.* 538–9.
9. *Hast.* 26, 28–9.
10. *Hast.* 29–30.
11. *Hack.* I, 49–50.

12. *Bac.* XIV, 192; *Hack.* I, 50.
13. *C.J.* 552; *C.D.* IV, 149; II, 212.
14. *Zaller.* 60; *Bas.MSS.* 54, no number.
15. *Clar.* I, 241; *Fiennes*; *Birch*, II, 319.
16. *L.J.* 36; *Dk.MSS.* 6.171; *Tann. MSS.* 94.267.
17. *Zaller.* 55.
18. *P.D.* I, 89, 103.
19. *Bac.* XIV, 192.
20. *L.J.* 54.
21. *Bac.* XIV, 225; *L.J.* 69.
22. *Sal.* 30 Mar. 1621, A.M. 4193; *Bas.MSS.* 54, no number; *Dom.MSS 14.* 119.69.
23. *Ch.* II, 356; *Tann.MSS.* 73.3v.; *L.D.* 63–4.
24. *P.D.* I, 286, 308–9.
25. *Cab.* 2; *Dom.MSS 14.* 121.136.
26. *Denmilne MSS.* 33.1.7, XXII.42; *Ch.* II, 302.
27. *L.J.* 121.
28. *Ch.* II, 369; *L.D.* 48, 52.
29. *Hast.* 33; *L.D.* 55, 57–9.
30. *Zaller.* 121–2; *Dom.MSS 14.* 121.54.
31. *L.D.* 82; *L.J.* 125; *Ch.* II, 374.
32. *L.J.* 76, 151; *Zaller.* 125.
33. *C.S.P.V.* XVII, 66; *Dietz.* 189; *Rush.* 36; *C.J.* 639.
34. *P.D.* II, Appendix; *Trum.MSS.* 18.60, 77; *Cab.* 259, 332; *Ch.* II, 438.
35. *C.S.P.V.* XVII, 162; *Add.MSS.* 36, 445.226.
36. *Sp.MSS.* 23.3.
37. *P.D.* II, 218; *Ch.* II, 412.
38. *Harl.MSS.* 1580.428, 401. The last word of 401 has been struck through, presumably by Goring.
39. *P.D.* II, 220.
40. *Rush.* 41–2; *P.D.* II, 269.
41. *Ph.MSS.* DD/PH 224/82. I should like to thank Conrad Russell for this reference; *C.S.P.V.* XVII, 173; *Ch.* II, 413.
42. *Add.MSS.* 36, 445.319v.–320. I am indebted to David Hebb, who first saw the significance of the intercepted letters, and to Conrad Russell, who brought this to my attention; *Trum.MSS.* 7.96.
43. *Sack.MSS.* ON.2461, 15; *Dom.MSS 14.* 127.1; *Ch.* II, 418; *H.M.C.(11).* 21.
44. *Harl.MSS.* 7000.66.
45. *Hack.* I, 107; *Sack.MSS.* ON.2417; *Carte MSS.* 30.135.
46. *Sack.MSS.* ON.28, 872, 22; *Trum.MSS.* 18.76.
47. *Harl.MSS.* 1580.369; *Havran.* 70; *Trum.MSS.* 18.87; *H.M.C.Coke.* 122.
48. *Trum.MSS.* 18.88; *Harl.MSS.* 1581.115; *Ch.* II. 470; *Eg.MSS.* 2533.63v.
49. *Preston.* 66, 69, 84.
50. *Hack.* I, 171, 173; *Laud.* 139; *Trevor.* 59–60.
51. *Birch.* II, 282; *Ch.* II, 419–20; *Eg.MSS.* 2594.109.
52. *Carte MSS.* 30.133.
53. *Sainty.* 27; *Ch.* II, 439; *Sack.MSS.* ON.8682; *Trum.MSS.* 18.82.
54. *Ch.* II, 439; *H.M.C.(12).* 467–8; *Dom.MSS 14.* 151.86–7.
55. *Cab.* 304–5; *Dom.MSS 14.* 127.97.; *H.M.C.(4).* 255.
56. *Rawl.MSS.* D.398.192; *Ch.* II, 476; *Man.* I, 314.

57. *D'Ewes.* 192; *Cab.* 262, 263.
58. *Ritchie.* Intro.; *Bac.* XIV, 327.
59. *Harl.MSS.* 7000.70; *Bac.* XIV, 329.
60. *Essays.* Dedication.
61. *Clo.MSS.* C.54.2515; *Bod.MSS.* D.111.411.
62. *Sack.MSS.* ON.2461; *Trum.MSS.* 18.66; *Ch.* II, 430, 434; *Bas.MSS.* 56.43; *Wil.* 727.
63. *Harl.MSS.* 6987.1; *Trum.MSS.* 18.82.
64. *Ch.* II. 441, 452; *Clo.MSS.* C.54.2493; *H.M.C.Supp.* 136; *H.M.C.Coke.* 122; Duchess of Lenox, Sept. [1624], *Sack.MSS.* uncat.; *Harl.MSS.* 1581.118, 120, 121.
65. *Bas.MSS.* 56.43; *H.M.C.Supp.* 115–16; *Goodman.* II, 231–3; *Dom.MSS 14.* 128.97; 129.50.
66. *Birch.* II, 301; *Ch.* II, 442; *Sack.MSS.* ON.7748; *H.M.C.Mar.* 133; *H.M.C.Supp.* 140.
67. *Bas.MSS.* 56.143; *H.M.C.Supp.* 145; *Trum.MSS.* 18.88; *C.S.P.V.* XVIII, 530; *Ch.* II. 479.

CHAPTER FIVE

1623: 'We shall go for the daughter of Spain'

I

James's hopes for restoring peace to Europe in 1622 depended upon a complex series of negotiations in a number of different places. The main line of communication was with Spain, for it was through Madrid that James planned to exert leverage on the imperial branch of the house of Habsburg. He therefore ordered Digby to leave immediately for Spain, in the hope that he would be there before the end of February. However, delays in preparing the ships for his voyage kept Digby waiting at Plymouth for many weeks, and it was not until the end of June that he eventually reached Madrid. But any irritation he may have felt at the tediousness of his journey was more than compensated for by the warmth of the welcome he received, and in early August he reported to Charles that 'I now make no doubt but that the prince [Frederick] shall entirely be restored, both to his territories and to his electorate, and this king, merely to gratify His Majesty, will make it his work.' He added that the marriage and the restitution were so closely linked 'that they would not make the match without resolving to restore the Palatinate, nor restore the Palatinate without resolving to make the match'. A few days later Digby reported that the Spanish council of state had unanimously decided that Philip IV should 'take this business upon him and procure His Majesty's entire satisfaction for his son-in-law, as well by the restitution of his electorate as of his territories'. James must have been delighted to receive this confirmation of his highest hopes, particularly when the usually cautious Digby wrote to tell him 'that which hitherto I have never said – that I am in great hope that God will . . . bless Your Majesty with such success as shall be highly to Your Majesty's honour and satisfaction'.[1]

The Spaniards were genuine in their desire to see the problem of the Palatinate resolved, so that they could concentrate their forces against their major enemy, the Dutch; and they recognised that Frederick must either be restored or compensated. But they were in no position to make a unilateral restitution of the Lower Palatinate, since they occupied only part of it: the rest was being fought over by Frederick's troops under the German mercenary, Count Mansfeld; the English volunteer force headed by Sir Horace Vere; and Maximilian of Bavaria's army under Count Tilly. The Spaniards could, in theory, have pulled out of that part of the territory which they did control, but in the absence of a general settlement this would have left the situation even more confused. It would have deprived them of the only bargaining-counter they possessed in Germany, and it would also have left their vital land route to the Netherlands dangerously exposed. In practice their best hope of achieving a satisfactory settlement was by bringing pressure to bear on the Emperor, but here again their influence was limited — although James and his fellow-countrymen, who were convinced that all catholic Europe danced to the Spanish tune, would have been the last to realise this. It was all very well for Philip's ministers to assure Digby that they would 'speak very plain language' at the imperial court, but the Emperor was not likely to take much notice of warnings from the Spanish ambassador. He had his own plans for the extension of Habsburg power in Germany, and he was not dependent upon Spain. His main creditor, in fact, was Maximilian of Bavaria, who demanded, as the price of his support, both the lands and the title of his kinsman, Frederick. This was a price which the Emperor would have to pay, since he had no alternative, and the Spanish ministers knew it. [2]

James may have overestimated the influence of Spain in German affairs, but he was correct in his assumption that without the support of Spain his own representations would merely be brushed aside. Spain had given encouragement to his suggestion that, as a prelude to a general peace conference, there should be a cessation of arms in the Palatinate, and the Emperor had agreed that if James were to send a representative to Brussels, the Infanta Isabella, the ruler of the Netherlands, should have full power to negotiate a truce. James chose his Chancellor of the Exchequer, Sir Richard Weston, for this task, and by the time Digby arrived at Madrid in the summer of 1622, Weston was already in the middle of his negotiations at Brussels. These proved to be long, tedious, and in the end frustrating. One of the major problems was that of Frederick himself. The Elector had never accepted the principle that he must abandon the use of force if he was to recover his possessions, and in the spring of 1622 he made an abrupt departure from the Hague and suddenly appeared at Mansfeld's camp, where he proposed to take charge of military operations in the Palatinate. This news aroused fears at Brussels, as elsewhere, that Frederick was not interested in a negotiated settlement, and discussions were virtually suspended. Not until Frederick's armies had been defeated did they get going again, for it was only then, in June, that Frederick gave his written agreement to abide by any terms that James accepted on his behalf.

Weston was now hopeful that rapid progress could be made, but there was still the problem of the auxiliary forces, including those of Mansfeld, which had gone to Frederick's aid. Would they observe a cease-fire, and if not, what action should be taken against them? James gave his reply to this in August, when he assured Isabella that he would 'be so far from permitting that the truce shall be any way infringed . . . that contrariwise he promiseth and declareth that he will join his arms with those of his imperial majesty against all such as shall attempt it'. Weston was convinced that the last obstacles to a cease-fire had now been removed, and he pressed for a speedy conclusion of the negotiations. This was particularly urgent in view of the fact that Frederick's possessions in the Palatinate had been reduced to the three towns of Heidelberg, Mannheim and Frankenthal, all of which were held by English garrisons. At this stage, however, it became clear to Weston that the imperial representatives were not acting in good faith. As the military situation changed in their favour, so their main concern came to be the spinning out of negotiations in the hope of winning a total victory in the field. Weston, in despair, announced his intention of playing no further part in this charade, and in September he took his leave. He returned to England, full of resentment and foreboding, at the same time as Digby's despatches with their assurances that all would be well were being received. Brussels and Madrid were obviously speaking with different voices.[3]

The direction of the various negotiations in which English representatives were involved was, as always, in the hands of the King, and Buckingham played only a subsidiary role. Domestic matters, such as the purchase of houses and the birth of his child, took up much of his time, as did attendance upon James. When Buckingham was in town he would usually pay his respects to Gondomar, who responded by presenting him and his wife with jewels and other gifts, but he did little more than echo James's declarations of continuing trust in Spain. However, at the same time as Buckingham observed these formal courtesies with the Spanish ambassador, he also kept in touch with the exiled King and Queen of Bohemia and did his best to improve their condition. In March 1622 he was asked by the Privy Council to urge James to make some further provision for them, 'knowing your good affection for His Majesty's children and to anything that concerneth their service'. Buckingham persuaded James to supply £5,000 for this cause, but in July the Privy Council asked his help in obtaining a further grant of £3,000 in order to pay Elizabeth's debts, and a regular allowance of £1,000 a month, 'being well acquainted with your readiness and zeal to join with us upon all occasions concerning her highness's service'. Elizabeth herself wrote to the favourite in July, thanking him for his letter and for the gift of a horse. 'I am exceedingly beholding to you', she told him, 'for the care you take in fitting me so well with horses, by which you continue to tie [me] to you, as you do by other many obligations.' Later that month she wrote to him again, urging him to press the King to take effective action before the Palatinate was totally lost. In fact Buckingham had already made a move in that direction, for in June he secured the appointment to the Privy Council of Sir Edward Conway, and he was now preparing the ground for Conway to replace Naunton as Secretary of State. Conway was a professional soldier with long and close connexions with the Dutch, who made no secret of his belief that diplomacy without the sword was unlikely to be of much avail. Buckingham's choice of such a man at this time indicated the direction in which his own attitude was developing.[4]

In September 1622 Gondomar, who was now back in Spain, wrote a friendly letter to Buckingham from Madrid, telling him what pleasure it would give him 'to walk with you in the open gallery which leads from Your Excellency's chamber to the palace on the Thames', and adding that although he could not enjoy the Marquis's company in person, he had a portrait of him in his room. Gondomar made only a passing reference to the marriage negotiations, since Sir Francis Cottington, who was returning from Spain with the latest Spanish proposals, would give the details, but he assured the favourite that Philip IV wanted the marriage to go ahead and that a great deal had already been done to advance it. Such assurances would normally have been well received in England, but there was increasing alarm at Court about the rapidly worsening situation in the Palatinate, and the suspicion was growing that Spain was not doing all that she promised. As early as July the Venetian ambassador had told his government that James 'and the favourite grow more determined not to suffer any more delay beyond a certain, limited time' and he made the interesting observation that, in the opinion of some people, 'the Marquis fears that all the blame and punishment will descend upon him if it ends in nothing after all this time, and accordingly he says openly that he wants to make an end'. With the news that Weston's negotiations were getting nowhere, and that Heidelberg was under siege, the King and Buckingham became even more impatient with the interminable delays in reaching agreement on the terms of the Spanish marriage, and in early September Kellie told Mar that 'if there shall be no more appearance of the rendering of the Palatinate . . . I much doubt what shall be the event of it'.[5]

James decided to increase the pressure on Philip IV. On 9 September 1622 he wrote to Digby, pointing out the contrast between the ambassador's optimistic despatches and the gloomy news from Germany. 'Our meaning', he said, 'is to carry all things fair with that king [Philip IV] and not to give him any cause of distrust or jealousy', but he was not prepared to wait indefinitely. Digby was therefore to insist upon a 'final resolution' before Christmas. Meanwhile Buckingham wrote a long letter to Gondomar, almost certainly at the King's command, setting out James's feelings. Everything necessary had been done in England, he assured the Count. The penal laws had been relaxed, and imprisoned priests and recusants had been set at liberty. 'Here is a King, a Prince, and a faithful friend and servant unto you . . . that long so much for the happy accomplishment of this match as every day seems a year unto us. . . . If we could hear as good news from you, we should think ourselves happy men.' Buckingham then went on to describe the difficulties which Weston had encountered, and the King's bitterness at the way in which he had been treated by the Emperor. In short, concluded Buckingham, 'we ever received comfortable words from Spain, but find such contrary effects from Brussels, together with our intelligences from all other parts of the world, as all our hopes are not only cold but quite extinguished here'.[6]

It was while Buckingham was entertaining the King and Prince at New Hall, in late September, 1622, that news arrived that Tilly's forces had overwhelmed the English garrison defending Heidelberg, killing the English commander, and had taken and sacked the town. As it happened, Sir Francis

Nethersole, Elizabeth's secretary, arrived at New Hall with messages for the King at much the same time as the news from Heidelberg, and in a letter to his royal mistress he reported Buckingham's reaction. The favourite had told him, said Nethersole, 'that the affairs are now come too near a period to admit of any dissimulation, and that he . . . was very confident the King . . . will make good all that he hath promised; that for himself, he will urge it with all the credit he hath with His Majesty, and beg of him that he may in person go to the wars'. Nethersole was convinced that Buckingham really meant what he said, and he added that the favourite intended 'to make Sir Edward Conway Secretary of State . . . and that he doth advise much and often with him about the ways of redressing the affairs and vindicating the King our master's honour'.[7]

II

James watched the mounting war fever with apprehension, particularly now that it had affected his son and his favourite – the two people who meant most to him. Matters did not improve when Weston returned empty-handed from Brussels, and the Prince decided not to join his father in the country but to stay with the Privy Council in London to work out proposals for an army of twenty thousand men which he intended to lead to the aid of his distressed sister. The King resolved to make one last attempt to bring the Spanish marriage – and with it, he assumed, the restitution of the Palatinate – into effect. He decided to despatch a special messenger to Digby, and his choice fell on Endymion Porter, a relative and close friend of Buckingham as well as one of the principal officers of the favourite's household. Porter was in many ways a good choice, for he had a Spanish grandmother and had spent a number of years in Spain in the service of the Count of Olivares, now Philip's chief minister. Porter, if anyone, should be able to penetrate behind the facade of Spanish assurances and see if James was being hoodwinked.[8]

It might be thought that Digby, with his long experience of Spain, would have been better placed to know how the Spanish mind worked. But Digby was in some way too much of a gentleman, too easily blinded by the polished surface of Spanish manners, to realise that he was being deceived. He was also the victim of the power structure of the Spanish court, in which decisions were made by the favourite in conjunction with the King, and members of the council of state were themselves frequently unaware of what was really going on. Olivares had only recently come to power in 1622, and he quickly discovered that he was faced with the problem of reconciling a number of policies that were mutually contradictory. The Infanta Maria's projected marriage with Prince Charles was one of these, for although Philip III had allowed negotiations to go ahead in order to retain James's friendship, he declared on his deathbed that he had never intended the marriage to take place. In view of this, Philip IV now asked Olivares for his advice on what course to pursue.

In his reply, Olivares made clear the dilemma confronting Philip. If he consented to the marriage he would have to agree to the restitution of the Palatinate, since the two were inseparable, and as a consequence he might well find himself, 'together with the King of Great Britain, engaged in a war against the Emperor and the Catholic League . . . a thing which, to hear, will offend Your Majesty's godly ears'. If, on the other hand, Philip consented to the marriage but did nothing to secure the restoration of the Palatinate, he would leave James 'offended and disobliged'. The English marriage, in short, would create more problems than it solved, and Olivares was of the opinion that it should not be proceeded with. A better solution, in his eyes, was that put forward by the imperial ambassador – namely, that Charles should marry one of the daughters of the Emperor Ferdinand. If this could be done at the same time as another of Ferdinand's daughters was married to the Elector Frederick's son and heir, the Emperor – who alone could sort out the intricate tangle of German politics – would be personally committed to finding a satisfactory solution to the Palatinate question.[9]

The scheme outlined by Olivares was basically sound, but among the many difficulties involved in bringing it to fruition was that of broaching it to Digby, and through him to James I. Digby had spent years negotiating marriage terms for the Prince of Wales, and was convinced that the last obstacles were about to be overcome. The temporal articles had been agreed on. As for the spiritual ones, these were at Rome, waiting to receive the assent of the Pope, who would then issue the dispensation for the marriage to take place. Philip's representative at Rome had been instructed to drag out matters as long as possible, but Digby, although he was unaware of this, became increasingly impatient over the lack of progress and insisted on an interview with Olivares, who gave him a formal assurance that Philip wished to see a speedy conclusion to the English marriage.[10]

This calculated deception of Digby was simply a bid to gain time, for the Spanish ministers could see no obvious way out of the impasse they were in, and could only hope that the course of events would itself resolve the situation. As far as German affairs were concerned they wished to await the outcome of the assembly of German princes which the Emperor had summoned to meet at Regensburg in January 1623. Meanwhile they were quite prepared to support English efforts to achieve a ceasefire in the Palatinate – particularly as this would give their own forces time to recover and would also enable them to strengthen their main front against the Dutch. Philip therefore wrote to the Emperor, pressing him to call off the sieges of Mannheim and Frankenthal – a request that he repeated more insistently in November, 1622, even though by that time Mannheim had fallen.[11]

While the Spaniards were genuine in their assurances to Digby that they were working for a cessation of arms in the Palatinate, they were less than straightforward in their reply to another of the demands which, at James's insistence, he made of them. James had given a formal assurance that the Elector Frederick, his son-in-law, would observe any terms which were agreed on for a cease-fire, and had also promised that in case either Frederick or his auxiliaries should refuse to lay down their arms, English forces would be used to compel them to do so. James now demanded that the Spaniards should make a similar commitment, by agreeing not only that the Palatinate should be restored to Frederick, but that Spanish forces would join with English ones to drive out imperial troops if the Emperor refused to make a peaceful hand-over. Olivares was reluctant to give any such commitment, but Digby was insistent and he was eventually accorded an audience of Philip IV at which the king gave his word of honour that Spanish troops would, if necessary, combine with English ones to clear the Palatinate. Digby pressed for written confirmation of this promise, but all he could obtain, in late October 1622, were letters from Philip giving orders 'that in case that the Emperor or Duke of Bavaria would not forbear those towns wherein His Majesty [James] had his garrisons, that the King of Spain's forces in the Palatinate should be employed in their assistance, and that they should not suffer any wrong to be done them by any other whatsoever'. This was far short of the commitment that Digby insisted had been made by word of mouth – though Olivares was later to tell Buckingham that Philip had never made any such promise. Nevertheless Digby sent the letters off to England, where they gave great satisfaction to James. The King had already shown his appreciation of Digby's services by creating him Earl of Bristol in September 1622, and now, in November, he assured him that 'we are well pleased with the diligent and discreet employing of your endeavours in all that concerns our service'.[12]

In an earlier letter, written in October, James had told Digby 'not to trouble yourself with the rash censures of other men in case your business should not succeed, resting in the full assurance of our justice and wisdom, that we will never judge a good and faithful servant by the effects of things so contingent and variable'. This was a great comfort to the ambassador, who was well aware that he was coming under heavy criticism in England for making promises about the restoration of the Palatinate that seemed to bear no relation to the realities of the deteriorating situation in Germany. Digby himself had doubts about the genuineness of the assurances he was being given, for in a letter to the Prince of Wales he told him 'there is here either a sincere intention of giving His Majesty and Your Highness full satisfaction, both in the business of the match and of the Palatinate; or they are the falsest people upon the earth'. In another letter, to his fellow-ambassador Sir Dudley Carleton, he outlined his attitude more explicitly. An ambassador's duty, he declared, was to carry out negotiations as ordered: 'if either intervenient accidents, want of obedience in the ministers that should execute, or deceit or unworthiness in the prince or state itself that gave orders, hinder the due performance of what is promised, it can have little reflection upon an ambassador'. His task, he maintained, was 'only faithfully to deliver his master's letters and to represent back (without cooling or warming it in the carriage) the answer he receiveth'. Digby was technically correct. It was indeed his function to keep open the lines of communication between England and Spain, while it was James's responsibility to evaluate the information he received by testing it against reports from other parts of the world. Yet Digby's narrow view of his role was in marked contrast to that of Gondomar, for instance, who never ceased to warn his government about the dangers of James's perfidy and to interpret the King's policies in an often unflattering light. Digby was too uncritical in his acceptance of promises which the Spaniards had no means of honouring, even if they had the intention. If James was willing to be duped, Digby unconsciously assisted the deception, for the assurances which he transmitted were, in the words of the Venetian ambassador to England, 'a narcotic to make them [the English] sleep the more profoundly this winter'.[13]

Endymion Porter's mission was designed to put an end to the long English slumber, for the despatch which James gave him to carry to Bristol required the ambassador to set a term of seventy days during which Philip was to secure a cease-fire in the Palatinate and the handing over to James of Heidelberg and any other major towns which had subsequently been captured by imperial forces. Bristol was also to insist on a formal agreement by the Spanish king that in the event of the Emperor refusing to comply with these just demands, he would either authorise Spanish troops to join with English ones in clearing the Palatinate, or at least allow the English free passage through his territories to attack the imperial army. The time limit for the receipt of this assurance was set at a mere ten days, but James qualified it by telling Bristol that in the event of an unsatisfactory reply he was not to take his leave immediately but was to report back and await further instructions.[14]

Endymion set out at full speed for Dover, where he boarded a ship to cross the Channel. Just off Calais, however, his vessel came into collision with a larger one, and Endymion only just escaped with his life. A broken shoulder kept him prisoner in Calais for a week or so, but his message was too important to await a full convalescence, and he was soon on the road again, riding post for Spain. He reached Madrid at the beginning of November 1622, and handed over his despatches to Bristol. The ambassador, it seems, was not best pleased with the arrival of this special courier, whose very presence in the Spanish capital seemed to betray a certain lack of trust in his own judgement. Bristol also feared that the Spaniards would not react kindly to ultimatums. As he told Carleton on 26 November, 'they here think it very strange that they should be bound in the greatest business of Christendom, whereby they are to declare a war to their own family . . . to declare themselves in ten days, and that they should undertake that Heidelberg and Mannheim should be restored in seventy days, in which time a post can scarcely go and return from the Emperor'. One minister even went so far as to tell Bristol that his action savoured of menace and that his insistence on having Philip's promise signed and sealed implied too great a distrust for friendly relations.[15]

Philip was determined not to be bound as far as the restitution of the Palatinate was concerned, and all he offered was a reiteration of his readiness to continue his good offices. Even Bristol found this answer unsatisfactory, but in accordance with his instructions he reported it to James, on 10 December, and left the King to decide what step to take next. But in a parallel letter to the Secretary of State – which, like the one to James, was carried by Porter on his return journey – Bristol said how impressed he was with the firm tone of the despatches which the Spanish king had sent to his imperial cousin, urging him to seek a peaceful solution of the problems of Germany. As for the Spanish ministers, added Bristol, 'I dare affirm it unto His Majesty for truth that I do not think he hath so many great men and counsellors in all Christendom so heartily affected to him and his service as in this court.'[16]

While Porter was making his painful way across Europe, a select number of James's Councillors were considering what action should be taken to prevent the total loss of the Palatinate. They were strongly in favour of the suggestion that the King should take into his pay the troops of the mercenary commanders, Count Mansfeld and the Duke of Brunswick. These would not only be useful as a stopgap. They would also provide the King with a very valuable body of cavalry – an arm in which his own forces were deficient – if he decided on direct intervention. But James knew only too well that armies cost money and that money on this scale could only be raised by summoning Parliament once again – an expedient which he was anxious to postpone as long as possible. Buckingham, who appreciated the need to maintain Mansfeld's forces if anything effective was to be accomplished, proposed that another benevolence should be collected, and offered to make a substantial contribution himself. But the Marquis's fellow-Councillors would not accept his suggestion. They feared, with some reason, that a voluntary contribution would merely delay the calling of Parliament, and in the long run lose valuable time. They wanted James to summon Parliament forthwith; the King, on the other hand, would not do so while he had hopes of Spain. As Sir Francis Nethersole commented, 'we are therefore now here at a loss till the game be put up again by Mr Porter'.[17]

No courier was ever awaited so eagerly as Endymion Porter, for upon his report would depend the future conduct of English policy and the decision between peace and war. He arrived in London on 2 January, 1623, and the next day the news spread rapidly that the marriage was as good as concluded and that Gondomar was to be sent to the Emperor to secure the restoration of the Palatinate. The King, not surprisingly, was delighted, since it looked as though his patient diplomacy was at long last bearing fruit. As far as the Palatinate was concerned the Spaniards were still offering no more than promises, but James was convinced that once the marriage had taken place, Philip – who would thereby become a kinsman of the dispossessed Elizabeth – would compel the Emperor to make a peaceful and honourable settlement.[18]

Buckingham almost certainly assumed, as did James, that the marriage was the best way to secure the restitution of the Palatinate – indeed the only way, in view of James's notorious reluctance to use force. During the course of 1622, however, he had become increasingly doubtful about the degree to which the Spaniards could be trusted, and Porter's account of his reception at the Spanish court can hardly have allayed his suspicions. Porter had orders to spend no more than ten days in Madrid, but in the event he had been kept kicking his heels for six weeks. Bristol had shown little eagerness to procure Porter the interview with Olivares which he had asked for, so Porter eventually took the initiative himself and went to see the Count. Olivares welcomed him as an old friend and asked him what he wanted. Porter said he had come for an assurance that Philip would fulfil the promise he had made to join his forces with English ones for clearing the Palatinate, or at least allow passage to English troops, if the Emperor proved obdurate. He can hardly have anticipated the reaction which his words caused. Olivares gave a start of astonishment, and then, recovering himself, declared that it was a preposterous demand, and that there could be no question of the Spanish king taking arms against the Emperor and the House of Austria. When Porter protested that Philip had already committed himself by a verbal promise to Bristol, Olivares answered that Bristol was a liar. As for the proposed marriage, he declared that he knew nothing about it.

Porter was so amazed by this revelation that he went immediately to Bristol and told him what had happened. Bristol was furious at the suggestion that he had lied, and declared that 'an earl of England is as good as a *conde* of Spain, and that the Conde de Olivares should give him satisfaction if he held this language with him'. A night's reflection, however, persuaded Bristol that more diplomatic methods should be tried, and in the course of conversations with Olivares over the next day or two he discovered the cause of the misunderstanding. It was, he told Porter, a consequence of Olivares's unwillingness to discuss state secrets with an envoy who was not formally accredited. This explanation may have satisfied Bristol – who, as befitted his station and long experience of Spanish customs, had a due appreciation of the niceties of protocol – but it can hardly have impressed Porter, who was no fool. Nor can it have offered much comfort to Buckingham, when Porter gave him an account of his mission, particularly as Porter added the significant detail that when he challenged Olivares with concealing from him what was known to the rest of the world, Olivares answered 'that he had reason to take it unkindly that he who being tendered and favoured of him as his child had communicated that with the Earl of Bristol which he had told him in secret'. Olivares's anger suggested that Porter had shocked him into speaking the truth, and Buckingham must have wondered yet again whether the assurances which Bristol had sent from Madrid were worth the paper they were written on. [19]

III

If the Spaniards could not be trusted where the Palatinate was concerned, could it be taken for granted that they were proceeding in good faith in the marriage negotiations? Matters could not be allowed to drag on indefinitely, for quite apart from the question of the Palatinate, which it was hoped the marriage would resolve, there was the consideration that Charles was now a full-grown man of twenty-two while his father was well into his fifties and not in the best of health. It was essential that the Prince should be married as soon as possible, so that the succession could be assured. There were also the Prince's own feelings to take into account, for Charles – despite his stammer, his reserve and his apparent blandness – was physically vigorous and needed an outlet for his natural passions. He was only too aware of what James, in his forthright Scottish fashion, called the 'codpiece point' and his desires had become focussed – failing any alternative – upon the Infanta Maria, despite the fact that he had never seen her. In January 1622 he started taking Spanish lessons, and later that year he asked Bristol to send him a portrait of the Infanta. Bristol was delighted to find that the course of his negotiations coincided with the Prince's own feelings, and did his best to keep the flame of Charles's passion well and truly alight. In December 1622 he told how he had closely observed the Infanta at a court entertainment. She 'danced as well as any that ever I saw [and] as soon as the dance was done, the Infanta unmasked herself and took her place by the King, sitting all the night in the same attire. And I dare boldly say unto Your Highness that it was not so seldom as an hundred times repeated that night *"Plugiera a Dios que el Principe de Inglatierra la viese. O que linda, que hermosa, que angel."*' [If only, please God, the Prince of England could see her. How exquisite, how beautiful, how like an angel she is].[20]

Charles was understandably full of impatience to set eyes upon this delicious creature, and in May 1622 he had told Gondomar, in great secret, that if the ambassador, on his return to Spain, sent word that he should go to the Spanish court in person and put himself into the hands of Philip IV, 'he will do so, and will reach Madrid incognito and only accompanied by two servants'. As negotiations proceeded, it looked as though there would be no need for such a romantic gesture. Bristol reported that he had made provisional arrangements for the Infanta to be handed over in the spring of 1623, in which case an English fleet would have to be sent to collect her, and Charles might well accompany it. In November 1622 Buckingham asked Middlesex, the Lord Treasurer, to provide money for setting out the ships, for 'in the spring we shall go for the daughter of Spain', and early in 1623 Chamberlain reported that ten ships were making ready, 'and I have it *di buona mano* (and under the rose) that the Prince himself goes in person'. Charles, however, had not forgotten his original proposal, and one of the objects of Endymion Porter's mission was to spy out the ground in Madrid and see if the Prince would be welcome. No wonder the Prince was on tenterhooks until he got the reply, and when Endymion at last returned with the news that the marriage negotiations were apparently in their closing stages, the Prince could not contain his impatience. He was constantly badgering Sir George Calvert, one of the Secretaries of State, to hasten the departure of despatches to Rome and Madrid. He wanted to know the name of the Spanish nobleman who would deputise for him in the marriage ceremony, and he asked for Bristol's advice on when would be a suitable moment for him to send love letters to the Infanta.[21]

On 14 February 1623, Kellie told Mar that the sole topic of conversation at Court was of Buckingham's 'going to Madrid for the Infanta, and the ships preparing for that purpose'. Nothing was said of the possibility of the Prince's going with him, nor was it suggested that the Lord Admiral would be leaving until it was known that Philip had received the necessary papal dispensation.

The Prince and the favourite were with the King at Theobalds, but when he set out from there for Royston on Monday, 17 February, they did not go with him. He had given them permission to spend a few days at New Hall, and when they came to take their leave he reminded them to 'be with me upon Friday night'. ' "Sir," said Buckingham, "if we should stay a day or two longer I hope Your Majesty would pardon us?" "Well, well," quoth the King; and so they parted.' That night the two young men spent at New Hall, but on the Tuesday morning they put on hoods and false beards, assumed the names of Thomas and John Smith, and rode off towards Gravesend. They were accompanied only by Richard Graham, Buckingham's gentleman of the horse. At Gravesend, where they crossed the river, they had nothing to give the ferryman but a gold piece. Generosity on such an extravagant scale was too much for the man, who took the money, of course, but promptly informed the officers of the town that suspicious characters were passing through. Orders were given for the travellers to be arrested, but by this time they were beyond Rochester. On the far side of the town they spotted the imperial ambassador and his train, en route to London, and hastily leapt over a hedge into the adjacent fields, to avert discovery. At Canterbury, where they changed horses, they were stopped by order of the mayor, and were only allowed to proceed when Buckingham took off his beard and revealed his true identity. He explained that he was paying a secret visit to the fleet, and did not wish his journey to be blazed abroad. The mayor, professing to be satisfied, let them go, and that evening they arrived at Dover, where they found Sir Francis Cottington, the Prince's secretary and James's former agent in Spain, awaiting them. Also at Dover was Endymion Porter, who had arranged for a ship to carry them across the Channel. By six o' clock on the Wednesday morning, after a stormy night, they were at sea, and that afternoon they landed at Boulogne. Both the Prince and Buckingham had suffered acutely from seasickness, but dry land saw their spirits recover, and they managed to ride three posts to Montreuil, where they spent their first night in France. On Friday 21 February – the day on which they were due to rejoin the King at Royston – they reached Paris.[22]

Meanwhile back in England the ports had been closed by order of the King, who was in the secret and had given his sanction, if not his blessing, to this romantic venture. James hoped to get the young men off to a good start by holding up the news of their departure as long as possible, but he could not prevent rumours from spreading, and as they did so they created a sensation. The Privy Councillors, who knew no more than the man in the street, rode post-haste to Newmarket (where the King was now in residence) and begged James to tell them whether the rumours were true. James – late in the day it may be thought – took them into his confidence and told them everything that had happened. He added 'that it was an action affected with much passion by his son, partly out of an earnest desire to see his mistress, and especially to give a final end to that business that had distracted His Majesty's other affairs so long a time'. It was for these reasons, said James, that he had given his consent, and he reminded his hearers that such a romantic journey was not without precedent, 'seeing that himself being then a king, and his father and grandfather before him, had gone out of the realm of Scotland to fetch their wives'.[23]

James had no doubt – or so he assured his Councillors – that God would crown his son's journey with success, but his views were not widely shared. The Venetian ambassador gave it as his opinion that 'England is now in the hand of Spain', and Dudley Carleton junior, when he reported the astonishing news to his uncle at the Hague, was equally pessimistic. 'If the marriage be in that forwardness that the Prince's presence in Madrid will bring on an immediate and full consummation thereof,' he argued, 'why then did he not go with an equipage suitable to the Prince, only son of his father and heir to so great dominions? Why not with a navy royal, and the great ones of the kingdom attending him?' If, on the other hand, 'the marriage still hang in the hedge of uncertainty, why was the journey undertaken? What need of so much adventure, so much hazard of his person, of his religion, of his honour, of all?'[24]

It was not long before the responsibility for this hazardous journey was being pinned on Buckingham, and Clarendon, when he came to write his *History of the Rebellion*, confirmed this interpretation. It was Buckingham, he said, who insinuated the whole idea into the Prince's head until Charles became 'transported with the thought of it and most impatiently solicitous to bring it to pass'. Clarendon derived his information from Cottington, who had been appalled when the King told him of the plan, and had tried to dissuade him from agreeing to it. Buckingham had rounded on Cottington 'with all possible bitterness of words', and had also (if Clarendon is to be believed) spoken roughly to the King, telling him that if he went back on his word nobody would ever trust him again. Other accounts, however, give a different version. Bishop Goodman, who knew many of the people involved, came to the conclusion that it was Charles's 'own invention and proceeded from himself'. John Hacket, in his life of Lord Keeper Williams, records Charles's later assertion that 'that heroic thought started out of his own brain, to visit the court of Madrid', and adds that the Prince persuaded Buckingham to plead his cause with James. This interpretation makes sense, for there is no doubt that Charles was – or at least imagined himself to be – deeply in love and had all the impatience of the ardent wooer. He was also somewhat afraid of his choleric father and would therefore have urged Buckingham, whose influence with James was likely to be more immediately effective, to prepare the ground for him. James, when he gave an account of these events to the members of the 1624 Parliament, declared that it was the Prince who 'being of fit age and ripeness for marriage ... urged me to know the certainty in a matter of so great weight .... I only sent the man whom I most trusted, Buckingham, commanding him never to leave him nor to return home without him.' It could be argued that this statement was designed to avert blame from Buckingham, but in June 1623, in a private letter to the Prince, who was then in Madrid, James reminded him that 'it was upon your earnest entreaty that I suffered you to leave me and make so far and hazardous a journey'.[25]

There was no obvious reason why Buckingham should have incited the Prince to go overland to Spain. Such a journey would, it is true, give Buckingham the opportunity to deepen his friendship with the Prince in a way that a sea trip, with its inevitable accompaniment of courtiers and attendants, would not. But close proximity under trying conditions is not always a recipe for harmony, and in any case Buckingham's relations with the Prince were already very close and friendly. He had no need of the Madrid venture to establish a reversionary interest, particularly since there was no indication that James's reign was nearing its end. The King, according to his doctor, bolted his food, ate too much fruit, drank more than was good for him and, as a result, suffered from insomnia and diarrhoea. But there was nothing new about any of these symptoms, nor any apparent reason for alarm. James seemed set to reign for many more years, especially as he laughed at doctors and held medicine to be of little use. Buckingham, with the Brett episode painfully fresh in his mind, would have been more concerned with re-establishing his hold over the old King than with preparing his ascendancy over the new. It might be that absence would make James's heart grow yet fonder, but it was far more likely that while Buckingham was miles away his enemies would move on to the attack and try to topple him by introducing a new favourite. Taking all these considerations into account, it seems highly unlikely that it was Buckingham who first put forward the idea of posting to Madrid. On the contrary, it may be that his haste to prepare a fleet for Spain was designed to blunt the edge of the Prince's impatience and persuade him to make a public rather than a private journey.[26]

Buckingham, however, was a born trimmer. He had been at Court long enough to be able to recognise the point at which opposition must give way to acceptance, and when he realised that the Prince was determined to go, he would have seen the danger of continuing his efforts to dissuade him. Everything then would depend upon James. If the King gave his consent, Buckingham would accompany the Prince. If not, the blame would rest on the King and not on the favourite. There was no question, of course, of the Prince going alone. He would need someone to speak for him, someone to advise him and to restrain him from ill-considered actions which his passion for the Infanta might drive him to. Above all, in the court of the Most Catholic King of Spain, he would have need of a staunch protestant to counter the wiles of the Jesuits and hold him firm to his faith. Such a man was Buckingham – at least in James's eyes – and in fact the favourite's conduct in Spain justified the high trust that James reposed in him in this respect. In the face of constant efforts to subvert the Prince's religion, Buckingham stood firm, and thereby earned the hatred of his Spanish hosts. Doncaster chose his words carefully when he commented approvingly on Buckingham's 'nobleness, wisdom and vigilance' during his stay in Spain; while Sir George Goring had nothing but praise for his patron's constancy. 'For such as have either suspected him for his religion or condemned him as one more wedded to his own ends than his country's good', he declared, 'God forgive them!'[27]

Clarendon may well be right in suggesting the Charles initially persuaded

James to accept the idea that he should go to Spain in person, and only then revealed his intention to make the journey overland. Such a journey would be full of risks, for foreign travel was hazardous at the best of times, but by posting to Madrid the Prince would gain the enormous advantage of surprise, since he would arrive in the Spanish capital unannounced and unexpected. Then, at long last, the Spaniards would be forced to show their true colours and either conclude the marriage or publish their perfidy to the world. As the Duke of Savoy commented, when he heard the news, 'there was no other way to come speedily out of the labyrinth of treaties in which His Majesty did stand'.[28]

In Paris the Prince and Buckingham took lodgings above a post-house, at the sign of the Grand Cerf in the Rue St Jacques. Buckingham, who had had seven falls during the ride from Boulogne, was weariest of all the travellers, but after a night's rest he felt sufficiently recovered to accompany the Prince to the French Court, where Louis XIII and his wife — Anne of Austria, the sister of the Infanta Maria — were dining in public. The two travellers were still plain John and Tom Smith, and for fear of being recognised they bought periwigs to cover their foreheads. By chance they overheard two gentlemen discussing a ballet that was to be given that evening, and at the appropriate hour they joined the throng of sightseers and asked to be let in. The queen's chamberlain took pity on them as strangers, and was so impressed by Buckingham, who played the part of the Prince's master, that he ushered them to seats from which they had a perfect view. Before going to bed that night they penned a hasty letter to James, telling him that they had seen 'the queen and madame, with as many as made up nineteen fair dancing ladies, amongst which the queen is the handsomest'. This, added Charles, 'hath wrought in me a greater desire to see her sister'.[29]

By four o'clock the next morning, Sunday, the five travellers were on the road again, and covered an average of sixty miles a day to the Spanish frontier. They were carrying £1,000 in gold, as well as bills of exchange for a further £25,000 — a rich prize for any highwayman — but luckily for them they passed through France unmolested. Their greatest problem was finding enough to eat, for it was Lent, and they could get no meat in any of the inns they stayed at. Near Bayonne, however, they came across a herd of goats, and Graham told the Marquis he would sneak up on one of the kids and capture it for their supper. The Prince, overhearing this, pretended to be shocked by such Scottish barbarism. ' "Why, Richard," says he, "do you think you may practise here your old tricks again upon the borders?" ' Graham took the hint and offered the goatherd money for the kid. But the poor beast had still to be caught, and Buckingham and Graham nearly wore themselves out chasing it round a haystack. It was left to the Prince to despatch it with his pistol.[30]

Beyond Bayonne the route across the Spanish frontier passed through a mountainous, sparsely populated region, where the danger from robbers was greatest. The Prince and Buckingham rode on ahead, as if they were the servants of the great man — Cottington — who was following on behind. In this way they reckoned they would be safe. And in fact they crossed the border without incident and found lodging for the night in an inn. The meatless days of Lent plagued them in Spain just as in France, and it was while they were broiling a piece of the kid in their room that they were discovered by Walsingham Gresley, *en route* to England with despatches from the Earl of Bristol. They immediately opened these and read all that they could without the aid of a cipher. As Buckingham told the King, they found nothing which 'made us repent our journey'. Despite Bristol's optimistic utterances the main business was 'so slowly advanced that we think ourselves happy that we have begun it so soon; for yet the temporal articles are not concluded, nor will be till the dispensation comes – which may be God knows when'. It is clear from this letter, and from another written a month later, that one of the principal reasons for the journey was to put an end to the long-drawn-out negotiations. In Buckingham's words, 'if we had not come here, you had been held on with long delays,' and God knows with what success'.[31]

On Friday 7 March the Prince and Buckingham reached Madrid, having taken just over two weeks for the journey from England. The postilion who accompanied them on the last stage took them to the house where Bristol lived, and Buckingham knocked on the door while the Prince stood in the shadows opposite. The door was opened by Harry Jermyn (the future Earl of St Albans), who in normal circumstances would have recognised the Lord Admiral, but never dreamed that the travel-stained Englishman who stood in front of him was Buckingham in person. Jermyn begged 'Mr Smith', who asked to see Bristol, to go up to the ambassador, but Buckingham excused himself on the grounds that he had had a fall and hurt his leg. He waited downstairs, therefore, while Jermyn went up to tell Bristol about the stranger. At this point Simon Digby, the ambassador's nephew, came to the door to see what was going on, and immediately recognised the Lord Admiral. He at once took him up to his own room, and then went down and fetched the Prince. It was there that Bristol found them, to his utter astonishment – for, as his wife explained to a friend, she and her husband were 'altogether ignorant of any intention that the Prince had of coming hither', and Bristol felt constrained to tell James that if he had been asked for his advice 'I should rather have dissuaded than given any such counsel'.[32]

Despite their long and exhausting journey, the Prince and Buckingham showed little sign of weariness. Bristol's main concern was to keep the news of their arrival secret until he could inform Philip IV, but on the Saturday morning the other members of the little party reached Madrid, and rumours began to circulate. Bristol therefore sent word to Gondomar that Buckingham had unexpectedly arrived in the Spanish capital, and Gondomar, before going to pay his respects, notified Olivares. The chief minister announced his intention of calling on Buckingham immediately, but when the Marquis heard of this he refused to permit it, for fear that the Prince – who was not yet ready to reveal his presence – might thereby be discovered. An alternative arrangement was accordingly devised, and later that afternoon Gondomar's coach came to fetch Buckingham and carry him to a private park where Olivares was waiting for him. The two favourites sat together for an hour and a half, with Bristol

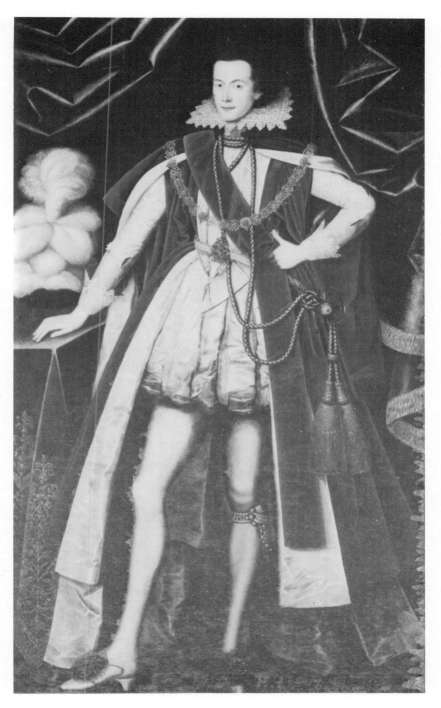

Buckingham as a young man, artist unknown

James I, by Paul Van Somer. Probably painted *c.* 1620, the portrait depicts James standing before the Banqueting House at Whitehall, which was then under construction

Prince Charles, by Daniel Mytens; painted in 1623, probably just after the Prince's return from Spain

Brooksby Hall, near Melton Mowbray, Buckingham's birthplace

New Hall, Buckingham's house in Essex, the only one of his properties which survives

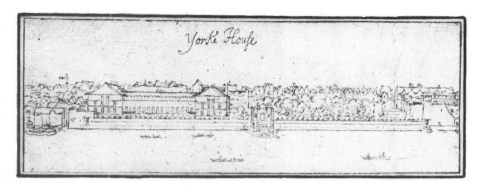

York House, Westminster, Buckingham's London home. The Water-Gate in the foreground still survives in Embankment Gardens

One of a pair of chairs, now in the possession of the Earl of Jersey, which once belonged to Buckingham

Fireplace from Apethorpe Hall, Northamptonshire, where Buckingham first met James I. The anchor and coronet are Buckingham's insignia, and the fireplace quite probably commemorates his return from Spain, with the Prince, in 1623

Sir John Coke, by Cornelius Jannsens

The Count of Gondomar (Spanish Ambassador to England), engraved from a drawing by G. P. Harding after an original painting

the busines requires, wee must euer and like
proctors of one busines, who leaues all his=
cases to conclude with there ... purposes, wee
shall with in this day ... two haue
another sight of oure ladie mistriss,
and wee promis you yous babe shall no
soner haue her in his armes but wee
shall make hast to throw him selfe at
your feete so crauing yor blessing
wee end

Madrid the 28 of October
1623.

your Majtie

and humble shall
... seruant and doge
Steenie

Humble and obedient sone
& seruant

Charles

Olivares, by Velazquez

Left: Autograph letter from Buckingham to James, while he and the Prince were in Madrid, 1623.

It is signed by the Prince:
   'Your Majesty's humble and obedient son and servant. Charles' And by Buckingham; who begins the letter:
   'Dere Dad and Gossope' [gossip = godfather] and ends it by describing himself as James's
   'humble slave and servant and doge [dog] Steenie'

Samson slaying a Philistine, Giambologna. Presented to Prince Charles by order of the King of Spain, after the Prince expressed his admiration for it when he saw it as the centre of a fountain at Valladolid. Following his return to England, the Prince gave it to Buckingham, and it stood in the Duke's gardens at York House

Buckingham on horseback, *c.* 1625. The recently rediscovered sketch on which Rubens based his equestrian portrait of Buckingham, formerly at Osterley, in Lord Jersey's collection, and subsequently destroyed by fire

and Sir Walter Aston (the resident English ambassador) acting as interpreters, 'within which time', according to Bristol, 'there passed so much expression of joy and so great a declaration of a grateful acceptation of this action as I dare confidently say . . . that whatsoever I have formerly written of their [the Spaniards'] professions hath been by many degrees exceeded'. By this time the news of the Prince's arrival had been officially announced, and Olivares assured Buckingham that he would write to the Pope immediately and tell him 'that the King of England hath put such an obligation upon this king, in sending his son hither, that he [Philip IV] entreats him to make haste of the dispensation, for he can deny him nothing that is in his kingdom'. Olivares added that if the Pope proved unwilling to comply with this request, the Spaniards would hand over the Infanta without waiting for the dispensation.

Olivares then led Buckingham into the private rooms of the palace for an audience of Philip. The seventeen-year-old king had his full share of Spanish gravity, but on this occasion he set it aside and spoke to Buckingham with great ease and warmth. When Buckingham referred to the Prince's love for the Infanta and his impatience to set eyes on her, Philip promised to take her driving in the Prado the following day – even though it was a Sunday in Lent – and Buckingham and the Prince, along with Gondomar, Bristol, Aston and Endymion Porter, were there to see the royal family. The visitors sat, in Buckingham's phrase, 'in an invisible coach, because nobody was suffered to take notice of it, though seen by all the world', and after the parade was over Olivares accompanied the Prince back to his lodgings and told him of the king's determination to call on him. Charles would not hear of it and declared his intention of going to the royal palace in person to pay his respects, but it was eventually agreed that Philip and his distinguished visitor should meet that night in the Prado. The Prince took the two ambassadors and Cottington, his secretary, with him. Philip insisted that Buckingham should go as his companion, with Porter to interpret. Olivares took Buckingham with him to the Prado, where they found Philip IV 'walking in the streets, with his cloak thrown over his face, and a sword and buckler by his side'. As soon as Buckingham arrived, the king 'leaped into the coach, and away he came to find the wooer in another place appointed, where there passed much kindness and compliment one to another'.[33]

The Spanish love of ceremony kept the Prince fully occupied for the next week, and not until Sunday, 17 March, did he make his formal entry into Madrid. He dined at the monastery of San Geronimo, where the king came in state to meet him in the late afternoon. From there they rode together through the streets, with the Prince on the king's right hand and Olivares and Buckingham following behind as Masters of the Horse. When they reached the royal palace the Prince was conducted to apartments that had been prepared for him, where more courtesies took place and presents were exchanged. For the rest of his time in Spain the palace was the Prince's home, and it was also Buckingham's. The Marquis shared to the full the warmth of the welcome given to the Prince, and Bristol told James that there have been such demonstrations made unto him, both by the king, the grandees and all the court, as I think have never been made to any subject. The night that the Prince came to the palace, the Conde of Olivares's lady sent him [Buckingham] a very noble present, and he is lodged in a quarter of his own, adjoining to the Prince's Highness, with a very plentiful diet, and nobly attended.[34]

Charles had, as yet, caught only a brief glimpse of the object of his affections through the windows of his coach, for Spanish etiquette was rigid, and lovers, however ardent, were not permitted to meet except under the closest supervision. The Infanta was reported to be far from enthusiastic about the proposed match. She cared deeply for her religion and had protested that she would take the veil rather than marry a heretic. According to one account, she showed the greatest stubbornness when the carefully contrived encounter with the English visitors took place, because while Charles was gazing out of the window to feast his eyes to the full, she looked steadily ahead and never so much as glanced in his direction. But Charles professed himself more than satisfied, and so did Buckingham. 'Without flattery,' wrote Buckingham to James, 'I think there is not a sweeter creature in the world. Baby Charles himself is so touched at the heart that he confesses all he ever yet saw is nothing to her, and swears if that he want her [i.e., cannot have her] there shall be blows.'[35]

Buckingham played the part of secretary throughout the whole time that he and the Prince were away from England, and nearly all the letters which James received from the two young men were in his hand. He wrote as he talked, swiftly and to the point, and while Charles always signed himself 'Your Majesty's humble and obedient son and servant', Buckingham preferred the more informal and intimate 'Your humble slave and dog'. The letters were directed, on the outside, 'To the best of fathers and masters', and inside they nearly always began 'Dear Dad and Gossip' [Godfather] – appropriately enough, since James had acted both as a surrogate father and a godparent to his favourite . They were not formal documents, nor were they designed to be read by any other than the King, and for this reason they give – along with James's replies – a vivid and accurate picture of the relationship between the lonely and heartsick King and his two 'boys'.

No sooner had the Prince and Buckingham set out on their journey than the King wrote to give them his blessing and pray for their speedy and safe return. He called them 'my sweet boys and dear venturous knights', and declared that they were 'worthy to be put in a new romance'. He assured Buckingham that he was looking after his affairs for him during his absence, and told how he had already written three letters to Kate and had received a fine reply from her. 'I have also written one to Su [Buckingham's sister, Susan Feilding, Countess of Denbigh] but your poor old Dad is lamer than ever he was, both of his right knee and foot, and writes all this out of his naked bed.' In another letter James reported a discussion with Buckingham's steward, Fotherly, who had told him the details of his master's indebtedness, as a result of which James had lately signed divers quillets of land for you . . . for which, he says, ye shall receive £18,000 in money. He will reduce the charges of your table to my allowance till your return . . . I have commanded him to come boldly to me whenever he hath occasion for any of your businesses, for I have taken the charge of them upon me. I have no more to say but that I wear Steenie's picture in a blue ribbon under my waistcoat next to my heart . . .[36]

IV

The two young visitors had not been long in the Spanish court before they realised that the joy shown at their arrival was due in large part to the assumption that the Prince had come to declare his conversion to Roman Catholicism. On Buckingham's second day in Madrid, he and Olivares drove out into the country, with only Porter to act as an interpreter. They began to discuss the marriage, and Olivares suggested – in the impulsive and outgoing manner that came naturally to him – that they should waste no more time waiting for the papal dispensation, but conclude the match forthwith. This was more even than Buckingham had hoped for, and he immediately agreed. But how, he wanted to know, could it be done? ' "The means", quoth the Conde, "is very easy. It is but the conversion of the Prince, which we cannot coinceive but His Highness intended upon his resolution for this journey" '. Buckingham, according to his own account, replied that they had come to Spain to conclude a bargain already made, not to embark upon new conditions, and he warned Olivares that if the Spaniards 'struck any more upon that string, they would mar all the harmony'. Buckingham recalled this conversation when he was giving his account to Parliament in the following year, and it might be thought that he was then only too anxious to embroider the story. But letters written from Spain show that he was telling no more than the truth, for on 17 March he informed James that while the Spaniards 'by outward shows' were as desirous of the marriage as the Prince himself, 'yet are they hankering upon a conversion, for they say that there can be no firm friendship without union in religion'. This, he assured James, 'we put . . . quite out of question, because neither our conscience nor the time serves for it'.[37]

The Spaniards were not the only people who assumed that the Prince had come with an intention to declare himself catholic. Bristol, when he turned over in his mind the possible reasons for this extraordinary journey, arrived at a similar conclusion, and was encouraged in this belief by Gondomar, who assured him that not only was it true but that Buckingham also was in the plot. Bristol went so far as to kneel before Charles one day when he was alone with him and ask him if this was indeed what he had resolved to do. If it was, then Bristol begged him to make his declaration as soon as possible, for all difficulties would thereby be removed and the match could go ahead. The Prince immediately rejected any such imputation, and made plain his astonishment that Bristol should ever have suspected him of inconstancy in religion. The embarrassed ambassador said no more, and from that time onwards did not question the Prince's adherence to the protestant faith. The Spaniards, however, kept up their relentless pressure, and constantly reminded Charles of the noble example set him by his grandmother, Mary, Queen of Scots, who had died a martyr for the Roman Catholic church. They seemed unable to accept that the Prince had come to Spain simply to conclude the last stages of a match that had already – or so he had been given to believe – been brought to the verge of completion, and even in late March the Venetian ambassador in Madrid was reporting the general belief that the Prince would become a catholic.[38]

When Charles and Buckingham realised that the match was not so advanced as they had been told, and that, failing the Prince's conversion, the major stumbling-block was the dispensation, they sent a messenger to Rome to hurry things along. Olivares also despatched an envoy to the Pope, with secret instructions to block the issue of the dispensation, in the hope that Charles, driven by passion and despair, would eventually agree to give up his faith for the Infanta. By the time the envoy arrived, however, the dispensation had already been approved and sent off to the nuncio in Madrid. It contained a recommendation that Philip – who would be responsible to the Pope for seeing that James's promised concessions to English catholics were put into effect – should take some security for this. When the news reached Rome that Philip in fact would like the issue of the dispensation delayed, it was decided – since the document itself could not be altered – to stiffen the conditions attached to its delivery. The nuncio was now instructed to insist on complete liberty of conscience for English catholics as a *sine qua non*, and also to express a strong wish (though not a formal requirement) that the marriage should not take place without the conversion of the Prince.[39]

Charles and Buckingham, of course, knew nothing of these manoeuvres, and although their journey had been prompted by distrust of Spanish intentions, they were basically well disposed towards Philip IV and his ministers. Their only first-hand knowledge of Spaniards, before their arrival in Madrid, had been through Gondomar, and the firm way in which he had conducted negotiations, refusing to yield one inch on matters of principle, had given them the impression that all Spanish ministers were frank and open in their dealings. Hence Buckingham's comment to the francophil Doncaster that he was going to Spain to deal with men who 'carried their business wisely, honestly, and constantly, and not like inconstant false monsieurs'. The friendly reception which he and the Prince had been given in Spain had so far confirmed rather than shaken his pro-Spanish sentiments, and he willingly accepted the suggestion of Olivares that while they were waiting for the dispensation 'no time should be lost in preparing all things ready here for our journey homewards'. It was in order to avoid further protracted negotiations – as well as to carry out James's explicit instructions – that Buckingham refused to be drawn into discussion of the Palatinate. The marriage must be concluded first. Only then would it be time to discuss the 'ends and effects of friendship'.[40]

Charles, meanwhile, was preoccupied with the problem of arranging a meeting with his bride-to-be, and on his instructions Buckingham requested the council of state to permit the Prince to visit the Infanta. The council discussed the issue, and a number of members were inclined to accept Gondomar's suggestion that in order not to offend Charles he might be allowed to see the Infanta in the presence of the Queen. They were not supported by Olivares, however, whose hard line in council was characteristic, and contrasted with the open and friendly manner which he adopted when talking to the English visitors. Olivares described how he had passed a whole morning battling over this point with Buckingham, and then, in the afternoon, spent a further two and a half hours discussing the matter with Buckingham and the Prince. He was firmly of the opinion that Charles should not be allowed to see the Infanta, but on this occasion he was prepared to bow to the will of the majority, which was apparently in favour of Gondomar's suggestion. When Buckingham wrote to James, therefore, on 28 March, he was able to tell him that 'we shall, within this day or two, have another sight of our lovely mistress'. He was already showing signs of impatience at Spanish dilatoriness, which threatened a much longer stay in the Spanish capital than either he or the Prince — or, for that matter, James — had ever envisaged, but he took comfort from the thought that 'your baby shall no sooner have her in his arms but Steenie shall make haste to throw himself at your feet'.[41]

April saw the beginning of Holy Week, and the Prince and Buckingham were able to watch the many ceremonies and processions which took place during this period. Buckingham, at least, was not impressed, and later made apparent his revulsion at what he called the superstitious observances to which the church in Spain was prone. But the Spaniards themselves were hoping that the fervent atmosphere generated in these days leading up to Easter would affect the Prince and crown with triumph their efforts to convert him. Olivares was losing patience over the length of time it was taking to achieve this, and now pressed Buckingham to agree that Charles should listen to arguments in favour of catholicism. Buckingham revealed that James had authorised him to permit such discussions, but he suggested that the first encounter should take place with him and not the Prince. Olivares agreed, and on Maundy Thursday the two favourites went off to the royal apartments in the monastery of San Geronimo, where Father Francisco de Jesus was waiting for them. The session lasted four hours, and Buckingham listened attentively, rebutting a number of the arguments put forward by Father Francisco. There were some points, however, on which he made no immediate comment, but first consulted a paper he had brought with him. Was this, perhaps, a defence of Anglican doctrine drawn up by James for use in just such a situation? Whatever it was, it confirmed the Spaniards in their impression that Buckingham was not a suitable subject for conversion. It also deepened the suspicion which was already forming in their minds that he was a major impediment to the Prince's acceptance of the catholic religion.[42]

In the third week in April a day was fixed for a formal discussion about points of doctrine in which the Prince, as well as Buckingham, was to take part. The defence of the catholic position was on this occasion entrusted to Philip IV's confessor, and he developed a powerful argument in support of papal supremacy that apparently shook the Prince. Charles – who was seated on a chair, apart, while the others sat on benches – turned to Buckingham for reassurance, but the Marquis 'was so disturbed by these demonstrations, slight as they were, that he at once went down to a place where he could be alone, in order to show his extreme indignation, going so far as to pull off his hat and to trample it under feet'. This was the end of the conference, and when Olivares proposed another, Buckingham declined. He had now, in the words of a Spanish account, 'begun to resist the firmness of the Count-Duke [Olivares] on any point of religion which might be connected with the marriage'. The Spaniards attributed this to malice, but it seems far more likely that Buckingham was worried about the Prince's susceptibility to catholic arguments and was carrying out the orders that James had given him.[43]

Although Charles and Buckingham knew by the end of April that the dispensation had reached the nuncio, they also knew that it was 'clogged with some new conditions' and that a certain amount of hard bargaining would have to take place before it was handed over. They would be severely handicapped if they had to refer everything to James for his approval, and since the whole point of their journey was to save time Charles wrote to his father asking him for a written commitment to accept and put into effect whatever the Prince promised in his name. 'I confess', added Charles, 'that this is an ample trust that I desire, and if it were not mere necessity I should not be so bold. Yet I hope', he added, 'Your Majesty shall never repent you of any trust ye put upon Your Majesty's humble and obedient son and servant.' His request was seconded by Buckingham, who reminded the King that he need have no doubts about Charles's discretion. 'And for the faith of myself,' he added, 'I shall sooner lose life than in the least kind break it.' James, in fact, had no doubts – or if he did, he did not reveal them. In a letter of 11 May in which he sent the required written engagement he expressed his confidence that 'such two as ye are will never promise in my name but what may stand with my conscience, honour and safety, and all these I do fully trust with any one of you two'.[44]

In the dispensation the Pope gave his formal consent and blessing to the proposed marriage between Charles and the Infanta Maria, and also expressed his approval of the articles agreed between Bristol and Philip in December 1622, though 'with fresh additions, alterations and explanations to some of them'. The nuncio was instructed, however, to demand that in return for the dispensation James should agree to allow English catholics to worship freely and openly – a concession which was to be approved, in the first instance, by the English Privy Council, and subsequently confirmed by Parliament. Once this concession had been obtained, the Spaniards were to press ahead with the conversion of the Prince, going as far as they possibly could. In order to encourage this process, the Pope had written directly to James, exhorting him to embrace the faith of his mother and expressing his conviction that the Spanish match was the silent word of the Holy Spirit, indicating the way in which James and his dominions could return to the bosom of the true church.[45]

The nuncio's orders were that the dispensation was not to be handed over until Philip IV had sworn a solemn oath that James and the Prince would carry out the articles of the amended marriage treaty. This was not an optional but a necessary condition, and without it the dispensation would not come into effect. Philip now had a good excuse for demanding further concessions from the English, and his hand was strengthened by the fact that the Prince was a virtual hostage in his court. In early May, therefore, the English and Spanish ministers held talks, at which the Prince was present, to consider the amendments to the articles of marriage and the demand for liberty of worship for English catholics. Charles gave a formal promise, in the name of his father, that the laws against recusants would be suspended, and that Parliament would in due course be invited not simply to confirm this suspension but to repeal the laws themselves. When pressed for a time limit within which this would be accomplished, he said it would not be longer than three years. However, the Prince refused to accept the demand that English catholics should have free access to the Infanta's chapel, since this, he said, would be tantamount to public toleration of the Roman Catholic religion, which was something James would never agree to. Catholics would be free, after the suspension of the penal laws, to worship privately in their own homes, so they would have no need to go to the Infanta's chapel. Yet if they chose to go secretly, no action would be taken against them.[46]

The Prince was convinced that he had now done whatever lay in his power to remove the obstacles to the completion of the marriage. Olivares professed his contentment at the Prince's attitude, but his true feelings were shown in a letter which he sent to Philip IV. In this he argued that James was not to be trusted. 'It is to be judged that he is acting without any fixed objective, and that he has not committed himself either to one side or the other, but is merely waiting to see what will turn out best for him. My opinion therefore is that, with respect to the handing over of the Lady Infanta, your majesty ought to act in the same manner; that is to say, that she should not be given up till either the engagement into which he [James] enters, or the actual state of the catholics in England, is such as to give us sufficient security.'[47]

When the council of state came to discuss the security, if any, to be insisted upon by Philip, members were of the opinion that the marriage should be concluded immediately, without waiting to see whether James carried out his promises. The one exception was Olivares, who argued that Philip IV's zeal for the catholic cause was 'the sole pillar upon which is founded the greatness and security of your mighty and extensive monarchy', and that it would be far better for the king to lose all his territories than to take the risks which might arise 'from the mere appearance of giving way on a single point of the rigorous observance of religion'. Spain, he went on, had no need of the English marriage, for friendship between states depended upon political, not family, considerations. How could Philip possibly bind himself to see that the conditions of the marriage treaty were put into effect when he was dependent for this upon the will of a heretic King and Prince? If James or Charles became catholic, or if the promised tolerance were confirmed by both Privy Council and Parliament, then the Infanta could be handed over and the marriage could take place. Failing this, she should be kept in Spain until such time as it became clear that the condition of the catholics in England was improving. This view, while it did not meet with the approval of the council of state, found support among the junta of theologians appointed by Philip to advise him on what security he should ask for. Philip followed their advice, and began by asking Charles to state exactly how far he was prepared to go towards meeting the conditions laid down by the Pope.[48]

V

Under the insistent pressure of repeated Spanish demands for further concessions, relations between Buckingham and Olivares deteriorated rapidly. According to one report, in mid-May, they had not spoken to each other for several days, and Olivares had been heard to declare that Buckingham was the enemy of the marriage and in secret league with the French. It was shortly after this that Buckingham spoke sharply to Olivares about the discourtesy shown to the Prince in keeping him dangling in Spain, after he had given such an unprecedented demonstration of his trust by making the journey to Madrid. Olivares replied that so far as the Prince's person was concerned they had treated and would continue to treat him with all honour, but that where matters of religion were concerned they would not give an inch for any human considerations. Many of Buckingham's contemporaries (as well as most subsequent historians) came to accept the Spanish view that he alone was to blame for the breakdown of good relations, and that it was wounded pride that drove him into confrontation with Olivares. No doubt pride came into it, and there may indeed have been a clash of temperaments between the two favourites, each (by virtue of his position) accustomed to getting his own way. But to assume that the whole matter was one of personalities is to misread the situation. The quarrel between Buckingham and Olivares was one of principle, and Buckingham would have betrayed the trust committed to him by his royal master if he had not opposed the Spanish attempts to win further concessions from the Prince.[49]

Buckingham realised that Charles was reluctant to take a firm stand for fear of losing the Infanta. But he was also aware that not only James but the entire English nation would hold him, Buckingham, responsible if the Prince yielded to Spanish pressure. From time to time the strain to which he was subject showed in his behaviour, but his actions were frequently misinterpreted. On one occasion, for instance, he met the papal nuncio by chance at the royal palace and urged him to do all he could to promote the marriage. The nuncio said he would like to, but was bound by his orders from Rome. 'I assure you', replied Buckingham, 'that if this marriage is not concluded, what little remains of catholicism in that kingdom [England] will be utterly rooted out, and they will proceed against the catholics with the utmost rigour.' The Mantuan ambassador reported this as an example of Buckingham's insolent behaviour and threatening carriage, but the Marquis was speaking no more than the truth: the fate of the English catholics did depend, to a considerable extent, upon the outcome of the negotiations in Spain, and Buckingham was trying to make the perfectly valid point that if the Spaniards demanded too much they were likely to lose everything.[50]

In early May the Prince gave his considered reply to the request that he should state just how far he was prepared to go. It was a reiteration of his former position, though he promised to do all that was in his power to secure parliamentary confirmation of the suspension of the penal laws. But he pointed out that if the risk of civil disturbance or seditious outbreaks in England was to be avoided, the improvement of the catholics' condition would have to be a gradual process. The marriage junta considered this reply in the presence of the nuncio, who then announced that he had no authority to alter one word of the articles as they had been amended at Rome. When Buckingham heard this totally unexpected and unpalatable news, he went to see the nuncio, and the two men argued into the early hours of the morning. Nothing was achieved. The nuncio refused to give an inch, and Buckingham became so angry that he told him that the only way to negotiate in future would be with a drawn sword held over the heads of the catholics.[51]

Olivares proposed two ways by which Charles and Buckingham might emerge from the dilemma they were in. Either they could send an agent to Rome to ask the Pope to modify the articles in line with what the Prince was ready to accept; or they could despatch a confidential messenger to James to see if he would agree to the Pope's demands. On 11 May the Prince told Olivares that there were great disadvantages in both proposals, and he pressed him once again to find some other way out of the labyrinth. What he had in mind was a change of heart by the Spaniards, but they still hoped that with time and persistence they could extort further concessions from the Prince and quite possibly bring about his conversion. Buckingham recognised this danger, and urged Charles to cut his losses and leave. Consequently the Prince announced that while he approved of the idea of sending an agent to Rome to ask the Pope to modify his demands, he also thought that he himself should return to England to persuade his father to make the necessary concessions. He therefore requested Philip IV to give him leave to go. Buckingham told Father Francisco de Jesus that although Charles had suffered a 'great sinking of heart' at the thought that he could not obtain the fulfilment of his desires, he was determined to leave, and that 13 May had been fixed as the day of their departure. The Marquis added that 'although they were much dissatisfied at having to go away after . . . failing to obtain that which they had hitherto looked forward to as sure and certain, they nevertheless wished that there might be no change in the friendship between them'.[52]

Father Francisco, who gives this account of the interview between him and Buckingham, adds that it was easy to see in the Marquis's face the indignation

149

with which his mind was filled. Buckingham, he says, had been confident of overcoming all difficulties in the way of the conclusion of the marriage by imposing on the Spaniards, through the Prince's sudden arrival in their court, a reciprocal obligation. Now that the Spaniards had failed to react as he anticipated, he had taken quite unjustified umbrage and 'looked upon all plain dealing as an injury to himself'. Father Francisco also makes clear his conviction that Buckingham was holding out against further concessions 'with the idea that if we put forth all our strength in obtaining their acceptance, we should have so exhausted our powers as no longer to be able to urge the principal point of liberty of conscience or the securities which we demanded'. Buckingham, in short, had called the Spaniards' bluff – or rather he had persuaded the Prince to do so – and he asked Father Francisco to tell Olivares of their resolution to leave. But the Prince's presence at the court of Philip IV was the Spaniards' trump card, and they had no intention of parting with it. Gondomar was therefore sent to tell the Prince that the love which Philip bore him 'and his desire of coming to a better arrangement in this business, obliged him urgently to beg His Highness to be so good as to refrain from taking any resolution in opposition to the plans which had been proposed'. The language was courteous, but the threat was unmistakeable. Philip was warning Charles that he would not be allowed to leave. The Prince had no option, therefore, but to agree to stay in Spain while a confidential messenger was despatched to England to warn James that he would shortly be confronted with new articles. The Prince was obviously deeply disturbed at the situation he was now in, and a few days later he sent his secretary, Cottington, to Olivares with a request that Philip IV should release him from his promise and allow him to return home to discuss matters with his father. Philip's reply was unequivocal. Charles must stay in Spain.[53]

One suggestion that the Spaniards made was that Buckingham should return to England, while the Prince remained behind until such time as he could take the Infanta home with him as his wife. If this suggestion had been accepted, the Spanish ministers would then have been free to conduct negotiations through Bristol, who, they felt, had a better understanding of their position – though in practice this meant little more than that he was prepared to accept their assurances at face value. Bristol had been eclipsed by the arrival of the Prince and the Lord Admiral, and he allowed it to be known that he resented his exclusion from the conduct of an affair in which he had been involved from the beginning. There were a number of incidents showing the ill-will between the ambassador and the Marquis which were duly reported back to England. One of these took place when Bristol and Buckingham were accompanying the Prince in a coach. Olivares arrived, and Buckingham suggested that Bristol should leave the coach in order to make room for him, since he wished to confer in private with the Prince. Bristol replied, 'My lord, I am in the commission of this business, and has [sic] dealt most of any man in it. I think, my lord, I must have the commandment of some other man than your lordship.' The Prince immediately came to the support of Buckingham and ordered Bristol to leave the coach, but it was clear that the joint commission which James had given to Buckingham and Bristol was causing more friction than it was worth. The King therefore sent Bristol word that he should take no further part in the negotiations but leave everything to the Marquis. Bristol, however, could not avoid the Prince's company entirely, nor could he refrain from offering his advice when asked. He and Buckingham had a serious difference of opinion over the tactics to be used in face of the latest demands made by the Spaniards, because while Buckingham wanted the Prince to announce his determination to leave, Bristol advised him to stay and continue discussions. It was probably at about this time that Buckingham began to suspect that Bristol had become so 'hispaniolised' and so certain of the correctness of his conduct that he was endangering the entire course of the negotiations.[54]

There is no doubt that by the end of May Buckingham had emerged as the major obstacle not to the accomplishment of the marriage but to its conclusion upon terms which, however, favourable to the cause of Spain and the English catholics, would be unacceptable to James and the greater part of his subjects. In particular he opposed the conceding of freedom of public worship for the catholics, on the grounds that James had always refused to agree to this. Those who knew the pressures to which the Prince and Buckingham were being subjected had nothing but praise for the stand which the Marquis was taking. Sir George Goring declared that Buckingham had given 'such proof of his courage, judgement, religion and true English heart, with such resolution of stability in all these, as the like, I believe, were never met with in any one person'. His views were echoed by Sir Henry Rich, Viscount Kensington, who described Buckingham's conduct as 'so brave, judicious and religious as not only his master has reason to put honour upon him, but also our nation hath cause to reverence and admire him, so careful hath he been to serve, and nobly to serve, his King and country with offices of a true and religious heart, giving way to nothing but what wisdom and honour directs him'. It was true, added Kensington, that the firm stand taken by Buckingham had lost him favour at the Spanish court, but that was simply because 'those great and powerful persons here . . . would have pressed unfit and unlooked-for conditions upon us'.[55]

VI

Buckingham's position would have been much weaker if he had not had the unswerving support and encouragement of James. There had been many people who assumed that once Buckingham was out of sight the King would quickly forget him and transfer his affections to someone else. But this proved not to be the case, and Sir William Beecher, writing to Buckingham at the end of March, commented 'that this is the only Newmarket journey for many years that we have not had so much as a whisper of a new favourite; so careful His Majesty hath been not only to preserve unto you his own heart but other men's opinion'. The many letters which the King wrote his two boys show the depth of his continuing affection for 'my bastard brat'. In mid-March he sent Buckingham 'a fair table diamond, which I would once have given thee before, if thou would have taken it. And I have hung a fair pear pearl to it for wearing in thy hat or where thou pleases. And if my baby [Charles] will spare thee the two long diamonds in form of an anchor, with the pendant diamond, it were fit for an admiral to wear, and he hath enough better jewels for his mistress!'[56]

The King continued to keep watch over Buckingham's interests, and his letters, as well as dealing with matters of public concern, were also – like those between members of any family – full of private gossip. Kit Villiers – whom Buckingham described, with justice, as 'my little-deserving brother' – had been elevated to the Earldom of Anglesey and given the means to maintain this dignity: 'thus was thou born in a happy hour for all thy kin'. Kate had been 'a little sick within these four or five days . . . . I hope it is a good sign that I shall shortly be a gossip [godfather] over again.' As for Mall, whom James called his 'little grandchild', she had four teeth and was well weaned. Nothing was too insignificant for the King to report to his absent favourite. In April, for instance, Buckingham was given the news that 'your bay Spanish mare with the black mane and tail hath an exceeding fair and fine horse-foal of ten days old, just of her own colour but that he hath the far foot white; and there is another of them ready to foal'.[57]

Although Buckingham was very fond of his little daughter, Mall, he longed for a boy to perpetuate his name and dynasty, and it is not difficult to imagine his feelings when he heard that his wife might once again be pregnant. In April Kate herself wrote to tell him that while she could as yet say nothing for sure, she was not out of hope. Kate missed her husband dreadfully. 'I protest to God,' she said, 'I have had a grievous time of this our grievous absence, for I am sure it has been so to me, and my heart has felt enough – more than, I hope, it shall ever do again.' She thanked him for his long letters, which could never be long enough for her. Her only comfort was to read them over and over again, and to reflect how privileged she was to be 'that happy woman to enjoy you from all other women'. She had already written him sixteen letters, but she longed to have him home again, and she was delighted with reports that negotiations were almost at an end. She was also pleased that the Prince had been so 'wonderfully taken' with the Infanta, for 'I think he will make a very honest husband: which is the greatest comfort in this world, to have man and wife love truly'. Of her own affections there could be no doubt, for, she assured him, 'you could never a had one that could love you better than your poor, true, loving Kate doth; poor now in your absence, but else the happiest and richest woman in the world'.[58]

There was a constant flow of messengers between Madrid and London – 'they go up and down like a well with two buckets' commented Chamberlain – and few if any went without a letter from Kate to her husband or from Buckingham to Kate. In July she sent him a present of some perspective glasses, commenting wryly that she was sorry that the Prince was kept at such a distance from his beloved that he had need of them to see her. She also craved her husband's pardon for not giving him enough news about his little daughter. 'She is very well, I thank God, and when she is set to her feet and held by her sleeves she will not go safely but stamp and set one foot afore another very fast, that I think she will run before she can go.' Mall loved dancing and was 'full of pretty play and tricks' and everybody agreed that she grew daily more and more like her father. Kate promised to send him Mall's picture as soon as Gerbier could complete it, as well as one of herself. She had also commissioned Gerbier to do a miniature of Buckingham, since the one which she already had, and which comforted her during her husband's absence, had been borrowed by the King.[59]

While Kate's letters to her husband are full of love and tenderness, those written by her father are more down to earth. In one of these he reminded Buckingham that he was in a hot country and that he should take great care how he behaved himself with women. 'If you court ladies of honour you will be in danger of poisoning or killing,' he warned him. 'And if you desires [sic] whores, you will be in danger of burning.' Buckingham was a notorious womaniser – though how much his reputation was based on fact and how much on malice and supposition is impossible to say – and when relations between him and the Spaniards deteriorated they charged him, amongst other things, with bringing strumpets into the royal palace for his own pleasure. It was even hinted that during his stay in Spain he contracted syphilis, which accounted for the sickness that struck him down shortly after his return. This last rumour was almost certainly false, and so were many of the others which clung to him. He was said to have made advances to the Countess of Olivares, but as Clarendon pointed out, she was then 'a woman so old . . . of so abject a presence, in a word so crooked and deformed, that she could neither tempt his appetite or magnify his revenge'.[60]

Buckingham's exceptional good looks, combined with his charm of manner, made him very attractive to women, and there is no reason to doubt that he made many conquests: the Jacobean Court was not notable for its high moral tone, and Buckingham, like his companions, was accustomed to take his pleasures where he fancied. But his marriage clearly gave him great contentment, and it is unlikely that his conduct in Spain was anything like so unbridled as his enemies gave out. Endymion Porter, writing from Madrid to his much-loved Olive, told her that 'my lord and I wish you were both here very often, for which I hope you will pardon us. We live very honest and think of nothing but our wives.' Kate had no fears about her husband's basic fidelity – or if she had she kept them quiet. 'Yourself is a jewel that will win the hearts of all the women in the world,' she told him, 'but I am confident it is not in their powers to win your heart from a heart that was and ever shall be yours till death. Everybody tells me how happy I am in a husband, and how chaste you are, that you will not look at a woman, and yet how they woo you.' She was delighted when Cottington told her that Buckingham had made a vow to touch no woman until his return home. She assured her husband in return that she had never doubted his constancy, 'yet it is so many cordials to my

153

heart when they tell me of it'. She needed cordials, for her hopes of being with child had proved to be unfounded. 'I would I had been so happy,' she confessed, 'but since it is not so, I hope I shall be often.'[61]

Kate saw a great deal of James, from whom she had received favours that were 'so infinite that I can never express my thankfulness to Your Majesty for them in words'. The King sent her frequent gifts, including dried plums, violet cakes, and chickens, as well as grapes, for which he and Buckingham had a great liking. It was clear from his every action that he loved and missed the young man whose warmth, charm and sheer vitality helped to fill days that otherwise dragged interminably. James was now a widower, and even during his wife's lifetime had never been very close to her. And although he loved his son, there was a certain formality about the relationship between them. Only with Buckingham could James relax, and the favourite could indulge in banter that Charles would never have risked, or condescended to. In a letter written in late April, for instance, Buckingham reproached his royal master for being niggardly in his despatch of jewels to the Prince. 'Hitherto you have been so sparing that whereas you thought to have sent him sufficiently for his own wearing . . . I, to the contrary, have been forced to lend him.' By way of contrast to the King's tight-fistedness, Buckingham, who knew and shared James's passion for unusual objects, was sending him four asses, five camels and an elephant, and also promised to 'lay wait for all the rare colour birds that can be heard of. But', he warned him, 'if you do not send your baby jewels enough, I'll stop all other presents. Therefore look to it!' James was highly delighted with this mock-severe tone, and wrote back at once to thank 'my sweet Steenie gossip . . . for thy kind drolling letter'. He also reminded him not to give away any of the jewels which Kate had sent him, 'for thou knowest what necessary use she will have of them at your return here; besides that it is not lucky to give away anything that I have given her'.[62]

James had already made clear to Buckingham his desire to advance him yet further in honour by making him a duke. 'Thou knowest I am ready when thou will give the word,' he told him. 'I say not upon thy request, but upon thy consent.' Buckingham, however, was not eager for advancement. He told James that it would cause envy and emulation at Court, and that his estate was not sufficient to maintain so great a dignity. He therefore asked the King to leave the whole matter until he was back in England. This was at a time when Buckingham anticipated a swift return, but as the negotiations dragged on and the atmosphere at the Spanish court became more and more tense, he began to appreciate the advantages that such an honour would bring him. At home it would help to hold in check what Endymion Porter described as 'those unruly factions which, since my master's coming away, have strived to find something to be discontented at', while in Spain it would be seen, rightly, as setting the seal of James's approval on the firm stand that Buckingham had taken. Buckingham therefore decided to leave the King free to act as he wished, and James's reaction was swift. By the end of May the patent conferring the dukedom had arrived in Madrid, and it was accompanied by a long letter in which James dealt with the objections earlier raised by the favourite. There could be no question of envy, he argued, since the only person who could claim a similar rank was his cousin, the Scottish Duke of Lenox, whom he had now raised to an equivalent rank in the English peerage, as Duke of Richmond. Not only this; he had also, at Buckingham's suggestion, given Richmond precedence. As for emulation, James had made it clear that Buckingham's elevation was in return for exceptional services and could not therefore be taken as a precedent.[63]

There remained the problem of the favourite's estate, but this, as Buckingham confessed in his letter of thanks, had already been solved by the King's generosity. 'You have filled a consuming purse, given me fair houses, more land than I am worthy of to maintain both me and them, filled my coffers so full with patents of honour that my shoulder cannot bear more.' All this was enough, and more than enough, but James – in the letter which he wrote with his own hand, despite the rheumatic pains in his arm – had gone even further, for 'you have furnished and enriched my cabinet with so precious a witness of your valuation of me as in future times it cannot be said that I rise, as most courtiers do, through importunity'. So far as titles of honour were concerned, Buckingham could go no further. The last dukedom to be granted to a commoner had been that of Sir John Dudley, created Duke of Northumberland by the boy-king, Edward VI, in 1551. The dukedom of Norfolk had, it was true, been revived in 1553, but it lapsed again after Thomas Howard, the fourth Duke, was attainted of treason in 1572. The only dukes in early Stuart England were the King's sons, Prince Henry being Duke of Cornwall and his brother, Prince Charles, Duke of York. Buckingham, then, was the first duke for nearly a century to have no trace of royal blood in his veins, and his elevation was a further indication that as far as James was concerned the favourite was to all intents and purposes a member of his own family.[64]

VII

At the time when he despatched Buckingham's patent of creation to Madrid, James was still optimistic about the probable outcome of the negotiations, but his mood changed to despair when Cottington reached England with the news that they were far from over and that Charles and Buckingham had no choice but to stay on in Madrid. This information, as James told his two boys, 'hath strukken me dead. I fear it shall very much shorten my days.' Now he blamed himself for ever letting them go, and declared that he would willingly abandon the marriage, the alliance, everything in fact that he had so long worked for, if only he could have them in his arms again. 'God grant it! God grant it! God grant it! Amen. Amen. Amen.' Prayers alone, however, were likely to be of limited effect, and James therefore wrote back immediately to guarantee that he would accept whatever changes in the marriage treaty the Prince and

Buckingham felt obliged to agree to. He urged them to conclude matters as soon as possible. The best solution would be for the Prince to marry the Infanta and bring her back with him, but if the Spaniards put difficulties in the way, let him be formally betrothed and then take his leave, on the clear understanding that his bride would be sent after him within a stated time. And if 'they will neither marry you this year, nor assure you, give the fairest words ye can to get home, and ye shall be heartily welcome'.[65]

According to Hacket, the messenger who brought the King's patent of dukedom to Buckingham also carried letters from his 'secret intelligencers . . . whom he had left behind to be, as it were, the lifeguard of his safety'. These told him that public opinion in England was deeply opposed to the match with Spain, and that since he needed the people's love as well as that of the King, he should either work against the marriage or at least couple it with the restitution of the Palatinate. It was this advice from the 'cabinet men at Wallingford House', says Hacket, that persuaded the Duke to change his tactics. Now he began 'to irritate the Spaniard, to shut out or to slight the Earl of Bristol in all counsels, to pour vinegar into every point of debate, to fling away abruptly, and to threaten the Prince's departure'. Hacket was in general well informed, and there is no reason to doubt that among the many letters that Buckingham received were some advising him to throw himself on the 'popular' side by opposing the match. But there was no sudden change of course, nor did Buckingham need the advice of distant friends to tell him the truth about the situation in Spain. His disillusionment with the Spanish ministers and with Bristol had begun well before the arrival of his patent of dukedom, and he had already become convinced that the only way in which to deal with ministers who ruthlessly exploited every advantage open to them, was to play their own game, to counter stratagem with stratagem and threats with threats.[66]

As for the coupling of the restitution with the marriage, James's orders had been explicit, and Buckingham was careful to observe them. But James, like his favourite, assumed that the marriage would be only a prelude to the settlement of affairs in Germany, not simply an end in itself, and in early April, when it seemed that the Prince was 'upon the conclusion of that happy alliance there' he authorised Buckingham to take up the question of the Palatinate. As Conway told Buckingham, 'it is therefore expected from His Highness and you – and the time and place is with you – to ease and help not only the honour of His Majesty but the state of those affairs; which is by declaration as well as expectation cast upon you'. In other words, it was not the 'cabinet men at Wallingford House' who persuaded Buckingham to link the marriage question with that of the Palatinate, but James himself.[67]

While Cottington was making all haste to England, Buckingham and the Prince were negotiating with the Spaniards about the disputed articles. Buckingham hoped that as soon as agreement had been reached on these the Spaniards would allow the marriage to take place and hand over the Infanta. But the junta of theologians which Philip had set up to advise him was still adamant that the only adequate security consisted in retaining the Infanta in

Spain until there was clear evidence that James was putting his promises into effect. Buckingham, as he told James, hoped 'to have the opinions of these beastly divines reversed' and he and the Prince were not afraid of using 'plain and sometimes rough language'. They drew up a long and well-argued letter to Philip IV in which they set out the reasons for allowing the marriage to take place sooner rather than later. The Prince, they reminded Philip, had exposed himself to great dangers in order to demonstrate his love for the Infanta and his desire for a union between the two crowns. It would be an aspersion on his honour if he had to return without his bride simply because the junta of divines was not prepared to accept as sufficient a solemn oath taken both by himself and his father to suspend the penal laws. He would have to 'leave his wife behind him in pawn, and with her the hope of his succession', and who was to say that during the interim between the betrothal ceremony and the handing-over there might not be further delays? This would be a hard case, after seven years' expectation and 'refusal of all other affairs in that kind'. The question was essentially one of trust, they argued, and at some stage the Spaniards would have to show their confidence in Charles and his father. Kings could not be bound in perpetuity, and generous and open treatment now was likely to provide a far more secure foundation for friendship than any 'securities' that could be devised. They ended by stating that if, in spite of all these arguments, Philip would still not consent to a speedy conclusion of the marriage, then the Prince would be forced to believe that there was 'some disesteem of his person'.[68]

Philip handed over the Prince's letter to the junta of divines and asked it to advise him on his reply. The junta duly considered the Prince's arguments, but saw no reason to modify its attitude. Charles, it said, was under the mistaken impression 'that if he only pressed hard he could make the obstacle give way; whereas it was certain that neither would the matter allow of any further concession, nor would they themselves dare to deduct a single day from the year which they had demanded for the execution of the conditions before the consummation of the marriage'. Buckingham complained bitterly about the barriers that were repeatedly placed in the way of a settlement, and in late June he told James that 'the foolery of the Conde of Olivares hath been cause of this long delay'. 'By this', he added, 'you may a little guess with what favour they proceed with us, first delaying us as long as possibly they can, then, when things are concluded of, they thrust in new particulars, in hope they will pass, out of our desire to make haste.' It was at about this time that the Prince sent a message to his father, telling him that he was still a virtual prisoner, and asking him for permission 'to depart from Madrid as secretly as he came thither', if he was not allowed to leave of his own free will. Should this attempt fail, he urged James to think no more about him but to 'reflect . . . upon the good of his sister [Elizabeth] and the safety of his own kingdoms'.[69]

James promptly wrote to the Prince, ordering him to return without delay. When his letter reached Madrid it gave Buckingham the excuse to appeal over the heads of both Olivares and the theologians direct to Philip IV. Buckingham drew up a draft of the declaration which the Prince intended to make. It began with a reminder of the dilemma confronting Charles, who had been ordered to return home, and was bound to obey, not simply out of filial duty but also out of natural feelings, since James had warned him that 'if you come not quickly, you shall not find me alive'. It continued with a complaint about the behaviour of Olivares, who 'at my first coming said if the Pope would not give you leave to give me the Infanta as a wife you should give me her as a mistress', but had now so far altered his opinions that he was prepared to risk 'the breach of the business of most consequence in Christendom'. Charles decided that before presenting this memorandum to Philip, he would tell Olivares of his purpose, but when he did so the Count asked him to take no action until further consideration had been given to his demand for an immediate betrothal. The Prince agreed, and that night, at the play, Buckingham went to Olivares and pressed him to state what was the uttermost concession Philip would make. Olivares then revealed that Philip's final terms were that the Prince should be betrothed upon the news of James's acceptance of the articles as amended; that the formal ceremony of marriage should take place at Christmas; but that the Infanta should not be handed over until the following spring.[70]

Buckingham and the Prince spent an entire night discussing what response they should make to this declaration. It was Charles who eventually broke the deadlock by deciding to accept the Spanish terms. He told Buckingham that while he thought they were unreasonable, his affection for the Infanta was so great that he was prepared to submit to them 'for her respect only'. No further obstacles now seemed to remain, and Buckingham told Middlesex on 8 July that 'our business here is at an end, all points concluded'. The Prince, meanwhile, informed his father that the Infanta 'sits publicly with me at the plays, and within this two or three days shall take place of the queen as Princess of England'. For four nights bonfires blazed in the Spanish capital, and, in the words of the Venetian ambassador, there was 'universal rejoicing and congratulations'.[71]

The Prince sent Sir George Goring to carry the news to his sister at the Hague. Elizabeth had been very upset when she first heard of the Prince's journey, assuming, as did so many other people, that James had decided to cast himself entirely into the hands of Spain. In April she was said to be 'in a pitiful case, almost distracted', and it was no doubt reports of his sister's acute distress that prompted Charles to transmit a message to her at the beginning of May, promising that he would not consent to the marriage until he had first obtained satisfaction for her. What little he could do, he did, and the Earl of Kellie – who presumably heard the story from James himself – described how 'the Prince, before the contract, was earnest that there might have been a treaty for restoring of the Palatinate; the King of Spain answered him he would treat nothing of that before the match was done, and, that being once done, he [Frederick] should be restored to all without any treaty – to lands, honours, and dignities'. Charles had good reason to know by this time that Philip's actions — at least where the Palatinate was concerned — rarely lived up to his words, but as this was obviously the only sort of promise he was going to get, he had to rest content with it.[72]

Buckingham had still not given up hope of persuading the Spaniards to modify their hard line and allow the Infanta to go back to England with the Prince. He suggested two ways in which this might be brought about. Either the junta of divines should be instructed to reconsider its verdict, or the Pope should be requested to free Philip from the responsibility for seeing the terms of the dispensation put into effect, now that both James and Charles had formally committed themselves to suspend the penal laws against the catholics. Olivares made encouraging noises, and told the Duke that he was 'working underhand with the divines, and under colour of the . . . Prince's journey makes preparations for hers [the Infanta's] also'. In fact, of course, Olivares was doing nothing of the sort. He was using his familiar carrot-and-stick technique of raising the Prince's hopes and then dashing them, on the assumption that frustration working on infatuation would eventually drive Charles into conversion to catholicism. As part of his strategy, he encouraged the Prince and Buckingham to go ahead with plans for their departure, and by the end of July it had been agreed that they would leave on 29 August.[73]

Olivares seems to have thought that the best way in which to achieve his objectives would be by separating the Prince from his intransigent companion. On 29 July, therefore, Philip IV made a formal promise in writing to Charles that if he stayed on in Spain until Christmas he would then be allowed to consummate the marriage. The Prince was reported to be favourably inclined to this suggestion, and it was no doubt to push him yet further in this direction that the Countess of Olivares made known the Infanta's grief at the thought that Charles might leave without her. The Infanta was so upset, added the Countess, that she had declared her intention not to go through the marriage ceremony until the very day of the Prince's departure. The Prince immediately sent Buckingham to the Infanta to assure her of his devotion and to explain that he 'never spoke of going but with this end, to get her the sooner away'. Buckingham took the opportunity to make clear to the Infanta that he also was devoted to her service and that all his thoughts were bent 'to gain her the love of that people whither she was to go'. He suggested that she should intercede with the Prince for a lightening of the burdens to which the English catholics were still subject, and assured her that she could expect a favourable response. What he was trying to show her was that she could accomplish far more for her fellow catholics through her presence in England at her husband's side than any number of formal conditions could ever do. If only he could convince her of this, he would then have a powerful ally in the campaign to persuade Philip to consent to an earlier marriage date. He had already offered to delay the Prince's departure until September as long as the Infanta would then be allowed to accompany him, but he would not for a moment accept that the Prince should stay on until Christmas — for this would inevitably be extended till March, and who knew what concessions the

Prince might by that time have been induced to make? It was no doubt to strengthen his hand in this matter that in a letter of 20 July he asked James to send 'peremptory commands to come away, and with all possible speed'.[74]

In this same letter Buckingham chided James because he had 'sent me no news of my wife, and have given her leave to be sick; and I conclude it the more dangerous because you dare not write the news of it'. Buckingham had been deeply disturbed by the news of Kate's illness, which turned him, as one observer noted, into a 'brick wall of reflection'. He wrote at once to tell her that if she had not recovered he would leave for home immediately (and since this was known to the Spanish ministers, it must have reinforced their hopes that they would at last have the Prince to themselves). Kate had, in fact, recovered by the time she received her husband's letter, but she confessed that she had looked and felt very ill and had at one time feared a consumption. She had kept this news from Buckingham in order to avoid adding to his troubles, particularly as the real reason for her sickness, she was convinced, was grief at his long absence. 'I hope', she told him, 'when once we are together again we shall have no more such partings, for if ever I should be so unfortunate again I am sure it would kill me. Then might you have a finer and a handsomer, but never a lovinger wife than your poor Kate is.'[75]

Kate's sickness was not the only reason which made Buckingham impatient to return home. Reports from his friends in England warned him that his long absence had given an opportunity for his enemies to combine against him. One informant was of the opinion that 'there will shortly be foul weather and that the storm will fall upon your lordship'. Another advised him to 'suffer no longer delays in Spain . . . . Your presence is most necessary here for home affairs, for your absence hath caused too great insolency in the Court by such as bear themselves very loftily and insult very much over yours.' Lord Keeper Williams was said to be among those who were intriguing against the Duke, and so was Lord Treasurer Middlesex. Williams was under particular suspicion because of the close ties between him and Bristol, who had become the focus of anti-Buckingham sentiment and had a 'great and more powerful party in Court than you imagine, insomuch that . . . were the King a neuter, he would prevail'. Bristol, of course, continued to maintain that the marriage negotiations had been on the point of completion at the very moment when the unexpected arrival of the Prince threw everything back into the melting-pot. He was also critical of Buckingham's conduct of these negotiations while he was in the Spanish court, and constantly advocated a softer line. In view of the charges frequently made against Buckingham of acting out of personal pride and pique rather than his country's interests, it is worth noting that Charles, looking back on the situation two years later, blamed Bristol in exactly these terms. Bristol, he said, had not done all that he might to persuade the Spanish ministers to allow the Infanta to leave at the same time as her husband. When Olivares and Buckingham were on good terms, 'you [Bristol] were very cold in soliciting that particular. But . . . as soon as the Conde and Duke were fallen out – which was not personal between them, but caused by the business and for His Majesty's service – your lordship was instantly friends with the Conde.' Charles added that this conduct had been evidence of 'much ill will in you to the Duke, and an aptness in you to be overconfident in the Spaniards when their promises concurred with your desires'.[76]

Buckingham managed, despite the opposition of Bristol, to prevent the Prince from making a total capitulation to the Spanish ministers, but he could never take his ascendancy over Charles for granted. The Prince had to be won over by persuasion, not threats, and in June the Venetian ambassador reported that Buckingham had modified his approach 'chiefly because the Prince . . . has signified that such is his pleasure, and he has even blamed the Duke for harshness in his methods'. The ambassador, who was generally well informed, added the significant information that the Prince had brought Bristol back into the negotiations. In the following month came rumours that Charles was dissatisfied with the lack of respect shown him by the favourite, and Williams, in one of his many letters to Buckingham, advised him 'to observe His Highness with all lowliness, humility and dutiful obedience'.[77]

In August 1623 the despatches of the Spanish envoys in England, confirming that James had sworn the requisite oaths to perform the marriage treaty, reached Madrid, and Charles and Buckingham took advantage of this further evidence of the King's goodwill to press for permission for the Infanta to accompany them to England. But the theologians, to whom Philip again referred the matter, were adamant and 'answered with a more fixed and determinate resolution than even before, that it was neither possible nor right to make any change in that which had been agreed upon on this point'. There was even some doubt about whether the marriage ceremony could now take place before the date set for the Prince's departure, since Pope Gregory, who issued the dispensation, had recently died, and although confirmation of it by his successor, Urban VIII, was said to be on its way, it had not yet arrived. Meanwhile the Prince was beside himself with impatience. He had already transgressed the bounds of decorum by leaping a garden wall in order to get a closer look at his beloved, and in mid-August an observer reported that he 'longingly expecteth the nuptial day when the business so long in treaty is to be consummated in the bed'. According to the Venetian ambassador, the Prince was determined not to leave for England unless and until he could take the Infanta with him, and if this was indeed the case Buckingham must have been a very worried man. No wonder he bitterly reproached Olivares for the lack of trust he displayed in refusing to allow the Infanta to accompany her future husband.[78]

The Spanish ministers were by now showing intransigence over the question of the Palatinate as well. Olivares told the council of state on 12 August that the best solution would be for Frederick's son to marry the Emperor's daughter and be brought up in the imperial Court. He could then, after the death of the Duke of Bavaria, recover both the estates and the electoral dignity of his father. No doubt James would agree to this, added Olivares, since he would see the advantages of having catholic rather than puritan grandchildren. Olivares was here being too cynical. James took a favourable view of the proposed imperial marriage, but he wanted at least a token restoration of lands and dignity to his son-in-law, and he would not agree to his grandson being sent to Vienna, except on condition that he should be brought up there as a protestant. When the Prince raised the question of Frederick's restoration with Olivares, the Count told him there could be no question of it. Bavaria would never agree to hand back either the electoral title or the Palatinate, nor would the Emperor undo what he had done. When the Prince asked for some assurance that the King of Spain would, as he had promised Bristol, join his troops with English forces to clear the Palatinate and restore it to Frederick, Olivares replied that it was a maxim of state in Spain that they would never take up arms against another member of the House of Austria. The Prince was said, by Olivares, to be very upset at this information. Whether or not he made any further comment at that time is uncertain, but when he returned to England he declared that he had told Olivares that 'if you hold yourself to that, there is an end of all; for without this you may not rely upon either marriage or friendship'. Even if he never spoke these words, they undoubtedly represented his feelings. He had gone to Spain to conclude the marriage as a prelude to the restoration of the Elector Palatine. Now, six months later, the marriage had still not taken place and even if it did there was little indication that it would lead to the desired political result.[79]

Olivares was still hoping to persuade the Prince to stay on in Spain until the spring of the following year, and offered, if he did so, to give him a blank sheet of paper with Philip IV's signature on it, upon which he could write his own conditions for settling the question of the Palatinate. But even the Prince, by this stage, had come to realise that Olivares's impulsive gestures were not to be taken at face value. It may have been at about this time that Buckingham, by remarking that the marriage could have been concluded many years earlier given Spanish goodwill, goaded Olivares into producing the letters exchanged between him and Philip IV in late 1622 which showed that Philip III had never intended the marriage to take place. If so, the incident can only have confirmed the Prince's distrust of Spanish promises and persuaded him to hold fast by his resolution to leave Madrid on 29 August. The one thing which was now likely to delay the journey was Buckingham's state of health, for the intense pressures to which he had been subject had brought on a fever. He was let blood, but this made him so weak that he could not walk and had to be carried in a chair belonging to the Countess of Olivares. Philip IV's own physicians were instructed to attend on him – and received from Buckingham the munificent gift of £200 for their trouble – as was an English doctor. Whether through their efforts or through natural processes the fever was checked, and Buckingham, though still not fully recovered, was able to prepare for his departure. He could scarcely contain his pleasure at the thought that the interminable delays were now nearly at an end. 'Sir,' he told James, 'my heart and very soul dances for joy, for the change will be no less than to leap from trouble to ease, from sadness to mirth – nay, from hell to heaven.'[80]

VIII

On 28 August the Prince and Philip both took solemn oaths to put into effect the articles of marriage concluded between them. The English and Spanish ministers took similar oaths, and Buckingham committed himself never to execute any law against any Roman Catholic. Gifts were then exchanged, and Philip gave Buckingham twenty horses with their saddle-cloths made of embroidered damask fringed with gold lace, as well as a number of colts and mares. He also presented him with a magnificent hatband set with diamonds. From Madrid the Prince and the king, accompanied by their suites, made their way out of the capital towards the great monastery-palace of the Escorial. There the Prince signed the document authorising his marriage to take place by deputy. The authorisation was valid until Christmas, and Charles handed it over to Bristol, with instructions to make use of it as soon as Urban VIII's dispensation arrived. It was also at the Escorial that Buckingham and Olivares had their last interview. Buckingham was still smarting from the fact that Olivares, in a final effort to dissuade the Prince from leaving, had advised him not to listen to Buckingham since the Duke had his own reasons for wanting to return home. Buckingham, when he heard of this, had been so angry that he had only with difficulty been restrained from challenging Olivares to a duel. Nevertheless he called on the Spanish favourite on the night of their arrival at the Escorial, taking with him Wat Montagu, the son of the Lord President, to act as interpreter. Buckingham hoped that in this interview he might achieve a reconciliation with the Spanish favourite, so that they could at least part as friends, but the differences between the two men were too wide to be papered over. When, at the end of their conversation, Olivares asked Buckingham for an assurance that their bad personal relations should not affect the business on which they had both been engaged, Buckingham gave it. But he added 'I tell you very frankly that I shall never be a friend to your excellency.' When the report of this declaration reached England it seemed to confirm the view of those who blamed the failure of the Spanish match on the rivalry and bitterness between the two favourites, but in fact the causes, as has been shown, went far deeper than this. Toby Matthew, who, as a leading English catholic, longed for the negotiations to succeed, had already expressed his despair at the realisation that 'reason prevails nothing with these people [the Spanish ministers]'. As for Buckingham's unpopularity, Matthew was of the opinion that it was 'impossible for any incorrupt great minister of state to have the love of a whole world when a part of that world hath affairs and ends which are contrary to his'.[81]

From the Escorial the Prince's party made its way north towards Santander. It was probably at Segovia that Charles and Buckingham met Sir Francis Nethersole, who had been sent from Elizabeth with a message to her brother, urging him not to conclude the marriage before he had received firm assurances about the restoration of Frederick to his lands and dignities. This was no more than Charles had already promised, yet he had committed himself to marry the Infanta without receiving any such assurance. It was perhaps this consideration which prompted him to a subterfuge. He sent one of Buckingham's trusted servants, Edward Clerke, back to Madrid with orders that he was to stay at Bristol's house until he heard that Urban VIII's dispensation had arrived. Then – and only then – he was to produce an undated letter from Charles to the ambassador, commanding Bristol not to proceed with the marriage until he had obtained security that the Infanta would not, subsequent to the formal betrothal, go into a monastery. Charles's fear may have been genuine, since the Infanta had earlier expressed her determination to take the veil rather than marry a heretic, but the significance of his manoeuvre was that the marriage would be postponed for some weeks while Bristol communicated with the Prince in England. This would give Charles time to consult with his father on what further steps should be taken to ensure that the Palatinate and the electoral title were restored to Frederick. It might have been more honest of him to give a direct order to Bristol to delay the marriage, but this would have been in contravention of his oath. As it was, by raising a legitimate query Charles could hold up the marriage without infringing the letter of what he had sworn. He had certainly not decided at this stage to abandon the marriage. But with every step he took away from Madrid he weakened the hold of the Infanta upon him and became increasingly conscious of those other obligations which he had come near to betraying.[82]

Nethersole carried a message for Buckingham as well as Charles. It was an invitation for him to act as godfather to Elizabeth's new-born son. This was a signal honour as well as a mark of confidence, and it was some time before Buckingham could gather his thoughts sufficiently to write an acknowledgement 'of my humble and thankful part for so unequal a favour, both for the giver and the receiver'. He could as yet, he told Elizabeth, send her 'nothing but obscure words, professions and protestations', but he assured her that he was her 'faithful servant and slave'. No doubt, he added, his enemies would judge whatever action he subsequently took on her behalf as a direct response to her generous gesture, but in fact it was his sense of duty which was driving him towards a more open commitment to her cause. As for Charles, he told her, she need have no fears about his constancy, for 'when he had most cause of confidence in the good success of his marriage, [he] protested he would not be engaged till he might judge what would become of your business, it being one of the chiefest causes of his journey'.[83]

On 12 September, as they drew near to the coast, the Prince and Buckingham met Sir John Finett, the assistant master of ceremonies at James's Court, who brought them the news that the English fleet sent to take them home had just anchored in the bay of Santander. The Prince was overjoyed, and Buckingham was so delighted that he embraced Finett, and 'drawing from his finger a diamond of above an hundred pounds' value' gave it him as a present. A week later the ships sailed, and on 5 October they entered Plymouth harbour. The Prince and Buckingham immediately went ashore, and by early the following morning they were in London, where they breakfasted at York House. From there they set out for Royston, where James was staying, while bonfires were lit and bells were rung to welcome the Prince's return. Chamberlain had never seen anything like it, and described how in the capital tables were set out in the streets 'with all manner of provisions . . . whole hogsheads of wine and butts of sack . . . . The people were so mad with excess of joy that if they met with any cart loaden with wood they would take out the horses and set cart and all on fire.'

At Royston, on Monday 6 October, the two travellers at last reached the end of their journey. As they were going up the stairs to the King's chamber, they met James coming down, and fell to their knees. The King embraced them both with tears of joy, happy and relieved beyond measure to see before him the two people he loved most in the world, and whom at one stage he had feared he might never set eyes on again. The Spanish journey had solved none of the problems confronting the King, indeed it had made them in many respects worse. Yet for the moment there was room in his heart for nothing but joy and gratitude. His son had returned, like Israel out of Egypt 'and the house of Jacob from among the barbarous people'. As for the Duke 'his carriage in all the business is much applauded and commended', reported Chamberlain, 'and sure, if it were altogether as is reported, it was brave and resolute'.[84]

NOTES

(Abbreviations are explained in the Bibliography, pp. 477–86)
1. *Sp.MSS.* 25.166, 168v., 182.
2. *Sp.MSS.* 25.169.
3. *Perr.MSS.* 4.113.
4. *Sp.Tr.MSS.* 26, no number; *A.P.C. 1621–23.* 164, 291; *H.M.C. (10).* 90.
5. *Goodman.* II, 238–41; *C.S.P.V.* XVII, 381; *H.M.C. Mar.* 133.
6. *Tann.MSS.* 73.178v.; *Cab.* 224–6.
7. *Holl.MSS.* 109. 106–8.
8. *H.M.C.Supp.* 138; *Endym.* passim.
9. *Sp.MSS.* 25.269, 275; *Cab.* 315; *Hecho.* 191–4.
10. *Est. MSS.* 7026.205–6; *Sp.MSS.* 25.241.
11. *Lon.* 334, 361.
12. *Brist.* 39; *Rus.* 139; *Dig.MSS.* 40.
13. *Dig.MSS.* 39; *Sp.MSS.* 25.261, 286v.; *C.S.P.V.* XVII, 502.
14. *Tann. MSS.* 73.240, 44.
15. *Goodman.* II, 249–51; *Sp.MSS.* 25.288, 302.
16. *Sp.MSS.* 94.327, 324v.
17. *Holl.MSS.* 109.205–6, 211.
18. *Birch.* II, 353.
19. *Endym.* 69–70; *Sp.MSS.* 30.160.
20. *Goodman.* II, 299; *Sp.Tr.MSS.* 26, no number; *Sp.MSS.* 25.261, 334.
21. *Sp.Tr.MSS.* 27.8; *Sack.MSS.* ON.7580; *Ch.* II, 472; *Tann.MSS.* 73.267, 269.
22. *H.M.C.Supp.* 150; *Holl.MSS.* 111.148; *Goodman.* I, 367–8; *Wot.* 212–13; *Fr.MSS.* 71.41.
23. *Holl.MSS.* 111.148.

24. *C.S.P.V.* XVII, 575; *Dom.MSS 14.* 138.99.
25. *Clar.* I, 13–14, 21; *Goodman.* I, 364; *Hack.* I, 114; *L.J.* 209; *Sp.MSS.* 27.22.
26. *Moore.* Appendix III.
27. *Denmilne MSS.* 33.1.10, 25; *Sp.MSS.* 26.228.
28. *Sav.MSS.* 10.58v.
29. *Trum.M̃SS.* 7.101; *Ch.* II, 491; *Wot.* 215; *Mareuil.* 173; *Harl.MSS.* 6987.11.
30. *Trum.MSS.* 7.101; *Wot.* 216.
31. *Hearne MSS.* 150.30–30v.; *Harl.MSS.*6987.19, 54.
32. *H.M.C.(8).* 215; *Harl.MSS.* 1581.352; *Denmilne MSS.* 33.1.10, 21.
33. *Denmilne MSS.* 33.1.10, 24 and 21; *Harl.MSS.* 6987.21
34. *Sp.MSS.* 26.93–8.
35. *C.S.P.V.* XVII, 611; *Sp.MSS.* 26.123; *Harl.MSS.* 6987.23.
36. *Harl.MSS.* 6987.13, 15.
37. *Hecho.* 204–5; *Rush.*120–1; *Harl.MSS.* 6987.33.
38. *Hecho.* 206–8; *Rush.* 252,291.
39. *Goodman.* II, 296; *Albion.* 28–31; *Est.MSS.* 7026.394–5; 1869.10.
40. *Harl.MSS.* 1581.332; 6987.44, 46.
41. *Pal.MSS.* Consultas y Otros Papeles sobre Cosas de Inglaterra. II.2167.30–2; *Est. MSS.* 2516.26–7.; *Harl.MSS.* 6987.48.
42. *Hearne MSS.* 150.7.34v.; *Reade MSS.* 4/3; *Hecho.* 209–10.
43. *Hecho.* 211.
44. *Harl.MSS.* 6987.73, 92, 90, 94.
45. *Hecho.*214; *Est.MSS.* 1869.16.
46. *Hecho.* 216–17; *Est.MSS.* 7026.400–1.
47. *Est.MSS.* 7026.401–401v.; *Hecho.* 67.
48. *Hecho.* 220–23.
49. *Pal.MSS.* II.2198.79; *Reade MSS* 4/5.819.
50. *Reade MSS.* 1/6.199; 4/5.819.
51. *Hecho.* 228–30.
52. *Hecho.* 230–32.
53. *Hecho.* 232–3, 241; *Rush.* 122.
54. *C.S.P.V.* XVIII.21; *H.M.C.Supp.*166, 169; *Birch.*II, 399; *Harl.MSS.*1580.126; *Wynn.* 1107.
55. *C.S.P.V.* XVIII, 20; *Sp.MSS.* 26.228; *Dom.MSS 14.* 145.39.
56. *Harl.MSS.* 1580.90; 6987.29; *Goodman.* II, 257–8.
57. *Harl.MSS.* 6987.37, 41, 63, 69.
58. *Harl.MSS.* 6987.117.
59. *Ch. II,* 495; *Harl.MSS.* 6987.119; *Goodman.* II, 260–7.
60. *Tann.MSS.* 73.289; *Clar.* I, 46–7.
61. *Endym.* 91–2; *Harl.MSS.* 6987.119.
62. *Harl.MSS.* 6987.223, 231, 78, 80.
63. *Harl.MSS.* 6987.63; *Sp.MSS.* 26.151.
64. *Harl.MSS.* 6987.153.
65. *Harl.MSS.* 6987.100; *Sp.MSS.* 27.24.
66. *Hack.* I, 125, 137.
67. *Goodman.* II, 273–5.
68. *Harl.MSS.* 6987.96; 1583.276–278v.; *Sack.MSS.* ON.250.
69. *Hecho.* 243–4; *Harl.MSS.* 6987.107; *Hack.* I, 137, 145.
70. *Sp.MSS.* 27.22; *Harl.MSS.* 1583.281–282v.; *Add.MSS.* 36,447.112–112v.

71. *Add.MSS*.36, 447.113; *Sack.MSS*. ON.8862; *Harl.MSS*. 6987.115; *Sp.MSS*. 27.102; *C.S.P.V*. XVIII, 73.
72. *Sp.MSS*. 27.106; *Knyvett*. 58; *C.S.P.V*. XVIII, 19; *H.M.C.Supp*. 176.
73. *Harl.MSS*. 6987.115, 126.
74. *Hecho*. 248; *Harl.MSS*. 6987.128, 126.
75. *Goodman*. II, 303–6, 309–14.
76. *Goodman*. II, 302–3; *Cab*. 122; *Dom.MSS 16*. 2.100.
77. *C.S.P.V*. XVIII, 53; *Cab*. 283.
78. *Hecho*. 249; *C.S.P.V*. XVIII, 37, 101; *Sp.MSS*. 27.173.
79. *Pal.MSS*. Consultas del Consejo de Estado 1623–4. II.2220; *Sp.MSS*. 28.123v. –124v., 125v.; *Side* II, 240; *Rush*. 123.
80. *Sp.MSS*. 29.114; *Holl.MSS*. 113.205; 114.231; *Hack*. I, 146; *Add.MSS*. 12, 528.9v.; *Harl.MSS*. 6987.164.
81. *Hecho*. 252–4; *Sp.MSS*. 28.223; *Reade MSS*. 4/5.837; *Goodman*. II, 303–6.
82. *Side*. II.260; *Harl.MSS*. 1580.274; *Sp.MSS*. 28.44.
83. *Harl.MSS*. 6987.151.
84. *Fin*. 121; *Pett*. 128–9; *Ch*. II, 515–16.

CHAPTER SIX

1624: 'St George on Horseback'

I

The return of the Prince was, in Sir Benjamin Rudyerd's striking phrase, 'the turn of Christendom', for it was to lead to English commitment to the great war against the Habsburgs. This was not immediately apparent, however, and the last three months of 1623 were taken up by complicated manoeuvres in which Buckingham played a difficult and dangerous part with great skill. His own attitude was quite clear. The journey to Madrid had given him the opportunity to study at first hand the men who moulded Spanish policy, and he had been made forcibly aware of the very real dangers that the expansion of Habsburg power offered to the western world. He was now in favour of war – not a holy crusade against the catholic enemy but concerted operations by all those states which were threatened by Habsburg ambitions, with the aim of forcing Spain and the Emperor to the negotiating table. James had made the mistake of treating with an olive branch in his hand. Buckingham now realised that the best way in which to win concessions from a powerful, unscrupulous and arrogant enemy was by the sword.[1]

The Duke had to tread carefully however. Policy-making was in the hands of the King, and James was not going to turn warrior overnight. Nor could Buckingham count on the support of the Councillors who advised the King. Some of them were committedly anti-Spanish; others, for various reasons, were still in favour of the Spanish marriage. Yet even those who were most inclined on political grounds to favour a harder line against Spain might well distrust the royal favourite. He had been too long associated with James's policies of appeasement for them to be easily convinced that he had really changed his views; and they were unwilling simply to become pawns in a power game that would raise Buckingham to an even greater eminence. The Duke would have to use all his skill to overcome their doubts and fears and all his charm to win over James.

He had one enormous advantage in the friendship of the Prince. The two young men had been on close terms even before they left England, but their time in Spain, despite occasional rifts, had created a bond between them that turned out to be not only unbreakable but even unshakeable. Buckingham had no longer any reason to fear that he would share the fate of most favourites, whose power ended with the life of their master. As Sir Henry Wotton observed, 'by so long and so private and so various consociation with a prince of such excellent nature he had now gotten (as it were) two lives in his own fortune and greatness; whereas otherwise the state of a favourite is at the best but a tenant-at-will and rarely transmitted'.[2]

Charles's political attitude, however, was as yet unclear. He had made a magnificent gesture by going to Spain to claim the Infanta's hand, but his trust and confidence had not been reciprocated. Philip IV had treated him with great courtesy, but when it came to the major business the Spaniards had not scrupled to extort from him and his father terms that they would never, in normal circumstances, have agreed to. The Prince resented this, and one of the first comments he made after boarding the English fleet at Santander was that the Spaniards had shown great 'weakness and folly . . . in that after they had used him so ill, they would suffer him to depart'. Yet he had not decided, at this stage, on a complete break. He still believed himself to be in love with the Infanta, and had made a binding promise to marry her, by proxy, as soon as the dispensation from the new Pope reached Madrid. But Charles was determined that Spain should give a firm undertaking to restore the Palatinate before he would finally commit himself to the marriage. He had hoped to gain time by sending Clerke with the message to Bristol, but Clerke had fallen ill at Bristol's house and had been persuaded to hand over the Prince's letter much earlier than intended. This gave Bristol the opportunity to press the Spanish ministers for a formal assurance that the Infanta would not take the veil, and having received this, he made such haste to inform the Prince that the message reached Royston at about the same time as Charles himself.[3]

Charles therefore wrote to Bristol telling him 'to try what the King of Spain will do concerning the business of the Palatinate before I be contracted'. Bristol's proxy was valid until Christmas, and a reply could easily reach England before then, so there was no reason, said Charles, to believe that his request for a 'positive answer' about the Palatinate would hold up the marriage. Just in case there should be any doubts about his intentions, he added that his purpose was 'in no ways to break the marriage but (in this dull interim of looking for my mistress) to put an end to the miseries of my sister and her children'. In another letter, this time to Sir Walter Aston, 'Honest Wat', the Prince made his position crystal clear. Bristol was not to hand over his proxy until the King of Spain had explained exactly what he was prepared to do about the Palatinate. If the Spaniards looked askance at this demand, Aston was to assure them that 'I do really intend and desire this match, and . . . so that we may have satisfaction concerning the Palatinate, I will be content to forget all ill usage and be hearty friends. But if not, I can never match where I have had so dry entertainment, although I shall be infinitely sorry for the loss of the Infanta.'[4]

While the Prince's wishes would obviously be given due weight by the ambassadors, their instructions could only come from James himself. The

King therefore wrote to Bristol at the same time, confirming Charles's statement that the marriage and satisfaction over the Palatinate were to go together, since he had never intended at the same time as he gave 'joy to our only son, to give our only daughter her portion in tears'. Bristol was instructed to seek an immediate audience of Philip IV and ask not only for 'a punctual answer what course that king will take for the restitution of the Palatinate and electorate to our son-in-law' but also for a clear statement of Philip's intentions 'in case that either the Emperor or the Duke of Bavaria will oppose any part of the expected restitution'. James recognised that the problem of the Palatinate could not be solved in a few weeks. All that he wanted was a positive commitment on the part of Spain; a formal obligation that Philip IV would be bound to honour.[5]

The major difference between Buckingham and the King at this stage was in their attitude towards Spain. James still professed his belief that Spanish promises could be relied on, but Frederick's representative in London described Buckingham as being 'utterly disgusted with the Spaniards. [He] now maintains that His Majesty had been given biased reports and that the King of Spain's intentions were not what they had been represented to be' Charles obviously shared Buckingham's doubts, for when the King pressed Elizabeth and Frederick to agree to the proposal for a marriage between their eldest son and the Emperor's daughter, Charles advised them to do nothing until they had heard from him by a confidential messenger. It was no doubt as a consequence of this initiative that Frederick, in due course, informed James that while he accepted the marriage proposal in principle, the restitution of his hereditary estates must come first.[6]

Charles's initiative was one of a number of indications that he was escaping from his father's tutelage and beginning to think and act for himself. It was also consistent with the general principle on which he and Buckingham were now working, that the time for promises had passed, and that no further negotiations should be entered into until the Spaniards had shown their goodwill by giving firm assurances about the restitution of the Palatinate. Their influence was shown in James's reply to a letter from Bristol pointing out that the marriage with the Infanta could not be delayed until Christmas because his proxy would by then have expired. James sent him a new proxy, with a later expiry date, but instructed him, before he delivered it, to

procure from that king . . . under his hand . . . that he will help us to the restitution of the Palatinate and dignity by mediation, or otherwise assist us if mediation fail, and within what time the mediation shall determine and the assistance of arms begin . . . . And to show you how we desire to comply with our dear brother of Spain, we shall be ready to propound good ways to satisfy the Duke of Bavaria in point of title and honour, and to continue our negotiations for the match of our grandchild '(the eldest son of our son-in-law) with the daughter of the Emperor.'

James's letter was in reply to a number from Bristol asking for clarification of the King's intentions. Bristol was genuinely puzzled. As far as he was concerned, the marriage had been agreed upon before the Prince left Spain, and could not be delayed after the arrival of the dispensation. By 13 November the dispensation had reached Madrid, and the Spanish ministers were pressing Bristol to agree upon a date for the marriage ceremony. Bristol did not see how he could refuse to hand over his proxy or ask for the ceremony to be delayed without besmirching his own and the Prince's honour. He was also convinced, as he told James, that 'the greatest assurance Your Majesty could have of the restitution of the Palatinate was the good proceeding of the marriage, to be a good pawn for the rest'.[8]

If Bristol perhaps had some excuse for professing uncertainty about the exact intentions of James and Charles, Aston had none, for Charles had told him explicitly that he would not marry unless and until he received watertight assurances about the Spanish commitment to restore the Palatinate. Yet Aston allowed himself to be overborne by Bristol and to agree that a day should be fixed for the marriage ceremony. When the Prince heard this news his anger drove him to prompt action. On 14 November he sent a brief note to Bristol, commanding him 'not to deliver my proxy until you hear farther from the King and myself. Make what shifts or fair excuses you will, but I command you as you answer it upon your peril not [to] deliver my proxy till you hear farther from hence.' He followed up this peremptory instruction with a longer letter, the following day, in which he made clear his exact intentions. Bristol was to press for an unequivocal answer from Philip IV within fifteen days. Failing this, he was to announce his intention to leave after a further five days. 'So that if within twenty days ye get no answer, ye must take your leave and break off the treaty . . . . But whatsoever answer ye get, ye must not deliver the proxy till ye make my father and me judge of it.' And just in case either Bristol or Philip IV should be in any doubt about what the Prince and his father wanted. Charles added that

except that king will promise some way under hand to help my father with his arms, in case mediation fail, to restore my brother-in-law to his honour and inheritances, there can neither be marriage nor friendship . . . . And if they will do all that my father desires, they may not only be sure of an alliance but of a hearty sincere friendship. Make no replies. Suffer no delays.'

English foreign policy was now being made by a trinity consisting of the King, the Prince and Buckingham, and at this particular stage the Duke was probably less influential than the other two. James remained the most important member of the trinity since he alone had the authority to take final decisions, but in early November 1623 he fell ill and was not able to keep his usual close control over affairs. He spent much of his time in his country houses at Royston and Theobalds, crippled by his old enemy, the gout — though Kellie was of the opinion, as were many others, that his sickness had been brought on by the conflicting pressures to which he was constantly subjected. The King was frequently in great pain, and Buckingham was in constant attendance. Meanwhile the Prince, as one observer noted, was 'entering into command of affairs . . . and all men address themselves unto him'.[10]

Whatever reservations he had about Spanish trustworthiness, Buckingham did not neglect his duties towards Philip IV's representatives in England. The King's recovery freed him to return to town, and on Tuesday, 18 November, he held a great feast in honour of the ambassadors at York House. Chamberlain described the 'superabundant plenty', with 'forty dozen of partridges [and] as many quails'. The King was said to have borne the cost of what was essentially a state entertainment, but Buckingham paid the royal musicians for performing in the masque that followed. One notable absentee was the Marquis de la Inojosa, the resident ambassador in London, who was engaged in a bitter quarrel over precedence with his fellow envoy and preferred to sulk at home rather than risk a public rebuff. Buckingham sent Endymion Porter to him, however, with a selection of the best dishes and a message of goodwill, to which Inojosa returned an appropriately courteous answer. These outwardly good relations did not last for long, though, for later that month Buckingham went out of his way to court the members of a delegation which had recently arrived from the (Spanish) Netherlands and 'did freely say to them that he did wonder they did with so much patience bear the tyranny of Spain'. If ever they chose to throw off the yoke, he assured them, they would find friends ready at hand to aid them.[11]

As the year 1623 drew to its close, James continued to hope, against all odds, that Philip would make a positive and constructive reply to his overtures about the Palatinate, which would enable him to fend off the mounting pressure for war. His optimism was not shared by the Prince, nor, of course, by Buckingham, who was concentrating his energies on strengthening English links with friendly foreign powers at the same time as he reconciled himself with leaders of the 'popular' or war party at home. In November he wrote to Elizabeth at the Hague, to express his regret that he could not attend the christening of her child and to explain that during all his apparent shifts of policy he had been seeking 'a good opportunity . . . to do you effectual service'. This letter was very well received, and Sir Dudley Carleton, writing from the Hague, declared that while 'I never knew Your Grace ill with this good and gracious princess . . . now you are so well settled in her good opinion and favour that I know none hath more interest therein'.[12]

Buckingham, although he had no military experience, was well aware of the fact that if England was to make any effective military or naval intervention in the war against the House of Austria in the following year, preparations would have to begin immediately. It was essential to win over the Dutch, for they were the foremost naval power in Europe, and if their fleet cooperated with that which Buckingham hoped to bring into being, the allies would be able to strike not simply at the main Spanish supply lines but at the Iberian peninsula itself. The Dutch also had long experience of fighting the Spaniards on land, and this would be very useful when it came to planning military operations to free the Palatinate. There was the further consideration that the only English regular forces were the regiments in Dutch pay, and if the two countries were formally allied, the Dutch might agree to release a number of English officers who could be used as a nucleus around which new armies could be built.

The Dutch would no doubt have welcomed formal offers of alliance from England, but there was no chance of James making these. He had little liking for the Dutch, and while Charles was in Spain he had ordered him to discuss with Olivares the prospects of joint Anglo-Spanish operations to put an end to the existence of the United Provinces and split them between the two crowns. Now that the situation had changed, he recognised the need to draw closer to them, but as a crowned sovereign he would not demean himself by soliciting assistance from republican burghers. It was up to the Dutch to make the first move, and in mid-December Rusdorf, the Elector Palatine's agent in London, informed his master that now would be an appropriate moment. The Dutch, he said, should stress that they had hitherto borne the burden of the struggle against Spain unaided, and that while they were prepared to continue the fight, they needed the help of other states whose independence was similarly threatened by the expanding power of the House of Austria. They should declare that if James was forced into war, they would give him all assistance and enter into a formal alliance if invited to do so. In this way, said Rusdorf, it would be possible, little by little, to detach the King from his pacific courses and win him over to more bellicose ones. He added that while his propositions were made with Buckingham's approval, the Duke's name was not to be mentioned.[13]

Buckingham did not confine himself to Rusdorf as an intermediary. He also instructed his close friend, Sir George Goring – who was being sent with a message to Frederick and Elizabeth – to seek an audience of the Prince of Orange and press him to make an approach to James. Orange's reply was that while he would make a positive response to any English overtures he dare not advise the States General to take the first step themselves for fear that James, having got an assurance of Dutch support, would simply use this as a lever with which to extort better terms from the Spaniards. This was not the first, nor the last, occasion on which James's reputation for deviousness, and his known susceptibility to Spanish influence, held up the formation of an anti-Habsburg league.[14]

II

During the King's illness in early November 1623, the Prince had turned for advice to what was described as a 'committee council' of leading ministers, to whom Buckingham made a full report of the course of his negotiations while in Spain. This body had to consider, among other things, whether or not to advise the King to summon Parliament, but there was considerable divergence of opinion among members. Buckingham was in favour, on the grounds that only Parliament could provide the financial sinews of war, but support for him was limited to Sir Edward Conway and James Hay, Earl of Carlisle (formerly Viscount Doncaster). Conway had long believed that war with Spain (preferably in alliance with the Dutch) was the only way in which to check the growth of Habsburg power, and that a close union between the King and his people, represented in Parliament, was the best guarantee of success. Carlisle was of the same opinion, except that he favoured a French alliance. Pembroke, the Lord Chamberlain, was committedly anti-Spanish and approved of the idea of summoning Parliament, but was deeply distrustful of Buckingham, as were a number of others. Arundel, the Earl Marshal, thought the best policy was one of peace with Spain, and was supported by Lord Treasurer Middlesex, who was aware of the intolerable strain that war would place upon the royal finances. Sir Richard Weston, the Chancellor of the Exchequer, saw no reason to abandon the pro-Spanish policy to which James had hitherto been committed; nor did Sir George Calvert, Conway's colleague as Secretary of State, who was a Roman Catholic. The only remaining member of this 'committee council' was John Williams, Bishop of Lincoln and Lord Keeper, who steered a typically devious course between the various interest groups but refused to be identified with any of them.[15]

Buckingham was faced with no easy task in trying to persuade this ill-assorted and mutually suspicious body to follow his lead, but he received powerful support from the Prince, who had by now given up hope of Spain. In late November 1623 Charles was said to have told his father that the Spaniards not only had deceived him but would continue to do so as long as he continued to negotiate with them. It was time now, he said, to take a stand, for the Spaniards were aiming at nothing less than the ruin of James and his kingdom. James, according to Rusdorf, wept at these words and asked the Prince 'Do you want to commit me to war in my old age and make me break with Spain?' This was indeed what the Prince wanted, and when, in mid-December, a despatch from Bristol arrived in which the ambassador spoke of his regret that the marriage had been broken off just at the very moment when it was about to produce all the benefits that had so long been hoped for, Charles dismissed this as 'an inflated bladder, wind without substance'. It was almost certainly knowledge of the Prince's atitude, combined with respect for his person and awareness of the fact that at some time in the not too distant future he would become King, that persuaded a majority of the committee-council to vote in favour of summoning Parliament. The King, unable to resist the combined pressure of his son, his favourite and his advisers, gave his reluctant consent, and on 28 December instructed the Lord Keeper to prepare the appropriate writs. Two days later he wrote to Bristol, telling him to leave the conduct of negotiations in the hands of Aston and to return home to explain 'your misconstructions of our directions'.[16]

Although the committee-council had decided by a narrow majority to recommend the King to summon Parliament, it had not thereby committed itself to war with Spain. The summoning of Parliament could be regarded as a means to win more favourable terms from Spain, since this was the way James had acted in the past. Buckingham, as he no doubt realised, was in a dangerously exposed position, and it was probably at this stage that he turned for advice to Bacon, who drew up a number of points for him to consider. There were, said Bacon, three main groups within the state, and none of them could be relied on to remain constant to Buckingham. There were

the party of the papists, which hate you; the party of the protestants, including those they call puritans, whose love is yet but green towards [you]; and particular great persons which are most of them reconciled enemies or discontented friends; and you must think there are a great many that will magnify you and make use of you for the breaking of the match or putting the realm into a war, which after will return to their old bias.

He therefore recommended Buckingham not to trust anybody, but 'to play your own game, showing yourself to have, as the bee hath, both of the honey and of the sting'.[17]

Buckingham had already begun the task of building bridges towards the leaders of the 'popular' party. In November 1623 he had been reconciled with the Earl of Southampton, and in the closing days of that year he secured the release from the Tower of the Earl of Oxford, after twenty months of imprisonment. On New Year's Day, 1624, Oxford married Lady Diana Cecil, thereby linking himself with a family with which Buckingham had close ties, and he wrote to the Duke to assure him that this 'noble and free beginning . . . binds me in a perpetual acknowledgement'. In the following February Buckingham persuaded the King to receive Lord Saye back into favour and allow him to take his seat in the House of Lords in the forthcoming Parliament. Later that year he signalled his pleasure at Saye's support of his policies by having him raised to the rank of viscount.[18]

It was relatively easy for Buckingham to demonstrate his change of attitude towards former opponents like Southampton and Oxford, but he was faced with a much harder task when it came to dealing with great ministers like Williams, the Lord Keeper, Middlesex, the Lord Treasurer, and Pembroke, the Lord Chamberlain. During his absence in Spain, Buckingham had heard that Williams was involved in plots against him, and his reaction, understandably, was one of resentment. He also resented the way in which Williams pressed him to make up his differences with Bristol, as though these were due simply to personal distastes and not to fundamental disagreements over policy. In his anger against the ingratitude of a man for whom he had done so much he announced that one of his first actions on returning home would be to drive Williams from office, and when the Lord Keeper came to pay his respects at York House, Buckingham declared that he was 'a man odious to all the world'. But Williams, who had a remarkable capacity for survival, protested his innocence and assured Buckingham that 'I never harboured in this breast one thought of opposition to hurt Your Grace'. Buckingham had his own view about this, but he realised that if a Parliament was to be held, he would need the support of the Lord Keeper, who had useful contacts with the 'popular' leaders in both Houses. He therefore reconciled himself to Williams, but he could never feel confident that the Lord Keeper was wholeheartedly committed to him. Williams, indeed, was careful not to commit himself to anybody, for he was keenly aware that great men are liable

175

to fall and that when they do so they bring down their adherents with them. 'To whom a man is obliged for his raising,' he told John Hacket, his biographer, 'it is expected he should run the same hazard with him . . . . This consideration seriously taken, he was afraid of that lord's [Buckingham's] continuance – the title of a *favourite* being so inauspicious in almost all examples.'[19]

Middlesex may well have had similar doubts about Buckingham's ability to survive, and during the Duke's absence in Spain he had taken the opportunity to entrench himself firmly in the good opinion of the King. Although Middlesex owed his rapid rise to Buckingham, and had been brought into the charmed circle of the Villiers connexion, he was too ambitious and too powerful a figure in his own right to be content to remain a mere client. Even before Buckingham set off for Madrid there had been the Brett episode, which had created suspicions in the favourite's mind that the Treasurer was not altogether reliable. His doubts had increased while he was in Spain, for Middlesex was reported to be among those who were intriguing against him. It is hardly surprising, in these circumstances, that Middlesex viewed the prospect of the return of the Duke with something less than unalloyed pleasure, and asked his friend, the Duke of Richmond, 'to clear all doubts or informations (if any there were) either in the Prince or my Lord of Buckingham'. Richmond's mission was apparently successful, for there was no open break between Buckingham and the Treasurer, but the Duke continued to receive reports that Middlesex was attempting to undermine him. In December 1623 the Treasurer was said to have 'stayed the passing of some things granted to the Duke of Buckingham, which makes them look strange upon each other', while at the same time, Lord Falkland, the Deputy of Ireland and a client of the Duke, wrote to warn him of the 'labour and art' that were being used there 'to withdraw the affections and dependencies of the men of war and ministers of state of this poor kingdom from you'. Falkland himself – or so he assured the Duke – remained firm in his commitment to 'the patronage of . . . Saint George', but the fact that he chose to emphasise this and to declare his intention never to 'quit my Saint George's for that of Sir Lionel's, whatever other men do', was a reminder to Buckingham that the patronage empire which he had carefully built up in Ireland was under attack from the Lord Treasurer.[20]

It is against this background of suspicion that Middlesex's open opposition to the policy of war with Spain must be set. Buckingham needed to win him over, if he possibly could, but Middlesex had none of the flexibility for which Williams was notorious. He was a proud, stubborn man, conscious of his own great ability and of the service he had done the King, and apparently confident in the support of his royal master. Had he come to terms with the favourite, as Williams did, there is no reason to assume that he would have been hounded from office – his financial talents were too good to be wasted unnecessarily – but he chose to break rather than bend.

Pembroke, the Lord Chamberlain, presented an even greater challenge to Buckingham than that which came from Williams or Middlesex. The Lord Keeper and Lord Treasurer held high offices, but they had only limited influence outside these. Pembroke, on the other hand, was a great landowner, with a power base in Wales and the west of England which gave him control over a number of Parliamentary seats. Through his clients in the House of Commons Pembroke would be able to influence the course of debates, and his cooperation, or at least his neutrality, was therefore of the utmost importance to the Prince and Buckingham. He was also a respected and influential figure in the House of Lords, who could, if he chose, act as a rallying-point for anti-Buckingham feeling. Pembroke could not be browbeaten, like Williams, nor could he be attacked through his office, like Middlesex, for he was not a minister. He owed his post of Lord Chamberlain to the King, and James never gave any indication of withdrawing his trust. Pembroke was essentially a King's man, and for this reason he distrusted Buckingham's policy of trying to force the King's hand, even though he was in agreement with the ultimate aim of committing England to the anti-Habsburg cause. He was also suspicious of the Duke's motives, and like other prominent courtiers he resented the monopoly of favour which Buckingham seemed set to establish and thought it high time 'to take down his greatness'. But here he came up against Charles, whose position and authority as the King's son he respected, and it was Charles who worked for a reconciliation between Pembroke and the Duke. In January 1624 the Venetian ambassador reported the success of Charles's efforts, but while some sort of uneasy peace was established there was no real meeting of minds or hearts. In February one observer reported 'some passages betwixt the noble Duke and the Lord Chamberlain', and it was hardly surprising that when the Spanish ambassadors decided that the time had come for them to throw their weight into the scale against the Duke, it was to Pembroke, among others, that they turned for help.[21]

Pembroke's advice to Inojosa and his colleague was that they should hasten the return from Madrid of the Earl of Bristol, for only he could provide the detailed background knowledge and the leadership to rally those elements which were in favour of continuing the negotiations with Spain. In December 1623 Bristol had written to Buckingham from Madrid, saying that in view of the fact that 'the present estate of the King's affairs requireth the concurrency and cooperation of all his servants', he was ready to make a 'tender of my service'. Buckingham responded to this offer with a letter in which he set out the terms for a reconciliation. Bristol would have to acknowledge his errors – thereby implicitly admitting that he had been misled by the Spanish ministers and had given too favourable a picture of the state of negotiations – but once he had done so there would be no barrier to his return to favour. This Bristol refused to do. He would not accept that he had ever committed any errors, and even as late as February 1624, when he was on the point of returning home, he gave his opinion that if James still really desired the match 'and by the help and mediation of Spain hopeth for an accommodation of the business of the Prince Palatine, there is yet means of reconciling those differences wherein affairs seem to stand at present'. James was only too likely to grasp at such straws, and the English ambassador to Brussels was expressing a widely-held opinion when he told Carleton that 'upon the Earl of Bristol's return into

England . . . all will be patched and made whole again'.[22]

The Prince and Buckingham had scored a major success by persuading James's advisers to recommend him to summon Parliament, but there were many more obstacles to surmount. When Parliament met it would clearly wish to discuss foreign policy, but this was a matter that came within the sphere of the royal prerogative, and James had shown in 1621 how sensitive he was on this point. In order to prevent another clash between the King and the Commons, it would be best for the King to confront Parliament with a clear statement of his intentions, and, in particular, of his decision to break off the Spanish negotiations. But James was still hoping for a positive response to his latest messages to Philip IV and wanted, as always, to keep open as many options as possible. The Prince and Buckingham could take some comfort from the fact that the Spaniards, instead of responding to James's advances, had retreated into a sullen silence, for this meant that there was no very obvious alternative to the course of action they were advocating. But in mid-January the Spanish ambassadors in England came forward with new proposals, offering to return the Lower Palatinate by the following August and to meet all James's demands about military cooperation in order to put the settlement into effect.[23]

James was delighted with these overtures. Not so the Prince and Buckingham. After James had given them an account of Inojosa's conversations with him, 'they were observed to come out very sad, and presently the Duke went to his bed'. James, of course, assumed that these new offers represented a vindication of his policy of negotiation, but it was possible to interpret the Spanish response in quite a different way. The Prince and Buckingham presumably regarded this latest manoeuvre as evidence that their hard-line approach was beginning to pay off. If mere talk of war had driven the Spaniards to make conciliatory gestures, there was every hope that war itself would compel them to negotiate in all seriousness. Instead of drawing back and letting another campaigning season slip away without accomplishing anything, James should press ahead with the construction of an anti-Habsburg league at the same time as he prepared his forces by land and sea. This was the course of action which Charles urged his father to adopt, apparently with some success; but he and Buckingham still had to win the majority of the Council over to their point of view.[24]

It was no easy task, particularly for two young men who had very little experience of fighting political battles. Buckingham was a master of the art of patronage, but in matters of policy he had until recently been little more than his master's voice. Spain had been the school in which both the Prince and Buckingham had been forced to serve their apprenticeship in statecraft, but as yet they were mere tyros. The Venetian ambassador was not alone in fearing that they would 'come off badly in opposing the obstinate will of a very crafty King and the powerful arts of the most sagacious Spaniards', and throughout the early months of 1624 the Prince and Duke were under great strain as they developed their campaign, often on several fronts simultaneously. The Prince, who was reserved by nature, with great inner sources of strength gave no indication that the strain was telling on him; but Buckingham, who was of a more volatile temperament and wore his feelings in his face, was driven into explosions of anger that could have harmed his cause had not the Prince been at hand to heal the wounds he inflicted. Shortly after the Spanish ambassadors made their new propositions, Buckingham met Lord Belfast in the gallery at Whitehall and rounded upon him with the bitter question 'Are you turned too?' He also attacked Lord Keeper Williams for siding with his opponents. It was not simply a question of ingratitude, he insisted, nor would he have blamed Williams for opposing him on grounds of 'conscience or affection to His Majesty's service'. What stung him to anger was the belief that Williams, like a number of other Councillors, had allowed personal considerations to override public ones. Instead of binding King and nation together to face the menace of Habsburg power, Buckingham's opponents were, as he saw it, pursuing a personal vendetta against him; and his friends and clients, who ought to be rallying to his and the country's defence, were holding back or even joining in the attack.[25]

Buckingham was, of course, discounting the legacy of suspicion which his long association with pro-Spanish policies had bequeathed him, but many people, both at Court and in the country at large, shared his view that at this critical juncture, when crucial issues of religion and politics, war and peace, were to be debated and resolved, faction fighting should cease. William Pelham, for instance, a Lincolnshire country gentleman, was amazed when he heard of Pembroke's attacks on the Duke, 'by reason I was ever of opinion, with many more, that the Earl favoured not the Spanish cause'. The Venetian ambassador went further, and suggested, in conversation with the Lord Chamberlain, 'that it was necessary to preserve Buckingham as the enemy of the Spaniards if for nothing else, and it would be sheer waste of time to enquire into and punish his actions, prejudicing the principal business and playing the Spaniards' game. But I found him very set in his opinions, namely that they must consider internal foes before external ones.'[26]

Buckingham's critics claimed that he, and not the Prince, was responsible for the breakdown of the Spanish marriage negotiations. Buckingham resented this, not only on his own account but on Charles's as well, for, as he told Williams, it was to 'throw dirt in the Prince's teeth' to treat him as if he was a mere cipher. In fact, as many observers noted, the Prince was a changed man after his return from Spain, and it became clear during the early months of 1624 that in the close alliance between the Prince and the Duke, Charles was as much the leader as the led. He seemed to shed his fear of his father along with his love for the Infanta, and at the end of January he told James categorically that he would not hear either of friendship or alliance with Spain. The King seems to have been genuinely undecided what to do in face of this firm stand by his formerly bland and malleable son. His instincts told him to keep the negotiations going, but he clearly could not force Charles into a Spanish marriage, and there was little point in pursuing a policy which was bound to be abortive. He chose, therefore, to let events take their course, and instead of returning to London to give a lead to his Councillors he stayed in the country, enjoying the delights of the chase in Buckingham's company. It was left to the Prince to take the chair at meetings of the Council, and he used the full weight of his position and authority to rally its members behind him. The Venetian ambassador summed up the situation with his usual acuteness: 'The balance of affairs leans to the side of the Prince; while Buckingham remains at Newmarket to prevent any harm, he stays here to achieve the good. Thus they both cooperate towards the same end, although with different functions, yet with a good understanding.'[27]

By the end of January 1624 the Prince's authority had prevailed, and the Council sent James its advice that he should make no response to the latest overtures from Spain but instead break off negotiations. However, it was still not clear if the formal break would be made by the King in Council or whether it would have to await the meeting of Parliament, which was now drawing near. Tillières, the French ambassador, gave it as his opinion that the Prince and Duke were uncertain which course to follow, but it seems more likely that Buckingham had already decided on taking the issue to Parliament and letting that body decide. One reason for this was his belief that the animosity felt towards him by many members of the Council would prevent them from arriving at a decision in accord with English interests. He was also determined that if they went ahead with an enquiry into his conduct, 'the greatest council in England may be judge of it, and the like he wisheth for other men's actions'. But the most important consideration was that Parliament would have to provide the money for war, and by engaging members at this early stage he could hope to win their confidence and open their purses. This would be no easy task for the favourite, who had come under heavy attack in the previous parliament, but in statecraft, as in so many other things, Buckingham was a quick learner. He was now the champion of war, which seemed to be a popular cause, and he planned to present his case to Parliament in the most dramatic and effective way. In other words he intended to revive that very close cooperation between government and Parliament which had been the secret of Elizabeth I's success. There was, however, an important difference, in that he was aiming to rally members in support of his own and the Prince's policy rather than the King's. Whether he realised it or not, it was a hazardous undertaking.[28]

III

Parliament was formally opened by the King on 19 February 1624, and Buckingham's first major intervention came five days later, on the afternoon of 24 February, when he addressed a joint meeting of Lords and Commons in the Banqueting House of the palace of Whitehall. The great room had been specially scaffolded for the occasion, and the serried ranks of members looked down on a long table, at one end of which sat the Prince, and on either side the principal lords. At the Prince's request Buckingham gave a long, carefully constructed speech in which he surveyed the whole course of the negotiations between England and Spain during the previous decade. His account has been described as 'an exercise in apologetics rather than a systematic review', but such a judgement is unduly harsh. There was only one major respect in which Buckingham told considerably less than the truth. He did not reveal the far-reaching concessions which the Prince had been prepared to make on behalf of English catholics in order to secure the Infanta. This was not simply to spare the Prince's blushes; it was essential that the Prince's honour should not be sullied, nor his judgement impugned, at this critical moment when he was breaking out from his chrysalis and showing hitherto unsuspected powers of leadership.[29]

Buckingham did not, of course, cite every letter that had passed between the courts of Spain and England – though the Lord Keeper, at his command, read summaries or extracts of the more important ones. But if his account is compared with other evidence, including that of his own letters home as well as those or Bristol and Aston, it becomes clear that while there were differences of emphasis there were no major divergences. Like any politician Buckingham put his own and the Prince's actions in the most favourable light, but he had no need to distort the truth in order to demonstrate the depths of Spanish duplicity since the facts were overwhelmingly on his side. It was in the light of this demonstration of Spanish untrustworthiness that he called on the assembled members to decide whether to advise James to continue with the negotiations or to recommend that 'these treaties set aside, His Majesty were best to trust in his own strength and to stand upon his own feet'.[30]

Buckingham's speech made a deep impression on the members of both Houses who had crowded in to hear it. He was now, in Hacket's phrase, 'the Alcibiades that pleased the commonwealth', and his popularity soared even higher when it became known that the Spanish ambassadors had protested to James against certain passages in his speech. He had, they said, used language about the King of Spain which was deeply dishonourable. If similar remarks had been made in Spain about the King of England, the offender would have lost his head. Buckingham promptly reported this to the Lords and called upon them to judge whether he had been guilty of any offence. The change of attitude towards him on the part of his former critics and enemies was immediately apparent. Pembroke declared his complete satisfaction with Buckingham's narration; Archbishop Abbot praised the Duke for 'his pains and hazard to bring these things to light'; while Southampton declared that Buckingham would have 'deserved very ill if he had shortened his narration'. The upshot of the debate was a unanimous resolution that Buckingham 'did deliver nothing in his said narration but what was fit for him to do and the matter led him unto'.[31]

At the Earl of Warwick's suggestion, the House of Commons was officially informed of the Lords' action and invited to join with them. In the debate that followed Sir Robert Phelips expressed the hope that Buckingham's head would remain on his shoulders much longer than those of his enemies, while Sir Edward Coke gave it as his opinion that 'never any man deserved better of his King and country'. The Lower House then added its own voice to that of the Lords by resolving that Buckingham should be 'acquitted from all blame for anything that was delivered by him at his last narration before both Houses; and that he hath merited a great deal of thanks of this House and the whole commonwealth for the same'. These resolutions of both Houses were, of course, a triumph for Buckingham. Not only had he turned the Spanish ambassadors' initiative to his own advantage; he had also silenced all those who had doubts about his motivation. Moreover he had demonstrated to the King the massive support he could line up behind him in opposition to the continuance of negotiations with Spain.[32]

Parliament had been summoned not simply to advise the King on what direction he should take in foreign policy, but also to strengthen his hand by giving him the means to fight if need be. Simonds D'Ewes was of the opinion that 'all men now seeing the treaty of the Spanish match and the peaceable restitution of the Palatinate broken off, verily hoped to see that recovered and the gospel again settled in Germany by the armies and assistances of the King of Great Britain'; but although James and his people were at one in their desire to secure the restoration of the Palatinate, they were widely apart in their views on how best to achieve this. The Commons were no more enthusiastic than they had been in 1621 about the idea of a military campaign in Germany. In view of English inexperience in land warfare, such an operation was likely to consume a great deal of money to little purpose. It would be far better to fight a war at sea, where England was strong and her enemies were weak. The Commons were convinced that the armies of the Emperor and the Duke of Bavaria, like those of Spain herself, were only kept in action by the bullion which flowed across the Atlantic to Seville from the silver mines of the New World. If this artery could be severed, the pressure on the Palatinate would be immediately relieved. And even if the capture or destruction of the Plate Fleet was too much for the English to accomplish, there was the certainty of financial gain from the letters of marque which the Lord Admiral was authorised to issue in wartime and which gave the holders permission to commit acts of piracy against enemy vessels. A sea war, in short, could be largely self-financing or even run at a profit, and thereby relieve the pressure on taxpayers. This was particularly important in view of the continuing economic depression. As Sir Edward Coke reminded the Commons at the opening of the 1624 session, the country had grown faint with 'want of trade and traffic, which is the lifeblood of the state . . . . And from the decay of that arises the want of money, which is the sinews of the body of a commonwealth. And from this want proceeds the third, which is want of labour and employment for the meaner people.'[33]

All decisions about strategy rested ultimately with the King, for although James had asked Parliament for advice on the particular issue of the Spanish negotiations, he had not committed himself to accept it, nor had he abandoned his prerogative right to map out the direction in which English policy should move. James was determined that he would not go to war unless and until he was assured not simply of adequate financial backing but also of the firm support of other anti-Habsburg states. Buckingham hoped that the Parliament which had just opened would reassure James on the one score, while negotiations with the Dutch and the French would satisfy him on the other. But neither of these projects would ripen overnight, and meanwhile the King was not prepared to sanction anything other than a limited military operation in the Palatinate itself, which he hoped would achieve his objective without involving him in general hostilities.

The maritime and land strategies were not mutually exclusive. Buckingham was already thinking in terms of a sea war against Spain, in association with the Dutch, but he was also planning a military expedition to the Palatinate. This was not simply in order to retain James's support, although it was true that without the King's approval he could do nothing. Buckingham also recognised that a military operation of this nature would be a way of demonstrating to the world that the long period of English inactivity had come to an end. And if other states – France, for instance – could be brought in as active partners, a firm foundation would have been laid on which to construct a league of anti-Habsburg powers. Buckingham, however, had to tread very carefully. Through his contacts with the leaders of the 'popular' party he must have been made aware of the fact that the Commons were not likely to provide substantial sums of money if they thought these would be thrown away in the Palatinate. Yet he knew only too well that if he campaigned openly for the sort of maritime war which the Commons wanted, he would antagonise James. He therefore had to treat the Commons much as he treated the Dutch and the French, working to some extent underhand and giving only nods and winks to indicate the directions in which he wanted to move. What he hoped for was an early vote of supply, preferably with no strings attached, since this would reassure James and make him more amenable to the idea of war. And once war had actually broken out, the lingering suspicions that clouded relations between the King on the one hand and Parliament and his potential foreign allies on the other, would, so the Duke hoped, be quickly dispersed.

Speedy and decisive action was, as Buckingham saw it, the key to success, and it was probably no coincidence that when the Commons began their debate on foreign policy the only two speakers who had any obvious connexions with the Duke took up these themes. Sir Miles Fleetwood, who was widely regarded as a client of Buckingham, called on the House 'to be humble suitors to His Majesty to proceed in no further treaty', while Sir John Eliot – who was Buckingham's Vice-Admiral for Devon and had only recently been released from prison by his patron's intercession – told members that it was now 'fitter for us to do than speak'. Let them press for the setting out of the fleet and vote an immediate supply of money. On this same first day of March, 1624, Buckingham was putting forward similar arguments in the Upper House, where he reminded his hearers that 'if we should lose the benefit of this spring, it would be irrecoverable'. He called on the Lords to appoint a committee to survey the state of munitions and of the forts, and to take appropriate measures to redress any defects – a proposition which the House willingly assented to. The Lords also confirmed the order which Buckingham

183

had issued, as Lord Admiral, to stop the sailing of a number of ships belonging to the East India Company. These vessels, or at least their crews, might be needed for defence against a Spanish invasion attempt, and even if this did not materialise the ban on sailing would encourage the company, one of the richest in England, to come to some arrangement with Buckingham about the prize money which he was claiming from them for their operations against the Portuguese in the Far East. Whether in fact his rights as Lord Admiral extended so far across the seas was a moot point, but money was desperately needed for the naval expedition which the Duke was now planning and he was not over-scrupulous about the means by which to raise it.[34]

The outcome of the Commons' debate was a decision to petition the King to break off negotiations with Spain. As soon as the Lords heard of this they proposed a conference to arrange for combined action by both Houses. The initiative for this came from the Prince and Buckingham, who were working in conjunction with a small group of lords which included not only friends of the Duke, such as Carlisle and Sir Edward Sackville (now Earl of Dorset), but also former enemies, in particular Oxford and Southampton. None of these peers was a minister, yet because of their close relationship with the Prince and Duke they could effectively by-pass such figures as the Lord Keeper and Lord Treasurer who had the nominal responsibility for presenting royal policy. In 1621 Buckingham and the King had stood firm against attacks by the 'popular' party in both Houses, and in general terms the division of opinion had been between Court and country. But in 1624 there was a state of undeclared civil war within the Court itself, and Buckingham, who had from the beginning of his career showed a remarkable capacity for mastering techniques, now used the methods of the 'opposition' of 1621 for his own purposes. His power base was the House of Lords rather than the Commons, for although he had links with influential figures in the Lower House, who acted in effect as 'undertakers' for him, he could not exert a sufficient degree of control over them (or they over the House) to ensure more than general agreement with the broad outlines of his strategy.[35] For the working out of tactics he depended upon the Lords, where he and his associates, with the authority of the Prince behind them, could usually sway the House. In this smaller, more intimate assembly they could use much greater finesse in timing and adapting their proposals to the prevailing mood than would have been possible in the Lower House. The Lords also had the advantage of exerting considerable influence over the Commons, both as a body and as individuals. The Upper House still had great prestige, and individual peers had their clients in the Commons – men who sat for boroughs they controlled or held offices which were in their gift. The Lower House was not, of course, a subservient body, nor were all its members clients of aristocratic patrons, but the Lords were well placed to restrain it, if they wished, and, to some extent, to guide it.

The joint committee of both Houses decided, at the Prince's suggestion, to ask Buckingham to arrange an audience for them with the King, at which they could proffer their advice to him about breaking off the treaties. But James was unwilling to receive the deputation. He had been in touch with the

Spanish ambassadors, and was veering once again towards his former policy of achieving a settlement by negotiations with Philip IV. Buckingham was very alarmed when he heard about this development. The King's wavering threatened not only the working out of the anti-Habsburg strategy to which Buckingham was committed, but also the very basis of his power, for the Spanish agent had been admitted to Court by the Earl of Kellie, who, in Weldon's vivid phrase, 'was the truest alarum to give warning of the downfall of a favourite'. Buckingham, who never concealed his anger, wrote to upbraid the King for his actions, but James accused him of using 'cruel, Catonic words' and of looking more to the rising sun of Charles than to the King his maker. A draft letter from Buckingham to James, hastily written and with numerous alterations, shows how perturbed the Duke was. 'If I should give myself leave to speak my own thoughts,' he protested, 'they are so many that though the quality of them should not grieve you, coming from one you wilfully and unjustly deject, yet the number of them are so many that I should not give over till I had troubled you. Therefore I will only tie myself to that which shall be my last and speedy refuge, to pray the Almighty to increase your joys . . . .'[36]

On 4 March Buckingham decided to go to Theobalds, where the King was hunting, to plead his case in person. He was reluctant to leave Westminster, but he dare not let the King slip into the embraces of the Spaniards once again, and so he contented himself with addressing the joint committee before he left and reminding them of the need to prepare the fleet. He spoke

of the vast ambitions of Spain after the western monarchy, which in part, and a great one, they had effected. But what remained must be gotten with arms – arms retained by money; money with the Indies; the profit of the Indies must come by sea; and if the King and the Low Countries join, they shall be masters of the sea and Spain's monarchy will have a stop.

Buckingham clearly hoped that by indicating his approval of a sea war against Spain he would encourage the Commons to be realistic and open-handed when they came to vote supply.[37]

The Duke's visit to Theobalds was successful, for the King not only agreed to receive the Parliamentary deputation but also based his reply to their message upon the suggestions which Buckingham had drawn up. Among these was a promise that if the Commons voted money for the recovery of the Palatinate, they should be allowed to appoint their own commissioners to see that it was employed for this, and no other purpose. However, James did not commit himself, in his reply, to accept the advice that had been tendered to him. He was not, as yet, satisfied in honour or conscience that he should break with Spain, and in any case his financial difficulties were so acute that he could not envisage war without the assurance of Parliamentary support. It was now up to the Commons to decide how much offer, and on 11 March the members resolved that once they had received a formal assurance that the negotiations with Spain were at an end, they would be ready 'to assist His Majesty with both our persons and abilities in a Parliamentary course'.[38]

The King, however, was not impressed by such unspecific promises, even though both Houses joined in making them. His attitude was almost certainly similar to that of Kellie, who described how members of Parliament 'will have him to discharge all treaties [i.e. break off negotiations], whereupon must follow a war; but as yet they will condescend to no other help but by the ordinary course of subsidies in Parliment, which is not able to do that business'. On 14 March, therefore, the King asked for a specific vote of five subsidies and ten fifteenths for the 'great business' plus one subsidy and two fifteenths to be paid every year until his debts had been wiped out. Since a subsidy was worth about £70,000 and a fifteenth £30,000, the King was demanding, in effect, about half a million pounds – a realistic sum in view of the costs of waging war in the seventeenth century, but infinitely greater than anything the Commons had ever considered.[39]

The Prince and Buckingham were shocked by the King's forthright and uncompromising reply to the message which the Houses had sent him. According to the Venetian ambassador 'they turned pale, and the Prince never uttered a word the whole day'. But later on, after he had recovered from the shock, Buckingham went to see the King and persuaded James to allow his answer to be modified in a way that would be more acceptable to Parliament. Armed with the King's permission he appeared before the joint committee again on the next day, 16 March, and worked out with the members the detailed modifications which he agreed to submit to the King. And in order that there should be no doubt this time about the King's response, he sent him a letter, addressed as always to 'Dear Dad and Gossip', in which he asked him for 'your plain and resolute answer, whether, if your people do resolve to give you a royal assistance as to the number of six subsidies and fifteenths, with a promise after, in case of necessity, to assist you with their lives and fortunes, whether then you will not accept it and their counsel to break the match, with the other treaties'. If James was agreeable to this, he asked him for permission to inform some of the members underhand and to reassure them that if they voted the sum required they would not thereby be putting an end to Parliaments by enabling the King to live without them; on the contrary, they would be making James so in love with Parliaments that he would be only too willing to call them together frequently to reform abuses and redress grievances.[40]

Not long after writing this letter, Buckingham made a lightning dash to Court. Perhaps he feared that without his own presence to reinforce the arguments of his letter, James would give way to other counsels. His stratagem was successful, and on 17 March he was able to inform the two Houses that the King had accepted the modifications to his answer which they had proposed. As a consequence, James had dropped his demand for regular payments to wipe out the crown debts and now wanted the Houses to vote six subsidies and twelve fifteenths [ca.£780,000] for the war. This was a great sum, but they would be able to control the expenditure of it through their own commissioners, and James promised them that if they went ahead with this supply, he would accept their advice and break the treaties.[41]

Once again Buckingham became a more or less passive spectator while the Commons debated the question of whether, and how much, to give. It soon became clear that they were unwilling to commit themselves to vote the entire sum that James had demanded, but they accepted the suggestion of one of the Privy Councillors in the House, Sir Thomas Edmondes, that they should vote half to begin with. It was therefore resolved, on 20 March, 'that after His Majesty shall have been pleased to declare himself for the utter dissolution and discharge of the two treaties [i.e. of marriage and restitution] . . . in pursuit of their advice given to His Majesty, and towards support of the war which is likely to ensue, and more particularly for those four points proposed by His Majesty — namely the defence of this realm, the securing of Ireland, the assistance of our neighbours the states of the United Provinces and other His Majesty's friends and allies, and the setting-out of His Majesty's Royal Navy — [the Commons] will grant, for the present, three subsidies and three fifteenths . . . to be paid unto the hands and expended by the direction of such committees or commissioners as shall hereafter be agreed on in this present session of Parliament'.[42]

Buckingham made yet another journey to Court, to arrange an audience at which the two Houses could give the King a formal proffer of their support. He took the draft declaration with him, to make sure that James should clearly understand what was in it. The King made no objection to the fact that he was being offered only half what he had asked for, but criticised a phrase referring to the necessity of a war for the defence of the 'true religion', on the grounds that this might deter catholic states from joining him. This was a sound point, and when Buckingham reported it to the Lords they agreed to advise the Commons to delete the phrase. The Commons did so, albeit reluctantly, and a few days later a delegation representing both Houses waited on the King at Whitehall and presented him with the declaration. At the same time they gave him a formal assurance that the sum they had resolved upon was but the 'first fruits of our hearty oblation' and that for the future he could rest confident in the knowledge that 'if you shall be engaged in a real war, we, your loyal and loving subjects, will never fail to assist Your Majesty in a Parliamentary way'. This was a point taken up by James in his reply, for at the same time as he announced the acceptance of their advice to break off the treaties he also made it clear that he would be committed to war only to the extent that the two Houses fulfilled their promise to assist him. As for the conduct of the war, that must be left to him alone. 'I desire you to understand, I must have a faithful and secret council of war that must not be ordered by a multitude, for so my designs might be discovered beforehand. A penny of this money shall not be bestowed but in the sight of your own committees. But whether I shall send twenty thousand or ten thousand, whether by sea or by land, east or west, by diversion or otherwise, by invasion upon the Bavarian or the Emperor — you must leave that to the King.'[43]

As the news spread that James had agreed to break off negotiations with Spain and prepare for war, there was widespread jubilation. The Duke was now the hero of the hour, and Conway's son was speaking little more than the truth when he declared that 'never before did . . . one man . . . have so much love of the King, Prince and people'. Buckingham had indeed been extraordinarily successful in bringing King and Parliament together in a commitment to war, but all his skill could not create a total identity of interest between them. The King had explicitly reserved to himself the right to direct operations, and he had made it clear that the three subsidies would have to be followed by others. As he told the delegates, their grant would be sufficient 'at least to make a good beginning of the war', but 'when the end will be, God knows'. Yet members of the Commons were aware that even if they were prepared to vote more and more subsidies, the country would be extremely reluctant to pay them. They pinned their hopes, therefore, on a speedy victory, and although their enthusiasm for war was genuine enough, they preferred not to contemplate the magnitude of the sums that might be needed to engage in effective combat with the greatest power-bloc in Europe.[44]

On 26 March Parliament went into recess for Easter, leaving Buckingham free, for the moment, to concentrate on the other major plank of his policy, the negotiation of a French marriage for Prince Charles. His friend and confidant, Sir Henry Rich, Viscount Kensington, had arrived in Paris in mid-February, and had sent a glowing account of Henrietta Maria, 'a lovely, sweet young creature . . . [whose] shape is perfect'. There was some suspicion at the French court that James was more concerned to extort better terms from the Spaniards than to marry his son to a French princess, but the queen mother was in favour of the marriage, 'for she hath now a clear sight of the pretensions of the King of Spain unto the monarchy of Christendom'. Her opinion was shared by La Vieuville, the chief minister of Louis XIII, who agreed with Kensington that as the power and ambition of Spain increased, so it became ever more necessary for England and France to join together. By early March Kensington was able to report that the French were ready to enter into negotiations. All he needed now was a formal commission empowering him to treat. Only the King could issue this, however, and it may be that James was reluctant to trust the entire course of the negotiations to Kensington simply because he was so close to Buckingham. When, therefore, he issued his commission at the end of March, he joined Carlisle with Kensington. They were to negotiate both a marriage for Charles and a treaty of friendship. Kensington had earlier given his opinion that they should begin with the marriage question, for this would create a good atmosphere, but the Prince, no doubt recalling his experience in Spain, thought the treaty of alliance should come first.[45]

February had also seen the arrival in England of the Dutch ambassadors, sent over in response to the covert but emphatic prompting of Buckingham. They were given an audience by the King and Prince, but before they could wait on the Duke, Buckingham went to see them, a signal mark of favour that indicated the importance he attached to good relations between the two states. He also told Dudley Carleton's nephew that the ambassadors were welcome 'and that there was no cause to fear but that we should agree together very well and roundly, unless the fault were in themselves'. But negotiations went ahead at a snail's pace, for Buckingham could do nothing until the King had

188

been brought to the point of declaring his intention to break off the treaties with Spain, and even then James, with his habitual caution, insisted on very favourable terms for the English alliance. By mid-April the Dutch ambassadors were so disheartened that they were only just prevented from packing their bags and going home. Commissioners, of whom Buckingham was one, were thereupon appointed to conduct negotiations, and a month later agreement was reached on a treaty of mutual defence. Nothing was said about offensive operations, but as early as the end of March Buckingham had discussed the possibility with the ambassadors, and one well-informed observer had commented that, although the King was opposed to the idea, 'the Prince and my Lord Duke will want of their will if they gain not that point also ere long'. Buckingham made a sudden dash to Chatham, ostensibly to review the defences there, but also to see what ships might be available for a joint expedition with the Dutch.[46]

IV

When Parliament reassembled on 1 April, Buckingham told the Lords about his visit to the fleet, and also informed them 'that the King of Spain had now in a readiness a far greater and stronger navy than that of '88 [i.e. the Armada]'. Parliament had agreed to vote supply for setting out the fleet, but the actual subsidy bill had not yet been prepared, let alone passed. Even after it became law the subsidies would not begin to flow into the Exchequer immediately, and Buckingham was of the opinion that other means would have to be employed to raise money at once, so that effective action could be taken before the year was out. He therefore proposed 'that certain monied men may be dealt with to disburse such a sum of money as for the present is requisite, and they to be secured for the repayment thereof by Parliament, out of the subsidies now intended to be granted'. The Lords agreed to inform the Lower House of the Duke's suggestion and ask for their reaction. At the same time Buckingham announced to the Lords, and through them the Commons, that when the Spanish ambassador was at Court the King told him of his intention to break off negotiations; and that James had also sent a despatch to Sir Walter Aston in Spain confirming this and instructing him to inform Philip IV.[47]

Buckingham's report about Spanish naval preparations and his suggestions for anticipating the vote of supply were given to the Commons on 1 April, not long after he had spoken in the Lords. Sir John Eliot, who had doubtless been briefed by Buckingham, stressed that this was a matter of great importance, and that no time should be wasted. The House was far from full, however, and at Sir Robert Phelip's suggestion it was agreed to postpone discussion of the matter until the following day. Phelips also indicated his own sense of priorities when he reminded members that 'Spain can do us no harm unless he have a party here in England' and called for a debate on the need to enforce the penal laws against the catholics. The Commons never, in fact, took more than passing notice of Buckingham's proposal about anticipating the subsidies. Had they accepted his suggestion they would have established a precedent that might subsequently be invoked to their disadvantage, and in any case their main concern was with the religious issue. This was not as peripheral as it might seem. James was clearly thinking in terms of military operations in Germany to recover the Palatinate – operations which need not lead to war with Spain. The Commons, on the other hand, wanted the war to be directed principally against Spain, and by making it first and foremost a war of religion they would be going a long way towards achieving their aims.[48]

The Commons drew up a petition against recusants, but as soon as James heard of this he sent word to Conway to hold up the despatch of his letter to Aston. He was determined not to be pushed into a war of religion, and if the Commons tried to force his hand by making the subsidy bill dependent upon his acceptance of their petition, he wanted to be free to turn once again to Spain. As he told Conway, 'if I may be sure that they mean to keep their promises to me, let the packet go on; otherwise it were no reason I should be bound and they leap free and leave me naked and without help'. When the Prince heard of his father's reaction he concentrated his efforts on making sure that the Commons' petition was substantially modified by the Lords, and in this he was successful. But a price had to be paid. Part of it was the abandonment of Buckingham's proposal about anticipating supply, for when the Lord Keeper reminded the Upper House about this on 5 April, the Prince suggested that no further action should be taken until agreement had been reached with the Commons about modifications to their petition. The House followed his lead, and reduced the petition, in effect, to a request that the existing laws should be put into effect. This was a point which Buckingham had emphasised: 'petition for the laws in force,' he advised the House, 'and avoid the objection of a war of religion'. He was strongly supported by Pembroke, who reminded his fellow peers that since the King had been careful 'not to give occasion to make this a war of religion, we ... [should] be careful not to move him to do any such act'.[49]

The other part of the price which had to be paid was a formal declaration by the Prince to the House of Lords 'that whensoever it should please God to bestow upon him any lady that were popish, she should have no further liberty but for her own family [i.e. household] and no advantage to the recusants at home'. Such a statement was well timed, for rumours about the concessions the Prince had been prepared to make in Spain had created suspicions in the minds of many members of the Commons that the same thing might happen all over again with France. These suspicions go a long way towards explaining the harsh tone of the Commons' petition on religion, for it was deliberately designed to restrict the freedom of manoeuvre of those who were negotiating the French marriage. The Prince was not opposed to such a restriction. Indeed, the original suggestion that it should be made came from Sir Robert Heath, the Solicitor-General, who was one of Buckingham's confidants. From the Prince's point of view, any Parliamentary ban on concessions to English catholics as part of a treaty for a French marriage would strengthen his bargaining position. This was a point well taken by Tillières, the French ambassador, who told La Vieuville that the English intended to trap the French negotiators in a stranglehold ['*tenir le pied sur la gorge*'].[50]

The Prince's manoeuvre was successful in so far as it helped persuade the Commons to accept the Lords' redrafting of their petition. Now that the two Houses had agreed on a text, the petition was ready for presentation, and the ceremony took place on 23 April. The King was in a conciliatory mood and agreed to do all and more than was asked. As for the request that no concessions to English catholics should be included in any future marriage treaty, he assured the delegates that 'I will be careful that no such condition be hereafter foisted in upon any other treaty whatsoever'.[51]

No sooner had the two Houses reached agreement on the question of religion than the Prince suggested that the Lords should 'put the Commons in mind that we be not now slack and not forward to proceed about subsidies'. He was immediately seconded by the Duke, who argued that 'it may breed a jealousy in the King of our slackness in it'. There were many members of the Lower House, however, who feared that James had not yet finally cut the links with Spain, and who wanted more than the assurances which Buckingham and the Prince had given them. In mid-April, therefore, Buckingham wrote to his 'Dear Dad and Gossip' to tell him 'that there is a jealousy raised in the Lower House how that yet the two treaties are not absolutely broken off. The Prince, Hamilton, Pembroke, Doncaster and myself, who have all seen your despatch to the King of Spain, thinks [*sic*] if that was showed to them that it would fully content them.' He therefore asked James's permission to communicate the substance of the despatch to Parliament, and James agreed. Consequently, on 17 April, Buckingham addressed a conference of both Houses and gave them 'a report of the King's letter', which Sir Edwin Sandys described as 'very exact and every word of great weight'. The Duke then urged members not to 'look for any more public or manifest declaration' but to concentrate upon the important business of providing the sinews of war. 'The King had granted divers commissions to treat with his ancient allies, [the] Low Countries, Venice, France and Denmark. Further, [he] was appointing a council of war to manage this great business.' The Spaniards were mustering their forces in Flanders, and Ireland was threatened. Now was the time for Parliament to provide for the nation's defence.[52]

Some days later the Commons took up the question of supply. Sir Robert Heath, on Buckingham's behalf, urged them to speedy action, and when some members still expressed reservations, Secretary Conway intervened to remind them of 'the necessity of going on with this. Very necessary. Delay will be very dangerous.' The House therefore gave a first reading to the subsidy bill on 22 April. There were now obvious signs that preparations for war were really going ahead. On 15 April the King named the commissioners who were to conduct formal negotiations with the Dutch, and the Venetian ambassador reported the current gossip that a joint expedition against Spain was planned, with the Dutch contributing twenty ships to a fleet of seventy sail under the flag of Frederick and Elizabeth. On 14 April the German mercenary commander, Count Ernst von Mansfeld, had arrived in London. D'Ewes described Mansfeld as a man who 'had done great service to the protestant party' and would have done even more to stop the 'bloody and tyrannous conquests' of the Emperor if only he had had the money. Mansfeld was treated with great consideration, and was lodged at St James's Palace in the apartments original-ly intended for the Infanta. His brief mission was highly successful, for the King agreed to give him command of a force of ten thousand infantry and three thousand horse, to be employed, under the joint direction of England and France, 'for re-establishing the public peace and recovering the Palatinate'.[53]

The warm reception given to Mansfeld during his brief visit to England was designed to achieve a number of different aims. It served, as Dudley Carleton told his uncle, the ambassador at the Hague, 'to despite the Spaniards so much the more and give contentment to the Parliament'. It demonstrated to France that the English were serious in their intention to break with the Spaniards and engage in military operations against the House of Habsburg, at least in Germany. It also enabled the Prince and Buckingham to commit the King further and faster than he would normally have gone, since the opportunity of intervening directly in the Palatinate was too good a one for him to let slip.[54]

V

The Spanish ambassadors in England, and their friends at Court, were by this time thoroughly alarmed. They had earlier regarded Buckingham as a political lightweight who would never be able to push a suspicious King and a wary Parliament into a warlike posture, but now they turned their broadsides on him. In early April the ambassadors informed James that Buckingham in-tended to shut him away in one of his country houses, and take over the direction of government in person. This was why he had 'reconciled himself to all the popular men of the state and drawn them forth out of prisons, re-straints and confinements'. If James wished to preserve his authority intact he should take action immediately 'by cutting off so dangerous and ungrateful an affector of greatness and popularity as the Duke was'. These charges were skilfully designed to arouse the King's anger and suspicion, for James was always very susceptible to fears that his authority was being challenged, and regarded 'popularity' as a grave crime. He told the Spanish agent that while he could not believe that the Duke was, in fact, affecting popularity he had had 'good cause to suspect [him] of late'. James also expressed some concern at the influence which Buckingham exerted over the Prince. When Charles set out for Spain, said James, 'he was as well affected to that nation as heart could desire, and as well disposed as any son in Europe; but now he was strangely carried away with rash and youthful counsels and followed the humour of Buckingham, who had he knew not how many devils within him since that journey'.[55]

The Spanish charges against Buckingham were so skilfully woven around a core of truth that James could not simply dismiss them as unfounded. Yet how could he proceed against a man who was the hero of the hour, 'St George on horseback', the darling of Prince, Parliament and people? The King needed allies, but they were not easy to come by. Buckingham had won over the 'popular' leaders, and Pembroke and Hamilton were now his political associates, if not his friends. As for Lord Keeper Williams, who might at one time have taken a stand against the Duke, he had been frightened off at the beginning of the Parliament when a number of petitions against him, said to be prompted by 'a great name', were presented to the House of Commons. This left only the Lord Treasurer, Middlesex, who had refused to abandon his opposition to the war policy which Buckingham was pursuing. The King's support, as well as the key office which he held, made Middlesex potentially a dangerous opponent, and Buckingham's fears can hardly have been allayed by the news that in late March Arthur Brett had returned from his voluntary exile in France. Early in April the Venetian ambassador reported that 'the Lord Treasurer is almost openly trying to oust Buckingham, assisted secretly by the Earl of Arundel. The method is by bringing forward a young kinsman of the Treasurer.' Shortly afterwards the King had a long conversation with Padre Maestro, who had been sent over by Philip IV with new propositions, and there was clearly more than an even chance that James, with the encouragement of Middlesex, might succumb once again to Spanish blandishments. It was to prevent this that Buckingham now decided to overthrow the Lord Treasurer, and it was one of his clients, Sir Miles Fleetwood, who, on 5 April, laid charges against Middlesex before the House of Commons. This move was also calculated to increase Buckingham's popularity, since the Lord Treasurer's greed and arrogance, as well as the firmness with which he enforced his policy of retrenchment, had made him much hated. It would, in addition, prove to the Commons that they could pursue their role of inquisitors-general of the nation at the same time as they cooperated with the Prince and Duke to prepare the way for war.[56]

Buckingham no doubt intended and assumed that he would be present in Parliament to watch over the development of the impeachment proceedings against the Lord Treasurer at the same time as he kept up the pressure on the two Houses to push the subsidy bill through its remaining stages. But the strain on him was enormous, for as well as attending to Parliamentary affairs – a full-time occupation in itself – he was engaged in negotiations with the Dutch and with Mansfeld. He was also actively supervising preparations for the naval expedition which, in the absence of Parliamentary supplies, he had largely to finance out of his own pocket – for as Kellie told Mar on 12 April, the 'Admiral has laid out of his own monies £15,000 for preparing the Navy, but as yet never one penny subsidy granted but in the general'. In addition to these preoccupations, Buckingham still had to oversee the workings of the patronage system of which he was the nerve centre, and was at this moment engaged in a highly complex operation which was designed to give the Provostship of Eton College to Sir Henry Wotton (in return for his twenty years of service as ambassador at Venice) while making alternative provision for Sir William Beecher, to whom Buckingham had originally promised the post. Buckingham really had more business on hand than he could cope with, but there was no one else on whom he could rely, for he alone had the prestige, the authority, and the degree of commitment that could overcome all obstacles.[57]

While Buckingham was not afraid of hard work and responsibility – and indeed welcomed them – the burden of so many affairs was bound to take its toll, particularly as he was deprived of the support of the King which had previously sustained him. James had publicly declared his disbelief in the accusations made against Buckingham by the Spanish ambassadors, but the fact that he had ordered his Privy Councillors to take a solemn oath that they had not been involved in any plot to overthrow him suggested quite the contrary. And although relations between James and the favourite were outwardly friendly, they were lacking in their old intimacy. This affected Buckingham profoundly, for whether he thought of the King as a surrogate father, a wise counsellor, or simply a doting admirer, he was deeply attached to him. The suspicion that the King's love for him was dead or dying was one further cause for worry at a time when he already had more than enough. Although he was a vigorous young man of thirty-two, his constitution was not strong, and at moments of crisis his health was liable to give way. There were signs that this was now about to happen, for on 7 April one observer reported that 'these two days he hath been ill at ease, and yesterday was let blood to prevent a fever'.[58]

Buckingham retired to New Hall for a brief stay, and recovered sufficiently to return to London. But on 20 April Padre Maestro had a long audience with the King, at James's request, during the course of which he made further and even more serious charges against the Duke. This time he alleged that Buckingham had broken off the Spanish match in return for an offer from the Elector Frederick to marry his son to the Duke's daughter, Mary Villiers. And now, by persuading Charles to make a public declaration that he would not consent to any improvement in the treatment of English catholics as a condition of a future marriage treaty, Buckingham had effectively ruled out the possibility of a French match. Charles would therefore remain unwed, and the throne would in due course pass to the Palatine. After Frederick died, his son would inherit the crown of England, and Mary Villiers would become Queen. There had for some time been rumours about a marriage between Buckingham's daughter and Frederick's son, and it is not inconceivable that Frederick, as a gesture of thankfulness for Buckingham's invaluable support and as an encouragement to him to remain firm in the same course, had proposed some such arrangement. But the rest of this devious plan to keep Charles unmarried may be dismissed as sheer fantasy, for it would have depended for its execution upon far too many imponderables. In any case there were good practical grounds for Charles's declaration, and all the reports from France suggested that the French would not insist upon better treatment for English catholics as the price of their alliance.[59]

Whatever James thought of these accusations, he was not prepared to deny the Spanish ambassadors access to him, and a few days later Inojosa – 'under cloak and pretext of zeal and particular care of his person' – gave James further details of the conspiracy in which Buckingham was said to have been involved. At the beginning of the Parliament, according to the ambassador,

the Duke of Buckingham had consulted with certain lords of the arguments and means which were to be taken touching the breaking and dissolving of the treaties of the Palatinate and match; and the consultations passed thus far, that if His Majesty would not accommodate himself to their counsels, they would give him a house of pleasure, whither he might retire himself to his sports, in regard that the Prince had now years sufficient to, and parts answerable for, the government of the kingdom.

The King was deeply disturbed by these revelations but was determined to keep them to himself for the time being, until he had resolved what to do. He was about to leave for Windsor, for the Garter ceremonies on St George's Day, but could not bear to take Buckingham in his coach with him. The Duke, sensing that something was wrong, pressed James to say what was the matter. Thereupon the King, bursting into tears, declared that he was the unhappiest man alive, to be treated with such ingratitude by those who were dearest to him, and told Buckingham of the charges made against him. The Duke, who could not restrain his own tears, protested his innocence and called for a full investigation to discover who had given the ambassadors this false information. But James drove off to Windsor, taking only the Prince with him, and the disconsolate Buckingham was left to return to Wallingford House where he retired to bed and refused to see anybody. Lord Keeper Williams, however, who had been given an inkling of what had occurred, forced his way into the Duke's chamber and urged him to leave for Windsor immediately. Buckingham followed this advice, and some sort of reconciliation took place at Windsor between him and the King. James agreed to the request for an investigation, and decided to administer formal interrogatories to all his Councillors, to try and find out what truth, if any, was contained in the ambassadors' accusations.

Buckingham was not happy about this procedure, since it seemed to imply that the King was not, as yet, persuaded of his innocence, but the Prince advised him, in a letter full of warmth and affection, to let the King have his way. Buckingham feared that some of the Councillors might perjure themselves in order to bring about his downfall, but the Prince reassured him on this score, 'for I cannot think that any man is so mad as to call his own head in question by making a lie against you when all the world knows me to be your true friend'. And if they all spoke the truth, Charles continued, Buckingham would have nothing to fear, for they could only tell the King what the Duke had 'avowed to all the world – which is that you think, as I do, that the continuance of these treaties with Spain might breed us much mischief'. In case Buckingham should have any doubts about the degree of the Prince's support, Charles was quick to reassure him: 'Now, sweetheart, if you think I am mistaken in my judgement in this, let me know what I can do in this or anything else to serve thee. And then thou shalt see that all the world shall daily know more and more that I am and ever will be your faithful, loving, constant friend.'[60]

On 5 May Buckingham returned to town with the King. He was sick in body as well as mind, and instead of accompanying James to Whitehall he retired to Wallingford House, where he once again took to his bed. Theodore Mayerne, the King's principal physician and one of the leading doctors of the day, was called in, and on 10 May he told James – who was by now thoroughly alarmed – that his favourite had passed a disturbed night, with feverish bouts. His pulse was regular but he was evacuating yellow bile, the colour of saffron, and it could not be taken as certain that he would survive. The King went to Wallingford House immediately, and spent three hours by the bedside of his sick favourite. In the days that followed Buckingham's condition rapidly improved, but there was no relaxing of the King's concern. Sir John Coke described how James 'hath shown great tenderness over him and sendeth unto him three or four times every day. Yesterday he sent him cherries; this day the eyes, the tongue and the dowsets [testicles] of the deer he killed in Eltham Park.' Buckingham's illness, in short, swept away all the clouds of suspicion and cross-purposes between him and James. The King's love for his favourite came flooding back, as strong as it had ever been, and he could not do enough for him.

With Buckingham's health steadily improving, suitors started flocking to Wallingford House, and the doctors became alarmed that their incessant importunities would cause a relapse. When the King heard of this, he immediately ordered a guard to be placed on Buckingham's lodgings, to keep away unwanted visitors. This, of course, gave rise to further rumours. The adherents of Spain declared that a guard was needed because the Duke had gone off his head, like his brother, and they attributed his lunacy to the judgement of God. Others were convinced that the King had ordered the guard because he did not trust the Duke and wanted to prevent him from further plotting.[61]

By the end of the third week in May Buckingham was well enough to be carried in a close chair to see the Prince at St James's, yet repeated blood-lettings had enfeebled him to such a point that he could scarcely stand. For some time he had been too weak to hold a pen, and had left it to Kate to write to the King and thank him for the melons, grapes, peaches and other gifts which James sent in such abundance. But as Buckingham's strength increased, he was able to write himself and give the King the good news that 'my grudgings have left me again', and that although 'the highness of my urine, with the yellowness of my skin betokens a yellow jaundice, [this] will be no great matter to cure if it prove so'. He showed some of his old spirit by chiding James 'for this new vein you have taken of losing of stags', but had to cut his letter short because of his faintness. A week or so later, however, he was feeling much stronger, 'what with your sweet cordial and my seasonable drawing of blood', and was looking forward to an early return to Court.[62]

On 25 May the King, who had been at Theobalds for a brief visit, returned to town in order to pick up the now-convalescent Duke and take him down river to his palace at Greenwich. Buckingham had at one time planned to go to Nonsuch, but his friends assured him that the air at Greenwich was much better, not least because 'the breath of a King did blow upon it'. They were afraid that James had not yet overcome all the suspicions about his favourite's conduct which the Spanish ambassadors had put into his mind. Yet all the outward indications were to the contrary. On the King's last visit to Walling-ford House he had knelt by Buckingham's bedside with raised hands and called on God either to cure his beloved Steenie or else to transfer the sickness to himself. And when Padre Maestro took advantage of the favourite's absence from Court to seek a further audience of James, the King would have none of it. 'If I admit Maestro,' he declared, 'it will kill the Duke with grief.'[63]

Where public affairs were concerned, Buckingham's illness had come at a particularly unfortunate moment, for without him to goad people on, lethargy and inefficiency were the order of the day. This was shown most clearly in the preparations for setting out the fleet, for this was an immensely complicated operation that involved the working out of detailed and interlocking time-tables. It was not simply a question of building or requisitioning ships and pressing sailors. Cattle had to be bought and arrangements made to slaughter them to provide meat for the projected voyage; hundreds of casks had to be ordered to store fresh water; clothes and shoes had to be provided for sailors who were often too poor to provide these essential articles themselves; sails had to be repaired, guns cast and powder manufactured. Very little of this could be done without Buckingham there to give the necessary orders and see that they were carried into effect. As Dudley Carleton's nephew told his uncle, 'until he be well again, all business suffers extreme delays'.[64]

Yet if Buckingham's eagerness to return to work was understandable, it was at the same time mistaken, for as Conway noted, he 'ventures abroad too soon, too much'. While Buckingham was with the King at Greenwich he was attacked by fever again, and had to retire to New Hall. His reasons were, as he told James, that

first, I find business and the sight of busy folks does me much harm; and though your extraordinary care and watchful eye over me would keep them from speaking with me, yet in a Court I must needs look many of them in the face. Then Theobalds House is now very hot and hath but few change of rooms – both inconvenient to a sick body. Then my Lord of Warwick tells me that by experience he hath found New Hall air as good a one to ride away an ague as any in England.

Buckingham spent the greater part of his days walking or riding in the park at New Hall, where he was planning improvements that would, he hoped, make it as fine as Burley. He enjoyed watching his lusty stags and his fat Spanish colts, and he took great comfort in the company of Kate, his wife, and his 'jovial fille' Mall. At his parting from James, the King had assured Buckingham that he loved and trusted him as much as ever and had no fears about his 'popularity'. He sent his absent favourite gifts of 'excellent melons, pears [and] sugared beans', as well as strawberries and raspberries and what

Buckingham referred to as an 'assurance of better fruit planted in your bosom than ever grew in paradise'. He also wrote loving letters, which Buckingham confessed were expressive of 'more care than servants have of masters, than physicians have of their patients . . . . Of more tenderness than fathers have of children, or more friendship than between equals; of more affection than between lovers in the best kind, man and wife.' What adequate return, he asked, could he possibly make to a King who was 'my purveyor, my good-fellow, my physician, my maker, my friend, my father, my all'? There was nothing left but to crave James's blessing and assure him that 'I can never be other than Your Majesty's most humble slave and dog, Steenie'.[65]

Buckingham may have felt fully confident that he once again enjoyed in fullest measure the King's favour, but other observers were not so sure. 'The eyes of this people', said one reporter, 'could not well be more fixed on a meteor than they have been upon the motions of the Duke, to see whether he diminishes in his light or hold still the same fulness in His Majesty's affection and favour.' It was noted that James had twice been the guest of Arundel at his house in Hampstead, and it was also said that he would have met the recently-returned Bristol and the Spanish ambassadors there, had not the Prince heard of this and taken steps to prevent it. Charles wrote to Buckingham to tell him that 'Bristol stands upon his justification and will by no means accept of my counsels'. He urged the Duke to use his influence with James to block Bristol's request for a speedy trial, for fear that 'if you be not with us, to help to charge him and to set the King right, he may escape with too light a censure'. This message must have alarmed the Duke. So must the news that Middlesex — who, following his impeachment by the Commons, had been sentenced by the Lords to loss of office, fine and imprisonment — had been released from the Tower by James's orders and was rapidly gaining favour, while his nephew, Arthur Brett, was to be seen frequently at Court. Although a number of Buckingham's friends, such as Conway, assured him that 'it shall be time enough to come upon the stage of business when you may act it well, without prejudice to your health', Buckingham knew that the longer he was away the more time his enemies would have in which to plot his destruction.[66]

VI

On 16 June Buckingham returned to Court, where he was 'received and embraced by His Majesty with all good testimonies of welcome'. He was still far from fully recovered, and Sir Thomas Wentworth described him as 'much discoloured and lean with sickness'. Yet although he was anxious to keep out of the way of suitors, this was only so that he could concentrate on the major businesses in hand, and in particular the negotiations with France. The initial reaction of the French government to the overtures of Kensington and Carlisle had been highly favourable, for as Ville-aux-Clercs (one of the French ministers involved in the marriage negotiations) told Tillières, Louis XIII detested the Spaniards and saw the need to 'restrain their unbridled passion for domination'. The most difficult aspect of the negotiations was that which concerned the English catholics, for despite the Prince's declaration about making no concessions, La Vieuville was determined that some provision for improving their condition should be included in the marriage treaty. This was not simply a matter of prestige, although Louis XIII, as the 'Most Christian King' of France, was anxious to demonstrate that he had the interest of religion at heart no less than his Spanish counterpart, the 'Most Catholic'. La Vieuville had also to take into account the strength of catholic feeling in France, particularly among the *Dévots*, who regarded an alliance with a heretic power with suspicion, and were only prepared to accept it if it held out hopes of reconciling England to Rome.

There were also the English catholics themselves to consider. They were traditionally hispanophil, but if their allegiance could be transferred to France they would give Louis XIII the capacity to intervene directly in English affairs, in a way that had hitherto been possible only for Spain. William Bishop, the leader of the English catholics, had written to Louis in April 1624 expressing 'the pleasure and hope which we have conceived in the alliance of our Prince with Madame your sister'; and Richard Smith, his successor, was even more francophil, having been for many years a member of the household of Armand de Richelieu, the future cardinal. Smith went across to France at the same time as Carlisle was making his more ceremonious and stately way, reached the French court before him, and pressed Richelieu – who was the queen mother's confidant – to insist on a substantial improvement in the condition of his co-religionists in England. Richelieu agreed, and in late May Smith was able to report that 'both the king and queen mother say they will never agree to the match unless they obtain as good conditions for catholics as Spain hath obtained'.[67]

By this time Richelieu was directly involved in the marriage negotiations, having been appointed to the council in late April. The news that a prominent ecclesiastic, and one who had been closely associated with the *Dévots*, had been brought to office, was likely to cause some apprehension in England, but Ville-aux-Clercs instructed Tillières to inform the English that Richelieu, although a churchman, was a gentleman by birth and a Frenchman to boot, and would be devoted to advancing the interests of Louis XIII rather than those of the Pope.[68]

In early June 1624, Louis stated his terms for the marriage. They included, among a number of provisions relating solely to Henrietta Maria and her household, the demand that James should commit himself, in the marriage treaty, to suspend the penal laws against the catholics. Carlisle and Kensington protested strongly against this, declaring that James would never accept such a condition, but Louis was not dealing solely with the ambassadors. He had also informed Tillières of his demands and instructed him to make them known to Buckingham. The French clearly hoped to outflank the ambassadors by opening up a direct line of communication with the favourite, but the

Duke also had alternative means of communication. He had despatched his friend, the Roman Catholic Earl of Nithsdale, to Rome to expedite the issuing of the papal dispensation for the marriage, and asked him to go via Paris and make clear to Louis and his ministers that there could be no question of including concessions to English catholics in the marriage treaty. The French realised that they would have to moderate their demands and therefore suggested that the suspension of the penal laws should be put in a secret article. At the same time they assured Nithsdale that they needed a written promise from James solely in order to procure the dispensation from the Pope. This assurance was also given to Carlisle, who added the welcome news that once the marriage articles had been agreed the French had promised to 'wholly espouse His Majesty's interests and *se jetter là-dedans à corps perdus*, as is their own language'. Carlisle, who had long been in favour of a French alliance, was optimistic about the possibility of restoring Christendom to the state it had been in during the days of Henri IV, when France held Spain in check, and he urged that French enthusiasm should not be allowed to cool through any slackness on the part of England.[69]

Further evidence of French goodwill came in late June, when Louis recalled his ambassador, Tillières, whom Kellie described as 'too much jesuited and not fit for our purpose'. He was replaced by the Marquis d'Effiat, to whom the Duke gave a warm welcome, declaring that now he had no further cause to fear the malice of his enemies. During the course of a long conversation at Windsor, Buckingham told the ambassador of the difficulties he had faced in detaching the King from Spain and of his promise to James that the French marriage would definitely be accomplished. If this did not happen, he declared, his good fortune would be at an end.[70]

It might seem that Buckingham, by these words, was placing his future in Effiat's hands and committing himself lock, stock and barrel to the French alliance. But the Duke knew what he was doing. By exerting his undoubted charm and flattering the ambassador, he might well be able, to some extent, to use him for his own purposes. And by emphasising that the achievement of the French match depended upon the continuance of his own favour he was reminding Effiat – and through him Louis and Richelieu – that the French needed him just as much as he needed them. The success of Buckingham's tactics was shown by the despatch which Effiat sent Louis XIII, describing the Duke as the unchallenged ruler of England. The King, said Effiat, loved him so deeply that he let him do what he liked and saw everything through his eyes. The Prince looked on him as the sole source of his happiness and contentment. And as for the ministers, they were all Buckingham's creatures and held their places only during his good pleasure. This was a very superficial and in many ways misleading description of the political situation, since Buckingham's power was certainly not unchallenged and rested on an unstable coalition of conflicting interests. But Louis accepted it at face value and wrote to the Duke in his own hand, addressing him as 'mon cousin' and telling him to trust in the friendship and support of France.[71]

Kensington returned to England for a brief visit in late June, 1624, and brought with him verbal assurances from La Vieuville that all James need offer, with regard to the English catholics, was a letter promising that they would not be persecuted, and that the French in fact did not care what happened once the dispensation had been issued. These assurances were most welcome to the King, the Prince and Buckingham, but when Kensington arrived back at the French court he found that La Vieuville had been dismissed. Not only this. Louis denied any knowledge of La Vieuville's informal undertakings and had appointed as his replacement Cardinal Richelieu, whose attitude was markedly different. Richelieu began by insisting that James should give a formal written promise about better treatment of the English catholics, which should form one of the articles of the marriage treaty, but the ambassadors managed to convince him that James would never consent to this, since it would amount to a breach of the promise he and his son had made to Parliament. Richelieu therefore lowered his sights and proposed that the concession should be contained in a separate and secret article.

There were good reasons for Richelieu's insistence on some sort of formal commitment on James's part, since the French ambassador at Rome reported rumours that the Pope would not issue the necessary dispensation unless the marriage treaty included provisions for the relief of English catholics. Richelieu was therefore fighting on two fronts, and at the same time as he urged the English ambassadors to accept the principle of a secret article he despatched Père Bérulle to Rome to explain to the Pope the necessity of issuing the dispensation even though the marriage articles were 'somewhat less advantageous for the catholic religion than those which had been made by the Spaniards'.[72]

Buckingham as yet knew nothing of these developments. He assumed that Kensington's return to the French court would lead to the speedy conclusion of the marriage treaty which would then be followed by an agreement on joint military action against the House of Habsburg. Everything, in fact, seemed to be going well, for his health was slowly improving and his enemies were in disarray. He still needed the occasional visit from a doctor, but in mid-July he signalled the end of the worst stage of his illness by paying his physicians £50 apiece for their pains. To celebrate his return to health he planned a great feast at Burley-on-the-Hill, at which the King would be the guest of honour, and in late July his household officials, under the direction of his steward, Mr Hopton, were hard at work, laying in great store of venison, game and fish, and buying delicacies such as musk melons and Colchester oysters.[73]

James's acceptance of Buckingham's invitation to Burley was an unmistakeable sign that the Duke had returned not only to health but also to favour. His enemies, perceiving this, had decided on one last, desperate throw involving Middlesex's relative, Arthur Brett, who had again been barred from Court. Sometime during the early summer of 1624 Brett was approached by Benjamin Valentine and William Coryton, who were to become notorious, a few years later, for their opposition in Parliament to the policies of Charles and Buckingham. They suggested that Brett should return to Court, this time under the protection of Pembroke, the Lord Chamberlain. They gave the impression that Pembroke as yet knew nothing of their proposal, though this may be doubted. Brett therefore approached Pembroke, who (as Brett later told Lady Middlesex) 'took it very kindly that I would address myself unto him', but after a day or two's consideration decided not to take part in the plot. Pembroke was not swayed by any kind feelings towards Buckingham but simply by the fact that, in Brett's words, 'he perceives the Prince to be so much for his grace'. Brett now decided to act alone, and in mid-July, when the King was hunting in Waltham Forest, he suddenly appeared before him, to plead his case in person. But the King would have none of it. Spurring on his horse, he commanded the Earl of Warwick to remove Brett from the field, and later sent a warrant to the Attorney-General ordering Brett's arrest.[74]

This incident put an end to all Middlesex's hopes of recovering the King's favour. As for other members of the anti-Buckingham circle, Bristol was still in limbo waiting to be called to trial, while Lord Keeper Williams, Arundel and Secretary Calvert had been dropped from the select committee which advised the King on foreign policy. Only Pembroke remained, and since he was too important and influential a figure to be openly challenged, Buckingham moved towards an accommodation with him. In mid-August rumours were circulating that Pembroke was to be made Lord Treasurer, while his brother Montgomery (an old friend of Buckingham) was to take his place as Chamberlain, and although the rumours proved to be unfounded they reflected the fact that Buckingham and Pembroke had come to terms. Buckingham was now firmly seated in power, and Archbishop Abbot commented sourly that 'no man goeth free that doth not stoop sail to that castle'. Another observer, after deducing that Buckingham's victory over Brett was 'a most invincible argument of his greatness', added that 'if you saw the fashion of his treating of suitors (whereof he is as full as ever), and with what elevation he comports himself with the greatest that have to do with him, you would say he hath gained *le hault bout*, and that he knows himself fixed past jeopardy of relapsing'.[75]

At the beginning of August 1624 the Court was at Apethorpe, in Northamptonshire, but when Secretary Calvert wrote from there to Carleton on the 2nd he ended his letter by telling him that 'this is removing day to Burley, and business proclaimed treason there'. Among the guests at Burley, however, was Effiat, and he had not gone there simply to enjoy the food and the company. During dinner he and Buckingham discussed the problem of concessions to the English catholics, and the Duke, although he protested that the French demands were exorbitant, eventually persuaded the King to write to his law officers, ordering them to suspend all prosecutions of recusants. He hoped, as he told Effiat, that this would open the way to agreement and enable France to join with England to recover the Palatinate. But at this point Effiat gave Buckingham the news of La Vieuville's dismissal, which he had just received. The Duke was so flabbergasted that for some time he said nothing, and Effiat had a hard job persuading first Buckingham and then the King that the alteration of ministers would make no difference to the progress of the negotiations.[76]

For their part the English ambassadors to France welcomed the fact that Richelieu, the new chief minister, was the confidant of Marie de Médicis, 'that good and blessed queen mother', whose affection to the match they had never doubted. But Carlisle was upset by the cavalier way in which Louis had repudiated assurances given in his name, and resented Richelieu's demand that James should provide a formal written undertaking not to persecute the catholics. Carlisle suggested that the English should take a very firm line on this issue, going so far, if necessary, as to threaten to break off negotiations, and he asked Buckingham for permission to return home to explain his attitude. The news of this sudden check to proceedings, just at the moment when everything seemed to be nearing conclusion, caused consternation at Court. Kellie told Mar on 12 August that 'it is now come to that which was expected and professed, that it would never be a match, neither was there any great hopes of it in the wisest sort of folks here'. If Buckingham had been at Court he might have been able to calm the furore, but he was again troubled by ill health, and he and his wife had gone over to Wellingborough to try the newly discovered spa waters there. The King and Prince were consequently left to make up their own minds about the significance of the French action, and Charles, at least, was clear that it boded ill. Louis's disavowal of La Vieuville had, he told Carlisle, 'made me a St Thomas for believing of any good issue of your negotiation. If you find they persist in this new way that they have begun in making an article for our Roman Catholic subjects, dally no more with them but break off the treaty of marriage, keeping the friendship in as fair terms as you can.'[77]

When Effiat heard of the sudden change in the English attitude he rushed over to Wellingborough to consult with Buckingham, and the two men returned together to the Court, which was then near Derby. On the way they met a courier carrying the King's reply (written by Conway) to the letter from his ambassadors which had announced La Vieuville's dismissal and Richelieu's insistence on harder terms. Buckingham was suspicious at the speed with which the reply had been drafted and sent off, suspecting that advantage had been taken of his absence from Court. He therefore intercepted the messenger, broke open the despatch, and read it over to Effiat, explaining its exact meaning as he went along. Later, when they reached Court, he procured the ambassadors' original letter from Conway, and showed this as well to Effiat. The two men then went through the King's reply, cutting out some two thirds of it and moderating its tone. By the time this was done, the King was ready to give Effiat audience, and in the course of a long, and at times stormy, interview, Effiat managed to calm James's anger and persuade him that the ambassadors had misinterpreted the French position. He also said he had heard rumours that the King's reply, which had already been drawn up, was couched in harsh and uncompromising terms, and that if this were the case it might be as well for James to have second thoughts. The King agreed, and told Buckingham to show the despatch to Effiat and let him take out whatever he thought fit, as long as the essentials were left in. Effiat did not, of course, reveal that this was what he and the Duke had already done.[78]

The ethics of Buckingham's action in showing Effiat both the ambassadors' despatch and the King's reply, without even asking James's permission, are open to question. But he had to act quickly, in order to prevent the reply from being sent, and he was genuinely anxious to clear up what he felt sure was a misunderstanding rather than a real breach. He now wrote direct to Louis XIII – nominally in reply to the letter which Louis had earlier sent him – and enclosed a draft of the secret undertaking which James was prepared to give. This, said Buckingham, was the limit of James's concessions, and he urged Louis not to press for more. If he did so he would risk driving James into breaking off the negotiations, which would leave the English catholics in a far worse position than they were at present.

Buckingham sent a copy of this letter to Carlisle and Kensington, carefully explaining that his direct intervention was no reflection upon their own competence, and telling them that they were to await Louis's reply – which would be sent to them – before deciding whether or not to continue the negotiations. He also, of course, showed his letter to James, who approved of it and later wrote to congratulate him on its good effect. James's opinion was confirmed by the ambassadors, who told Conway that this 'fair and free dealing of the Duke of Buckingham's in his so well tempered letter' had caused the French to change their attitude and had smoothed the way to renewed negotiations.[79]

In his conversations with Effiat, Buckingham put the blame for the near breakdown on the hardline approach of Carlisle, but his anger against the Earl may well have been simulated, for some weeks later he encouraged Effiat in his attempt to obtain the Garter for Carlisle. Buckingham probably welcomed the opportunity of demonstrating to Effiat that while he personally was working for a successful outcome to the negotiations between the two crowns, there were other, more intransigent, forces pulling in a different direction. The implication of this was that the French, if they wished to take advantage of Buckingham's influence and preserve his power, must be prepared to make concessions. Effiat showed that he had learnt this lesson when he advised his own government not to be too inflexible, and the point was driven home by Buckingham in a personal letter to Richelieu. Beneath the superficial flattery was the warning that Buckingham had done all that he possibly could. It was now up to the French to make the appropriate response.[80]

Kensington, who had been away from the French court on account of illness, did not share his colleague's belief that they should 'carry all with a high hand', for in his opinion 'there is ten times more to be gained by kindness and love'. He gave greater weight to the private comments of French ministers than to the formal wrangling over the wording of articles, and was convinced that while the French were determined to get the best terms they possibly could, they were also genuine in their desire to cooperate with England to check the advance of Habsburg power. While other people thought of Richelieu first as a cardinal and ally of the *Dévots*, Kensington, who moved at ease in the circle around the queen mother, believed that he was more of a politician than a priest. For this reason he advised James not to be misled by pessimistic reports. It was true that Richelieu was now in effect ruling France, but he 'will (in my poor conceit) do it wisely and worthily, and so as Your Majesty shall have no cause to regret that the secular sword comes to be wielded by a spiritual hand'.[81]

Since Kensington was Buckingham's confidant it seems likely that the Duke accepted his interpretation of Richelieu's attitude, and this would explain why Buckingham was not over-concerned about the exact wording of articles, secret agreements, and so on. His main purpose was to bring about an effective political and military alliance between England and France as the basis of a union of anti-Habsburg states, and he believed that once the two parties were fully engaged in the common cause, many of the doubts and misgivings would fade away. Events were to show that his optimism was unfounded, and that the legacy of suspicion between the two countries was too great to be got rid of overnight. While Richelieu shared Buckingham's conviction that the expansion of Habsburg power threatened the whole of Christendom and must be halted, his own position as Louis XIII's chief minister was as yet insecure. He was hated by the great nobles, who feared (and had good reason to do so) that he intended to curtail their freedom of action; he was watched with suspicious eyes by the *Dévots*; and he was regarded with alarm and dread by the French protestants, the Huguenots. He could not even take the continuing support of the King for granted. If Richelieu never appreciated the limits on Buckingham's freedom of action – limits imposed by the need to consolidate his position at Court while preserving his links with an aggressively protestant Parliament – neither did the English appreciate the checks on Richelieu. The Cardinal simply was not able, at this early stage, to give the sort of whole-hearted response to English overtures which might have transformed the tentative Anglo-French alliance into a really effective and powerful anti-Habsburg league.

Nevertheless, by the end of September 1624 the marriage negotiations had virtually been completed, and James had agreed to give a written promise about freeing his catholic subjects from persecution. This was to be countersigned by the Prince and a Secretary of State, but it was not to form part of the marriage articles. It was referred to, in fact, as an *Ecrit Particulier* and its exact status was by no means clear. There is little reason to believe that Buckingham attached much importance to it. He was no lover of persecution, particularly since so many of his relatives and friends were catholics, but he would have preferred to see the religious issue left out of the negotiations altogether. Since this proved impossible he was content to have persuaded the French to accept a form of engagement that bound James in general terms without tying him to particulars.

The French professed to believe that they had won a signal victory by persuading the English to make any concessions at all, and congratulated themselves on the skilful way in which they had turned Buckingham into their agent. Nobody encouraged this belief more than Buckingham himself, with his insistence that his life and fortune depended upon the achievement of the French match and his carefully calculated revelations to Effiat. In fact there is no reason to suppose that Buckingham would have been ruined if the French negotiations had collapsed. The King and Prince would almost certainly have stood by him; Parliament would have been delighted; and the war could still have gone ahead, with the Dutch and Denmark as allies. It was not self-preservation which drove Buckingham to push so strongly for a French alliance. It was his belief that the essential interest of the two states consisted in checking Habsburg attempts at domination of the western world. And if the French really had secured a great triumph by their conduct of the negotiations, this was certainly not apparent to hard-line French catholics. Against the charge that Buckingham allowed himself to be outwitted by Effiat should be set the judgement of Tillières. 'Buckingham,' he wrote,

in choosing the Marquis for his confidant, wanted to make him believe that he kept nothing from him and that he loved him like his own soul; although on other occasions and during his absence from the Court he spoke of him with the greatest disdain. If the Marquis d'Effiat had not been duped by these pretences of friendship he would never have given way to the Duke, as he did, in so many matters which were prejudicial to religion and the honour of the king.[82]

VII

It could be argued that the French had inflicted a defeat on themselves rather than gained a victory, since by insisting on concessions to English catholics they had forced James to go back on the promise Charles had made in the Lords, and had thereby undermined the fragile union between Parliament on the one side and the Prince and Buckingham on the other which offered the best chance of effective English participation in the war against the Habsburgs. As early as mid-September Kellie told Mar that 'the business does not now relish so well with the Parliament as it did before, since they begin to hear that matters for the catholics here must be in the same course that was concluded with Spain'. Fortunately for Buckingham, Parliament was not in session. He hoped that by the time the two Houses did come together again the fruits of Anglo-French cooperation would be so apparent that all criticism would be stifled. For this reason he now concentrated on what had always been, for him, the major objective of the *rapprochement* with France, namely a military alliance. In late September Mansfeld returned to England, bringing with him assurances that the French were ready to aid him as soon as the English translated their promises into men and money. The King was quite prepared to do this, but wanted something more specific from the French, particularly in view of their attitude over the *Ecrit Particulier*. Conway therefore wrote to the ambassadors on 5 August to tell them of James's 'immoveable position: that the hand of his dear brother, the French king, must declare his conjunction in the action before he put in execution anything'. Mansfeld himself saw no sense in making such a demand. James's contract, he pointed out, was with him, not with France, and if he, as commander of the force, was prepared to accept Louis's word, why should not James do so?[83]

James saw matters differently. He did not trust the French and he feared that they intended to engage him in a war and then leave him in the lurch. James also suspected that Louis might encourage him to provide men and money for the relief of the Palatinate, and then persuade Mansfeld instead to undertake operations for freeing the Alpine passes from Spanish control. For these and other reasons he wished to tie Louis down by a formal written engagement. But Louis was determined not to be tied. His distrust of James was at least equal to that of James for him, and in any case he believed that an open military alliance with a major protestant power would lower his credit with the catholic princes of Germany – who might otherwise be persuaded to cooperate in an anti-Habsburg war – and would also damage his chances of obtaining the dispensation from Rome. Louis was already putting his position at risk by agreeing to provide troops for Mansfeld's army, but at least he could always deny that he had ever officially authorised Mansfeld to levy these. If, on the other hand, Louis gave a written commitment to James, he would be providing him with the opportunity to publish his perfidy to the world. This was why, when the English ambassadors, in accordance with their instructions, pressed for a written commitment, the French told them that 'they meant it not under writing but by such a real and actual performance as they presumed would be more satisfactory than all the articles in the world'.

When the King received the despatch in which Carlisle and Kensington reported Louis's refusal to give a written commitment, he was so furious that he threatened to suspend all further negotiations. Perhaps he was encouraged to do so by the news that Gondomar was on his way back to England, with fresh Spanish proposals for settling the problem of the Palatinate. The Prince had to remind him most forcefully that he would never consent to a Spanish marriage and that if the French one were rejected he would be left without a bride. The King, now in a calmer state, recognised the validity of this argument. He also listened to the ambassadors' messenger, who enlarged on their despatch and emphasised the binding nature of the verbal commitment which the French were prepared to give. James eventually decided to accept this, and Conway wrote to tell the ambassadors 'that we prize words spoken to you equal with letters graven in marble'.[84]

The French had agreed to meet half the expenses of Mansfeld's army for at least six months. They had also committed themselves to provide three thousand cavalry. These would be waiting in northern France, where Mansfeld would land with his twelve thousand English infantry, and the combined force would then make its way to the Palatinate. There was much to be said for the French claim that joint action of this sort would demonstrate their commitment to the common cause and bind them more effectively than any formal undertaking. Buckingham certainly thought so, and now bent all his efforts towards ensuring that men and money should be forthcoming. At the end of October the Privy Council wrote to the Lord Lieutenants of all the English counties, giving them orders to conscript soldiers for this service. They were to take special care to choose men who were 'of able bodies and years meet for this employment', but were not to recruit members of the trained bands, whose presence would be needed at home to repel possible Spanish invasion attempts. The trained bands were that section of the county militia that was supposed to receive regular instruction in the use of arms, and although in practice they were poorly disciplined and ill equipped, at least they had some acquaintance with military matters. The same could not be said of the untrained, unskilled dregs of society who were forcibly recruited for service with Mansfeld. They were an army only in name. In every other respect they were a rabble.[85]

Mansfeld, however, was used to turning raw recruits into soldiers; it was his profession and his livelihood. And whatever the quality of the English conscripts, the very fact that twelve thousand men were to be assembled at Dover and shipped abroad for military operations was a sign that England was waking from her long sleep. Frederick and Elizabeth were pinning their hopes on Mansfeld and his army, because they believed that whatever it did on the battlefield it would have the effect of encouraging other German princes to commit themselves to the common cause. This was also the assumption of Conway, who told Rusdorf that once the King had drawn his sword he would soon find allies, for it was inconceivable that the German princes would be content to remain under the imperial yoke once they were offered the chance to free themselves.[86]

There were many people in England who felt it to be a slight on the nation's honour that an English army should be commanded by a German mercenary. Sir Edward Cecil, for instance, told Buckingham that he intended to retire from the military profession now that 'strangers get the command . . . which was never heard of before amongst men of our occupation'. His annoyance was understandable, but he ignored the fact that the colonels of the infantry regiments under Mansfeld were all Englishmen. In any case Mansfeld's expedition was not simply an English affair, and the French might well have refused to cooperate if the overall command had gone to an English officer. There was the further consideration that, as Kensington had told La Vieuville some months before, Mansfeld's knowledge of Germany and his experience of fighting there were unrivalled. And although his reputation for spreading destruction wherever he went was so notorious that his very name struck terror into the inhabitants of those parts which were threatened by him, this was an advantage in so far as it would increase the pressure on the Habsburg powers to negotiate rather than fight.[87]

By December 1624 the two negotiations, for marriage and alliance, had both been brought to completion, though with a good deal of ill-feeling and suspicion on both sides. Carlisle and Kensington (who had now been elevated to the Earldom of Holland) gave their formal approval to the marriage articles in November. But before the ceremony of signing took place, they had an audience of Louis XIII at which he made three solemn promises concerning Mansfeld. These were, to pay him for six months, to employ him solely for the relief of the Palatinate, and to give him permission to land, with his troops, either at Calais or Boulogne. Carlisle told Buckingham of his disappointment that the French had not agreed to enter into an offensive and defensive alliance, as the English had hoped. He attributed this to 'the inconstancy and perfidiousness of those with whom we had to do', but took comfort from the reflection that 'before it be long, the necessity of their own engagements will force them to seek unto us, whom they might now have obliged with a better grace'.[88]

James accepted the marriage articles at a ceremony at Cambridge on 12 December, at the same time as he and the Prince gave their undertaking, in the form of an *Ecrit Particulier*, to free the catholics from persecution. Observers commented on the fact that only the King, the Prince, Buckingham and Conway took part in the ceremony on the English side. The other Councillors were bitter at their exclusion from the negotiations. They knew so little about what was going on that in late November, when they saw the flames of celebratory bonfires lighting up the winter skies, they had to send out their servants to discover the cause – which was the conclusion of the French marriage. The Archbishop of Canterbury was reported to have said that there were now two Councils in England, of which 'that of Newmarket was the higher', and Kellie, commenting on the Cambridge ceremony, told Mar that the lords of the Council were not pleased at the neglect of them. One reason for confining the negotiations to such a small group was, no doubt, to avoid dispute over the concessions to catholics, which would almost certainly have been opposed by Abbot and a number of other Councillors. Yet the *Ecrit Particulier* could not be kept completely secret, for in order to put its provisions into effect the King had to instruct the appropriate ministers to cease all proceedings against catholics. 'This makes men believe that the same course goes on now with the French that was concluded with the Spaniard,' wrote Kellie. And he added the pertinent comment that 'how pleasing these things shall be to the Parliament, men are doubtful'.[89]

Shortly before the signing of the articles at Cambridge, Pembroke wrote to Carleton at the Hague to tell him of the steady progress that was being made towards effective intervention on behalf of the Elector Palatine. He gave it as his opinion that 'it were better for the general cause that this war be styled by us rather a particular war for the kingdom of Bohemia than a war for religion, though I know in the consequence these cannot be severed'. Pembroke, like Carleton, was genuinely devoted to Elizabeth of Bohemia and was delighted that James had at long last decided to support his daughter and son-in-law with deeds rather than words. He took it for granted that his enthusiasm was typical, for he assured Carleton that 'I never saw this kingdom so affectionate in any business'. Yet in fact there was little evidence of popular support for the actions to which James had so far committed himself. What most people wanted was war with Spain; anything less they regarded as unnecessary or even harmful to the greater cause. The French marriage, in particular, was unpopular. D'Ewes was expressing a moderate opinion when he wrote that 'the English generally so detested the Spanish match as they were glad of any other which freed them from the fear of that', but even he felt bound to add that 'wiser men feared much danger would ensue to the gospel and true religion by this marriage'.[90]

There was even less enthusiasm for Mansfeld's expedition. One commentator, referring to the raw levies that were to go with Mansfeld, said that he could not imagine 'what miracles can possibly be wrought now by them (being untrained and undisciplined), and in this rotten time of winter', particularly since they would be up against some of the finest and most experienced soldiers in Europe. The troops themselves seem to have shared his doubts, for they deserted in droves. Those that stayed and made their way, under escort, towards Dover, were far from disciplined or orderly. They 'straggle up and down', reported the Privy Council, 'and not only spoil and take what they list, but do also terrify the poorer sort of inhabitants and molest and offend all that pass upon the highway'. Nothing was safe from the marauding troops. They even intercepted official despatches, and they caused such havoc upon the coasts that one exasperated naval captain declared they were worse than the Dunkirk privateers. If war meant the terrorising of peaceful and law-abiding English men and women by the dregs of the country, there was no enthusiasm for it among the inhabitants of Kent and adjacent counties. They were learning what the peoples of continental Europe had long known from bitter experience, that involvement in open hostilities was detrimental to the maintenance of civilised patterns of behaviour, and that the cost of war was not to be measured in money alone.[91]

One of the reasons why the troops plundered the civilian population was that they were unpaid. The King had agreed to give Mansfeld £15,000 to purchase arms and other equipment for his army, and £20,000 a month to enable him to keep it in the field. Such sums were not easy to come by, but on the strength of the Parliamentary subsidies, which had been voted but not yet collected, James managed to raise a loan of £55,000 which he handed over to Mansfeld. The Count, however, was always reluctant to part with money — since, as a mercenary, he had to run his armies at a profit — and denied any financial responsibility for the troops until they reached Dover. Sir William Beecher, who had been appointed treasurer for Mansfeld's army, was at his wits' end and told Conway that he did not know what to do. 'Yet I should not despair that all might be accommodated,' he added, 'if my Lord Duke were come (as he hath been looked for hourly these three days).' Buckingham in fact reached Dover shortly afterwards, and persuaded Mansfeld that £6,000 should be deducted from the sums already allotted him, and used to pay the costs of conducting the troops to the rendezvous. As Beecher told Conway, the Duke's presence 'hath dispelled the clouds that hung upon this expedition'.[92]

VIII

Buckingham could not solve all his financial problems so easily. Money was needed desperately, not only for Mansfeld but also to set out the fleet, but none would be forthcoming until the Parliamentary subsidies reached the Exchequer. The Duke had realised that this would be the case; hence his suggestion to Parliament that a number of rich men should be asked to make substantial advances on the security of the subsidies. This suggestion had not met with approval, however, and as a result the preparations for war had to be made with whatever sums could be scraped together from loans, gifts and other sources. When Mansfeld pressed, in December, to be paid four months' advance, he was told there was no possibility of this, and Rusdorf, who had seconded his request, informed Frederick and Elizabeth that he would never have believed that there could be such a shortage of money in England.[93]

Buckingham knew better than anyone else the crippling effect that financial weakness would have on England's capacity to act as a great power, and was toying with a number of different projects designed to raise money. He considered selling off the remaining crown lands, until Williams pointed out that if he did so he would merely furnish Parliament with an excuse for not voting further subsidies, and that in any case 'the money got thereby will not be much, and will instantly be gone'. He discussed with Laud the possibility of sequestering the Charterhouse and devoting its rich endowments to the maintenance of a standing army of some ten to twelve thousand men which would be always available for the defence of the kingdom against surprise attack. Laud, however, dissuaded him from this course. A standing army would cost more than the Charterhouse could provide, he pointed out, and its very creation would arouse doubts about Buckingham's intentions. If defence was the primary need, it would be better to select certain members of the trained bands and have them ready at an hour's notice for any service at home or abroad. This idea, or something similar, had already been put forward by Conway, who, as a former professional soldier, appreciated just how inefficient the military organisation of England was, and in August Buckingham had written to him from Burley to say that the King had resolved 'to set the militia of England in that course which you propounded, and for the present to have a certain number out of every trained band to be in such readiness as shall be within a few hours' warning at any place appointed'. Such a scheme, however, needed money, and money was simply not available.[94]

Buckingham can hardly have failed to reflect from time to time upon the curious attitude of the House of Commons which, in 1621, had declared its readiness to 'adventure the lives and estates of all that belong unto us . . . for the maintenance of the cause of God and of His Majesty's royal issue', but now that it had been given the opportunity, was unwilling to provide funds on an appropriate scale. What he was witnessing was the fulfilment of a prophecy made by the anonymous author of a letter to the King, urging James to stand firm in his policy of peace on the grounds that 'those very tongues which in the last [Parliament] did cry "War!" "War!" "War!" will now curse him that urgeth for one poor subsidy to raise a war; and miserable is he that is to make a war, or to defend against it, with money that is to be given or gathered from them'. Buckingham's state was not yet miserable, but in order to find money for the war he had to use his own and the Prince's credit. From 1624 onwards it becomes increasingly difficult to disentangle Buckingham's personal finances from those of the state, because he advanced large sums from his own purse to get military and naval preparations off the ground, and looked to the King to reimburse him as and when he could. The £10,000 which he persuaded the East India Company to pay him as consolidated prize money for their plundering expeditions against the Portuguese was all spent on the fleet, and it seems likely that a good deal of the money obtained from the sale of honours was used for the same purpose. Money had also to be found for the journey which Buckingham was planning to make to France, to bring back Henrietta Maria and to put the finishing touches – or so he hoped – to the Anglo-French alliance, and in late November 1624 it was reported that 'the Prince doth borrow £20,000 to give him towards his charges. And besides there are some barons to be made, to pay the Duke's debts, which amount to £40,000 or £50,000.'[95]

If the state was near bankruptcy and compelled to live on credit, much the same was true of Buckingham himself. At the time he left for Spain, in February 1623, his debts amounted to £24,000 and the journey itself and the long months of attendance upon the Prince at the Spanish court cost him another £13,000 (which was not repaid by the crown until 1627). By selling some of his lands in 1623 he wiped out the debt of £24,000, but bills of exchange for Spain, as well as the cost of running his various households, meant that by the end of 1623 his debts had reached the figure of £25,000. Sir Robert Pye, one of the commissioners charged with the supervision of Buckingham's finances, wrote to tell him that 'your steward, gentleman of the house, clerk of the kitchen, have neither money nor credit to pay when you go abroad, and your lady hath no money for her house[keeping] . . . . Your lordship hath so little credit as every man is weary, and will be worse unless the disposing of your money be better ordered.'[96]

Although Buckingham's annual income by 1624 was nominally £15,000 and in practice probably nearer £20,000, a great deal of it was appropriated to specified purposes. £3,000 went to the Duchess for her housekeeping expenses and £2,000 to Buckingham's mother, the Countess. Attendance at Court cost the Duke some £2,500 a year, while his stables ate up another £1,200. He disbursed £1,000 annually on wages and pensions for his servants, and £500 on the maintenance of his houses. Clothes, on which he spent lavishly – particularly for Court functions and foreign embassies, when he was required to shine – cost him £1,500; tilting another £1,000; while incidental expenditure, which ranged from large sums for the purchase of works of art and gambling at one end of the scale to a steady trickle of small amounts dispersed by way of tips and alms at the other, amounted to £2,000. In mid-1623 the Duke's annual expenditure was only a little less than his annual income, a state of affairs which, as his commissioners pointed out, 'differs from all prudent rules, for not to spend above two parts of the certain yearly revenue hath always been used by such as desire to leave behind them a fair patrimony to their posterity'. By October 1624, however, Buckingham was spending more than he received, and the interest charges on his debts, which now stood once again at £24,000, came to well over £1,000 a year. Nor was this all. The Duke owed £13,000 on bills of exchange for his Spanish journey; he had spent

£20,000 on building and furnishing his various houses as well as improving their parks; his 'extraordinary feasts and entertainments' during the previous three years had cost him £8,000; and he had run up debts to tradesmen amounting to £28,000, to be paid off over four years at an interest rate of thirty to forty per cent. If this was not depressing enough, he had £30,000 worth of bills still to be settled. In these circumstances it is hardly surprising that his commissioners recommended him to 'know how to raise money before you enter into any vast charge of purchasing or building', and also to appoint 'some particular persons to buy and take in all your provisions'. Only then would they be able to give him a true picture of his debts, 'which now, by [reason of] many buyers and providers, we are unable to do'.[97]

It is doubtful whether Buckingham paid much attention to the sober and careful advice which his commissioners gave him. He continued to live in the lavish and carefree style that he and his contemporaries took for granted in a great magnate, and worked on the assumption that means would somehow be found to pay for his expenditure – an attitude which, however reprehensible by twentieth-century standards, was widely shared at the Stuart (and, for that matter, the Elizabethan) Court. At the very moment when his commissioners' report reached him he was engaged in building operations at York House. This property did not become officially his until late 1624, since an act of Parliament was needed to confirm the transfer of ownership from the Archbishopric of York to the crown. It was James who had pressed Buckingham to take York House, and in May 1624 the King went in person to the Lords to assure them that the Duke had provided suitable alternative accommodation for the Archbishops. The King was followed by Lord Keeper Williams, who pointed out that no Archbishops had in fact lived in York House since Mary's reign, and that the transaction would benefit them financially since their rent from the house came to no more than £11 a year, while the crown lands they were being offered in exchange could be made to yield £700.[98]

Williams also reminded their lordships that York House was in a very ruinous condition. This was so much the case that Buckingham had ordered work to be started on it even before he became the lawful owner. Balthazar Gerbier, his adviser on art and architecture, later described how there was at first 'much daubing and breaking through old, rotten, decayed walls'. But it soon became clear that this would not suffice to create 'rooms to entertain (according to the dignity of a prime minister of state) foreign princes and ambassadors'. Buckingham, who at that time was still feeling the effects of his serious illness, and was not in the best of tempers, declared that 'he would have the house pulled down and built anew after another fashion', but this could not be done at once, partly because of shortage of money. He was helped by the King, who gave him a gift of two thousand tons of stone (at a cost of £1,800), but even so it looks as if he decided to adapt the existing house until such time as he could afford to build a totally new one. The pace of activity now became frenetic, and Gerbier reports how 'the ceilings of rooms [were] supported with iron bolts, balconies clapped up in the old wall

[and] daubed all over with finishing mortar'. Sir Thomas Wentworth watched the alterations taking place in June 1624 and also described the setting up in the garden of 'a goodly statue of stone . . . bigger than the life, of a Sampson with a Philistine betwixt his leg, knocking his brains out with the jawbone of an ass'. This was in fact a magnificent composition by Giambologna, which had originally been commissioned by the Medici ruler of Florence in 1568, and sent to Valladolid in 1601 as a gift for the Duke of Lerma. There it stood, as the centrepiece of a fountain, until it was admired by Charles on his journey homewards to Santander. The Spaniards, only too anxious at that time to put the Prince in a good humour, promptly offered it to him, and it was crated up and brought to England. Charles presumably intended to keep it as a memento of his great romantic adventure, but subsequently, as his affection for Spain and the Infanta declined, he handed it over to his friend and former travelling companion.[99]

Buckingham had already decided to become a collector of works of art on a major scale. He was not the first, by any means. Charles, like his elder brother, Prince Henry, was a patron of the arts, but the greatest of all English connoisseurs was the Earl of Arundel, with his magnificent collection of Greek marbles, and it may well have been the galleries at Arundel House which provided the model and inspiration for Buckingham. The Duke chose as his agent and adviser Balthazar Gerbier, who had been born in Holland of Huguenot parents, and commissioned him 'to choose for him rarities, books, medals, marble statues, and pictures great store'. Gerbier told Buckingham that he was delighted with his orders to 'view the paradise of Europe under the happy title of servant of your greatness', and in 1621 set off for Italy on a buying expedition. His taste was for Caravaggio and the Bolognese school of painters, but in Venice he came to admire Titian and paid £275 for a 'great piece . . . of Pilatus' – the magnificent 'Ecce Homo', now in Vienna. He also bought a Tintoretto, the 'Woman taken in Adultery', and two works by Jacopo Bassano.[100]

Buckingham's visit to Madrid in 1623 gave him the opportunity to see with his own eyes one of the finest collections of paintings in Europe and he returned to England with a determination to assemble a collection of pictures that should rival, in its scale and its quality, anything that the rest of the world had to offer. Hitherto English taste had been directed towards France and the Netherlands, but the Duke was captivated by the Italians. After seeing Titian's portrait, 'Charles V on Horseback', at the Escorial, Buckingham ordered a copy to be made to hang in the great hall at York House, and as his collection expanded it became a major influence on English attitudes to art. In 1624 Gerbier was in France, where he compiled a list of the principal paintings in private collections. 'I never could have thought that they had so many rare things in France', he wrote to Buckingham, and he rejoiced that so many of them would be available when the Duke made his visit. Gerbier reported that he had made a down payment on a Tintoretto study of 'Danae, a naked figure, the most beautiful, that flint as cold as ice might fall in love with it'. This, along with a painting by Titian, cost £60, but the purchase which pleased Gerbier most was Titian's 'Portrait of a Secretary'. He later told Buckingham how Inigo Jones went to see it at York House and 'almost threw himself on his knees' in front of it.[101]

Inigo Jones was 'surprised and abashed' at the splendour of York House itself, where Gerbier had decorated a number of rooms with rich velvet hangings. At the same time Gerbier was preparing designs for New Hall where Buckingham was busy planting trees in the park and improving the water supply — no doubt with an eye to fountains. Buckingham was also planting heavily at Burley, and in November welcomed the arrival there of a thousand walnut trees sent as a gift from the Earl of Northumberland. In an age when great men were 'rewarded' for their services by offerings of one sort or another, Buckingham became the recipient of countless presents. In October 1624, for instance, his friend Lord Salisbury sent him a picture, which the Duke promised to set up 'as a monument of your love to me and of mine own obligation ever to remain your humble and faithful servant'. In September Sir Dudley Carleton, still hoping to be brought back from his honourable exile at the Hague, asked his nephew's opinion whether this would be an appropriate time at which to offer Buckingham the gift of a 'gate and chimney of marble'. His nephew thought the gate would fit very well into the new front at York House, and Carleton therefore instructed him to go ahead with the offer. But he reminded him to 'use care and discretion, for they are of too great value to be cast away, especially considering my hard estate. Wherefore first weigh with yourself how you find the Duke to continue affected towards me, then what intention he hath or means to favour me.' Later that year Lady Carleton went to Middleburg to see the goods which the Dutch had taken from a Spanish prize. 'Here are very rich and rare things,' she told her husband, 'sufficient to make my Lord of Buckingham a wonderful sumptuous present', and in due course the ambassador wrote to the Duke to tell him that he had sent off a number of pictures, including 'a Christ *in scurzo* which hath been adored here even by Brownists and Anabaptists'.[102]

The splendour of York House and the magnificence of its contents were symbols of Buckingham's greatness, and he was treated with a deference normally reserved for members of the royal family. Conway, for instance, who as Secretary of State was one of the King's chief ministers, always addressed Buckingham as 'gracious patron' and insisted on giving him the title of 'excellency' even though the Duke asked him to refrain. Theophilus Field, the ever-hopeful Bishop of Llandaff, who had obtained his see through Buckingham's favour and yearned for greater (and richer) preferment, went one stage further. He not only dedicated to him a treatise on holy communion which he wrote in 1624, but hailed him as 'high and illustrious prince'. Towards the end of November 1624 rumours were current that Buckingham was to be given even greater honours. One letter-writer reported that he was to be created 'Prince of Tipperary in Ireland, with the high command of Lord High Lieutenant of that kingdom'. The Venetian ambassador heard much the same story and added that Buckingham would enjoy many sovereign rights such as justice and coining money. Sir Edward Peyton, in his violent attack on the

House of Stuart, published after Charles I's execution, declared that 'the Duke's drift was, after King James's death, to make himself King of Ireland, and therefore he was styled Prince of Typeraria, an appendix to that throne'. These rumours were apparently unfounded, although it was the case that Buckingham had close links with Ireland. He had established something of a monopoly over appointments to high office there; he encouraged James to expand the Irish peerage; he was in receipt of a substantial income from the Irish Customs; and he had been granted lands in Ossory and Leitrim which he administered through one of his many agents in Ireland, Sir William St Leger. Furthermore Buckingham's half-brother, Sir Edward Villiers, was to be appointed President of Munster in January 1625.[103]

It is not totally out of the question that James intended to advance his favourite to yet further heights, but in fact the only addition to Buckingham's titles in 1624 came in the autumn, when he purchased the Lord Wardenship of the Cinque Ports from old Lord Zouch. Buckingham's acquisition of this office was prompted by more than vanity. The Cinque Ports were a nursery of seamen, whose services were essential to the nation in time of war. But the Ports were exempt from the jurisdiction of the Lord Admiral, who could not press men within their confines, and the Lord Warden had a number of other privileges which led to constant disputes between him and whoever was Lord Admiral. By the seventeenth century this 'second Admiralty', as Wotton correctly described it, had become an anachronism, and Buckingham's assumption of the office effectively put an end to the clash of interests and united the entire naval administration of the country under one head. The advantages of this soon became apparent, for in December 1624 Buckingham took steps as Lord Warden to provide shipping for Mansfeld's expedition, which he could not easily have done under the old dispensation.[104]

By the end of 1624 Buckingham was clearly chief minister in all but name. Parliament had given him its confidence. His enemies in the Council had been routed. The Prince was content to leave the execution of policy in his hands because he trusted him, recognised his capacity for getting things done, and was satisfied that the course which Buckingham was steering was the one which he and the Duke had sketched out during and after their return from Spain. As for the King, although in November 1624 he had been described as 'more gaillard' and in better health than he had been for many years, he suffered renewed attacks of leg pains in the following month, rarely stirred from his chamber, and was said to be very melancholy. Yet James had not abandoned the reins of government, and because he was the most obvious focus of national loyalties as well as the man who, in the last resort, either made or sanctioned decisions, his approval of proposed policies was essential. This was one of the reasons why Buckingham wanted an offensive and defensive alliance with France. James was as yet hesitant, looking over his shoulder longingly towards Spain and deeply distrustful of French intentions. Although he had broken the links that bound him to Madrid he had not yet forged new ones with Paris, and he felt isolated and afraid in a hostile world. With France behind him, however, James might well recover his old self-assurance and direct English policies against Spain as effectively as he had earlier guided them towards her.[105]

Buckingham saw no reason why France should not join fully in the anti-Habsburg league that he was working to bring into existence. It was true that James cared principally for the Palatinate while Louis's main interest was the Val Telline, the Alpine pass through which Spanish forces in Italy had to march in order to reach Germany and the Netherlands. But both crowns were equally threatened by Habsburg ambitions, and the logic of the situation demanded a close alliance between them. In case there were any lingering doubts among Louis and his ministers about the attitude of England, Buckingham planned to go in person to Paris. The nominal object of his voyage was to bring back Henrietta Maria as Charles's bride, but he also hoped to return with an assurance of total French commitment to the common cause.

NOTES

(Abbreviations are explained in the Bibliography, pp. 477–86)

1. *Spring MSS.* 11 Mar. 1624. I am most grateful to Colin Tite for the loan of a microfilm of this and other Parliamentary diaries.
2. *Wot.* 219.
3. *Harl.MSS.* 1581.31.
4. *Dig. MSS.* 55; *Sp.MSS.* 28.138.
5. *Sp.MSS.* 28.134.
6. *Reade MSS.* 4/3, no number; *Rus.* 136, 143; *Holl.MSS.* 114.224.
7. *Sp.MSS.* 29.11.
8. *Sp.MSS.* 29.210.
9. *Dig.MSS.* 62,63.
10. *H.M.C.Supp.* 183; *Dom.MSS 14.* 154.10.
11. *Ch.* II, 527, 530; *C.S.P.V.* XVIII, 157; *Add.MSS.* 12,528.12; *H.M.C.Supp.* 184; *Fin.* 130–1.
12. *Gy.MSS.* 29.356–7. The draft of Buckingham's letter is in Conway's hand; *Holl.MSS.* 115.73.
13. *Rus.* 151–3.
14. *Holl.MSS.* 115.102, 151.
15. *Dom.MSS 14.* 154.2; *C.S.P.V.* XVIII, 149; *Dissolving.* 299; *Ruigh.* 33.
16. *Rus.* 146; *C.S.P.V.* XVIII, 177; *Ruigh.* 35; *Sp.MSS.* 28.193.
17. *Bac.* XIV, 442.
18. *Trum.MSS.* 18.110; *Ch.* II, 537; *Dom.MSS 14.* 158.74; *Cab.* 274.
19. *Hack.* I, 148, 39; *Cab.* 274.
20. *Sack.MSS.* ON.8884; *Dom.MSS 14* 156.3; *Carte MSS.* 30.157.
21. *Rowe.*; *Briley.*; *Ch.* II, 542; *C.S.P.V.* XVIII, 202; *Dom.MSS 14.* 159.28; *Ruigh.* 264.
22. *Harl.MSS.* 1580.136; *Dig.MSS.* 77; *Sp.MSS.* 30.90; *Flan.MSS.* 17.15.
23. *C.S.P.V.* XVIII, 207.
24. *Ch.* II, 539.
25. *C.S.P.V.* XVIII, 208; *Cab.* 197, 319.
26. *Dom.MSS 14.* 159.28; *C.S.P.V.* XVIII, 216.

27. *Cab.* 319; *Bas.MSS.* 58.15; *C.S.P.V.* XVIII, 210.
28. *Bas.MSS.* 58.21; *Cab.* 319.
29. *Dom.MSS 14.* 159.76; *Ruigh:* 162.
30. *Rush.* 125.
31. *Hack.* I, 179; *L.J.* 232; *D.L.* 2–4.
32. *C.J.* 721.
33. *D'Ewes.* 242; *Spring MSS.* 24 Feb. 1624.
34. *C.J.* 722; *A.P.C. 1623–5.* 156; *L.J.* 237; *D.L.* 14.
35. The links between Buckingham and members of the Commons are discussed in *Russell.* 166–71, 175–6.
36. *Ruigh.* 189; *Wel.* 155; *H.M.C. Supp.* 195; *Harl.MSS.* 6987.196.
37. *Spring MSS.* 4 March 1624.
38. *Harl.MSS.* 6987.202; *Spring MSS.* 11 March 1624.
39. *H.M.C. Supp.* 195; *L.J.* 266.
40. *C.S.P.V.* XVIII, 255; *Harl.MSS.* 6987.200.
41. *Ruigh.* 215.
42. *Spring MSS.* 19 March 1624; *C.J.* 744.
43. *Ruigh.* 229; *L.J.* 275, 283.
44. *Dom.MSS 14.* 161.30; *L.J.* 282.
45. *Harl.MSS.* 1581.39, 26, 47; *Fr.MSS.* 72.50, 83.
46. *Holl.MSS.* 116.186; 117.31, 48, 220; *Dom.MSS 14.* 161.61.
47. *L.J.* 284–5.
48. *C.J.* 751–2.
49. *Dom.MSS 14.* 163.30; *Ruigh.* 239–44; *D.L.* 52, 55–6.
50. *C.J.* 756, 752; *Crisp MSS.* 1.19.
51. *L.J.* 318.
52. *D.L.* 64; *Denmilne MSS.* 33.1.7.XXII.67; *C.J.* 769–70.
53. *Ruigh.* 248; *C.J.* 772; *Holl.MSS.* 117.48; *C.S.P.V.* XVIII, 286; *Rus.* 281; *D'Ewes.* 244; *Ch.* II, 556; *Dom.MSS 14.* 214.118.
54. *Dom.MSS 14.* 163.16.
55. *Cab.* 275–6.
56. *Hack.* I, 190–91; *H.M.C. Supp.* 197; *C.S.P.V.* XVIII, 268; *Ruigh.* 272–3; *Spring MSS.* 5 Apr. 1624; *Young.*
57. *Holl.MSS.* 116.31; *H.M.C.Supp.* 199; *Dom.MSS 14.* 162.13.
58. *Trum.MSS.* 18.114.
59. *Ruigh.* 279–81.
60. *Ruigh.* 282–4; *Cab.* 13; *Sp.MSS.* 30.224; *Hack.* I, 196–7; *Dom.MSS 14.* 164.12; *Harl.MSS.* 6987.211.
61. *Laud.* 152; *Add.MSS* 19,402.162; *H.M.C.Coke.* 162–3; *Trum.MSS.* 18.119.
62. *Arch.Cam.* 16–17; *Denmilne MSS.* 33.1.7.XXII.73,72,69.
63. *Dom.MSS 14.* 165.43; *Trum.MSS.* 18.120, 121.
64. *Dom.MSS 14.* 164.91.
65. *Fr.MSS.* 72.267; *Denmilne MSS.* 33.1.7.XXII.77, 79, 87, 88; *Add.MSS* 12,528.14.
66. *Trum.MSS.* 18.122; *Arun.* 232; *C.S.P.V.* XVIII, 343–4; *Harl.MSS.* 6987.207; *Dom.MSS 14.* 167.3, 4.
67. *Trum.MSS.* 18.123; *Str.P.MSS.* 21/23; *Crisp MSS.* 1.1v.; *Allison.* 165, 171.
68. *Crisp MSS.* 1.72.
69. *Harl.MSS.* 4594.45, 64v.; *Cab.* 304; *Fr.MSS.* 72.312; *Goitein.* passim.
70. *H.M.C.Supp.* 206; *Goitein.; Bas.MSS.* 59.157.

71. *Crisp MSS.* 2.14v.–15.
72. *Rich.* IV, 94, 66–8; *Aven.* II, 28; *Fr.MSS.* 73.5–7.
73. *Add.MSS.* 12,528.14v.–16v.
74. *Sack.MSS.* ON.245; *Ch.* II, 571.
75. *Dom.Add.MSS.* 43.73; *H.M.C.Supp.* 206; *Dom.MSS 14.* 171.49, 59; *Trum.MSS.* 18.128.
76. *Holl.MSS.* 119.2; *Bas.MSS.* 59.173–182v.
77. *Holl.MSS.* 119.79; *Fr.MSS.* 73.1, 40; *H.M.C.Supp.* 209.
78. *Bas.MSS.* 59.197–206.
79. *King's MSS.* 134.II.251; *Fr.MSS.* 73.105; *Harl.MSS.* 6987.192.
80. *Bas.MSS.* 59.207; 60.253; 59.209.
81. *Fr.MSS.* 73.65, 103.
82. *Till.* 83–4.
83. *H.M.C.Mar.* 211; *Holl.MSS.* 120.125v.–126v.; *Fr.MSS.* 73.225; *Rus.* 374–5.
84. *Fr.MSS.* 73.229–30, 250, 247.
85. *A.P.C. 1623–5.* 351–2.
86. *Rus.* 339–40, 358–60.
87. *Cab.* 170; *Fr.MSS.* 72.204; *Flan.MSS.* 17.409.
88. *Fr.MSS.* 73.293–6, 299.
89. *Ch.* II, 591; *Trum.MSS.* 18.138; *H.M.C.Supp.* 216.
90. *Dom.MSS 14.* 176.34; *D'Ewes.* 257.
91. *Trum.MSS.* 18.140; *A.P.C. 1623–5.* 409; *H.M.C.Coke.* 178.
92. *Holl.MSS.* 120.197; 121.124; *Ashton.; Stearns.; Dom.MSS 14.* 175.49, 54.
93. *Rus.* 404.
94. *Hack.* I, 202; *Laud.* 154 and Vol. VI, Pt I, 1–4; *Dom.MSS 14.* 171.34.
95. *Zaller.* 137; *Cab.* 255; *C.S.P.C.* 246 *et seq.; Goodman.* II, 346–8; *Dom.MSS 14.* 175.7.
96. *Dom.MSS 14.* 149.91; *Devon.* 357; *Harl.MSS.* 1581.125.
97. *Dom.MSS 14.* 149.91; *Cod.MSS.* 218.87v.–88v.
98. *Dom.MSS 14.* 161.54; 165.61; *D.L.* 94.
99. *Gerb.* 27–8; *Arch.Cam.* 17; *Devon.* 286–7, 291–2; *Str.P.MSS.* 21/23. The statue is now in the Victoria and Albert Museum, London.
100. *Bet.* passim; *Tann.MSS.* 73.119.
101. *Goodman.* II, 326–45, 356–61.
102. *Add.MSS.* 12,528.16v.–17; *H.M.C.Sal.* 196; *Dom.MSS 14.* 173.83; *Holl. MSS.* 120.155v.; 121.58, 222.
103. *Sp.MSS.* 26.115; *Field.* Dedication; *Trum.MSS.* 18.136; *C.S.P.V.* XVIII, 499; *Peyton.* 38; *Carte MSS.* 30.161, 163.
104. *Dom.MSS 14.* 170.16; *Wot.* 220; *Corbett.* 164–5; *Dom.MSS 14.* 176.14; *McGowan.* passim. I should like to record my gratitude to Dr McGowan for the guidance I have obtained from this excellent study.
105. *Holl.MSS.* 121.117v.; *Dom.MSS 14.* 176.66; *C.S.P.V.* XVIII, 537–8.

PART TWO

Buckingham in Power

CHAPTER SEVEN

1625: 'Your Glorious Match with France'

I

James had agreed to Mansfeld's military operations in the Palatinate on the assumption that these would not involve him in war with Spain, for although Spanish troops were in occupation of part of Frederick's territories they were there in the name of the Emperor. No doubt Spain could make a *casus belli* out of Mansfeld's intervention if she wished, but there were good reasons for supposing that she would prefer to maintain peace with England. The Emperor's attitude, however, was less predictable, and it was for this reason that James was so insistent upon French cooperation, for he had no intention of becoming involved in hostilities in Germany without the support of powerful allies.

Louis's refusal to commit himself openly to an anti-Habsburg alliance had done nothing to lessen James's suspicions; in fact they were increased when, in November 1624, Louis despatched Ville-aux-Clercs to England with instructions to sound out the King, Prince and Duke about the possibility of sending Mansfeld to the relief of Breda. On the face of it there was much to be said for this suggestion. The loss of Breda, which had been under siege since August, would be a great blow to Dutch hopes and would encourage those elements within the United Provinces which were in favour of making peace with Spain. The Dutch struggle for independence had been going on for half a century, and during that time Spanish forces had been tied down and great quantities of Spanish treasure consumed. Should the Dutch now withdraw from the war the power balance in Europe would be tilted heavily in favour of the Habsburgs just at the moment when France and England were preparing to throw their weight into the opposite scale. If Mansfeld could prevent this by relieving Breda he would make a major contribution to the common cause. It was true that his soldiers were only raw levies, but the Spanish besiegers were suffering from sickness and were on the verge of mutiny because of lack of pay.[1]

James, however, was not prepared to sanction this change of plan. The troops besieging Breda were operating under the direct orders of Philip IV, who was likely to regard any action against them as a *de facto* declaration of war. Sir Walter Aston, the English ambassador in Madrid, had already told Buckingham that the Spaniards were threatening to retaliate, possibly by invading Ireland, and similar warnings came from Jacques Bruneau, the Spanish agent in London. Early in January 1625 Bruneau demanded a formal assurance that Mansfeld's army would not be used against forces belonging either to Philip IV or the Infanta Isabella. James made no difficulty about giving the required assurance, for he had now instructed Mansfeld to go direct to the Palatinate, without passing through any Spanish territory.[2]

James's action, which was prompted by mistrust of France as well as fear of Spain, provoked counter action from Louis XIII, who was convinced that James had now effectively crippled Mansfeld's expedition. The shortest and most direct route from France to the Palatinate was through the Spanish Netherlands, and if Mansfeld was forbidden to take this he would either have to make a much longer journey along the French frontier towards Lorraine, or else encamp somewhere near Calais while an agreed strategy was worked out. Louis did not relish the thought of Mansfeld's undisciplined soldiers descending like locusts upon his own fair land. Quite apart from the damage they would cause in France itself there was the question of their effect upon public opinion abroad. The Pope, for instance, was being pressed by Louis's envoys to issue a dispensation for the English marriage and also to withdraw his garrisons from the Val Telline — the gateway from Italy to Germany — which they were, in effect, keeping open for the passage of Spanish troops. Urban VIII, who was more aware than many rulers of the dangers of Habsburg expansion and had no wish to become a Spanish chaplain, was inclined to favour the Most Christian King of France, but only on condition that Louis's orthodoxy was not publicly impugned, and this would hardly be the case while the king was maintaining a protestant army within his borders. There was also the consideration that the Huguenots were becoming restless once again, fearing that Richelieu's accession to power meant a triumph for the *Dévots* and an end to the policy of coexistence, and it was not inconceivable that they would look for support from their fellow protestants in Mansfeld's army. Louis could have cut the Gordian knot by telling Mansfeld to ignore James's instructions and to strike through the Netherlands towards the Palatinate. But if he did so the responsibility for the breach of peace would rest on France alone, and Louis might thereby call down upon his northern border the full weight of Spanish military power. Even if this did not happen, the delays in assembling and despatching Mansfeld's troops had given the Infanta Isabella time to strengthen her defences, and if Mansfeld tried to force a way through it was more than likely that he would be defeated. Louis would then be faced with the problem of what to do with a defeated, demoralised and broken army spilling back into his own territories. It was not a prospect that appealed to him.

Buckingham and the Prince realised that James's limitation upon Mansfeld's freedom of action cast doubt not simply upon the success of the expedition itself but also upon the whole future of Anglo-French cooperation. They therefore pressed him to change his mind, but James — who was still playing for time in hopes that Gondomar's arrival would solve his problems for him —

refused to give way. He did make one limited concession, however, by authorising Mansfeld to ask the Infanta Isabella for permission to pass peacefully
through her territories. If permission was refused – which James professed to
think unlikely – he might then use a minimum of force to protect his army as
it made its way towards the Palatinate. But as the Prince told Buckingham,
James's explicit orders were that Mansfeld was 'not to go near Breda by any
means', and if, in defiance of those orders, he attempted to lead his men there,
the English were to refuse to follow. James was acting quite logically according to his own lights, and his suspicion and caution were founded upon a
lifetime's experience of kingcraft. But consciously or unconsciously he blighted Buckingham's policy just as it was coming into flower. Louis had, in fact,
made a considerable concession by agreeing to cooperate in Mansfeld's expedition and but for James's restrictive orders he would probably have kept his
promise. As it was, suspicion bred suspicion, and when Louis heard that
James would not withdraw his limitations on Mansfeld's freedom of action, he
cancelled the permission he had previously given for the Count to land in
France. This unwelcome news was conveyed to Buckingham by Ville-aux-
Clercs in early January, 1625. The Duke could not hide his anger and disappointment, but confined himself to the bitter observation that Louis had
broken his solemn pledge. Buckingham assumed that there was now no question of joint operations, since the English infantry could not link up with the
French cavalry, but Ville-aux-Clercs suggested that Mansfeld should sail direct
to Holland, where he would be joined by the French horse (as long as the
English supplied ships to transport them). When Buckingham hesitated, Ville-aux-Clercs pressed him to leave the decision in Mansfeld's hands. Buckingham eventually agreed, since – as he told Conway, who was also present –
they could count on Mansfeld refusing to accept such a last-minute change of
plan. What he did not know, however, was that Mansfeld, after he received
James's restrictive order, had made up his mind to go to Holland instead of
France, and had formally proposed this to the Dutch.[3]

Buckingham, working on the assumption that Louis would revert to the
original arrangement if only Mansfeld stood firm, stepped up the pressure on
the mercenary commander to sail without delay and land in France. When
Mansfeld complained of lack of money, he sent him some from his own pocket
and also arranged to divert to him part of the funds that had been set aside for
the Navy. Mansfeld then asked for more ships, so that he could go to Holland, but the Duke replied that there were none available. 'His Majesty is at
the end of his patience,' he told Mansfeld. 'Provisions are being wasted, and
the whole design will go up in a puff of smoke if your excellency does not take
a decision to leave immediately for Calais.' This letter was sent on 16 January,
and on the same day Buckingham wrote to Aston to reproach him for the way
in which he had reported the news of Gondomar's mission. Gondomar, he
reminded the ambassador, 'was the instrument to abuse my master, the
Prince, and the state, and if now, by your means, the King should be fetched
on again upon a new treaty, the blame would light upon you'. Buckingham
knew that time was running against him. He was in sight of achieving his

great aim of creating a coalition of powers, catholic and protestant, united in the common cause against the Habsburgs, and delay would be highly dangerous. The Dutch were exhausted by the strain of their long war, but would be revived if England and France came to their aid. The King of Denmark was prepared to commit himself the moment France did so. Gustavus Adolphus of Sweden was also offering his services, and hoped to bring with him into the alliance his brother-in-law, the Calvinist Elector of Brandenburg (who was married to Frederick's sister). Brandenburg's lead might well be followed by the Lutheran Elector of Saxony, and the common cause would then form a great power block with which the Habsburgs would have to come to terms.[4]

Buckingham, more than any other individual in England or Europe, was responsible for calling into existence – even though, as yet, in only an embryonic form – this alliance of anti-Habsburg states. A great deal more than his own fortune, therefore, depended upon his continuation in power and favour. Yet he had many enemies. Some opposed him on grounds of policy; some shared his basic assumptions but suspected him of being prompted by personal rather than political considerations; others simply wished to get rid of him so that they could take over his authority. The Privy Council was so split that it was an impediment to action rather than a promoter of it. When the Elector of Brandenburg's agent asked for a conference at which to discuss the Swedish proposals for a military alliance, Conway had to explain that while some Councillors would be well disposed towards them, others would not. If the King deputed only those who were in favour to participate in a conference, the rest would take offence. Yet if all were deputed, the common cause might well receive prejudice. It was for this reason, said Conway, that matters of policy were now decided by the triumvirate of the Prince, the Duke and himself.[5]

Buckingham derived great strength from the continuing support of the Prince, and Kellie noted in a letter of 12 January that 'infinite is the affection betwixt the Prince and him'. He could also feel reasonably sure of the King's love, for later that month Charles, who was with his father in the country, wrote to tell him that James was suffering once again from pains in his arms and legs, and longed for 'your coming merrily hither . . . [to] make him a whole man again'. But he knew that his enemies were still intriguing against him. A number of them (of whom Arundel may have been the most important) were in close touch with Bruneau, the Spanish agent, and did not conceal from him their hopes that ill success would attend all Buckingham's ventures, including Mansfeld's expedition and the great fleet that was being prepared. They were openly resentful at the way in which they had been excluded from policy-making since the Prince's return from Spain, and Bruneau described one occasion, in January 1625, on which they showed it. A number of Councillors came into a room where the Prince was present, just as he was about to leave to join the King at Newmarket. The Prince took the occasion to remind them of the good work which was now coming to fruition, and to ask for their help in maintaining and promoting it. The Councillors replied with a sullen silence, only broken by Arundel, who declared that while they could indeed see what was happening around them, they had no knowledge of how or why the decisions had been arrived at: only when they were fully informed and taken into the Prince's confidence would they be in a position to tender their advice. The Prince left the room without comment – which was comment enough – but the very fact that a detailed account of this incident was given to Bruneau demonstrates the dangers that the Prince and Buckingham would have faced in discussing policy matters with the Council as a whole. They undoubtedly made a mistake in drawing too narrow a circle around the number of their advisers, but war demands secrecy, and there were few men they could trust. They had hoped that the Court and the country as a whole would unite behind them in a popular war, but factions and cabals were increasing in intensity rather than fading away. To one observer, Dudley Carleton's nephew, the situation in early January appeared so unsettled that he advised his uncle to sell his marbles and make money from them, rather than risk presenting them to a favourite whose power was perhaps on the wane. 'A great tempest is approaching,' he told him, 'able to overwhelm our greatest ships and greatest pilots here; and they most secure that have the least to do in the government.'[6]

It is hardly surprising, in view of the many pressures to which Buckingham was subjected, that his health began to give way again. In late January he was said to be taking physic, and the King urged him to get 'out of that filthy town as soon as your pressing occasions will permit you'. But the Duke could not leave London with so many problems still unresolved. It was therefore the Prince who attended the King in the country, while Buckingham stayed in town, dealing with a great variety and complexity of affairs. His three secretaries were kept fully employed, for in addition to his normal business of interviewing suitors, filling offices, running his estates, keeping in touch with political figures and a hundred and one other things, the Duke was conducting negotiations with foreign powers, which involved frequent meetings with their representatives in England as well as correspondence with English ambassadors abroad; he was keeping up the pressure on Mansfeld to carry his army across the Channel; and he was also pushing ahead with preparations for the great fleet that was to be England's major contribution to the common cause. Bruneau reported that every day Buckingham's house was awash with captains and masters of vessels summoned there to give the Lord Admiral their knowledge of the coasts of Europe, particularly Spain, and advise him on possible locations for a landing in force.[7]

Although Buckingham had a few really good administrators to assist him – Sir John Coke, for instance – he could have done with many more. The long Jacobean peace had left the English pitifully unprepared, both in mind and body, for the realities of a major war. There was no standing army and only a small Royal Navy. The Ordnance Office was notoriously inefficient; the dockyards specialised in producing leaky, unseaworthy vessels that could be easily outsailed by their opponents; the victuallers were more concerned with making fat profits than supplying wholesome provisions; and waste, corruption and incompetence were endemic in the entire system of administration. There was nothing new about this, of course, nor was it unique to England; but while such a system could cope with the limited requirements of peace, it could not respond in any adequate way to the imperative demands of war. Buckingham quickly came to learn a truth which Chamberlain also noted, that 'we are but young warriors, and there goes more to the furnishing and setting out of an army than bare pen and ink'.[8]

Buckingham was still trying to persuade Mansfeld to take his English regiments across the Channel, but Louis had written to the Count to warn him that there could be no question of their landing in France. He should ship them instead to Holland, where the Dutch had expressed willingness to receive them. Mansfeld thereupon wrote to Buckingham, asking for clear and explicit instructions. He could not, he pointed out, sail up and down the Channel, waiting for the two kings to sort out their differences, and if Buckingham really wished the expedition to have a good chance of success, he ought to allow it to follow the prevailing winds to Holland. If this were not done, warned the Count, his army would melt away, the money spent on it would be wasted, and all the fine hopes which had been built up would crumble into nothing. Mansfeld also reminded Buckingham that the eyes of Europe were on this army and that people were looking to it for their salvation. If it was simply to wither away they would regard it as a sinister omen. The enemy would claim the glory without even having to fight for it.[9]

These arguments were calculated to make a strong impression on Buckingham, who was concerned above all to commit England and France to action. But he was angry at the way in which the French and Mansfeld had apparently deceived him. 'This is such a false practice in Mansfeld,' he told Charles in a long letter describing the tortuous course of his negotiations, 'such a strange act of the French king, as may raise strange doubts of the other part of the treaties.' There was no simple way out of the dilemma. If Mansfeld attempted to land in France and was driven off, it would be an affront 'almost irreparable, and hazard the rest of the treaty'. If, on the other hand, his army was disbanded, the inhabitants of Dover and neighbouring areas would be once again at the mercy of 'a collection of the scum of the countries and city'. There was no doubt in Buckingham's mind that this change of heart by Louis had been brought about by Spanish threats and the intrigues of the *Dévots*. Nothing would delight them more than a pitched battle between English and French troops if Mansfeld attempted to land. They would also be pleased if the whole enterprise went up in smoke. In these circumstances, suggested Buckingham, it would perhaps be best, 'as well to avoid this extremity as to preserve these troops from utter loss and their oppression to the country', for James to give in to Louis's pleas and allow Mansfeld to go direct to Holland.[10]

Sir John Coke carried this long letter to Charles and no doubt gave him a verbal report about Buckingham's views. It was left to Charles to win over the King, and this he did successfully. James, he told the Duke,

fully approves the course ye have taken and directions ye have given hitherto. He is likewise of your opinion that this juggling proceeds from the importunity of the

Jesuits and Spanish faction with that king . . . . He also fully approves of your opinion for the remedy, for if by no means the troops may be gotten to land in France without apparent hazarding of them, there is no other safe way but that ye have set down, that they may land in Holland.

There was no question of Mansfeld's troops being used for the relief of Breda, of course. They were to sail to Holland and then make their way, by force if necessary, through the lands of the prince-bishops along the Rhine, until they reached the Palatinate.[11]

As soon as Buckingham received the King's authorisation, he instructed Mansfeld to transport his army direct to Holland, and on the last day of January the Count sailed out of Dover — much to the relief of the long-suffering inhabitants. When the small armada arrived off Flushing, Carleton wrote with delight to his fellow ambassadors to tell them that he never thought 'to have seen so fair a presentation to this state of so royal an assistance of my countrymen, levied and paid by the King my master'. But his later despatches told a different story. The Dutch did not have enough ships available to send all the troops to their quarters at Gertruidenberg, due north of Breda, so half the men were put ashore on Walcheren. They were the lucky ones, since they were provided with reasonable accommodation. The remainder, who went by sea to Gertruidenberg, were caught in a severe frost that compelled them to stay on board, where infection soon set in. They died by the hundreds, and their bloated corpses, which were unceremoniously dumped overboard, created such a stench on the beaches where they were washed up that huge plague pits were dug to bury them. Those who survived were sent into winter quarters, but even there they were not free from trouble, for the quarters had only recently been vacated by the Prince of Orange's men, who had stripped the whole region bare of everything necessary to sustain life. Lord Cromwell, who was with Mansfeld's army, wrote in despair to Conway to tell him that 'we die like dogs', and the Venetian ambassador, in somewhat more diplomatic language, referred to 'that natural fatality of this nation the moment they leave their own country'. Carleton tried to put a brave face on things. It was true, he admitted, that the 'army hath already suffered much, many being dead, some fled, and a great part of the remainder sick', but great actions 'are usually subject to such hard beginnings' and were not therefore to be abandoned. The very fact that the Kings of England and France had committed themselves to Mansfeld was an encouragement to 'other princes who have long fainted for fear and groaned under the burden of servitude', and every effort should be made to reinforce the Count rather than abandon him.[12]

Mansfeld's army was not the only one facing difficulties through lack of money and supplies. The Infanta Isabella wrote to Philip IV to warn him that the Spanish troops besieging Breda had not been paid for weeks, and were on the verge of mutiny. The intervention of Mansfeld's force, half-starved and plague-ridden as it was, might have served to tip the balance in favour of the Dutch, but James still refused to modify his orders. Conway told Rusdorf that he, the Prince and the Duke had done all they possibly could to change the King's mind, but to no effect. James remained adamant, and Mansfeld's army crumbled away without achieving anything. When the news reached England there was an outcry against the dreadful waste of men and money and scapegoats were sought. Buckingham believed that Mansfeld was to blame, since it was his secret agreement with the French which had led to the last-minute change of plan. If only the original proposals had been adhered to, there would have been no need for the troops to spend so long on board ship, first off the English coast and then off the Dutch, with all the risk of infection that this entailed. But the more general opinion was that expressed by Chamberlain, who held that the responsibility for the failure of Mansfeld's expedition rested on those that 'should have made better provision and taken better order for them' — of whom Buckingham was, of course, the foremost. The Duke had hoped that this first venture would not only be successful in itself but would spur on his fellow-countrymen to greater efforts. In fact it had the reverse effect, for as Chamberlain commented, 'it will quite discourage our people to be thus sent to the slaughter, or rather to famine and pestilence'. He added that there had been a time when an English army 'would have done somewhat and made the world talk of them', but now 'the basest of people in matter of courage dare brave and trample upon us'.[13]

II

Buckingham did not hide his disgust with the French, who, he told the Venetian ambassador, had 'deceived him by their double dealing about Mansfeld and by their equivocations over their promises'. But at this stage he was prepared to stifle his anger for the sake of advancing the mutual interest of the two crowns, and when Louis requested the loan of a number of English ships, he welcomed the opportunity to show his goodwill by making a positive response. The suggestion that English and Dutch ships should be lent to the French had first been made in the closing weeks of 1624, when France and Savoy were planning a spring campaign against the Spanish satellite state of Genoa. The French navy was so small that it could not effectively blockade Genoa from the sea, and Louis, working on the assumption that a Spanish defeat in Italy would be welcome to his English and Dutch allies — who happened to be the two greatest maritime powers in Europe — had no hesitation about asking for their assistance. In January 1625, however, the nature of the request changed, for the ships were needed nearer home. The French Huguenots were uneasy at the accession to power of a cardinal and apparent *Dévot*, and suspected that the armies which were being raised nominally for service in Germany and Italy might be turned against them. The inhabitants of La Rochelle, in particular, feared that it would be only a matter of time before their independence, and with it their religious liberties, was extinguished. Louis XIII had already made one attempt, in 1621–2, to subdue this Huguenot stronghold and incorporate it completely into his kingdom, but his action had sparked off a widespread protestant revolt under the leadership of the Duke of Rohan. Louis was not strong enough to deal with this, and by the Treaty of Montpellier, in October 1622, he had reluctantly agreed to restore the *status quo*.[14]

The treaty provided, among other things, for the destruction of the fort which had been built immediately outside the walls of La Rochelle, but this provision was never put into effect, and Fort Louis remained as a perpetual reminder of the danger hanging over the Huguenot communities of France. In late 1624 there were rumours that Louis's government, now under the direction of Richelieu, was planning to renew the war against the Huguenots, and was assembling ships in the port of Blavet in order to cut off La Rochelle from the sea. The citizens of the town appealed for help to Rohan, and on 8 January 1625 his brother, the Count of Soubise, put into execution a plan he had long been preparing. He sailed into the port of Blavet and seized the ships that were lying at anchor there. Louis immediately asked the English and the Dutch for their assistance in bringing Soubise to heel, and on his instructions Effiat pressed Buckingham for the loan of eight vessels. Buckingham promptly agreed, and sent a courier to James to ask for his approval. James, who had no love for rebels, was quite happy about assisting his brother monarch, and suggested that if eight warships were not available, because of the demands of Mansfeld's expedition, ships belonging to the East India Company might be commandeered.[15]

It may seem, at first sight, that Buckingham had fallen into a French trap by opening the way for English ships to be used against French protestants, but there were good reasons for his action. For one thing, the Rochellois had not come out in support of Soubise. In fact their first response was to disavow his action, which they feared might bring down Louis's wrath upon them. Soubise claimed to be acting for the sake of religion, but in practice he seemed more like a rebel and a pirate. There was a second and even more important consideration. France was about to begin military operations against the Spaniards in northern Italy, in association with Savoy, and the French Constable, Lesdiguières, had been appointed to command Louis's forces. Lesdiguières, who was himself a Huguenot, saw the need to check Soubise's rebellion before it flared into a full-scale religious revolt, because he knew that Louis XIII would never commit himself to fighting the Habsburgs abroad while he was threatened by unrest at home. Buckingham shared the Constable's belief that Soubise, by his precipitate action, was putting a brake on a most hopeful and promising development, and was giving encouragement to the pro-Spanish *Dévot* group at the French court. If English ships could serve to restore him to obedience and enable the Italian campaign to get under way, they would, in Buckingham's opinion, be well employed.[16]

In February 1625 Sir George Goring — who had been sent over to Paris by Buckingham to sort out the remaining problems connected with the marriage of Prince Charles and Henrietta Maria — reported that Louis was about to issue a declaration giving Soubise and his followers one month in which to submit. Goring added that in his view this offer was unlikely to be accepted, since La Rochelle had now decided to give its support to Soubise unless the government agreed to demolish Fort Louis. The Constable had tried to defuse the situation by suggesting that Rohan should have joint command with him of the operations against Genoa while Soubise should second him by sea, but if his proposal was turned down it seemed more likely that the Italian campaign would be called off and the Constable would be ordered to lead his troops not against Genoa but against La Rochelle. If this were to happen there would be, in Goring's words, 'such a blaze in these parts as will not easily be quenched, the which will not a little serve to the prejudice of our present affairs and consolation of our enemies'.[17]

Buckingham was alarmed by the suggestion that Lesdiguières might be recalled from Italy, and feared that there was some connexion between this and the delay in sending the French cavalry to join up with Mansfeld. He therefore called on Effiat to remind Louis of the dangers of fomenting war within his own kingdom instead of carrying it into the territories of his enemies – dangers, added the Duke, which threatened not only Louis himself but 'the common good of all Christendom'. He was no doubt relieved to hear, in early March, that Louis, far from recalling the Constable, had sent reinforcements to him, and that Lesdiguières had already joined forces with the Duke of Savoy. Buckingham presumably hoped that the English ships might not after all be needed, since the Huguenots, alarmed by the mere fact that they had been offered, would draw back from aiding Soubise. James, however, took a much simpler line. These Huguenot rascals, he told Effiat, must be treated as rebels, and he would be prepared to go in person to help exterminate them. As for the ships, Louis was welcome to have them for as long as he liked and to use them for any purpose. In this respect, as in so many others, James significantly altered Buckingham's policy.[18]

If Buckingham expected the French to show gratitude for the way in which he had responded to the request for ships, he was mistaken. The attitude of some of Louis's ministers, and in particular Ville-aux-Clercs, was that the Duke's goodwill should be exploited in such a way as to gain the maximum advantage for France. This was shown when the news reached Paris, early in February 1625, that the Pope had at last issued the dispensation for the marriage of Henrietta Maria, but had asked for a number of changes in the articles agreed on between Louis and James. Louis now wrote to Effiat, instructing him to use all his powers of flattery to persuade Buckingham to accept these changes. Let Effiat remind the Duke, said Louis, that his arrival in France was eagerly expected and that his propositions about joint operations would be welcomed. Let him also be assured of Louis's affection for him, and asked to demonstrate his goodwill by procuring these relatively minor changes in the treaty.[19]

Buckingham, however, had other sources of information about the motives of the French king and his ministers, and these told a very different story. From Paris, Goring wrote to warn him that Ville-aux-Clercs was publicly boasting that he could get from Buckingham what the English ambassadors would never concede and that 'no negatives grow in England'. 'If in time you look not to this people and their ways,' Goring added, 'they will so encroach upon His Majesty's, His Highness's, and Your Grace's goodness as [it] will be impossible for you to quit yourselves without much loss both in honour and safety.' Similar warnings came from the English ambassadors, Carlisle and Kensington. 'These unworthy, false ministers,' they declared, 'are grown to that indiscreet and insolent presumption upon the taste which they have had of your lordship's infinite goodness and nobleness as to say that your lordship's honour and fortune was so far engaged for the conclusion of their alliance as they were confident to prevail in whatsoever your lordship's power could procure.' They urged Buckingham therefore to stand firm and reject the French demand.[20]

Buckingham needed little persuasion. The negotiations over Mansfeld had taught him to look sceptically at French promises, and in February 1625 he reminded the English ambassadors that in any future discussions they should 'trust not to words only, but procure it under their hands in writing'. In any case his friend, Lord Nithsdale, had by now returned from the Vatican, bringing news that the dispensation had been issued 'free and unclogged'. The French, it seemed, were using the Pope as an excuse to extort more favourable terms, and this was the view of Kensington and Carlisle. 'We are confident,' they said, 'that all these new conditions have been forged here', and they recommended that James should give 'a sharp, stout negative' to the French demands. James was not surprised by this evidence of French perfidy, since he had never expected anything better. 'Where is your glorious match with France?' he asked his favourite sarcastically, 'and your royal frank *Monsieurs?*' Buckingham's reply was to call the French 'shitten mouths' and to advise James that he should 'roundly let the ambassador know you so much prize your honour that neither in a circumstance nor form will you make any alteration'. When Effiat had an audience with James to discuss the proposed alterations, Buckingham was conspicuously absent. The King eventually agreed to minor modifications in the wording of certain articles, but on the substance he stood firm, and this time it was the French who had to give way.[21]

Buckingham had taken a considerable risk in allowing the negotiations over this issue to reach breaking point. His hand was strengthened by the fact that the marriage was so near fulfilment, that the French were engaged in military operations against the Spaniards in Italy, and that they needed English assistance to settle their differences with the Huguenots. Buckingham also reminded Effiat that if the French remained obdurate, James would have no alternative but to call another Parliament, in which case 'the wit of men could not foresee the dangers that would be cast in by the Spanish party (who would have but too much cause to hope it would be no match) . . . and by the puritans, who, out of fear that it would prove a match, might, with as just cause, seek to hinder it'. The reference to 'the Spanish party' was more than an idle threat, for letters from Gondomar, addressed to the King, the Prince and Buckingham, had just reached the English Court, and once again there were rumours that the problem of the Palatinate would be solved without war – in which case there would be no need for the French alliance. One observer declared that Gondomar 'brings peace and the Palatinates in his pocket' and that the only struggles he intended to engage in were peaceful ones. Gondomar told Buckingham in his letter from Madrid that he did 'appoint for the field of our battle Your Excellency's gallery over the Thames', and he swore that he had been, and ever would be, 'a faithful and true servant and friend to Sir George Villiers, Duke of Buckingham'. Whether the favourite placed much reliance on these assurances may be doubted, but he had a long interview with Gondomar's secretary, and told James 'I am sure you now begin to laugh in your sleeve to see yourself so courted of all sides'.[22]

III

Now that the dispensation for the French marriage had been issued and the articles agreed on, all that remained was for Buckingham to go over to Paris and bring back Henrietta Maria. In mid-March 1625 he sent off his coaches towards Dover, but before he could follow them he received the news that James was seriously ill at Theobalds. He immediately changed his plans and rode post-haste to the King's bedside. Despite the fact that James was in many ways a restraint upon his freedom of action, Buckingham had never lost his love for 'the best of masters', as he styled him. In the letter in which he gave the King an account of his interview with the French ambassador, he expressed his regret that his duties kept him away from James's company. 'Dear dad,' he told him,

since I cannot come tonight, let this hasty letter give thanks for that true, favourable and most affectionate interpretation of my staying here, and God never relieve me when I haye most need if it be not a separating of myself when I am from you. And in lieu of having comfort and my heart's ease by you, to serve you I give myself nothing but trouble and vexation.

James's letters to Buckingham show the same warmth of affection, and make it plain that his love for his favourite was no less now than it had been in the early days of their acquaintance. Towards the end of 1624 when James was ill and out of sorts, he wrote to Buckingham to tell him how much he was looking forward to his visit and how he hoped

that we may make at this Christmas a new marriage, ever to be kept hereafter. For God so love me as I desire only to live in this world for your sake, and that I had rather live banished in any part of the earth with you than live a sorrowful widow's life without you. And so God bless you, my sweet child and wife, and grant that ye may ever be a comfort to your dear dad and husband.[23]

James's wishes were fulfilled, for when in March 1625 he fell dangerously ill, his favourite as well as his son was at Theobalds, watching by his bedside. The doctors employed their usual remedies, but to little effect, and Buckingham's mother tried a plaster manufactured by an Essex doctor who had attended upon Buckingham. This was attached to the King's wrist and was supposed to eat down into his stomach to cure his fever, but it seemed only to make James's condition worse. Buckingham then had a julep, or 'posset-drink', made up by one of his servants, and gave this to James to drink, but the King was too weak to take more than one or two sips. James, in fact, was dying, and nobody could save him, but this did not prevent some of the doctors from arguing that the plaster and the julep should never have been administered. Other of the King's attendants went so far as to claim that Buckingham and his mother had murdered James. Buckingham, who was physically and emotionally exhausted, was deeply distressed by this slander, but there was little he could do to stop it spreading. It soon became an article of faith to many people that the Duke had killed his master, and years later, in 1648, Parliament accused the defeated and imprisoned Charles of having allowed Buckingham to hasten James's end by giving him poison.[24]

It may well be that the remedies which Buckingham administered did more harm than good, but he acted with the best intentions. It was not Macchiavellian cunning that prompted him, but simply a desire to ease the sufferings of his 'dear dad and gossip'. Buckingham loved James – not, perhaps, in the same way, or with the same physical intensity, that James loved him, but with a depth of affection that created a firm bond between them. Commentators, both at the time and since, have found the relationship between the ageing King and his youthful and handsome favourite at times absurd, at times embarrassing, and generally distasteful. No doubt it was all of these – as many human relationships are – but it was also genuine, profound, and, on occasions, moving. If 'true love' is, as Sir Walter Raleigh defined it, 'a durable fire, in the mind ever burning', then the reciprocal affection between James and Buckingham falls within that category. The Duke felt bereft by the King's death and could not hide his grief. Soon after he returned to London he fell ill and had to be carried to his lodgings in a chair. On this occasion, as on a number of others, Buckingham's physical collapse shows that the strains upon him had become intolerable.[25]

There was widespread speculation about whether the accession of a new king would affect Buckingham's position. He had been on close terms with Charles as Prince, but would Charles as King feel the same need to rely on him? Favourites were nearly always the flowers of one reign only, and as for the affection of princes, there were many people at the Stuart Court who had seen Shakespeare's *King Henry IV*, and remembered what had happened to Falstaff. But Charles, far from disowning Buckingham, tied the bonds of friendship between them even more closely. 'I have lost a good father and you a good master,' he told the Duke, who was in tears at James's death. 'But comfort yourself, you have found another that will no less cherish you.' Charles took Buckingham with him in his coach to London, and ordered lodgings to be prepared for him at St James's, next to his own chamber. He confirmed the Duke in all his offices, and gave him a golden key as symbol of his right to enter the royal palaces at any hour of the day or night and go where he wished. This confirmation of Buckingham's position as favourite was unwelcome to all those who had hoped that his influence would end with the death of James. Kellie told Mar that 'there is some that does fear my Lord of

Buckingham's power with him [Charles I], and I assure you that it is not pleasing to most men'.[26]

In general, however, the comments on Charles's accession were favourable. Towards the end of April the Venetian ambassador reported that 'the King's reputation increases day by day. He professes constancy in religion, sincerity in action and that he will not have recourse to subterfuges in his dealings.' The Countess of Bedford described how Charles never failed, 'morning and evening, coming to prayers . . . [and] being an attentive hearer at sermons'. He had already changed the tone of the Court from the lax morality of James's days 'very near to the same form it had in Queen Elizabeth's time', and her general impression was that 'there is all good signs that God hath set him over this kingdom for a blessing'.[27]

Although Buckingham remained the King's confidant, Charles showed that he wished to heal the factions that had risen at Court by associating some of its leading figures more closely with his policies. In early April, for instance, he pardoned Middlesex, and when he went to York House to call on Buckingham – who was confined to his chamber, taking physic – he asked Pembroke and Montgomery to accompany him. They spent three hours in conversation with the Duke, and a few days later Pembroke was appointed, along with Buckingham, Conway, Lord Brooke (Fulke Greville) and the Lord Treasurer (James, Lord Ley), to a committee to advise the King on all aspects of foreign policy.[28]

Among the subjects which this 'cabinet-council' (as Chamberlain called it) was instructed to consider was the proposed offensive and defensive alliance with France. Buckingham was optimistic about the chances of bringing this into effect, for he had long since received assurance from Richelieu that Louis approved of the propositions he had made for joint action and was looking forward to discussing them with him. Buckingham hoped that by going in person to the French court he would be able to lessen Louis's dependence on the pro-Spanish *Dévots* – whom he regarded as responsible for the misunderstandings which had crippled Mansfeld's expedition – and thereby open the way to the creation of a formal league between the two crowns. His mission was all the more urgent in that the Pope's nephew was already en route to Paris, with instructions to remind Louis of his duties as a catholic sovereign and to bring about an end to the hostilities between France and Spain in Italy.[29]

IV

Buckingham could not leave as early as he would have liked, since James had not yet been buried. The funeral took place on 7 May, and Buckingham, as the late King's Master of the Horse, walked in the procession. He was dressed in a long black robe with a black hood, and the horse which he led was covered with black velvet embroidered with silver and pearls. After paying his last respects to his royal master, Buckingham had no further reason to delay his departure for France, and on the day of the funeral Goring returned from Paris with the news that Henrietta Maria was ready to set out. The marriage ceremony, in which Charles was represented by his kinsman, the Duke of Chevreuse, had taken place in Notre Dame on 1 May, and all that remained was for the young Queen to be escorted to the coast, where she would embark for Dover and her new life. On 12 May, therefore, Buckingham set out for France, taking with him, apart from a handful of servants, only the Earl of Montgomery, Sir George Goring and Sir Albert Morton, the newly appointed Secretary of State. In order to save time he left instructions that his carriages and the sumptuous clothes which had been specially made for him should follow on after. The crossing from Dover took four hours, and Buckingham, unlike Montgomery, survived it without being sick. The master and crew of the ship that carried them were £70 the richer for their pains, thanks to the Duke's generosity, and at Boulogne he gave £30 to the postmaster's wife and daughter for their kindness to him and the Prince when they had landed there over two years earlier, en route to Spain.[30]

From Boulogne, Buckingham and his company rode post to Paris, where they arrived on 14 May. The Duke had been given sumptuous lodgings in the Hôtel de Chevreuse, and during his week's stay in the capital there were endless festivities, in which Buckingham appeared in all his finery. Although he delighted in displaying his grace of person, the Duke was not prompted solely by vanity. He was in Paris as his king's representative, and to maintain the honour of England he had to outshine all competitors – even when, like the Duke of Chevreuse, they were bedecked with so many diamonds and precious stones that their radiance was said to turn night into day. One member of Anne of Austria's household described Buckingham as 'the best made man in the world, with the finest looks', and told how 'he made his appearance at court with so much charm and magnificence that he won the admiration of all the people. The ladies of the court were filled with joy (and something more than joy); the court gallants were openly envious; and all the husbands at court were consumed by jealousy'. Such was the rage for everything English that even the hunting-cap which Buckingham wore – and which looked for all the world like a modern deerstalker – became the height of fashion for a time and was naturalised under the name of *un boukinkan*.[31]

The week that Buckingham spent in Paris was not entirely given up to dancing and feasting. He also had long discussions with Richelieu, in which he urged him to bring France into a league of anti-Habsburg powers and to promise not to make a separate peace with Spain. Richelieu, however, would give no such commitments. If France were to ally openly with protestant states, he argued, she would drive the catholic princes of Germany into the arms of the Emperor – the very thing that both he and Buckingham wanted to avoid. And as for a separate peace with Spain, there was no possibility of France concluding this, and no need, therefore, for him to make any binding promises. Buckingham then suggested that if a formal league was out of the question, the two crowns should at least unite their strategy by linking the problem of the Palatinate with those of the Val Telline and Genoa, in such a way that there would be no settlement of the one without the other. But Richelieu would not accept this either. The war in Italy, he pointed out, was in its closing stages, whereas the war in Germany was only just beginning.[32]

What Richelieu did not say – but what Buckingham almost certainly suspected and feared – was that the French were considering making peace with Spain over Italy so that they would be free to deal with the Huguenot threat. It was in order to prevent such a development that Buckingham offered to try to bring about an agreement between Louis and his Huguenot subjects. But this, like the Duke's other proposals, was unacceptable to Richelieu. The Huguenots' defiance of royal authority was in no way justified, he insisted, especially as Louis was not threatening their freedom of worship. For a foreign ruler to intercede on behalf of rebels was to countenance rebellion itself, and this was something that no prince should do.

Buckingham, realising that he would get nowhere on the Huguenot issue, returned to broader questions, and warned Richelieu that if France was not more forthcoming in her response to the propositions he had made for joint action, there was a danger that his master would listen to Spanish overtures and procure the restitution of the Palatinate by treaty rather than by arms. If, on the other hand, Louis agreed to cooperate with Charles, there was no limit to what might be done. While the great fleet which was being prepared in England would ravage the coasts of Spain, another fleet could land an English army in Flanders. With the aid of French cavalry this could take possession of Dunkirk, link up with Mansfeld, and conquer Artois for France. But Richelieu refused to take this bait. His only reply was that the English must make their own decisions and act accordingly. Louis would continue his payments to Mansfeld and would also contribute towards the maintenance of a Danish army in Germany if Christian IV decided to invade. But he would not enter the proposed league of anti-Habsburg states.

Buckingham, according to Richelieu, kept his temper throughout these discussions and behaved with perfect courtesy. But there is little doubt that the Cardinal's response to his overtures was a bitter disappointment to him. He had built his strategy around the French alliance, and had been encouraged to believe that his propositions would be favourably received in France. But that was before the Huguenot revolt. Now the French government was obsessed with the threat to its security at home, and, as Richelieu observed, 'so long as the Huguenots in France are a state within the state, the king cannot be master within his realm or achieve great things outside it'. Buckingham could have disowned the Huguenots, of course, and treated them merely as rebels. He had been prepared to do this when it was simply a case of Soubise acting for himself, but early in May 1625 the inhabitants of La Rochelle, who had earlier kept aloof from Soubise, made common cause with him. Not only this. Rohan wrote to Buckingham on 5 May to assure him that there was no question of private ambitions concealing themselves under the mask of public interest, nor was there any truth in the rumours, assiduously propagated by the *Dévots*, that Rohan and his brother were in Spanish pay. The sole reason for their revolt, he told Buckingham, was that Louis had refused to put into effect the solemn promises he had made in the Treaty of Montpellier, and was now threatening to blockade La Rochelle by sea as well as land. Rohan repeated the offer which he and his brother, Soubise, had already made, to put their services and their lives at Louis's disposal, to be used against the foreign enemy, on sole condition that the threat which hung over La Rochelle and other Huguenot communities was removed. Rohan's plea to Buckingham was seconded by the mayor and chief inhabitants of La Rochelle itself. Recalling their earlier contacts with Buckingham, when he had, on James's instructions, expressed sympathy for their cause, they declared that all they were now seeking was the restoration of tolerable conditions for the Huguenot churches in France and confirmation of the ancient privileges of their own town. Once these were assured, they told him, 'all our forces will be . . . turned against the common enemy'.[33]

Buckingham would have been happy to see an end to the Huguenot revolt, but only on honourable terms. Quite apart from his own religious sympathies, there was the question of his reputation, for his enemies would be quick to make capital out of any suggestion that he had betrayed the protestant cause in France. If Richelieu's response to his propositions for joint action had been generous and forthcoming, he would no doubt have used his considerable influence to calm down the Huguenots and bring them to an accommodation. But he now had to consider the possibility that Richelieu, despite the optimistic assurances of Kensington, was himself a *Dévot*, or at least their instrument. He was, after all, a cardinal of the Roman chuch who had risen to power with their support and encouragement. What was more likely than that he would put religious considerations first? If this were the case, there was nothing to be gained from negotiations. English policy would be better directed towards the overthrow of Richelieu, in the hope that he would be replaced by someone more amenable to *raison d'état*.

Buckingham had not, at this stage, completely turned against Richelieu. But his suspicions about the motives behind the Cardinal's conduct can only have been increased by his long discussions with him. Carlisle, who was basically francophil, made no secret of his disgust at Richelieu's policy, and his opinions can hardly have failed to influence the Duke. Buckingham was careful to preserve an outward appearance of equanimity, but he told the Venetian ambassador in Paris of his disappointment at the French response. 'God and the world', he declared.

knew the extent of his goodwill to France and his interest in the common welfare. He had frequently proposed a right and generous line of action to the French ambassadors and here, but they would never consent. He did not know what more he could do, except leave it in God's hands, and apparently it was not His will that such a union should be made to abate the Spanish monarchy.[34]

Buckingham left Paris a frustrated man, for although he had achieved one half of his programme, the French marriage, he had not achieved the other. Marriage and political alliance had been intended to go together, and the marriage by itself was worth little. Henrietta Maria, instead of being the symbol of the league between the two crowns, was an irritating reminder of what had not been accomplished, and it may be that Buckingham's attitude towards her reflected in part his bitterness against her brother, Louis. Yet the week in Paris had not been without its compensations, both minor and major. On a minor scale Buckingham had enjoyed the ministrations of the Duke of Chevreuse's barber, a man who was such a master of his craft that Buckingham paid £100 to take one of his assistants back to England with him. He had also acquired a number of rare plants which his gardener, John Tradescant, would carry home to enrich the grounds of New Hall and Burley. Higher up the scale, he had met Peter Paul Rubens, the greatest painter in Europe, and had commissioned an equestrian portrait from him, at a cost of £500. In a different sphere altogether it is possible that he had met, through the mediation of Carlisle, some of the Huguenot representatives in the French capital. He had also, in the course of his social round, come into contact with many of the leading nobles, including the princes of the blood, and had been made aware of their discontent at the rule of Richelieu, whose avowed intention to elevate the royal authority was a threat to their privileged and irresponsible position.[35]

Among those elements at the French court which were most opposed to the Cardinal was the queen regnant, Anne of Austria. A woman of great charm, still in her early twenties, Anne was the sister of Philip IV of Spain. Her marriage with Louis XIII had been arranged to cement the alliance between the two major catholic states of Europe, and personal considerations had not entered into it. For a time the young couple had been happy together, but they soon drifted apart. Louis's deepest passions were stirred only by male beauty, and although he prized Anne as an ornament of his court, and was jealous of her, he was only in a nominal sense her lover.[36]

Richelieu treated the queen with cold disdain. According to many observers his attitude was the reflection of his own thwarted love for her, but whatever the cause the effect was to make Anne a focus for anti-Richelieu intrigues. By virtue of her position she had close contacts with the leading dissidents among the magnates (including the king's brother, Gaston), who were only waiting for the opportunity to oust the Cardinal and take over the direction of French policy themselves. How much of all this became known to Buckingham during his stay in Paris is uncertain, but his future policies were to be based on a sensitive appreciation of the complexities of the power struggles within France. Where Anne of Austria was concerned, however, his interest was not simply political. Among Anne's confidantes was the Duchess of Chevreuse, who was a born intriguer and a great admirer of handsome men. Her many lovers included Sir Henry Rich, now Earl of Holland, who was a close friend of Buckingham and had described Anne's beauty to him in terms that made the Duke impatient to see the queen. At the same time Holland and Madame de Chevreuse had inflamed Anne's curiosity by telling her of the charm and magnificent physical presence of the Duke. As a result, when Anne and Buckingham first met each other, in Paris, they were already more than half acquainted. Their meeting exceeded all that Holland and Madame de Chevreuse could have hoped for. Buckingham was notoriously susceptible to the beauty of women, and it was hardly surprising that he found Anne irresistible. Anne, perhaps because of her strict Spanish upbringing, kept her emotions under tighter control, but it soon became clear, and not only to her intimates, that she found the Duke extremely attractive.[37]

In the rooms and galleries of the Louvre, thronged with courtiers, household officers and servants, there was little or no chance of a private meeting between the Duke and the queen regnant. Buckingham's chance came on the return journey, at Amiens. Henrietta Maria was being escorted on her way to the coast by her sister-in-law, Anne, as well as her mother, Marie de Médicis, and at Amiens Anne stayed in a house which had a large garden running along the river Somme. In the warm May evenings she took pleasure in walking there, and on one particular occasion she was accompanied by Buckingham. Holland followed some distance after, with Madame de Chevreuse on his arm, and they in turn were followed by the ladies and gentlemen of their suites. Anne and Buckingham, strolling on ahead, turned off the main avenue into a tree-lined path where the light was already fading, and for a few minutes were out of sight of all the others. What happened then is not clear. The Duke made some gesture – perhaps he tried to kiss Anne or to embrace her? – which took the queen by surprise and caused her to cry out. Her attendants came running up, to find her flushed and ill at ease, while Buckingham, taking advantage of the gathering darkness, had disappeared.[38]

There was an epilogue to this scene a week or so later. The queen mother was unwell, and stayed behind at Amiens, where Anne of Austria kept her company. The rest of the party conducted Henrietta Maria to Boulogne, where English ships were meant to be meeting them. The ships had indeed arrived, and had disembarked the welcoming party, which included Buckingham's mother, the Countess, as well as his sister, Su Denbigh. But a storm was raging and there was no question of setting sail for England, particularly with such precious cargo. While they waited at Boulogne for the tempest to die down, a flow of correspondence was kept up between Madame de Chevreuse and Anne of Austria – for the queen regnant, who was by nature coquettish, had thoroughly enjoyed the glittering progress towards the coast, with its touches of gallantry and hints at something more, and was frankly bored by Amiens. Buckingham knew this, of course, and when a small boat managed to beat its way through to Boulogne with despatches from England, he took the opportunity to go back to Amiens, nominally to discuss with the queen mother the possibility of using English ships against Genoa. When he arrived, Marie de Médicis was still in bed, but she immediately received her distinguished visitor and spent some time with him in discussion of political matters.[39]

Buckingham then went to pay his respects to Anne of Austria, who was also in bed, having just been bled. She was surrounded by the ladies of her chamber, one of whom offered the Duke a chair, but he waved it aside and instead knelt by the bed, fondling the sheets and speaking softly and tenderly to the queen. The attendant ladies, embarrassed by this unprecedented style of address, tried to persuade Buckingham to adopt a more conventional position, but he told them that it was the English custom to kneel to queens, and that he preferred to observe the conventions of his own country rather than adopt those of his hosts. He stayed kneeling, therefore, until he had said enough – or as much as he dared – and then took his departure. He never saw Anne again, but they exchanged messages during the few remaining years of his life, and the queen later confessed that she had not found Buckingham's advances displeasing, and that 'if an honest woman might love someone other than her husband, then he would have been the only one who could have been acceptable to her'.[40]

These two incidents at Amiens were soon reported to Louis, and his jealousy of Buckingham and determination not to allow him to return to France became yet another twist in the already tangled skein of Anglo-French relations. Buckingham's behaviour had been, to put the most favourable gloss upon it, undiplomatic, yet it needs to be placed within the context of its time. In James's Court standards of morality were notoriously low, and according to some accounts the King encouraged and abetted the favourite in his amorous exploits. The tone was not much higher at the court of France, as was indicated by the career of Madame de Chevreuse, and there was only a thin line that divided gallantry from licentiousness. Buckingham had been indiscreet, but only because he misread the queen's natural coquettishness. Underneath Anne's veneer of gallantry was an innocent and ingenuous nature, and it was this which betrayed her. Had she not cried out, the incident in the garden would have remained, like many others, locked up in a few private memories. Marie de Médicis, the queen mother, put the events at Amiens in perspective by insisting that they amounted to nothing. The queen regnant, she pointed out, could not have behaved improperly even if she had wished to, since she was always surrounded by attendants. And if Buckingham had been unable to conceal his admiration for her beauty, was there anything surprising or wrong about this? There had been, recalled Marie, many such occasions in her own youth . . . Louis, of course, did not take so light-hearted a view of what had occurred, but his relationship with Anne was a complex one, and the bad feelings between the young couple were fomented by Richelieu, who did not want a rival policy-maker in the king's bedchamber. As for Buckingham, he retained not only the memory of a passionate encounter, but also an important link with all those elements in France which he might one day need in order to oust the Cardinal from power.[41]

Henrietta Maria crossed over to England on 12 June and spent her first night in the apartments at Dover Castle which Buckingham, as Lord Warden, had ordered to be prepared for her. The next day the King came to greet his bride and take her to Canterbury, where the marriage was to be consummated. The Duke and Duchess of Chevreuse had accompanied the new Queen to England, but Marie de Médicis was not able to do so because of her indisposition. She wrote to Charles from Amiens, however, to say that while she was unable to convey her good wishes in person, as she had wished, she would do so by the agency of Buckingham, 'who has conducted himself here in a most worthy manner and given great satisfaction'. French appreciation of Buckingham's goodwill and his services to the common cause were shown by the presentation to him of a circlet of diamonds; but this was little compensation for his failure to bring about a military and political alliance, particularly as he would shortly have to defend his policy in Parliament.[42]

V

It was taken for granted that the beginning of a new reign would shortly be followed by a meeting of Parliament. In this case there was the additional incentive that money was needed on an enormous scale to meet the various commitments into which Charles I had entered. Lack of money was holding up everything, and one of the first actions of the new King had been to ask the City of London for a loan of £60,000 on the security of certain crown lands. This was only a stopgap measure, however, until such time as the two Houses came together at Westminster, for as Conway told Carleton in April 1625, 'the Parliament will supply all for the kingdom and those affairs into which they have engaged His Majesty upon good grounds for the surety of the state'.[43]

Buckingham had some reason to assume that Parliament, when it met, would be easy to handle. In the previous Parliament he had been acclaimed as a hero, and no man had done more than himself to bring the country to the brink of war with Spain, which was what members had been calling for since 1621. The new King, moreover, had served his apprenticeship in the House of Lords, had supported Buckingham's policy of breaking off the Spanish negotiations, and could not be held responsible for the errors of his father. As Charles reminded the two Houses in his opening speech on 18 June 1625,

the business that is to be treated of at this time . . . is no new business, being already happily begun by my father of blessed memory . . . . It is true that I came into this business willingly, freely, like a young man, and consequently rashly; but it was by your entreaties, your engagements; so that, though it were done like a young man, yet I cannot repent me of it . . . I pray you remember that this being my first action and begun by your advice and entreaty, what a great dishonour it were, both to you and me, if this action, so begun, should fail for that assistance you are able to give me.[44]

There is something in the tone of Charles's speech that suggests he was not entirely confident about the response it would meet with. The omens were in many ways unpromising. The trade depression produced by the outbreak of war on the continent and consequent currency fluctuations was still causing widespread dislocation in the English economy, and matters had been made worse by the disastrous harvest of 1622 and the famine months of the following spring. Then, in 1625, as if to cast a shadow over the new reign at its very beginning, plague struck London. As members assembled at Westminster the dreaded infection was gathering strength; one member of the Lord Mayor's household was attacked by it, and the Mayor himself had to flee from the city. Over ninety people were said to have died of plague in the week preceding the opening of Parliament, but the popular belief was that numbers were being deliberately underestimated, to avoid causing panic, and that the true figure was twice as high.[45]

The general gloom would have been lightened by good news from the battle fronts, but God had not, it seemed, blessed the arms of England and her potential allies. Twelve thousand unwilling conscripts had been despatched to the continent under the command of Mansfeld, but on 17 June, the day before Parliament opened, Lord Cromwell, writing from the Count's headquarters, reported that a mere six hundred were left, and even they were only kept alive by eating horses and cats. The King referred in his opening speech to 'the fleet that is ready for action', but it was all too apparent that, despite the large sums expended on it, the fleet was far from ready. A great deal of the meat and beer provided for it had been found to be rotten, and time, as well as money, was needed to replace them. The King's ministers had spoken of aiding the Dutch, but once again there were few signs of success for their endeavours. Charles, as soon as he ascended the throne, freed Mansfeld from all restrictions on his freedom of action, but this came too late to save Breda, which capitulated to the Spanish besiegers at the end of May 1625. The Dutch were further disheartened by the death of their leader, Prince Maurice of Orange, and there were rumours that they were trying to negotiate peace with the Spaniards.[46]

When the gloomy situation at home and abroad is taken into account, it is hardly surprising that the members of Parliament who assembled at Westminster in June 1625 were in a sombre frame of mind. They had no enthusiasm for the war (as yet undeclared) into which they were being led. For many of them the greatest cause at stake was that of religion, and they wanted an anti-catholic crusade. Yet the penal laws against the catholics had been relaxed, and there was a widespread suspicion that despite Charles's promise to Parliament in 1624 some concessions to English catholics had been agreed on as part of the French marriage treaty. As if to confirm members' worst fears, a popish Queen, accompanied by a numerous and all-too-apparent retinue of popish priests, had now arrived in London. No wonder God had shown his displeasure by sending the plague.[47]

There was little welcome in Parliament for the French marriage, which, in the general opinion, was only marginally preferable to the dreaded Spanish one. Nor was there much support for Buckingham's view that an alliance with France was essential to English interests. Most members would have preferred to leave the continent to look after itself, while they concentrated on a sea war against Spain, for they clung to their belief that this had been the policy of England in the great days of Elizabeth. In fact, the privateering campaign against Spain with which the names of heroes like Drake and Hawkins were inseparably linked, had nearly always been of secondary importance. The main thrust of Elizabeth's strategy had been directed towards keeping the Netherlands free from Spanish control and maintaining the anti-Spanish elements in France. It was because she blocked the achievement of his continental ambitions that Philip II had sent the Armada against the Queen; not because she threatened to cut his lifeline with the New World or to strangle Spanish trade.[48]

Buckingham's policy was in one sense more realistic than that of his critics, for he recognised that major land powers could only be effectively challenged on land, and that since England could not, by herself, provide armies large enough to match those of Spain and the Emperor, she would need foreign allies. While they bore the brunt of the fighting – assisted, where necessary, by English money – the main contribution of England to the war would be by sea. Buckingham was already planning, in association with the Dutch, to impose a permanent blockade on the Spanish coast – an elaboration of a scheme originally put forward in Elizabeth's reign by Sir John Hawkins. This would deprive the Spaniards not only of silver from the New World but also of naval stores and grain from the Baltic, and would inevitably weaken the effectiveness of Spain and her allies in military operations. But while this strategy was realistic in that, if put into effect, it would have shifted the balance of power in Europe decisively against the Habsburgs, it was in another sense unrealistic. Buckingham assumed that Parliament, under the stimulus of war, would supply money on a sufficient scale to translate his plans into effective action, but in this belief he was totally mistaken. He was to find out from bitter experience the truth of Sir Julius Caesar's assertion in 1610 that 'the Commons are so sure of their safety, as that they refuse to enlarge themselves to the provision of things necessary for the maintenance of the name of England'.[49]

There was nothing surprising about Parliament's reluctance to provide money on an adequate scale. The Commons, who alone could vote supply, were not involved in the formulation of policy. This function, by long tradition, was reserved to the crown, and even when they were called on for their advice – as in 1624 – they were given no assurance that it would be taken. There is little evidence that the majority of members of the Lower House resented their subordinate role or would have welcomed a closer and more permanent involvement. Had such a development taken place they would inevitably have been committed to paying for the policies they formulated, and this would have been unacceptable to their constituents, whose main concern was to make ends meet at a time when the economic situation was quite bad enough without adding the further strain of war taxation. The members of the Commons were very conscious of their representative role and regarded it as one of their principal duties to redress the ills that afflicted the local communities. They were not unaware of national issues, but they looked at these from the point of view of the taxpayer, and believed that the best policies were those which cost least.[50] On the continent, representative assemblies had largely disappeared or had been emasculated, for the religious conflicts and power struggles that had convulsed Europe since the Reformation in the sixteenth century demanded a concentration of authority and resources in the hands of the ruler in order to produce and maintain the armies that were essential for national survival. The English were lucky in that they were defended by the great moat with which nature had endowed them, and Parliament could therefore look critically at government appeals for financial assistance, happy in the knowledge that there were no enemy armies poised on the frontier.

The 1625 Parliament was typical in this respect, for while the King had summoned it principally in the hope of obtaining a speedy grant of supply, the Commons were more concerned with economic and religious issues. Their attitude might have been somewhat different if only they had been given more specific information about the King's policies and needs, but the crown's spokesmen in the Lower House confined themselves to generalities. This is puzzling, in view of the energy and skill which Charles and Buckingham had displayed in marshalling support during the 1624 session. Perhaps they assumed that the accession of a new monarch, and one, moreover, who was committed to the carrying out of the policies which the 1624 Parliament had advocated, would sweep away all doubts and hesitations. But in this they were mistaken, for the Commons, left to determine their own order of priorities, put religion first and called for a more rigorous enforcement of the penal laws against the catholics. From the point of view of Buckingham's general strategy their timing could not have been worse, for as one observer noted, 'to move these things in the face of the French, while the great ambassador is here, and during the joy of the [marriage] feast, was not so much of able judgement in the movers as out of passion and ignorance in state business'.[51]

On 30 June Sir Francis Seymour — who favoured an exclusively maritime strategy, and thought that the best way of committing the King to this was by denying him the resources to do otherwise — suddenly proposed that the House should vote one subsidy. Sir Benjamin Rudyerd, who had been acting as the King's mouthpiece, immediately intervened to point out that such a sum — amounting, with the customary fifteenth, to about £100,000 — would be 'too little both in respect of want and of his [the King's] reputation'. He failed, however, to indicate what he thought would be a more appropriate level of supply, and the House eventually accepted Sir Robert Phelips's suggestion that two subsidies should be granted. This 'gift', he assured his fellow-members, would 'express the affections of the subjects more than the value. . . . There is no cause for more, and [he] hopes no man will press for more. They diminish the King that think money can give him reputation. The hearts of his subjects are his greatest honour and reputation.'[52]

Phelips was at this time on quite close terms with Buckingham — through whose influence he was hoping to be appointed ambassador at the Hague, if Carleton was recalled — and he may have thought that by proposing a grant of two subsidies, when opinion in the House was apparently running in favour of one, he had demonstrated his usefulness to his patron. No doubt he also regarded two subsidies as a generous grant — even though it would hardly suffice for a minor campaign, let alone a major one. Buckingham, however, took a different view of Phelips's speech and believed that his 'swelling language' had served only 'to cool the desire of speedy supplying the King with monies'. He knew that two subsidies would fall far short of the King's needs; and he had cause to doubt Phelips's high estimation of the value of the subjects' goodwill in view of the fact that the Commons had voted the Customs duties (Tunnage and Poundage) for one year only, instead of following precedent and making the King a life grant. The Commons regarded their action as justified on the grounds that Charles was continuing to collect what they regarded as unconstitutional additional duties on trade ('Impositions'), but it seemed a strange way of expressing their affection for a new King who was about to engage in a great war of which they supposedly approved.[53]

When Buckingham heard that the Commons had decided upon a vote of a mere two subsidies, he immediately rode to Hampton Court – where the King had retired in order to escape the plague – and persuaded Charles to allow him to ask for more. By the time he returned to York House it was nearly midnight, but he sent for as many of his friends and clients in the Lower House as he could get hold of, and they discussed the best strategy to follow. It was eventually decided to raise the question of further supply in the House on the following day, 8 July, but when, next morning, other of the Duke's advisers got to hear of this, they did their utmost to dissuade him, on the grounds that the only result of such a manoeuvre would be to poison relations between him and the Commons. Sir Humphrey May was one of these advisers, but his efforts were unavailing, and so he turned to Sir John Eliot. Eliot was at this time Vice-Admiral of Devon and on reasonably close terms with Buckingham: he had, for example, written to the Duke at the beginning of April to assure him of the 'great desire I have unto Your Grace's service' and of his regret that he had not had the opportunity to 'express the character of my heart, that only takes of your impression'. Eliot was already a prominent member of the House of Commons, and May presumably felt that Buckingham would pay careful attention to his warnings. At May's suggestion, therefore, Eliot went to call on Buckingham at York House. The Duke and his wife were in bed, but on the news of Eliot's arrival the Duchess withdrew, and Eliot was admitted to the bedchamber. There he deployed his arguments against Buckingham's proposed course of action. The King, he pointed out, had already accepted the offer of two subsidies and expressed his satisfaction. It would be dishonourable for him now to demand more, particularly at a time when the House was three-quarters empty, since the majority of members had left London to escape the plague. Buckingham's own reputation would also suffer, argued Eliot, since he, rather than the King, would be blamed for reopening a question that had apparently been closed, 'of which imputation what the consequence might be nothing but divinity could judge, men that are much in favour being obnoxious to much envy'.

Buckingham, however, rejected Eliot's arguments. Elaborating, consciously or unconsciously, upon a point that Phelips had earlier made in the House, the Duke claimed that the King had accepted the subsidies only as a gift, a symbol of his subjects' love; he had never regarded them as sufficient for his needs. As for the thin attendance in the Lower House, this was the fault of

those members who had left early, and 'their neglect must not prejudice the
state . . . . The honour of the King stood upon the expectation of the fleet,
whose design would vanish if it were not speedily set forth: money there was
wanting for that work, and therein the King's honour was engaged, which
must outweigh all considerations for himself.'[54]

Eliot's conversation with the Duke took up some two hours, but his arguments were of no avail and he had to return to the Commons empty-handed.
His spirits can hardly have been lifted by the knowledge that the man chosen
to put the government's case to the Lower House was his rival for Buckingham's favour, Sir John Coke. As soon as Coke heard that Eliot's mission had
failed, he stood up in the House and announced that he had a message to
deliver from the King. He then gave details of the heavy expenditure to which
the crown had been subject since the last Parliament. 'There hath been disbursed for Ireland, to confirm the peace of that kingdom, £32,000. For the
Navy (the preparation for the enterprise now in hand not computed) £37,000.
The office of the Ordnance and forts £47,000. For the support of the regiments in the Low Countries £99,000. The charge of Mansfeld's army
£62,000.'[55]

These figures, which are confirmed by the accounts of Parliament's own
treasurers, show the inadequacy of Parliamentary supply when measured
against the needs of the crown. Of the three subsidies and three fifteenths
granted by the 1624 Parliament, only £23,000 remained unspent. The two
subsidies (without fifteenths) which had now been voted, eventually brought
in £127,000. In other words, Charles had a total of £150,000 with which to
carry out his engagements. But this sum would not even cover the £113,000
still needed for the fleet and the £40,000 he had promised to pay Christian IV
of Denmark 'to draw him into Germany'. Where was he to find the money
with which to meet his subsequent commitment to pay Christian £30,000 a
month and Mansfeld £20,000 to keep their armies in the field? He would
need at least six more subsidies and fifteenths if he was not to plunge yet
further into debt.[56]

Coke reassured the Commons that the King was not asking for this additional supply immediately. What Charles wanted was a resolution that they
supported his policies and that when they returned from their recess they
would be 'willing to relieve His Majesty in some farther proportion'. When
Coke had finished his speech there was a marked lack of response from the
Privy Councillors in the House, who would normally have been expected to
support government measures. Buckingham had either failed' to consult them
or failed to win them over, and presumably they shared Sir Humphrey May's
opinion that the proposition should not have been made at this particular
time. Where Privy Councillors declined to lead, other members were in no
haste to rush in, and Coke's motion was left to die a natural death. Neither
Buckingham nor the King, however, was prepared to concede defeat on this
issue. With more than half a million pounds to find they could not afford to
do so. And almost as important as the question of money was that of confidence. The anti-Habsburg league which Buckingham had been struggling to

create was beginning to take shape, and representatives of interested powers had been invited to a conference at the Hague later in the year. Everything now depended on a clear lead from England, and Charles was already moving towards an open declaration of war against Spain. But this, by itself, would be insufficient. Foreign powers had learnt from past experience that English Kings could only act effectively when they had their people behind them. If Parliament could now be persuaded to make a further grant, however small, and to renew its assurances of support for the future, Charles would have a much stronger negotiating hand.[57]

On 10 July the King held a meeting of Councillors at Hampton Court to consider the question of whether and when Parliament should reassemble. A proposal had been made, presumably by Buckingham, that it should be summoned to Oxford, which was at that time free from plague, for 1 August. John Williams, the Lord Keeper, opposed this suggestion. He argued that in a time of infection men were reluctant to leave their homes and assemble together, and that if members did gather at Oxford they would be ill-tempered, discontented and generally in no frame of mind to advance the King's business. He also pointed out that it was not the custom for Parliament to make more than one grant in a session, and that a meeting at Oxford, or elsewhere, would still technically be part of the same session. Buckingham was impatient at what seemed to him to be hair-splitting and argued that 'public necessity' made the recall of Parliament essential. Williams then asked leave to speak to the King in private and revealed knowledge of a plan among the Duke's enemies in the Lower House to bring charges against him if they were summoned to Oxford. What folly it would be, he argued, 'to continue a session that had no other aim but to bring the Duke upon the stage'. It would be far better to wait for the plague to abate, during which time tempers would cool and Williams himself would be able to mediate with the leading critics of royal policy in the House of Commons and win them over to more constructive courses. His proposal, therefore, was that Parliament should not reassemble until after Christmas. Charles's reaction to Williams's revelations was to ask him why he had not made them earlier to Buckingham. Williams said he would have done so, but that he feared the Duke's wrath. In the event his fears were justified, for Buckingham interpreted Williams's devious proceedings as a subtle bid for power and regarded his links with the more intractable leaders of the Commons as evidence of guilt by association.[58]

The Lord Keeper's professions of willingness to do the King service by smoothing the passage of measures through the Lower House were put to the test at a much earlier stage than he had advocated, for Charles decided to accept Buckingham's advice and recall Parliament. Sir John Coke had already warned the Commons that the King's 'important occasions concerning his own honour and estate, and the estate of Christendom, do require our meeting very shortly'. It was left to Williams, as Lord Keeper, to inform both Houses on 11 July that the King required them to assemble again at Oxford on 1 August.[59]

VI

During the Parliamentary recess Buckingham was, as usual, kept very busy dealing with the multiplicity of affairs for which he was responsible. He found time, however, to write a brief note in his own hand to Dudley Carleton, at the Hague, giving him the assurance that 'all things succeed here as I could wish' and instructing him to 'tell the Queen of Bohemia that when she thinks me farthest off, I am then nearest her service'. Such optimism might seem unfounded, in view of what Conway summarised as 'the King's great expenses [and] the scanty provision made by Parliament'. There were some grounds, however, for Buckingham's optimism. Mansfeld's army was still in existence, even though it was by now largely made up of recruits from Germany, and at the end of June 1625 the King gave orders for the levying of four thousand Scots soldiers to be sent over to reinforce it. Mansfeld had not accomplished anything very positive, but the mere existence of his army acted as a check upon Tilly (who commanded the forces of the Catholic League) and made it easier for Christian IV of Denmark to begin military operations in north Germany. Mansfeld assured Charles, in a letter written at the beginning of August, that if only he were paid his arrears he would increase his numbers and undertake operations against Tilly. But money was vital, 'and unless I have the full amount I shall be unable to do anything worthwhile. Past experience has shown that the furnishing of money in driblets and at long intervals is the surest way to lose and waste it to no purpose.'[60]

There were grounds for optimism, too, where the Dutch were concerned. Buckingham had sent Sir Albert Morton to the Hague to press them to enter an offensive and defensive league, and although they had not yet decided to do so, they had agreed to provide twenty ships for the fleet that Buckingham was assembling in England. The destination of this fleet had not yet been clearly decided on. While James was alive it had been impossible to make open preparations for an assault upon the Spanish coast, though this was one of Buckingham's main objectives, and much depended upon the time of year at which the fleet set out. Buckingham had offered to use it against the ports of Flanders, as an inducement to the French to commit themselves, and he had made a similar offer to the Dutch to employ it against the Spanish naval and privateer base of Dunkirk. The Dutch had rejected this suggestion, perhaps because they suspected that the fleet would not be ready before the campaigning season was over, but their agreement to provide ships of their own was more than a goodwill gesture: it was a commitment to the sort of joint action that Buckingham had long been pressing for.[61]

As for the fleet itself, progress depended upon the rate at which money became available, and it was the realisation of this that made Buckingham so anxious to obtain a further grant from Parliament. There was already a great deal to show for his pains. The French ambassadors, in a report to Louis XIII in mid-June, expressed their astonishment at the size of the fleet and the magnificence of its equipment: 'the Thames', they told him, 'is covered with sails'. Buckingham had also picked a commander for the expedition – or rather a deputy-commander, since he was intending to take charge of the whole operation himself if his health would permit. His choice lighted upon Sir Edward Cecil, whom he had earlier recommended for the command of the English volunteer force in the Palatinate. 'It hath pleased His Majesty,' Buckingham told Cecil in a letter he sent him in early May, 1625.

in contemplation of the extremity in which he sees his dear brother and sister . . . to think of the ways to remedy the necessities they are in . . . . It is resolved upon that a fleet of ships may be employed, accompanied with ten thousand land soldiers, which may do some notable effects to move those that have dispossessed His Majesty's dear sister of her inheritance to loose that prize.

Buckingham gave Cecil no details at this stage of the objectives of the expedition, but he dropped a broad hint that the Spanish Plate Fleet might be one of the prizes, for he told him to choose as officers men who were 'covetous to measure gold by their hats, and other spoils by ships' lading'. He also instructed him to ask the Dutch to release from their service two thousand experienced English soldiers, in return for a supply of new recruits. These could then be brought over to England to train the conscripted rabble who would shortly be making their reluctant way towards the rendezvous at Plymouth. Buckingham ended his letter by reminding his old friend 'that I have put into your hands the first infinite trust and pawn of my goodwill that ever I had in my power to bestow'. Cecil, in reply, assured him that his confidence was well founded. 'I do promise myself Your Excellency will have no cause to doubt or repent you of your favours,' he said. 'I will seek nothing but to please you and to honour you, and, if God say Amen, to make the world speak of your design as much (I hope) as ever our nation hath given cause.'[62]

With the naval preparations going ahead, with the assurance of Dutch cooperation, and with the knowledge that both Mansfeld and Christian IV were now operating in northern Germany, Buckingham had good grounds for some measure of optimism. He had access to the complete picture, of which the general public, including members of Parliament, knew little. Where they saw only waste, corruption, inefficiency and failure, he was conscious of the gradual fitting together of the pieces which might, with good luck and judgement, make a coherent whole. He was also learning, by experience, what needed to be done if the English were to be made capable of waging war. It was not simply a question of tinkering with the machinery of government. Deeper changes were required, which might well affect the structure of English life. The county militias, for instance, would have to be adequately armed and trained, and a special rate raised for this purpose. The Navy would have to be expanded and sailors' pay improved, to make the service more attractive. New dockyards would have to be built in southern and western ports so that the King's ships would not be dependent, as they were at present, on the vagaries of wind and weather for their journey down Channel from Deptford. More vessels would be required to guard the coasts against Dunkirk privateers and Barbary corsairs, and some way would have to be found of spreading the cost of this in order to relieve the maritime towns and counties which were already overburdened. In these and a hundred and one other ways long-cherished habits and attitudes would have to be modified, for there was more than a modicum of truth in the view – which, according to Trumbull, was widely held in the Spanish Netherlands – that the English were 'effeminate, unable to endure the fatigations and travails of a war; delicate, well-fed, given to tobacco, wine, strong drink, feather-beds; undisciplined, unarmed, unfurnished of money and munitions'. Trumbull might well have added that the English aristocracy and gentry were also deeply conservative, tenacious of precedent, and liable to react violently against anyone they suspected of innovation.[63]

In the second half of July 1625, while members of Parliament were enjoying their brief respite from public duties, Buckingham was trying to sort out the problems involved in the French alliance. There was, firstly, the question of the Queen and her household. Henrietta Maria was not yet sixteen years of age when she became Queen of England, and although she was a high-spirited and capricious young woman, she had been taught to show unquestioning obedience to her spiritual advisers. Following the marriage ceremony in Paris she retired to a convent to await the day of her departure, and there she meditated upon her spiritual duties, as the catholic wife of a heretic prince. Her guide and counsellor was Father Bérulle, founder of the Oratorian order, and it was he who drew up the letter of instruction which Marie de Médicis handed to her daughter shortly before she left for her new life in England. In this letter Henrietta Maria was reminded that God had singled her out for a great purpose. She was to pray daily that Charles would be converted to the catholic religion, and she was to use all her influence to improve the condition of her fellow-catholics in England. She must, of course, obey her husband and concur with his wishes in all those aspects of life in which her conscience was not involved. But on matters of religion, said Bérulle, she was 'to show from the very beginning such constancy and determination that you need not fear telling him boldly and openly that you would rather die than give way on even the slightest point'. Such rigidity was hardly calculated to make for easy relations between Henrietta Maria and Charles, but this was not, of course, Bérulle's concern. Indeed, Richelieu later claimed that Bérulle deliberately strengthened the young bride's initial aversion to her husband for fear that otherwise she might give way to Charles's own preferences in matters of religion, and thereby endanger her immortal soul.[64]

Henrietta Maria's household, which she brought with her to England, included a substantial number of religious advisers. They were headed by her grand almoner, the Bishop of Mende, who was assisted by four ordinary almoners, three chaplains, two clerks of the chapel, and twelve Oratorians. In addition to all these there was Bérulle himself, who had been appointed as the Queen's confessor. Such a collection of papist priests was not welcome to the good citizens of London, especially since, as one resident noted, 'they perambulate the palace in their clerical habits and say mass daily in the little oratory'.[65]

There was trouble over the Queen's household from the moment of her arrival in England, for when the King came to take her to Canterbury he invited the leading English as well as French ladies to accompany her in his coach. This meant there was no room for Madame de Saint-Georges, a former governess to the Queen and now her lady of honour. Henrietta Maria, alarmed at the prospect of being parted from one of her few sure landmarks in a strange country, asked the King to include her. Charles refused to do so, and it was only at the insistence of the French ambassadors that he eventually changed his mind. This was a slight which the sensitive young Queen did not easily forget. But the question of who was to be in attendance on her involved more than etiquette. If the marriage between Charles and Henrietta Maria turned into one of affection, the Queen would be in a very influential posi-tion. Richelieu realised this, and the French household was intended from the very beginning to be a political centre in its own right, with close connexions with the English catholics. Buckingham also realised it and took steps to ensure that his own interests should not be overlooked, by asking for his mother and his wife to be appointed Ladies of the Queen's Bedchamber. Richelieu was at first prepared to accept this, and wrote to Father Bérulle to tell him so. But a few days later he changed his mind. It would be unwise, he now thought, to make any concessions, for fear that this would be taken as a sign that the French were either too weak or too lacking in religious zeal to insist upon an exact fulfilment of the treaty obligations. Tillières put the responsibility for this hardening of the French attitude upon the Queen's almoner, the Bishop of Mende (a relative of Richelieu), who had developed an intense hatred for Buckingham and blamed him for all the ill-treatment to which the catholic community in England was subjected. Once again the religious issue had soured Anglo–French relations and interposed itself between Buckingham and the achievement of that close union of the two crowns which he so much desired.[66]

Even those gestures which had been calculated to inspire goodwill had a way of turning into matters of contention. Louis's request for the loan of a number of English ships was one of these. Buckingham had made a swift and generous response, and Louis was offered one King's ship, the *Vanguard*, and given permission to hire seven merchant vessels. Early in May 1625 Bucking-ham, as Lord Admiral, signed warrants to the captains and masters of these ships, requiring them to sail to whatever port should be indicated by the French ambassador, Effiat. A week later he was in Paris, where one of his principal objectives was to bring about a satisfactory settlement between Louis and the Huguenots. He knew that Parliament was due to meet in the near future and that he might well come under attack for the failure of Mansfeld's expedition. He did not want to lay himself open to the additional charge of allowing English ships to be used for the suppression of French protestantism. His hope was that by the time the ships actually reached France the Huguenots would have made peace with Louis, and Captain John Pennington, the commander of the small force, was therefore instructed to delay his depar-ture as long as possible. In case he should be in any doubt about his duties, Coke wrote to make the position clear. There were no clauses in the agreement between the ambassador and the Navy Commissioners, he pointed out, which could be interpreted in such a way as to

> embroil you and the ships and companies under your command in the civil wars of France . . . or against them of our religion in that kingdom or elsewhere . . . . The true intention of your employment is to serve the French king against the foreign enemies and opposers of his honour and state and the interests of both kingdoms and of the common cause of their confederacy with us at this time.[67]

Pennington set sail, at last, on 9 June 1625, and a few days later his squadron arrived off Dieppe. The French admiral, Montmorency, was still in Paris, but when he eventually reached Dieppe he found that there was to be no simple transfer of the English ships. Penningon raised difficulties over the number of soldiers who were to be put on board. Buckingham, he insisted, had told him that not more than half his crew were to be replaced by Frenchmen, but now the French wanted to take over completely. Pennington also had doubts about Montmorency's assurances that 'the design was merely against Monsieur de Soubise' and he decided therefore to return to England and seek clarification of his orders. Meanwhile Thomas Lorkin, Charles's agent at the French court, was impressing on Richelieu the need for a peaceful settlement with the Huguenots: the King, he said, was full of apprehension at seeing Louis, 'upon whose friendship and assistance he partly built those great designs he had in hand, embroiled in civil wars at home'. Lorkin was also pressing the Huguenots to take a more conciliatory attitude, reminding them 'what an unseasonable conjuncture of time Soubise had took to begin his enterprise, which was sufficient to have ruinated utterly His Majesty's affairs, not only with this king and state but abroad likewise'. No one could doubt Charles's care for them, he added, but 'the churches of Germany were equally, at least, considerable with those of France, towards whom all generous designs would be made fruitless by their dissensions'. Lorkin, in his letter reporting on his negotiations, held out some hope that the result of his efforts would be an early peace, and it was presumably on the basis of this forecast that Buckingham ordered Pennington to return to Dieppe, where Effiat was now waiting to receive the ships from him.[68]

Buckingham was very anxious to maintain good relations with the ambassador, whom he recognised as being well affected to the common cause, and he hoped that a prompt delivery of the ships would reinforce those elements at the French court which looked to England rather than Spain. He managed to persuade both Effiat and Chevreuse that he was really on their side and working to overcome all obstacles, but in fact he was determined to delay the handing over of the ships until such time as Louis had concluded peace with the Huguenots. He therefore engaged in a subtle game of bluff and counter-bluff, in which his naval secretary, Edward Nicholas, was his main agent. Nicholas was sent over to Dieppe with instructions that he should give every appearance of hastening the delivery of the ships, while at the same time covertly encouraging Pennington to raise as many difficulties as possible. Meanwhile Pennington had been instructed to pay little heed to any peremptory missives he might receive from the King or the Lord Admiral, and to take his orders solely from Nicholas by word of mouth. If all else failed, he was to allow his crew to mutiny and carry him back to England, supposedly against his will, rather than hand over his ship.[69]

Buckingham was waiting for confirmation from Lorkin that the Huguenots had agreed to make peace, and this reached him in late July. Lorkin reported that Louis's ministers and the Huguenot deputies had at last come to terms; he added that the ambassadors of Venice and Savoy were 'confident that if the peace were firm . . . all those forces would be sent into Italy and attack the Spaniard on his own dunghill'. This was just what Buckingham wanted to hear. French operations in and beyond the Alps had, in fact, been going extremely well. The Val Telline had been cleared of its papal garrisons, and sovereignty over the area restored to the Grisons (one of the Swiss cantons which looked to France rather than Spain for protection). In Italy, a combined Franco-Savoyard army, over twenty-five thousand strong, had forced its way to the outskirts of the city of Genoa, which was a Spanish satellite. Its advance was only checked by its lack of naval support, and also by the French reluctance to risk open war with Spain while the Huguenots were in revolt. But now (if Lorkin's report was correct) it looked as though both restraints might be removed simultaneously, for with peace at home Louis could risk war abroad, and his naval forces, including the ships loaned to him by his Dutch and English allies, could then be turned against Genoa. With these considerations in mind, there was no point in delaying yet further the transfer of the English vessels, and on 28 July Pembroke wrote to tell Pennington that 'the King is assured that war will be declared against Spain for Milan, and the peace is made in France for the religion. Therefore his pleasure is that you peremptorily obey his last direction.' Pennington received another message from Buckingham, to the same effect. There were to be no more delays in handing over the ships, the Lord Admiral told him, 'and you may do it, and so may assure the merchants, with the better courage and alacrity, the peace being made with those of Rochelle and the rest of the religion, as we have newly received certain advice'. Pennington thereupon set sail once again for Dieppe, taking his small fleet with him, and on 3 August sent a note to Nicholas, who had all this time been patiently waiting for him, to say that he was willing to hand over the *Vanguard* without further delay, 'and to cause the rest to do the like, or sink by their sides'.[70]

Charles and Buckingham were acting in good faith, but in fact no firm peace had yet been made between Louis and the French protestants. When the Huguenot deputies arrived at Fontainebleau in July 1625, the King gave way to most of their demands, but at Richelieu's insistence he stood firm on his refusal to demolish Fort Louis. This combination of what the Abbé Scaglia, the Duke of Savoy's ambassador to Louis, described as the bad faith of the French ministers and the stubbornness of the Rochellois, brought into question once again the purpose for which the English ships had been lent to France. Now that they had actually been handed over, the French would be able to employ them as and where they wished, and Charles would be free only to protest. This had been foreseen by Richelieu, who deliberately spread optimistic reports about the progress of peace negotiations with the Huguenots in order to deceive the English. Richelieu wanted to demonstrate to the French protestants that their expectation of assistance from across the Channel was a delusion, and that English sea power was more likely to be turned against them than used in their defence. He hoped that when the Huguenots realised this they would quickly come to terms, thereby freeing him to concentrate on his major objective of destroying Habsburg power. This objective was one which Richelieu and Buckingham had in common, but cooperation depended upon trust, and Richelieu's methods were so devious that the suspicion which they aroused became a barrier in itself. Whatever Buckingham may have felt about the Huguenots, he could not simply stand aside while their political and religious liberties were taken from them. To have done so would have meant the end of all chance of winning the cooperation of Parliament, upon which the success of his policies ultimately depended.[71]

VII

The two Houses reassembled at the beginning of August, and as members arrived at Oxford they were greeted with the unwelcome news that the plague had come with them. The King referred to this in the speech which he made in Christ Church hall on 4 August. Members must decide for themselves, he said, what was greater, 'the danger of the sickness or of the reputation of the kingdom'; but he made clear his own opinion that public matters, and in particular the provision of further monies for the fleet, should take precedence over all other considerations: 'it were much better the Navy should come home beaten by the enemy, and half lost', he told them, 'than not go out at all'. Charles, as always, kept his speech short. He left it to Conway and Sir John Coke to give the two Houses the details of his commitments and requirements. Conway was an obvious choice, since as Secretary of State he was closely concerned with the formulation of policy. Coke, however, held only a minor office, and although he had a detailed knowledge of naval affairs he could not speak with the authority of a minister of state. Indeed, until the very last moment he was not sure whether he would be called upon to speak at all; it was only on the morning of 4 August, when members were already assembling in Christ Church hall, that, as Coke himself records, the final resolution was taken, 'so as a greater charge, with so little warning and many changes, could hardly have been laid upon so weak shoulders'. No doubt the choice reflected Buckingham's confidence in Coke, and also, perhaps, his assumption that the Commons would pay greater attention to a statement by one of their own number, who had no formal responsibility for policies, than to a speech by a Privy Councillor.[72]

Conway opened proceedings with an optimistic account of the international situation. The King now had allies, he said, who were only waiting for a firm lead from England before taking action. 'The honour and safety of this nation and religion are at the stake. If we now grow cold, the princes of Germany will divide; the King of France come in as a party to the Catholic League; the King of Denmark make his peace with the Emperor.' It was up to Parliament to give such a lead, above all by enabling the fleet to go to sea, for which some £40,000 was still needed. Coke, who followed Conway, covered much the same ground, only in greater detail. He reminded his hearers that the King had summoned Parliament not as a formality

but to consult with you how these businesses may be proceeded in, and to let you know that what you have given he accepts graciously, but that these affairs require a further supply. The fleet is now at the sea, going to the rendezvous at Plymouth, where there lie ten thousand men at pay; for which action His Majesty is deeply engaged in respect of his own honour, the cause of religion, and support of his allies.[73]

When the Commons debated the question of supply on 5 August it soon became apparent that those members who, in Nethersole's phrase, 'usually stand stiffest for the country' were not impressed by the arguments that had been put forward. Sir Francis Seymour declared that the whole point of the meeting was to produce a clash between King and Parliament, and had been devised by 'those who, knowing their own faults, seek occasions to lay blame upon us'. Members had been informed that Louis and the Huguenots had come to terms, but it was well known that the French king was still in arms against his protestant subjects. Subsidies had already been voted and wasted. 'Nothing hath been done. We know not our enemy. We have set upon and consumed our own people.' Seymour was careful not to name the person he held responsible for the ills and failures that had afflicted the country, but his fellow members can have been in no doubt as to whom he was aiming at. 'Since princes must see and hear with other eyes and ears,' he commented philosophically, 'how happy is that king who reposeth his counsel upon men of worthiness, and how unhappy he who resteth upon one or two, and they such as know better how to flatter and to beg of him than how to give him good counsel.' Seymour was supported by Sir Edward Coke, who observed that 'the office of Lord Admiral is the place of greatest trust and experience' and that it had been the wisdom of former times to appoint to such offices men who were worthy of them.[74]

Sir Edward also argued that there was no point in granting further subsidies, since they could not be collected in time to affect the going out of the fleet. The Commons would be better employed in analysing the causes of the crown's shortage of money, and taking steps to remedy fundamental weaknesses. In this he was echoing Sir Robert Phelips, who had called upon the House to 'look into the estate and government, and, finding that which is amiss, make this Parliament the reformer of the commonwealth'. Phelips, who spoke with a passion and vigour that carried the Commons with him, had also obliquely attacked Buckingham. 'In the government there hath wanted good

256

advice,' he declared. 'Counsels and power have been monopolised.' In Phelips's view, reformation should begin at home with the enforcement of the penal laws. Could it be that there was some secret understanding with France which prevented this first and vital step? 'What the Spanish articles were, we know. Whether those with France be any better, it is doubted. There are visible articles and invisible: those we may see, but these will be kept from us.'[75]

Against this torrent of criticism the Privy Councillors in the Commons struggled bravely but in vain. Sir Humphrey May declared that 'if the King's plate or jewels, or the plate and jewels of some others whom he hears dashed upon, could have procured money, we had not met here now', and he urged the Commons to give all that was asked for, so that they could not be held to blame if things went wrong. Sir Richard Weston, the Chancellor of the Exchequer, echoed Conway's words about the need to support the common cause at this, its most promising time. 'We have engaged all the princes of Christendom. They anger, they hate, they fear with us. And will they not grow cold with us?' The King's revenues, he said, were all anticipated and he had mortgaged his lands in order to raise money. He concluded with a proposition for a vote of two subsidies and two fifteenths. Sir Francis Nethersole, a former secretary to the Queen of Bohemia and very much her spokesman, also begged the Commons to fulfil their promise to aid the King. If they did not, he warned them, they would merely discourage their friends abroad and give heart to their enemies.[76]

By this time the day was far spent and passions were running high. The decision was therefore taken to adjourn the debate, but not before Sir George Goring had suggested that 'the great Lord who hath been touched may come to clear himself'. Nethersole, in a letter written a few days later, reported that this suggestion was not liked by the House, 'and as little by my Lord Duke, as I hear', but Goring always kept in close touch with Buckingham during Parliament time, and since the Duke had been present in the House of Lords on that day – where he proposed that some action should be taken to relieve the poor of London who were badly hit by the plague – it seems likely that Goring was acting on instructions.[77]

In the debates on 5 August the Commons were apparently moving towards an open attack upon the favourite, but on the following day there was a marked change of tone. This was almost certainly because consultations had taken place between Buckingham and influential members of both Houses who preferred compromise to confrontation. The timing and nature of these consultations cannot be precisely established, nor can it be assumed that a definite 'bargain' was agreed on, by which Buckingham promised to modify his policies in certain directions while his new advisers undertook to dampen down opposition to him. What seems more likely is that discussions were going on all the time, with different groups, and that Buckingham adjusted his tactics in such a way as to secure – or at least try to secure – the maximum support. He was aware of what his critics wanted. He was also aware of what he, the King and, he believed, the country needed. Between these two poles he steered his course, adjusting it as best as he could to the prevailing winds.[78]

The issue of religion was, as always, a cause of dissension. The wrath of the Commons had been directed, at Westminster, against an Essex clergyman, Richard Montagu, who in two trenchant and provocative books had not simply upheld high-church Arminian doctrines but – in the words of the Commons' committee charged with investigating his offence – had laboured 'to put a jealousy betwixt the King and his well-affected subjects by saying there is a potent prevailing faction in the kingdom, etc; and these he calls puritans, but doth not define a puritan, and yet he saith a puritan is worse than a papist'. The Commons ordered Montagu to be handed over to the custody of the serjeant-at-arms while they considered how best to proceed against him, and when Montagu heard this he was, understandably enough, highly alarmed. He had already made the acquaintance of Buckingham, who had treated him with his accustomed courtesy, and now he declared to one of his confidants that 'my hope, next to God, must be in the Lord Duke'. Montagu wrote this letter on 10 July, but the first step in saving him from the wrath of the Commons had already been taken. On the previous day the Solicitor-General revealed to the House, by royal command, that Montagu had been appointed one of the King's chaplains and should therefore be set at liberty: the King, not Parliament, would deal with any complaints against him.[79]

The good news was given to Montagu by Buckingham, yet it does not follow from this that Buckingham had been responsible for the King's action. Clearly the relationship between the Duke and Montagu had gone beyond mere acquaintance, for in a letter written at the end of July Montagu thanked him for the way in which he had been 'pleased to tie me unto your excellent not only self but also most honourable sister, in that bond of obligation as never was poor scholar to such worthies'. The mention of Su Denbigh is significant, for Buckingham was deeply attached to his sister and, it may be assumed, paid careful attention to her views. Lady Denbigh was still, at this time, a member of the Church of England, but she was an intelligent and thoughtful woman who did not take her faith for granted. Her mother, after all, was a catholic, and her friends included Lady Falkland who, in the following year, 1626, announced her conversion to Rome. By that time, and quite possibly a good deal earlier, Susan Denbigh herself was wavering in her religion, and among those to whom she turned for guidance and support was John Cosin, a close friend of Montagu and a committed Arminian. It seems likely, then, that Lady Denbigh's household was already something of an Arminian centre by mid-1625, and in view of Buckingham's closeness to his sister he must have been well informed about Arminian doctrines. He was also frequently in touch with William Laud, who joined with his fellow Arminians, the Bishops of Rochester and Oxford, to launch a counter-attack on Montagu's behalf. At the end of July, 1625, they wrote to Buckingham to inform him that 'the opinions which at this time trouble many men in the late book of Mr Montagu are some of them such as are expressly the resolved doctrine of the Church of England'. As for the beliefs of those who denounced Montagu, 'we cannot conceive what use there can be of civil government in the commonwealth, or of preaching and external ministry in the church, if such . . . shall be publicly taught and maintained'. In other words the anti-Arminians – or so Laud and his colleagues maintained – were not simply the enemies of the church; they were also, whether they realised it or not, the enemies of the state and of its royal governor.[80]

At the time of the Oxford Parliament, then, Buckingham was under considerable pressure from the Arminians. But other contacts drew him in the contrary direction. John Preston, who stood on the opposite wing of the church, was still among Buckingham's advisers. Preston, as well as Laud, had comforted the Duke during the testing time of James's last illness, and when Buckingham accompanied the new King to London, he took Preston with him. Another of Buckingham's close advisers was Sir John Coke, who was strongly opposed to the Arminians and openly combated their growing influence. And Lord Keeper Williams noted that Lord Saye and Sele, Sir William Stroud, and Sir Nathaniel Rich – all of them committed opponents of the Arminians – 'were never out of my Lord Duke's chamber and bosom' at Oxford. Williams himself occupied something of an intermediate position. He was not an Arminian and he had no time for Laud, whom he regarded as an upstart as well as a dangerous rival in the competition to win the confidence of Buckingham. Yet at the same time Williams had a lofty view of the episcopal office and lived in style, as befitted a great prince of the church. He was avid for political power, and devoted considerable time and skill to extending the range of his political contacts. When the Oxford session opened, Williams kept in touch with some of the more influential members of the Commons. Phelips was one of those he spoke with, though Williams claimed that this was with Buckingham's knowledge and approval, and another was Sir Thomas Wentworth, who sat for Yorkshire. The Lord Keeper was also on close terms with Pembroke, the Lord Chamberlain, who was far from being one of Buckingham's admirers. When, on one occasion in Christ Church hall, Buckingham reproached Williams for his lack of loyalty, Williams was said to have replied that he and Pembroke had come together 'to labour the redress of the people's grievances', and added that he was 'resolved to stand upon his own legs'. Williams later assured the King that he was innocent of the charge of plotting against the Duke and consorting with the 'stirring men' at Oxford. Apart from Phelips and Wentworth 'the rest are all strangers to me', he declared, 'and I never spake with any one of them concerning any Parliamentary matters'. All this may be true, in form at any rate, because Williams probably used intermediaries. But by his own confession he was close enough to Buckingham's critics at Westminster to know that they were planning to attack the Duke at Oxford, and it would seem unlikely that he suddenly dropped all these valuable contacts.[81]

Williams's links were not confined to members of Parliament. He also had a connexion with the French household of Henrietta Maria, which was already a source of much ill-will against the Duke. He was on good terms with Father Bérulle, the Queen's confessor, who regarded Buckingham with abhorrence, and it is not without significance that when, towards the end of August, Louis decided to send the Sieur de Blainville on a special mission to England, he told him to cultivate the friendship of the Lord Keeper, who was a lover of France. It was perhaps this French connexion that led Williams to advise the King that he should observe the terms of the marriage treaty with regard to the English catholics, and not subject them to renewed persecution in an attempt to win the cooperation of Parliament. Williams's 'soft' line on catholics, and his robust defence of episcopal rights, made him unpopular with the anti-Arminians, and some of his political actions also angered them. He took care to uphold the royal prerogative and for that reason he opposed the suggestion that Tunnage and Poundage should be voted for only one year. This proposal was, in Williams's own words, 'the darling of the active part in the House of Commons', and by securing its rejection he lost not only their good will but also that of Lord Saye, who had championed it in the Lords.[82]

There are some indications that Buckingham – having learnt the lesson at Westminster that he could not simply rely on Parliament's goodwill, but must resort to management – decided to follow at Oxford the tactics which had succeeded so brilliantly in 1624. This involved sacrificing an unpopular minister, in order to give the Commons a *quid pro quo* for supply, and it looks as though Williams was chosen as the scapegoat. No sooner had the Commons begun their proceedings than the question of a royal pardon issued to a Jesuit was raised. Sir John Eliot, who declared that the blame must rest not upon the King but on his ministers, insisted that an enquiry should be made to see who was responsible. He was clearly aiming his shaft at Williams, who had promised members in the King's name, before the end of the Westminster session, that there would be no relaxation of the laws against catholic priests. Eliot was still, at this stage, a client of Buckingham, and was presumably acting on his instructions. Other members had also been approached to see if they would join in the attack – among them, if Williams is to be believed, Sir Francis Seymour. But the Lord Keeper, whose contacts in the Commons would have warned him about the impending assault, took effective counteraction by showing that the pardon had been sealed not at his request but at the insistence of Buckingham. Williams apparently went further and – in the words of Laud's biographer, Peter Heylyn – 'so applied himself to some leading members that he diverted them from himself to the Duke of Buckingham, as a more noble prey, and fitter for such mighty hunters than a silly priest. Nor was his overture proposed to such as were either deaf or tongue-tied.' Heylyn, who was a confidant of Laud, may well have been repeating hostile gossip, but there can be little doubt that this view of Williams's activities was shared by Buckingham.[83]

Although Eliot failed to pin the blame for the shortcomings of the royal government upon the Lord Keeper, he did not abandon his efforts to serve, and if necessary save, Buckingham. In a speech on 6 August he referred to the great expedition which was being prepared and which would, he hoped, 'have a prosperous going forth, and a more prosperous return'. Eliot argued that the Commons had engaged themselves to provide funds for the fleet, but he did not accept that an immediate vote of supply was needed. 'Our land soldiers were pressed in May last, and our seamen in April, and our victuals prepared; and all this spent with lying-to this time, to no purpose. If necessity, why stay they here to hinder the action, consume victual, and lose the season of the year?' This barbed reference to the delays in furnishing the fleet might seem to reflect on the Lord Admiral, but Eliot was careful to absolve him from responsibility. 'I dare, in my conscience, clear and vindicate the noble lord who hath had some aspersions laid upon him': the blame should light instead upon the Commissioners for the Navy. Eliot was not entirely disinterested in trying to shift responsibility in this way, since the most prominent of the Navy Commissioners was Sir John Coke, whom Eliot would have been glad to see discredited. But Sir John immediately rose to protest that 'this tax of the Commissioners is an artificial condemning of my Lord Admiral. The King's Navy is the most potent Navy of Christendom and if there [be] any thanks deserved, it is all due to my Lord Admiral.'[84]

Eliot was followed by Sir Nathaniel Rich, one of the leaders of the anti-Arminians in the Commons, the cousin of the Earl of Warwick (with whom Buckingham was at this time on quite close terms) and a frequent visitor to the Duke's lodgings at Oxford. Rich put forward what amounted to a middle-group programme, designed to win the support of Parliament for the crown, provided that royal policies were modified in certain directions. Rich asked for a reply to the petition on religion which the Commons had presented to the King at Westminster, and obviously assumed that if the King took a strong line against both recusants and Arminians he would go far towards winning over the House. He called for a declaration of war against 'the enemy', and supported a proposal for another meeting of Parliament later in the year at which the whole problem of the weakness of the royal finances could be looked into. Much of this programme would have been acceptable to Buckingham. The Duke had cultivated his links with the anti-Arminians and when the question of what reply should be given to the petition on religion was discussed in Council, he urged the King to make an answer that would satisfy the House, and brushed aside Williams's objection that the terms of the marriage treaty forbade the enforcement of the penal laws. Buckingham was also in favour of naming the enemy, for he had earlier told the Venetian ambassador that too much money was being spent to no purpose, 'and instead of secretly helping others, the King would ultimately have to make war for himself'.[85]

In some ways, then, Rich's speech may be seen as an olive branch held out by the middle group to Buckingham. But the Duke could not simply accept it, without reservations. Rich asked, among other things, that the King should 'use grave counsellors in the government of these great affairs', which clearly implied that Buckingham must be prepared to share power. And the talk of reforming the royal finances was not without its dangers to the Duke, because there was every likelihood that someone would propose that as a first step the crown should take back those lands that had been granted away, principally to the favourite. Eliot and Rich may have been intending to assist Buckingham, even if only by providing him with an escape route, but their speeches also contained implied criticisms of his conduct of policy, and these were enough to bring Edward Clerke to his feet. Clerke, who had previously been Bristol's servant, was now a client of Buckingham, and he rose to protest 'that some of this House did use some particularities with bitter invectives, not fit for this time, and that against the greatest officer of state in this kingdom'. Clerke was not allowed to continue, however. Members declared that his complaints against their conduct were an insult, and he was committed to the custody of the serjeant-at-arms until such time as the House should decide how to deal with him.[86]

This was virtually the end of business for that day, Saturday, 6 August. Parliament was not due to meet again until the Monday, and during the brief interval Buckingham was besieged by members offering him advice. Clerke's fate, it was suggested, was a foretaste of what the Commons might have in store for him, and he was urged to come to an accommodation with them on the lines indicated by Eliot and Rich: 'that the disorders of the Navy might be imputed to the officers; that the want of counsel might be satisfied by a free admission to the [Council] Board'. The greatest difficulty, as Eliot later recalled,

was conceived to rest in religion and the fleet. For the first, the jealousy being derived from his protection given to Montagu; for the latter, that it had so unnecessary a preparation and expense; and yet, in both, that there might be a reconciliation for himself. Sending the fleet to sea and giving others the command was propounded as a remedy for the one . . . . For the other, it was said that the leaving of Montagu to his punishment and the withdrawing that protection would be a satisfaction for the present.[87]

Buckingham was prepared to accept some of these proposals, but not all, and not necessarily in the way they were propounded. He decided that he would first take up the suggestion put forward originally by Goring, that he should make a public defence of his actions and policies. The King showed his approval of this course not simply by commanding both Houses to be present in Christ Church hall to hear Buckingham speak, but also by instructing the Duke to give a detailed reply to the petition on religion — a manoeuvre that Eliot was later to describe as 'like to pills that have some sweetness over them to make their reception the more easy'. The core of the Commons' petition was contained in the request that 'all the laws now standing in force against Jesuits, seminary priests and . . . popish recusants [should] be duly executed'. Buckingham was able to announce that the King had given his consent to this request and had ordered that the laws should be strictly enforced. He had done so, declared Buckingham, not to please members of Parliament and encourage them to be open-handed, but 'to discharge his conscience' and also to carry out the instructions of his father that he should 'show unto the world as soon as he was married that he did not marry her religion but her person'.[88]

Buckingham then turned to naval matters, but before going into details of what had been done, he recalled the occasion, a year earlier, when he had had the honour and happiness to address both Houses. 'I call it honour and happiness,' he told them, 'because upon that which I said then were grounded these

counsels and resolutions that have made so marvellous a change in the affairs
of Christendom . . . . Now having the same heart to speak with, and the same
cause to speak in . . . I doubt not but to have the same success and approba-
tion.' The change in the state of affairs that had taken place during the previous year had been, Buckingham asserted, little less than miraculous. The
Val Telline had been freed, the French were fighting the Spaniards in Italy,
the King of Denmark was in the field, and other princes were taking heart and
preparing to stand firm against the advance of Habsburg power.[89]

Buckingham went on to assure his audience that he had not changed his
attitude in any way, but was still the same man they had applauded in 1624.
He then turned to the critical questions that had been asked about his conduct, and gave detailed answers. The first question that he dealt with was 'by
what counsels this great enterprise hath been undertaken and pursued?' It was
Parliament, said Buckingham, that had advised the King to undertake the
policy which he was now following; and three of the four points specifically
mentioned by the Houses in their vote of supply in 1624 – namely the defence
of England, the securing of Ireland, and the aiding of the King's friends and
allies – had been immediately put in hand. Only the fourth, the setting out of
the fleet, had proved difficult, and this was because of shortage of money.
Buckingham recalled how James wrote to tell him that 'I have no money in
my coffers, but I would have you engage yourself, your own estate and your
friends' to set it forward'. This, said the Duke, he had been only too glad to
do, since all that he had came from the King. 'Hereupon I went to it with
alacrity . . . and held it a happiness that I could once say to the King: "Sir,
you may see all that you gave me floating in your service."' As far as strategy
and tactics were concerned, Buckingham insisted that he had acted only with
the advice of members of the council of war. 'I never spake almost of the
business but with them. I never came to town but I met with them . . . I
never thought of alteration, nor resolved of anything, but in their company.'[90]

The Duke then turned to the question of why no open war had been declared
in 1624, when the subsidies were voted. There were, he said, several reasons
for this. Time was needed for English merchants to withdraw their ships and
goods from Spain. And as war could not be started at once, there was no point
in declaring it, since this would merely have encouraged the enemy to build
up his defences. Also the potential allies of England, seeing war declared but
nothing happening, would have suspected that the naming of the enemy was a
mere formality and that nothing of substance was intended.[91]

The third question concerned the apparent waste of much of the money
which had been provided for the fleet, and the suspicion that the King did not
really intend to send his ships to sea. To this Buckingham replied that all the
expenditure had been managed by the proper officers, and that Sir John Coke
was ready to show members the accounts. At this point Coke intervened to say
that Buckingham had already laid out £44,000 of his own money, while the
Treasurer of the Navy had contributed £50,000. The Duke went on to
confirm that only £40,000 was now needed to get the fleet to sea – a sum
which the King would have raised but for the fact that his credit was ex-

hausted. As for the rumours that the fleet was never intended for use, why should the King spend so much money to no purpose? 'What should my master gain? . . . Certainly he would never have employed so great a sum of money but that he saw the necessity of the affairs of Christendom require it; and it was done with an intention to set it out with all the speed that may be.'[92]

Buckingham then took up the question of why the want of money had not been foreseen. It had been foreseen, he answered, but a series of 'unfortunate accidents' had caused delays and prevented the consideration of the matter until now. These accidents included James's death and funeral, 'then the journey into France, and the marriage, which made more delays than were expected'. But the new King, when he addressed the Houses, had 'told you plainly that this sitting must be not for counsel but resolution. And when he understood the grant of two subsidies, he conceived that money to be but a matter of custom, to welcome him to the crown, and intended, when you should present them unto him, to dilate of the business more at large, as afterwards he did by Sir John Coke.'[93]

The next question, said Buckingham, was who was responsible for advising the King to summon Parliament to Oxford at a time of plague. The answer, he declared, was 'the business itself and the necessity of it'. He had perhaps been mistaken in advising such a meeting, but 'if it be for my master's honour (which is now budding), your own good and the kingdom's, why should a particular man's mistaking cause it to miscarry?' It had been argued, said Buckingham, that the King should have used his own resources rather than call on Parliament once again, but this was to ignore the fact that the King had already spent more than he could afford. As for the assertion that it was too late in the year for the fleet to accomplish anything even if it were despatched, the Duke claimed that 'there was not one only but three ends proposed of this service, and the time of year is yet seasonable for either of them'.[94]

Buckingham then dealt briefly with relations with France, beginning with the claim that the ships which had been loaned to Louis had been paid for out of the subsidies voted by Parliament and were to be employed against the Huguenots. In fact, said the Duke, the charge of setting out these ships was born by Louis. As for the purpose for which they were loaned, 'it is not always fit for kings to give account of their counsels. Judge the King by the event.' Then there was the charge that the conditions of the French match were worse, from the English point of view, than those which had been insisted on by Spain. This, asserted Buckingham, was not the case. The King's answer to the petition on religion would provide sufficient proof, especially since the commitment which the King had now given to enforce the penal laws entailed no breach of 'any public faith'.[95]

To those who claimed that he had broken off the Spanish match out of personal malice against Olivares, Buckingham replied that he was not vindictive by nature, and in any case had good cause to thank Olivares for making clear to him the way in which the Spaniards had been deceiving James. As proof of his lack of vindictiveness Buckingham pointed to his readiness to forgive 'one of his own nation that concurred with Olivares' [i.e. Bristol]. But he warned his critics that if they persisted in raising this matter it would 'prove a lion to devour him which was the author of it'.[96]

For the last two questions which he proposed to answer, Buckingham turned to the naming of the enemy and the fear that the King's financial commitments to his allies were too heavy for the country to bear. On this last point Buckingham called on his audience to provide the resources which were needed if English sea power was to be used to maximum effect. Naval operations, he insisted, should not be limited only to privateering. 'Let the King our sovereign be master of the wars elsewhere and make a diversion; and let the enemy be compelled to spend his money and men in other places; and our allies . . . will be suddenly and unperceivedly strengthened.' As for the question of who was the enemy, this, said the Duke, was for Parliament to decide. If they enabled the fleet to sail, then the King would allow them to name the enemy themselves. 'Put the sword into his hands and he will maintain the war. Make but once an entrance, it may afterward be maintained with profit. When the enemy is declared, you may have letters of marque. None shall be denied . . . I shall make propositions of venturing whither you yourselves may go and shall have the honey of the business.'[97]

Buckingham was followed by the Lord Treasurer, who gave a detailed account of the King's expenditure and commitments, and then the two Houses returned to their separate meeting places. In the Commons, the Privy Councillors took advantage of the good impression which they hoped had been created by Buckingham's speech to press for an immediate vote of supply, but the House decided to postpone further discussion until the next day. According to Eliot's account, written some years later, the Duke had not won over all his critics. 'Many things of arrogance were observed,' notes Eliot, 'as in the narrative which he made of that great change in Christendom, usurping that work unto himself which time and providence had effected, turning fortuities into glory.' Eliot also records the unfavourable impression that was created by rumours deliberately circulated at this particular moment that Buckingham's account of the motives inducing the King to summon members to Oxford had concealed the difference of opinion between him and other Councillors, in particular the Lord Keeper. These secrets, said Eliot, were let out because of 'private disgusts among the courtiers', and he refers to those who 'for the preservation of themselves, studied his [Buckingham's] subversion'. Eliot gives no names, but Williams was the obvious source of this particular information, and Buckingham was also said to believe that Archbishop Abbot, Arundel, and Pembroke, the Lord Chamberlain, were actively plotting against him.[98]

On 10 August the King sent a message to the Commons, delivered by Sir Richard Weston, the Chancellor of the Exchequer, urging them to resolve upon supply before it was too late. If they delayed much longer they would not simply prevent the fleet from accomplishing anything effective; they would also risk being struck down by the plague themselves. The King, however, did not ignore the proposals which had earlier been made by Rich. These had been partly answered by his replies to the petition on religion, but he now thanked members for taking into consideration 'divers heads concerning King and commonwealth' and gave them his royal word that if they made an immediate vote of supply they should meet again later in the year 'and stay together till you may bring to maturity those things which were propounded'. Sir Robert Naunton, Master of the Court of Wards, immediately rose and made a speech urging the Commons to do what their own, as well as the King's, honour demanded of them, and he was supported by a number of other speakers. But Sir Robert Phelips asserted that the King's honour consisted in taking good counsel, and that if Parliament committed itself to voting supply more than once in a session it would be creating a dangerous precedent. 'We are the last monarchy in Christendom that retain our original rights and constitutions,' he reminded members. 'Let them not perish now. Let not posterity complain that we have done for them worse than our fathers did for us.'[99]

Phelips proposed that a committee should be appointed to draw up an answer to the King, explaining why the Commons could not, at this time, grant further supply. He also referred obliquely to Buckingham's claim to have acted at all times by good advice by asking the House to hear what Sir Robert Mansell — who was a member both of the Commons and the council of war — had to say on the matter. This suggestion was taken up, and Mansell revealed that the last meeting of the council of war which he attended had taken place the previous February and had only discussed the broad outlines of strategy. Mansell, of course, had his own private reasons for attacking Buckingham, since the favourite's appointment as Lord Admiral had ended his lucrative career as a naval administrator. He had only avoided probable dismissal by selling his Treasurership to Sir William Russell — a man of much· greater probity — and although he was employed in 1620 to command the fleet which was sent against the Barbary corsairs, he was never able to regain the influence in naval matters which he had enjoyed under Nottingham. Mansell, like Eliot, felt that he had been eclipsed by Sir John Coke, and now he saw his chance to pay off a number of old scores. He returned to the attack the next day, 11 August, when the House considered complaints that the coasts of England were infested with pirates and that the King's ships did nothing about it. The timing of such complaints, which reflected upon Buckingham as Lord Admiral, suggests more than coincidence, and Mansell drove the knife home by asserting that if such matters had been brought to the consideration of the council of war it would have taken effective action. This provided an opening for Sir Francis Seymour, who, in Eliot's words, 'took off all vizards and disguises in which their discourses had been masked' and openly named Buckingham as the cause of all these ills. 'Then in plain terms,' continues Eliot, 'the jealousies were expressed which hindered the satisfaction of the King. His nearness to His Majesty was too much; his greatness and exorbitance offensive; his power and practice were both doubted and disliked. In his person was contracted the cause of all those miseries.'[100]

Buckingham and his supporters had not yet abandoned hope of leading the

Commons into a more constructive attitude by rebutting the charges made against him. On the next day, 12 August, the Solicitor-General, Sir Robert Heath, informed the Commons that Mansell's assertions had been misleading. It was true that he had been absent from the council of war since the preceding February, but this was by his own choice. He had made a number of suggestions about using the fleet, which, while they seemed highly persuasive to himself, did not evoke the same enthusiasm among fellow councillors. Mansell had thereupon declared that 'if he might not have his own desire, he would meddle no more with the business' and stayed away from all further meetings. Other councillors continued to attend, however, and 'all things were debated and agreed upon by the council and the officers'. Heath's attack brought Mansell to his feet, but he made a rather rambling reply, 'as many men conceived with some variation from what he had delivered the day before'. The House, however, was no longer very interested. Members feared, with good reason, that their session was about to be ended, and they therefore spent the rest of that day drawing up a remonstrance in which they asserted that they were and always would be 'most loyal and obedient subjects to our most gracious sovereign lord King Charles', and that they would be ready, 'in convenient time, and in a Parliamentary way', to reform the abuses in the state and to 'afford all necessary supply to His most excellent Majesty'. They asked the King to 'rest assured of the true and hearty affections of his poor Commons . . . and to account all such as slanderers . . . that shall dare to say the contrary'.[101]

The King had already decided to dissolve Parliament. The question was discussed at a meeting of the Privy Council on the afternoon of 11 August at which opinions were divided. Lord Keeper Williams pressed the King not to part in anger with this, his first Parliament, and warned him that if he did so he would in due course have to summon another, and that 'the next swarm will come out of the same hive'. According to Hacket the majority of the Councillors supported Williams, but could not prevail against Buckingham, who was determined upon dissolution. Eliot, however, tells a different story. He describes how the Duke argued strongly in favour of keeping Parliament in being, and went on his knees before the King to plead his case. Eliot dismisses this as a piece of play-acting, which it may have been. But the action of Sir Robert Heath – a client of Buckingham – in refuting the charges made by Mansell, suggests that even at this late stage Buckingham was still concerned to clear his name and open the way to cooperation with Parliament. Buckingham, though hot-tempered, was rarely impulsive when it came to matters of policy; as Dudley Carleton's nephew once commented, 'he never did anything in his life with post-haste, but when he went into Spain'. Buckingham was always ready to search for a compromise solution to problems, no matter how intractable they seemed, and in this respect he was very different from the King. Charles felt himself betrayed by Parliament. He had committed himself to the policy which both Houses had urged on the crown in 1624, but now, at the outset of his reign and with his honour at stake, the Commons were apparently preparing to impeach his close friend and chief minister, who had been guilty of nothing but loyal and devoted service. In such circumstances, Charles, unlike Buckingham, would have seen no point in continuing the session, and he brought it to an end on 12 August.[102]

VIII

The King, on Buckingham's advice, had gone a long way towards accepting the reform programme put forward by the 'middle group', yet there had been no positive response. The only major demand which Rich had made and which Charles had not explicitly accepted was that 'grave counsellors' should be used to determine policies. But this was only because, in the opinion of the King and Buckingham, the range of consultation was already wide enough. The whole question of who advised the Duke – and through him the King – was a prickly one, and caused a great deal of suspicion, but the facts are not easy to determine. Contemporaries talked about the Duke's 'privados' but rarely named names. Perhaps Sir George Goring was among them. He had been brought up at Court, and was described by Weldon as one of James's 'chief and master fools'. Buckingham made frequent use of him – sending him to France, for instance, to sort out differences that had arisen between Carlisle and Holland, the English ambassadors. He also used Wat Montagu, the second son of his old friend, the Earl of Manchester. But while Goring and Montagu were in the Duke's confidence, and were trusted with the execution of policy, it seems unlikely that they played a major part in formulating it. The Earl of Holland may have been more important in this respect, for he accompanied Buckingham to the Hague later in the year, but his role in policy-making seems to have been essentially that of a supporter and encourager rather than an initiator. Carlisle may have played a more creative part, particularly in the period following the conclusion of the French match. Carlisle was a courtier and a notorious spendthrift, but he was well versed in European politics through his numerous embassies and was far from being a lightweight, whatever his enemies might assert.[103]

Among the other men to whom Buckingham turned for advice were Sir Edward Conway – an old soldier with a record of long service in the Netherlands, who could certainly not be described as frivolous – and Sir John Coke – a dour puritan now over sixty years of age, who had spent a great part of his life in naval administration. In view of Buckingham's dependence on men of this gravity, who did Rich have in mind as more suitable counsellors? Perhaps he would have put forward his cousin, the Earl of Warwick, or Lord Saye. Other people would have nominated Pembroke, or Arundel, or Lord Keeper Williams, while in the Lower House Sir Edward Coke clearly thought of himself as well fitted to advise on matters of state. And no doubt Sir Robert Phelips, now nearing forty, and Sir Thomas Wentworth, who was only just turned thirty, would have welcomed the opportunity to counsel the Duke, if he had only been prepared to listen to them.

Buckingham was, in fact, ready to go a long way to win over his critics and add them to his already wide circle of advisers, but he could not do so unless there was some common ground between them. Before the Oxford Parliament, for instance, he approached Sir Thomas Wentworth through an intermediary, and offered him his 'good esteem and favour' if only Wentworth would agree 'to comply with his ends'. Wentworth, who wanted power, replied that he honoured Buckingham as a person and would be ready to serve him 'with quality of an honest man and a gentleman'. The Duke was pleased with this reply and sent his thanks to Wentworth, but it became clear, after the session was over, that Buckingham still regarded Wentworth as an opponent. Wentworth felt aggrieved at this, particularly since he had, in his own words, 'performed what I had professed'. This phrase gives the clue to the difficulties which Buckingham – or any other chief minister for that matter – was liable to encounter when he tried to arrange a political bargain. Wentworth was no doubt genuine in believing that he had done what he promised, for in his speech on 10 August he had been careful not to attack Buckingham. But he opposed the grant of supply on the grounds that although the sum asked for was small, it would create a dangerous precedent. He wanted 'the business of the commonwealth' to be dealt with first, and he denied that the Commons were in any way committed to meet the King's necessities, for 'the engagement of a former Parliament bindeth not this'. Buckingham might well feel that with friends like Wentworth he had no need of enemies, for Wentworth, while scrupulously refraining from any personal criticism of the Duke, had knocked away most of the planks on which Charles and Buckingham had built their strategy.[104]

The same phenomenon was to be observed in Sir Robert Phelips, who apparently regarded himself, at the beginning of the 1625 Parliament, as one of Buckingham's clients, but allowed himself – and with him the Commons – to be carried away by violently anti-French sentiment at the very moment when the alliance with France, which was the cornerstone of Buckingham's policy, was coming into effect. What the Duke wanted in return for favour was loyalty to himself as a person and commitment to the policies which, as the King's chief minister, he was responsible for carrying out. What Wentworth, Phelips and others were, in effect, offering was an alliance of equals in which their views would carry as much weight as anyone else's. There is something very attractive about their independence of spirit and their refusal to become mere yes-men, but it should not be assumed that they differed from Buckingham on principle. Once in office Wentworth was to show a passion for the King's service (as well as for his own enrichment) that was at least equal to Buckingham's, and in consequence he inspired much the same hatred that the Duke had formerly endured. There is no reason to believe that Phelips, or, for that matter, Arundel, Pembroke, Williams or Saye, would have been any the less autocratic if ever they had attained power. Nor would they necessarily have been more effective as administrators, for there was not a great deal wrong with Buckingham's policies other than the lack of money with which to carry them into effect, and the attitude of Parliament towards the voting of supply would not have been fundamentally altered by a change of ministry.

The two subsidies voted by the 1625 Parliament eventually brought in £127,000, but because of the time needed to collect them they could provide no immediate relief for the desperate financial situation in which the crown found itself. The shortage of money was acute, and yet the demands for payment were endless. In mid-August, for instance, the mayor of Plymouth informed the Privy Council that money was urgently needed to pay for the billeting of the troops who were arriving in the town for employment in the expedition under Cecil; while Carleton wrote from the Hague to point out that funds would have to be provided not only for Mansfeld's men but also for the English troops in Dutch service, and that 'nothing can serve but supply'. Later that month John Evelyn, who had a virtual monopoly of gunpowder manufacture, announced that he was unwilling to provide any more on credit. He was already owed above £2,500, and complained that the Lord Treasurer, 'howsoever he hath been pressed by the council of war, by the Lord Admiral, by the Upper House of Parliament and by the King himself, yet hath directly answered that there be no monies for him'. On 29 August the Treasurer revealed that he had only £600 left in the Exchequer, and that there was no prospect of replenishing the stock of money until the first subsidy payments started to come in, during October.[105]

Money was needed not only for overseas commitments but also for the defence of England itself. The east coast was threatened by privateers from Dunkirk, while the south and west were plagued by 'Sallee and Turkish' pirates from the Barbary shore of north Africa. Already, in June 1625, Buckingham had taken action. Having learnt that 'the inhabitants upon the western coasts are put in continual fear of the burning their houses, loss of their goods and captiveing their persons', he ordered Sir Francis Stewart, who was with the fleet at Plymouth, to take his own and another warship to sea, along with a number of Newcastle colliers – which, with their shallow draught and sturdy build, were thought to be good for off-shore operations – and to range the waters from Plymouth westwards. But a handful of ships was only of limited effectiveness against much larger numbers of pirates, and Sir James Bagg, Buckingham's Vice-Admiral for Cornwall, wrote to warn him at the beginning of August that questions were likely to be raised in Parliament about the lack of adequate protection for the coasts.[106]

It was, in fact, during the closing stages of the Oxford session that John Glanville, one of the burgesses for Plymouth, declared 'that the King's ships do nothing, going up and down feasting in every good port'. He was supported by other members, one of whom asserted that Sir Francis Stewart and his ships had stood idly by while a barge was captured in full sight of them. Sir Francis, when he heard of these public criticisms, reacted strongly. If these complaints were just, he informed Buckingham, 'and that I should so abuse the trust Your Grace hath committed unto me, I should judge myself fitter for Wapping [where pirates were hanged] than to command the meanest ship in the fleet'. Stewart declared that as soon as he heard that pirates were off the coast, he sent a warship and four Newcastle colliers to sea to hunt for them, but they spent 'ten days' unprofitable and dangerous wallowing against wind and weather' with nothing to show for it. They did spot a number of pirate ships, and gave chase, but were outstripped. Stewart suggested that if Parliament wanted to improve the effectiveness of his squadron it should pass an act for fair winds, but the Lord Admiral took the view that additional ships were needed, and in late August he asked the Council to provide one more vessel to join the four that had already been allocated for coastal protection. The Council agreed, but since it might be some time before royal ships could be made available, Buckingham authorised his officers to press any merchantmen with ten or more guns and use them for defensive operations. [107]

When Sir Francis Seymour made his barely concealed attack on Buckingham in his speech to the Commons on 5 August, he dismissed reports of Spanish invasion preparations with the comment that 'the rumour of the flat-bottom boats we heard the last meeting'. But these reports were not a figment of Buckingham's imagination. After the Spanish victory at Breda, Philip IV had taken the somewhat surprising decision to stand on the defensive as far as military operations were concerned, and concentrate his resources upon a naval war against the Dutch and English. He ordered his successful commander, Spinola, to take charge of these preparations, and advised the Infanta Isabella to assemble a fleet of fifty ships in the ports of Flanders. By early September, 1625, the Infanta was able to report that the concentration of ships was going ahead according to plan, and that nineteen had already been assembled at Mardyck. Trumbull, the English ambassador, had not been slow to give notice of these preparations. On 25 August he warned Conway that the ships at Dunkirk were designed for use against either England or Ireland, and in another letter of the same date he said that Harwich was the likely target. [108]

Buckingham had already despatched a number of ships to Dunkirk, where they joined up with the Dutch squadron that was blockading the port, and when he received the news of invasion preparations he detached two more from the fleet at Plymouth and sent them off to tighten the blockade. He was also considering the possibility of blocking up the harbour by sinking some 'old hoys or other vessels laden with great stones' or of setting fire, by some means, to the ships inside. The need for effective action seemed urgent, for in early September he was informed by one of his officers that the Dunkirkers had 'sixty flat-bottom boats, all tallowed and made fit'. In order to beat off any possible invasion attempt, instructions were given to strengthen the fortifications of key places. The Earl of Warwick was sent off to Harwich, to take all necessary precautions – which included mustering the trained bands. But he reported that a great deal needed to be done and that there were no resources available. 'That which of all other wants is the greatest, and for which we are already reduced to some straitness, is that we have no money.' Harwich was not exceptional in this respect. The inhabitants of the parishes of St John and St Peter in Thanet sent a petition to the Lord Admiral informing him that the fortifications which had been erected there in Queen Elizabeth's time were now in urgent need of repair, and they asked him 'to be a means for us unto His Majesty that the same may be done and maintained at His Majesty's charge'. Meanwhile Lord Clifford was reporting from the north that 'the forts and other places of strength . . . are very meanly provided for defence'.[109]

Money was needed above all for the ships and soldiers assembled at Plymouth. While, in the closing debates of the Oxford session, some members were claiming that the fleet was not intended to sail and that all talk of 'necessity' was unfounded, Sir Edward Cecil was at Court, with his officers, for a final discussion on the aims and objectives of the expedition. From Plymouth, however, came reports that 'men, monies and clothes of all sorts are wanting to make this body complete and in vigour to move upon any enterprise'. This poor impression was confirmed in early September by Sir William St Leger, who told Buckingham that 'the army, both by sea and land, be in a very miserable condition for want of clothes'. He did not despair, as he put it, of licking the bear whelp into some reasonable shape, but said that this could not possibly be done until 'we shall be enabled . . . with money and new supplies of men'. The Privy Council had already instructed the commissioners at Plymouth, at the end of June, to supply shirts, shoes and stockings to 'the poorer sort of soldiers', and even breeches in cases of dire need. Two months later it agreed, at Buckingham's suggestion, to provide £3,000 for the replacement of rotten victuals, but in order to find the money it had to deduct this amount from the £20,000 set aside for the Navy.

When Sir Edward Cecil at last reached Plymouth he saw for himself the condition of the expeditionary force. The wants of the fleet, he informed the Lord Admiral, 'are many, begotten out of so long a peace'. As for the army, it hardly existed except on paper. The men had been billeted over a wide area, which made it impossible to concentrate and train them, and since they were not allowed to keep their arms with them, for fear that they would terrorise the local inhabitants, they had little or no idea how to use them. But 'the impediments that will most hinder our proceedings', wrote Cecil, 'will be want of money and the revictualling of our ships'. He added that in his opinion it would now be an appropriate time for the King to call for loans from his richer subjects. With the army and fleet nearly ready to depart, let those who 'doubted the action would never go on' show their 'affections to the cause of their country'.[110]

Charles had already decided on this course of action. In the few months since he came to the throne he had been compelled to raise money for the war by further impoverishing the crown. The £60,000 which he had borrowed from London cost him eight per cent a year, and the City had only agreed to advance the money after Charles paid off the capital and interest still owing for loans transacted by James. As a consequence, lands worth considerably more than £200,000 were transferred to the City, and the income from the crown estates showed a significant decline. Charles had received a windfall in the shape of the Queen's dowry of £120,000 and at first intended to hold it in reserve for use in emergencies. But by June the financial pressures on him were so great that he could no longer keep to this resolution, and the dowry was used in large part to finance the expeditionary force at Plymouth. After the dissolution of Parliament, however, Charles turned to the old-established practice of levying forced loans, and privy-seal writs were sent out to selected gentlemen calling on them to contribute 'for supply of some portions of treasure for divers public services which, without manifold inconveniences to us and our kingdom, cannot be deferred'. The sums demanded were approximately the same as those that would have been paid for a Parliamentary subsidy – Sir Thomas Wentworth, for instance, was asked for £20 – but it soon became clear that payment would be made reluctantly, if at all. The reasons for this were not necessarily political. Sir George Paul, who was one of Buckingham's financial advisers as well as a member of Parliament, protested against the folly of asking for forced loans at this juncture, especially as the two subsidies voted by Parliament were about to be collected. Freeholders and farmers, he declared, were in such straitened circumstances that they could

neither furnish themselves with money for their present necessary uses, much less pay their rents to their landlords – who, knowing not how to remedy themselves, nor where to borrow (by reason of London's poverty and departure of the chief citizens thence) must undergo the censure of their non-payment of these loans, as many begin already to protest they shall be enforced to do.*

Charles recognised the validity of these arguments, and he did not, at this time, press ahead with the project for loans. Instead he turned to the international financier, Philip Burlamachi, who was rapidly assuming the unenviable role of royal banker, and borrowed £70,000 from him. With this he was able to meet his immediate commitments and get the fleet ready for sea.[111]

Despite the expenditure of sums that amounted in the end to nearly half a million pounds, the fleet and army at Plymouth were still short of arms, clothing and victuals, and the officers of the expedition referred in contemptuous terms to the 'beggarliness' of it. The main reason for this was that long years of peace had left the English unprepared for the organisation of an operation on this massive scale. The Navy Commissioners had performed their peacetime task well, but now they were called upon to supply ships at a rate and on a scale that were unprecedented. The same was true of the victualling and ordnance offices. Matters would have been easier if only regular funding had been possible, but the 1624 Parliament had not accepted Buckingham's suggestion about anticipating the subsidies, and in consequence the financing of the expedition had to be conducted on a hand-to-mouth basis, and work frequently came to a halt for lack of money. Not until the subsidies voted in 1624 began to replenish the Exchequer did regular working become possible, and during the time that had elapsed men had deserted, victuals had rotted,

* Paul, who was in a position to know, stated that Sir Edward Coke had suggested the resort to loans. Coke had been prominent among those who at Oxford opposed a further grant of supply, on the grounds that the country could not afford it. Yet he had offered to contribute £1,000 out of his own pocket [D.N.B.]. Was Coke hoping that a generous response to the King's request for loans would persuade Charles that the hearts of his subjects were in the right place, and that all he needed to do to win their full cooperation was to change his advisers? If so, he had miscalculated. Paul's acid comment was that Coke, 'with other his adherent, (might) have better furthered the supply of this want by a Parliamentary course than by the way that it is now brought into'.

and ships had been diverted to other purposes.[112]

Buckingham had come under great pressure at Oxford, from Sir John Eliot and others, not to lead the expedition in person, and had decided to accept their advice. His health was still not fully recovered, and in any case his presence was needed in Holland, where the representatives of the common cause were due to meet shortly to seal their alliance. The Duke may also have felt that his lack of experience in military matters would put the success of the expedition in jeopardy at a time when it already had enough drawbacks to contend with. He therefore handed over the command to Sir Edward Cecil, and went down to Plymouth in person to hasten him away. There, in Cecil's own phrase, he 'played the General' to such effect that he accomplished in one week what would otherwise have taken three. Cecil was assisted by the Earl of Essex, as vice-admiral, and the captains and colonels of the expeditionary force, who included Buckingham's brother-in-law, the Earl of Denbigh, and another of his kinsmen, Sir Alexander Brett. These senior officers constituted a council of war, from which Cecil was required to take advice, and they had the day-to-day management of the ten thousand soldiers and five thousand seamen who were carried in the fleet, which consisted of fourteen King's ships, thirty merchantmen and over forty Newcastle colliers. Cecil's orders were that he should destroy the King of Spain's shipping, and, if possible, take possession of some port on the Spanish coast. San Lucar was suggested as a possible objective, but the choice was left to him and the council of war, since much would depend on wind and weather and the degree of opposition – if any – that they encountered.

Buckingham had already ordered a second fleet to be prepared, and was thinking in terms of a permanent blockade of the Spanish coast. Mansell's expedition had shown that a fleet could stay at sea for a considerable time, and Buckingham had received assurances that the states of the Barbary coast – which were the enemies of England in so far as they committed acts of piracy, but shared a common interest in curbing Spanish power – would cooperate with the English. Cecil was also given orders to look out for the Plate Fleet, in the hope that by its capture he would not only cripple the Spanish war effort but also more than cover the costs of the expedition. He was to take due care not to hazard his ships unnecessarily, since they were – as Charles put it in his instructions – 'the principal honour and bulwark of our kingdom'; but he was not on that account to refrain from undertaking 'any enterprise that may be dangerous, as long as it be by the advice of the council of war, for we know very well that there is no great enterprise can be undertaken without danger'.[113]

Cecil was far from optimistic about the prospects of success. The time of year was too late, he thought, and the fleet was likely to be dispersed by storms. Also the soldiers were likely to succumb to sickness, 'being raw men and by nature more sickly, even in summer, than any nation of the world'. But he comforted himself with the reflection that 'no navy, in the most stirring time, so full of wants and defects, was ever made more ready at so short a warning than this', and he set about drafting instructions for the officers and men under his command. These included an injunction to avoid 'the drinking of new wines and eating new fruits and fresh fish', which showed Cecil's awareness of the fact that the enemy was not the only peril to which his troops would be exposed.[114]

The King, who journeyed to Plymouth to inspect the fleet, was pleased with what he saw. Conway reported that the 'gallant ships in good equipage and exceeding well provided of all necessaries, and able persons of men wanting neither courage nor alacrity in the service, kept His Majesty amongst them a full week longer than was designed'. Cecil had obviously put on a brave face and shown the King only what he thought it fit for him to see, but even Sir John Eliot, who had observed the preparations at first hand, seemed to be quite optimistic. Writing to Conway, whose son was colonel of one of the regiments, he told how the Dutch ships had just arrived, and commented that this timely conjunction was taken as 'a prediction of fortunate and good success to the whole undertaking'.[115]

Cecil — who, at Buckingham's request, had been promised a peerage, under the title of Viscount Wimbledon — took his fleet out of harbour early on the morning of 5 October, much to the relief of Buckingham and of Sir John Coke, who had been driven to distraction by his attempts to deal with all the problems that were referred to him. Coke's relief was of short duration, however, for on the 6th he heard that the fleet had returned to port. He immediately wrote to Cecil to warn him that 'it concerneth much your honour to suspect those that give advice to lose time or which pretend the safety of the ships to frustrate the voyage'. With the King's instructions in mind, Coke added the telling comment that 'the wars require hazard, so it be with judgement, and if the safety of your ships had been most to be respected, the way had been to have kept them at Chatham'. He urged him to admit no further delay. 'The Lord Admiral,' he reminded him, 'in his own person hath given an example of diligence and resolution'; it was now up to Cecil to follow it. Cecil, in reply, assured Coke that he would make all haste, and on the afternoon of 8 October the fleet set sail once more.[116]

IX

Until such time as the expedition returned, Buckingham had many other matters to occupy his attention. One of his major concerns, as always, was the distribution of offices among those he favoured. In September, for instance, following the death of Sir Albert Morton, Sir John Coke had been appointed Secretary of State. His place as Master of Requests was taken by Thomas Aylesbury, a distinguished mathematician who was one of Buckingham's secretaries for naval affairs. Such appointments could be defended on the grounds that the persons concerned had given proof of their ability and their capacity for hard work, but it did not pass unnoticed that they were Buckingham's men. 'The Duke . . . disposes of all more absolutely than ever,' observed Sir

John North, who was himself a member of the royal household. And some time later he added the sour comment that 'my Lord Duke's creatures are the men that rise, the King's servants having little hope of preferment'. It was indeed the case, under the new king as under the old, that the surest way to advancement was through Buckingham's favour, and Goring pointed out to Carleton that one of the reasons for his failure to win promotion was that 'your dependencies have been fixed upon persons averse to my Lord Duke and his undertakings'.

However, it was relatively easy to enter the circle of Buckingham's patronage. All that was needed was the will to do so, and the readiness to support the Duke and his policies. Buckingham did not pursue vendettas. When Yelverton, who had openly attacked Buckingham in the 1621 Parliament, expressed his wish to Conway that 'that most noble Duke may not shut his ears so much upon me', he was soon received back into favour, and a few months later Buckingham informed him that he was to be made a judge. Even Bristol could have effected a reconciliation had he wished it. All Buckingham required him to do was to acknowledge that he had been mistaken in his policies. He was quite content that Bristol should emphasise that these mistakes were the result not of malice, nor want of faith, but of 'an earnest and misled zeal to endeavour by all means his master's ends'.[117]

Bristol, however, was adamant in his refusal to acknowledge that his conduct had been in any way mistaken, and he remained a focus of intrigue against Buckingham. When the Lord Chamberlain, Pembroke, and his brother, Montgomery, were on their way to Plymouth, they turned off to dine with Bristol at Sherborne – an action that upset the King, since it was an indication of Pembroke's ill-will towards Buckingham, and seemed to confirm suspicions that the Chamberlain had been in touch with the Duke's enemies during the recent session of Parliament. Pembroke, however, liked to remain in the background and operate through intermediaries. Among them – or so, at least, it was widely believed – was the Lord Keeper, John Williams, and his dismissal from office in October 1625 was, among other things, a warning shot across Pembroke's bows. It was also a demonstration of Buckingham's power – which was such, Kellie told Mar, 'that none could have made me believe if I had not seen some of it' – and of his willingness to punish those who betrayed his trust.[118]

The dismissal of Williams was a calculated blow against the factious men who, in Buckingham's view, had destroyed the prospect of cooperation between King and Parliament during the recent session. The Arminians claimed that those whom they called puritans had been mainly responsible, but this was not Buckingham's view. He regarded the opposition to him as springing from self-interest, not religious principles, and he planned to demonstrate the truth of this by isolating his critics and strengthening his links with the anti-Arminians. In this way he hoped to restore the harmony which had characterised the successful session of 1624. Buckingham therefore offered the vacant Lord Keepership to John Preston, Master of Emmanuel College, Cambridge, and one of the leading 'low-church' divines. Preston, however, did not want political office, so Buckingham turned to Sir Thomas Coventry, the Attorney-General. Coventry, who was one of the governing body of Emmanuel College and had defended it in a legal action against Lord Keeper Williams, was on good terms with Preston and well thought of by the anti-Arminians, so his appointment secured Buckingham's political aims. It also enabled the Duke to advance another of his clients, Sir Robert Heath, to the post of Attorney-General.[119]

At the time these changes were taking place, there were rumours of even more major ones. It was said that Buckingham would give up the office of Master of the Horse, and that Pembroke would become Lord Steward, leaving the vacant Chamberlainship to be taken over by his brother, Montgomery. These rumours proved to be without foundation at this particular time, but they almost certainly reflected Court intrigues in which Buckingham and his allies — in particular Carlisle and Holland — were trying to come to terms with Pembroke. Sir Benjamin Rudyerd observed, in early November, that the King's attitude towards Pembroke was somewhat warmer than it had been of late, and mediation between the two groups was eased by the personal friendship between Buckingham and Montgomery. But it looks as though the Duke was insisting that if Pembroke became Lord Steward, Carlisle should take his place as Chamberlain, and this was an arrangement which Pembroke was unwilling to agree to. It would have left him in too isolated a position, on a pinnacle of honour surrounded by Buckingham's men. He preferred that things should stay as they were until such time as Buckingham — who was by now on his way to the Hague, accompanied by Holland — should propose more acceptable terms.[120]

Buckingham was at New Hall, preparing for his journey, when news reached him that a great storm had dispersed the Anglo-Dutch squadron blockading Dunkirk. This had allowed an enemy fleet — said to consist of twenty-two ships with four thousand soldiers on board — to slip out to sea. The Lord Admiral immediately sent orders to Pennington, who was lying in the Downs, to pursue the Dunkirkers, while the Council warned the maritime counties to hold their trained bands in readiness. Pennington reported that he was ready to put to sea with four King's ships and two Dutch ones, but that he was short of gun-carriages, since the manufacturer would not supply any more until he had received payment. The want of money, he added, 'makes all things go very poorly forwards'. Of the seventeen ships which Buckingham had appointed for guarding the coast only five were ready for service, and now that four of these were to be sent in pursuit of the Dunkirkers, there would only be one ship left. No clearer indication could have been given of the way in which shortage of money was threatening the essential defences of the kingdom. Fortunately for the Lord Admiral some prize ships had just been brought into Dover, suspected of carrying contraband goods, and several thousand pounds which had been found on board was now used, by Buckingham's direction, to purchase powder and guns.[121]

The Duke, by this time, was no longer at New Hall. As soon as he heard about the escape of the Dunkirkers he dashed over to see the Earl of Warwick, who was charged with the defence of the east coast, and told him to commandeer as many ships as he possibly could. He then went on to Ipswich, where he inspected the trained bands, which had already been mustered. The captain – a local man, not versed in Court etiquette – grasped the Duke's hand instead of kissing it, but was rewarded with twenty gold pieces for declaring that he and his men would know how to deal with Spinola if he landed! Buckingham spent some days at Ipswich – where, it was noted, he attended a sermon by Samuel Ward, a local clergyman of strongly anti-Arminian views, who had earned a certain notoriety by complaining to the Commons about Montagu. From Ipswich Buckingham went on to Harwich, where he waited for the ships that were to carry him across to Holland. Time did not hang heavy on his hands, however, for there was the threat of the Dunkirkers still to be dealt with. He wrote to the Lord Deputy of Ireland to warn him that the enemy might attempt a landing, and he told Conway that he had written to London 'to see what shipping can be had there, and so all along the Thames'. He added that 'some of the Dutch fleet that I stayed from going with the fleet to Spain are come, and I hope that His Majesty's ship which comes from Plymouth to guard the prizes will soon be here'. He asked Conway to send to Plymouth, 'lest the King's ships should yet be there, to hasten them away'. After this frenzy of activity it was hardly surprising that Buckingham was, in his own words, 'wearied with writing of letters and signing of warrants'.[122]

By the end of the first week in November the squadron of ships which was to convoy Buckingham to Holland had reached Harwich, and the Duke and his party (which included his nephew, Lord Feilding, as well as the Earl of Holland) duly embarked. They had a rough passage, and only two ships finally straggled into Helvoetsluys. From there Buckingham made his way directly to the Hague, where he paid his respects not simply to the Prince of Orange and the States General, but also, of course, to the exiled King and Queen of Bohemia. There had been indications of strained relations between Elizabeth and the Duke. Her agent, Nethersole, was out of favour with him, and she was said to believe that his dilatoriness in despatching Cecil's expedition, as well as his conciliatory attitude towards English catholics – which had caused the breach between King and Parliament – were responsible for the lack of progress in her affairs. If Buckingham could now win her active support he would be able to dispel some at least of those suspicions which had clouded relations between him and Parliament. It was even rumoured that he was asking her to agree to a marriage between one of her sons and his daughter Mary, and that in this he had the full support of the King.[123]

Officially, however, Buckingham's purpose in going to the Hague was to conclude the treaties which would bring the alliance of anti-Habsburg states into formal existence. The basis for this had been laid two months earlier, in September 1625, when England and the United Provinces agreed on the terms of the Treaty of Southampton, which bound them together in an offensive and defensive league. Approaches were then made to France, Denmark, Sweden and Venice, inviting them to become members, and although only one state, Denmark, made a positive response, the decision was taken to hold a further conference in December, at the Hague, in the hope that by that time the other countries might have been persuaded to participate. This hope turned out to be unfounded, for as Conway sourly observed, many princes were forward with words but backward when it came to deeds. Gustavus Adolphus of Sweden expressed his willingness to join, but did not send a plenipotentiary to the Hague, and was in any case too involved in war with Poland at this stage to be able to render effective assistance to the allies. As for Louis XIII, he gave general assurances, through his ambassador, of his willingness to cooperate informally, but would not consider participating in the league as a full member. Buckingham and his Danish and Dutch colleagues therefore went ahead by themselves, and on 4 December 1625 set their signatures to the Treaty of the Hague, by which they bound their respective countries to work together to contain Habsburg power, secure the restoration of the Palatinate, and preserve the liberties of the German princes. In order to achieve these aims, Christian engaged himself to increase his army to thirty-six thousand men, while Charles promised to contribute £30,000 a month to their upkeep. The Dutch, whose resources were under strain because of the long war they had fought against Spain, agreed to provide a further £5,000 a month for Christian; they also gave a formal assurance that if he were under pressure from the enemy they would launch a diversionary attack. As far as naval operations were concerned, England was to prepare a second fleet, to which the Dutch were to add a number of vessels. Finally all the signatories declared their intention to act together for their mutual assistance and not to consider any peace proposals from the enemy except in consultation with their partners.[124]

The Treaty of the Hague had been drawn up with great care, to make it acceptable, in Buckingham's phrase, to the most delicate tastes. He was thinking primarily of France, and intended to go on from the Hague to Paris, to make one more attempt to overcome French doubts and hesitations. But his proposal met with a distinctly chilly reception from the French government. There were a number of reasons for this. Louis had received reports – no doubt exaggerated – about Buckingham's conduct towards Anne of Austria during his first visit, and on personal grounds had no wish to see him make a second. This objection could doubtless have been overcome if Richelieu had been convinced of the political advantages to be gained by such a visit. But he was jealous of Buckingham's success in establishing a league which included among its objectives the restoration of German liberties, for this was a traditional aim of French policy and he had no wish to see the German princes look to Charles rather than Louis for their salvation. He was also afraid that Buckingham's presence in France might encourage the Huguenots to adopt a more intransigent attitude, and would increase the likelihood of magnate discontent. For Richelieu was not, as yet, firmly established in power. The nobles in general hated him and were involved in constant plots to overthrow him. It was rumoured that the plotters included not merely the King's brother, Gaston, Duke of Anjou (who was heir to the throne), but the queen regnant also, and it needed little imagination to see how easily and effectively Buckingham would be able to re-establish his links with these opposition elements and

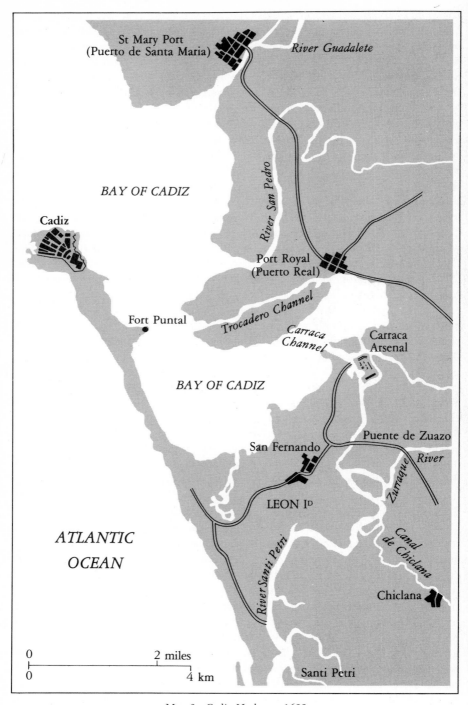

St Mary Port
(Puerto de Santa Maria)

River Guadalete

BAY OF CADIZ

Cadiz

River San Pedro

Port Royal
(Puerto Real)

Fort Puntal

Trocadero Channel

Carraca Channel

Carraca Arsenal

BAY OF CADIZ

Puente de Zuazo

San Fernando

Zurraque River

LEON Iᴰ

River Santi Petri

Canal de Chiclana

ATLANTIC OCEAN

Chiclana

| 0 | | 2 miles |
| 0 | | 4 km |

Santi Petri

Map 3. Cadiz Harbour, 1625

thereby make himself the arbiter of Richelieu's fate and of French policy. Richelieu needed all the support he could get, and he therefore made approaches to his former allies, the *Dévots*. But they demanded that he should show the genuineness of his intentions by giving religious considerations priority over secular ones. This meant, in effect, withdrawing from the English alliance, for there was no sign that the marriage between Charles and Henrietta Maria had had any effect in improving the treatment of the catholics in England. On the contrary, Charles had ordered the strict enforcement of the penal laws, in an effort to win back the goodwill of his subjects after the dissolution of Parliament, and in December 1625, at the very moment when Buckingham was pressing for permission to go to France, the Florentine resident in England reported that 'the position of the catholics becomes worse and worse'. In these circumstances Richelieu felt that he had no alternative but to discourage the projected visit, and he instructed the French ambassador at the Hague to make this clear to the Duke. The ambassador did so, with a most undiplomatic lack of tact, and Buckingham took the decision as a personal affront. He therefore changed his plans and returned direct to England.[125]

X

On the evening of 7 December Buckingham reached Hampton Court, but the joy at his return was shortlived, for an hour later the Earl of Essex arrived with the news that Cecil's expedition had failed miserably. The fleet, far from staying on the Spanish coast to keep up a permanent blockade, was straggling back into English and Irish harbours. The ships, battered by wind and weather, were leaking like sieves, and their crews were so crippled by sickness that they were barely able to move the sails. Buckingham could have suffered no more telling blow, for he had pinned his hopes and his reputation upon a successful outcome to this enterprise. The Florentine resident had noted, in November, how people were boasting that the great days of Elizabeth had come again, and if Cecil had returned triumphant, popular enthusiasm for the war would have infected even members of the House of Commons, and the clouds of ill-will which hung over Westminster, Whitehall, and, in particular, York House, would have been dispersed. Now, on the contrary, Buckingham's enemies would have yet more fuel for their indignation, and the public mood, instead of soaring upwards into elation and commitment, would plunge down into cynicism, bitterness and despair.[126]

Cecil had managed to reach the Spanish coast, and as he drew near he summoned the council of war on board his flagship, the *Anne Royal*, to decide where to strike. In discussions at Plymouth, when the King had been present, experienced seamen had recommended San Lucar as a place that could be captured without much opposition, but now the ships' captains and masters declared that 'it was a barred haven, and not to be entered without a very skilful pilot'. Cadiz, which was the obvious alternative, was said to be too strongly defended, so the decision was taken to anchor off St Mary Port, opposite Cadiz, where the troops could be landed and the ships could fill up with fresh water. A number of colonels asked Cecil to draw up contingency plans for an assault on St Mary, but Cecil insisted that his main purpose in going there was to water the ships and that he would wait and see how things developed before he issued his instructions. This, in effect, deprived the Earl of Essex of a great opportunity to emulate his father and gain the glory which he longed for. As the fleet sailed into Cadiz Bay he saw a number of Spanish ships lying at anchor there, and immediately set his course towards them. He assumed that other ships in his squadron would come up to support him, but because no orders had been given they hung back, and the frustrated Essex had to withdraw from his exposed position and watch the Spanish vessels make their escape towards Port Royal. 'It was thought,' wrote John Glanville, Cecil's secretary, 'that if my Lord of Essex had been more immediately seconded, and have attempted it, he might have prevented the enemy's ships from gaining Port Royal, and taken them in the Bay of Cadiz. But his lordship had no special order other than only to come to an anchor hereabouts and expect the resolution and direction of a further consultation; which he did.'[127]

On 22 October Cecil held another council of war to determine what to do. Some members wanted an immediate assault on Cadiz, for they had received a report – which, as it happened, was correct – that the town was poorly defended and short of provisions. But the ships' captains were more concerned for the security of their vessels and 'it was held a vain thing to consult or think of attempting Cadiz or any other place until we had provided a safe harbour for our ships, the chief bulwarks of England and only hope of our return'. There was a secure harbour further into the Bay of Cadiz, but the approach was guarded by Fort Puntal, which had therefore to be captured. Some Dutch ships and Newcastle colliers were appointed to bombard the fort that night, but although the Dutch showed great bravery in carrying out this task, the colliers hung back. Their masters were in most cases the owners as well, and they did not relish the prospect of losing both their ships and their livelihoods. 'Not a collier appeared in the service the whole night through,' complained Cecil, 'nor would have done at all, had I not next morning forced them to it myself and brought them upon it with threatening and cudgelling.'[128]

The bombardment continued during part of the next day, and then eased in order to allow the landing of an assault force under Sir John Burroughs. Its chances of success were limited by the inadequacies of the commissariat, for although scaling ladders had been loaded on board the ships at Plymouth they were only located at the last moment, by which time it was too late to distribute them among the men. As for grenades to lob over the walls of the fort, these were never located at all, and Burroughs had to land without them. The Spanish commander of Fort Puntal announced his determination to hold out until death, and might well have done so. But fortunately for the English his men were not of the same mettle, and instead of keeping up their resistance they 'held out their handkirchers' in sign of surrender. The commander was forced to follow suit, and by nightfall Fort Puntal was in English hands. Meanwhile Essex had taken his squadron up to Port Royal, determined to capture or destroy the Spanish vessels that had fled to safety there. But the enemy had blocked the entrance to the port with sunken ships, and the weather was so bad that Essex could not force his way through. He therefore returned to Puntal, where the disembarkation of the infantry had by now been completed.[129]

Cecil had at last decided to assault Cadiz, but his men had been landed in such haste and confusion that many of them were without food or water. The weather suddenly turned very hot, and the exhausted soldiers were in desperate need of drink. They came across some deserted farmhouses, which contained great vats of wine, and Cecil – despite the instructions he had originally issued – now gave permission for the casks to be broached. The result was disastrous, for within a brief space of time the English army was turned into a drunken rabble. 'The worser sort', Glanville recorded,

set on the rest, and grew to demand more wine, in such disorder and with such violence that they contemned all command . . . not respecting my Lord Lieutenant himself. . . . No words of exhortation, no blows of correction, would restrain them, but breaking with violence into the rooms where the wines were, crying out that they were King Charles's men and fought for him, caring for no man else, they claimed all the wine as their own . . . . The whole army, except only the commanders, was all drunken and in one common confusion, some of them shooting at one another amongst themselves.

There was no question now of continuing the assault on Cadiz. As Sir William St Leger told Buckingham, a mere five hundred of the enemy 'would have cut all our throats. And there was no hope to see things in a better condition, for our men were subject to no command. Such dissolute wretches the earth never brought forth.'[130]

When the men were sober enough to move, Cecil ordered them to return to Puntal and go back on board ship. A week after landing at Cadiz, the fleet was once more at sea, this time with no clear idea of its objective. The troops, with their inexperience of shipboard life and lack of hygiene, had brought infection with them; sailors as well as soldiers were falling sick, and water and beer were running short. Everyone was disheartened by the failure at Cadiz and the evident impossibility of accomplishing anything worth while.[6] I confess our men are no men, but beasts' wrote St Leger to the Lord Admiral,

but the truth is, more might have been done. But the action is too great for our abilities, of which I am so much ashamed that I wish I may never live to see my sovereign nor Your Excellency's face again . . . . God send you hereafter a better account of your future employments than you are like to have of this.[131]

Cecil's ships sailed out of the Bay of Cadiz on 29 October, and the council of war decided that they should cruise up and down in search of the Plate Fleet. Two days later, in squally conditions, they caught sight of a number of ships making their way towards Cadiz, but were unable to intercept them.

What they had seen was, indeed, part of the fleet which was bringing to Spain the silver from the New World. Its capture would, even at this late stage, have turned disaster into triumph on a legendary scale, but this opportunity, like so many others, was let slip.[132]

Cecil's original intention was to stay at sea until the second fleet, which Buckingham had assured him was in preparation, arrived to relieve him. But his captains reported that infection was spreading very rapidly among their crews, and that the damage caused by a violent storm on the way out would not enable their ships to stay at sea much longer in winter conditions. On 16 November, therefore, the council of war decided that the fleet should make all haste for England. From then on it was every vessel for itself. On Cecil's flagship drink was so short that the allowance per man was cut to a third, and so many of the crew were sick that there were hardly enough to handle the sails or keep the pumps going. When they eventually reached the Scillies the master gave his opinion that they would be best advised to aim for an Irish port, since they would never reach England. And so, on 11 December, they made their way into Kinsale, 'not having seamen enough in health for the fitting of our ship to come to an anchor without assistance'.[133]

The great armada which Buckingham had built straggled home in disgrace, beaten not by the enemy but by its own deficiencies. The search for scapegoats started even before the ships reached harbour. One captain, Sir George Blundell, told Buckingham that the Navy Commissioners were to blame for sending ships to sea that were only 'patched up' and unfit for service. 'We were told (so was Your Grace) that everyone had six months' victuals and good drink fit for men, but I believe you will find it nothing so . . . I am afraid you have been much wronged and abused. Everyone looks to his own commodity and regards not the King's service.' Blundell's complaints were echoed by a fellow captain, Sir Michael Geere, who declared that the meat provided for his men was so rotten that 'no dog of Paris garden I think will eat it'.[134]

If the Cadiz expedition is considered in isolation, it seems like a typical early Stuart piece of bungling. Yet in fact many of the problems which contributed to its failure were inherent in such operations and had already been experienced in the retrospectively glorious days of Queen Elizabeth. Combined expeditions were notoriously difficult to manage, as Drake and his fellow commander found in 1589. They set sail with 150 ships and 18,000 men to attack Lisbon, but were defeated by the same combination of inexperience, disease and supply failures which affected Cecil. There was certainly nothing new in complaints about rotten victuals. When Fulke Greville — who, as Lord Brooke, was one of the council of war which advised Charles and Buckingham in 1625 — was on patrol in the Channel in 1599, he was appalled at the poor quality of the provisions which his ship's company was supposed to live on. 'Our drink, fish, and beef is so corrupt as it will destroy all the men we have,' he reported, 'and if they feed on it but a few days, in very truth we should not be able to keep the seas.'[135]

The immediate problem confronting Buckingham and the Privy Council was what to do with the hundreds of half-naked, half-starved and diseased men landing in west coast ports. The Council's first reaction was to order the soldiers to stay with their colours so that they could be used for other operations, but it was soon made to realise that the army was no longer fit for service. On 22 December the commissioners at Plymouth reported the arrival of some four thousand soldiers, in 'such miserable condition and state, in respect of their wants and sickness, as the consideration does much trouble us'. The £5,000 assigned by the Privy Council would not, they feared, be sufficient, for the men were 'so poorly clad that they have hardly wherewithal to cover their nakedness; which has been . . . the greatest cause of their sickness and mortality'. The commissioners were not exaggerating, for Sir John Eliot told Conway that 'the soldiers . . . are in great numbers continually thrown overboard, and yesterday fell down here seven in the streets'. St Leger's description was even more vivid. 'They stink as they go,' he said, 'and the poor rags they have are rotten and ready to fall off.' Sir James Bagg tried to persuade the local gentlemen to advance money for the immediate relief of the sick men, but they refused to do so. And money was needed, of course, not only to provide for the needs of the returned fleet but also to prepare a new one: military and naval operations could not simply be halted, especially now that the King had committed an act of war against Spain and had become a member of the anti-Habsburg alliance set up at the Hague. But where was the money to come from? Buckingham had assured the Dutch that a Parliament would be summoned to meet early in the new year, but even if this agreed to vote supply it would be many months before the money came in. So desperate was the need for ready cash that Charles had decided to pawn some of the crown jewels, and one of Buckingham's objectives in going to Holland had been to prepare the way for this. Now, on his return to England, he wrote to Sackville Crowe — a member of his household who had been entrusted with this delicate mission — telling him 'to endeavour to raise upon the said plate and jewels, as well His Majesty's as mine, the sum of £300,000'. Carleton, who had come back to England with the Duke, added an appropriate postscript in a letter of his own, written shortly before Christmas. 'For your business you have all things needful,' he told Crowe. 'I pray God you find money as ready, for you are expected here like the Spanish Plate Fleet.'[136]

XI

By the time Carleton wrote his letter, Buckingham was on his way to Burley, and meanwhile, as the former ambassador noted, 'all affairs hang in suspense'. There were good reasons for Buckingham's journey to his Rutland home. Early in 1625 his sister-in-law, Lady Purbeck, gave birth to a boy who, since Buckingham had no son of his own, would be the heir to his titles and dignities. It was widely rumoured, however, that the boy's father was not Buckingham's brother, Viscount Purbeck, but Sir Robert Howard, a younger son of the Earl of Suffolk. Lady Purbeck asserted her innocence, but the whole matter quickly became a public scandal, and there were rumours of sorcery as well: Kellie, for instance, reported that 'there has been witchcraft in hand, and . . . the Duke of Buckingham's picture, in wax, is found'. Buckingham was so furious at his sister-in-law's conduct — by which, he claimed, she had 'forfeited that honour which might otherwise give her pre-eminence and protection' — that he wanted her imprisoned and the marriage annulled. In March 1625 Lady Purbeck and her lover had been ordered to appear before the Court of High Commission, to answer charges of adultery, and the law slowly ground into operation. In May, however, Chamberlain gave Carleton the news that 'the Duchess of Buckingham is said to be with child, which is no small joy'. This rumour was well founded, and on 17 November, while her husband was on his mission to Holland, Kate gave birth to a baby boy. He was named Charles, after the King, and as soon as Buckingham had returned to London and dealt with the urgent matters that demanded his attention, he dashed north to see his much-loved wife and his new-born child. Now at last he had a son of his own to inherit his estates and dignities and carry his name down into future generations. It was the one bright spot in a year that had opened so auspiciously and had ended in disaster.[137]

NOTES

(Abbreviations are explained in the Bibliography, pp. 477—86)

1. *Bas.MSS.* 60.285v.; *Lon.* 633.
2. *Harl.MSS.* 1580.58; *Est.MSS.* 7035.378, unpag.; *Sp.MSS.* 31.282.
3. *Gy.MSS.* 32.26; *Harl.MSS.* 6987.203; *Ville.* 392—4.
4. *Dom.MSS* 14. 214.185; *Gy.MSS.* 32.39; *King's MSS* (in French). 135.272v.— 273v.; *Sp.MSS.* 32.6; *Dk.MSS.* 6.4v.
5. *Rus.*425.
6. *H.M.C.Supp.* 218; *Harl.MSS.* 6987.203; *Est.MSS.* 7035.378, unpag.; *Holl.MSS.* 22.16v.
7. *Harl.MSS.* 6987.203; *Est.MSS.* 7035.378, unpag.
8. *Ch.* II, 596.
9. *Gy.MSS.* 32.37, 40, 42.
10. *Fr.MSS.* 74.40—40v.
11. *Harl.MSS.* 6987.203.
12. *Dom.MSS* 14. 183.9; *Holl.MSS.* 122.86—86v.; 126.1, 42v., 3; *Fort.* 212—13; *Peck.* 467; *C.S.P.V.* XVIII, 598.
13. *Lon.* 692, 693; *Rus.* 499; *Holl.MSS.* 126.15; *Ch.* II. 601—2.
14. *C.S.P.V.* XVIII, 575; *King's MSS.* 135.240.
15. *Rich.* V, 4; *Roh.* 147; *Clarke.* 120; *Bas.MSS.* 61.26, 31.
16. *Rich.* V, 18, 38—9.
17. *Harl.MSS.* 1580.442.
18. *King's MSS* (in French). 135.449, 419.
19. *King's MSS.* 135.399—402v., 406v.—413v.
20. *Fr.MSS.* 74.58—9, 60—61.

21. *Hard.* I, 558; *Denmilne MSS.* 33.1.7.XXII.90; *Fr.MSS.*74.60–61; *H.M.C.*(9). 427.
22. *H.M.C.*(9). 427; *Birch.* II, 501–2; *Harl.MSS.* 1580.87; *Denmilne MSS.* 33.1.7.XXII.84.
23. *Trum.MSS.* 7.175; *Denmilne MSS.* 33.1.7.XXII.84; *Goodman.* II, 379.
24. *Fuller.* 365; *H.M.C.Supp.* 226; *C.S.P.V.* XXVIII, 44.
25. Sir Walter Raleigh: 'As You Came from the Holy Land'; *Fort* 213–14; *Chas.* 4; *Ch.* II, 609.
26. *Trum.MSS.* 7.175; *Sal.* 3; *H.M.C.Supp.* 227.
27. *C.S.P.V.* XIX, 26; *Corn.* 125–6.
28. Herman, 9 April 1625. *Sack.MSS.* uncat.; *Ch.* II, 611.
29. *Dom.MSS 16.* 1.43; *King's MSS.* 135.263; *Rich.* V, 83–4.
30. *Sal.* 16, 14; *Trum.MSS.* 7.179; *H.M.C. Coke.* 196; *H.M.C.Sid.* 439; *Dom.MSS 16.* 2.54; *Add.MSS.* 12,528.21v.
31. *Merc.* XI, 365–6; *Rich.* V, 16; *Porte.* 7; Gilles Ménage: *Dictionnaire Etymologique* (Paris, 1694).
32. *Rich.* V, 85–9.
33. *Burck.* 208; *Tann.MSS.* 72.32, 34.
34. *C.S.P.V.* XIX, 59–60.
35. *Add.MSS.* 12,528.23–4.
36. *Chev.* 256–61.
37. *Roche.* 381; *Bat.* 50.
38. *Roche.* 382; *Porte.* 7; *Retz.* 302–3; *Motte.* 14–16.
39. *Motte.* 17–18; *Roche.* 382; *Ville.* 404–6; *Porte.* 8.
40. *Motte.* 15.
41. *Peyton.* 43–4; *Porte.* 8.
42. *Sal.* 21; *Harl.MSS.* 1583.244.
43. *Sal.* 9; *Holl.MSS.* 126.173.
44. *L.J.* 435–6.
45. *Ch.* II, 623; *Sal.* 21.
46. *Holl.MSS.* 127.240; 126.173v.; *L.J.* 436; *C.S.P.V.* XIX, 76.
47. *Sal.* 24, 25.
48. *Andrews.* passim.; *Howard.* I am grateful to David Hebb for calling my attention to this lecture.
49. *Hawkins.* 451; S.R. Gardiner (ed.), *Parliamentary Debates in 1610* (Camden Society, 1862). 169. I am grateful to Pauline Croft for this reference.
50. *Russell.* 218 *et seq.*
51. *Trum.MSS.* 18.146.
52. *Debs.* 30, 31–2.
53. *Ph.MSS.* 221312. I am grateful to Conrad Russell for lending me a photocopy of this letter; *Holl.MSS.* 127.144; *Eliot.* I, 78.
54. *Eliot.* I, 110–11; *Dom.MSS 16.* 1.25; *Ball.* passim; *Oxford.*
55. *Debs.* 56.
56. *Dom. MSS 16. Addenda*, 521.83; *Dietz.* 227.
57. *Debs.* 59; *C.S.P.V.* XIX, 128.
58. *Hack.* II, 13–14.
59. *Debs.* 67; *L.J.* 465.
60. *Holl.MSS.* 128.69; *C.S.P.V.* XIX, 106, 117; *Chas.* 40; *Gy.MSS.* 33.154B.
61. *Gard.* V, 406.
62. *King's MSS.* 335v.; *Holl.MSS.* 127.22; *Cab.* 168–9.

63. *Flan.MSS.* 18.164v.
64. *Ber.* 3, 9; *Rich.* V, 275–82; IX, 88–9.
65. *Ber.* 22; *Sal.* 25.
66. *Ville.* 408; *Ber.* 27–9; *Rich.* V, 144–5; *Till.* 64.
67. *Imp.* 174–5.
68. *Imp.* 181–2, 203, 205–11; *H.M.C.Coke.* 204.
69. *Imp.* 220–21, 245–6, 249; *Dom.MSS 16.* 43.43.
70. *Fr.MSS.* 75.189; *Dom.MSS 16.* 4.134, 137; 5.7.
71. *Fr.MSS.* 75.311v.; *Rich.* V, 39 et seq., 52.
72. *Wynn.* 1358; *Debs.* 73; *Dom.MSS 16.* 5.30; *H.M.C.Coke.* 208.
73. *Debs.* 74, 76.
74. *Dom.MSS 16.* 5.30; *Debs.* 78, 85.
75. *Debs.* 81–2.
76. *Debs.* 78–9, 83, 89.
77. *Eliot.* II, 48; *Debs.* 89; *Dom.MSS 16.* 5.30; *Relf.* 61.
78. *Thomp.* 76–9.
79. *Debs.* 49, 62; *Cos.* 22, 78.
80. *Cos.* Appendix I, 295; *C.S.P.I.* 178–9; *Heyl.* 164; *Cab.* 105.
81. *Preston.* 111; *Hack.* II, 17–18; *Rush.* 198.
82. *Hack.* II, 17–18; *Bas.MSS.* 62.121.
83. *Eliot.* II, 10; *Hack.* II, 15, 18; *Heyl.* 133.
84. *Debs.* 137–8, 90.
85. *Debs.* 91; *Thomp.* 78; *C.S.P.V.* XIX, 143, 128.
86. *Debs.* 91, 139.
87. *Eliot.* II, 53–4.
88. *Eliot.* II, 56; *Debs.* 95.
89. *Debs.* 95.
90. *Debs.* 96–8.
91. *L.J.* 482.
92. *L.J.* 482; *Debs.* 98–9.
93. *Debs.* 99. *L.J.* 483.
94. *Debs.* 100; *L.J.* 483.
95. *L.J.* 483; *Debs.* 101.
96. *L.J.* 483.
97. *L.J.* 484; *Debs.* 102.
98. *Eliot.* II, 77–9; *Knowler.* 28.
99. *C.J.* 813; *Debs.* 106–7; 109–10; *Eliot.* II, 82–4.
100. *Debs.* 110, 115, 117; *Eliot.* II. 94.
101. *Debs.* 122–3; *Dom. MSS 16.* 5.42; *Rush.* 190–91.
102. *Hack.* II, 16; *Eliot.* II, 104; *Dom.MSS 14.* 176. 67.
103. *Eliot.* II, 110; *D.N.B. sub* Goring.
104. *Knowler.* 34, and rough draft in *Str.P.MSS.* 40/50; *Debs.* 113; *C.J.* 814.
105. *Dom.MSS 16.* 5.35, 85v., 95; *Holl.MSS.* 128.175.
106. *Dom.MSS 16.* 1.48; 5.6.
107. *Debs.* 117; *Imp.* 9–10; *Dom.MSS 16.* 5.84, 102.
108. *Debs.* 78; *Lon.* 724, 726, 729; *Flan.MSS.* 18.216, 218.
109. *Add.MSS.* 37, 816.45, 46; *Dom.MSS. 16.* 1.48; 6.42, 44, 45, 46 I.
110. *Dom.MSS 16.* 5.42, 70; 6.37; *A.P.C. 1625–6.* 105, 140; *Dalton.* II. 129–30.
111. *Crown.* 127–9; *Dietz.* 223; *Rush.* I, 193; *Dom.MSS 16.* 8.34.

112. *Cab.* 371.
113. *Dalton.*II.142;*Dom.MSS 16.* 17.49;*Eg.MSS.*2541.47−9;*Harl.MSS.* 1581.320.
114. *Dalton.* II.142; *Dom.MSS 16.* 11.22.
115. *Holl.MSS.* 129.137; *Dom.MSS 16.* 7.31.
116. *Dom.MSS 16.* 7.9, 29.
117. *H.M.C.Sid.* 440, 441; *Dom.MSS 16.* 6.35; *Dom.MSS 14.* 182.63; 183.13; *Ch.* II, 616.
118. *H.M.C.Sid.* 440; *Preston.* 115; *H.M.C.Supp.* 235.
119. *Preston.* 117, 92−3.
120. *Chas.* 57−9; *Dom.MSS 16.* 9.22; *H.M.C.Supp.* 236−7.
121. *Dom.MSS 16.* 8.22, 28, 47; *A.P.C. 1625−6.* 213.
122. *Dom.MSS 16.* 8.47 and *Addenda.* 522.29; *Chas.* 61−2.
123. *Gy.MSS.* 33.225; *Holl.MSS.* 130.18, 56; *Dom.MSS 16.* 7.44; *C.S.P.V.* XIX, 201; *H.M.C.Supp.* 237.
124. *Dumont.* 478, 482; *Rus.* 628.
125. *Dk.MSS.* 6.218; *Rich.* V, 162; *Ville.* 424; *Sal.* 40.
126. *Dom.MSS 16.* 11.32; *Sal.* 37.
127. *Harl.MSS.* 1583.37; *Glan.* 33−6, 39.
128. *Glan.* 41−2; *Dalton.* II, 211.
129. *Add.MSS.* 6703.45−45v.; *Harl.MSS.* 1583.37; *Dalton.* II, 203−4.
130. *Add.MSS.* 6703.46−8; *Glan.* 59−60; *Dalton.* II, 200.
131. *Dalton.* II, 201−2.
132. *Dom.MSS 16.* 11.22; *Dalton.* II, 225; *Plaja.* 134−5.
133. *Glan.* 106 *et seq.*: *Dom.MSS 16.* 11.22.
134. *Dalton.* II, 206, 226.
135. *Rebholz.* 119.
136. *A.P.C. 1625−6.* 264; *Dom. MSS 16.* 12.35, 38; 11.64; 12.10, 31; *Dalton.* II, 236; *C.S.P.V.* XIX, 257.
137. *Dom.MSS 16.* 12.31; *H.M.C.Supp.* 220; *Dom.MSS 14.* 183.52; 184.7; *Cab.* 281−2; *Ch.* II, 619; *Laud.* 175.

CHAPTER EIGHT

1626: 'The Chief Cause of these Evils and Mischiefs'

I

Buckingham can hardly have been surprised by Louis's refusal to become a member of the league of anti-Habsburg states which was created at the Hague in December 1625. Some months earlier, before leaving for Holland, he had told the Venetian ambassador of his belief that the *Dévots* were now in the ascendant in France and had persuaded Louis to commit himself to the destruction of the Huguenots rather than the containment of Habsburg power. The evidence certainly seemed to confirm this pessimistic prognosis, for on 5 September a French naval squadron (which included English and Dutch elements) encountered the Huguenot fleet off the Ile de Ré, within sight of La Rochelle, and in a two-day battle virtually annihilated it. Soubise, with a handful of ships, fled to Falmouth, where he was given protection against his French pursuers. Meanwhile Louis's army occupied Ré and the neighbouring island of Oleron, and cleared the way for the blockade of La Rochelle itself. The destruction of Soubise's fleet meant that La Rochelle was no longer at sea power in her own right and was now almost totally dependent upon England for the maintenance of her independence. The leading citizens of the town realised that they would have to make their peace with Louis, but they called on Charles to guarantee the terms of any settlement they might conclude and to promise his assistance in case Louis subsequently refused to implement them.[1]

It was very much in the King's interest to preserve the quasi-independence of La Rochelle, since this provided him with a convenient lever which he could use to bring pressure to bear on the French government. There was also the important consideration that the Rochellois were protestants and had the sympathy of their co-religionists in England. An anonymous pamphlet called 'Tom Tell Truth', which made its undercover appearance in the closing years of James's reign and took the form of a letter to the King, put the matter succinctly:

As long as God hath any children in France we shall be sure to have brethren there.

But they once gone, your brother of France will quickly show whose child he is . . . . Since then the tie you have upon that prince's friendship is of so loose a knot, what can Your Majesty do better for yourself and yours than to keep his enmity still clogged, by cherishing and maintaining so good a party in his country as those of the religion?

These sentiments were widely shared in Parliament, and both the King and Buckingham were aware that if La Rochelle were allowed to fall they would lose whatever chance they had of winning the cooperation of the two Houses. For all these reasons, then, the King was inclined to favour the Huguenots and assure them of his continuing protection.[2]

There were, however, other factors to be taken into consideration. The most important of these was the French refusal to engage simultaneously in war at home and abroad. If English support encouraged the Rochellois, and the Huguenots in general, to keep fighting in the hope that they would eventually extract better terms from Louis, then the prospect of France joining in the anti-Habsburg crusade would be even more remote. It was essential to preserve the protestants in France but not at the expense of the protestants in Germany and elsewhere. Charles therefore pressed the Huguenots to make their submission to Louis at the same time as he urged the French king to offer them reasonable terms. His assumption, and that of Buckingham, was that once Louis had peace within his kingdom he would turn his attention towards Italy and Germany. But could this, in fact, be taken for granted? There were many voices, not least among the Rochellois, which expressed a different opinion. According to them the French government was preparing to cooperate with Spain to achieve the total destruction of protestantism. If such indeed were the case, then the best policy for England would be to strengthen the Huguenots and enable them to defend themselves. It would not be difficult to do this, since Soubise was pressing for an audience with the King, and asking for ships and money with which to continue his fight. Charles refused to see him, hoping thereby to demonstrate to Louis that while he supported the legitimate claims of French protestants he drew the line at rebels. Yet such an attitude did not endear him to his subjects, especially as the Rochellois had many links with England and were skilful in putting over their case. In the last resort, then, Charles and Buckingham had to feel their way by instinct rather than reason. Like soothsayers they observed the omens closely and adjusted their policy accordingly. While on the one hand they appeared to accept Louis's assurances and encouraged the Huguenots to sue for peace, they also, on the other, kept open the lines of communication with Soubise and the protestant leaders within France and made preparations to aid them if necessary. In the circumstances of late 1625 this was almost certainly the best policy, but the hedging of bets, which was born out of suspicion, generated suspicion on both sides of the Channel.[3]

One of the major immediate causes of ill-will between France and England was the issue of the ships which had been loaned to Louis earlier in 1625. The Dutch were also involved, and were less well placed than the English, since the ships which they (unlike Buckingham) had handed over according to schedule played a major part in the battle off Ré, and after the news of the Huguenot defeat it was reported from Holland that 'the preachers and common people here do ascribe the misadventures at sea by tempest and otherwise unto the judgement of God revenging their having employed their ships against them of their own religion'. Buckingham, by delaying the transfer of the *Vanguard* and the merchant vessels until the last possible moment, had ensured that although the English ships were present at the battle they took no significant part in it. But this was not widely known or appreciated in England, and the general opinion was very similar to that in Holland. Fulke Greville, Lord Brooke, for instance, wrote to his friend and former client, Sir John Coke, to ask him 'how this change of wounding our own church with our own weapons stole in since the first instructions, which so providently restrained that French-desired liberty'. And Kellie, writing to Mar in November 1625, reported that Buckingham was 'much blamed for those ships that went from hence'.[4]

Charles made repeated attempts to secure the return of the loaned ships, on the grounds that they had done all that was expected of them and were now urgently needed at home for coastguard and trade protection duties. He brought the matter up with the Sieur de Blainville, whom Louis sent over to England as his special envoy in the closing months of 1625, but Blainville gave a temporising reply. His view was that the longer English ships were seen to be in Louis's service, the greater would be the effect in lowering Huguenot morale. And there was the unresolved problem of Soubise, who had brought with him to Falmouth one of Louis's vessels, the St Jean, which he had captured at Blavet. If Charles wished the English ships to be restored, said Blainville, let him first instruct Soubise to hand over the St Jean.[5]

A swift return of the English ships might have done much to improve Anglo-French relations. Repeated equivocations, on the contrary, deepened the already acute suspicions about French policy at the English Court and strengthened the hand of those who believed that strong action was now required. Sir John Coke, for instance, wrote to the Duke in Holland to give him his opinion that until Louis and his ministers had lost all hope of gulling England into acquiescing in the destruction of the Huguenots they would never 'really and vigorously pursue the war beyond the Alps. And if once they extinguish the religion in France they will, for many respects, be to us worse neighbours than the Spaniard.' Reinforcement for Coke's views came from Henry De Vic, who had been sent to France by Conway to report on the situation there. In his despatches of November 1625 he told how the Huguenot deputies had arrived at Court and asked for peace on the same terms as they were offered before the defeat off Ré. Louis was prepared to grant this to other Huguenot communities, but not to La Rochelle, and when the deputies insisted that the great port should be included 'he answered "Non! Non! Non!", but with such indignation, shaking his head and stretching out his arms, as is beyond the expression of words to represent'. The deputies therefore decided to return home, and the French government began the construction of fortifications on the island of Ré, which could well be the prelude to a blockade of La Rochelle. De Vic attributed the intransigence of the French ministers to the prevalence of the *Dévots* at Court, and pressed Charles to take a firm stand, since a conciliatory approach would be interpreted as a sign of weakness; only loud remonstrances, he said, could 'prevail in that court and break the knot of the contrary faction, which hath taken a settled resolution, almost past recovery, to extirpate the protestants, unless speedy and powerful remedy be applied'. In case any doubt should remain in English minds about the seriousness of the threat facing the protestants in France, the citizens of La Rochelle sent a delegation to London in December 1625 to inform the King of their desperate state and to urge him to give all the help he possibly could. Charles referred the matter to the Privy Council, which, after due deliberation, advised him that English assistance should be offered to the Rochellois.[6]

By this time Buckingham had returned to Court, having completed his mission to the Hague, but there is no reason to suppose that he was responsible for the hardening of the English attitude. Before he went to Holland he had told Blainville of his annoyance at the way in which time and energy were being wasted in trivial disputes which simply held up the achievement of the major objective, the creation of 'a great union of all the states which are apprehensive about the power of Spain'. He had hoped to go on from the Hague to Paris, in order to resolve all these differences, but although he had been angered by the French refusal to allow this visit his influence was still on the side of moderation, for he saw no reason to change his assumption that only through the cooperation of the two crowns could the threat of Habsburg domination be lifted from Europe. Yet he could not ignore public opinion in England, which was highly critical of the attitude of the French government towards the Huguenots. Nor could he count on the King to stem the mounting tide of indignation, for Charles held the French responsible even for the dis-harmony of his private life. He was convinced that Henrietta Maria's advisers were ruining his marriage by preventing the growth of that trust between man and wife on which any successful relationship must be based. Henrietta Maria took her religious duties seriously, and looked for guidance to Father Bérulle and Madame de Saint-Georges. She could hardly ask Charles for his advice, since in her eyes he was a heretic, yet her failure to do so made the King frustrated and angry. Even Richelieu felt that the Queen was somewhat too rigid in her attitude, for he asked Marie de Médicis to write to her and suggest that she should show greater flexibility. Marie did so, and her letter was apparently effective, for in October 1625 Charles told Buckingham that 'my wife begins to mend her manners'. But he showed his distrust by adding 'I know not how long it will continue, for they say it is by advice.'[7]

Charles also gave Buckingham the welcome news that the *Monsieurs* (which was the pejorative term the King used to describe the members of the Queen's household) were about to return to France. In this, however, he was mistaken, for men like Bérulle regarded it as their sacred duty to stand by the Queen and protect her from all the unwholesome influences that abounded in a heretical land. This placed them in something of a dilemma where the King was concerned, for while they held it to be a wife's duty to obey her husband, they did not wish Henrietta Maria to succumb to Charles's blandishments for fear that she might thereby endanger her immortal soul. They found an easy way out of this dilemma by blaming Buckingham, rather than themselves, for the lack of harmony between the royal couple. That this was not the case is shown, among other things, by a letter from Charles to Buckingham (who was then in Holland), in which he described how he had patiently endured his wife's ill-treatment of him, 'overcome by your protestations to me that my kind usages would be able to rectify those misunderstandings', but added that the situation, far from improving, was growing daily worse. In another letter, written at about the same time, he told the absent Duke that the *Monsieurs* were guilty of 'attempting to steal away my wife or . . . making plots with my own subjects', and that he could no longer endure it. He was determined to send them packing, but he promised to do nothing until he heard from Buckingham. The Duke's reply is not preserved, but the fact that the *Monsieurs* were suffered to stay on in England for some months longer suggests what the tenor of it must have been.[8]

As if there were not problems enough to hinder the establishment of good relations between France and England, a new difficulty arose in the closing months of 1625. The Treaty of Southampton, concluded between England and the Dutch, contained an article declaring that all contraband goods – such as provisions, arms, money, minerals and naval stores – which were being transported to any part of the dominions of the King of Spain, were lawful prize, along with the ships that carried them. This article made good sense in the context of the strategic plan to blockade Spain and force her to the conference table, but it could only be put into effect by exercising a right of search over the ships of neutral nations, and chief among these, by reason of its proximity to Spain, was France, The ink was hardly dry on the treaty before news came in that an English squadron had seized eleven ships en route from Spain 'laden with merchandise, with boxes of coin, amongst which are a good many golden doubloons'. Six of these ships were French, and their masters claimed that all the goods they were carrying belonged to subjects of Louis XIII. If this was indeed the case then there were no grounds in law for detaining either the goods or the ships. But it was common practice for Spanish traders to make use of a French agent, so that their goods could be carried unharmed to Calais, from where they went overland to the Netherlands. The only way of deciding whether the articles in question were genuinely French or 'fraudulently coloured' was by examining all the bills of lading and other documents, which could be a time-consuming task. When perishable goods were involved it was common practice to sell them, on the understanding that if, after due process in the Court of Admiralty, they were declared not to be contraband, the owners could claim compensation. Non-perishables were, in theory, left on board or stored, but this was seldom the case with bullion. The English government was too poor, and had too many demands upon its very limited resources, to leave gold or silver untouched, and a substantial part of the monies found in the prize vessels in 1625 was used to pay the soldiers who were sent on the Cadiz expedition. The rest, as one observer noted, was taken to the mint and re-coined, 'and besides the alteration in its character which this involved, it has passed into private hands'. These proceedings, he added, as well as 'the offence given to the French courtiers in attendance on the Queen, increase beyond measure the prevalent bad temper, and cannot fail to counteract the good effect which was anticipated from the matrimonial alliance'.[9]

II

If relations had continued to deteriorate as rapidly as they were already doing, England and France would soon have found themselves at war. But neither side wanted this. Buckingham, despite his anger at being barred from France, was willing to respond to a conciliatory gesture, and this came at the very end of 1625, when Richelieu sent one of his gentlemen to England to assure Buckingham of his continuing esteem and affection and to make it clear that if he still wished to go to France he would be welcome. Buckingham was not prepared to make such a visit until he knew more about the climate of opinion in Paris, but he immediately arranged for the despatch of two special ambassadors. He chose for this important mission his close friend, the Earl of Holland, and Sir Dudley Carleton, whom he had brought back with him from the Hague. They were instructed to do all they could to persuade Louis to grant an honourable peace to his protestant subjects, including the inhabitants of La Rochelle. They were also to press for the immediate return of the English ships which had been loaned him. As for more general issues, they were to welcome any inclination Louis might show to make a formal offensive and defensive alliance with England. But if, as seemed probable, he declined to commit himself to this extent, they were to encourage him to join the league which had recently been created at the Hague.[10]

Holland and Carleton arrived in Paris early in January 1626, and the Earl wrote to Buckingham to tell him that 'though beauty and love I find in all perfection and fulness, yet I vex and languish to find impediments in our designs and services for you'. The references to 'beauty and love' were meant for Buckingham's eyes alone, since he had entrusted Holland with the delicate task of conveying assurances of his continuing passion to Anne of Austria. Buckingham had not seen her since that day in June 1625 when he knelt by her bedside to take his farewell, but the memory of her beauty still stirred him. He hoped shortly to set eyes on her again, but Holland's report was not encouraging. 'I have been a careful spy how to observe intentions and affections towards you,' Holland told him. 'I find many things to be feared, and none to be assured of a safe and real welcome. For the [King] continues in his suspects, making (as they say) very often discourses of it, and is willing to hear villains say that [the Queen] hath infinite affections, you imagine which way.' As for Anne's own attitude, 'you are the most happy unhappy man alive, for [the Queen] is beyond imagination right, and would do things to destroy her fortune rather than want satisfaction in her mind'. Whether this somewhat gnomic utterance made sense to Buckingham must remain a matter for conjecture, particularly as Holland did not venture a clear opinion. 'Do what you will,' he told the Duke, 'I dare not advise you. To come is dangerous. Not to come is unfortunate.' In the event, Buckingham decided not to go.[11]

Public affairs made no better progress than private ones. Richelieu told the ambassador that while Louis was prepared to give covert assistance to the Hague allies he would not enter openly into any league as long as he had trouble from the Huguenots at home. As for the ships, Louis was willing to return the *Vanguard* but only on condition that the *St Jean* was handed back to him.

The ambassadors had been instructed, among other things, to make contact with the Huguenots and find out what was happening in and around La Rochelle. Their report gave small grounds for optimism, because it confirmed that the French government was planning to blockade the great Huguenot stronghold by land and sea. Buckingham had already envisaged this eventuality and, despite the acute shortage of money from which Charles's government was suffering, had taken steps to avert it. He had instructed Pennington to prepare a fleet of thirty sail – the usual mixture of King's ships and merchantmen – and to make ready as many of Soubise's vessels as were seaworthy, so that they could carry corn, butter and other provisions for the relief of the threatened city. 'I intend myself to convoy them,' added the Duke, 'and to see them safe (God willing) unto Rochelle.'[12]

Buckingham clearly felt that there was now little to hope for from France, and on 23 January he wrote to the ambassadors, telling them that they should make one last attempt to secure the immediate return of the loaned ships, and then take their leave. On that same day, however, the ambassadors sent the unexpected and welcome news that they had persuaded the Rochellois to come to terms with Louis. In fact the peace treaty was signed at Paris three days later. The Rochellois agreed to receive a royal commissioner into their town, to dismantle the fortifications they had erected, and to refrain from building any new warships. In return Louis pledged himself to demolish the strongholds that had been built outside the gates of the city, including the fort that bore his name, but only after the Rochellois had given proof of their good intentions. These terms were marginally better than those which Louis had originally offered, but they did not give La Rochelle the guaranteed security which its deputies had demanded. Indeed it seems likely that both the Rochellois and the Huguenots in general would have preferred to continue fighting rather than accept what was in many ways an unsatisfactory settlement. What made them change their minds was the intervention of the English ambassadors, who as Richelieu observed, acted more like parties to the dispute than independent mediators. Their aim was to restore peace within France so that Louis could commit himself to war abroad, and they would not allow the Huguenots to stand in their way. They were prepared to accept the French ministers' assurances of goodwill and to work on the assumption that as long as the Huguenots showed themselves to be loyal subjects of Louis XIII he would have no desire to deprive them of their special status. But they also gave the Huguenots a formal, written guarantee that Charles I would uphold the treaty and, if necessary, intervene to enforce its provisions. It was this guarantee that persuaded the Rochellois to accept the proffered terms.[13]

The initial reaction in England was distinctly unfavourable. Soubise wrote to Charles, declaring that he was unable to hold back his grief at the news that the deputies of La Rochelle, under pressure from Holland and Carleton, had made a peace which would destroy the liberty and safety of their city and of the protestant churches throughout France. He called on Charles to disavow the ambassadors and to maintain his former resolution of sending aid to the threatened port. The King and his advisers had considerable sympathy with Soubise's attitude, and when Conway wrote to the ambassadors to acknowledge their despatch, he expressed the prevailing disquiet at their action. The King, he told them, found it 'something strange that your lordships had concluded the peace with so little surety for those of the religion, for aught appears here'.[14]

Holland and Carleton were alarmed at the hostile reaction to what they regarded as something of a triumph, and protested that they had got the best terms they possibly could — a view that was shared in the United Provinces, where the general opinion was that they had preserved the Huguenot cause from utter ruin and prepared the way for effective cooperation between France and the Hague allies. Carleton was particularly anxious to know what Buckingham's attitude was. 'My care is, since His Grace put me into this employment, to make it appear I have done nothing to discredit his choice' he told Goring. He went on to say that provided Buckingham was satisfied he did not doubt that he and Holland would 'stand upright *in curia*', but that it was not for this reason only that he hoped for the Duke's approval. 'I protest unfeignedly I tender his satisfaction more than all men's else, under His Majesty, and this not so much for fear of my fortune as love of his favour, which when I shall lose, I shall lose what I esteem most.' Carleton's fears were not unfounded, but neither was his confidence in Buckingham's protection. The King had been very annoyed when he heard about the action of his ambassadors, and threw their letters into the fire. Eventually, however, he was persuaded by Buckingham to accept the *fait accompli*, and it was, appropriately enough, one of the Duke's confidants, Wat Montagu, who carried the good news to Holland and Carleton. In late February they wrote to Buckingham to express their 'humble thankfulness . . . [for] your favour in standing betwixt us and displeasure whilst our doings were questioned, and setting us again upright in His Majesty's gracious opinion'.[15]

There were a number of reasons which persuaded Buckingham to support the ambassadors and accept the treaty. The perennial lack of money was one of these. The Cadiz expedition had shown how risky it was to send fleets to sea without adequate preparation, and there could be no certainty that Pennington's squadron, which the Duke intended to command in person, would be any better equipped. Pennington had already spent more than £1,300 on fitting up his own and Soubise's ships, but said that more was needed. Men and provisions also were in short supply, and there was no easy way of remedying either of these deficiencies. Buckingham, who was always quick to learn from experience, realised that one of the basic causes of sailors' reluctance to enter the King's service was the poor pay that they were offered. In late 1625 he had made a formal proposal to the Privy Council that rates of pay for all those serving in the King's ships should be substantially increased, and in January 1626 the Council gave its approval. The ordinary seaman stood to gain between £4 and £8 a month as a result of the Lord Admiral's initiative, but this measure could not take immediate effect. So acute was the shortage of money that seamen could not even be paid the old rates, let alone the new, and there seemed no obvious way of filling the royal treasury. The Duke had pinned his hopes on pawning his own and the King's jewels, and had received some sort of assurance from the States General, when he was in Holland, that they would be prepared to advance several hundred thousand pounds upon this security. In early February 1626, however, Sackville Crowe reported that the Dutch were no longer willing to honour their verbal promise. They were unhappy about the King's legal right to dispose of jewels which belonged to the crown, and feared that Parliament, when it met, would press for their return. In fact, said Crowe, the only jewels which were likely to raise anything were the Duke's own, and these would not bring in more than £40,000. With such a small sum it would not be possible for the King even to fulfil his obligations to his foreign allies. There would certainly not be enough money to provide for the needs of the fleet. [16]

In view of the serious financial problems with which he was confronted, the King had decided to summon Parliament. It was due to meet in February 1626, and this consideration was among the most important of those which Buckingham took into account when he persuaded Charles to accept the terms of the peace settlement which Holland and Carleton had mediated. Buckingham had good reason to fear that the question of the loaned ships would be raised in Parliament, and he hoped that one of the first fruits of an agreement between Louis and the Huguenots would be a swift return of the *Vanguard* and the merchantmen. This would take the wind out of the sails of his enemies, and if Parliament subsequently agreed to cooperate fully in the financing of the war, the gains to the common cause would far outweigh the losses to the Huguenots.

Buckingham was now more optimistic about the possibility of open French commitment to the struggle against the Habsburgs, for on 17 January Holland and Carleton reported that Richelieu – who showed great contentment 'for the good success in our treaty of pacification' – had promised that 'all other things should follow according to our wish: that our ships shall be speedily restored, and this king enter – in effect if not in title – into our German league'. A week later they had a long interview with Louis's ministers in which these general assurances were given precise definition. The English ships would be sent back as soon as a few formalities had been completed. As for the Treaty of the Hague, Louis was reluctant to become an open adherent, for fear of offending Roman Catholic opinion, but the French promised to contribute money underhand and to continue their operations in Italy, in conjunction with Venice and Savoy. They still declined to fuse the two leagues – for Italy and for Germany – but they made a major concession in offering to link them by a formal agreement between Louis and Charles. They also proposed that a new Anglo-French army should be raised to intervene in Germany and relieve the pressure being built up against Denmark. These proposals must have sounded sweetly in Buckingham's ears, for they promised the fulfilment of all the high hopes he had placed on the French alliance. The common cause at last was moving forward. The Prince of Piedmont, son and heir to the Duke of Savoy, was in Paris, urging the French to commit themselves fully to the proposed campaign against the Spaniards in Italy, and he wanted Buckingham to go over to concert strategy with him. The Savoyard ambassador, the Abbé Scaglia, who had recently visited England and done much to prepare the way for the *rapprochement* with Louis, wrote to assure Buckingham that his presence would be welcome in France. The Queen Mother, said Scaglia, was about to send him a formal invitation, and the King had made it plain that he had nothing against him. The disputes over Henrietta Maria's household and the treatment of English catholics still rankled, but the French were hoping for a solution even to these problems, and in order to facilitate it had decided to recall their ambassador, Blainville, and replace him with a less rigid negotiator. [17]

It seemed that the conclusion of peace between Louis and the Huguenots really had opened a new chapter in the history of Christendom, one in which all those states which had reason to fear the encroachment of Habsburg power would join together for their mutual defence. From Turin the English ambassador reported the Duke of Savoy's delight at the prospect before him. 'The news of the peace', he said, 'doth make us hope that shortly we shall fall to action . . . and we have here in Piedmont above 20,000 foot and 5,000 horse effective, besides new levies . . . that are expected and which do daily arrive.' Savoy was prepared to undertake operations against the Spanish satellite state of Genoa, while the Constable Lesdiguiéres, in command of a French army, invaded the Spanish duchy of Milan. It seemed certain that Philip IV would have to divert men and money to Italy to meet this threat, and this would relieve the pressure on the Dutch. Since Mansfeld was still in the field, and Christian of Denmark was preparing to invade Germany, there was a good prospect of pushing back the forces of the Emperor and the Catholic League and of recovering the Palatinate. If, at the same time, Anglo-Dutch naval power could be used effectively to blockade the Iberian peninsula and cut off the supply of war materials to Spain, Philip IV would be compelled to open peace negotiations. [18]

What Buckingham did not know, any more than Savoy, Venice or the other allies or potential allies of France, was that the grandiose plans for joint operations in Italy were mere castles in the air. The French ambassador in

Spain had been authorised to hold talks with Olivares on the settlement of outstanding differences between the two crowns, particularly over the Val Telline, and in the closing days of 1625 he signed an agreement on behalf of Louis XIII. When news of this reached Paris it was kept a close secret, particularly since certain of the articles were regarded as unsatisfactory. The ambassador was ordered to obtain better terms, and did so, but the Treaty of Monçon, which he eventually concluded on 23 February 1626, did not differ substantially from the earlier draft. The treaty restored control over the Val Telline to the Grisons, who were clients of France, and to this extent it could be expected to satisfy France's allies. But it was not so much the terms of the treaty as the way in which it had been negotiated and the fact that it had been concluded at all that caused anger and dismay as the news spread. By settling her differences with Spain, France had effectively committed herself to peace in Italy at the very moment when major campaigns were about to open there. No wonder the Duke of Savoy expressed his horror at 'the perfidiousness of this treason, which is the greatest of all that were ever seen in like cases amongst Turks or any other more barbarous or more perfidious nation'. When the Prince of Piedmont heard the news he left France in disgust. As for the English ambassadors, they were appalled. Carleton had earlier given his opinion that the French were so closely tied to the alliance with England that they could not possibly make peace with Spain, yet now the unthinkable had occurred. Richelieu assured the ambassadors that peace with Spain in Italy would leave France even freer to pursue the war in Germany, but they were not impressed. Nor was the English government. Sir John Coke, writing to Holland and Carleton on 17 March, told them that 'if all their [the French] discourses hang together like the dreams of sick men and can give no hopes of bringing your endeavours to better pass, you have very great reason to repatriate'. The ambassadors took the hint, and before the end of the month they were back home.[19]

III

The news of the secret agreement between France and Spain caused an outcry in England, and Buckingham, as the principal architect of the French alliance, has more cause than other men to feel betrayed. This was the latest in a long series of French deceptions, and he came to the conclusion that there could be no hope of any real friendship with France so long as Richelieu was Louis's chief minister. Buckingham already knew of the plotting that was taking place among the dissident nobles in France. If he could renew the traditional connexion between disaffected magnates and apprehensive Huguenots that had earlier brought France to the verge of anarchy, he might be able to create a situation in which Louis would either have to disavow Richelieu or risk losing his throne. Buckingham was encouraged to pursue this course by the Duke of

Savoy, who had close links with the discontented elements inside France and was hopeful of bringing about a change of French policy through a change of ministers. Savoy by itself was too small a power to accomplish anything of significance, but if it had the support of other peripheral states, such as Lorraine and the Venetian Republic, and the backing of England, it might well be able to bring considerable pressure to bear on Louis at just the right moment. The tactics with which to put this general strategy into effect were not easy to work out, because of the many miles that separated London from Turin, but there was a steady exchange of information between the two capitals. Buckingham had not abandoned his major aim of containing Habsburg power, but since this could not be achieved without France, and France under Richelieu was unable or unwilling to cooperate, he concentrated his efforts on bringing about the redirection of French policy.

While these long-term plans were slowly maturing, Buckingham had to deal with a whole range of immediate problems, all of them exacerbated by shortage of money. Among the most pressing, and the most intractable, was that of providing effective protection for the English coasts. In January 1626 Buckingham wrote to Sir Henry Palmer, his commander in the Channel, to make known his displeasure at a report that there had been no officers on board his ships during Christmas. This was not to happen again. 'I will that you also presently give order to all captains and masters of His Majesty's and others' ships now employed in His Majesty's service in the Narrow Seas, that they instantly repair aboard their several ships and that they command that all their officers do apply themselves to their several charges.' The Lord Admiral also ordered that all the ships in Palmer's fleet were to 'ply up and down (as wind and weather will permit)', not simply to intercept pirates but also to exercise their right of search over all vessels bound to or from the ports of Spain or her dependent territories.[20]

Palmer indignantly rejected the charge that his officers had not been on board over Christmas, but there was no end to the pressure on him. Buckingham wrote to ask why it was that 'notwithstanding my many orders and directions given you to send out ships to secure the Narrow Seas and preserve His Majesty's subjects from being made a prey to the enemy' there were daily reports of the capture of English and Scottish vessels. He reminded Palmer that he had at least twelve merchant and prize ships under his command, and that three-quarters of these should always be at sea. Early in February the Duke wrote again, telling Palmer to stir up the captains of his ships at Harwich 'and let them understand that I expect a better account from them of the trust committed to their care'. The Lord Admiral added that 'it seems very strange to me that in all the time of the employment of the ships under your charge there hath been nothing effected by them on the enemy!' A month later, after complaints from merchants that Palmer's ships did nothing but lie in port and consume their provisions, the Duke wrote him an even more sternly-worded letter, and this time instructed him to send up his journal for inspection. 'I have relied much on your care and vigilancy,' Buckingham reminded him. 'I know you cannot but well judge of the importance of the charge committed to you, as I am very sensible of the prejudice and dishonour that by the carelessness and remissness which is used doth fall on His Majesty, the state and myself.'[21]

Palmer was swift to defend himself. Most of his ships, he told the Duke, were at sea, and the complaints against him were without foundation and inspired solely by malice. The main problem, as he made clear to Buckingham's naval secretary, Edward Nicholas, was lack of men and provisions: 'our wants . . . grow so apparently upon us as [to] threaten ruin without speedy relief, and for service we are able to do none farther till we receive supplies'. This plea for help was made in March 1626, but the government had no money and Palmer and his men were left to shift for themselves. In July he reported that he had 'of late suffered more trouble and affliction to keep those men under my charge from dangerous mutinies, for want of victual and clothes, than I have ever been acquainted with'. There were occasions when Palmer could no longer contain his indignation at being blamed for what was not his fault. 'You write to me that my lord would have me send some good force to Dunkirk and some also to the westward,' he told Nicholas, 'whereas you know I have only with me four ships, the rest (according to His Grace's commands) being disposed of elsewhere, and how I can do several services without ships you know is impossible.'[22]

Given the circumstances it is surprising that Palmer and other senior officers kept their patience as long as they did, and never wavered in their loyalty to the Lord Admiral. When Palmer's wife gave birth to a son, he waited on Buckingham to ask for permission to christen the boy George. And in May 1626, when Buckingham was under strong attack in Parliament for not maintaining an adequate guard in the Narrow Seas, Palmer told Nicholas that he had not been unaware 'how much envy hath aimed at him whose least misfortune had been to me the worst of chance . . . . I have suffered from the malice of some because I would not address myself for the service elsewhere, but I am so his as I know not the way of falsehood.' Buckingham repaid loyalty with consideration. In July 1626 he decided to remove Palmer from his key post of Admiral of the Narrow Seas and restore it to a former holder, Sir Henry Mervyn. In the letter announcing this, however, the Duke added a postscript in his own hand. 'It shall be in your choice whether you will be Vice-Admiral in the Narrow Seas or the West. And could I have stayed you longer in your employment . . . I should not at all [have] removed you.'[23]

For offensive operations Buckingham relied on John Pennington, a hard-working, experienced and highly competent seaman who embodied all that was best in the English naval tradition. Buckingham had originally intended to use Pennington's fleet for the relief of La Rochelle, but after the conclusion of peace between Louis XIII and the Huguenots he decided that it should be employed in enforcing the blockade against Spain. Buckingham attached great importance to this policy, because it was now England's major contribution to the common cause, and, if successful, would build up the pressure on Spain to such a degree that Philip IV would be compelled to negotiate a settlement of all outstanding problems, including that of the Palatinate, It also offered a good chance of profit from the sale of prize goods — one tenth of which went to Buckingham as Lord Admiral. The income from captured ships and goods became a significant element in the royal finances, for on 15 February 1626 Sir William Russell, the Treasurer of the Navy, was appointed receiver of prize monies and instructed to issue these 'for maintenance of the Navy and wars, as the King shall direct or the Duke think expedient'. It may be that in the long run the English lost more than they gained by commerce-raiding, but the short-term advantages were considerable. Prize money may have amounted to some £50,000 during the course of 1626, and while this was admittedly less than a Parliamentary subsidy would have produced, there were no Parliamentary subsidies in that year. The prize ships were also invaluable, since they were allotted to coastal defence and other services.[24]

Prize money alone, however, could not sustain a naval war on the scale which was needed, and offensive as well as defensive operations were crippled by the government's poverty. In February 1626 Pennington wrote to Buckingham from Portsmouth, urging him 'to take some speedy course for our supply; otherwise we must be constrained to discharge our men and let the ships ride destitute, for without victuals we cannot keep them'. Since no money was forthcoming, Pennington scraped together what supplies he could by engaging his own credit, and in early March was able to report to Buckingham that he had managed to assemble a small fleet of some thirty vessels manned by sixteen hundred sailors. The ships were ones which had returned from Cadiz, but, said Pennington proudly, I 'wish Your Grace were here to view them, not doubting but that you would find them better fitted than at their last going out'. Victuals were a problem. He was using up the stores that had come back with Cecil's expedition, but they were so rotten that they caused the men to fall sick. This, added to lack of clothes and lack of pay, said Pennington, explained why the sailors deserted faster than the press gangs could recruit them.[25]

Pennington, like Palmer, sometimes despaired and complained of the impossible task that had been given him, of organising a fleet without any money to pay for it. But, again like Palmer, he remained loyal to the Lord Admiral. Indeed on one occasion in March 1626, after a long silence from Buckingham — who was waiting to hear the outcome of the negotiations over La Rochelle, and was in any case distracted by the mounting attack on him in Parliament — Pennington expressed his feelings with unexpected warmth, though characteristic bluntness. 'It is now full six weeks since I received any packet from my lord,' he told Nicholas,

which I must confess hath almost broken my heart. And whereas you write it is for want of money, it is true I am infinitely troubled and perplexed for want of that. But the other troubles me ten times more. For I do not only honour my lord, but love him, as a young man doth his mistress, and am jealous of his favour or the contrary.[26]

303

IV

The King and Buckingham hoped that the Parliament which had been summoned for February 1626 would put an end to the financial stringency that was crippling the war effort. The first parliament of Charles's reign had been a disaster, but there could be no question – at this stage, at any rate – of ruling without one. Quite apart from the need for money, a nation at war needed to demonstrate its unity even more than a nation at peace, and a successful Parliament would give notice to the rest of Christendom that the King and his people were at one in their commitment to the common cause. Since Charles's policy in 1625 was substantially what he had promised, and been praised for, in 1624, he could not understand why Parliament had changed its attitude of approval into one of criticism. There was only one obvious answer to this puzzling question, and that was given by young Sir Edward Conway, who declared that the 1625 session had been 'spoiled by some few factious men'. Charles had already taken steps to see that this should not happen again. Among the most factious men in the Commons – or so at least he believed – were Sir Edward Coke, Sir Francis Seymour, Sir Robert Phelips and Sir Thomas Wentworth. All these he pricked as sheriffs for the year 1626, thereby effectively excluding them from the Commons, since a sheriff had to reside in his county throughout his term of office. The King also created a number of earls – among them Buckingham's friend Thomas Howard, Viscount Andover, who now became Earl of Berkshire. Rudyerd described the new earls as 'so many cardinals to carry the consistory, if there be occasion', but the list was not confined to Buckingham's supporters. Lord Sheffield, for instance, who now became Earl of Mulgrave, was to be numbered among the Duke's leading opponents in the House of Lords during the ensuing session.[27]

Buckingham, despite the fact that he owned considerable estates in Rutland and Essex, was not a major Parliamentary patron in his own right. As Lord Warden, however, he had great influence over the Cinque Ports, and in 1625 he had secured the return of eight of his nominees. Yet in the elections of 1626 Buckingham let his chances slip. His chief agent, Sir John Hippesley, who was Lieutenant of Dover Castle, wrote to remind him on 8 January that polling was to take place on the following day. 'I marvel that your letters are not come down to all the Ports for those men that you intend to put in,' said Hippesley, 'for the writs for the Parliament I have sent four days since, and this is not to be delayed except you intend to lose your right.' It was only on 10 January that Edward Nicholas, who was Buckingham's secretary for Cinque Ports affairs, sent the formal letters of recommendation, and by then it was too late. Of the eleven candidates nominated by the Lord Warden, a mere five were returned.[28]

Buckingham's failure to exploit his electoral advantages in the Cinque Ports may have been caused by overconfidence, for his advisers professed to believe that he would have sufficient supporters in the Commons 'to keep him from all offence, as well in his honour as in his person'. Or it may simply have been that the pressure of the various businesses he was involved in – particularly the negotiations with France – left him insufficient time to attend to supervision of elections. Yet the Duke, despite his naturally buoyant temperament, can have been in little doubt that he would require all the strength he could muster in the forthcoming session, for his enemies were preparing their ground with great deliberation. The most dangerous of these was, as always, the Lord Chamberlain, the Earl of Pembroke, whose seat at Wilton was the centre of a network of patronage that covered the whole of the west country. Sir James Bagg, writing to Buckingham shortly after Parliament had opened, warned him that Pembroke would not be operating, as before, through recognised dependants such as Benjamin Rudyerd, but through lesser figures. William Coryton, 'his Vice-Warden [of the Stannaries], Deputy-Lieutenant [of Cornwall] and Custos Rotulorum', was one of these, and Dr Turnour, the member for Shaftesbury, was another. Pembroke's influence in the Lower House was reinforced by that of his friends and allies in the Lords. George Abbot, Archbishop of Canterbury, who had lived to regret the way in which he had advanced the fortunes of young Villiers, was among the most important of these. Abbot's brother, Sir Maurice, was governor of the East India Company and as such was aware of the heavy pressure which Buckingham, with James's backing, had exerted on the Company in order to secure the payment of £10,000 prize money. By revealing this information to the Commons later in the session Sir Maurice provided the basis for one of the impeachment charges against the Duke. There were also close links between the Abbots and another of Buckingham's accusers, Sir Dudley Digges, for George Abbot had been Digges's tutor, while Sir Maurice was one of his business associates.[29]

Pembroke and Archbishop Abbot were identified with the 'protestant interest' which had never liked the idea of the French marriage. Their views were shared by John Preston, who tried to persuade Buckingham not to go ahead with it. The Duke argued that 'there was not a protestant to be had, and to marry with a subject had always been unhappy and fatal to the Kings of England', but Preston was not convinced. He agreed that French popery was not quite so evil as Spanish, but it was popery all the same, and he doubted Buckingham's assurances that the French would not be so rigid in their religious demands as the Spaniards had been. Preston, like the majority of his contemporaries, was deeply shocked by the news that English ships had been loaned for use against La Rochelle. He took the charitable view that Buckingham had been left with little choice, but from this time, as his biographer records, Preston 'doubted of the saintship of the Duke of Buckingham'[30]

Preston was also alarmed by the increasing influence of Laud and the Arminians. When Buckingham left for Spain in 1623 he had asked his wife and his sister, Su Denbigh, to watch over Preston's interests, which they duly did. But Preston discovered, to his chagrin, that William Laud was also a welcome visitor at Lady Denbigh's, and later on Richard Montagu, the *bête noir* of the anti-Arminians, found his way there also. Buckingham had deliberately courted Preston, for he hoped to gain through this friendship the support of the 'protestant interest' both in Parliament and the country at large. These tactics paid off handsomely in 1624, but the first Parliament of Charles I's reign had been a major setback. Buckingham had cause to reflect that either the leaders of the 'protestant interest' were insincere in their professions of friendship, or their influence was not sufficient for them to win popular support for the war strategy. The Arminians, on the other hand, were able to argue that their commitment to the King and his policies was unshakeable, and that dependence on them, rather than on their opponents, would yield greater fruit.[31]

Buckingham was under pressure from the leading anti-Arminians among the bishops to come down clearly on their side. The opening of a new reign was traditionally a time for a restatement of doctrine, and what the anti-Arminians wanted more than anything was a formal commitment on the part of the King and the church to enforce the decrees of the Calvinist synod held at Dort, in Holland, in 1619. These decrees, which condemned Arminian attitudes, had never been officially accepted in England, despite the fact that James's representatives at the synod had cooperated in drawing them up. Their adoption in 1626, at the opening of a new reign, might have caused a split in the English church, and Buckingham was therefore anxious to avoid a showdown. So also was Preston, but with Parliament about to assemble the pressure became irresistible. It looks as though Buckingham gave way at last because of the pleading of the Earl of Warwick and Lord Saye. What they offered in return is not known, but it seems highly likely that they promised their support for the Duke in Parliament if he would agree to arrange a debate at which the major religious issues in dispute could be thrashed out. From this initiative came the conference which was held at York House on 11 and 17 February 1626.[32]

Buckingham opened the proceedings by showing how the conference had arisen as a result of 'some private speeches that had lately passed between my Lord of Warwick and him concerning sundry matters that were said to be erroneous and dangerous in Mr Montagu's works'. Knotty doctrinal problems such as these were not to be resolved without expert advice, and Buckingham explained that he had therefore invited representatives of both sides to argue their case before a select audience that included Pembroke, Warwick, Saye and Carlisle, as well as Sir John Coke, whose anti-Arminian views were well known. At the first session of the conference the attack on Montagu was led by Thomas Morton, Bishop of Lichfield, a man of moderate views who had earlier published 'A Defence of the Innocence of the three Ceremonies of the Surplice, the Cross in Baptism, and Kneeling at the Blessed Sacrament', which he dedicated to Buckingham. Morton took a number of statements from Montagu's writings and attempted to show that these were incompatible with protestant beliefs, but by all accounts he made a poor showing, and Buckingham did not conceal his impatience. One of Morton's charges was that Montagu had impugned the royal supremacy by denying that princes could exercise authority over the church, but Montagu's defenders challenged this and pointed to a number of passages in which he had justified such authority.

Buckingham read out one of the passages himself and commented that 'this accusation might well have been spared, for we are all of Mr Montagu's mind, and if you be not so likewise, my lord of Lichfield, you are much to blame'. Morton, accepting defeat, said he would drop this point and move on to another one, but the Duke called on him to 'let it be to some purpose . . . for hitherto nothing hath been said that is of any moment'.[33]

As the first session was drawing to its close, Preston made a belated appearance, and joined in the disputation on Morton's side. The two men argued the case for predestination, but did it in such a way that they appeared to deny the efficacy of the grace which is conferred by the sacraments. Buckingham, whose long apprenticeship to James I had given him practice in following theological arguments, immediately pounced upon this point and asked Morton why children were baptised if they received neither grace nor remission of sins from baptism. He added that in his view Morton had 'much disparaged his own ministry and did not only dishonour the Church of England but also debase the sacrament through this opinion which he maintained'. At this point Saye and Coke came to Morton's rescue by formally proposing that the rulings of the Synod of Dort should be made binding upon the Church of England. But the Duke would have none of it. 'This is not the first motion that hath been made for the Synod of Dort,' he told them, 'but I have been assured by divers great and learned prelates that it can neither stand with the safety of this state nor church to bring it in.' Carlisle observed that 'in England we have a rule of our own', and his implied assumption that the English did not need foreign theological importations received warm support from Buckingham. 'We have nothing to do with the Synod,' he declared. 'It is all about the hidden and intricate points of predestination, which are not fit matters to trouble the people withal.'[34]

At the second session of the York House Conference, on 17 February, Montagu came in person to answer the charges against him, which were presented once again by Morton and Preston. The debate lasted some six hours, and it was past eight at night before Buckingham eventually brought proceedings to a close. The general verdict seems to have been that the anti-Arminians had the worst of it, though this view was not shared by Saye and Warwick. As for Pembroke, he gave his opinion that no one came away from the debate an Arminian who had not already been so before he went there. But if the York House Conference was in some ways inconclusive, there were other respects in which it was decisive. It showed that there was to be no firm stand taken against the Arminians, and left Warwick, Saye and others to draw the conclusion that where the King was unwilling to act, the responsibility must pass to Parliament. It also marked the end of the alliance between Buckingham on the one side and Preston and the 'protestant interest' on the other – an alliance which, even though it had not prevented the attack upon the favourite in the Parliament of 1625, had served to restrain his enemies within certain bounds. These restraints were now removed, with consequences that became all too apparent in the ensuing session.[35]

Buckingham's comments during the debates at York House suggest that his sympathies were with the Arminians but this could well have been for political as much as religious reasons. The Arminians were a minority among the bishops and within the church as a whole, but it soon become clear that Charles approved of them, and this must have been one of the considerations that Buckingham took into account as he plotted his course. Charles showed his Arminian preferences by picking Laud to officiate at the coronation, which took place in February 1626. He also demonstrated his continuing favour to Buckingham by appointing him Lord High Constable of England for that day. It was Buckingham, therefore, who, on bended knee, presented the King with the regalia; and after the crowning he had the honour, as Master of the Horse, of putting on the King's spurs. Arundel – who, as Earl Marshal, was responsible for organising the coronation – had arranged that the royal party, which came by barge to Westminster, should land at Sir Robert Cotton's house, where a stone staircase led directly up from the water. The steps were duly covered in carpets, but when the royal barge appeared, it swept past and made its way instead to a much dirtier and more inconvenient place near the back yard of the old palace of Westminster. This affront was assumed, no doubt correctly, to be the work of Buckingham, who had recently come across the notes on the English constitution which Cotton had produced as a justification for the attack upon him in the 1625 Parliament. It was also, and perhaps intentionally, a snub to Arundel, whose friendship with Bristol and proposal to put an end to the sale of honours had ranged him openly among the Duke's opponents. The change of plan must, however, have been sanctioned by the King, and there could be no doubt of Charles's continuing affection and support for the man who was virtually his only close friend. Simonds D'Ewes, who watched the royal party arrive at Westminster Hall, recorded a dramatic illustration of the depth of the King's feelings. As Charles approached some steps on to a wooden platform which had been specially constructed for the occasion the Duke stretched out his hand to assist him. But the King immediately put his own hand under the Duke's arm and 'whether he would or not, led him up the stairs, saying "I have more need to help you than you have to help me." '[36]

V

On 9 February, a week after the coronation, Charles rode in state to Westminster to open the second Parliament of his reign. Buckingham also rode in the procession, as Master of the Horse, and it was observed by those with a taste for omens that 'his bridle would not hold upon his horse's head, but . . . fell quite off, with the plume of feathers, to the ground'. Buckingham's commitment to the anti-Habsburg cause had not dimmed, nor had his recognition that without the full support of Parliament – a support that he and the King believed had been promised in 1624 – such a war would never achieve its objectives. He still hoped to persuade Louis XIII to throw his weight on the side of the allies, and at that very moment there was a letter *en route* from Holland and Carleton in France reporting that 'for Germany the purpose here is certainly good . . . but unless we will concur with them they show no willingness to undertake anything of themselves'. The ambassadors expressed their hope that with the meeting of Parliament the King would be enabled to respond fully to the French initiative, in order 'to engage this crown in the German war'. What remained to be seen was whether, in fact, Parliament would support royal policy as long as Buckingham was the King's chief minister. At least one member of the Commons believed that it would, for the King's action in pricking the Duke's principal critics as sheriffs seemed to have left the Commons leaderless. 'We shall have a tame House,' wrote this observer, 'and the King will master his own ends without much ado.'[37]

The House of Commons still included a number of fiery spirits, however, and no one could inflame passions more effectively than Buckingham's former friend and client, Sir John Eliot. The Oxford session of 1625 had seen a rift opening between Eliot and his patron, and by 1626 the gap was too wide to be bridged easily, if at all. Eliot had been appalled by the failure of the Cadiz expedition, and in a speech to the Commons on 10 February he called for a full enquiry into the reasons for it. 'Is the reputation and glory of our nation of a small value?' he demanded. 'Are the walls and bulwarks of our kingdom of no esteem? Were the numberless lives of our lost men not to be regarded?' He was careful not to attack the Lord Admiral personally, but his listeners can hardly have been left in doubt about where he pinned the blame. 'Our honour is ruined,' he thundered, 'our ships are sunk, our men perished, not by the sword, not by an enemy, not by chance, but . . . by those we trust.' Eliot did not stop here. He pressed the Commons to initiate a strict enquiry into the expenditure of the Parliamentary subsidies voted in 1624, and to consider the ways in which the crown's income could be increased. 'The treasure of the King,' he declared, 'is the life of the subject,' but successive Kings had weakened the crown's finances through their open-handedness, and royal revenues had been diverted into private pockets. If this process could be halted and reversed, then the King would not have to burden his subjects with repeated demands for extraordinary supply. To restore the crown to financial health might well entail the taking back of what had already been granted away, but earlier Parliaments had shown how this could be done. 'What resumptions of lands, what accounts of officers, what infinite restitutions have been by that means made to the crown', Eliot reminded members, and left them to draw their own conclusions.[38]

Eliot's speech, even though it did not evoke an immediately favourable response, set the tone for the whole session – what Hacket called 'a long discontent of eighteen weeks [which] brought forth nothing but a tympany of swelling faction and abrupt dissolution'. The Commons had set up a committee of grievances to gather evidence about the various ills that were afflicting the country, and among the topics that were brought to its attention was the seizure of English merchant ships in France. On 22 February, Eliot, reporting from the committee to the House, traced the events that had led up to this

309

hostile gesture on the part of a nominally friendly state. During the course of 1625 a number of French merchantmen had been arrested by English warships on the grounds that they were carrying prohibited Spanish goods. Among them was the *St Peter* of Havre de Grace ('Newhaven'). The owners of this vessel had petitioned for its release, and in January 1626 the Court of Admiralty agreed that it should be handed back. But the *St Peter* got no further than Gravesend before it was once again arrested, by order of the Lord Admiral. It was this action, according to Eliot, which had goaded the French into taking reprisals. On 1 March, therefore, the Commons decided to send a message to the Duke, asking him to explain 'why, after a legal discharge of the *St Peter*, the same was again stayed?' If they did not get a satisfactory reply they were determined to present their complaint to the King, as a public grievance.[39]

One member of the Commons recorded his private opinion that they were wasting their time, 'for he [Buckingham] will easily answer it to the King and Upper House, though we be deaf to him'. The Duke, however, could not count on the automatic support of the Lords, as was shown by an episode towards the end of February 1626. It was a custom of the House for lords who could not be present for the session to give a proxy to a peer of their choice, and Buckingham had in this way amassed a total of thirteen proxies – more than any other peer. This meant that he could command fourteen votes in his own person, and in a relatively small House, where opinion might be evenly divided, this voting strength could be decisive. On 25 February, however, the Lords' Committee for Privileges recommended that in future Parliaments the number of proxies should be limited to two, and a spirited debate took place on this proposal. Buckingham opposed it, as did Sir Edward Sackville, a former member of the Commons and a frequent critic of royal policy, who had succeeded to the Earldom of Dorset in 1624 and was now among Buckingham's most stalwart supporters. But Lord Saye expressed himself strongly in favour of the change and argued that although the existing system had so far worked well, it was the 'greatest wisdom to prevent an inconvenience before we feel the smart of it'. Saye was supported by Arundel, Mulgrave, Russell and Clare, among others, and in the end it was his opinion that carried the day. As John Chamberlain commented, the Duke had 'had one feather plucked from his wing'.[40]

The Lords' action spurred on Buckingham's critics in the Commons, and in late February a committee was set up to enquire into the evils with which the country was afflicted, to identify their causes, and to propose remedies. This Committee for Evils, Causes and Remedies, as it was soon called, became in effect the nerve centre of the Commons, receiving information from all over the country and planning the strategy of the developing attack upon the feared and hated favourite. Among the measures it considered was one originally suggested by Eliot, namely the examination of members of the council of war, to see if they had used the subsidies voted in 1624 in accordance with the objectives laid down in the act. No doubt the committee expected to find that the greater part of the subsidies had been spent on Mansfeld's expedition, which, it could be argued, did not come within the prescribed categories. But it was also decided to ask the individual councillors what advice they had given, presumably with the aim of pinning responsibility for unsuccessful operations on Buckingham in person. This line of attack was foiled by the King, however, for although he was prepared to allow councillors to answer questions about the expenditure of money he would not permit them to reveal the details of discussions that had taken place about strategy. The conduct of the war was his own responsibility and in Heylyn's phrase 'he saw himself wounded through the Duke's sides'. Charles told one of the councillors that 'it is not you that they aim at, but it is me upon whom they make inquisition', and when it was pointed out to him that unless he gave way the Commons would never agree to vote supply, he made the significant observation that 'gold may be bought too dear'.[41]

The Commons eventually abandoned their attempts to interrogate the councillors of war, but they were determined to call Buckingham to account for specific actions, starting with his arrest of the *St Peter* of Newhaven. In their enthusiasm they paid too little heed to the susceptibilities of the House of Lords, for when Buckingham informed his fellow peers that the Commons had required him 'to answer his actions in public', and that it would give him the greatest happiness to do so, their lordships took the view 'that for a member of this House to be sent unto to give satisfaction there [in the Commons] might be derogatory to their privileges'. Not until the Commons had modified their request, in such a way as to leave the decision whether or not to respond entirely in Buckingham's hands, did the Lords give him leave to reply. He did so through the agency of Sir Robert Heath, the Attorney-General, who on 6 March gave the Lower House a detailed defence of Buckingham's conduct. The French prizes, he explained, had been released in late December 1625 only on the understanding that they and their cargoes were indeed French. But in the following month Sir Allen Apsley, the Lieutenant of the Tower, informed Buckingham that while the goods appeared to be French they were in fact Spanish, and therefore lawful prize. The Duke asked him specifically whether this applied to the *St Peter*, and hearing that it did so, he informed the King, who ordered the ship once again to be stayed. He also consulted with the Admiralty judge, Sir Henry Marten, who told him that a ship could legitimately be stayed upon the receipt of new evidence, but that no final decision could be given in this case until the Admiralty Court had considered all the proofs. In February, therefore, the *St Peter* was again released, after its owners had given security to abide by whatever decision the court eventually reached.[42]

Heath continued his statement by pointing out that the seizure of English ships in France had been ordered before the re-arrest of the *St Peter* took place, and could therefore have had nothing to do with it. The French action had been prompted by a general dissatisfaction with the slow pace of legal proceedings in England, and Heath reminded the House that 'our prejudicating this cause here may do us hurt abroad [and] will hinder the seizing of victuals etc. carried . . . into Spain'. The French had already set up a staple at Calais, from which Spanish goods could be transported into the Netherlands, and if this trade was allowed to continue it would seriously weaken the English blockade.[43]

Heath's refutation of the accusation made against Buckingham was so powerfully argued that for the time being the Commons could go no further along this course. Meanwhile, Buckingham had taken the initiative in the Upper House. On 6 March, while Heath was addressing the Commons, Lord Montagu of Boughton – presumably taking his lead from the Duke, with whom he and his family had long enjoyed close and friendly relations – rose in the Lords to remind his fellow-peers that they had sat a whole month without considering 'the arduous and urgent business for the defence of the kingdom', and called on them to take appropriate action forthwith. This motion met with a very good reception, and the House appointed a committee, of which Buckingham was a member, to draw up propositions which could then be presented to the Commons as formal recommendations. Warwick – who at this stage was still among Buckingham's allies – suggested that the committee should concentrate on three specific topics, namely naval preparations, the strengthening of the forts, and the training of the militia. Buckingham supported him, but urged that there should be no restriction on the committee's competence 'to treat of anything else that might be thought of for the defence of the realm'. The House agreed to this, and the committee was instructed to meet early the next morning.[44]

Now that the Lords had been persuaded to take the initiative, the government kept up the pressure on them to continue the good work. On the following day, 7 March, the Lord Keeper reported that the King had commanded him 'to give their lordships all very hearty thanks for their zeal herein to his honour and the safeguard of the realm, and doth desire them to proceed with all alacrity and speed'. As it happened, the committee members needed little prompting, for on that same morning they concluded their deliberations and returned to the House with a number of propositions. These were that one fleet should be immediately set out 'against the King of Spain, to annoy him and to prevent the invasion of this kingdom'; that another should be prepared for coastal defence and trade protection; and that all necessary steps should be taken to provide for the maintenance of Mansfeld's army and that which Christian IV of Denmark was raising. When the House debated these proposals, Pembroke spoke strongly in favour of them, and was supported by Buckingham and Warwick. There is every indication that these speeches, and indeed the whole course of the debate, had been carefully orchestrated, and that the King had used his influence to procure a united front between the Duke and the 'protestant interest'. These tactics were successful, for the Lords approved of the propositions and decided to present them to the Commons. Their choice of speakers symbolised the new-found unity among the King's advisers, for Archbishop Abbot and Pembroke, the Lord Chamberlain, were yoked with Buckingham and his old friend Carlisle.[45]

The Commons did not make any immediate response to the Lords' recommendations, but appointed a committee to consider them. They now came under government pressure similar to that which had spurred the Lords into action, and on 10 March the Chancellor of the Exchequer delivered a message from the King calling on members to let him know 'without further delaying of time, what supply you will give him for these his present occasions, that he may accordingly frame his course and counsel'. The Commons, however, were less malleable than the Lords and were determined not to commit themselves to voting subsidies until they had secured the removal of Buckingham – or at least prepared their case against him. The only result of the King's message, therefore, was to make them speed up their investigations into the Duke's conduct, and on 11 March Dr Turnour, the member for Salisbury, rose from his seat to declare that there must be a *causa generalissima* for all the ills from which the nation was suffering, and that 'common fame presents one man to be this cause'. He listed the evils for which he held Buckingham responsible. The Duke had allowed England to lose control of the Narrow Seas; he had weakened the crown's finances through excessive gifts to himself and his kindred; he had accepted so many offices that he could not adequately carry out the duties attaching to them; he had upheld recusants; he had sold honours, judicial appointments, and places in the church; and he had chosen to stay at home even though, as Admiral and General, he should have led the expedition against Cadiz in person.[46]

Turnour had put into words what many members felt, and when the Commons drew up their reply to the King's message they made it plain that they wanted a *quid pro quo* for any monies they voted. They assured Charles that 'no King was ever dearer to his people than Your Majesty' and 'no people more zealous to maintain and advance the honour and greatness of their King'. They intended to show their love by assisting him 'in such a way and in so ample a measure as may make you safe at home and feared abroad', but they asked him first to allow them to reveal the causes of 'these great evils which have occasioned Your Majesty's wants and your people's grief', and to propose appropriate remedies. Charles's reply, which he gave the Commons in an audience on 15 March, was conciliatory in tone. He thanked them for their 'full and satisfactory answer' and assured them he would be no less willing than his predecessors to redress their grievances. But he made it plain that he would not allow any questioning of his servants, especially 'such as are of eminent place and near unto me'. In former times, he reminded them, 'the old question was "What shall be done to the man whom the King will honour?"' but now some people seemed more ready to criticise than to respect those whom the King had singled out for favour. 'I see you specially aim at the Duke of Buckingham,' said Charles. 'I wonder what hath so altered your affections towards him?' In the 1624 Parliament, he reminded his hearers, the Duke had earned universal praise by being the instrument to break off the treaties with Spain, and all the honour that could be conferred upon him was held too little for his deserts. 'What he hath done since to alter and change your minds, I wot not; but [I] can assure you he hath not meddled or done anything concerning the public or commonwealth but by special directions and appointment, and as my servant.'[47]

The Commons listened to the King's warning but did not heed it. They were persuaded that there could be no reformation, no hope of success for the future, unless Buckingham was removed from power. The Committee for Evils, Causes and Remedies therefore pressed ahead with its self-appointed task of preparing a massive indictment against the Duke, and Eliot, in particular, was very active behind the scenes, With his interest in and knowledge of naval matters he had a good deal to contribute, and it was largely through his advocacy that accusations of loaning ships to the French king to extirpate the Huguenots and leaving the Narrow Seas unguarded were added to the list. The debate on the latter charge on 24 March shows the difficulties under which Buckingham's defenders laboured. Sir John Coke, who knew from his own experience just how much the Duke had done to improve the state of the Navy, put the blame squarely upon lack of money, and called on members to consider 'how unjustly these things are laid upon the Lord Admiral'. Eliot immediately complained that Coke's comment was a reflection on the work of the sub-committee which had been investigating this charge, and the out-flanked Secretary had to 'explain himself'. Sir Robert Mansell then gave his opinion that there had been more complaints of lack of care in the execution of naval matters in this Parliament 'than ever since the Conquest'. This implied criticism of the Lord Admiral was refuted by Sir Richard Weston, the Chancellor of the Exchequer, who pointed out that 'it cannot be made the Duke's fault, the not guarding of the seas. Commands from the Council Table are according to the necessities of the times, but if there wants [sic] means to perform them, neither they nor who they command are in fault.'[48]

Eliot, however, would not accept the argument that shortage of money was to blame. 'We know it too well,' he declared, 'there is no want of monies. Massy and great sums of money; and the ships sent to Rochelle were sent away in the very time of complaints of the west country at Oxon . . . . If there was want, it was want of endeavour in him to inform the King and seek for means to effect it.' Sir Humphrey May did not allow this statement to pass unchallenged. 'We are daily deceived in generals,' he said. 'The ships sent to Rochelle cost not the King or state one penny.' But May — who did not count himself among the Duke's clients, and had, on this occasion, spoken no more than the truth — had much the same reception as Coke, for he was accused of casting aspersions upon the sub-committee which had looked into this matter. Nevertheless the Duke's supporters kept up their defence and tried to disprove some of the more obviously outrageous accusations. Sir Peter Heyman, for instance, calculated that Parliamentary grants, loans, and prize money had brought in more than £1,500,000 a year, but Pye, even though he could not produce figures, assured members that the King's actual income was under half this amount. In these discussions there was all the appearance of reasoned argument, but in fact the committee was not engaged in an impartial search for truth. Its members knew already what their verdict was; all they needed now was sufficient evidence to substantiate it. The majority attitude was made clear by William Coryton. 'We must of necessity lay the fault upon somebody,' he said. 'Upon the King we cannot, seeing his care and great wisdom. And upon the Council we cannot. But on nobody but the Lord Admiral.'[49]

By 25 March the Committee for Evils, Causes and Remedies had produced a draft list of accusations against Buckingham, and decided to notify the Duke of these so that he could, if he wished, make his reply before the House formally considered them. At this point, with the initial stages of the campaign against Buckingham completed, the Commons at last turned to the question of supply, and on 27 March considered a proposal that they should offer three subsidies and three fifteenths to the King. It was during the course of this debate that Eliot made one of his most passionate and effective speeches. Since it was the anniversary of the King's accession, Eliot took the opportunity to survey the whole course of events in the reign so far, and as he unfolded the tale of misfortune he focused the blame upon one person. Buckingham, he declared, had rotted the entire structure of the state by his unscrupulous and avaricious conduct. The King's

treasures are exhausted, his revenues are consumed, as well as the treasures and abilities of the subject. And though many hands are exercised and divers have their gleanings, the harvest and great gathering comes to one. For he it is that must protect the rest. His countenance draws all others to him as his tributaries, and by that they are enforced not only to pillage for themselves but for him, and to the full proportion of his avarice and ambition . . . . This cannot but dishearten, this cannot but discourage, all men well affected, all men well disposed to the advancement and happiness of the King. Nor, without some reformation in these things, do I know what wills or what abilities men can have to give a new supply.[50]

Eliot had referred to precedents from Henry III's and Richard II's reigns, to show that Parliament could force the dismissal of an unpopular minister by withholding supply, and the House followed his lead by determining to grant the three subsidies and fifteenths 'as soon as we have presented our grievances and received his [the King's] answer to them'. Charles, who recognised the danger inherent in this sort of bargaining, immediately sent a message to the two Houses ordering them to attend him at Whitehall on 29 March. When the members were duly assembled the Lord Keeper made a speech setting out the King's reasons for discontent at the way in which the Commons had behaved. They had publicly declared their determination to maintain him in honour and safety, but now they had settled upon a sum which fell far short of his requirements. 'His Majesty findeth it so far from making himself safe at home and feared abroad, as contrariwise it exposeth him both to danger and disesteem.' Nor was this all. The Commons had continued their attacks upon Buckingham despite the King's express order to the contrary. 'His Majesty hath commanded me to tell you that himself doth better know than any man living the sincerity of the Duke's proceedings . . . and therefore His Majesty cannot believe that the aim is at the Duke of Buckingham, but findeth that these proceedings do directly wound the honour and judgement of himself.'[51]

When the Lord Keeper had finished speaking, Charles added a few words of his own. He reminded the Houses that it was with their full support that he had persuaded his father to break off the treaties with Spain, and to embark upon the course of proceedings in which he was now engaged. At that time nobody was in greater favour with them than Buckingham and he could not understand why the Duke should now be under attack. The only possible explanation seemed to be that the Commons were using the excuse of Buckingham to criticise and undermine his own rule. But he warned them that this was a dangerous course. 'Now that you have all things according to your wishes, and that I am so far engaged that you think there is no retreat, now you begin to set the dice and make your own game. But I pray you, be not deceived. It is not a Parliamentary way, nor it is not a way to deal with a King.' Charles reminded members that it was up to them to decide whether or not Parliament should continue in session. If they took due heed of 'the distressed state of Christendom' and gave him sufficient means to cooperate fully with his allies in the anti-Habsburg league, then he would have no reason to dispense with it. But if they chose another course then it would be of no further use to him. 'Remember', Charles told them, 'that Parliaments are altogether in my power for their calling, sitting and dissolution. Therefore, as I find the fruits of them good or evil, they are to continue or not to be.'[52]

The forceful, almost brutal, tone of the King's speech seemed likely to have the opposite effect from that which had been intended, for the Commons, when they debated the matter on the following day, decided to suspend all further business until they had drawn up a remonstrance which they could present to the King as a justification of their actions. But before they could begin work on this they were summoned to the Lords to hear Buckingham give an 'explanation' of the King's speech. Buckingham, who was speaking with Charles's full authority, showed how the door was still open to agreement. The King was quite prepared to allow the Commons further time for their deliberations so long as they used this constructively and not to rake over old sores. Buckingham made it clear that Charles still insisted on a larger grant, since 'that which is proposed is so little that when the payment comes it will bring him to a worse estate than now he is in', but he added that the King acknowledged the Commons' right to present grievances and was also willing to permit a select committee of both Houses to undertake the examination and reformation of the royal finances.[53]

One of Buckingham's strengths as a politician was his flexibility. Another was his readiness to explain and defend his conduct, in the hope that reason might prevail over passion. The joint meeting of both Houses on 30 March gave him the chance to justify his actions and he seized it. He reminded all those who doubted the strength of his adherence to the protestant faith that he had given ample witness of this during his time in Spain. He assured those who condemned him for acting without taking sufficient advice that the Council had been fully consulted over the question of whether or not the Cadiz expedition should sail, and had also been closely involved in the negotiations for an offensive and defensive alliance with the United Provinces. As for the complaint that during his special embassy to the Hague he had committed the King to a scale of contributions to the common cause that the kingdom could not possibly sustain, Buckingham pointed out that the commitment was much greater in appearance than reality. The Dutch had been persuaded to give up the military assistance they received from England and to pay a fourth share of all joint naval operations. The Danes, likewise, had agreed to offset against Charles's promised subventions the cost of any diversionary action undertaken not simply by English arms but also by French — if only France could be persuaded to support the league.[54]

Buckingham then turned to the charge that through his negligence he had allowed command of the Narrow Seas to slip out of English hands. He referred to the poor state of the Navy at the time of his appointment (though he was careful, with his accustomed tact and courtesy, to absolve his predecessor from all blame), and described the work done by the Navy Commissioners, under his patronage, in cutting the annual cost from £54,000 to £30,000 while regularly building two ships a year. He informed members that there were now, as there had been ever since the war started, twelve ships assigned for coastal defence, even though the official allowance was only for four. A fleet of thirty vessels was ready victualled at Portsmouth and another ten needed only supplies. Besides all these, there were twenty Dutch ships waiting to come over. What more could he be expected to do with the money available? 'If any can show me a project how to maintain a war against Spain, Flanders, and the Turkish pirates with less charge, he will do a great work and good service.' The Duke ended with a plea for an end to all bitterness. 'Gentlemen,' he told them, 'it is no time to pick quarrels one with another. We have enemies enough already, and therefore [it is the] more necessary to be well united at home.'[55]

Buckingham's speech made some impression on his audience, and one report, which described it as 'fair and submissive', said that the Duke had answered the accusations against him so well 'that those who were indifferent, or not much his enemies, seemed then well satisfied'. But although Buckingham had a nucleus of firm supporters in the Lower House, they could not persuade their fellow members to abandon the idea of a remonstrance. Work on this therefore went ahead, and it was formally presented to the King on 5 April, after which both Houses went into a brief recess over Easter.[56]

VI

Buckingham had been an assiduous attender at the House of Lords during the first part of this Parliamentary session, and had also been involved in preparing and delivering speeches, partly in an attempt to rebut the accusations made against him. But there was no slackening in the pressure of the many other businesses in which he was involved. Naval matters took up a great deal of his time, and in the month of March alone Edward Nicholas sent out, on the Lord Admiral's instructions, close on a hundred letters. The fishermen of Suffolk and Norfolk had asked for 'such number of ships for the defending and wafting their ships to Iceland and North Seas about their fishing, as the danger and uncertainty of these times requireth'. Buckingham duly appointed two of the King's ships for this purpose, instructing them on their return 'to range the seas over, to free those parts of the Dunkirk ships which now frequent the same and do much daily spoil on His Majesty's subjects and their goods'. The Dunkirk pirates were a perpetual problem, and at the very moment when the Duke was being attacked in Parliament for neglecting the guard of the seas, he was writing almost daily to the hapless Sir Henry Palmer, ordering him to perform miracles with the limited resources at his disposal. Yet even when ships were available they were rarely able to catch the fast-sailing Dunkirkers and Buckingham therefore recommended the Navy Commissioners to construct a vessel specially designed for coastal defence. He wanted six of these 'tartans' but the Commissioners replied that in view of the pervailing shortage of money they could only put two in hand.[57]

Shortage of money held up everything. The soldiers who had returned with the fleet from Cadiz, and were billeted in the west country, were still without pay, food and clothing. The fleet being prepared at Plymouth was confined to harbour because there was no money with which to victual it, and Sir Thomas Button wrote to his fellow captain, Sir John Pennington, to commiserate with him. 'I am sensible of your insufferable troubles and wish for my soul you might be, to your content, eased of them . . . . It is hoped that the Parliament will take a course to see things better settled. Howsoever I wish, till that may be, that I and those that I love were quit of their employment.' Buckingham assured Pennington that he was aware of the desperate shortages which were sapping his confidence and effectiveness, 'but the delays in Parliament hath caused delays in other affairs that require most expedition'. Pennington could not restrain his anger at the way in which the safety of the kingdom was being neglected by those who, in the last resort, were responsible for it. 'I am heartily sorry that the Parliament is no more sensible of the consequence of this fleet,' he told Sir John Coke, 'as also of a further preparation, considering how patiently our great enemy, the Spaniard, prepareth against us'.[58]

Palmer and Pennington were not the only people who were clamouring for money. Mansfeld was asking for an immediate payment of £40,000 in order to hold his army together, while Christian of Denmark had sent an ambassador to London to press for the honouring of the promises that had been made to him at the Hague. By March 1626 the English contributions to him were seven months in arrears, and Christian needed the money desperately to pay his army and keep its courage up. He told Sir Robert Anstruther, the English ambassador to Denmark, that if Charles was unable to maintain the war which he had undertaken it would be far better to sue for the best peace terms that could be got. This was no doubt a realistic piece of advice, but with the steady advance of Habsburg power in Germany it seemed that only by their combined exertions could the Hague allies save themselves from destruction.[59]

The strain on Buckingham was so great that his health once again gave way. On 14 April Laud recorded in his diary that 'the Duke of Buckingham fell into a fever', and a few days later the Lord President told the Privy Council that the Duke was still indisposed and had therefore asked him to report on the urgent need to repair and supply the forts on the Thames and elsewhere. Buckingham made a swift recovery – fortunately for him, since his enemies were intensifying their campaign against him. He took advantage of the Easter recess to make private approaches to a number of members of the Commons, to see whether some way could be found to divert their energies into more constructive channels.[60] He was also considering the use of the Upper House once again to give a lead to the Lower. But the mood of the Upper House became distinctly less favourable towards the royal government after Charles's action in sequestering Arundel from it, early in March, and sending him to the Tower. The nominal reason was that Arundel had allowed his son to marry a royal ward, against the King's wishes. In fact, however, Charles had known of this clandestine marriage for some time, and had taken no action. His decision to remove Arundel from both the Council and Parliament seems to have been prompted by political considerations. Arundel was clearly not going to be numbered among Buckingham's supporters. He voted against the Duke over the proxies issue, and he was also pressing for his friend, the Earl of Bristol, to be allowed to take his seat in the Lords. In a narrowly divided House Arundel's votes could have been of key significance for the royal government, and rather than risk having them used against it Charles preferred to remove him from the scene. Did he perhaps thereby intend to give a warning to equally intransigent but less easily removable figures, such as Pembroke and the Archbishop? Arundel was sequestered on 4 March, only two days before Montagu's motion in the House of Lords which marked the beginning of the royal initiative. It could be that Arundel had been invited to support this initiative – along with Pembroke and Archbishop Abbot – but had declined to do so.

Whatever the reason, however, the House was restive at this action against one of its members, and Saye persuaded his fellow peers to appoint a committee to look into the precedents. The committee reported just before Easter, and Saye tried to capitalise on the situation by securing a petition to Charles asking for Arundel's release. Buckingham marshalled his strength against this proposal, and Saye's motion was defeated, though only by thirty-four votes to thirty-one. After Easter, however, Saye and his allies took advantage of Buckingham's absence through illness to secure the passage of a resolution that no peer should be imprisoned or restrained while Parliament was sitting, unless at the order of the House. On the following day, 19 April, while Buckingham was still absent, the Lords decided to present a remonstrance to the King, asking for Arundel's release. They also authorised the reading of a petition from the Earl of Bristol, complaining that he had been wronged in point of liberty and honour for two years 'by the industry and power of the Duke of Buckingham, to keep him from the presence of Their Majesties and the Parliament, lest he should discover many crimes concerning the said Duke'.[61]

Meanwhile, in the Commons, repeated attempts to focus attention upon the King's needs and to procure a vote of supply had failed. On 20 April the House resolved to ' proceed in the business in hand concerning the Duke of

Buckingham, forenoon and afternoon, setting all other businesses aside till that be done', and on the following day they accepted Digges's motion to appoint a sub-committee 'to consider the state of the great business now in hand and to reduce it into form'. In earlier judicial proceedings, such as those against Bacon and Mompesson, the Commons had secured detailed evidence from witnesses and transmitted this to the Lords along with their charges. But such a procedure was barely possible in the case of Buckingham, for his power was so great that few people would be prepared to risk offending him, and in any case the King had specifically forbidden members of the council of war to disclose confidential information. The Commons therefore decided to proceed on the grounds of 'common fame', which amounted to an assertion that the facts of which they were complaining were already so well known that they did not require detailed proof. On 24 April the House resolved that Buckingham was responsible for eight of the evils which had been called to its attention. A day or two later a select committee revealed that it was in receipt of information showing that Buckingham had administered certain medicines to James in his last illness without the sanction of the King's physicians. It was suggested that the House should immediately turn itself into a committee to consider the implications of this revelation, but members were clearly not of one mind. Eventually a division was called, and while one hundred and fifty members voted against any further investigation of this particular issue, one hundred and ninety-one voted in favour. This gives some indication of the support Buckingham had in the House – though it may be presumed that on this particular question a number of moderates voted for him. It also, of course, shows the strength of the majority against him, and this was confirmed on the next day, when the House resolved that Buckingham's administering of the medicine was 'an act of a transcendent presumption of a dangerous consequence', and that it should be annexed to the charges against him. A further charge was added on 1 May, when the old complaint about the re-arrest of the *St Peter* was resuscitated and voted to be a grievance: on this occasion just under a hundred and fifty members voted in favour of the Duke.[62]

On 2 May the House debated whether or not to transmit the charges against Buckingham to the Lords. There was a significant body of opinion which thought they should be presented to the King, and Buckingham's friends and clients in the Commons did their best to procure this. Goring reminded members that their actions were leading in one of two directions: they could secure either the Duke's removal or his reformation. As far as the first was concerned, the King had made it clear that he would never consent to it. As for the second, they need have no fear: 'a heart so generous will reform itself . . . . If we look for amendment, let us give some time.' Sir Robert Pye echoed this plea 'for pity and mercy', while Sir William Beecher declared his belief that Buckingham 'may prove a faithful minister hereafter'. But they could not carry the majority with them, and the House resolved to transmit the charges to the Lords.[63]

While the Commons were putting the final touches to their accusations against Buckingham, the favourite was coming under direct attack in the Upper House. The King had instructed Bristol to appear there as a delinquent, and on 1 May the Attorney-General, in the King's name, charged the Earl with high treason. Bristol was brought to the bar of the House to hear this charge, but interrupted it by asking the Lords to hear his own accusations against Buckingham and Conway. The Lords assented, and Bristol thereupon presented twelve specific charges against the Duke, accusing him, among other things, of taking Charles to Spain in 1623 in order to convert him to popery. Bristol called on the peers to give him and Buckingham equal treatment when it came to the hearing of their respective cases, and the Lords were considering this request when a message reached them from the Commons, asking for a conference. The Lords agreed, and on the afternoon of 8 May representatives of the two Houses met in the Painted Chamber of the Palace of Westminster.

Although no reason had been specified for the conference, everyone knew that the Commons had asked for it so that they could make a formal presentation of their charges against Buckingham. Eight speakers, each with two assistants, had been appointed by the Lower House to carry out this great business, and they acted with a due sense of their heavy responsibility. Proceedings were opened by Sir Dudley Digges, who, after a brief prologue, read the formal indictment.

For the speedy redress of great evils and mischiefs, [he declared] and of the chief cause of these evils and mischiefs which this kingdom of England now grievously suffereth . . . the Commons in this present Parliament by the authority of our said sovereign lord the King assembled, do by this bill show and declare against George, Duke, Marquis and Earl of Buckingham, Earl of Coventry, Viscount Villiers, Baron of Whaddon; Great Admiral of the kingdoms of England and Ireland . . . . Master of the Horse of our sovereign lord the King; Lord Warden, Chancellor and Admiral of the Cinque Ports and of the members thereof; Constable of Dover Castle; Justice in Eyre of the forests and chases on this side the river Trent; Constable of the castle of Windsor; Gentleman of His Majesty's bedchamber; one of His Majesty's most honourable Privy Council in his realms both in England, Scotland and Ireland; and Knight of the most honourable order of the Garter; the misdemeanours, misprisions, offences, crimes and other matters comprised in the articles following; and him, the said Duke, do accuse and impeach of the said misdemeanours, misprisions, offences and crimes.[64]

After this introduction the first three charges were read out, and then enlarged on by Sir Edward Herbert (a kinsman of Pembroke). They dealt with the excessive number of high positions which the favourite held, 'whereof every one would employ the industry of an able and provident man', and accused the Duke of paying money for the offices of Admiral and Lord Warden of the Cinque Ports. The fourth article, charging him with failing to guard the Narrow Seas, and the fifth, which covered the case of the re-arrest of the *St Peter* of Newhaven, were expounded by the distinguished lawyer, John Selden, and he was followed by John Glanville, who addressed himself to the sixth charge, of extorting money from the East India Company; the seventh, of delivering English ships into the hands of the King of France; and the eighth, of allowing these ships to be used against the protestants of La Rochelle, to the 'great and most apparent prejudice of the said religion'.[65]

By the time Glanville had finished speaking the Lords were exhausted, for it was a hot day and the strain of following the long and intricate speeches must have been considerable. The conference therefore adjourned, but although, on the following day, Buckingham pressed for a speedy resumption, this was not possible because of the sickness of one of the Commons' spokesmen. The Commons therefore spent part of the morning in a discussion on whether or not to demand the Duke's arrest. Several speakers referred to Buckingham's proud carriage as he listened to the reading and exposition of the charges against him, Christopher Wandesford, who had chaired the Committee of Evils, declared how ashamed he had been to see the Duke 'sit there with a greater confidence to hear his charge than I should be to deliver it'. It was not fit, he asserted, 'for us to see him thus outface us'.

Not everyone agreed that Buckingham's conduct had been arrogant. One member pointed out that a man could hardly defend himself if he was not present, and said that in his opinion Buckingham's expression had shown cheerfulness rather than scorn. Such moderation, however, was far from welcome to the Commons. Pym thought he could detect 'an influence from the great man upon some men, when they shall dare to speak in his defence in so high a strain', and the foolhardy member was ordered to withdraw from the House. The feeling of the majority was expressed by Sir Dudley Digges when he gave his opinion that it was 'too much favour that he [Buckingham] should be suffered to come to affront us who came to accuse him . . . . It is both just and necessary to commit him. There is such a precedent of power in the Duke as cannot be precedented in Parliament.' When a vote was taken, just over a hundred members voted in Buckingham's favour, but more than double that number wanted him to be imprisoned. It was therefore decided that a delegation should be sent to the Lords to request this, but only after the completion of the major business which was still outstanding.[66]

On 10 May the presentation of the charges was continued and concluded. The ninth and tenth articles, which were concerned with the sale of honours and offices, were expounded by John Pym, who took occasion to remark, in the course of his speech, that Buckingham seemed to be the patron of the Arminians. Pym also dealt with the eleventh article, accusing Buckingham of procuring titles of honour for his kindred, 'whereby the noble barons of England, so well deserving in themselves and in their ancestors, have been much prejudiced, and the crown disabled to reward extraordinary virtues in future times'. The twelfth article, which covered the 'exhausting, intercepting and misemploying the King's revenues', was presented by Christopher Sherland, who went into great detail about the various ways in which the Duke had profited from the royal bounty. 'If we look upon the time past,' said Sherland, 'never so much came into any private man's hands out of the public purse. If we respect the time present, the King never had so much want, never so many foreign occasions important and expensive; the subjects have never given greater supplies, and yet those supplies unable to furnish these expenses.' Buckingham, he said, had made known to both Houses that, despite the royal largesse from which he had benefited, he was £100,000 in debt. 'If this be true,' expostulated Sherland, 'how can we hope to satisfy his prodigality? If false, how can we hope to satisfy his covetousness?'[67]

There was only one more article, the thirteenth, and this concerned the Duke's action in administering medicine to James I during his last illness. Christopher Wandesford, in a relatively brief speech, sketched in the details and summarised the legal position. It was then left to Sir John Eliot, by way of epilogue, to tie up the various threads into one massive indictment. Eliot spoke, as always, with passionate conviction and a marked lack of restraint. He compared Buckingham to 'the beast called by the ancients *Stellionatus*: a beast so blurred, so spotted, so full of foul lines, that they knew not what to make of it'. The Duke, he said had consumed the revenues of the crown 'not only to satisfy his own lustful desires but the luxury of others, and by emptying the veins the blood should run in, he hath cast the body of the kingdom into an high consumption'. Buckingham had been the recipient of enormous sums of money, far exceeding the value of supplies voted by Parliament, yet they had been spent 'upon costly furniture, sumptuous feasting and magnificent building, the visible evidences of the express exhausting of the state'. Buckingham, continued Eliot, was the canker which ate up the King's treasure, the moth which consumed all the goodness of the kingdom. His power was such that it could hardly be paralleled, except perhaps by that of Sejanus, the unscrupulous favourite of the Emperor Tiberius.[68]

The King had not, of course, been present when the Commons delivered their charges against his chief minister and confidant, but he kept in close touch with the proceedings and made plain his anger at those who had been responsible for them – particularly when, like Eliot, they compounded their offence by the use of unbridled language. On the very next day Charles took his barge from Whitehall to Westminster accompanied not only by Buckingham but also by Rutland, Dorset, Carlisle, Holland and Conway – the hard core of the Duke's friends and supporters in the Upper House. Addressing the Lords, Charles told them that an attack on any of their members was an attack upon himself. 'I have been too remiss heretofore,' he said, 'in punishing those insolent speeches that concerned myself . . . for that Buckingham, through his importunity, would not suffer me to take notice of them lest he might be thought to have set me on, and [so that] he might come on the forwarder to his trial, to approve his innocency.' Charles now called on the Lords to be as tender of his honour as he was of theirs, and then quitted the House. If the Lords were puzzled about the purpose of the King's intervention they were not left long in doubt, for he had hardly left Westminster before Digges and Eliot were arrested and committed to the Tower.[69]

Meanwhile the Commons had sent a message to the Lords asking for the immediate imprisonment of Buckingham. Before the Upper House took any decision on this, however, it first listened to the Duke speaking in his own defence. Buckingham began by pointing out that if he remained silent he would seem to be admitting his guilt; yet if he replied to the accusations against him he would be accused of arrogance. Whatever he did, he could not win. Nevertheless, in view of the nature of the charges he felt impelled to state his own case. He did not deny that he had committed errors, for he was not 'an angel amongst men'; yet much the same could be said of all great office-holders, and the King would have no one to serve him 'if, for their reward of service . . . they shall be given up, in the times of their master's wants, for a grievance or a sacrifice'. But the Duke insisted that he had never done anything that deserved public condemnation. 'My lords,' 'I speak not this arrogantly, nor will I speak anything else to cast dirt at those who have taken pains to make me foul.' He reminded his hearers of the dishonour cast on his name and person, both at home and abroad, by the accusations levelled against him, and called on them to press speedily ahead with his trial in order to put an end to his suffering. It had been his intention, he added, to absent himself from the House while it discussed what to do; but now that the Commons had gone so far as 'to prescribe your lordships the manner of my judgement, and to purge me before I am heard, I shall not give way in my own particular to any of their unjust demands, but yet submit myself in this and all things else to your lordships' consideration.'[70]

The Lords decided to postpone any decision on the Commons' request — which amounted to a victory for Buckingham. They also agreed that the Duke should answer only the formal charges against him, and not the 'aggravations' which had been added by Digges and his colleagues when they delivered their accusations. When Buckingham asked for permission to consult learned counsel, they granted this, but they were not prepared to do everything that the King and Duke wanted. For example, they insisted on giving Bristol permission to take legal advice, even though the King had made clear his objections to this. They also declared their opinion that Digges appeared to have done nothing that merited imprisonment — and the King subsequently released both Digges and Eliot. However the subject which more than any other drove the Lords and the King apart, at a time when he stood in great need of their support, was Arundel's arrest. Feeling rose to such a pitch that on 26 May the Lords declined to consider any further business until their missing member was restored to them. Not until 8 June, when Arundel once again took his seat in the Upper House, did the Lords resume their discussions.[71]

Arundel held five proxies, which gave him a total of six votes, and it seemed highly likely that when Buckingham came to judgement before the Upper House, these votes would be cast — perhaps decisively — against him. The King therefore took steps to redress the balance in Buckingham's favour. The Duke's relative and client, Oliver St John — a former Lord Deputy of Ireland, who held the Irish title of Grandison — was given an English barony to enable him to take his seat in the Upper House. Dudley Carleton, also a loyal servant of Buckingham, was raised to the peerage as Lord Carleton of Imbercourt; while Edward Montagu, the eldest son of Buckingham's old friend and ally Sir Henry Montagu, Earl of Manchester amd Lord President, was summoned to the Lords by one of his father's titles, Baron Montagu of Kimbolton. The Florentine resident reported the current opinion that 'with these additions, when at last they come to conclusions with him [Buckingham], he will have two thirds of the votes in his favour'. But in fact the Lords were evenly split and there could be no certainty about the outcome of Buckingham's trial if it was allowed to go ahead. He had a solid core of supporters on whom he could rely, but, as Salvetti noted, there was increasing dissatisfaction within the House as a whole towards the Duke and his 'swelling and arrogant authority'.[72]

VII

At this very moment, when Buckingham was under attack for holding too many offices, he added another to his collection. On 28 May the Earl of Suffolk died, leaving vacant the Chancellorship of Cambridge University. Twenty-four hours later the Bishop of London's chaplain arrived in Cambridge to canvass on Buckingham's behalf and to assure members of the university that the King would be most gratified if they elected the Duke. Buckingham could count on the support of Matthew Wren, master of Peterhouse, and Leonard Mawe, master of Trinity, who had been sent out to Spain by James I in 1623 to act as chaplains to Prince Charles, and had thereby become closely acquainted with the Lord Admiral. He could also rely on the high churchmen, since Richard Neile, Bishop of Durham and one of the most prominent of the Arminians, had written letters on his behalf. For a day or two it looked as though Buckingham's election would be uncontested, but then his opponents rallied and put forward an alternative candidate. In the event the election was a close-run thing. Buckingham won by a small majority, and even that result may only have been achieved by a less than scrupulous counting of votes. Nevertheless he was now Chancellor of Cambridge University, and his election was a calculated rebuff to the Commons.[73]

The affronted members lost no time in discussing the matter, and Pym expressed the view that it was part of 'a conspiracy to bring in Arminianism'. The House decided that a letter should be sent to the university authorities, expressing displeasure at the action they had taken and requiring them to send up one of their number for interrogation. But at this point Charles intervened with a message to the Commons forbidding them to question the decision of the Cambridge electors. If the House felt that during the brief period of canvassing its honour had been impugned, then he agreed that it might legitimately enquire into this. It had no right, however, to investigate the election as such. Cambridge, like other corporations, derived its privileges from the crown, and Charles made it clear that he was determined to uphold them.[74]

The Commons were not prepared to risk an open clash with the King on this issue, especially as the time of Buckingham's trial seemed to be drawing near. On 8 June, when the Lords decided to resume work, Buckingham presented a detailed reply to the charges made against him by the Commons. He had taken great pains with this document, looking for advice on the legal implications to the Attorney-General, Sir Robert Heath, who had long been a client of his, and to Nicholas Hyde, a future chief justice. He also consulted William Laud, who had already assisted the King in the preparation of a number of his speeches and was only too glad to perform a similar service for the Duke.[75]

Buckingham began by reminding the Lords that 'what is my cause now may be yours and your posterity's hereafter', and went on to express his regret that 'my business should be the cause of the loss of this year for foreign attempts, and the hinderer of those resolutions that would have comforted our friends abroad and secured ourselves at home'. He made it plain that he bore no malice towards his accusers. The House of Commons had acted out of the best motives, but had been misled by 'common fame' – that poor opinion of himself and his activities which was grounded upon nothing more substantial than misinformation and misunderstandings. He hoped that once he had cleared his name he would be able to regain the good opinion of the Commons, for nothing had afflicted him more than the loss of it. He rejected totally the charge that he had acted against the interests of the state. On the contrary, he had been born and bred in the state's service.

I have been raised to honour and fortunes in it (I freely confess) beyond my merit. What I have wanted in sufficiency and experience for the service of it I have endeavoured to supply by care and industry, and could there be the least alienation hereafter of my heart from the service of the state for anything that hath passed, I should be the ungratefullest man living.[76]

Buckingham then turned to the specific allegations made against him in the Commons' articles, and dealt with them one by one. As far as plurality of offices was concerned, only three of the posts he held – those of Lord Admiral, Lord Warden of the Cinque Ports, and Master of the Horse – were really major ones; the others were, he said, 'rather titulary and additions of honour'. Two of these offices had been bestowed by the King's free gift, without any pressure on his part; but in any case it was not without precedent, even in recent times, that one man should hold a number of high offices – an obvious reference to Robert Cecil, Earl of Salisbury, who had been simultaneously Lord Treasurer, Secretary of State and Master of the Wards.[77]

Buckingham then dealt with the accusation that he had committed an offence by offering money as an inducement to office-holders to surrender their places to him. He took two specific cases: those of the Earl of Nottingham, his predecessor as Lord Admiral, and Lord Zouch, from whom he had acquired the Wardenship of the Cinque Ports. It was true, said Buckingham, that Nottingham had been granted a pension of £10,000 a year after giving up office, but this was a reward for his long and faithful service to the crown and not a precondition. As for Lord Zouch, he had insisted on compensation for giving up the Lord Wardenship and had already agreed to part with it to the Duke of Richmond for £1,000 down and £500 a year. After Richmond's sudden death, Buckingham stepped into his place and accepted the same terms. He made no excuse for doing so, for what other way was there by

which 'an ancient servant to the crown, by age and infirmity disabled to per-
from his service, can, in an honourable course, relinquish his place?' As Buckingham pointed out, 'if the King himself give the reward, it may be said it is
a charge to the crown. If the succeeding officer give the recompense, it may
thus be objected to be within the danger of the law.'

Buckingham defended his acquisition of the Lord Wardenship on the
grounds that the existence of two Admiralties in England was a hindrance to
the King's service. In the same way he defended his tenure of the office of
Admiral by pointing to the marked improvement in the condition of the
Navy that had taken place during that time. A principal function of the
Navy was to guard the Narrow Seas, and neglect of this duty was one of the
charges against Buckingham. But the Duke denied that he had been lax in
carrying out this duty. He had increased the number of ships assigned for
coastal defence, and he had sent an English squadron to join with the Dutch
in blockading Dunkirk. Only a sudden storm had put an end to this
effective method of controlling the menace of the Dunkirkers, and although
it was true that once they were at sea the enemy ships could outsail the English ones, he had given orders for the construction of faster vessels specially
designed to catch them. The Barbary pirates were a different matter, and it
was not easy to prevent surprise attacks; nevertheless he had taken steps to
strengthen the coastal defences against them, and the King, by his advice,
was engaged in negotiations with the states of the Barbary coast in an effort
to put an end to this scourge by treaty.[78]

Turning to the charge that he had illegally detained the St Peter of Newhaven, Buckingham showed how the re-arrest of that ship had been consequent upon the receipt of new information that the goods it was carrying were
really Spanish. Not until the King's officers had satisfied themselves that there
was insufficient proof of this allegation was the ship finally discharged. It was
true that money found in the ship had been confiscated, but it was used for
the King's service; not a penny, said the Duke, went into his own pockets. As
for the suggestion that the restraint of the St Peter was directly responsible for
the embargo of English goods in France, this was clearly not the case, since
the embargo had already come into effect before the ship was stayed. In any
case the French were bound by treaty not to lay an embargo on English goods.
The correct course, if they felt themselves aggrieved, was to complain to the
King, and even after that, if they did not receive satisfaction, they were only
permitted by the treaty to take specific and limited retaliatory action, not to
impose a general embargo.[79]

Buckingham, in dealing with the St Peter case, had confined himself to the
legal position, and it does indeed seem that his statement was well grounded
in law. Sir John Coke, writing to Holland and Carleton at Paris in March
1626, had set out the English attitude with great clarity. The French ships
and goods which had been seized by the English had come from Spain at a
time when French merchants had been forbidden by their own government to
trade there. The assumption was, therefore, that the lading of these vessels
had been done with the cognisance of the Spaniards, and this supposition was

strengthened by the fact that the French merchantmen were guarded for part of their journey northwards by Spanish warships. The goods in question were all consigned to Calais, where the Spanish factor for the Netherlands had established himself, and were of a type suitable for the Netherlands but not for France. It was now the task of the Admiralty Court to sort through all the evidence and decide whether the goods were genuinely French (in which case they would be restored) or Spanish (in which case they would be confiscated).[80]

Buckingham may have been guilty of misjudgement in his treatment of the *St Peter* of Newhaven, but no evidence was produced that he had broken the law. Much the same was true of the Commons' charge that as Lord Admiral he had illegally extorted money from the East India Company. Buckingham, in his defence, pointed to the fact that his claim for prize money had been prosecuted by due course of law before the Court of Admiralty, and that the Company, rather than risk an adverse judgement, had agreed to make composition with both James I and himself in return for a royal pardon. It was the King, said Buckingham, who negotiated with the officers of the Company about the amount that should be paid, and he himself had no hand in it. In any case, all except £200 of the money he received was borrowed by James and spent on the Navy.[81]

Buckingham then dealt with the charge that he had loaned ships to the King of France for use against the Huguenots, and declared his readiness (with Charles's consent) to reveal the details of the secret negotiations over this business, which would exonerate him completely. The next article, the ninth, accused him of forcing Lord Robarts to buy a baronage at the cost of £10,000. This, said Buckingham, was quite untrue. Robarts wanted a title and had previously offered a great deal more than this for it. He obtained it at his own solicitation, and there was no question of compulsion. The Duke also denied selling judicial offices, which was the tenth charge against him, and declared that in the two particular instances that were cited – Mandeville's purchase of the Lord Treasurership for £20,000 and Cranfield's reputed payment of £6,000 for the Mastership of the Wards – he 'neither had or disposed of a penny thereof'.[82]

The eleventh article accused the Duke of procuring honours for his kindred. Buckingham pointed out that a number of these honours – those bestowed on his mother and his brothers, for instance – had been granted without his intercession. But even if it were true that he had asked the King to honour his kindred, was there anything wrong in this? 'The law of nature and the King's royal favour, he hopeth, will plead for his excuse. And he rather believeth he were to be condemned in the opinion of all generous minds if, being in such favour with his master, he had minded only his own advancement and had neglected those who were nearest unto him.'[83]

Of the two remaining articles, the twelfth dealt with the grants of land and money which Buckingham and his relatives had received. The Commons had included a schedule of these in their charge, but the Duke now submitted one of his own which, he said, gave a truer picture. There could be no doubt, of course, that Buckingham had profited enormously from the favour shown him by James and Charles, but however undesirable such lavish generosity might have been from the public point of view, it was not illegal. As Buckingham observed in his reply, 'the King's liberality cannot be imputed as a crime to the Duke'.[84]

The last charge concerned Buckingham's administering of medicine to the dying James, and this he rebutted by describing what had in fact happened. James, knowing that Buckingham had recently recovered from a serious illness with the skilled assistance of the Earl of Warwick's physician, who had given him a 'plaster and posset drink', asked to have the same remedy provided for himself. Buckingham was reluctant to do this, but the impatient King sent the Duke's servant to fetch the medicine. Buckingham, who was about to leave for London, urged the King not to take any of it without first consulting his own doctors, but when he returned to Court he found that James had in fact sampled the posset. Not only this : the King now asked Buckingham to give him some more. The Duke did so, in the presence of the King's physicians, some of whom had tasted it themselves. 'Afterwards, when the King grew somewhat worse than before, the Duke heard a rumour as if this physic had done the King hurt, and that the Duke had ministered that physic unto him without advice. The Duke acquainted the King therewith, to whom the King, with much discontent, answered thus: "They are worse than devils that say it".'[85]

Buckingham concluded his defence by acknowledging that his youth and inexperience might have led him to commit many errors during the ten years in which he had had the honour to serve the King. 'But the fear of almighty God; his sincerity to true religion established in the Church of England (though accompanied with many weaknesses and imperfections which he is not ashamed humbly and heartily to confess) . . . and his love and duty to his country, have restrained him and preserved him (he hopeth) from running into heinous and high misdemeanours and crimes.' Since Buckingham's case never came to trial, there is no way of knowing how impressed the Lords would have been by his defence, but unless they had abandoned all pretence of judicial impartiality it is difficult to believe that they could have convicted him. The case against Buckingham was essentially political. He was the King's chief minister, yet he did not have the trust of Parliament or the nation at large. His continuance in office and favour made impossible the achievement of that harmony between King and people which alone could give England the chance of unity at home and success abroad. On these grounds Charles might have been well advised to dismiss the Duke from his counsels, as the Commons urged in their remonstrance. But since the King refused to do so, the Commons had no alternative to proceeding by impeachment, which could only work if a minister could be convicted of criminal, and not simply political, offences. Buckingham, however, was not a criminal. A number of his actions fell within that hazy area which lay between the boundaries of law and morality, but so did the actions of many, if not most, of his contemporaries, including members of both Houses of Parliament. For this reason, if for no other, the Lords would doubtless have pondered very carefully before condemning Buckingham.[86]

In the event, however, they were not called upon to pass judgement. On 10 June Buckingham urged the Lords to hasten proceedings as much as possible so that the business of the nation could be attended to. He also announced that until his case was decided one way or the other he would forbear to take his seat in the Upper House. On that same day the Commons decided to send for the record of Buckingham's speech to the 1624 Parliament about the course of his negotiations in Spain during the previous year. The re-opening of this particular question, especially now that Bristol was back in England, was a most alarming development from the King's point of view. Not only would it consume many more weeks at a time when Parliament had already sat far too long; it would also focus public attention upon Charles's own conduct during his time in Spain, and might well reveal what Buckingham had managed to obscure – namely the extent to which Charles had been prepared to make concessions on matters of religion if only he could be assured of the Infanta.[87]

The King had warned the Commons, on 9 June, that unless they passed the subsidy bill by the end of the following week he would be forced 'to take other resolutions'. The Commons, however, decided that they would first complete work on the remonstrance which they intended to present to him, and they also gave the second reading to an act 'concerning divers privileges of Parliament'. On 14 June they concluded their articles of impeachment against Richard Montagu, whom they regarded as the promoter of Arminianism, and gave further consideration to an anti-Arminian bill 'for the better continuance of peace and unity in the church and commonwealth'. Such actions were hardly likely to meet with the approval of Charles, who was sympathetic to the Arminians, and in fact he was already considering a dissolution of Parliament. However, at a meeting of the Council which was held to discuss this proposal, Buckingham argued strongly against it. Given the continuing shortage of money, he said, the King could not afford to dispense with Parliament, and although it might well be desirable in the long run to reduce the power of this assembly, now was not an opportune moment. Buckingham's view was shared by a number of other Councillor, who argued that if Charles broke with Parliament the King of France would seize the opportunity to crush the Huguenots. It was therefore decided to keep Parliament in session, and the King was said to have assured Buckingham that either the Lords would find him innocent or else he, Charles, would raise him up again as soon as the promised subsidies had reached the Exchequer.[88]

After further reflection, however, the King changed his mind and decided to dissolve Parliament. It must have been clear to him by this time that he stood little or no chance of gaining any subsidies from Parliament as long as Buckingham remained his chief minister. Yet if he were to dismiss Buckingham, who else could he turn to? Charles was not somebody who gave his trust easily; nor was he a man who liked being browbeaten. When he was confronted with the stark choice between Buckingham or Parliament, he preferred Buckingham. On 15 June, therefore, the Lord Keeper informed the Upper House of the King's commission to dissolve Parliament. Lord Montagu of Boughton – who may have been speaking on Buckingham's behalf as well as his own – proposed 'that the whole House move the King to make a pause of this, for that it may be of a most dangerous consequence', and it was decided to send a delegation to Charles to ask him to reconsider his decision. The Lord Chamberlain, Pembroke, was appointed to this, since he was known to carry great weight with the King, and so was Montagu's relative, the Earl of Manchester, who held the office of Lord President. It may be significant that the other two members were both close associates of Buckingham, namely Carlisle and Holland. Yet the combined pleading of all four men was of no avail. When they pressed the King to allow Parliament to sit just a few days longer, Charles was said to have replied 'Not a minute!'[89]

VIII

The end of Parliament meant the suspension of Parliamentary privilege, and there was widespread apprehension that the leaders of the opposition to Buckingham would now feel the full force of the King's anger. But while Arundel was ordered to retire into the country, and Bristol was once again imprisoned in the Tower, there was no general purge of the Duke's enemies. The Earl of Warwick, it is true, lost his place as Lord Lieutenant of Essex, and it was said that all those members of the Commons who had shown themselves to be hostile to Buckingham were to be removed from the Commission of the Peace. But such changes were dictated more by prudence than a desire for revenge, since Buckingham's critics had also, by definition, been critics of the war policy with which the crown was identified, and now that Parliament had been dissolved, without granting subsidies, the King would be even more dependent upon the goodwill of the local rulers. As one country gentleman reminded Buckingham, there was much to be said, when considering the appointment of Justices of the Peace, for 'making choice of men known to be well affectioned to His Majesty's service in every county, and the sparing of others not well disposed', for upon their lead would depend the attitude of the county community as a whole.[90]

It was hardly to be expected that Buckingham would continue to show favour to those who had led the attack upon him, particularly when, like Sir John Eliot, they had gone out of their way to whip up angry passions. In October 1626 Buckingham ordered an investigation into complaints that Eliot had committed 'divers misdemeanours, abuses, and unjust exactions' in the execution of his authority as Vice-Admiral of Devon, and later that month the Privy Council decided that he should be sequestered from office. There was nothing necessarily final about Eliot's disgrace. The punishment of ingratitude was simply the negative aspect of patronage, and an offender could usually work his way back into favour if he so wished. Eliot is often portrayed as a patriot motivated by principle, which in some ways he was. But he was also a man who was ambitious for office, and part of his anger towards Buckingham sprang from his resentment at the fact that Sir John Coke had been advanced above him. A similar mixture of motives is to be found in the attitude of Sir Thomas Wentworth, who took as an affront the goodwill which Buckingham showed to his Yorkshire rival, Sir John Savile. Wentworth had been pricked, as sheriff of Yorkshire in 1626, and thereby prevented from serving as a member of Parliament. But despite this outward mark of disfavour (or perhaps because of it) he had eagerly accepted Weston's offer to try and bring about a reconciliation between him and the Duke, for he described himself as being 'infinitely ambitious not of mere employment, but much rather to live under the smile than the frown of a sovereign'.[91]

It was because political attitudes were in practice far less rigid than they appeared to be that Buckingham did not despair of coming to terms with his enemies and thereby winning the cooperation of Parliament once again. The tone of his reply to the Commons' charges against him suggests that he would have welcomed a public trial as an opportunity to exonerate himself. The dissolution of Parliament prevented this, but steps were taken to bring both Buckingham and Bristol before the Court of Star Chamber, where their cases could be dealt with in a calmer atmosphere. Whether Star Chamber proceedings would have had much effect on public opinion is doubtful, since the judges of that court, apart from the two chief justices, were members of the Privy Council and therefore likely to be more amenable to royal and ducal pressure than the House of Lords. Nevertheless a formal trial and sentence in the Star Chamber would have prevented Parliament from reopening the impeachment proceedings and thereby cleared the way for a more constructive relationship between the King and the two Houses. This plan broke down, however, because the managers of the Commons' impeachment, when they were examined by the Attorney-General and asked to reveal the names of witnesses to the crimes alleged against Buckingham, declined to go beyond the evidence given when they presented their charges to the Lords. Without witnesses no prosecution could be sustained in a court of law, and the Duke was therefore never brought to trial.[92]

Despite this setback there were indications that Buckingham was still thinking in terms of a renewed appeal to Parliament. In August he submitted to the Privy Council a list of grievances complained of by the Commons, and urged his colleagues to take effective action to remedy them. His pressure apparently had some effect, for in early September one letter-writer described how 'the best of the grievances hath lately been perused and fair answers framed thereunto', and gave it as his opinion that it would not be long before a new Parliament was summoned. Some weeks later the Venetian ambassador reported that Buckingham and his supporters were pressing the King to have recourse once again to Parliament, but that Charles remained obdurate.[93]

Buckingham could not be certain, of course, that a new Parliament, if ever it met, would abandon the path of confrontation marked out by its predecessor. But he was aware that his critics in the Commons had derived strength and guidance from certain dissident lords, and that if he could break this alliance he would be far better placed to win support for his policies. The key figure in the opposition to him was, as always, the Lord Chamberlain, the Earl of Pembroke, and what Buckingham now proposed was a treaty of friendship and cooperation, based on a marriage alliance. Pembroke had no son of his own, but had left his estates to his nephew, the seven-year-old child of his brother, the Earl of Montgomery. In July 1626 it was agreed that this young boy, Lord Charles Herbert, should be formally engaged to Buckingham's four-year-old daughter Mary, and the articles were signed in early August. Pembroke agreed to provide £10,000 a year for his nephew, in addition to the £2,000 a year which Montgomery would give. Buckingham committed himself to pay a dowry of £20,000, but the first half of this was not to be handed over until Mary became fourteen.

The marriage contract was drawn up on conventional lines and contained no hint of the arrangements for sharing power between the two families. These implicit arrangements were the really essential ones, however, for it was they which made the marriage alliance both necessary and possible. They also held out hope of an end to the enmity between Pembroke and Buckingham, and for this reason the King was happy to give not merely his blessing but his active cooperation. He agreed that Pembroke should be appointed to the dignity of Lord Steward of the royal household, which he had long coveted. His place as Lord Chamberlain was to be taken by his brother Montgomery. This meant that the Herberts were now firmly ensconced at Court, but the Duke's friends were also advanced. Carlisle and Holland were appointed Gentlemen of the King's Bedchamber, while the Earls of Salisbury, Dorset and Bridgwater were sworn as Privy Councillors.[94]

The *rapprochement* between Pembroke and Buckingham was immediately followed by attempts to reconcile the Duke with Bristol, and in mid-August a rumour ran round the capital that Bristol's son was to be married to one of the Duke's many female relatives. This turned out to be false, but in the following month Bristol was released from the Tower and allowed to return to his country house at Sherborne in Dorset. This act of grace was largely Pembroke's work, though Buckingham, when he heard of it, expressed regret that he had not thought of it himself. Only a few months before, Bristol and Buckingham had been open enemies, hurling charges and counter-charges against each other. Now all was sweetness and light – on the surface at any rate – and Bristol wrote to the Duke to thank him for his kindness. 'I understand by my Lord Steward,' he said, 'that Your Grace hath been so far from opposing that you have with much readiness assisted and furthered my humble suit unto His Majesty of having leave for some small time to go into the country; the which . . . I cannot but ingeniously acknowledge to be a nobleness and generousness in Your Grace, and therefore return unto you my humble thanks for so free a favour, which shall not be only acknowledged but met with all due respects.'[95]

IX

No sooner had the King put an end to faction in his Court than he made a bid to end the wrangling which marred his private life by dismissing the French household of his wife, Henrietta Maria. Buckingham had hoped to make this unnecessary by freeing the young Queen from her excessive dependence upon her French advisers. To this end he introduced his own relatives into her entourage, and he also wrote to Marie de Médicis, suggesting that she should instruct her daughter to pay careful heed to what he told her. Marie did so, and Buckingham thereupon went to see Henrietta Maria and, after assuring her of his desire to promote her best interests, offered to persuade the King to invite her to meetings of the Privy Council, so that she could become fully involved in affairs of state. The Queen turned, as always, to her French advisers, and Blainville — who was at that time Louis's ambassador in England — warned her to have nothing to do with such proposals, on the grounds that they were simply snares to bring her into the Duke's net.[96]

In January 1626, therefore, the Queen politely but firmly rejected Buckingham's offer; and in the following month she announced her intention not to take part in the coronation ceremony, on the grounds that it would be carried out by a protestant bishop. This caused great offence to Charles, and his scarcely suppressed anger burst out into the open a week or so later. The Queen wanted to watch her husband ride in state to open Parliament, and had agreed to do so from the Countess of Buckingham's apartments in Whitehall. On the day itself, however, it was raining, and Henrietta suggested that instead of crossing the muddy garden to the Countess's lodgings she should view the procession from her own gallery. The King agreed, but with an ill grace, and later sent Buckingham to tell her how offended he was at her sudden change of plan. Blainville, who was in attendance on the Queen, advised her to mollify the King's wrath by going over to the Countess of Buckingham's rooms, which Henrietta promptly did. But this only made matters worse, for it seemed to confirm what Charles had long suspected, that his influence over his wife was as nothing compared with that of her French attendants. He therefore sent Buckingham to order her to return at once to her own apartments, and later that day he made the Duke transmit a further message to the effect that unless she mended her ways he would expel Madame de Saint-Georges and all the French household.[97]

Buckingham regretted the ill-feeling between the King and the Queen, and told the Venetian ambassador how sorry he was that things had come to such a pass. 'He had nothing whatever to do with it. The King had done everything himself', Buckingham added. The French, however, believed that the Duke had fomented the bad blood between Charles and Henrietta in order to preserve his monopoly of influence over the King. They pointed to the many occasions on which he had carried curt orders or reproachful messages from Charles to his wife as evidence of Buckingham's true feelings, for they assumed that Charles was entirely under the Duke's influence and had no will of his own. In fact this was far from the case, as Holland explained to Marie de Médicis. 'I told her', he wrote to Buckingham, 'that she must distinguish between what you say as commanded by the King, and what you say of yourself: for if it be his pleasure to make [you] the instrument to convey his will upon any occasion of his displeasure, you are not to dispute but to obey his command, in that and in all other things.' This was confirmed by Dudley Carleton, after the expulsion of the French household had actually taken place, for he told the Bishop of Mende – who clung to the belief that the Duke was responsible – that the decision was Charles's own. Carleton, who was speaking from personal knowledge, went on to say that when Buckingham heard of the King's intention he did his utmost to dissuade him, but without effect. This account of events is supported by a surviving letter from Charles to Buckingham, written on 7 August. 'Steenie,' wrote the King,

I have received your letter by Dick Graham. This is my answer. I command you to send all the French away tomorrow out of the town – if you can, by fair means, but stick not long in disputing; otherwise force them away, driving them away like so many wild beasts until ye have shipped them. And so the Devil go with them.

Just in case the Duke should still have doubts about his master's intentions, the King added a peremptory further sentence: 'Let me hear no answer but of the performance of my command.' Whatever Buckingham's personal feelings or reservations, he clearly had no choice but to obey.[98]

The expulsion of Henrietta Maria's French attendants came at a moment when relations between the two crowns were more than usually complicated. The English had been deeply shocked by the news of the Treaty of Monçon, and Buckingham was looking for some way of pushing the French and Spaniards once again into open hostility in Italy. He pinned his hopes on Savoy, for Charles Emmanuel, the ruler of that Alpine duchy, had proposed an assault either on Genoa or Milan – the one a client state of Spain, the other a Spanish duchy. The attraction of this plan was that such an attack would inevitably provoke a reaction from Spain, and once the Spaniards had intervened it would be difficult for France to remain neutral. In this way the two great powers might be brought into conflict even against their will.[99]

The English welcomed this evidence of Savoy's constancy in the struggle against Spain, but Charles had to make clear that he was in no position to give direct aid. In July 1626 he was engaged in the setting out of two fleets, but one of these was to guard the Narrow Seas while the other undertook offensive operations against Spain. There were no ships to spare, especially in view of Spanish preparations to invade England from the Netherlands. Nor was there any money available, now that Parliament had been dissolved without granting subsidies. Charles therefore instructed Sir Isaac Wake, his ambassador to Savoy and Venice, to try to persuade the Venetians to subsidise Charles Emmanuel. Wake was also to stir up the protestant Swiss cantons to reject the terms of the Treaty of Monçon, and thereby effectively nullify it. While these diplomatic exchanges were taking place, the Duke of Savoy's agent, the Abbé Scaglia, was in England for discussions with Buckingham on the international situation. The two men agreed on the overriding need to make France fulfil the promise she had made to support the anti-Habsburg states, but they had different opinions about what means to use. The best way, thought Scaglia, would be to force France into war with Spain, but this would not be possible unless Spain was willing to fight and she would be reluctant to do so as long as she was at war with England. Scaglia therefore suggested that Savoy should act as mediator to bring about peace between England and Spain, on the assumption that once this had been arranged, Spain would feel free to take a more aggressive line against France. Buckingham did not agree with this, however. While he shared Scaglia's desire to foment hostilities between France and Spain, he was sceptical about the chances of an Anglo-Spanish settlement in view of the fact that the Spaniards were at this very moment preparing to invade England. In any case, as he pointed out, if England were to make a separate peace with Spain she would be guilty of the same treachery towards her allies that she reproached in the French.[100]

This was the end of the matter for the time being, and Buckingham was hopeful that events within France itself would push Louis into more belligerent policies without recourse to such devious methods as those outlined by Scaglia. For some time there had been rumours of growing unrest in France, involving not only the Huguenots but also the dissident nobles, and Richelieu's continued tenure of power could not be taken for granted. Buckingham and the Duke of Savoy were in secret touch with the malcontents, and they had some reason to hope that the Cardinal would either be forced to throw in his lot with them or else be replaced by a more amenable minister. The plots centred round Louis XIII's brother Gaston, Duke of Anjou, whom the queen mother and Richelieu wanted to marry off to the Princess of Montpensier. Anjou, however, had no inclination to wed, and he was strengthened in his resolve by the principal magnates, who feared that if he were to marry and produce children their own chances of inheriting the throne would be impaired. The ladies of the court were also involved, for the queen regnant, Anne of Austria, felt that she was already despised for being childless, and would become the object of even greater derision if Anjou had children while she and Louis had none. Moreover, if, as rumour had it, the plotters intended to depose Louis and put him in a monastery, she would be free to marry Anjou herself – but only if he were still unattached. Anne confided in Madame de Chevreuse, through whom, it may safely be assumed, Buckingham learnt the details of what was being plotted. Madame de Chevreuse also had the confidence of the young Count of Chalais, who, as well as being Louis XIII's favourite and one of her many lovers, was also the avowed opponent of Richelieu.[101]

In late April, 1626, Richelieu struck at the plotters by ordering the arrest of Anjou's close friend and adviser, the Marshal d'Ornano, who had acted as intermediary with Savoy and (through his friendship with the Earl of Carlisle) with England also. However, Ornano's arrest did not put an end to the intrigues against Richelieu. Anjou was furious at the loss of his friend and contemplated withdrawing from court and setting himself up as a quasi-independent prince in one of the provinces. Brittany was a possibility, since its governor, the Duke of Vendôme, was another of Anjou's intimates. Once established in Brittany, Anjou would be well placed to secure support by sea from both the English and the Huguenots, and with this formidable strength behind him, as well as that of Savoy and his fellow nobles, he would be able to dictate his own terms to Louis XIII. Among those terms was certain to be included the dismissal of Richelieu.

Buckingham stood to gain a great deal from these involved manoeuvres. If Anjou carried through his revolt, and replaced his brother on the French throne, he was likely to be far less rigid than the Cardinal in his attitude towards the Huguenots and far more amenable to suggestions that France should commit herself fully to the anti-Habsburg league. If, on the other hand, he drew back and accepted a compromise, he ought still to be strong enough to make his voice heard in the formulation of policy. Buckingham was anxious to know what the outcome of the power struggle in France was likely to be, and in late June 1626 he sent Wat Montagu over to Paris, nominally on a mission to Marie de Médicis, but really to spy out the land. By mid-July Montagu was back in England with the report that everything in France was in turmoil, and it may have been this which persuaded Charles that the moment was ripe to get rid of his wife's French attendants.[102]

Any rejoicing on Buckingham's part would have been premature, however, for the conspiracy against Richelieu was on the point of collapse. In July 1626 Richelieu had Chalais arrested, and during the course of his interrogation the full extent of Anjou's involvement in the plots against Louis XIII was revealed. Anjou took fright and made his peace with his brother, who demonstrated his forgiveness by giving Gaston the duchy of Orleans. On 26 July the new Duke of Orleans married the Princess of Montpensier, and two weeks later Chalais was executed. On the same day as Chalais went to the block, Madame de Chevreuse was ordered to leave court, and rather than remain under the risk of further penalty she left France altogether and took refuge in the neighbouring duchy of Lorraine. For the time being at any rate Richelieu had routed his opponents.

The English – as the Bishop of Mende reported to Richelieu – were disappointed and alarmed by the news of Gaston's marriage, for they realised that it meant at least a temporary setback to their hopes of overthrowing the Cardinal. In the long run, of course, it was to become clear that Richelieu was as anti-Habsburg as could be desired, but Charles, Buckingham, and the other formulators of English policy did not have the advantage of hindsight. They had to judge Richelieu by his actions, and the evidence seemed to point clearly in one direction: Richelieu, under the cover of friendship with the English and the Dutch, seemed to be working towards an alliance of catholic powers which would establish a Franco-Spanish hegemony over the western world. In the words of an English state paper, drawn up in early October 1626, the King of France was so 'overawed with the fear of damnation, [and] is so enraged against our religion, that he believeth there is no way of honour or merit but by the ruin thereof . . . . The Cardinal keeps the king in his power, qualifieth the princes {i.e. holds the magnates in check] and keeps interest in the clergy and in the see of Rome by pretending [i.e. aiming] to supplant the protestant religion in that kingdom and to produce the same change amongst us which Spain did attempt.'[103]

English fears about Richelieu's ultimate aims were increased when the Cardinal turned his attention to the French navy. He was determined to make Louis XIII master of La Rochelle, but he could not do so without a fleet, and the public outcry in England and the United Provinces against the loan of ships to France meant that he could no longer rely on these two states for assistance. Richelieu therefore decided to create a large royal navy in France. He gave orders for the construction of a number of vessels in Dutch yards; he expanded ship-building facilities in France itself; and he began the process of concentrating French naval administration – hitherto divided up among a number of aristocratic admirals – into his own hands. Richelieu's aims may have been limited, but the transformation of France into a major naval power had implications that went far beyond La Rochelle. As the Archbishop of Bordeaux was later to declare, on 'the power of the sea' depended not simply the 'ruin of the Huguenots' but also 'the lowering of the pride of England [and] Holland'. It is therefore hardly surprising that, as Mende told Richelieu in June 1626, 'they [the English] are extremely apprehensive . . . about the resolution you have taken to make yourself powerful at sea, being cerain that if ever you have forty warships you will give the law to these nations which are predominant only through your neglect'.[104]

X

In the early summer of 1626 Richelieu set up a trading company based in the new port of Morbihan, in southern Brittany. This company, which was given the right to build ships and cast its own guns, was also granted extensive powers to develop trade with the East and West Indies, North America and the Levant. In other words Richelieu's plans envisaged not just the creation of a powerful French navy and mercantile marine for use in home waters, but also the entry of France, as a major contender, into the struggle for the acquisition and control of colonies and trading posts in the New World and the Orient. This constituted a challenge which no English government, and in particular no Lord Admiral, could possibly ignore. Carleton, who was sent on another mission to France in late July, told Buckingham that, as far as he could make out, Richelieu's plans were 'of three or four years' continuance' and might well be abandoned before they could come into effect. 'Yet,' added Carleton, 'for the interest His Majesty hath in this, it is not to be neglected.'[105]

There was little danger of Buckingham neglecting such a threat, for he had already called it to the attention of the council of war, which was holding daily meetings throughout June. But his more immediate concern was with the threat of Spanish invasion, and on 6 June he informed the council of reports that the Spaniards were preparing to send over two hundred ships and forty thousand men to effect a landing in England or Ireland. The members decided to consult with 'certain of the best and most experienced captains and seamen' and ask their advice on whether the fleet of thirty ships which the King had got together, and which was to be reinforced by twenty Dutch vessels, should be kept in the Narrow Seas or sent off to Spain or Flanders to destroy the shipping assembled there. Shortage of money, however, was a crippling limitation upon the English capacity to take effective action, and it was no coincidence that a few days later, on 9 June, the King sent an ultimatum to the House of Commons, telling them that he was 'daily advertised from all parts of the great preparations of the enemy ready to assail us' and that they must therefore pass their subsidy bill forthwith. Indeed it is more than possible that it was the Commons' refusal to do this, and their insistence on pressing ahead with the charges against Buckingham at the very moment when he was fully occupied with defence preparations, that prompted the King to dismiss Parliament.[106]

With the ending of Parliament went all hope of solving the crown's financial problems, and the council of war was left with the impossible task of providing for the nation's defence without having the funds to do so. It therefore suggested that the King should exercise his prerogative right to raise ships from the seafaring section of the population, and at the end of June 1626 the Privy Council sent letters to all the port towns, instructing them 'to furnish ships at their own charges for the defence of the kingdom, as they did in the year 1588' – when the Spanish Armada was on its way. Many of the ports, however, were unable to comply with this order, since war had disrupted their trade and they had suffered heavily from the depredations of pirates. The Council therefore decided to call on the adjoining counties to give financial assistance to the ports, but this immediately provoked opposition. The Justices of the Peace of Dorset, for instance, wrote to the Council to complain that they could not 'find any precedent for being charged in a service of this nature'. The Council was exasperated by such quibbling over legal niceties at a time of national peril. 'This kind of return upon the commands of His Majesty and this table, we are well assured, is without precedent,' it replied, 'and therefore we cannot but much marvel thereat and reprove you for it, letting you to know that state occasions and the defence of a kingdom in times of extraordinary danger do not guide themselves by ordinary procedents.'[107]

In his search for money after the dissolution of Parliament, the King at first contemplated asking for a benevolence, or 'free' gift, from his subjects – even though such demands had been declared illegal by a statute of Richard III. It soon became apparent, however, that his appeal would go largely unheeded, and so he turned to the equally traditional, and even less popular, device of a forced loan. But this in its turn aroused resistance, particularly from those who feared that if the King were successful in raising money by this means he would have no need ever again to summon Parliament. The loans came in so slowly that Buckingham, far from pressing ahead with the setting out of two fleets, had to use all his efforts to keep the ships already in commission adequately manned. Seamen deserted in large numbers rather than starve in the King's service, and commanders had to spend their energies suppressing mutinies instead of attending to their professional duties. Early in June 1626, John Pennington was trying to prepare his ships for sea in order to meet the imminent threat of Spanish invasion, but at this particular juncture the men of the *Red Lion* mutinied and determined to march on London to put their case in person to the King and the Lord Admiral. When their officers pressed them to stay, they replied that 'their wives and children were like to starve at home and themselves to perish abroad for want of clothes and other necessaries'. The Privy Council promptly sent orders to the Deputy-Lieutenants of Surrey to stop the mutineers getting any farther than Kingston. They were instructed to do everything in their power to persuade the men to return peacefully to their ships, but if all else failed they were to punish them by martial law. Draconian measures such as these were not to the liking of peaceful country gentlemen, however, and the whole business of the mutinies merely confirmed their dislike and disapproval of the policies which led to them.[108]

As money trickled in to the Exchequer it was used to pay the sailors and soldiers in England, as well as those abroad, but wages remained heavily in arrears. In July Buckingham informed the Privy Council of the need to provide more ships to guard the Irish coasts, since only one of the three provided for that service was now available. The Lord Treasurer said he had no money but would see what could be done. He gave the same reply to Buckingham's other requests: for more ships to secure the northern coasts of England against the Dunkirkers; for supplies to be sent to the vessels guarding the Narrow Seas; and for replacements to be provided for those ships which had been keeping watch at the mouth of the river Elbe, to stop the supply of contraband goods from the Baltic to Spain. There was little, in fact, that the Lord Treasurer could do, and Buckingham's attempts to enable the Navy to fulfil its responsibilities ran in tandem with reports of new mutinies provoked by lack of money. In July the sheriff of Hampshire intercepted three hundred sailors who had left their ships and were marching on London. They had been without pay for sixteen months and more, and their wives and children were near starvation. Their only hope, they declared, was in the King, and they were going to Court in order that 'their case might truly be made known to His Majesty'.[109]

Buckingham was still trying to get a fleet of thirty ships ready for sea, so that it could join forces with the Dutch, who were beginning to complain that their vessels had been kept waiting to no purpose. But there were endless delays, particularly in supplying the victuals without which the fleet could not sail. In July 1626 Buckingham wrote to the commissioners at Portsmouth, stressing the importance of seeing that the fleet being assembled there was well supplied. He instructed them to 'view, survey and search all provisions of beer, beverage, biscuit, beef and peas, pork, butter, cheese [and] oil', and see that these were 'sweet and wholesome'. They were also to provide rice, oatmeal and sugar for the the diet of seamen who fell sick, as well as shoes, stockings and shirts of the best quality for the sailors –

who were to pay for them by deductions from their wages. Furthermore, the commissioners were to see that adequate quantities of vinegar were made available for cleaning the ships, since Buckingham had been informed that the lack of vinegar had been one of the main reasons for the rapid spread of infection in the vessels which accompanied Cecil on the Cadiz voyage.[110]

Despite all this close and detailed supervision, the supplies still proved defective, and Buckingham therefore appointed a commission to find out what had gone wrong. This reported that the main fault was the long delay in sending provisions from London, and it implied that Sir Allen Apsley, the Victualler of the Navy, was to blame. But Apsley, as Buckingham well knew, was hampered by the prevailing lack of money. Indeed, without Apsley's readiness to pledge his own credit even less would have been accomplished, and Buckingham recognised this when he wrote to the Victualler in August 1626 to thank him for his 'extraordinary forwardness to supply (even beyond your own abilities) the great wants of the ships'. The Navy could not dispense with either Apsley or his credit. I 'would not press you to lend your help any further,' Buckingham told him, 'but that His Majesty's present occasions urge it for relief of the poor mariners who have long served His Majesty without wages and are now in great misery for want of victuals'. He added that if Apsley could find 'some good and present means to supply the ships in the Downs with victuals . . . your care and help at this pinch will add much to the merit of your care of His Majesty's service'.[111]

By the end of August Apsley was at Portsmouth, where he gave assurances that all the victuals which the fleet needed would be made available within ten days. But he could do nothing about the lack of sails, rigging, anchors and many other things for which he was not responsible. One exasperated captain, writing to Nicholas, declared that he 'never did see such confusion of business as is in this', and gave his opinion that 'there are too many that hath the managing of it, and too few that understands what belongs unto it'. He added that the blame for these faults was bound to light on Buckingham, and that it grieved him 'to see the government of this business, which so much importeth my Lord's place and honour' carried on in such a way as to bring the Lord Admiral nothing but opprobrium.[112]

Buckingham was by now coming to the opinion that the responsibility for the bad management of the Navy lay with the Commissioners. He had worked with them ever since he became Lord Admiral, and they had done wonders in cutting the costs of the peacetime Navy while increasing its strength. But they apparently could not cope with the exigencies of war, and although lack of money was part of the reason it was not – or so Buckingham thought – the only one. In September he wrote to the Commissioners to express his concern about the continuing delays to the fleet at Portsmouth, and did not hide his irritation.

When I wrought and pressed you for despatch of the fleet, it was ever answered all things were ready except the victuals; but my brother Denbigh . . . was forced to go away only with one suit of sails and not necessaries fitting to carry His Majesty's ship from port to port. If these provisions be not presently furnished, I must acquaint the state with it, that the blame thereof may not lie on me . . . . I am heartily sorry to see such coldness and remissness in a service so much importing the good of His Majesty and the state. It was not wont to be so, neither can the want of money excuse this fault.[113]

Although Denbigh — who was vice-admiral of the fleet — had taken his squadron to sea and beaten his way westwards as far as Land's End, he was far from happy, since his victuals were rotten and the beer stank so much that it was 'not fitting for any Christians to drink'. Meanwhile Lord Willoughby, who had been appointed to command the expedition, was still fretting at Portsmouth, waiting for the long-promised supplies to arrive. They reached him at last on 12 September, but he still could not sail, for his fleet had no pinnaces or fireships. When Buckingham heard of this he called on the Navy Commissioners for an explanation. They informed him that money had run out and they had been forced to discharge the shipwrights employed on this work. Nevertheless they promised him that they would now hasten the ships away 'by forcing men to work with threatenings, having no money to pay them'. They added a warning, however, that the Victualler's credit was exhausted and that he could do no more unless he received immediate payment. When Buckingham reported this to the Privy Council, it decided that Willoughby should sail without either fireships or pinnaces, and that the latter, when they were eventually made ready, should be employed on coastal defence duties instead.[114]

It might have been better for Willoughby to stay at home, but Buckingham was determined that the time and money spent in preparing his expedition should not be totally wasted. It was not too late for Willoughby to carry out his principal task of intercepting the Plate Fleet, which was due to reach Spain in the late autumn with the treasure of the New World in its hold. It was bearing a larger and more valuable cargo than usual, for in addition to its own consignment of bullion it was carrying that of the previous fleet, which had been held back for fear of English attack. Acute shortage of money had already caused distress in Spain, and above all in the Spanish Netherlands, from where Rubens reported that 'all payments have been postponed until [the fleet's] arrival, and meanwhile we have pawned even our shirts'. The capture of the Plate Fleet, upon which, as Rubens noted 'depends the fortune of Spain', would have been a great triumph for the common cause. Not simply would it have crippled the Spanish army operating against the Dutch and checked Spinola's plans to expand the privateer base at Dunkirk; it would also have interrupted the flow of Spanish silver which kept Habsburg armies marching throughout Europe.[115]

At this very moment, however, when Buckingham was doing his utmost to mount an operation which, if it were successful, would have repercussions throughout the entire western world, he was himself under attack. In August a mob of mutinous sailors surrounded his coach in London and would not let him go until he promised them payment of their arrears. A few days later, presumably as a consequence of this, the Privy Council instructed Sir William Russell, the Treasurer of the Navy, 'to cause the said mariners and seamen to be paid the old pay . . . until the 24th of April last'. But there was simply not enough money available to meet all the pressing needs. In September, for instance, the Navy Commissioners told Buckingham that they needed £14,000 to pay off a number of ships which it was costing the King £4,000 a year to keep on his books to no purpose. They also needed a further £6,000 to discharge the vessels returning from the river Elbe and the squadron of six ships which had been convoying east-coast fishermen. If this money – amounting in all to some £20,000 – were not forthcoming, 'the necessities of these poor men', they warned him, 'will force them to mutinous courses; for we find these in the river [Thames] so unruly already that we cannot meet to advise touching His Majesty's service without clamour and danger to our persons, threatening to break down the doors upon us as we set about our business'.[116]

The Commissioners were not being alarmist, for disorders committed by unpaid and mutinous soldiers and sailors were now a daily occurrence. In October 1626 Buckingham's coach was again attacked, and this time smashed to pieces, by a mob of unpaid sailors, while the Duke was sitting in Council. Next day a proclamation was issued, ordering all 'mariners, soldiers and loose people' to return to wherever they had come from, under pain of martial law, and a guard was appointed to keep watch over Buckingham's house. These measures, however, did not go to the heart of the problem, which was the poverty of the royal government and the consequent distress of unpaid soldiers and sailors. Spurred on by hunger the men continued to mutiny and flock to London. In early November Sir William Russell, the Treasurer of the Navy, informed the Privy Council 'that divers mariners belonging to His Majesty's ships riding at Chatham, to the number of about three hundred, were come up to London in a tumultuous manner to demand their pay'. Thereupon the Council, thoroughly alarmed, directed that monies coming in from the forced loan and other sources should be assigned for the payment of sailors' wages. A few days later it wrote to the commissioners for the forced loan in the home counties, ordering them to speed up collection. Meanwhile, to prevent further disorders, it instructed the Lord Mayor of London to 'cause strong and continual watch and ward to be kept, as well by day as by night' and to provide for a guard on Sir William Russell's house as long as 'it shall be needful for the repressing the insolency of mariners'.[117]

The poor Treasurer of the Navy had been driven to distraction by the threats made against him. Three hundred discharged sailors had been given tickets, or promissory notes, since there was no money with which to pay them, but they were far from satisfied and marched on Sir William's house, broke open his gates, and, in the words of one observer, 'would have plucked him out by the ears, had he not given them fair words'. Russell estimated that he needed nearly £50,000 to meet arrears of wages, quite apart from the sums required to replenish naval stores and keep skilled craftsmen in employment. All that the Exchequer could produce, however, was £3,000. The Privy Council therefore instructed Russell to use this to pay off all those sailors who had been lawfully discharged. As for the others, who had left their ships without permission, a proclamation was to be made 'with the sound of drum, that upon pain of death they make present repair to the ships wherein they are in His Majesty's service. And that if at any time hereafter any shall presume to leave their ships and come up in this manner, they shall be reputed runaways and have the laws on that behalf executed upon them, which is not only loss of wages but of life.'[118]

Buckingham, despite his guard, was not free from the clamour of the mutineers. One day, while he was sitting at dinner in his lodgings at Whitehall, a number of army officers who had served in Ireland and had been months without pay, forced their way in and demanded redress. They complained that such things had not happened in the time of the King's predecessors, and that it must therefore be his fault. When the Duke warned them that, under the terms of the royal proclamation, their lives would be at stake if they persisted in coming to Court, they replied that 'if they were hanged there were more others to be hanged with them for company; and from this proceeded to such uncouth language as His Excellency was fain to yield and to promise them upon his honour they should, and speedily, be satisfied'.[119]

It would hardly have been surprising if, in such adverse circumstances, Buckingham had abandoned all hope of getting Willoughby's fleet to sea; but he had the patience, the energy and the determination with which to perform the impossible. On 13 October he sent Willoughby orders to cruise off Cadiz in wait for the Plate Fleet, and to do his best 'to take, spoil or sink all such ships . . . of the enemy's as are now in the Bay of Cadiz'. Willoughby by this time had left harbour and reached Torbay, where he joined up with Denbigh, but his ships were so unfit for service that he had to send back a number of them. The *Vanguard* – which was the flagship of John Pennington, the rear-admiral of the fleet – was one of these, and Pennington confided to Nicholas his wish that he could have returned to base along with it, 'for I must confess I have no hope of the voyage, the time of year being so far spent and we being now victualled but for ten weeks'. Willoughby was equally pessimistic about the chances of success, but put a brave face on it, and declared that now he was at sea he was 'resolved to try the event'. He never reached Cadiz, however. In the Bay of Biscay his fleet was struck by violent storms, and he had to make all haste back to England while his ships were still afloat and able to sail.[120]

When Buckingham heard the news he did not blame Willoughby. 'It is God's doing,' he said, 'and we may not repine at it.' But he was astonished at the fact that the King's ships proved so defective, and he ordered Willoughby and his fellow commanders to come to Court 'to the end that judgement may be made, as well by whose default they proved leaky, as which of them may be soonest made ready again for service'. Buckingham also informed the Privy Council of the need to take into consideration the whole question of the government of the Navy, and on 29 October it ordered the principal officers – the Treasurer, the Surveyor and the Victualler, who had hitherto been subordinated to the Commissioners – to 'take a perfect survey of the Navy and all things thereunto belonging, and certify the true state thereof'. The officers must have acted with great speed, for only a few days later Buckingham was ready to make his report to the Council. Substantial sums of money were owed to the workmen in the dockyards he told its members: £10,000 was needed to pay the wages of the crews of ships assembled in the Thames, while the fleet which Willoughby had brought back would eat up a further £30,000. The owners of merchant vessels which had been loaned for the King's service would want £20,000 and another £20,000 would have to be found to meet the debts of the Victualler of the Navy. In view of the fact that heavy expenditure had been incurred for so little return, Buckingham proposed that a commission should be appointed under the great seal to enquire into 'the present state and condition of the Navy in general, and particularly what was the cause His Majesty's ships lately employed under Lord Willoughby proved so defective as that they were not able to endure a storm'. These special commissioners would also be responsible for advising on some 'effectual and speedy course' not simply to rectify what was amiss but also to replenish the stores and pay all outstanding arrears. The Privy Council approved this proposal, and at the end of November Buckingham himself, the Lord Treasurer, and nineteen other persons – including a number of experienced captains – were appointed to the new commission. By early December the 'Council of the Sea', as one reporter called it, was hard at work, and although Buckingham's many other commitments – in particular his plans to go over to France – kept him from regular attendance, there could be no doubt where the drive and determination behind the commission came from. As the Earl of Totnes, the Master of the Ordnance, told him, 'I know no man that loves the King with more zealous affection, or more seriously takes to heart the good of the state, than yourself.'[121]

XI

The despatch of Willoughby's expedition and the reform of naval administration were not the only subjects that occupied Buckingham's waking hours during the closing months of 1626. There was the unresolved problem of relations with France to be dealt with, and in particular that of how England should react to the French bid for naval supremacy. As early as 21 June the council of war took into consideration 'the Cardinal de Richelieu's purchasing the office of the Admiral of France from the Duke of Montmorency . . . and having since by secondary means bought divers governments of the coast towns in Brittany'. The Cardinal, so the council was informed, had given orders for the building of 'twelve great ships of war at Amsterdam, and others in sundry places of France'. These were said by the French to be needed for the protection of the merchant vessels which they intended to set out for the East Indies, but the council considered that they were more likely to be used 'for the usurping of an absolute or equal dominion with His Majesty upon the

British Ocean, to the great prejudice of His Majesty's regality and the ancient inheritance of his imperial crown'. The members of the council were afraid that the French might try to surprise the Channel Islands or the Isle of Wight, for in view of the peace recently concluded between France and Spain it seemed likely that 'both those Kings may, with other princes and states of the Roman religion, conspire against His Majesty's realms'. There was little that could be done for the present, other than to accelerate the defensive preparations already on foot, but the councillors showed their awareness of the gravity of the threat which England now faced by recording a formal resolution 'to be left for a memorial to posterity, that this state, for reason of state, shall oppose the growth and strength of shipping in Flanders and France, to prevent the encroaching upon His Majesty's regality of the British Ocean'. Buckingham was present at the meeting which drew up this declaration, and it may well be that the initiative for it, and even the very wording, came from him.[122]

Buckingham was also a member of a small committee – which included the Lord Treasurer, Carlisle and Conway – appointed by the King to advise him on what steps should be taken to counter French plans. In their report the members gave their opinion that the Cardinal's projects were 'laid upon strong and ambitious foundations of state and pursued with great zeal'. They went on to say that if these projects were carried through to completion the French king would acquire the means not only to take over those 'sea towns and ports which are of the party of the reformed religion' (which they thought Charles should do his utmost to prevent), but also to challenge England for 'the mastership of the Narrow Seas – an honour, right and surety which Your Majesty's crowns had enjoyed many ages'. In their view this threat was so great that it should be countered by all the resources at the King's disposal.

And although they held it fit by all possible means to keep amity between the two crowns – the rather at this time and in the present conjuncture – yet they judge it more advantageous for Your Majesty to enter into a war now that you have advantage at sea in a superlative degree than to be constrained to make or suffer one when there should be more equality of shipping.[123]

Buckingham was obviously considering a pre-emptive strike against France, but he had not ruled out the possibility of a peaceful settlement, and was still toying with the idea of going over to Paris so that he could deal directly with Louis and his ministers. French support for the common cause was more than ever necessary, for the anti-Habsburg alliance was in a bad way. At the beginning of the the campaigning season in 1626 hopes had been high, for three armies were ready to take the field against the Emperor in Germany. But one of these broke into fragments without accomplishing anything, while another, under Mansfeld, was heavily defeated at the battle of Dessau in April 1626. Only the Danes were left in the field, and they were now faced with the full might of the imperial armies. Meanwhile the Spaniards, taking advantage of the advance of the Emperor's arms, were planning to establish a naval base in the Baltic, so that they could squeeze the Dutch simultaneously from north and south. Buckingham hoped to persuade the French that it was in their own best interests to resist these developments, for if the whole of Germany were to come under the Habsburg yoke, and the Dutch were unable to continue their resistance, 'the power of Spain will be as a girdle of mischief and offence encompassing France'.[124]

Although Buckingham would have liked to go to the French court to put his case directly to Louis and Richelieu, the late summer of 1626 was hardly an appropriate moment, since the atmsophere had been soured by the expulsion of Henrietta Maria's attendants. He therefore sent over Sir Dudley Carleton, but the reception accorded to the ambassador confirmed his worst fears, for Carleton was treated very coldly and denied an audience with Louis XIII. Carleton attributed this to the dominance of Richelieu and the *Dévots* in Louis's counsels. 'The Marquis Fiat [Effiat] depends wholly on the Cardinal,' he reported. 'The Marshal Schomberg was ever an enemy to the English amity; the Secretary D'Herbault an old bigot, and Marillac, the new Garde des Sceaux, altogether Jesuitical.' He added his opinion that 'amongst men of this mould (which are all the chief ministers of state) it might easily be guessed what this young king would be carried unto, were it not in respect of the present constitution of this kingdom, full of faction and discontent'. In other words, the fomenting of discord within France was still the best policy for England.[125]

Buckingham had sent Wat Montagu back to France in order to report on the state of affairs following Gaston's marriage, the execution of Chalais and the flight of Madame de Chevreuse. This time, however, Montagu's mission was unsuccessful, for no sooner was his presence known to the Frech ministers than they ordered him to return at once to England – a tit for tat, as Carleton observed, for the expulsion of Henrietta Maria's attendants. Montagu, however, was not the only agent despatched by Buckingham, nor was his mission as important as that of Henry De Vic, who was sent to make contact with the Huguenot leaders and assure them of Charles's continuing support. De Vic told the Duke of Rohan that Charles resented the way in which his intervention had been exploited by Richelieu to deceive the Huguenots, and now realised that Louis intended to crush the French protestants rather than honour his obligations to them. If they were to make a formal complaint to Charles, this would give him the moral right, as guarantor of the peace of January 1626, to demand redress from the French government and to use force if he did not receive satisfaction. While De Vic was conveying this message to Rohan, Buckingham was engaged in secret negotiations with Rohan's brother, Soubise, who arrived in London in late September. The intention behind all these manoeuvres was to encourage the Huguenots to keep up their resistance and to revive magnate discontent within France. After the apparent failure of Carleton's mission, there seemed to be no other way in which to bring about a change in the direction of French policy.[126]

While France remained inactive on the European stage, the brunt of the fighting fell on Denmark and the Dutch, who both looked to England for support. The English King – as the Elector Frederick reminded Buckingham in a letter he sent him in mid-August 1626 – was 'the first mover and the great wheel which can and should give movement to the others'. Charles accepted this responsibility in principle but did not see what action he could take to put it into effect: as he told the Danish ambassador, the failure of Parliament 'doth constrain him to suspend the execution of those good resolutions and designs which he had projected for the public good'. When Sir Robert Anstruther, Charles's envoy to Christian, heard of the dissolution of Parliament, he did not dare inform the Danish King, for fear that Denmark, seeing there was now no hope of effective aid from England, would make a separate peace. Without Denmark there would be no way of halting the Habsburg advance in north Germany, thwarting Spanish plans to establish a naval base in the Baltic, or relieving the pressure on the Dutch. The despatches of Spinola, who commanded the Spanish forces in the Netherlands, make clear just how much he feared Danish intervention in the summer of 1626. His own army was mutinous for lack of pay, and he would not risk any major operations until he knew what Christian would do. Meanwhile revolt had broken out in the Habsburg heartlands in Austria; the Marquis of Baden had offered to put an army in the field against the Emperor; and Bethlen Gabor, the protestant Prince of Transylvania, had declared his willingness to mount a diversionary campaign in the Balkans if only he were given subsidies and invited to join the Hague alliance. By late summer it really did seem that the anti-Habsburg cause might gather renewed strength. But so much depended upon the full commitment of England, and this was out of the question given the desperate state of the crown's finances. As Conway told Frederick's representative, 'we have no money, and no ways or means of finding any . . . . The Duke cannot manufacture money, and his personal credit is exhausted.' There was talk of summoning another Parliament, but such a course seemed likely only to engender more frustration and anger, since there was no reason to suppose that the two Houses would show any greater readiness to finance the King's policies now than they had in the session which had recently ended. To an exasperated foreign observer, the Venetian ambassador at the Hague, the attitude of the Parliamentary leaders appeared incomprehensible. He could only conclude that they were 'all partisans of the Spaniards and Jesuits', whose activities would result in 'the dissemination of ruin on the top of disgrace'.[127]

Whatever hopes there were that the common cause might be about to revive were dashed to the ground by the news of Christian's defeat at the battle of Lutter on 17 August. The first reports reached England in September, and Charles could not hide his grief nor conceal his conviction that he had been partly responsible by urging Denmark on with promises he had not been able to fulfil. The Privy Council decided to raise a forced loan to subsidise Christian and keep him in the field, and it also proposed to transfer to Denmark the four English regiments serving with the Dutch. Neither of these measures, however, was likely to bring about a dramatic change in the situation. Indeed, the half-hearted nature of the response merely confirmed what Buckingham had known from the beginning, that without the commitment of France the Hague allies would lack sufficient strength to attain their objectives. However the news of Lutter had at last awoken the French to a realisation of the danger they were in, and English despair was lightened to some extent by Carleton's reports that there had been a sudden change in the attitude towards him. Instead of coldness there was now 'sweetness and mildness', and French ministers were making 'fair promises' of assistance once again. This was confirmed by De Vic, who, in a despatch written at the end of September, described the French as being 'very sensible of the daily progress of the Spaniards, and whatever show they have or do make of the King of Denmark's overthrow, they take it to heart more than is imagined, and will contribute as largely and as speedily to raise him up again as their abilities will give them leave'. [128]

The French were also alarmed at the rumours which were beginning to circulate about secret peace negotiations between England and Spain. They professed to believe that there was no substance in these rumours, and that if any contacts had taken place they were designed primarily for propaganda purposes. This was indeed one of the objects of English policy, to frighten France into a closer relationship by letting it be seen that otherwise England might come to terms with Spain. But there was another important factor which the framers of English policy had to consider. If it looked as though Philip and Louis were preparing to unite their forces against Charles, then peace negotiations with Spain would have to take place in earnest, for the prospect of fighting two major powers simultaneously was far from appealing. There was nothing fanciful or unlikely about the idea of joint action by the two catholic crowns. In early August 1626 Louis made a formal proposal to this effect, and at the end of the month he received a letter from Philip warmly welcoming the suggestion and promising his full cooperation. Buckingham may or may not have been aware of this agreement, but there is little doubt that he knew that secret exchanges were taking place between Madrid and Paris. The Franco-Spanish negotiations, like the Anglo-Spanish ones, contained an element of deception, and were not necessarily to be taken at face value. But there was always the danger that what had started out as bluff might turn into something more substantial. The states of western Europe were engaged in a war of nerves, as they tried to adjust to the rapidly changing military and political situation, and suspicion and fear created a climate of acute distrust. If, in the closing months of 1626, Buckingham's policy became increasingly devious and difficult to interpret, that is because he had to keep pace with the equally devious and complex policies of his counterparts in France and Spain. [129]

French fears that the continued deterioration of relations with England might lead to war, at a time when the anti-Habsburg cause needed strengthening, led to the decision to send a special ambassador to England, and Marshal de Bassompierre was chosen for this purpose. Bassompierre arrived in London on 27 September 1626, and that very night received an unheralded visit from Buckingham, who had driven over from Hampton Court for the purpose. On the following day Bassompierre went to see the Duke at York House and from then on he and Buckingham were in close and constant contact. Observers commented on the courtesy with which Buckingham treated

349

the ambassador, and interpreted it, correctly, as evidence of the Duke's desire to bring about a good understanding between the two crowns. Not all was plain sailing, and relations between Bassompierre and Charles were very strained, because the King was determined never again to allow the French to impose their household officers upon his wife. On one occasion the King and the ambassador grew so heated that Buckingham had to step between them, and for some weeks Bassompierre had so little hope of a successful outcome to his mission that he asked to be recalled to France. Buckingham, however, was determined to reach an agreement, and he and Wat Montagu spent many hours in negotiations with the ambassador. By 24 October they had settled all outstanding matters, and on that day Buckingham celebrated their accord by taking his daughter, Mall, to call on Bassompierre. The Privy Council had still to approve the terms, which included a provision that a bishop and twelve catholic priests should be restored to the Queen's household, but this was accomplished, largely through pressure from the King and Buckingham, before the end of the month. The rest of Bassompierre's stay was devoted to enjoyment, and on 5 November the Duke gave a magnificent feast at York House in his honour, at which the King and Queen were also present. After the supper was over the whole company watched a masque in which Marie de Médicis, the Queen Mother of France, was portrayed 'sitting on a regal throne amongst the gods, beckoning with her hand to the King and Queen of Spain, the Prince and Princess Palatine, and the Prince and Princess of Piedmont, to come and unite themselves with her there amongst the gods, to put an end to all the discords of Christianity'. The symbolism may have been crude, but at least the message was clear: only on the basis of friendship between England and France could security, and with it peace, be restored to Europe.[130]

Not everybody was happy about the agreement concluded with Bassompierre. Even though it had been laid down that, apart from the Queen's confessor, no Oratorians or Jesuits were to be included among the returned priests, the more extreme protestants in England objected on principle. They blamed Buckingham for making these concessions, for in the words of the Venetian ambassador, 'as he is universally detested, his measures, whether good or bad, do him equal harm, envy assigning evil consequences to every event'. In France, on the other hand, Bassompierre was accused of giving too much away, and Louis charged him with having been 'overwrought and gained' by the Duke. At the time, however, both Bassompierre and Buckingham had good reason to be pleased with the fruit of their labours, and Buckingham planned to capitalise on this success by making his long-delayed visit to the French court. In the instructions drawn up for him in the King's name he was told to assure Louis of Charles's desire for closer relations 'by the necessity of our mutual conjunction in the common cause, which otherwise would undoubtedly suffer, as well in disturbing the general affairs of Christendom as by our disabling one another to resist that growing power which, by this only means, may prevail against us both'. Buckingham was also to press Louis to carry out his promises to the Huguenots, by withdrawing his forces from around La Rochelle and demolishing the forts he had built there. The

Huguenots would then have no cause for further resistance, and Louis would be free to turn his attention to 'the restitution and settling of the peace and freedom of Germany by that confederacy which was publicly promised to be performed not in words but in effects'. Finally, if the French showed a 'real inclination' to join England and those other powers which had come together at the Hague to oppose the Habsburgs, Buckingham was authorised to 'offer to our dear brother to be the head of that league'.[131]

Buckingham's embassy was all the more important in view of a sudden worsening of Anglo-French relations just at the moment when they seemed to be improving. In September 1626 Buckingham's brother-in-law, the Earl of Denbigh, who was cruising off Ushant, arrested three French ships which he suspected of carrying prohibited goods from Spain. This action aroused intense resentment in France, and in November the *Parlement* of Rouen ordered the seizure of the goods of English merchants trading in the town. By taking this precipitate action before the judicial process had been allowed to function, the French made the situation very much worse, for when the English merchants petitioned the Privy Council for redress, that body decided 'that an arrest and stay should be forthwith made of all such ships and goods as shall be found here belonging to any the subjects of the French king'. Early in December the Council went further and ordered Buckingham to instruct his captains to arrest all vessels belonging to France or carrying French goods. By this time, however, the French had committed themselves to retaliation on a massive scale, for they seized the entire English wine fleet, amounting to some two hundred ships, which was lying fully laden in the river mouth at Bordeaux. The Venetian ambassador reported that the population of London was 'practically frantic', for it was estimated that in the City alone some five to six thousand families gained their living by the wine trade. The King was said to be furious and wanted the merchants to be issued with letters of marque, authorising them to fit out privateers against the French. But the Council dissuaded him from hasty action on the grounds that it was 'not credible that France, for fifteen ships only which still remain for judgement, should seize property to the amount of more than three millions'.[132]

It was left to Buckingham, as Lord Admiral, to take appropriate counter-measures, and in December 1626 he ordered John Pennington to assume command of the fleet of twenty vessels reluctantly provided by the City of London in response to the Privy Council's demand for ships, and to seek out and destroy a number of French vessels which were lying in the port of Havre de Grace. Pennington was delighted with his commission – though he described the London fleet as one of the worst he had ever had the misfortune to command – and assured the Lord Admiral that he relished the opportunity of letting 'the Frenchmen know that their insolencies are not well taken, neither shall pass unrevenged'. Buckingham, however, was motivated by more than simple desire for vengeance. The ships at Havre de Grace were some of those which had lately been built in the Low Countries for the rapidly growing French navy, and there was reason to fear that they would be used, in conjunction with Spanish ships, for operations against England. The threat which

Richelieu's ambitious plans for maritime expansion posed for England was steadily increasing. In September 1626 Louis had suppressed the office of admiral and had appointed Richelieu to supervise maritime affairs, with the title of *Grand Maître, Chef et Surintendant général de la Navigation et Commerce de France*. In the following December Louis summoned an Assembly of Notables, at which Richelieu took the opportunity to expound his policy. The support of the state was needed, he said, not only to revive French commerce − which without it would dwindle into insignificance − but also to build the warships which alone would enable France to defend herself and attack her enemies, 'some of whom, separated from us by the sea, have treated us with contempt because they can inflict harm upon us while we are powerless against them'. There could have been no clearer justification for Buckingham's belief that the expansion of the French navy threatened not merely La Rochelle but the very foundations of the power and security of England.[133]

By the end of 1626 Buckingham had come to the conclusion that only by a personal appeal to Louis XIII and Richelieu could he restore good relations between England and France and check the drift towards war. He therefore went down to Canterbury to discuss the details of his projected visit with Bassompierre, who was held up there by bad weather. But by this time Bassompierre was aware that the French government was dissatisfied with the outcome of his negotiations and in no mood to welcome Buckingham. He therefore urged the Duke to postpone his visit until he had sent over a confidential agent to spy out the land. Buckingham was taken aback at the sudden change of tone on the ambassador's part, for he had pinned his hopes on this visit, but he eventually agreed to do as Bassompierre suggested. Instead of going to Paris, therefore, Buckingham returned to London, where not long afterwards he received the news that the agreement which he and Bassompierre had painstakingly worked out, and which seemed to provide a basis for harmonious relations between the two crowns, had been repudiated by Louis. If he had needed further evidence of continuing French ill-will, this was it.[134]

NOTES

(Abbreviations are explained in the Bibliography, pp. 477−86.)

1. *C.S.P.V.* XIX, 154; *Fr.MSS.* 75.359.
2. 'Tom Tell-Troath', in *Harleian Miscellany* (1744), II, 441.
3. *Fr.MSS.* 75.368; 76.50; *Roh.* 170.
4. *Gy.MSS.* 33.225; *Dom.MSS 16.* 27.10; *H.M.C.Coke.* 217; *H.M.C.Supp.* 238.
5. *Harl.MSS.* 1583.252; *Bas.MSS.* 62.186.
6. *Tann.MSS.* 72.26; *Harl.MSS.* 1580.349; *Fr.MSS.* 76.202; *Bas.MSS.* 62.203.
7. *Bas.MSS.* 62.159−159v.; *Aven.* II, 93; *Harl.MSS.* 6988.5.
8. *Harl.MSS.* 6988.3, 1.
9. *Dumont.* 478; *Sal.* 35, 39; *A.P.C.1625−6.* 290.
10. *Fr.MSS.* 76.267.

11. *Cab.* 233. Holland uses the symbol of a crown for Louis XIII and a heart for Anne of Austria.
12. *Fr.MSS.* 77.16; *Dom.MSS 16.* 18.1, 11, 13, 24: *Add.MSS.* 37,816.58v.
13. *Fr.MSS.* 77.53, 55, 85; *Rich.* V, 230–31; *Roh.* 174–5.
14. *Fr.MSS.* 77.174, 178.
15. *Fr.MSS.* 77.250, 282; *Holl.MSS.* 131.65; *C.S.P.V.* XIX, 325.
16. *Dom.MSS 16.* 20.66, 60; *A.P.C.1625–6.* 333–4.
17. *Fr.MSS.* 77.95, 166,187; *Harl.MSS.* 1583.204–205v., 208; *Sav.MSS.* 12.40.
18. *Sav.MSS·* 12.37–37v.
19. *Sav.MSS.* 12.58; *C.S.P.V.* XIX. 331–2; *Fr.MSS.* 78.138–9.
20. *Add.MSS.* 37,816.54v.
21. *H.M.C.Coke.* 250; *Add.MSS.* 37,816.60, 60v., 66, 79v.
22. *Dom.MSS 16.* 23.73, 70; 31.105; 24.21.
23. *Dom.MSS 16.* 32.67; 27.4; *Add.MSS.* 37,816.142.
24. *C.S.P.D. Appendix,* 15 Feb. 1626; *Kepler; Dietz.* 237.
25. *Dom.MSS 16.* 21.80; 22.33.
26. *Dom.MSS 16.* 23.25.
27. *H.M.C.(14).* 20; *Sal.* 45; *Dom.MSS 16.* 20.23.
28. *Gruen; Dom.MSS 16.* 18.28.
29. *Hack.* II, 65; *C.S.P.D.Addenda,* 1625–49. 77.
30. *Preston.* 108–9.
31. *Preston.* 103–4; *Cos.* Appendix I. 295, 101.
32. *Preston.* 118–19; *Laud.* 182.
33. *Tann.MSS.* 303.33–46.
34. *Tann.MSS.* 303.39, 45–6.
35. *Tann.MSS.* 303.46; *Fuller.* 387.
36. *Trevor.* 76–7; *Fuller.* 383; *D'Ewes.* 292–3.
37. *Corn.* 143, 144; *Fr.MSS.* 77.187.
38. *Eliot.* I, 155, 152–3. Eliot's role in this Parliament is analysed by J.N. Ball, 'Sir John Eliot and Parliament 1624–29', in *Sharpe.*
39. *Hack.* II, 71; *C.J.* 823, 827–8.
40. *Corn.* 193; *D.L.* 114–15; *Ch.* II, 630.
41. *C.J.* 826; *Heyl.* 144; *Dom.MSS 16.* 22.51.
42. *L.J.* 513; *C.J.* 831.
43. *C.J.* 831.
44. *H.M.C.Bucc.* III, 272.
45. *L.J.* 519; *D.L.* 122–4.
46. *Rush.* 215; *Cam.MSS.* 37.
47. *Rush.* 216–17.
48. *Cam.MSS.* 17v., 16v.
49. *Cam.MSS.* 15v., 14v.
50. *Gard.* VI, 80; A slightly different version is given in part in *Hulme* (2). 118.
51. *C.J.* 842; *Rush.* 224, 223.
52. *Rush.* 225.
53. *Rush.* 226.
54. *Rush.* 227–9.
55. *Rush.* 228–30.
56. *Chas.* 93; *C.J.* 843–4.
57. *Dom.MSS 16.* 22.13; 23.15; 25.91.
58. *Dom.MSS 16.* 25.71; 23.76; 24.56; *Add.MSS.* 37,816.89; *H.M.C.Coke.* 266.

59. *C.S.P.V.* XIX, 404; *Dk.MSS.* 6.34; 7.46.
60. *Laud.* 188; *A.P.C.1625–6.* 440; *C.S.P.V.* XIX, 390.
61. *Case*; *D.L.* 138–40; *L.J.* 563.
62. *C.J.* 847, 849–52; *Tite.* cap.VII·
63. *Gros.MSS.* 2 May 1626. I am grateful to Colin Tite for lending me a microfilm of a typed copy of this dairy from Yale University Library.
64. *L.J.* 576–7; *Rush.* 303.
65. *Rush.* 308–14.
66. *H.M.C.Bucc.* III, 288; *L.J.* 590; *Gros.MSS.* 9 May 1626.
67. *Rush.* 335–50.
68. *Rush.* 350–55.
69. *Chas.* 101–2; *L.J.* 592.
70. *L.J.* 592–3.
71. *D.L.* 205, 210; *H.M.C.Bucc.* III, 294–5; *L.J.* 627, 652.
72. *Sal.* 70, 72.
73. *Mul.* 53–9; *Tann.MSS.* 82.268.
74. *Gros.MSS.* 3 June 1626; *Rush.* 373.
75. *Gard.* VI, 116.
76. *L.J.* 655–6.
77. *L.J.* 656–8.
78. *L.J.* 658–9.
79. *L.J.* 659–60.
80. *Fr.MSS.* 78.81–82v.; *Marsden.*
81. *L.J.* 660.
82. *L.J.* 661–2.
83. *L.J.* 662.
84. *L.J.* 625, 664–7.
85. *L.J.* 662.
86. *L.J.* 663.
87. *L.J.* 672; *C.J.* 870.
88. *L.J.* 670; *C.J.* 870–71; *Bas.MSS.* 63.39.
89. *D.L.* 231; *Chas.* 112.
90. *Sal.* 75, 76; *Sainty.* 20; *Chas.* 125; *Dom.MSS 16·* 37.5.
91. *A.P.C. 1626.* 328–9; *Add.MSS.* 37,816.170v.; *Hulme.*; *Str.P.MSS.* 40/50.
92. *C.S.P.V.* XIX, 462; *Sal.* 76; *Chas.* 116; *Eg.MSS.* 2978.14–15; *Memorials.* 7.
93. *A.P.C. 1626.* 212–13; *Chas.* 145; *C.S.P.V.* XIX, 558.
94. *Elm.MSS.* 1352/4 I am indebted to Conrad Russell for this reference; *Wynn.* 1428; *Fr.MSS.* 79.202v.
95. *Chas.* 140, 148; *Dig.MSS.* 102.
96. *Blain.* 188–9.
97. *Blain.* 194–5; *Fin.* 171.
98. *C.S.P.V.* XIX, 328; *Cab.* 232; *Fr.MSS.* 79.269; *Harl.MSS.* 6988.11.
99. *Sav.MSS.* 12.85v.
100. *Sav.MSS.* 12.123–4, 113, 117.
101. *Roh.* 184–96; *Bass.* 242–54; *Rich.* VI, passim.
102. *Rich.* VI, 231.
103. *Bas.MSS.* 64.120; *Fr.MSS.* 80.70.
104. *Absolutism.* 83; *Bas.MSS.* 63.107v.
105. *Fr.MSS.* 79.238v.
106. *Trum.MSS.* 48; *L.J.* 670.

107. *Dom.MSS 16.* 28.10; *A.P.C. 1626.* 130–31.
108. *H.M.C.Coke.* 273, 274; *Dom.MSS 16.* 30.48; *A.P.C. 1626.* 40.
109. *A.P.C. 1626.* 129–30; *Dom.MSS 16.* 31.112.
110. *Holl.MSS.* 132.31; *Add.MSS.* 37,816. 131–131v., 137, 140v.
111. *Dom.MSS 16.* 33.28; *Add.MSS.* 37,816.152v.
112. *Dom.MSS 16.* 34.39.
113. *Add.MSS.* 37,816.161.
114. *Dom.MSS 16.* 35.102, 104; 36.60; *A.P.C. 1626.* 296–7.
115. *Rub.* No. 95.
116. *Chas.* 141; *A.P.C. 1626.* 206; *Dom.MSS 16.* 41.44.
117. *Chas.*158; *C.S.P.V.* XIX, 587; *A.P.C. 1626.* 306, 360–61, 366, 370–71, 390.
118. *Chas.* 175; *Dom.MSS 16.* 39.78; 40.52; *A.P.C. 1626.* 386.
119. *Chas.* 176–7.
120. *Add.MSS.* 37,816.173; *Dom.MSS 16.* 37.49,20.
121. *Add.MSS.* 37,816.175; *A.P.C. 1626.* 338–9, 350–51; *P.S.* 472; *Chas.* 182; *Dom.MSS 16.* 42.15.
122. *Trum.MSS.* 48.
123. *Dom.MSS 16.* 34.87.
124. *Fr.MSS.* 79.178v.
125. *Fr.MSS.* 79.252v.–253.
126. *Fr.MSS.* 79.284; *C.S.P.D. Charles I. Appendix.* 15 Sept. 1626; *Roh.* 197; *C.S.P.V.* XIX, 560.
127. *Harl.MSS.* 6988.12; *Dk.MSS.* 7.156, 160; *Lon.* 854, 882, 879; *Rus.* 732–3; *C.S.P.V.* XIX, 464–5.
128. *Rus.* 736–7; *A.P.C. 1626.* 268; *Fr.MSS.* 80.30, 54, 61.
129. *Sal.* 87; *C.S.P.V.* XIX, 592; *Rich.* VI, 289–90, 270–73; *Fr.MSS.* 80.71.
130. *Bas.MSS.* 64.154; *Bass.* 257–8, 264, 268–70, 274, App.X; *Fr.MSS.* 80.126; *Sal.* 89, 94–5.
131. *C.S.P.V.* XX, 20–21; *Fr.MSS.* 80. 223, 229.
132. *Dom.MSS 16.* 36.31; *C.S.P.V.* XIX, 588; XX, 68; *A.P.C. 1626.* 323–4, 364–5, 391–2.
133. *Dom.MSS 16.* 42.67, 68, 79, 81, 100, 115; *Rich.* VI, 297.
134. *Bass.* 280.

CHAPTER NINE

1627: 'An ambition to serve faithfully both my King and country'

I

Buckingham blamed Richelieu for the repudiation of the agreement which Bassompierre had concluded on Louis XIII's behalf, and his view was widely shared, both at home and abroad. Writing from Paris, the Venetian ambassador told his government that to disinterested observers it seemed that Bassompiere had shown exceptional skill and prudence in carrying out his difficult task. Indeed it was these very qualities that had brought about his downfall, for 'Cardinal Richelieu wants to rule this kingdom alone and cannot support the growing fortune of the Marshal'. This belief, that Richelieu's main concern was to preserve his shaky hold on power, was confirmed by William Lewis, one of Buckingham's agents in Paris. 'The Cardinal,' he reported, 'finding no safety in the envies of this court and the variability of this prince's favour, sought out his props at Rome, where he is now established.' Lewis added that the marked change of course on the part of Richelieu – whom he had earlier heard described as a man who put reason of state in the saddle and religion in the crupper (*l'état en selle et la religion en crouppe*) – must indicate that Richelieu had decided to throw in his lot with the *Dévots.* Whereas previously there had been nothing of the cardinal about him except his red hat, now he was truly the Pope's agent: he might talk of reason of state, but this was only a mask to conceal his true intentions.[1]

Buckingham's close friend, the Earl of Holland, had come, however reluctantly, to the same conclusion. Holland had originally encouraged the Duke to have confidence in Richelieu, but now he was of the opinion that the Cardinal's 'private interests, the incentives of Rome and of ambition make him swerve from his original path. He thinks solely of extirpating the Huguenots.' It seems likely that one of the main reasons why Buckingham wanted to go over to France was to meet Richelieu once again and find out for himself what exactly the Cardinal was after. But Richelieu could not risk such an encounter. The pressures on him were already too great for comfort, and he had taken refuge within the labyrinth of his own policies. Any clarification of the pattern at this stage would almost certainly have been to his disadvantage.

He therefore sent a letter to Buckingham proposing that the English should make a number of concessions in order to open the way to a renewal of negotiations. Neither the King nor the Duke would consent to this, however, for as Buckingham informed the Cardinal – in a letter which, in its style of address and lack of conventional courtesies, matched Richelieu's own – the King regarded the public disavowal of an accredited ambassador as cutting the treaty links between the two crowns and freeing him from all obligations to Louis.[2]

Buckingham's letter was carried to Paris by Balthazar Gerbier, who had been instructed to go on from there to Brussels, where he was to meet Rubens. The ostensible reason for this meeting was so that the two men could work out the details of Buckingham's plan to buy the painter's magnificent art collection, but Rubens was also being employed by the Archduchess Isabella, ruler of the Netherlands, as a diplomatic agent. Rubens and Gerbier had earlier been in touch about the possibility of arranging a peace between England and Spain, and it was apparently Rubens who suggested this latest encounter. Buckingham was only too glad to make a positive response. He was being urged by Savoy to come to terms with Spain, and although he was not yet convinced that this was either desirable or possible, he appreciated that while such negotiations were in progress the Spaniards might be less inclined to take hostile action against England. There was the further important consideration that if, as seemed inevitable, the French came to hear of these overtures, they might well be shocked into moderating their harsh and uncompromising attitude. Gerbier was therefore given a letter from Buckingham to Rubens, in which the Duke promised that if the Archduchess was authorised by Philip IV to negotiate a general truce with the Hague allies – England, Denmark and the United Provinces – he would do his best to bring it about.

These tentative contacts with Spain did not imply that Buckingham had abandoned his major aim of gaining the restoration of the Palatinate. He had never wanted war for its own sake, only as a prelude and a means to genuine negotiations, and the overture from Rubens could be interpreted as a sign that his tactics were succeeding. He therefore emphasised that England was not interested in a separate peace and that any agreement would have to provide at least a measure of satisfaction for the Elector Palatine, still a refugee at the Hague.[3]

Negotiations with Spain, then, were part of the process of checking the spread of Habsburg power and securing the restoration of the Palatinate, but to many people they seemed to be proof of Buckingham's inconstancy. Among these was the Palatine ambassador, Rusdorf, who had come to believe that the Duke was no true friend to his master and mistress. Rusdorf preferred the more simplistic approach of the 'protestant interest' and was on close terms with Archbishop Abbot. The Archbishop professed the utmost contempt for Buckingham, whom he described as '*ce mignon*', and declared that the Duke could not bear honest men about him for fear that they would uncover his deceitful dealings. In view of Rusdorf's links with Buckingham's opponents it is hardly to be wondered at that the Duke distrusted him. He accused the ambassador, among other things, of being too intimate with the French representatives in London – a charge that is substantiated to some extent by Richelieu's own memoirs. But Rusdorf's main offence, in the Duke's eyes, was that he was causing Frederick and Elizabeth to doubt Buckingham's goodwill towards them. In January 1627 Buckingham secured Rusdorf's recall, but this did not put an end to reports that relations between the Duke and the exiled rulers at the Hague were far from cordial. In March, therefore, Buckingham despatched one of his relatives, John Ashburnham, to Holland to explain his policies, and Elizabeth subsequently wrote to thank him 'for the care you continue to have of our businesses, where I see your affection to me, which I shall never forget, nor be unthankful for it'. Rumours about her attitude continued to circulate, however, and in July she sent another letter to the Duke. 'Be still confident that I do not change in the good opinion I have of you,' she told him. 'I pray be assured of it. This I hope will put you out of doubt of her that is ever your most affectionate friend.' Despite these reassuring words, however, Elizabeth was puzzled and alarmed by Buckingham's secret negotiations with Spain, for she feared that any agreement that was reached would be at the expense of her and her husband. Yet Buckingham's obvious concern to preserve her friendship is in itself evidence that he had not forgotten the Palatinate or abandoned the cause of its unhappy rulers.[4]

Denmark was another power which felt itself threatened by the peace feelers between England and Spain, and here again Buckingham blamed Rusdorf, through his links with the Danish ambassador, for much of the misunderstanding. Christian was demanding payment of the large sums of money which were owed to him under the terms of the Hague treaty, and when Elizabeth wrote to Buckingham at the beginning of April 1627 she urged him 'if it be possible, get the King my uncle money as well as men, for that he hath most need of'. Christian held Buckingham responsible for the delay in fulfilling the treaty obligations, and declared that if the Duke was really his friend he could easily lay hands on £100,000 to send to Denmark. He was apparently unaware of the acute shortage of money following the dissolution of Parliament, or at any rate unwilling to accept that Charles I simply could not fulfil his obligations, however much he wished to do so. However, in March 1627 Buckingham informed Christian that his close friend, the Earl of Nithsdale, had offered to take over three thousand Scots to serve in the Danish armies, and this evidence of goodwill did much to dissipate Christian's suspicions. The English ambassador to Denmark wrote to assure Conway that 'what mistaking soever was afore betwixt this king and my Lord Duke, if any were, upon my credit it is wholly taken away'.[5]

The doubts and uncertainties generated by the news that England and Spain had started talking to each other created fears at home as well as abroad. The Duke was said to be under the influence of the Jesuits who frequented his mother's house, and to be planning to make himself 'the head and protector of the catholics, because his greatest hindrances proceed from the . . . puritans'. As Lord Admiral and Lord Warden he held the ports, the keys of the kingdom, in his hand, and with his connivance it would be easy for Spanish forces to land and impose a catholic despotism. The King, it was said, could do nothing to prevent this, since he was kept in ignorance of what was going on, and in any case was completely under Buckingham's influence. The prevailing opinion was that while Charles had the trappings of sovereignty, real power was vested in the Duke, and popular imagination seized on incidents, true and imagined, to build up its own fantasies. One story circulating in early 1627 told how Buckingham was carried in a litter to St James's to play tennis, while the King walked at his side. It was also reported that when Buckingham came late to a play which was being given at Christmas, the whole performance had to start again, even though the King was present and had already sat through the first act. Such stories are of little value in themselves, but they reveal the acute, almost paranoiac, suspicion which every move and gesture of Buckingham generated. Clearly the Parliamentary campaign against the Duke, culminating in the impeachment proceedings of 1626, had succeeded in convincing the public at large that he was an ogre. Perhaps for this reason the law officers of the crown were going ahead with plans to bring Buckingham to trial in Star Chamber, so that he could make a public defence of his conduct. In January 1627 the Privy Council authorised Sir William Beecher to answer any questions which might be put to him, involving Council business, if he was called as a witness, and later that month one observer reported that 'it is expected daily that His Grace should be accused of some of these matters in the Star Chamber, that so he might be judicially acquitted and clear himself'.[6]

II

Buckingham did not, of course, sit idly by while he waited for the opportunity to demonstrate his innocence. As Lord Admiral he was responsible for the defence of England against invasion and for the assertion of English naval supremacy against any power that dared to challenge it. The major threat still seemed to be that from France, for in January 1627 the Assembly of Notables, following Richelieu's lead, decided to maintain a fleet of nearly fifty ships in the Channel, and two months later the *Parlement* of Paris confirmed Richelieu's appointment as *Grand-Maître, Chef et Surintendant général de la Navigation et Commerce de France.* He was now formally responsible for building up French maritime strength, and his correspondence shows that he took these duties seriously, and set on foot the construction of ships not only in France itself but also in Amsterdam. The English had good reason to be alarmed by these preparations, and when William Lewis wrote to Buckingham in January 1627 he reminded him of the need to take counter-measures before it was too late. 'Fears, necessity and loss are the best rhetoric to persuade them [the French] to reason; and the dissipation of their naval designs (which may be done yet with Your Grace's least breath as well as with a tempest) the . . . best preface of agreements.'[7]

Buckingham had already taken steps to curb the growth of French power at sea. In January 1627 he ordered Pennington to assume command of the London fleet and cruise off the French coast to intercept shipping, but Pennington was hampered by vile weather and by the poor quality of his vessels and their crews. 'The ships themselves', he told the Lord Admiral,

are not capable to do service, for the most of them have ill ordnance and [are] ill conditioned ships and goes [*sic*] basely . . . . I think they could not have picked up so many more base ships in the river of Thames. And for the men, a great part of them were rogues taken up in the streets, that hath neither clothes nor knows anything.

Buckingham had originally intended to keep on at least part of the London fleet in the King's service after the expiry of the term originally set, but at the end of January – in view, perhaps, of Pennington's strictures on the City ships – he changed his mind. He was planning an operation to free the English wine fleet, which was still held at Bordeaux, but he now decided that this action should be carried out by Pennington, with one King's ship and nine specially-hired merchantmen.[8]

Buckingham was also preparing another operation, for in early January he ordered that twenty of the most serviceable ships on the King's books should be made ready by the end of the following month. He did not specify the purpose for which they were to be used, but it seems likely that he was already thinking in terms of an expedition to La Rochelle. In order to avoid the sort of delays that had held up earlier fleets, Buckingham asked the Privy Council – with which he was working in close collaboration – to arrange for the payment of the arrears outstanding to the Victualler of the Navy, so that he could embark on the task of equipping the twenty ships. The Privy Council agreed and decided that the money should be taken from the sums raised by the sale of crown lands; in due course it could be repaid by the proceeds of the forced loans. Money was also needed for the workmen in the dockyard at Chatham who had received no pay for twelve months and had now 'forsaken their works and . . . gone in great numbers towards London to demand their said arrearages'. Nearly £8,000 was owing to these key workers, and Buckingham pressed the Lord Treasurer to do all he could to find this amount so that the preparation of the expedition could go ahead. Meanwhile the special commissioners enquiring into the Navy informed the Lord Admiral that fourteen ships could be got ready by the end of March, but only if £3,600 was sent down to them immediately. They warned him, however, that by giving priority to this expedition he would be holding up the programme of fundamental reform which they had set on foot. In particular they would not be able to deal with the vessels lying more or less derelict at Chatham, since 'time will not permit that they may have that done to them which, by survey, was found most necessary'. A week or so later they sent a further warning, that the stores at Chatham were exhausted and that they had no funds with which to replenish them. They also needed money to pay the shipwrights, who would otherwise have to be laid off.[9]

Shortage of money remained a perennial problem. The forced loans were expected to bring in substantial sums to the Exchequer, but there was considerable resistance to them from certain sections of the community. The loan commissioners for Northamptonshire reported that a strong combination of the principal gentlemen of the county was not only frustrating the business in Northamptonshire itself but planning to 'infuse the confidence of contradiction' into neighbouring shires. Nor was resistance confined to the gentry. The Earl of Lincoln, who had earlier opposed Buckingham in Parliament, was summoned before the Privy Council to account for his refusal to pay, and the Earl of Northumberland was also said to be unwilling to contribute. Buckingham, who described himself as 'a faithful friend and servant' of Northumberland, urged him to think very carefully before making 'an absolute refusal . . . [which] cannot advantage you in the opinion of others, but much prejudice you in the opinion of His Majesty, with whom I have ever endeavoured to do your lordship and your children all the best offices I could'.[10]

No one knew better than Buckingham how much the naval effectiveness of England depended upon the success of the forced loans, and in January 1627 he went in person to his own county of Buckinghamshire and to the adjoining one of Berkshire to press matters forward. He returned to town perfectly satisfied, having met with only one refusal, but his detractors spread the rumour that everything had been arranged beforehand, in order to produce the required effect, and that the Duke 'covertly supplied the means for consenting to many who were resisting'. As fast as the loan money came in it was spent on the Navy, and much of it was used to pay the arrears of the seamen, who were once again in a mutinous state. Early in February 1627 the King ordered the captains of the trained bands to 'use all means of force, as shot or other offensive ways' to suppress those 'mariners and other loose people' whose insolency had reached such heights that they were a threat to all authority. This action was prompted by the news that five hundred mutinous sailors had smashed the windows of Sir William Russell's house and were threatening to wreak much greater havoc if their demands were not met. Some days later they held a rally on Tower Hill where they declared that unless the promises to pay them were carried out they would cut off the Lord Admiral's head.[11]

While Charles and his ministers were struggling to maintain a semblance of order at home, the enemies of England were preparing for concerted action against her. At the beginning of February 1627 Philip IV wrote to the Infanta Isabella, ordering her to hasten the building up of the fleet in the Netherlands. He was planning an invasion of Ireland later in the year, and although the Infanta and Spinola poured cold water on the idea he was not prepared to abandon it altogether. As for Richelieu, at the very moment when he was assuring the apprehensive Rochellois that the military preparations being made in the islands of Ré and Oleron were for defence against English attack, he was pressing ahead with his plan to subdue the city by cutting it off from both land and sea. The construction of a French navy was an essential part of this plan, but it would take time, and Richelieu's estimate was that France would not be strong enough to risk an open break with England until mid-1627. It was therefore essential, as he saw it, to secure the friendship of Spain, and on 10 March an agreement was signed between the two crowns committing them to joint operations against England. [12]

Buckingham may not have known of this treaty but he was well aware of the need to guard against invasion attempts, and this meant strengthening the number of ships appointed to keep watch in the Narrow Seas. Ships without sailors were of little use, however, and until the men were paid they would run away rather than serve in the King's fleet. Early in February 1627, at a time when his own house was under guard to protect him from the unwelcome attentions of the mutineers, Buckingham held a meeting with the special commissioners and asked them to go on board every ship and find out exactly what wages were owing. It was presumably as a result of this initiative that the King gave orders for the payment of the sailors in rotation, so that, in due course, all the men would receive their due. This did not put an end to the mutinies, however, for the sailors knew, from long and bitter experience, that royal assurances about payment were rarely translated into deeds, and in any case mere promises would not buy food for themselves and their families. The disorders continued, and in March a crowd of angry sailors rioted outside York House and threatened to pull it down unless they received their arrears. The Privy Council now ordered the appointment of Provost Marshals for the counties adjoining London, to assist the sheriffs and constables in the execution of their duties. However, there were doubts concerning the extent of the Provost Marshals' powers, for when Buckingham asked Sir Henry Marten, the Admiralty judge, what action could lawfully be taken against mutineers, he was informed that they could only be punished with whipping and ducking. If sterner measures were required, then commissions of martial law would have to be issued. The Council, in fact, had already issued these to a number of Lord Lieutenants, but it looks as though they – or at least their deputies in the counties – were reluctant to use such draconian measures. The Council therefore spurred them on. In April, for instance, when it heard that the Provost Marshal of London had captured four deserters, it ordered Buckingham, as Lord Lieutenant of Middlesex, to see that his deputies brought them to the gallows. There they were to be made to dice for their life, and the unfortunate loser was to be hanged, as a warning to any others who might be thinking of following his example. [13]

While stern measures were necessary to repress disorders, the principal aim of the government was to get the sailors back to their ships, for without them nothing effective could be done. In early April the Council wrote to the mayors of ports on the east coast to tell them that 'we have received frequent advertisements of the daily running away of the mariners imprested for His Majesty's ships and other ships in His Majesty's service . . . by which means His Majesty's preparations are very much cast back'. It therefore instructed the mayors to make careful enquiries about sailors who had recently returned to their towns, to arrest 'such as you shall find to have been of late times in His Majesty's service', and to send them back to the fleet at Chatham. At about the same time the Council also authorised the Lord Admiral to restrain all shipping until such time as the King's fleet was ready to sail, and to press seamen from merchant vessels in the river Thames and south coast ports. Meanwhile Buckingham appointed Sir Henry Mainwaring 'to go presently aboard [the ships] preparing for His Majesty's present fleet, and to hasten by all possible means the fitting, furnishing, arming, victualling and full manning of every of them'. In short, everything was being done that could be done within the limits of acute financial stringency. But in the last resort it was shortage of money that was decisive, and on 18 April the Lord Admiral was informed that the money received by the Treasurer of the Navy upon the estimate for this fleet is already disbursed . . . . The ships are unprovided and the whole service at a stand.' Sir William Russell, who had the doubtful privilege of holding the office of Treasurer of the Navy, had frequently used his own resources and pledged his personal credit in order to keep ships in service. However, the strain upon him had become too great, and at the end of March 1627 he was replaced by Sackville Crowe, who was one of the principal members of Buckingham's household and acted as his controller of accounts.[14]

While shortage of mariners was a major problem, it was not the only one, for ships also were in short supply. It was to overcome this deficiency that the King had ordered the ports of England to provide vessels for his service at their own expense. Such a command, however, was far from welcome to seacoast towns that were often quite poor and had suffered from the depredations of pirates as well as the dislocation of trade caused by the war. Poole, for instance, which was required to supply a ship of two hundred tons, declared that it simply could not do so. Two years earlier, the inhabitants pointed out, there had been over twenty fishing smacks in Poole harbour, but now there were only four. Over two hundred Poole sailors had been killed or taken prisoner, and the town had to look after some four hundred fatherless children. How could it possibly find the money to set out a ship for the King? Similar protestations came from Plymouth, which had been ordered to supply two ships but declared that it could not meet its own needs, let along the King's. The Privy Council was not without sympathy for the ports, since it recognised that they had suffered more than inland communities, and it had already instructed the maritime counties to assist those ports which lay within their boundaries. But such a break with tradition was still provoking angry reactions. The Justices of the Peace for Essex, who had been called on to subsidise Colchester, protested that there were no precedents for such a demand, and therefore refused to pay. But the Council gave a stern and unyielding reply. The Justices were informed that 'the occasions of state and defence of a kingdom in times of extraordinary danger are not tied to ordinary and continued precedents', and were ordered forthwith 'to raise and levy within that county such sums of money as may supply to the town of Colchester a full moiety of the charge of setting out one ship for His Majesty's service'. Here was yet another example of the way in which the imperative demands of war fractured the conventions of English government and forced the King into actions that appeared to threaten the traditional liberties of his subjects.[15]

Buckingham was not alone in recognising that the King's dependence upon

merchant vessels to meet his naval requirements was anachronistic and undesirable. Among the proposals put forward for consideration by the Lord
Admiral in the early months of 1627 was one for the establishment of a truly
royal Navy, consisting of seventy large ships and thirty pinnaces. Buckingham
approved of this, and wanted construction work to begin immediately. The
big advantage of designing ships specially for war was that considerations like
speed and manoeuvrability could be given first place. Merchant ships were too
cumbrous and slow to deal with the Dunkirk privateers, for instance, and the
Cadiz expedition had shown that even where they could be usefully employed
their owners were reluctant to hazard them. A permanent fleet would also
enable a much more effective guard to be maintained in the Narrow Seas, and
this was an objective that came very high in the Lord Admiral's order of
priorities. He asked the special commissioners to advise him on how many
ships would be needed for this purpose, and of what shape and size. Lord
Harvey, an old and experienced seaman, proposed four or five squadrons
amounting in all to twenty ships, but when Buckingham called for an estimate of the cost of such a fleet he was informed that some £70,000 would be
needed to build the ships in the first instance, and £6,000 a month to pay
their crews. [16]

Such sums were simply not available. Indeed there was not enough money
even to provide the minimum guard of six ships which the Navy Commissioners had recommended. At a meeting of the Privy Council, in March 1627,
Buckingham complained that no assignment had been made for the Ordinary
of the Navy for the current year, and that the £30,000 provided for the
previous year was £10,000 too little. Without some assured income he could
not carry out the duties with which he was charged, and he therefore requested the Council to enter in its register his solemn protestation 'that he
cannot promise and cause to be maintained at sea the said six ships . . .
according to the necessity and importance of the service for the securing of the
coasts and protecting of His Majesty's subjects from spoil and depredation of
enemies and pirates'. These tactics were successful, for a month later, when
Buckingham once again pressed the Board for a fixed assignment for the
Ordinary, the Lord Treasurer announced that he had 'agreed for this present
year upon an assignation of £30,000, and of £10,000 more for the same
service out of the monies arising upon the sale of French goods'. At a subsequent meeting it was decided that the Ordinary was so important for the
defence of the kingdom that it should be assigned upon some permanent and
certain source of income instead of upon 'casualties', as had been the case
hitherto. The Customs duties were chosen 'as the most proper revenue for that
service', and the Council also expressed the wish that the additional £10,000
'shall be likewise assigned upon some settled and constant part of His Majesty's revenues'. [17]

While the Lord Admiral was considering plans to transform the Navy into
an efficient fighting force – if only the necessary funds could be provided – he
had to make do, for practical purposes, with the limited resources immediately available to him. Vessels were needed to transport the troops that were

The Constant Reformation, so named, by King James, to inaugurate Buckingham's career as Lord Admiral, and to witness the ambition to which both James and Buckingham had committed themselves

Gateway to the Citadel of St Martin, which Buckingham besieged but was unable to capture during his expedition to the Ile de Ré in 1627. The fort was subsequently reconstructed by Vauban, but on the original plan

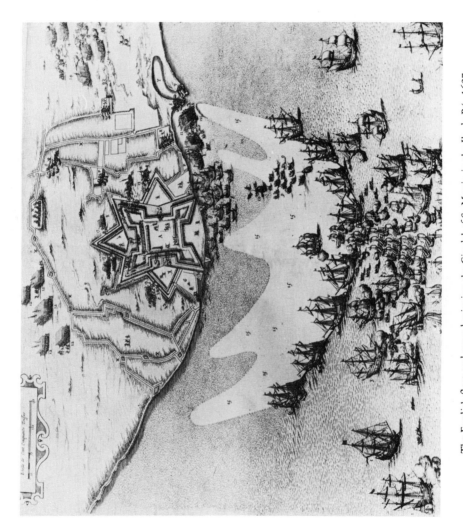

The English fleet and army besieging the Citadel of St Martin in the Ile de Ré, 1627

The Villiers family, artist unknown, 1628
Left to Right: Susan, Countess of Denbigh; Katherine, Duchess of Buckingham; Mary, afterwards Duchess of Richmond and Lenox; George, First Duke of Buckingham; George, Earl of Coventry, afterwards Second Duke of Buckingham, with his nurse; John, Viscount Purbeck; Mary, Countess of Buckingham; and Christopher, Earl of Anglesey

'Ecce Homo', Titian, formerly in Buckingham's collection

Felton's declaration. Felton, the assassin of Buckingham, wrote out this declaration and stitched it into the lining of his hat, so that if he was struck down after killing Buckingham the world would at least know what his motives were (for a transcription see pp. 458–9)

The memorial to Buckingham in Portsmouth Cathedral, put up by his sister, Susan Feilding, Countess of Denbigh

The house in Portsmouth High Street, formerly called the Greyhound Inn, in which Buckingham was assassinated

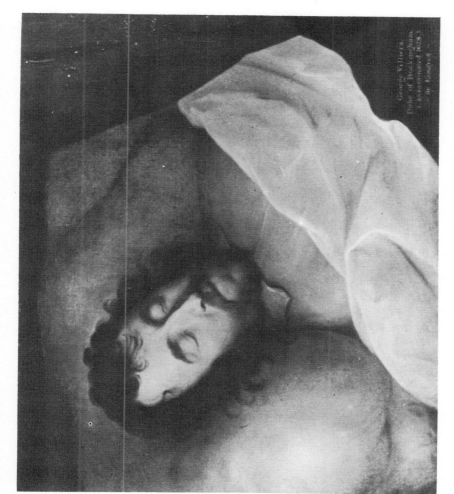

Buckingham on his deathbed, Van Dyck

Buckingham's tomb in Westminster Abbey

being sent to the aid of Denmark, and Buckingham appointed two King's ships and one merchantman for this service. They could then stay on at the mouth of the Elbe to keep up the blockade on seaborne traffic from the Baltic region to Spain. Ships were also needed to protect the east coast fishing fleet, which was ready to set out by the end of February 1627. Buckingham had given orders that two ships should be provided immediately, and a further two at the end of March, but now he was informed that none of the ships would be ready before late March. This led to a protest from the bailiffs of Yarmouth, who pointed out that the town had not been able to despatch its fishing fleet the previous year, and that 'a great part of our inhabitants, and specially of our fishermen, upon hope of such waftage, have very willingly and cheerfully brought to us His Majesty's loans . . .'. A similar protest came from the Justices of the Peace of Norfolk, who informed the Privy Council in February that the county had made a prompt response to the King's request for loans on the assumption that the money would be used to secure its inhabitants from the attacks of Dunkirkers. But nothing had been done, and the pirates were more of a menace than ever. They had recently 'burned upon our coasts two of our ships . . . and do daily show themselves in a most insufferable, braving and threatening manner near unto our shores, in such sort as our seamen dare not issue out'. In March it was the turn of Newcastle to complain about the Dunkirkers, but Buckingham had no ships to spare. All he could do was to suggest that a sub-committee of the Privy Council should be appointed to confer with the citizens of Newcastle and see whether, if some way were thought of to assist them, they would be prepared to contribute.[18]

Even when ships were available they were not always able to carry out the tasks allotted them. Sometimes this was because of their innate deficiencies. In April, for· instance, the captain of the ship which had been convoying the fishermen reported that he had spent the greater part of the day in chasing a Dunkirker, 'but he goes too well for any Newcastle ships [i.e. colliers] to fetch him up'. Another Dunkirker, which was hovering on the edge of the fleet, had ten oars on either side, which meant that 'upon any calm he may do much mischief, and we in sight and cannot come up to help it'. On other occasions the commanders seemed to be at fault. The long exchange· of letters between the Lord Admiral and Sir Henry Palmer had ended in the latter's dismissal and the appointment of Sir Henry Mervyn as commander of the King's ships in the Narrow Seas. But Mervyn did not long remain in favour. In April 1627 Buckingham sent him a stinging letter. 'Upon confidence of your care and vigilancy in performance of His Majesty's service,' he wrote, 'I thought that charge could not be committed to a better man. But my expectation therein hath failed, for I understand you have never been a-shipboard since your readmittance, which is now near twelve months.' Buckingham ordered Mervyn to go on board his flagship immediately and to carry out the instructions that had been despatched to him. 'If your other occasions are such as that they hinder and keep you from this your charge,' added the Lord Admiral, 'I will and must then appoint some other, for I cannot answer to His Majesty or the state the great neglect that is and hath been used therein by you.'[19]

There was a marked contrast between the tone of this letter and one which Buckingham wrote to Pennington a few days later, telling him that 'I have received much contentment and joy in your industrious performance of His Majesty's service committed to your care.' But Pennington fell within the category of 'diligent, honest and sufficient' captains, whom Buckingham admired and advanced. Too many of the others, unfortunately, fell into the other category, which Buckingham described as 'the slothful, negligent, mutinous and insufficient'. He did his best to weed out commanders of poor quality, and for this reason, among others, he would have welcomed the creation of a permanent Royal Navy with all that it could offer in the way of an attractive career to men of dedication and ability. There was no doubt about his own commitment, for his range of personal supervision extended from major matters of strategy and policy at one end of the scale to minor details of administration at the other. He pressed ahead with his plan to build a dry dock at Portsmouth, for instance, since naval operations were all too often hampered by the concentration of supply and repair facilities along the Thames, where ships could be imprisoned by bad weather or contrary winds for weeks or even months at a time. One of Buckingham's supporters was Captain Richard Gifford, who wrote to congratulate him on his firm stand and to assure him that 'you have taken more pains and care to have all things reformed concerning the Navy as never was the like done by any Lord Admiral'.[20]

The justification for this eulogy is to be found on nearly every page of the papers of Buckingham's naval secretary, Edward Nicholas, for there are repeated examples of the Lord Admiral's industry and attention to detail. In May 1627, for example, he wrote to John Hippesley — the Lieutenant of Dover Castle and his representative in the Cinque Ports — to enquire about provisions for the fleet. He wanted to know

how many tons of beer you have and how many gallons you account to a ton, either beer or wine measure, for that it is all to be delivered by gage. Next, how long your beer hath been brewed, and for what time your brewers have conditioned it should last; of what sort it is — either 36 or 40s. a ton more or less — and whether the cask be butts or pipes or hogsheads, and how much of either; whether it be in ships or cellars. And likewise whether the beef be dry-salted or pickled and whether cut in 2 or 4 lb. pieces, and what number of pieces you have in the whole. If your beef be pickled there must be great care that the casks be new dryen before they be shipped, to make it light. And also how many pounds of bacon you have . . . . Also what time the biscuit is conditioned to last, and how long it hath been baked . . .

This was a side of Buckingham that his critics knew (and cared) nothing about. They dismissed him as a frivolous courtier and an inexperienced young man occupying a position for which he was totally unfitted. Yet Buckingham's record as a naval administrator compares very favourably with that of his predecessor, the Earl of Nottingham, despite the fact that Nottingham had commanded Queen Elizabeth's Navy and had served a long apprenticeship at sea.[21]

Such praise might seem unjustified in view of the deficiencies in naval administration revealed in the 1620s, but these were caused by the sudden switch from a peacetime to a wartime footing and the uneven flow of funds from the Exchequer to the Treasurer of the Navy. Had it not been for the patience, energy and determination shown by the Lord Admiral during these years the administration of the Navy would have broken down altogether. The astonishing thing is that despite difficulties that would have overwhelmed a lesser man the Duke did not simply plan operations but carried them into effect. He also secured the appointment of the special commissioners who were charged with making a searching enquiry into every aspect of naval adminis- tration and producing proposals for fundamental reform. But, as so often, short-term needs forced the postponement or abandonment of long-term objectives. By the spring of 1627 Buckingham had decided to suspend the enquiry. He was preparing an expedition in support of La Rochelle, and it was essential to get the fleet ready for sea. If the Navy Commissioners and the officers under them were subjected to continuous and rigorous examination, the result would be further delays. Fundamental reform must therefore await a more suitable opportunity. The immediate concern was to provide the men, the ships, and above all the money, without which the expedition would never be able to leave England. Buckingham, despite the princely scale on which he lived, had personal experience of financial stringency. In August 1626 his stablemen complained that they had received no wages for one and a half years, and in that same month the Duke ordered Wallingford House and his residence in the Tiltyard to be put up for sale, while Dalby Park, in Leicester- shire, was to be let. All jewels, other than 'such as His Grace shall make especial choice of' were to be sold, and in February 1627 Buckingham raised £1,500 by having the buttons cut off his pearl suit. The greater part of this was paid, by Buckingham's order, 'for the use of His Majesty's Navy', and with Sackville Crowe serving both as his own treasurer and the Treasurer of the Navy, the distinction between personal and public expenditure became ever more blurred.[22]

Naval operations could not, of course, be maintained solely from Bucking- ham's own resources, yet the Exchequer was so denuded that they could hardly have been carried on at all had it not been for the income from the capture of French prizes. Much of this went to Philip Burlamachi, the international banker who acted as financial agent to the crown. In March, for instance, the Privy Council decided that £4,000 of prize money should be handed over to him to pay for the transport of Scottish troops to Germany, to aid Christian IV of Denmark. Later that month he was assigned a further £15,000 with which he was to equip the five regiments being raised for the Rochelle expedi- tion. In order to maintain the flow of prize money, Buckingham instructed Pennington to keep watch off the French coast, 'to intercept and take . . . all French, Dunkirkers' and Spanish ships and goods as shall come out of the Low Countries for the use of the French king'. By the end of March Pennington was ready to leave, but was held up by a lack of compasses and oars as well as sailors. Buckingham immediately wrote to the Navy Commissioners, urging them to remedy these defects, and a few days later he wrote again, in even stronger terms, requiring them to take immediate action so that 'the fleet may not, through your neglect and for want of a few necessaries, lie fruitlessly in the river, spending their victuals before they get to sea'. He added that while he was aware that they had a great deal of business on their hands, 'this is of such consideration and consequence as that it will bear no longer delay'.[23]

These remonstrances obviously produced the required effect, for by April 1627 Pennington was at sea, and towards the end of that month he wrote to the Lord Admiral to give him the welcome news that he had captured a number of rich prizes. 'I cannot acquaint Your Grace with the true value of these prizes,' he told him, 'but I dare undertake to put in security to give the King £70,000 for them.' Pennington returned to the west country where he went from port to port, picking up captured ships, French and others. By the time he arrived in the Thames in May 1627 he had with him a small fleet of some seventy prizes, and the delighted Buckingham persuaded the Privy Council that £1,140 of the money raised from the sale of their cargoes should be distributed among the crews of Pennington's ships as a reward for their good service and an encouragement to others to do likewise.[24]

It could not be taken for granted that all the seized ships and goods would be adjudged lawful prize. Sir Henry Marten, who presided over the Court of Admiralty, was an experienced and respected lawyer who was determined not to let considerations of expediency affect his judgements. Shortly after the arrival of Pennington's fleet, Marten announced his intention to resign, and gave as his reason the fact that Buckingham 'would have all to be judged good prize that the King's ships did take'. Buckingham, while admitting that he would have liked Marten 'not to be too easy in adjudging the prizes from the King', denied this charge and declared that Marten had a rancorous heart; but his anger was, as usual, of brief duration, for a week or so later he returned Sir Henry Marten's patent to him with an assurance of his love and satisfaction. Marten had made his point and kept his independence, along with his office.[25]

It was estimated that the total value of the goods brought in by Pennington and others was nearly £130,000, and to Buckingham and the hard-pressed Navy Commissioners this was like manna from heaven. The money was assigned even before the ships reached London. Burlamachi was instructed that the great fleet being made ready for the Rochelle expedition should be victualled for five months instead of the two previously stipulated, and that the £10,000 needed for this purpose should be taken from the prize money. A further £10,000 was to be added to the Ordinary of the Navy, to bring it up to £40,000. Such methods were no doubt somewhat irregular, but war made demands that had to be met, and England was not the only country in which extraordinary expedients were resorted to. Rubens, writing at this very time, commented upon the 'dire need and general penury of the princes'. It was incredible, he said, that they should all be reduced to such extremities, but it was self-evident that 'they are not only deep in debt, with all their resources pledged, but can hardly find any new expedients in order to keep breathing somehow and to extend their credit, which is already so strained that it seems it cannot last long'.[26]

III

In these early months of 1627 Rubens was engaged in a complex series of negotiations with a view to bringing about a truce between the Hague powers and Spain. The Duke of Savoy, who, through his ambassador, the Abbé Scaglia, had urged Charles and Buckingham not to reject the idea out of hand, was confident that such a truce could be concluded, and in May 1627 Rubens and Scaglia spent some time together in Brussels, discussing possible courses of action. There is no doubt that the Infanta Isabella would have welcomed a truce, for the Netherlands were suffering acutely from the strain of war. She was trying to bring about a reconciliation between the Emperor and Christian of Denmark, and at the same time she was pressing Philip of Spain to make peace with England rather than France, on the grounds that the French could not be trusted. Buckingham, on behalf of Charles, had made it clear that while the question of Denmark might be left for separate consideration – because it concerned the Emperor – there could be no question of England negotiating without the Dutch. He wanted Isabella herself to preside over the negotiations and to ask for authority from Spain to conclude a binding agreement which should also cover the Palatinate. Isabella was more than willing to do this, but could not act without Philip's authorisation. She was supported by the Spanish commander, Spinola, who declared that his forces were so enfeebled that the most they could do would be to stand on the defensive. What the Infanta did not know, however, was that Philip had already committed himself to a French alliance. He ratified the treaty with France on 10 March but not until 22 May did he write to Isabella to inform her of this. In his despatch – which he backdated in order to avoid infringing the letter of his agreement with France – Philip sent Isabella the requisite authorisation to treat with Charles I, but he ruled out negotiations with the Dutch. He told her that if England refused to consider a separate peace, she was simply to spin matters out as long as she possibly could. In other words the object of Spanish policy towards England in 1627 was what it had been prior to 1623 – to let negotiations drag on indefinitely while the military situation altered in favour (it was hoped) of the Habsburgs.[27]

If Buckingham could have brought about a peace with Spain which would have included the Dutch and also provided an honourable and satisfactory settlement of the problem of the Palatinate, he would have been glad to do so, for this had been the object of his policy ever since his return from Spain. However, the main thrust of his diplomacy was concentrated on a renewed attempt to topple Richelieu and thereby open the way to a wholehearted French commitment to the common cause. In March 1627 he despatched Wat Montagu on a mission to Lorraine and Savoy. Charles III, the young and ambitious Duke of Lorraine, welcomed Montagu to his court – where the exiled Duchess of Chevreuse had already fomented anti-Richelieu feeling – and promised that if there was a rising of malcontent princes in France accompanied by intervention by foreign rulers, he would be among the first in the field. Charles Emmanuel, Duke of Savoy, was also full of promises, and he had with him one of the greatest of all the French malcontent nobles, Louis de Bourbon, Count of Soissons, who was a prince of the blood. By the end of May 1627 Montagu had knit together the various threads of a plot designed to overthrow Richelieu and change the direction of French policy. An English expeditionary force was to effect a landing in western France, in the region of Bordeaux. At the first news of this the Huguenot leader, the Duke of Rohan, would muster all his forces and – once he had been supplied, as promised, with cavalry from Savoy – would strike westwards to link up with the English. If the cavalry failed to arrive, however, he would seize Montauban, roughly halfway between Nîmes and Bordeaux, and use this as a rallying-point for all the Huguenots of the Languedoc. Meanwhile the Count of Soissons would make his way to the independent principality of Orange, inside France, from where he would deliver a formal protest to Louis XIII in the name of the French nobility, calling on him to dismiss the Cardinal. If Louis refused, Soissons would put himself at the head of an army – to be provided by Savoy with financial assistance from England – and enforce his demands at the sword's point. He was confident that other princes, including quite possibly Louis's brother Gaston, Duke of Orleans, would flock to join him.[28]

Before the scheme could be carried into effect there were a number of snags to be overcome. The Duke of Savoy was reluctant to act until he had made peace with Genoa, but there was a good chance that this could be brought about through Spanish mediation, and Scaglia had instructions to negotiate a settlement of this dispute in Brussels. Soissons showed a similar reluctance to commit himself until he could be sure of somewhere safe to fall back on in case things went wrong. Orange would have been suitable for this purpose, but it belonged to the Prince of Orange. However, the English were hoping to persuade the prince either to sell or pawn it to Charles I, who would then hand it over to Soissons. No doubt this was one of the considerations that prompted Charles to appoint the Prince of Orange to the Order of the Garter in May 1627. He also hoped to link Soissons more firmly to the common cause by arranging a marriage between the Count and the eldest daughter of Frederick, Elector Palatine. As for Soissons's hopes that the Duke of Orleans would be among his supporters in France, these seemed unlikely to be fulfilled in view of Gaston's marriage and reconciliation with his brother. However, in May 1627 the Duchess of Orleans died in childbirth, and this event, in the words of Bassompierre, 'changed the face of the court and opened a whole new range of possibilities'.[29]

A plan which depended for its success upon the coordination of a number of separate enterprises, and upon the cooperation of princes who were unwilling to take action until someone else had made the first move, was not by any means sure of success. Yet it stood a reasonable chance, especially if a clear lead came from England. Buckingham planned to provide just this, with an expedition to La Rochelle, and he had been assured by Rohan and his brother, Soubise, that the Huguenots were only waiting for an English landing in order to commit themselves. Rohan had sent a gentleman named Saint Blan-cart to act as his agent in London, and early in March 1627 the Venetian ambassador reported that Saint Blancart and Soubise were engaged in frequent conferences with Buckingham. He added the information that 'they talk of an expedition . . . to be commanded by the Duke in person', and that the four regiments of infantry designed to go on it would be under the command of Colonel Burroughs, 'an Englishman who fought in the Palatinate and was at the surrender of Frankenthal'. This information was remarkably accurate, for although Buckingham had not yet appointed anybody to command the army he did so on the first day of April, and his choice lighted upon Sir John Burroughs.[30]

The Venetian ambassador showed the same degree of accuracy when he said that the purpose of the expedition was to link a number of foreign princes with 'the malcontents and Huguenots in France' to form 'a powerful party which shall force the Cardinal, on the pain of ruin, to become prudent and to adapt his views to the common welfare'. But although this was Buckingham's main aim, it was not his only one. He was also well aware that by mounting an expedition in aid of the French protestants he would be countering the unfavourable impression created by his apparent sanction of the use of English ships against the Huguenots in 1626. Buckingham was said to have told one of his fellow Councillors that he intended to perform an action which would win him back the affection of the people, and according to another report he was confident that before the summer was over he would be more honoured and beloved of the Commons than ever the Earl of Essex – Elizabeth's favourite and the leader of the successful 1596 expedition against Cadiz – had been. Buckingham had now decided to take Pennington with him, and to include the freeing of the English wine fleet among the objectives of his expedition. But his principal purpose – apart from setting his 'master plan' in action – was to succour La Rochelle and to deal a crippling blow to French ambitions to establish their power at sea. Buckingham was deeply concerned about the possible effect on England of Richelieu's projects for maritime expansion and did not dare stand aside while they were put into effect. He would have preferred a peaceful agreement, but Richelieu had apparently blocked the way to this. As the French agent in England informed his government, if only they had allowed the Duke to visit the French court and had given him satisfaction about 'the business of Navigation and Commerce, the English would be far more yielding and would not take the hard line they do at present'.[31]

It was widely assumed in England that when the fleet was ready to sail, Buckingham would hand over command to a deputy, as he had done in 1625, and stay at home. But the Duke had learnt his lesson from the Cadiz failure and was determined that this time he would be present to provide the leadership and spirit so conspicuously lacking in Wimbledon's expedition. He was in reasonably good health, and as the time of departure drew near he took purges and passed some days in bed to gather his strength. He knew the risks he ran in leaving England, and in particular the Court, for his enemies would be quick to take advantage of his absence. But he could count on a number of good friends as well as clients to watch over his interests, among them

Theophilus Howard, the new Earl of Suffolk, whose growing influence was signalled by his appointment to the Order of the Garter in May 1627. In the same month William Laud, now Bishop of Bath and Wells, was made a Privy Councillor. The initiative in this promotion probably came from the King, who favoured the Arminians, but the Duke had cause to welcome it. Laud seems to have been acting as Buckingham's adviser on religious matters, for when the Countess, who was now a professed Roman Catholic, gave her son a paper about invoking the saints, he handed it over to him. And it was to Laud that Buckingham turned in March 1627 at a moment of personal tragedy, when his young son and heir died, and he entrusted him with the melancholy task of burying the boy. Laud was also appointed to draw up a form of prayer, to be read in churches throughout England, asking for God's blessing on Buckingham's expedition. In short, the Duke could feel confident that his concerns would not be forgotten or overlooked while Laud was at the King's side: as the bishop's biographer commented 'it was not thought either safe or fit that the Duke himself should be so long absent without leaving some assured friend about His Majesty, by whom all practices against him might be either prevented or suppressed, and by whose means the King's affections might be always inflamed towards him'.[32]

Buckingham could also trust men such as Conway, Sir John Coke and Edward Nicholas to watch over his interests in their respective spheres, and to prevent the administrative machine from grinding to a halt. Nicholas was a relative newcomer to the Buckingham circle, having formerly been secretary to Lord Zouch, the Duke's predecessor as Lord Warden. It was at Zouch's suggestion that Buckingham kept Nicholas on to deal with Cinque Ports affairs, but Nicholas proved so competent that he became Buckingham's principal secretary for naval matters also. During the second half of 1627, when Buckingham was with the expeditionary force in France, Nicholas wrote to him regularly, and one observer reported how the Duke always read his secretary's letters before any others, and ended his perusal of them 'with a large discourse of "Honest Nicholas" '.[33]

By the spring of 1627 preparations for the expedition were well advanced — at any rate in appearance — and in early April the Duke instructed the Navy Commissioners to provide silk flags and pennants suitable for a Lord Admiral of England commanding a royal fleet. Despite this and other signs, however, it was still widely assumed that at the last moment Buckingham would find some excuse for staying behind. But later that month the Florentine resident reported that 'people now begin to believe that he really means what he says and that he will command in person . . . . His serious intention is also shown by the military costume which he wears, with an immense collar and magnificent plume of feathers in his hat.' Such panache was no doubt calculated to impress onlookers, but they could know nothing of Buckingham's hard work, attention to detail and incessant harrying of lethargic or inefficient administrators that alone made it possible to mount a major expedition. At the end of May Buckingham instructed the Navy Commissioners to let him know how many ships were still not ready, 'and for what they stay, to the end I may take some course for their speedy despatch, for I assure you it much imports His Majesty's service to have all the fleet to be instantly at sea'. A week later he wrote again. 'Notwithstanding the importance and haste of His Majesty's service, the long time spent in making ready of the ships, and my daily commands for expedition,' he told the Commissioners, 'there is such remisness used as if it were not intended the fleet should go forth this year . . . . I see such carelessness in this weighty and important service as that I must complain of it for mine own safety and justification . . . . I pray take this business into your serious consideration and cause a speedy repair of this neglect.'[34]

The Commissioners, in their replies, protested that they were handicapped by shortage of money, because the Ordinary of the Navy had not been settled, and by shortage of stores and many other deficiencies. Buckingham riposted by reminding them that he had 'daily importuned His Majesty, the lords of His Majesty's Privy Council and the Lord Treasurer' to take these matters into consideration, as the Commissioners well knew. He had done all that he could and had secured the issuing of the necessary orders; now it was their responsibility to keep up the pressure, 'and if the services required be not performed, they cannot be excused with alleging that I provided not monies for them. I gave directions for what is fit, and if they perform it not, at their peril be it'. As for the shortage of stores, this was inevitable when great expeditions were being prepared. 'It is good to have the King's stores replenished,' observed the Lord Admiral, 'but stores are ordained for use and service in a time of action, and not to be kept to be only looked on.'[35]

Buckingham made his own preparations for the expedition as well as supervising operations in general. He spent several thousand pounds on linens, silks, and gold and silver buttons, and took with him £50 worth of books as well as a musician and a harp. More money was disbursed on wine and groceries and on what one observer described as Buckingham's 'living store of provision' – oxen, milch cows, goats and poultry. The Duke was accompanied by a retinue of servants, and these were a further drain on his purse. He took with him one of his most sumptuous coaches and ordered his gentleman of the horse to send along with it the richly embroidered clothes that had been provided for his coachmen, footmen and pages at the time of his journey to Paris in 1625. Not all these trappings of glory reached their journey's end, however, for a number of the satin and velvet suits were mislaid somewhere between the shore and shipboard at Portsmouth and were never recovered. But more than enough remained to sustain the dignity of a Lord Admiral and to point the contrast between private affluence and public poverty. Buckingham spent more than £10,000 on equipping himself and his household for the expedition – a sum that would have maintained an entire regiment of infantry for over six months. Individual expenditure on such a scale at a time when the royal Exchequer was empty seems, by present-day standards, to be not simply unjustified but positively immoral. But in early seventeenth-century Europe, and indeed until much later, it was taken for granted that poverty among the rank and file could coexist with spendthrift magnificence on the part of magnates. Indeed one of the functions of a great man was to distribute his wealth through largesse, thereby creating employment and relieving at least some of the symptoms of distress. If there was a difference between Buckingham and other 'magnificoes' it came in his concern for the well-being of the men under him. Several hundred pounds was set aside, for instance, for drugs and medicaments, and the Company of Barber Surgeons found difficulty in supplying sufficient surgeons to meet Buckingham's demands. Also much greater care than usual was taken to prepare for the reception of sick and wounded men at Portsmouth and Plymouth when the expedition returned. Buckingham provided for the spiritual as well as the physical needs of his men by appointing chaplains, among them the poet Robert Herrick. As it happened, Herrick was not the only representative of English literature on the expedition, for one of the army officers was George Donne, whose father, the poet Dean of St Paul's, had accompanied Essex to Cadiz in 1596.[36]

On 14 May Buckingham gave a feast at York House to take his official farewells. The King and Queen were the guests of honour, and the entertainment included a masque 'wherein first comes forth the Duke; after him Envy, with divers open-mouthed dogs' heads representing the people's barking; next came Fame; then Truth'. However Buckingham did not leave town immediately, for there was still a great deal of work to be done before the fleet could sail. Among other problems was that of the poor quality of the men impressed to serve as infantry. Sir George Blundell, serjeant-major of the expeditionary force, had complained to Buckingham (in words that echoed Falstaff's) that the Hampshire levies were 'such creatures as I am ashamed to describe them'. The Deputy Lieutenants had sent these 'poor rogues and beggars' without any money, clothes or shoes, and Blundell protested that he was at his wits' end to know what to do. Buckingham took the matter up with the Privy Council, and orders were thereupon sent to the Lord Lieutenants requiring them 'to take the more care to send young and able-bodied men, well clothed and fit for service, and to send them under the charge of an able conductor'.[37]

At the very end of May, just as the King was about to leave London to inspect his ships and soldiers at Portsmouth before they set out, news arrived that a big fleet, thought to be Spanish, had been sighted making its way up the Channel. Buckingham immediately rode to Dover, gathered all the ships available there, and led them to sea in pursuit of the 'enemy'. However, the fleet turned out to be one of Dutch merchantmen bound for La Rochelle, and the Duke therefore landed at Portsmouth and posted back to London. It was at such moments of crisis that Buckingham showed his best qualities – in particular his speed of action and resolution. He went so fast that he outstripped Nicholas, who was left behind at Dover. The secretary had to content himself with writing to congratulate Buckingham on the fine example he had set, and to assure him that it would have very good effects. 'Your Grace's sudden departure and personal forwardness in this expedition hath so quickened all officers,' reported Nicholas, 'as I believe (the wind favouring) all ships whatsoever belonging to the fleet will be by the end of the next week at Stokes Bay [near Portsmouth].'[38]

The King left for Portsmouth on 5 June, taking Soubise in the coach with him. A week later he inspected the fleet and dined on board the flagship, the *Triumph*. He told Sir John Watts, its captain, that according to Buckingham she had good sailing qualities but was a little too hard in her helm – thereby showing that he had at any rate been well briefed. But Charles, unlike the Lord Admiral, took no pleasure in routine administration, and he found time hanging heavily on his hands. He wrote to 'Steenie' to tell him how much he missed his company, but he put a brave face on things by adding that 'the life I lead here . . . is not so wearisome yet as you imagine, and if it were worse than it is it would not weary me since I see it hastens the business'. The King did not have long to wait, however, for early on the morning of 12 June the Duke left town, accompanied by the Earl of Holland, and rode hard towards Portsmouth. No sooner had he arrived than he gathered up the threads of outstanding business and tied them firmly together. A week later the expedition was ready to leave.[39]

The army which embarked on board the ships waiting at Portsmouth consisted of seven regiments, each containing about a thousand men. The colonels of the regiments included Buckingham's kinsman, Alexander Brett, whom the King knighted; Charles Rich, son of the Earl of Warwick; and Sir Edward Conway, eldest son of the Secretary of State. Sir Edward had served in the disastrous Cadiz expedition, and placed the blame for failure upon inadequate leadership. Things would have been very different, he thought, if the Duke had gone with them, and he had told Buckingham at the time that he hoped one day to see him 'in the head of a gallant army'. When that day came, he added, 'no man shall follow you with a more earnest desire to your service'. Now at last his chance had come. The General of the army was Sir John Burroughs, who had also fought at Cadiz. Buckingham had picked out Burroughs as early as 1624, when he thought of appointing him as second-in-command of Mansfeld's expedition, and although he changed his mind, Conway assured Sir John that the Duke would continue to favour him since he 'loves worth wheresoever he finds it'. A year later Buckingham wrote to Burroughs, at that time serving with the English regiments in the United Provinces, 'to summon you to come over to go in an employment wherein I shall labour to advance you and give you contentment'. This was the Cadiz expedition, in which, as it happened, Burroughs found little glory or satisfaction; but he retained the Duke's goodwill, as was shown by Charles's decision to grant him a pension of £200 a year in November 1626. Now, less than a year later, Burroughs had the rare opportunity (given the infrequency of English military operations) of a major command. It was on men like Burroughs and Sir Edward Conway – and also Sir William Heydon, the master of the expedition's ordnance – that Buckingham relied in the first instance for advice on military matters. He had also offered a regiment to the Earl of Essex, but Essex declined. He had made clear in the previous year that while he would willingly accept employment if it were offered him by the King, he was not prepared to serve under Buckingham.[40]

The infantry were said to be in very good condition, and the King was delighted at 'their perfectness in their orders and in their unexpected readiness of the use of their arms and firing'. He was likewise impressed by the skill of the hundred or so cavalry, largely raised from among Buckingham's friends and followers. Buckingham himself was already winning some of the popularity he coveted, and one observer commented that 'by his real setting of sail' he had 'converted many men's curses into prayers'. But the number of converts was limited, and the more general attitude was expressed in scurrilous poems which had a wide circulation. Among the most notorious of these was one that began:

> And wilt thou go, great Duke, and leave us here
> Lamenting thee, and eke thy pupil dear,
> Dread Charles? Alas, who shall his sceptre sway
> And rule his kingdoms when thou are away?
> Are there no maids in Court to stay thee? Must
> Thy hate to France and Spain exceed thy lust?

and ended:

> Most graceless Duke, we thank thy charity,
> Wishing the fleet such speed as to lose thee,
> And we shall think't a happy victory.[41]

While there were many people who would not shed a tear if Buckingham failed to return from the expedition, his friends, and above all his family, grieved at his departure. His mother wrote to commend him 'to God's good pleasure, assuring myself He that hath done so much for you will make you a happy instrument of His further glory'. Buckingham, in reply, told the Countess how it had gladdened his heart 'not only to receive so hearty a blessing from you, but so courageous a farewell'. He had no doubt, he said, that God's blessing would go with him, 'since my intentions are not guided by spleen nor malice, but by an ambition to serve faithfully both my King and country'.[42]

Buckingham's wife, Kate, could not bear the thought of her husband's departure, particularly at this moment when attacks of morning sickness made her hope she was once again pregnant. Buckingham had promised Kate that he would see her before he departed, but in the event he broke his word. He must have known that a leave-taking at such a time would deeply disturb his wife — who needed quiet and rest — and might well shake his own resolution. But he could not escape Kate's reproaches. In a long and passionate letter she told him that

now I do plainly see you have deceived me . . . I confess I did ever fear you would be catched, for there was no other likelihood after all that show but you must needs go. For my part I have been a very miserable woman hitherto, that never could have you keep at home. But now I will ever look to be so till some blessed occasion comes to draw you quite from the Court, for there is none more miserable than I am now, and till you leave this life of a courtier – which you have been ever since I knew you – I shall ever think myself unhappy. I am the unfortunatest of all other, that even when I am with child I must have so much cause of sorrow as to have you go from me . . . . If

I were sure my soul would be well, I could wish myself to be out of this miserable world.

She tried to master her feelings and wish her husband a safe and prosperous journey, but she could not hold back either her love or her anger. 'Never whilst I live will I trust you again, nor never will put you to your oath for anything again . . . I pray God never woman may love a man as I have done you, that none may feel that which I have done for you.' At the end of her letter she begged her husband to burn it and to forgive her for writing as she had done,

for my heart is so full I cannot choose, because I did not look for it. I would to Jesus that there were any way in the world to fetch you off this journey with your honour. If any pains or any suffering of mine could do it, I were a most happy woman. But you have sent yourself and made me miserable. God forgive you for it![43]

Although it was true, as Kate complained, that Buckingham had sent himself away, by planning the expedition in the first place and then deciding to lead it in person, he was acting in the name of the King and under Charles's written instructions. These began by sketching in the history of the quarrel with France, culminating in the French threat 'to dispossess us of that sovereignty in those seas to which our kingdoms of Great Britain have given denomination, and which all our ancestors have enjoyed time out of mind'. They then developed the theme of Louis's perfidy in breaking his solemn pledges to his protestant subjects, and concluded by commanding Buckingham to take the English army to La Rochelle. On his arrival he was to inform the inhabitants that he had come solely for their protection, and was to demand an immediate answer whether they would be prepared to 'reciprocally oblige themselves to enter into action'. If the Rochellois gave a positive reply, he was to hand over the army and supplies to them; if not, he was to declare that Charles had done all that could be expected of him, and then send back the bulk of his force. Buckingham was also instructed to try and free the English wine fleet, still held at Bordeaux. Once he had accomplished this and opened a free passage to La Rochelle, he was to take his fleet to the coast of Spain to raid commerce and destroy shipping.[44]

These instructions are remarkable in that they contain no reference to what was in fact to be Buckingham's main objective, the Ile de Ré, off La Rochelle. This does not mean that no consideration had been given to the possibility of effecting a landing there. Wat Montagu had already told Rohan that Ré would be one of the targets for attack, and the capture of the island had much to be said for it from the English point of view. Ré was near enough to La Rochelle for reinforcements to be sent both to and from the town, as required. It was also conveniently placed halfway along the sea route from England to Spain, and would therefore be a valuable base for English warships keeping watch over the trade routes from the Baltic to the Iberian peninsula.[45]

The immediate aim of the expedition was to put an army into La Rochelle and attack and destroy Fort Louis – which, according to one French source, could easily have been done, since the fort had only a tiny garrison in it. But there was no certainty that La Rochelle would open its gates to the English. Soubise had assured Buckingham that it would, but many of the inhabitants were fearful of provoking Louis yet further, and among the leading figures in the town there was considerable disagreement about what was the best course to follow. If La Rochelle did not immediately commit itself, there was much to be said, from the English point of view, for occupying one of the nearby islands until such time as the citizens made up their minds. There was the further consideration that possession of a piece of French territory would be an invaluable bargaining counter when, as Buckingham hoped and assumed, the French agreed to negotiate. No doubt it was for these and other considerations – not least among them the uncertainty that attended all expeditions in days when wind and weather could play havoc with aims and objectives – that the King's instructions to Buckingham left him free to take whatever course seemed to him to be expedient once he arrived off the French coast.[46]

IV

On 20 June Buckingham ordered the troops at Portsmouth to begin embarkation, and two days later he stood by the King's coach to take his leave. The King departed for London on the 23rd, and on Sunday the 24th the Duke took up his quarters on board the *Triumph*. The fleet was disposed in five squadrons, of which the first, consisting of eight men-of-war and some thirty merchantmen, was commanded by Buckingham as admiral of the expedition. The second squadron was entrusted to the vice-admiral, Lord Willoughby, who had recently been created Earl of Lindsey, and the third to the rear-admiral, Lord Harvey. Buckingham's brother-in-law, the Earl of Denbigh, had charge of the fourth squadron, while the fifth was in the capable hands of John Pennington. The whole fleet numbered close on a hundred ships – forty of them royal ones – and by the evening of the 24th it was ready to sail. But before it did so, Buckingham went back on shore to round up laggards and deserters. He discovered a number of army officers skulking in their lodgings, and drove them on shipboard. One, who gave him an 'unmannerly answer', he ordered to be cashiered. He spent the night on shore, and the next morning rejoined the fleet. Two days later, when the wind began to blow in the right direction, he led his ships to sea. He knew that he had embarked on a venture which would expose him to great danger, so before the fleet sailed he made his will. 'Intending by the permission of Almighty God a voyage to sea, and considering the many casualties and dangers that the life of man is subject unto', he bequeathed his soul into the hands of God, 'trusting to have it saved by the merits, death and passion of my alone Saviour and Redeemer Jesus Christ'. As for his body, he asked that this should be interred in King Henry VII's chapel in Westminster Abbey.[47]

By the last day of June 1627 the expeditionary force was off Ushant, and a council of war was held at which the majority of members recommended an

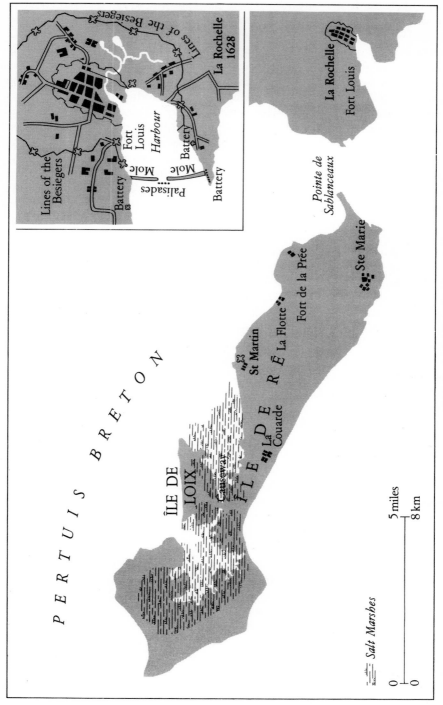

Map 4. Ile de Ré, 1627

La Rochelle 1628

Lines of the Besiegers

Lines of the Besiegers

Battery

Battery

Fort Louis

Harbour

Mole

Mole

Palisades

Battery

Battery

La Rochelle

Fort Louis

Pointe de Sablanceaux

Ste Marie

Fort de la Prée

St Martin

La Flotte

Î L E   D E   R É

La Couarde

Causeway

ÎLE DE LOIX

P E R T U I S   B R E T O N

Salt Marshes

5 miles

8 km

0

0

attack upon Bordeaux. But the wind dropped and the ships lay becalmed until the following day, when a fleet of some thirteen sail was sighted. Buckingham despatched one of his ships to interrogate the strangers, but although the captain caught up with them they refused to identify themselves, and merely observed that if the English fleet was bound for Bordeaux it would find a very hot reception waiting for it. The English captain thereupon returned to the main body of the fleet, gave Buckingham this information, and added his opinion that the strangers were probably Dunkirkers. Buckingham immediately ordered his fleet to give chase, but although the pursuit continued for two days the strangers outstripped the cumbersome English vessels. By the time the chase was abandoned, on 4 July, Lord Harvey's squadron had become separated from the rest of the fleet, and Buckingham summoned another council of war, which recommended him to sail direct to La Rochelle. By the night of the 8th they were off Belleisle when a violent storm blew up, which drove the *Triumph* into shallow waters where she was in danger of floundering. The ship's master was so despondent that it seemed that only a miracle would save the ship, and Buckingham, on the advice of his chaplain, called on the crew to join together in public prayer. But he remained remarkably untroubled by the prospect of imminent death, and when the chaplain took too long over his heartfelt pleas for divine intercession, Buckingham cut him short with the comment 'it is not long prayers that doth it'. He also told those around him that 'there's nothing grieves me in all this but [that] the rascals in England will say "It was the just judgement of God upon him" '.[48]

Fortunately for the expedition the storm blew itself out before it had caused too much damage, and by 10 July the greater part of the fleet was at anchor off La Rochelle, where it was joined on the 11th by Harvey's squadron. On that same day Buckingham sent Sir William Beecher to La Rochelle with a message to the mayor and council. But they were celebrating a fast, and used this as an excuse to delay talking to him. Beecher returned to the flagship in a bad temper, with the unwelcome news that the Rochellois were not prepared to allow entry to anyone. Buckingham decided that he should go back to the town on the following morning, this time accompanied by Soubise and Saint Blancart. But when, on Thursday 12 July, they presented themselves at the gates of La Rochelle and demanded admittance, the mayor was still unwilling to allow them in. He reminded Soubise what fearful consequences for the town might follow upon his entry there, and begged him to go away.

At this critical moment, however, Soubise's mother, the dowager Duchess of Rohan, who had taken up residence in La Rochelle, appeared at the gate and, taking Soubise by the arm, led him back with her. The mayor did not dare block their path, and Soubise and his mother made a triumphal progress to her house, where he summoned the town council to attend him. Once all the members had arrived he called on Beecher to address them. In his speech Beecher showed how Louis had fallen under the influence of 'the Jesuit and Spanish faction', which intended not only the destruction of the Huguenots but also the ruin of Christendom. When Charles I realised this, declared Beecher, he decided, in response to appeals for help from Rohan and Soubise, to send an expedition under Buckingham to offer the Rochellois powerful assistance both by land and by sea, on condition that they joined him in the fight. The King, so Beecher assured his listeners, had no aims or interests other than those of his fellow protestants in France, and he gave them a copy of Buckingham's manifesto, which stated unequivocally that Charles had taken up arms 'solely for the defence of the [Huguenot] churches'. It was now up to the Rochellois to decide whether to accept the proffered aid, but Beecher warned them that if they rejected it the King would hold himself free from all further obligations towards them. And, Beecher added, they must make up their minds quickly so that Buckingham could decide on how best to dispose his forces.[49]

Beecher's speech was well received, and if popular opinion had carried the day the Rochellois would have committed themselves there and then. But the leading citizens took a more cautious view and refused to be rushed into a decision. Instead they sent delegates to Buckingham to tell him that they could not give him an immediate reply but must first consult the other Huguenot congregations throughout France: meanwhile they wished him all success. The delegates were accompanied by Saint Blancart, who carried a private message from Soubise, assuring the Duke that the Rochellois were well disposed, despite their initial reserve, and that he should do nothing as yet. Buckingham, however, was not prepared to wait indefinitely. In any case he knew from the experience of former expeditions that it was dangerous to leave soldiers too long on shipboard. He had hoped for an immediate and positive response from La Rochelle, and had he received it he would have sent his army into the town. But in view of the inhabitants' apparent reluctance to commit themselves to their liberators, he had decided – with the approval of the council of war – to effect a landing on Ré. The best place seemed to be the Pointe de Sablanceaux, a finger of land pointing towards La Rochelle, for the English ships would be able to surround this from the sea and give covering fire while the troops landed. This, then, was the battle plan for Thursday 12 July.[50]

Buckingham was up well before daybreak, and after receiving the sacrament at five o'clock he conferred with Soubise before the latter set off for La Rochelle. He then instructed Richard Graham, his gentleman of the horse, to take a boat with a party of musketeers, and land a boy on the Pointe to see whether the French had prepared any defences there. The boy swam naked to shore and then ran inland for a mile or so, finding no trace of the enemy except three scouts on horseback who, as soon as they spotted him, chased him back to the boat. By ten o'clock the boy was on board the *Triumph*, where he gave Buckingham an account of what he had seen. The Duke then went by barge to all the warships in the fleet, issuing precise instructions about where they were to go and what they were to do. He also arranged for landing craft to take up their position on either side of the Pointe, under the cover of the big ships and as close inshore as possible.[51]

When all was prepared – by which time it was well into the afternoon – Buckingham climbed to the top of the mainmast on one of the ships and, looking across to the Pointe, spotted a large body of French infantry, with supporting horsemen, drawn up about a mile away from where the landing was to take place. He ordered the ships to open fire on these and to keep up a hail of shot while the first regiments went ashore. Sir John Burroughs and Sir Alexander Brett, whose troops consisted mainly of veterans experienced in the Dutch wars, had the honour of leading the assault, and Buckingham went with them to make sure they landed in the right place. The men were jaded after days on board ship and lingered in the refreshing water, but the Duke took a cudgel in his hands and drove them on shore, where they were quickly drawn up in battle array ready to face the enemy. Sir William Courtenay's regiment was due to land next, but his men were even more laggard and he called on the Duke to assist him. Buckingham ordered his bargemen to row up and down among the soldiers in the water so that he could urge them on, but while he was doing this he heard the sound of firing, and turning back towards the shore saw that the French had launched their counter-attack with several troops of cavalry. The horsemen had created confusion among the English, many of whom were running away or being forced back into the sea. Buckingham promptly left Courtenay to get his men ashore

and very bravely himself drew his sword and turned his barge, attended by Mr Graham and Mr Ashburnham, and thrust himself upon the revolters, and railing and threatening that he told them he hoped not that they came with an intent but [to] adventure themselves as far as he would lead them. Whereupon he thrust himself on to the shore, and they followed slowly. And encouraging of the other foot (which were run into the water), the most of them leaped out of the water, and upon the General's words, thrust themselves forward, as if they would have fought bravely.[52]

By this time, however, the brief but bloody battle was almost over. The enemy cavalry had advanced 'with all speed, furiously, most French-like' and had charged home despite the hail of shot that fell on them from the ships. The English infantry, consisting of well over a thousand men, reeled and scattered at the first blow, but quickly recovered. The French horsemen found they were powerless against the barricade of pikes, and as the English musketeers opened up 'they wheeled and made a hasty retreat, leaving many of the forwardest men behind them'. Now it was the turn of the French infantry, numbering about 1,500 men. They advanced slowly but in good order, and, when they came within range, shot off their muskets. Then they 'fell to it with swords and push of pike, until they were breathless on both sides. The French, finding our pike to be longer than theirs, threw away their pike and went to it with stones, and so did our men. But ours beat them out with stones and made them fly away very disorderly.' The French losses were heavy, particularly among the cavalry, and the greater part of the officers were wounded. Marshal Toiras, who commanded the island for Louis XIII, lost a brother in the action, and Baron de Chantal, the father of Madame de Sévigné, was killed riding in to the attack. The English losses were much lighter. None of the soldiers had been killed, though some thirty to forty were drowned, but fourteen officers, who had exposed themselves to danger as they rallied their men, had been slain. The worst loss from Buckingham's point of view was that of Sir William Heydon, an experienced soldier whose advice on military matters would have been invaluable. Another casualty was Saint Blancart, who, when he realised that the landing was going to take place despite Soubise's request for further delay, insisted on taking part in it. Saint Blancart had played a key role in negotiations between Buckingham and the Huguenots, and there was no one to take his place.[53]

Despite these losses, however, Buckingham had good reason to be pleased. He had successfully carried out that most difficult of operations, landing an expeditionary force in the face of enemy attack, and had won credit for his own conduct. One young officer told his father that 'our General hath behaved himself so courageously and nobly that his very enemies speak well of him', and it now seemed that nothing stood between the English and the conquest of the whole island. Toiras did not risk another engagement, but withdrew to the town of St Martin, where he and his disheartened army shut themselves up in the yet uncompleted citadel. If the English had kept hot on their heels they might well have swept Toiras and his men out of the island altogether. But the English did not know this. As far as they were aware, the French might attack again at any moment, and they therefore threw up palisades to protect themselves while they completed their disembarkation. Two whole days were spent in this, and meanwhile the French, with Buckingham's permission, were burying their dead. As for the French wounded, three barons who had been hurt in the charge asked him for leave to go to the mainland to have their wounds dressed. This gave Buckingham an opening for the sort of chivalrous gesture in which he delighted, and not simply did he give the necessary permission but he sent the wounded officers in his scarlet-lined barge with his musicians to soothe their pain.[54]

Buckingham was still hoping for a positive commitment from the inhabitants of La Rochelle, and it may have been for this reason, as well as the need to rest his men, that he wasted valuable time. Soubise returned from the town, bringing with him some three hundred volunteers, but it was quite clear that he had misjudged the mood of the populace. In his conversations with Buckingham in England he had assured the Duke that at the first sign of the English fleet the citizens would rush out to greet him as their liberator. But now that Buckingham had actually arrived they were more concerned with getting in their corn and avoiding any action that might bring a French army down upon their heads: as Rohan commented bitterly, the mayor was in the pay of the French court, while the common people were lacking in vigour or courage. Nevertheless Buckingham's victory had encouraged those elements among the citizens who wanted a more positive response, and messengers were swiftly despatched to Huguenot centres in Guienne and Languedoc to give them the good news and ask them for their advice on whether or not to accept Charles's offer of assistance.[55]

On Sunday 15 July the English army moved out of its temporary encampment, along the road that runs south towards Ste Marie. In some ways this was an odd choice, for it might have made more sense in military terms to take the northern route, and seize the small Fort de la Prée on the way. This fortress, standing on the edge of the water, had been battered by the English warships as soon as they arrived off the island, and had only a small garrison inside it. While it was of no great value at this stage, there was much to be said for denying it to the French, who might otherwise be able to use it as a base from which to challenge the English mastery of the island. Orders had in fact been given to assault the fort, but at the last moment they were cancelled. The reasons for this are not at all clear. Some accounts imply that while Sir John Burroughs wanted to capture Fort de la Prée, the Duke was anxious to press on to St Martin and exploit his initial success. Other accounts blame Burroughs for the decision not to assault the fort. He was said to be opposed to the whole idea of lingering on Ré, and simply wanted to plunder the island before moving on to the larger one of Oleron, where there were no forts capable of offering any resistance and only a small French defending force. Burroughs, according to these accounts, feared that if Fort de la Prée were taken it would encourage Buckingham to besiege the citadel at St Martin, which was a far bigger undertaking. Sir John may also have been influenced by his memories of the Cadiz expedition, in which he had attempted to storm Fort Puntal but had been beaten off. Whatever the reason, however, Fort de la Prée was left to its own devices, and the English army made its circuitous way south-west to Ste Marie before turning due north towards the town of La Flotte.[56]

As Buckingham and his troops approached La Flotte, on Sunday 15 July, a large force of enemy cavalry and infantry made its appearance, but retired without giving battle. Buckingham then took formal possession of the town – which the mainly protestant inhabitants were only too glad to surrender to him. He did not allow his men to stay within its walls, however, but quartered them in the open fields, where he likewise spent the night, on a camp bed, with one cloak over him and another serving as his pillow. On the following day he went back into La Flotte, accompanied by Soubise, for the burial of Sir William Heydon, whose body was interred in the protestant cemetery there. Buckingham's nephew, young Lord Feilding, was one of the pallbearers, and the whole ceremony was carried out 'in the best manner my Lord General could devise'.[57]

Buckingham and his army spent the night of the 16th also in the field, but were woken in the early hours by torrential rain – a sudden change from the hot weather they had hitherto enjoyed. On the morning of the 17th, however, the skies gradually cleared and by midday the soldiers were once again on the march. Buckingham and Soubise were at the head of the column, more than a mile long, which wound its way west towards St Martin. As they drew near the citadel, which stands on the sea's edge at the eastern corner of the town, they saw enemy horse and foot coming out, as if to give battle. Buckingham therefore turned inland and skirted the town so that he could approach it from the far side, where the guns of the citadel could not reach. A small force of French cavalry ventured forward to reconnoitre, but beat a hasty retreat when the English ordnance opened up on them. The inhabitants of the town, most of whom were protestant, then sent out a flag of truce and offered to surrender. By late afternoon Buckingham was master of St Martin.[58]

V

Toiras and his army had retreated to the citadel, which squatted like a huge petrified starfish at the water's edge. At the point of each of the four stars was a bastion, and on the landward sides the citadel was protected by a deep ditch. But although it looked imposing, the citadel, which had only been started a year earlier, was far from finished. In some places there was no parapet, and since the roofs had not been constructed as yet there was very little shelter for the garrison. Water was in short supply, and while Toiras had taken advantage of the delay in the English advance to gather in provisions from the surrounding countryside, he did not have sufficient for a long siege. In fact his men were so disheartened that they would have welcomed some good excuse for abandoning the citadel. An immediate English assault might have done the trick, but Sir John Burroughs, who surveyed the fort with a practised (and jaundiced?) eye, gave his opinion that it was too strong to be taken by storm. He also thought that it was too well provisioned to be easily starved out, and again suggested that the best thing to do was plunder the island and cross over to Oleron. Buckingham, however, thought otherwise. It would be a dishonour to quit the island while its chief stronghold was unsubdued, and he was not convinced that it would be a long job to starve the citadel into surrender, particularly as his captains assured him that they would maintain an impregnable blockade from the sea. If he could follow up his initial victory at the Pointe de Sablanceaux by capturing the citadel of St Martin, he would not only win glory for himself and redeem the reputation of English arms. He would also give the signal that the Huguenots, the foreign princes and the malcontent nobles were all waiting for. English victory on the battlefield would set the ball rolling that would, he felt sure, topple the Cardinal and bring down with him the Jesuit party that was leading France into alliance with Spain and the Habsburgs. This was certainly the view of Rohan, who was later to write that the success of the English in landing on Ré had created a great stir at the French court, and that if it had been followed up swiftly by the capture of the citadel, 'there was every probability of a great change in the face of affairs'. Richelieu's many enemies were only awaiting the outcome of the operation in order to declare themselves openly. Montagu had returned to England with news that the rulers of Savoy and Lorraine were 'ready to assist the King's actions', and had been sent back again to urge them to respond immediately to the English initiative. Meanwhile the Venetian ambassador in France was reporting that 'there is no Frenchman who does not rejoice at the success of the English against his country, such is the universal detestation of the government'. Nobody knew better than Richelieu himself how important it was for his survival that the citadel should hold out. He persuaded Louis to write to Toiras and give him his royal word that no effort would be spared to send him supplies. He also issued orders that all the ships' captains in the neighbourhood should be asked for their advice on how best to get provisions into the citadel. He set them a time limit of 5 August.[59]

By that date, however, if all went according to Buckingham's plans, substantial reinforcements would have arrived for the English army. The Duke had enough troops to cope with the immediate task of besieging the citadel, but if operations continued for any length of time he would need more men to replace the sick and wounded and also to guard the coasts of the island against French relief attempts. In the short run, however, the major impact of the arrival of English reinforcements would be on the enemy, for the appearance of several thousand additional English troops would demonstrate to the disheartened garrison that while their own king was powerless to aid them, the English, with their mastery of the seas, could come and go at pleasure. The effect of this on the morale of the citadel's defenders was easy to calculate.

Buckingham had foreseen that 'upon some probable success he might have, there might be cause of supplying him', and before he left England he had made arrangements for a further four thousand men to be sent him, half from Ireland and the other half from England. This was one of the last matters he had discussed with Charles before he left Portsmouth, for it was up to the King – with the assistance of Buckingham's friends and servants – to make sure that the Duke's absence did not result in any slackening of the pace of proceedings at home. On 2 July, while Buckingham was still at sea, Conway wrote to the Lord Treasurer, reminding him of the need to 'consider of all necessaries for sending the two thousand men to the Duke', and a few days later it was reported that the reinforcements were to be ready within six weeks, if only money could be found. The major source of money was the forced loans, which were levied with even greater strictness after the Duke's departure, and those who refused to pay were arrested and imprisoned. Yet although the forced loans had brought in nearly £250,000 by mid-July this was far from sufficient for the needs of the royal service. When the Lord Treasurer was pressed for money he announced that he had none, since Buckingham had taken it all to Ré, and Sir John Coke observed that while 'the inferior orbs of action are ready enough for motion . . . money, the *primus motor*, doth retard us all in our ends'.[60]

Charles fully appreciated the need to speed up the supply of funds for the expedition, and wrote a peremptory letter to the Lord Treasurer in his own hand, telling him that his delays 'makes [sic] me impatient, even almost beyond patience'. Charles was not simply unloading on to one of his ministers the blame for his own negligence, for he had already initiated a number of schemes for improving the royal finances. As he told Buckingham, in a letter written at the end of July, 'I have set the project for the Mint on foot, and the raising of my Customs, which I hope will prosper well; as likewise the loans, which upon your going, in hope of oversight, went on somewhat slowly, but now, seeing the contrary, mends [sic] their pace again.'[61]

No steps had yet been taken to press more soldiers. As Conway told Carle-

ton, 'the counties in which those two thousand men shall be levied are designed, and letters ready written to them, against we shall hear of the success
of the fleet'. There was obviously much to be said for waiting for definite news
of the fortunes of the expedition before sending away reinforcements, but no
reason – other than a lack of any real sense of urgency – for delaying the
preliminary impressment, which was likely to take several weeks, if not
months. Buckingham assumed that the men would be ready and waiting to go
as soon as he called for them, and on 18 July he sent Sir William Beecher to
England to give an account of his initial success and to hasten the despatch of
supplies and reinforcements. Beecher arrived at Plymouth on the 27th, and
four days later the Privy Council sent off orders to the Lord Lieutenants to
raise two thousand men. Everything now depended on the speed and efficiency
with which this was done. Meanwhile Buckingham was optimistic about his
chances of victory, and told Conway that the citadel was being cut off from
the land by entrenchments. When this was completed, the enemy would, he
hoped, 'be so well penned in, both by sea and land, that they will receive no
assistance from either. For all our shipping is so dispersed round about the
island that unless some fatality happens, which cannot yet be foreseen, no
considerable succour can come unto them.' The citadel, he added, although it
was unfinished, was so strongly built on rocky ground that there was no
possibility of undermining it. The garrison would have to be starved out, and
this might be a long job. But if the operation was successful then the other
elements of the plan would begin to operate and 'a strong party [of the
Huguenots] will come in of itself, which is one of the commodities that would
be gained by this conquest'. These hopes were well grounded, for at the end of
July Rohan wrote to his brother Soubise to tell him that he would take up
arms at the beginning of September, whether or not he received the promised
cavalry from Savoy. By October he hoped to be well ensconced at Montauban,
with a force of six thousand foot and six hundred horse, and if, as Montagu
had apparently assured him, an English landing took place in Guienne, near
Bordeaux, he would be well placed to support it by attacking the enemy in
the rear. 'The rude beginning in the Isle of Ré,' he added, 'hath put our
enemies, even in these parts, into a fear. It is the fairest action done in our
days. Therefore we must not leave off in so fair a way.' Rohan also told
Soubise that he had advised the Duke of Savoy to commit himself to the fight.
Charles Emmanuel had a substantial army of four thousand cavalry and ten
thousand infantry, and Rohan had assured him that if he chose to invade
Provence and Languedoc, where the protestants were thick on the ground, he
would meet little or no resistance.[62]

Buckingham did not rely upon starvation alone to drive the citadel to surrender. He ordered his cannon to be set up and was assured by his master
gunner that in a very short time the defenders would be battered into submission. The French were very alarmed when the English shot began to fall near
the windmills on which they relied for their corn, and immediately opened
counter fire. It soon became clear that the master gunner's optimism had been
unfounded, for it was the English batteries which were bombarded into

silence. No doubt if Sir William Heydon had been alive he would have ensured that the batteries were better sited. But mistakes were not confined to the artillery. The officers responsible for entrenching, for example, carried on their operations so far from the citadel that the enemy were able to push out counter-defences in front of the walls. Only after some five or six weeks was it decided to take the English trenches closer in, whereupon the French 'cheeringly told us that they thought we had been lost and wondered where we had lay hidden all the while'. Buckingham had chosen a skilled engineer, a man who had 'the experience of all forts', to go with him on the expedition, but his other officers were lamentably inexperienced in such matters. One of them, though he was described as a chief engineer, was said to have been 'never but a simple overseer of pioneers before', while another was so unskilled 'as he cast up the trench the wrong way'. It is hardly surprising that Buckingham wrote to Conway to tell him that more engineers 'would not be unwelcome to us', and also to Coke, to ask him to persuade 'Cornelis, the Dutch engineer' to join him in Ré. Meanwhile he conscripted into service his own gardener, John Tradescant, who had a good eye for the lay-out of a park and no doubt found this useful when it came to designing trenchworks.[63]

Back in England the King was keeping up the pressure on his ministers and officers to send Buckingham reinforcements as quickly as possible. He again wrote to the Lord Treasurer, this time in even more peremptory terms. 'I look to hear that those things I sent Beecher to you about are despatched,' he told him.

For if Buckingham should not now be supplied, not in show but substantially, having so bravely and (I thank God) successfully begun his expedition, it were an irrecoverable shame to me and all this nation; and those that either hinders or, according to their several places, furthers not this action as much as they may, deserves to make their end at Tyburn.

A day later the Privy Council formally requested the Treasurer and the Chancellor of the Exchequer 'to advise and consider by what means a present provision of money may be made to defray the charges both of the transportation of the said two thousand men for one-and-twenty days, and likewise for the supplying of them with victuals for their service'. The Council also sent a sharply worded letter to the Lord Deputy of Ireland, asking him why the troops which were supposed to have been sent from there to Ré had not yet set sail. They reminded him 'how much His Majesty may suffer in his honour, being now engaged in so important an action', and expressly required him 'to hasten the sending away of the aforesaid troops by all possible means'.[64]

Buckingham was already suffering from shortage of manpower, for several regiments had to be deployed along the coast, keeping a lookout for any French forces that might land there. The rest were fully employed in manning the trenches that cut off the citadel, and the long hours which they had to spend in the open, exposed to the endless rain of that exceptionally wet summer, produced 'catarrhs, diseases of the lungs, burning fevers and dysenteries' which rapidly reduced their numbers. In order to relieve the pressure on those who were still fit enough to carry out their duties, Buckingham took five hundred mariners from his fleet and formed them into an infantry company. But this brought into the open the latent hostility between soldiers and sailors. 'The land commanders, especially the younger ones, took it in great snuff' reported one observer, 'and so belaboured it as . . . [the sailors] were shortly after returned to their old quarters aboard'.[65]

Buckingham's main concern was to ensure that no enemy vessels should get in to the relief of the citadel. A few small boats had, in fact, slipped through the arc of English warships, and Buckingham therefore ordered the construction of a floating stockade, made out of masts and long pieces of timber fastened together with iron chains. One end was embedded in the shore on the far side of the citadel, and from that point the stockade swung out in a half moon to the near side, where it was also firmly fixed to land. Had it survived, it would have cut off the citadel completely from the sea, but the impact of the waves on its rigid structure was too great for it to bear, and it rapidly disintegrated. A more flexible barrier was then created by taking a number of ships and linking them with thick cables, on which were threaded empty barrels and small boats. This floating dyke, which moved up and down with the waves, seemed to have solved the problem of blockading the citadel from the sea, and Buckingham delightedly announced that only birds would now be able to get in to the defenders. But he had reckoned without the gales and storms which churned up the waters and made the barrier swing so violently that it became a menace to the entire English fleet and had to be hastily dismantled. A similar lack of success attended the floating island, constructed of overturned ships, which was designed to shelter English gunners and bowmen as they beat off relief vessels. At first it was thought to be 'of great moment for keeping the enemy from our shore. But at last, it being bruised and shattered with the winds and force of the waves, it came to nothing.'[66]

On 14 August Buckingham wrote to the absent Beecher to ask him why he had not heard from him. 'Our provisions grow low,' he said, 'and our men decrease', and he therefore pressed him 'to use some diligence in your solicitation of supplies, both of men, monies and munition'. Beecher had not as it happened been backward in this respect, and the ponderous administrative machinery was at last creaking into action. On 13 August Charles sent a letter to the Duke to tell him that 'I have made ready a supply of victuals, munition, four hundred men for recruits, and £1,400 ready money, to be brought to you by Beecher — who, by the grace of God, shall set sail within these eight days. Two regiments of a thousand men apiece . . . shall be embarked by the tenth of September . . . I hope likewise ye shall have two thousand men out of Scotland, under the command of my Lord Morton and Sir William Balfour.'[67]

Not all of Buckingham's correspondents, however, shared the King's optimism. The Earl of Dorset wrote to warn his friend that some people were 'diabolically disposed to hinder and distract these courses'; while Middlesex — who had by now been reconciled to the Duke — told him that all his designs would come to nothing 'without an ample and present supply [of money], which is not to be hoped for in your absence'. He therefore advised him to return home as quickly as possible, but Buckingham was determined not to leave the island until reinforcements arrived. As he told his mother, 'till I have means from England wherewithal to settle this army here, I cannot with my honour leave them'. His letter was in reply to one from the Countess that must have confirmed his worst fears. 'I am very sorry you have entered into so great business and so little care to supply [your] wants,' she told him. His pleas for urgent assistance were little regarded in England, 'where all is merry and well pleased', and the relief ships were not even 'victualled as yet, nor mariners to go with them. As for monies, the kingdom will not supply our expenses, and every man groans under the burden of the times.'[68]

Buckingham was so short of money for his own and his army's needs that he asked his wife and his mother to lend him some. The Duchess immediately instructed her steward, William Bold, to use £200 of her housekeeping allowance 'for the preparation of provision for my lord at the Isle of Ré'. The Countess, though she wanted to help, was unable to do so. 'If I had a world, you should command it', she told her son, but she reminded him that she had recently, and with his full consent, laid out all her available capital on the purchase of a new property. 'I never dreamed you should have needed any of my help, for if I had, there should have wanted all, and myself, before you.' Edward Nicholas reported that Buckingham had spent £2,700 of his own money to pay for the victuals that were to go with Beecher, but more than £3,000 was still needed. Lord Treasurer Marlborough promised to provide this, but everything depended upon the farmers of the petty Customs, who were negotiating to buy a year's extension of their lease, and who were 'so scrupulous and dilatory that we cannot possibly draw the money from them'. Nevertheless Marlborough was hopeful that enough would be forthcoming to pay for the four hundred men and the provisions that Beecher was to take back to Ré. As for the two thousand men who were supposed to follow at the beginning of September, assignments had been made for the estimated cost of £7,700, but 'there is now a surcharge of £3,700, besides above £3,000 to the office of the ordnance. This makes the work much more difficult.' The truth of the matter was that the King could not, from his own resources, provide sufficient funds to keep the military operations going, even though they were on a far smaller scale than those undertaken by other European powers. In late August, therefore, the Privy Council sent letters to county and municipal authorities throughout England to remind them that 'whatsoever His Majesty hath hitherto raised upon his plate, jewels, lands, loans and sales is already issued and employed for the public. And now, being in open action, his fleet and army abroad, which by God's goodness have prosperously succeeded, honour and reason require to have the undertaking seconded and supported.' In view of these considerations it was their clear duty, the Council declared, to hasten the collection of all outstanding loans.[69]

The four hundred men whom Beecher was to take back with him were ordered to be at their assembly point by 20 August, but although they arrived on time there was no trace of the provision ships which were to accompany him, nor of the money that he had been promised. When the King heard of this he wrote yet another angry letter to the Treasurer. 'It did make me much wonder,' he said, 'to understand from Beecher that at his coming to Portsmouth neither ships, munition nor money met him, as was agreed and (as I was made believe) were certainly ta'en order for.' Charles announced that he was sending the Earl of Holland

to know the cause and authors of this fault, and to hinder the like in time to come — at least, to give a fair warning to those [to] whom it may appertain that I am and shall be displeased to see business of great consequence so ill handled. I say no more, but I expect a better account of the two thousand men, not looking that ye should neglect the rest because I do not mention them.

This letter was sent on 23 August. On the following day Buckingham wrote to Nicholas from St Martin to remind him 'how nearly it concerns me to have speedy supplies out of England, both of men, monies and victuals . . . that are daily expected by our army, which, in hope of some ease out of England, hath hitherto performed extraordinary duty'. If only the supplies and reinforcements had been sent him, as promised, 'I had by this time forced the citadel [and] disposed of part of my fleet upon the coasts of France and Spain'.[70]

The provision ships for which Beecher was fretting at Portsmouth were still in the Thames in late August, waiting for the arms and munitions which the ordnance office had undertaken to supply. But the ordnance office was notoriously inefficient, and the Privy Council therefore gave orders that whatever equipment was available should be despatched at once to Portsmouth. The rest could go with the two thousand men who were to be sent off later under the command of the Earl of Holland. All Beecher now needed was £14,000 to pay Buckingham's army and keep it in the field. On 28 August Sir John Coke wrote to Conway to tell him that agreement had at last been reached with the farmers of the petty Customs and that they had promised to provide this amount forthwith. However £4,000 of it would have to be used to meet the demands of Burlamachi, so the Duke would have to make do with £10,000 for the time being. The remaining £4,000 would go with Holland.[71]

It was on 18 July that Buckingham had sent Beecher to England. He expected him back within a few weeks, but when September arrived and there was still no sign of him, the Duke began to lose heart. He poured out his feelings to Robert Mason, his secretary,

protesting that never his despatches to divers princes, nor the great business of a fleet, of an army, of a siege, of a treaty, of war, of peace, both on foot together and all of them in his head at a time, did not so much break his repose as a conceit that some at home, under His Majesty, of whom he had well deserved, were now content to forget him.

If Buckingham had any doubts of the strength of Charles's affection, however, they were unfounded. In late August the King wrote to assure him that 'no distance of place nor length of time can make me slacken, much less diminish my love to you'; and, in an unusually reflective passage, he advised Buckingham to act the miser and gloat over his riches. 'I think it is not unacceptable to you to bid you look of that that I esteem to be the greatest riches, and now hardest to be found – True Friendship; there being no style justlier to be given to any man that that to me, of being your loving, faithful, constant friend.'[72]

The King had been very upset by the news that an attempt had been made to assassinate Buckingham. From time to time soldiers from the citadel gave themselves up to the besieging forces, and one of these, when he was brought in to the Duke for questioning, looked so guilty that Ashburnham ordered him to be searched. He was found to be carrying a poisoned dagger, and under threat of torture confessed that he had been sent out expressly by Toiras to kill the Duke. When Toiras heard of this, he protested his innocence, with 'deep oaths and imprecations'. It may be that the whole story was an invention, designed to whip up public opinion at home in Buckingham's favour – though the Duke's letters suggest that he himself thought it was true. Whatever his opinion, however, he did not break off contact with Toiras. In late August, hearing that Toiras was asking if there were any melons in the island, he sent him twelve as a gift. Toiras riposted by presenting Buckingham with half a dozen bottles of orange-flower water and some boxes of Cyprus powder. The Duke sent these back to England as a present for his wife, but Kate, fearing that they might be poisoned, like the dagger, did not dare use them. However she thanked her husband for his kind thoughts and gave him the welcolm tidings that 'my child begins to stir strongly'.[73]

The exchange of courtesies between Buckingham and Toiras was so frequent and so marked that the two men seemed more like friends paying respects to one another than enemies. The English colonels, who made up Buckingham's council of war, were mystified by the constant parleys, particularly as the Duke never revealed what was discussed in them. But these civilities concealed a serious purpose. Buckingham knew that the defenders of the citadel were short of food and water, and he made their condition worse by sending a party of troops to burn some of their windmills and poison their wells. He also ordered that all the Roman Catholic women in St Martin who had husbands in the citadel were to be driven out of the town and left under the walls of the fortress. As he anticipated, the defenders opened their gates to let them in, and the pressure on limited supplies grew markedly worse. Toiras had to set guards over the remaining wells, and bread was rationed. This was particularly serious since most of the inhabitants of the citadel had nothing to live on except bread and water. They were also exposed to the weather, for there were no tiles to cover the quickly constructed wooden huts, and the incessant rain turned the earth floors into lakes of mud that rose halfway up their legs. The aristocratic officers in the citadel, on whom Toiras relied to maintain morale, were not used to such privations and did not share their commander's determination to hold out at all costs. They did not dare show their feelings openly, but they gave covert encouragement to the discontented soldiers who were pressing Toiras to come to terms. Buckingham knew all this from the many deserters who fled to the English, and the object of his frequent exchanges with Toiras was to open the way to a negotiated surrender.[74]

By the beginning of September it seemed as though the situation was developing in Buckingham's favour. On the 1st the inhabitants of La Rochelle at last accepted the offer which Beecher, on Buckingham's behalf, had made to them seven weeks earlier, and committed themselves openly to support the English. A day or two later a squadron of ships from Ireland anchored off the island and landed more than two thousand troops under Sir Ralph Bingley. The arrival of these 'long-expected succours' made an immediate difference. Previously the soldiers had been compelled to keep watch every other night, but now they were on duty only one night out of three. Two thousand additional troops were still not enough for safety, but they were a sign that the army in Ré had not been abandoned, and there were hopes that Beecher would shortly arrive with another two thousand men. Colonel Conway, writing to his father on 4 September, showed how the mood of the army had changed. 'The weakness of our troops hath been such', he told him, 'that we could not make approaches to force the enemy. Now that the Irish troops are come we shall go roundly to work with them.' He added a tribute to the way in which Buckingham had kept up the spirits of the army. Without him, he said, 'we should certainly have been discouraged. Our wants, and the appearance of what the enemy would do, did make some of the best to think of their safety. His good affection to the honour of the King and good of the religion made him despise the danger.' In another letter a few days later, Conway told Sir John Coke of plans to put a garrison of five hundred men into La Rochelle, and at least as many more when Beecher arrived. But he estimated that the town would need a force of eight or ten thousand men if it were effectively to withstand a siege, and this could not be provided until the citadel was taken. The arrival of the Irish made a successful conclusion to the siege more likely, but there were still many obstacles to overcome, and continued assistance from home was essential. 'Our engineers would in Holland be accounted ignorant, our provision to work small, our number of men few . . . . Winter comes on; our men will fall sick; but if we lose this island it shall be your faults in England . . . '[75]

The arrival of the Irish troops, which sent spirits soaring among the besiegers, had a correspondingly depressing effect upon those inside the citadel. They had had no certain news from the mainland and felt that they were forgotten men. The situation was so desperate that Toiras called for volunteers to swim to the mainland. Three men came forward and set out on their hazardous expedition. One was drowned; another gave himself up to an English ship; but the third arrived, exhausted, on the coast near La Rochelle, and was carried to the Duke of Angoulême, who commanded the army which had been assembled to invest the rebellious city. Angoulême immediately sent a despatch to Louis, to tell him that the citadel could not could hold out much longer, and that if he wished to preserve Ré as part of his dominions he would have to raise yet another army and send it across to Fort de la Prée. This would have to be done before further English reinforcements arrived, since otherwise there would be little chance of the French regaining control of the island.[76]

At the same time as he sent the swimmers to the mainland, Toiras also accepted Buckingham's suggestion that representatives of each side should go to Paris and try to persuade Louis to accept a negotiated settlement. Buckingham chose his relative, John Ashburnham, for this delicate and difficult task, and he set off in company with Toiras's delegate, the Baron de Saint Surin. But Louis, at Richelieu's prompting, refused to give audience to Ashburnham and declared that he would not listen to any overture of peace until the invaders had withdrawn from his territory. Richelieu argued that the English were negotiating from a position of weakness. Buckingham, he told the king, 'has received his reinforcements which do not amount to much. Now he asks for peace. It is a sign that he does not feel himself strong enough to make war.'[77]

The problem of Toiras and the citadel still remained, however, for Toiras had supported Buckingham's proposal in the hope that it would bring an honourable end to the tedious and exhausting siege. Richelieu therefore wrote to tell him that there could be no question of negotiating while English troops remained on French soil. The King was going to La Rochelle in person to take command of the army assembled there, and no effort would be spared to ensure that the citadel of St Martin was relieved. At the same time, Richelieu wrote to Gaston, Duke of Orleans, announcing that the King had given him overall responsibility for the operations against the English in Ré. This was a gesture of trust on Louis's part, for his brother had been among the leading malcontents and was thought in some quarters to have been privy to Buckingham's plans.[78]

When the Duke of Savoy heard of Ashburnham's mission to Paris he professed great alarm, on the grounds that Buckingham was trying to negotiate a separate peace in spite of promises not to do so. Charles Emmanuel made this an excuse for not carrying out his own promises both to aid Rohan and to intervene directly in France, but in fact he was waiting to see how events developed before committing himself. If the citadel had fallen, he might well have acted. But he was reluctant to make any move until he had some assurance that the Spaniards would not stab him in the back from Milan. This was why he had pressed the English to open negotiations with Spain, and even as late as the first week of September Scaglia, who was still in the Netherlands, was of the opinion that the Spaniards were genuinely interested in a settlement and would prefer a peace with England to one with France. But Philip IV had already concluded a secret agreement with France, and at this very moment was demonstrating his commitment to it by ordering that a squadron of Spanish ships should be sent to Ré to aid his new allies. A copy of the Franco-Spanish treaty was given to the Archduchess Isabella by a special Spanish envoy at the beginning of September, and she now notified Rubens, who had hitherto been kept in ignorance of it. Rubens immediately wrote to Gerbier, telling him 'that I find my masters very much agitated in this affair. They feel annoyed and affronted by Olivares, whose passion has prevailed over all reason and consideration . . . . The majority of the council of Spain were of our opinion, but its head has forced all to accept his.' Rubens also wrote to Buckingham to assure him that the Archduchess and Spinola had negotiated in good faith. He hoped that it would be possible to continue the discussions, but from the English point of view there was nothing to be said for this. At the beginning of October, therefore, Gerbier was instructed to break off what Coke described as 'those delusory treaties by which we have been so often abused'.[79]

Meanwhile Wat Montagu, who had returned to Turin, was trying to spur England's allies into concerted action. In late September he wrote to Rohan to assure him that the Duke of Savoy and the Count of Soissons were still of the same mind and would shortly commit themselves. As for the planned English landing in Guienne, this would not now be possible, but he suggested that Rohan should make for the Rhone, where he would be well placed to communicate with Savoy. He would also be near Orange, whose governor had already given evident signs of goodwill and would presumably provide a refuge for Soissons when the Count at last declared himself. Rohan had no objections to following this course, but he was not free to do so. He was having great difficulty in winning over a number of important Huguenot centres in Languedoc. They feared reprisals from the French government and they also suspected that Rohan was motivated more by personal ambition than concern for his fellow protestants; as the magistrates of one town informed him 'they knew no reason of state or religion which would permit them to embrace his party and that of the English'. Rohan, then, remained bogged down in Languedoc, while Savoy and Soissons waited for a good augury — such as the fall of the citadel — before intervening. The only signs of activity came from Lorraine, where the young duke was arming rapidly. But Louis XIII — who could command men and money on a scale that made English efforts seem derisory — raised a powerful force and sent it to the frontier of Lorraine to hold the duke in check.[80]

By mid-September it was clear to Buckingham that the fulfilment of his master plan depended upon the capitulation of the citadel, and he bent all his efforts to achieve this. He was eagerly awaiting Beecher's return, because he took it for granted that Sir William would bring with him not simply money and provisions but also two more regiments, which could swing the fortunes of war decisively in favour of the English. But Beecher had only four hundred men with him, and as late as 13 September he had still not left Portsmouth. He was held up by the usual shortage of mariners, who fled from the King's service like the plague, and also by contrary winds. It looked as though he might not reach Ré before the other reinforcements which the Council had given orders for. The two thousand English recruits who were to make up the two new regiments had been instructed to rendezvous at Plymouth not later than 10 September, while a further two thousand troops, this time from Scotland, were due at Dover by the 15th. On 11 September, however, the mayor of Plymouth informed the Council that not all the new recruits had arrived. 'Most of the conductors have left upon the way a part of the numbers committed to their charge,' he reported. He added that there could be no question of these deficiencies being made up locally, and that in any case no officers had arrived to take charge of the men.[81]

Nicholas was, as always, doing his best to overcome the inertia of the administrative system. On 17 September he wrote to the ordnance officers to remind them that arms and munitions for the new recruits must be provided at all costs. 'If there be any stop in any of these services for want of money or otherwise, you are to make it known, and I have order to attend my Lord Treasurer to supply you.' Ten days later he instructed one of his officers to go aboard the ships in the Thames which had been appointed to carry the English troops to Ré, and find out why they were still there. The Earl of Holland, he reminded him, was ready to leave for Plymouth to take command, but there was no sense in his going there if the troop transports had not arrived. Nicholas told the officer to send up the names of captains who had been negligent, and not to accept any excuses about shortage of men, since the ships' commanders had already certified that they had full complements. 'You know the importance of this service, and how expedient it is that all diligence be used in hastening those supplies to His Majesty's fleet,' Nicholas reminded him. 'Therefore I pray fail not to employ your best care in the expedition hereof.' This letter has the authentic Buckingham ring, but without the presence of the Duke himself matters progressed at a snail's pace.[82]

Buckingham meanwhile was fretting in St Martin and scanning the horizon for signs of Beecher. He had to try to keep up the spirits of his troops, who 'now give themselves for men neglected and forgotten in England', and he was not helped by the loss of Sir John Burroughs, who was killed by enemy fire on 11 September. Burroughs and Buckingham had not seen eye to eye on strategy, and there was probably a good deal of truth in De Vic's comment that Burroughs — who was not a young man and had learnt his trade in the defensive campaigns that the Dutch were compelled to fight — was 'fitter for . . . the keeping of a place already gotten than to find out or prosecute (with requisite activeness) a design upon the enemy'. Nevertheless it was very useful for an inexperienced commander like Buckingham to be able to draw on the accumulated wisdom of older, battle-tried officers. Sir William Heydon had been one of these, but he was drowned at landing, and now Sir John Burroughs had gone. In their place Buckingham turned for advice increasingly to the German, John Dalbier, who had previously served as paymaster to Count Mansfeld. Dalbier was not lacking in experience, having spent many years in the profession of arms, but as De Vic noted, he was 'not of that strength of understanding and other parts as are necessary to those that will have a power with His Excellency'.[83]

It was Dalbier whom Buckingham chose, in mid-September, to go to England with a letter to the King, pressing for the despatch of the two regiments from Plymouth with all speed. The Duke also repeated his demand for more engineers, and for wooden planks and spars with which to carry out mining operations. The timber, he suggested, should be sent on ships of shallow draught, which could then be used as artillery carriers to beat off enemy attempts to re-victual the citadel, because the English warships were so high out of the water that their shot often passed harmlessly over the enemy's masts. As for what would happen after the citadel was taken, Buckingham was thinking in terms of a garrison of two thousand men. This would be big enough to repel any French assault, and with the English fleet in control of the seas around the island the French would think twice about committing too many of their forces to operations there. Buckingham said nothing about attacking other parts of the French coast, but he had only postponed, not abandoned, his plan for a landing in force near Bordeaux, and perhaps it was for this reason that he asked Charles to provide a further four thousand men, in addition to the English and Scottish troops now supposedly ready to leave. He also asked for more money with which to pay the larger army. The £14,000 which Beecher was bringing would not suffice for this. He would need a further £16,000.[84]

On 20 September Charles replied to the Duke, and told him that he approved all his designs. 'Be confident of what secourse [succour] these fro-ward times can yield,' said Charles, 'which though they cannot be according to mind, yet by God's grace shall be enough for your fortune to maintain a just cause.' He chided his friend for exposing himself too rashly to danger, 'there being more inconvenience in it than I (almost) dare write', and express-ed the hope that within a week of receiving his letter Buckingham would be able to welcome the Earl of Holland with the longed-for reinforcements. In fact it was Beecher who arrived first, returning to Ré on 23 September, nearly ten weeks after he had left on what everybody imagined would be a fleeting visit to England. He brought with him a mere four hundred men – which, as one soldier commented, would not go far to meet the needs of 'this poor handful of an army' – and provisions and money 'much less than were ex-pected'. Nevertheless the defenders of the citadel were disheartened by this further evidence of English determination, especially since they had no certain news of any attempts to relieve their own dire necessities. Toiras's men were on the verge of mutiny, and in order to pacify them he sent his deputy to Buckingham to know on what terms the garrison would be allowed to surren-der. It was at this crucial juncture that Buckingham's inexperience and lack of sound advisers showed through. Had Burroughs or Heydon been alive and present they would no doubt have drawn up the terms on the spot. But the Duke merely professed his admiration for the courage of the garrison, gave assurances that he would treat them well, and invited the deputy to come back on the following day – which meant a valuable respite for Toiras. However, when the deputy reappeared on the 27th, Buckingham informed him that he wished Toiras to draw up his own terms of surrender, and would give him three hours in which to do so. Toiras replied that he would need at least twenty-four to prepare his conditions, and Buckingham agreed to allow him this. The defenders thereby won a further respite.[85]

On the mainland, at Sables d'Olonne, Richelieu and his assistants were straining every nerve to prepare a relief fleet for the citadel. They were spurred on by Louis XIII, who could think of little else and had a pocket compass made for him so that he could tell which way the winds were blowing. By the night of the 27th everything was ready, and a squadron of thirty-five small boats, crammed with men and provisions, set out to make the dangerous crossing. Their password was *Vive le roi. Passer ou mourir*. It was a very dark night with a high tide and strong current pushing the boats towards St Martin. They were also helped by the wind, which that morning had shifted direction and begun to blow from the north-west. Buckingham was on the lookout and had warned his men to be ready. He had secret intelligence that the French would make for the western tip of the island and sent a number of ships to intercept them. But at the last moment the French decided to sail direct for St Martin and go straight through the blockading fleet. These tactics worked superbly. The small boats slipped silently past the towering English warships in the black night, and even when they were spotted and the alarm was raised there was such confusion, with guns firing and ships moving in all directions, that twenty-nine boats reached the shelter of the shore outside the citadel.[86]

Buckingham, when he realised what was happening, took charge of a number of small English vessels that he had specially deputed to keep watch, and led them in a desperate attempt to destroy the French boats before they could unload their precious cargo. But he was ill seconded, for the sailors, on whose vigilance and courage he had relied, hung back, and 'many of them did very ill perform their duty'. Buckingham still did not give up hope, however. As day broke he ordered the English warships to keep up heavy fire on the French boats (which were still fully laden) while a fireship was prepared. When this was ready it was 'with great hazard and resolution . . . set on fire and put in among the barques'. But as luck would have it the wind dropped, and the soldiers in the citadel were able to use long poles to push the fireship out to sea, where it burnt harmlessly. That night the French boats were unloaded, and the next morning the besieging English troops were greeted with the sight of chickens, turkeys, hams and tongues, stuck up on pikes above the parapets by the delighted and triumphant French garrison.[87]

There could have been no greater blow to English hopes, for the citadel had been relieved at the very moment when it was about to capitulate. De Vic summed up the effect on the besiegers. 'It was impossible for me to have imagined so sudden and so great a change as I saw in us upon the coming of the last succour to the citadel,' he wrote. 'Such an alteration there was upon that unhappy accident, of joy into sadness, confidence into despair, triumphs to retreats, as I can hardly conceive the same spirits had been capable of so much contrariety.' Buckingham summoned a council of war, and his colonels were of the opinion that the English army should pull out of Ré while it was still able to do so. They argued that

by the late coming of their succours and supplies they were kept in such continual weakness that they could not advance their works . . . . That by the extreme duties, and the immoderate eating of grapes (which no care could prevent), the soldiers were so wasted as there do not now remain above five thousand able men and two thousand five hundred sick men, and the disease runs on so violently as worse is daily to be feared.

They would perhaps have arrived at a different conclusion if they could have been assured of prompt and continuous assistance from England, but the sad truth, which they were forced to acknowledge, was that 'their succours from home arrived always so late as they served only to keep them in lingering weakness'.[88]

The insufficiency of English relief efforts was demonstrated by the fact that the two regiments which had so long been promised had not yet set sail. The King was doing his best to hasten them on. He ordered Sir John Coke to bring him 'an exact account of the state all things stand in belonging to the expedition to the Duke', and he kept up his pressure on the Treasurer and other officers to remove the remaining obstacles to Holland's departure. When Charles wrote to Buckingham on 1 October he told him that the major impediments were 'the hardness of getting mariners, and the slow proceeding of the Commissioners of [the] Navy (which all commissions are subject to), money being readilier furnished than I could have expected in these necessitous times'. He asked Buckingham's forgiveness for the delays and assured him that 'by the grace of God ye shall have no more cause to complain of us; for now we know how to prevent those faults which we, without some experience, could hardly foresee'.[89]

There could be no doubt about the genuineness of Charles's intentions, but goodwill was no substitute for good administration. Sir Humphrey May told Buckingham that the real difficulties occurred when attempts were made to translate desires into actions. 'Our first consent and resolution is quick and speedy,' he said, 'for it is easy for us to set down in paper ships and money and arms and victuals and men. But to congest these materials together, especially in such a penury of money, requires more time than the necessity of your affairs will well permit.' Another of Buckingham's correspondents, the Earl of Dorset, urged him to return at once, for 'your being here would breathe a new life into most men. There is a kind of languishing in all proceedings here . . . . By your absence I perceive how necessary your presence is for the advancement of all actions.' The King had urged Buckingham not to be 'disheartened with our by-past slowness, for by the grace of God it is all past'. Dorset, however, was not so sanguine. 'I fear that all future succours will arrive, both in time and number, far short either [of] your expectation or desert,' he told the Duke. He could not accuse anyone in particular of failing in their endeavours. 'They all seem to intend your good. Yet . . . the care is here to transfer faults, not to remedy them.'[90]

Buckingham was reluctant to abandon Ré, and he did all that was in his power to keep the army in good heart. One foreign observer reported that 'the soldiers themselves do pity him. He is commonly every night in those boats or in the trenches till midnight.' But the fortunes of war were controlled by logistics rather than personal valour and in this respect the English were deficient. Buckingham therefore bowed to his colonels' pressure and agreed to pull out. But no sooner had he done so than Soubise and the representatives of La Rochelle made a powerful plea to him to stay. They promised the English army all the assistance they could give in the way of men and provisions, and the protestant inhabitants of the island did likewise. While Buckingham was considering what to do, Dalbier returned from England with the news that the relief force under the Earl of Holland was at last on its way. The Duke therefore decided to stay on, and accepted the Rochellois' offer to provide ships to strengthen the blockade of the citadel and cut off Fort de la Prée, where it was feared that enemy reinforcements would otherwise be landed. Buckingham still had just enough men to control the landward approaches to the citadel, and once the defenders had consumed the supplies brought in on the 27th the pressure on Toiras to surrender would be intense. But the Duke had no soldiers to spare for operations against an invading enemy force. This was where Holland's regiments would have made all the difference, for if the French relieving army had been thrown back into the sea at the same time as the citadel was held in an iron grip the English would have been assured of victory. Everything depended upon Holland's speedy arrival and, until then, upon the capacity of the English and Rochellois ships to stop the enemy from landing.[91]

Events were to show that this capacity did not, in fact, exist. Despite all attempts to stop them, the French managed to send in small boats to Fort de la Prée, thereby turning it into a bridgehead from which to launch their counter attack. Buckingham could no longer postpone his departure, since there was still no sign of the reinforcements and his men were dying in increasing numbers. But he determined to make an attempt to storm the citadel before he left. Runaways from the garrison had reported that in many places the walls were still unfinished and could be easily scaled, and that their comrades were so disheartened that at the first signs of assault they would surrender. Buckingham therefore gave orders for an attack upon the citadel to be launched on 27 October. The English troops prepared themselves by singing the psalm 'Let God arise and let his enemies be scattered', and then, at the sound of four cannon shot, attacked the citadel from all sides. Under a hail of musket fire they drove the enemy from his outworks, placed their scaling ladders against the walls, and attempted to storm the fortifications. But the scaling ladders were too short, and the defenders pelted their assailants with wooden logs, barrels filled with stones, and anything else that came to hand. The English soldiers fought bravely but their attempt was suicidal, 'for when they almost attained the height of their ladders, and had no further means to go on, casting their threatening eyes about they remained unmovable till they were shot and tumbled down'. The fight lasted some two hours before the retreat was sounded, and the English left several hundred dead on the counterscarp and in the ditches that surrounded the still unvanquished citadel.[92]

For Buckingham and his army there was no question of any further delay. Marshal Schomberg had arrived in the island to take charge of the French relief force and unless the English moved quickly they would be in danger of total annihilation. Buckingham had already decided to make his retreat from the Ile de Loix, which lay to the west of St Martin and was joined to Ré by a narrow causeway flanked by salt marshes. He had given orders for the causeway to be protected by ramparts, but although the engineers had constructed an earthwork they had placed it on the far side of the causeway; in other words it would hold back the enemy from the ships, assuming they got that far, but it would not stop them from forcing their way on to the causeway in the first instance. This example of the engineers' incompetence and lack of experience was confirmed by their failure to put rails on either side of the causeway to stop soldiers falling off.[93]

The English army made its slow way through the hamlet of La Couarde, where Buckingham had placed his musketeers to cover it, and by the late afternoon the vanguard had reached the near end of the causeway, which was some five hundred feet long and only four feet wide. About half the army had passed safely over into the Ile de Loix when the French launched a fierce attack, overran the rearguard, and forced a passage on to the causeway. The result was panic and confusion. The English troops who were massed on the causeway started fighting each other as they struggled to get through to the far end, and hundreds toppled into the salt marshes, where they were either drowned or piked to death by the advancing French. Buckingham, who was already in the Ile de Loix preparing for the embarkation, ordered all the small boats which were at the shore's edge to return to their ships, so that his men should see there was no way of escape by sea, and then returned to the causeway to try and stem the panic flood. He ordered Sir Ralph Bingley and his Irish troops to hold the redoubt which protected the far end of the causeway, and commanded those regiments which had already crossed over to face about and engage the enemy. For one brief moment the battle hung in the balance, as the French troops, pikes at the ready, charged off the causeway and on to the island. But the English officers managed to rally their men, and the French were halted and then thrown back. It was now their turn to flee across the causeway, pursued by the English. They were saved by the gathering darkness and by Buckingham's orders to abandon the chase. His losses had been heavy. More than forty officers had died in the action, seven of them colonels, and among them was his kinsman, Sir Alexander Brett. Another relative, Lord Mountjoy, who commanded the cavalry, had been taken prisoner along with twenty other officers. The French had also captured forty-four standards, which were later carried in triumph to Paris and hung in Notre Dame. As for the losses among the men, it was estimated that about five hundred had been killed and as many more drowned. When these were added to those who had been killed by the enemy or struck down by sickness since the opening of the campaign, the total may well have come to five thousand or more.[94]

Once his army had embarked, Buckingham summoned a council of war to decide what to do next. He was strongly in favour of putting in to La Rochelle, where his men could be used to garrison the town while they awaited the arrival of Holland with the reinforcements. There was little support for this proposal, but the Duke sent a letter to La Rochelle making a formal offer either to enter the town with his army or to return to England and prepare a new expedition. He spent nearly a week waiting for a reply, but like the Earl of Holland it never came. He did not dare wait longer, for bad weather would play havoc with his ships, and there was a danger of infection spreading among the undernourished soldiers. In any case his men had lost the will to fight. They had spent sixteen weeks in the field under exhausting conditions, and during all that time they had received little from England except promises and token supplies. As Sir Allen Apsley wrote to Nicholas from his sick bed on board the *Nonsuch*, 'my soul even melts with tears to think that a state should send so many men and no provision at all for them'.[95]

By a cruel irony the long-promised supplies and reinforcements were at last ready. Holland arrived in Plymouth on 21 October and immediately went on board. Contrary winds kept him fretting in harbour for a further two weeks, but on 6 November his fleet was able to weigh anchor, and on the 8th Sir James Bagg wrote to tell Conway that the ships were out of sight. It was on that same day that Buckingham turned his back on Ré and set sail for home. The winds that held back Holland sped him towards England, and by the 12th he had reached Portsmouth, where he transferred to a smaller vessel in order to go to Plymouth and supervise the reception of the sick and wounded. He had met Holland just off the English coast and had ordered him to return to harbour.[96]

It never occurred to the King to blame Buckingham for what he felt to be his own shortcomings. 'With whatsomever success ye shall come to me,' he wrote to the Duke, 'ye shall be ever welcome, one of my greatest griefs being that I have not been with you in this time of suffering, for I know we would have much eased each other's griefs.' He expressed the same feelings in another letter and gave his opinion 'that in this action you have had honour. All the shame must light upon us here remaining at home.' In order that the whole world should see that he attached no blame to the Duke, Charles sent the Lord Chamberlain, the Earl of Montgomery, to him with yet another letter, bidding him 'to bear these misfortunes with that courage that thou hast showed in all this action', and not to 'make this ill fortune to me irrecoverable by punishing thyself for our faults'. These sentiments were echoed by other of Buckingham's friends. The Lord President, the Earl of Manchester, urged him to 'be not discouraged . . . for no captain or general could play his part better. Would God you could say so by us; then neither seconds nor supplies should have failed you.' And Sir Richard Weston, the Chancellor of the Exchequer, declared that 'the number of your friends and servants who are gone out to meet you, to congratulate your safety, and the personal honour you have gained to yourself, will secure Your Grace that ill fortunes here are not accounted faults'.[97]

Despite the warm reception given him by the King and his friends, Buckingham can have been in little doubt that public opinion was more opposed to him than ever. His wife, Kate, noted sadly that 'by this action he is not any whit the more popular man than when he went'. And Sir Thomas Wentworth – who had been imprisoned for refusing to contribute to the forced loan – expressed a widely-held view when he recorded his belief that the whole affair had been 'ill begun, worse ordered in every particular, and the success accordingly most lamentable . . . . This only every man knows, that since England was England it received not so dishonourable a blow.' Sir Simonds D'Ewes, who was at this time a young lawyer, described the 'sadness and dejectedness almost in every man's face' when the news of the English defeat reached London, and told how the hatred of Buckingham was so intense that 'his coming safe home occasioned almost as much sorrow as the slaughter and perishing of all the rest'. There were reports that Buckingham had deliberately mismanaged the expedition in order to cripple the Huguenots and leave La Rochelle exposed to the fury of Louis and Richelieu. John Rous, a Suffolk clergyman, confided to his diary a rumour current among his parishioners that Toiras and Buckingham had been in league together, and that the whole campaign had been so managed as to give the impression that it was a protestant crusade when in reality it was part of a popish plot. When the sceptical Rous pointed out to the tale-spreaders that many French nobles had been slain in the campaign – which hardly suggested that they were collaborators – he was informed that those who had been killed were nearly all protestant! Rous also recorded a rumour that Buckingham had been sent to the Tower, and referred to the many 'strange rhymes and songs' about the Duke and the Isle of Ré – which, according to one letter writer, was now called 'the Isle of Rue, for the bitter success we had there'. Among the most popular songs was a mock-heroic epic in rhymed couplets that began:

> And art returned again with all thy faults,
> Thou great commander of the all-go-naughts,
> And left the Isle behind thee? What's the matter?
> Did winter make thy teeth begin to chatter?

It accused Buckingham of lack of personal valour as well as sheer incompetence, and urged him in future to stay where he belonged – at Court.

> Let valiant skilful generals be chose
> That dare in blood confront their proudest foes.
> Then there's some hope we may repair our losses
> And make our enemies to end our crosses.
> These things have lost our honour, men surmise:
> Thy treachery, neglect and cowardice.[98]

The object of this vilification was meanwhile attending to the needs of the men who had returned with him. Before leaving on the expedition he had made arrangements for the care of the sick and wounded, and on 20 November he wrote to Sir James Bagg at Plymouth, telling him to 'take an especial and pious care [of them] and let not any reasonable charge be spared that may procure their recovery'. A week later Buckingham ordered rice and oatmeal and some sugar to be sent to Portsmouth to supplement the diet of all those who had fallen sick since their return, and one letter-writer described how 'His Grace hath been all this week going to Portsmouth, to comfort and refresh the relics of our once-flourishing army'. Buckingham also pressed the Privy Council to provide funds for clothing the soldiers, who were in desperate need of stockings and shoes now that winter was drawing on. The board agreed that £1,000 should be set aside for this purpose, but the Duke instructed Captain Robert Mason, the paymaster of his forces, to make use of 'money of mine own . . . to give the better contentment and satisfaction to the country, officers and soldiers for the present, till further order can be taken'. Mason was now able to pay the householders who had troops billeted upon them — and it seems to have been lack of regular payments rather than any objections in principle that caused complaints over billeting — and to make arrangements for shifting the soldiers, now numbering 4,500, to Surrey, Somerset, Wiltshire and Kent, in order to relieve the pressure on the west country.[99]

VI

There could be no question of disbanding the army, despite the strain placed on royal finances by keeping it on foot, since it might have to be used in the near future for renewed operations against France. There had been no change in the circumstances which prompted English intervention in the first instance, except that the situation of the Rochellois was now even more desperate and their appeals for help from Charles I all the more insistent. In a conversation with the Venetian ambassador early in December Buckingham expressed his views very clearly. 'We are still of the same mind', the Duke told him, and 'if the Most Christian [King of France] will unite in earnest with us and other Christian powers, such as Denmark, Sweden, the United Provinces, the most serene republic [Venice], the Duke of Savoy and others, who desire reparation for Germany, and . . . entirely renounce his friendship with the Spaniards, we would make peace at once'. The object of the English action, Buckingham emphasised, 'was certainly not to injure the common cause, but to benefit it by proving to the French that it was neither honourable nor profitable to break faith and act contemptuously by the other friendly powers', as they had done by making peace with Spain in Italy and by breaking their promises over Mansfeld and the Huguenots.

The affairs of Christendom are brought to such a pass that unless a vigorous remedy be applied they must perish. It is clear that if the powers act one by one they will but destroy themselves. All must conspire for one end. If France, which is the vital part of this body, fails us, it will be proper to harass her, so that if she refuses to do good she may be prevented from doing harm.[100]

Buckingham's views may have been erroneous, but they were not based upon prejudice, ignorance or private passions. The affairs of Christendom were indeed in a bad way from the point of view of all those states which did not wish to live under the domination of one or other branch of the Habsburg House of Austria. In Germany the Emperor Ferdinand II's armies were triumphant. The protestant Elector of Brandenburg, who might just possibly have been a focus of opposition, had been forced into submission when Wallenstein's troops occupied his territories, and there were no other rulers of any consequence who had the courage or the ability to stem the Habsburg advance. Christian IV of Denmark had earlier given a lead, but he had now been driven out of Germany altogether and had to watch powerlessly while Tilly and Wallenstein took possession, in the Emperor's name, of Holstein, Schleswig and Jutland. As for Bethlen Gabor, the protestant ruler of Transylvania from whom much had been expected, he had been compelled to make his peace with Ferdinand. There was no salvation to be looked for, either, from the mercenary leaders who had earlier played a significant role in the anti-Habsburg campaigns, for Mansfeld was dead and so was Christian of Brunswick. The only possible saviour of the cause of German liberties – a cause which extended far beyond the geographical boundaries of Germany itself – seemed to be Gustavus Adolphus of Sweden, but his energies were fully occupied in his struggle against Poland. The Spanish contribution was important here, for the weak Polish monarchy was strengthened and rendered capable of resistance by money supplied from Spain. The Spanish and imperial branches of the House of Austria were not, as their enemies frequently assumed, putting into operation a detailed plan for the mastery of Europe which they had worked out in consultation with the Pope. But Spanish money supported the Emperor and his allies, and the progress of imperial arms in Germany was welcomed in Madrid. Philip IV hoped that Ferdinand's troops would in due course join in the struggle against the Dutch, and in October 1627 he told his envoy at the court of the Archduchess Isabella to press forward with negotiations to achieve this. The circumstances at the moment were very favourable, he commented, what with the alliance with France, the success of Habsburg arms in Germany, and the effect of Spanish aid to Poland in holding Sweden and Denmark in check.[101]

The Franco-Spanish alliance, as Philip's letter shows, was no mere figment of Buckingham's fevered imagination, but a reality which threatened the independence of England. Spanish ships had been sent to aid the French at Ré, even though they arrived only after the English had departed, and in October Philip asked the Infanta for her views on what time would be most suitable for a combined Franco-Spanish invasion of England. The Infanta replied that the spring of 1628 would be the best moment and that an army of thirty thousand foot and three thousand horse would be needed. The men for this could probably be provided by the Emperor and the Catholic League, but Spain would have to supply the warships. She added the comment that victory over England would, of course, leave the Dutch at Philip's mercy. Philip pursued the idea of joint operations, and in December 1627 informed the Infanta that a special envoy had arrived from Louis XIII to draw up plans for these. It was therefore hardly surprising that in English political circles it was widely assumed that Richelieu had put religious considerations before secular ones, or at any rate was intending to construct the greatness of the French monarchy upon the ruins of protestantism throughout Europe. In the words of an English state paper drawn up at about this time, the Jesuits had persuaded Louis that just as 'the King of Spain made his way to a monarchy by the zeal and support of the Roman Catholic cause', so 'if it were as vigorously pursued, the

Most Christian King would cast that lot of monarchy upon him [self]'.[102]

This was the reasoning which prompted Buckingham's belief that naval and military intervention was still needed to save La Rochelle and force Richelieu either out of government or into more acceptable courses. He had some hopes of reviving the alliance of secondary states which he had called into being as a prelude to the Ré expedition, and at the beginning of December it was decided to send the Earl of Carlisle to Lorraine and Savoy to bring this about. But Carlisle's mission was postponed when news came that Wat Montagu, who was in Lorraine on his way back from Savoy, had been seized by French troops, in a swift dash across the frontier, and taken to Paris for questioning. It could only be a matter of time before Richelieu secured detailed evidence of the plots that had been made to unseat him. In such circumstances there was little point in trying to set the conspiracy on foot once more.[103]

Buckingham's overriding and immediate concern was to provide for the defence of the kingdom, and to build up naval and military strength to a level consistent with the interests of England as a major power. In November he told Carleton that 'I am now in hand to repair the army and the fleet, and by the next spring, and sooner, I hope all things will be in readiness, that we may give accommodation to the affairs of Germany'. In the following month he took the opportunity of one of the many Privy Council meetings which he attended to

lively express the present state of the public affairs of Christendom, and how necessary it was that His Majesty should now take the same into his princely consideration, and resolve in this winter season what number of ships should be prepared and made ready against the next summer to scour the seas, defend the coasts of his kingdoms against the attempts of his enemies, and assist his friends and allies.

The King was present on this occasion and gave his approval to the proposition that a fleet of one hundred ships should be prepared, of which twenty were to be his own and eighty hired from merchants. He also gave orders that the trained bands of the counties should be brought to a much higher level of efficiency. The King and the Council were at last coming to realise what Buckingham had already appreciated, that the effective waging of war demanded a radical rethinking of traditional attitudes and assumptions. Whether the bulk of the English people either knew or accepted this was, of course, another matter.[104]

.The main obstacle in the way of strengthening the armed forces of the kingdom was, as always, shortage of money. When Buckingham called on the Navy Commissioners to give him a report on the state of their affairs they informed him that the stores were low and must be replenished; that ships must be paid off, since they were costing the King £5,000 a month to keep in service; and that the merchants who had been persuaded to loan their ships for the Ré expedition must have their accounts settled. Meanwhile the usual complaints were coming in about the poor condition of the sailors and the desperate need to supply them with the necessities of life. Sir Henry Mervyn, for instance, described the miserable state of his men at Plymouth, and warned that 'the winter employments will eat out more of them than the enemy unless better provision be made for clothes for them'. From Portsmouth Sir John Watts reported that 'divers ships' companies . . . intend to forsake their ships and to march up to the Court'. He found the greatest difficulty in obtaining victuals for more than a week at a time, and although, as he assured Buckingham, 'I purpose to use all diligence in performing all Your Grace's commands . . . I humbly pray Your Excellency to take to consideration how hard a business it will be for me to procure men without pay'.[105]

Buckingham reproached the Navy Commissioners for assuming that shortage of money relieved them of the responsibility for doing anything. Despite his instructions they had not sent shipwrights and carpenters to Plymouth to carry out essential repair work on the ships that had arrived there, and he found it difficult to believe that they could think themselves 'free from further care of that business till money were paid . . . for you well know the delay of a business of this nature may be loss of His Majesty's ships that are there distressed'. He added – in a sentence that has the typical Buckingham flavour and shows how and why he could get the administrative machine to work when others could not – 'I pray take this business more to heart, and give such expedition herein as may be for the preservation of His Majesty's ships and answerable to the wonted care of the Commissioners of the Navy'. He did not, of course, assume that the Commissioners could carry on their work without any money at all – indeed, as he told them, he had already secured an order for £500 for this particular task – but if they waited until they had the cash actually in their hands it would be too late. They must do what all seventeenth-century administrators were compelled to do (and not simply in England) – namely, employ their credit and their powers of persuasion to get work done without immediately paying for it.[106]

While he was goading the Navy Commissioners into making pennies do the work of pounds, Buckingham was pressing the Privy Council to provide for the long-term needs of the Navy. In mid-December the board decided that the paying-off of sailors should have first call on the King's resources. They also accepted Buckingham's suggestion that the Ordinary of the Navy for 1628 should be fixed at a higher level than the current year, and that it should be assigned on the same revenues. But where was the money to come from in the first instance? The King was hoping to negotiate a substantial loan from London on the security of crown lands, but this proposal aroused little enthusiasm. Sir George Goring attributed the poor response to the fact that the City was 'so infested by the malignant part of this kingdom as no man that is monied will lend upon any security if they think it to go the way of the Court'. There was some truth in this, but the crown had a bad record in repaying its debts, and there was the further consideration that Parliament, if and when it met, would almost certainly express its disapproval of the continued alienation of crown lands and press for the resumption of those that had recently been disposed of. The King was reluctant to summon Parliament again in view of his experience of the two previous ones, but as the Earl of Westmorland commented, 'which way will so great supplies be had as the maintenance of so great an army and navy will require? . . . A Parliament must of necessity be called, and that, I think, very speedily.' Buckingham himself was said to be in favour of another Parliament, and to have gone on his knees before the King, begging him to summon it. The Duke was essentially a pragmatist, prepared to compromise and make deals in order to achieve his ends. He knew that he had friends in both Houses who could be used to good effect if only they were organised; he was confident of his ability to win over his enemies in open argument; and he was convinced that the policies which he espoused were in the best interests of England. Parliament might, indeed attack him, as it had done before, but he was not lacking in courage when it came to facing his critics. [107]

The decision on whether or not to summon Parliament rested in the last resort with the King, and Charles came down against a meeting at this particular stage. As a consequence Buckingham was left to provide for the military and naval requirements of a state at war, without the financial means to do so. Fortunately for him he was by this time considerably experienced in such operations, and he had a remarkable buoyancy of spirits. He was no doubt cheered by the thought of his wife's pregnancy and the possibility that he might, once again, have a son of his own. There was no longer any question of his titles and dignities going to the children of his sister-in-law, Lady Purbeck, for in August 1627 the King ordered that if the Duke died without male heirs his rank and honours were to be inherited by his daughter Mary. Nevertheless the conduct of Lady Purbeck remained a cause of scandal and offence. [108]

In late November 1627 she again appeared before the Court of High Commission, and evidence was given that 'Sir Robert Howard came often unto her at evenings, crossing the water to York House, there being a private and secret passage to her chamber; and that he was seen often coming away very timely in the morning'. Lady Purbeck was found guilty of adultery and condemned to do public penance as well as suffer imprisonment. She made her escape, however, with the assistance of some of the Savoy ambassador's attendants, who dressed one of their number as a woman and sent him off in Lady Purbeck's coach as a decoy, while she disappeared, unnoticed, in another direction. Buckingham was furious with Scaglia when he heard of this, and it took all the efforts of Carlisle and Holland to bring about a reconciliation. The Duke's anger was understandable, for the whole episode was, as he told Scaglia, 'to his no small prejudice and scorn in a business that so nearly . . . concerned him . . . she being wife to his brother and bringing him children of another's begetting; yet such as by the law (because begotten and born while her husband was in the land) must be of his fathering'. [109]

VII

York House, where Lady Purbeck had her lodgings, was by now the Duke's principal London residence, and was sometimes referred to as Buckingham

House. He still kept Wallingford House, despite orders given in August 1626 that it should be sold, and he also had the great mansion at Chelsea, where Sir Thomas More had once lived and which later became the property of Lionel Cranfield, Earl of Middlesex. Buckingham acquired Chelsea as a result of complicated transactions involving the reduction of Middlesex's fine, and his main motive seems to have been that his mother, the Countess, was in love with it and wanted it for her own use. In July 1626 Buckingham feasted the King and Queen at Chelsea, but it was not until a year later that letters patent were issued granting him the house in perpetuity. For official business – meetings of the Navy Commissioners, for example – Buckingham still used his lodgings at Whitehall, but on more ceremonial occasions, such as that on which he entertained the Vice-Chancellor and heads of Cambridge colleges, he made use of York House, with its magnificent state rooms and fine garden. Although York House faced the Strand on one side, the principal approach to it was from the river, and in order to provide an appropriately noble entrance Buckingham commissioned Nicholas Stone to build him a new water-gate in 1626. Stone's design, which may have been influenced by Gerbier, was for three arched openings separated by heavily-rusticated columns and surmounted by a broken pediment flanked with lions. The keystones of the smaller side arches were engraved with anchors – as befitted a Lord Admiral – while the central one bore the arms of Villiers impaling Manners beneath a ducal coronet, and on the frieze was inscribed the Villiers motto *Fidei coticula crux* [the cross is the whetstone of faith].[110]

One of the great attractions of York House was the magnificent art collection which Buckingham assembled there. Gerbier told the Duke in 1625 that 'sometimes when I am contemplating the treasure of rarities which Your Excellency has in so short a time amassed, I cannot but feel astonishment in the midst of my joy; for out of all the amateurs and princes and kings there is not one who has collected in forty years as many pictures as Your Excellency has collected in five'. This was no exaggeration, for by the time Buckingham died he had well over three hundred pictures in his possession, most of them originals. There were the usual portraits, including those of James and Charles, but far fewer than there had been, for instance, in the Earl of Leicester's collection half a century earlier. Buckingham took great delight in Venetian painting, and his collection included more than twenty Titians, seventeen Tintorettos, sixteen Veroneses, two Corregios and one Giorgione. He possessed one painting by Michaelangelo, two Raphaels, and three Leonardos, of which one was a copy. He also had a number of pictures by Caravaggio, whom he greatly admired, and by lesser painters who had come under Caravaggio's influence. Among these was the Italian artist Orazio Gentileschi, whom Buckingham lured to England from the French court in 1625. Gentileschi was given lodgings at York House, where he decorated the ceiling of the grand saloon with his painting of the Nine Muses, and was frequently in the Duke's company: in November 1626, for instance, he was one of the party which Buckingham took to dine with the departing French ambassador, Bassompierre.[111]

Among contemporary painters Buckingham set the highest valuation on Rubens, whose magnificent equestrian portrait of him hung at York House. Buckingham had first met Rubens in Paris in 1625, and for the next two years he was negotiating to buy the famous collection of paintings and sculptures which the artist had assembled. By the end of 1627 the greater part of this collection was in York House, in return for payments said to have totalled £10,000. Among the treasures which Buckingham acquired by this transaction were the antique marbles and statues which Rubens himself had purchased from Sir Dudley Carleton. No doubt Buckingham was consciously vying here with the Earl of Arundel, who was renowned as a connoisseur of classical sculpture. Buckingham made a number of visits to Arundel House, 'to see the pictures', but where paintings were concerned his own collection was incomparably superior to that of Arundel: indeed, the Earl was so envious of one particular item in Buckingham's possession, 'a capital picture of Titian, called the Ecce Homo', that he was said to have offered the Duke £7,000 for it. In marbles, however, the reverse was true, and Buckingham therefore wrote to Sir Thomas Roe – one of his clients who was now ambassador at Constantinople – and asked him to procure columns, statues and other relics of antiquity. Roe did his best, and had hopes at one stage of obtaining the sculptures from the Golden Gate at Constantinople. He had bribed the appropriate officials and had been assured that the coveted pieces would shortly be his; but when the inhabitants heard of the proposed desecration they became so violent that the whole plan had to be dropped, and Roe commented sadly that the sculptures 'on Port Aurea are like to stand till they fall with time'.[112]

Roe was hampered by the fact that when it came to classical remains his artistic judgement was unsure. He was also forced to use agents 'who think every figure an antiquity'. Since he did not wish 'to lade Your Grace with ungraceful stones' he was compelled to move cautiously, but he hoped to avail himself of the skills and pertinacity of the Reverend William Petty, who arrived in Constantinople in early 1625. Petty, as Roe informed Buckingham, 'is able to judge of pieces of worth, and spares no labour . . . . He hath gotten many things, going himself into the islands.' Unfortunately from Roe's (and Buckingham's) point of view, Petty was Arundel's chaplain, and in May 1625 the Earl wrote to Roe to remind him 'that Mr Petty shall search only for me'. The harassed ambassador proposed that Petty's finds should be shared between his two noble patrons, but Arundel would have none of it; Petty, he declared 'directs all his labour of collecting for this house alone, which I must never think to break, but keep entire'.[113]

Roe was not the only ambassador through whom Buckingham enriched his art collection. Sir Dudley Carleton sent him a number of gifts from Holland, as well as the marble fireplace that eventually found its home in York House. And from Venice Sir Henry Wotton sent the Duke a present of a bed and some pictures, and also acted as his agent in purchasing a number of paintings of high quality. 'One piece is the work of Titian,' Wotton told Buckingham, 'wherein the least figure – namely the child in the Virgin's lap, playing with a bird – is alone worth the price of your expense for all four, being so round that I know not whether I shall call it a piece of sculpture or picture, and so lively that a man would be tempted to doubt whether nature or art made it.' Wotton's successor at Venice, Sir Isaac Wake, continued the practice of keeping a look-out for items that might be acceptable to Buckingham. He used the services of a Dutch merchant, Daniel Nys, who later played a significant part in acquiring the Mantuan collection for Charles I. In 1625, for example, Wake wrote to Gerbier to say that he and Nys spoke of him often and hoped to see him back in Venice in the spring. Meanwhile Nys had been fruitfully employed 'in gathering together some fine pieces for His Excellency's cabinet'.[114]

Buckingham did not restrict himself to ambassadors when it came to collecting works of art, nor did he confine his interests to paintings and sculptures. He was living at a time when the frontiers of knowledge were expanding at an unprecedented rate. The sixteenth century had seen not only the revival of antiquity but the discovery of the New World, and one of the results of this expansion of mental horizons was an insatiable curiosity about natural objects. Cabinets of 'rarities' became a feature of civilised life in Europe, and Buckingham spent a great deal of time and trouble in assembling one of his own. It was typical of his attitude that he took part in barrow digging on Salisbury Plain and kept a silver-tipped bugle-horn which he found there 'in his closet, as a great relique'. He also sent orders to merchants, especially those trading with the New World, to furnish him 'with all manner of beasts and fowls and birds . . . or seeds, plants, trees or shrubs'. As for those who ventured to the East Indies, they were to look out for 'shells, stones, bones [and] eggshells'. It was therefore no coincidence that John Tradescant, the Duke's gardener, who acted as his agent and adviser in the collection of rarities, should have established one of the earliest museums in England.[115]

Buckingham also spent a good deal of money on books. Sometimes these were for his own use, such as those he took with him to Ré, but on at least one occasion he was acting as a public benefactor. When he was in Holland in 1625 to sign the Hague Treaty, he heard that 'a collection of certain rare manuscripts, exquisitely written in Arabic and sought in the most remote parts by the diligence of Erpenius, the most excellent linguist', was for sale. He immediately offered to buy it, and paid £450 for the entire collection. At that stage he may have intended the manuscripts for York House, but after his election as Chancellor of Cambridge he decided instead to present them to the university, and although he was killed before he could put his design into effect, the Duchess carried out his wishes and handed them over in 1632. When, in March 1627, Buckingham made a formal visit to Cambridge, to preside over the degree ceremonies, he announced his intention to contribute £7,000 towards the building of a much-needed library. His assassination, and the heavy debts which he bequeathed to his wife, made it impossible to carry out this promise. But during his lifetime he presented the university with a tangible reminder of his interest in the shape of two new staves for the bedels, made out of silver, with his own and the royal arms sculpted on them. Although Buckingham was no scholar himself, he was not an inappropriate choice as Chancellor of Cambridge, for he had a genuine respect for learning and those who practised it. It was noted that during his visit to the university he was 'wonderful courteous to all scholars of any condition', and on another occasion, this time at Oxford, he ordered £10 to be given to 'a kinsman of his lordship's, a scholar that presented him with a Latin petition in verse'.[116]

VIII

As Buckingham's prestige increased, so did the drain on his purse, for at all times and under all circumstances he had to spend money. He took great delight in tournaments, which were a very costly form of entertainment, and in tennis, which could also be expensive, since bets were often laid on who would win: in January 1627, to take one example, he had to pay £200 to the Chevalier de Jars after losing several sets to him at St James's. More money went on gambling at cards: on Twelfth Night 1627 Buckingham took £200 to see him through, but he obviously had a run of bad luck, for he had to borrow a further £200. In addition to the occasional large sums spent on amusements such as these, there was the steady drain of payments for services rendered. When he went to see the Earl of Arundel's pictures, he paid the housekeeper twenty-two shillings. Ten shillings went to his boatman for rowing him from York House to Chelsea. Another ten shillings was given to Sir Henry Wotton's man who brought some gilt hangings to New Hall. A journey to Burley cost Buckingham £4 in coach hire, and there were payments of several shillings to the bell-ringers who welcomed him to the towns he passed through en route. When he stopped at Chelmsford on his way to New Hall he had to pay forty-seven shillings for his dinner, not to mention five shillings to the maids and five more to the trumpeters who played for him. Dinner at Henley, on another occasion, was considerably cheaper, a mere thirty shillings, but he had distributed 4s. 6d. in alms on the way there, and paid the fiddlers five shillings for entertaining him while he ate. Messengers were always rewarded for their pains, and no service, however trivial, went unacknowledged. When Buckingham was staying with the Earl of Northumberland he even ordered twopence-halfpenny to be given to the man who rolled the bowling-green for him. Sackville Crowe had charge of all this incidental expenditure, and during the course of four years he disbursed well over £40,000 on his master's behalf.[117]

It is hardly surprising that Buckingham, despite a considerable income, was perpetually in debt – though this was a characteristic he shared with many of his contemporaries. In July 1625 the Duchess had announced her intention to live very quietly for a while and 'redeem ourselves out of debt', and when Middlesex approached her to see if she would care to buy some of his jewels so that he could pay his fine, she announced that she had too many jewels already and no money with which to purchase any more. From time to time the Duke made efforts to put his financial affairs in order, and in July 1627 he approved of the suggestion made by his financial advisers that he should mortgage the greater part of his property and establish an order of priorities for the settlement of outstanding debts. Sir Robert Pye and Thomas Fotherly, who were two of his closest advisers, advanced considerable sums themselves, but the Duke also made use of the services of City merchants who had moved into the money-lending business. Sir William Courteen, for instance, loaned him £4,500 on the security of one of his Rutland properties, while the castle, manor and lordship of Oakham were pledged to Edward Wymark in return for £6,200. These emergency measures made it possible for Buckingham to avoid bankruptcy, but they did nothing to alter the fundamental weakness of his financial position. This was summarised simply and starkly by his advisers when, in 1626, they produced 'A brief declaration of Your Grace's yearly revenues'. They reckoned that his lands brought him in a net profit of about £5,000 annually; the Clerkship of the King's Bench £3,800; the Irish Customs £3,000; and pensions and fees for the offices he held £1,200; giving a total of £13,000. This figure did not include his income from the tenths which he received as Lord Admiral – which, in wartime, may have run into several thousand pounds. Nor did it take into account his profits from such things as the sale of honours: in late 1626, for instance, some eighty-five new baronetcies were created, and most of these were 'arranged' by the Duke or his family. It may be that Buckingham's real income was nearer £20,000 a year, but against this had to be set an expenditure of £23,000. Of this enormous sum, £5,000 went in interest charges, £2,000 on servants' wages, and £6,000 on housekeeping. The Duke spent £3,000 a year on clothes, his stable cost him £500 more than the allowance he received as Master of the Horse, and he annually distributed £500 in bounty. Yet the figure for Buckingham's expenditure, like that for his income, has to be qualified, for it does not include the considerable sums he spent on improving the houses and parks that belonged to him; on buying works of art; on entertaining – particularly foreign ambassadors; and on the King's service. The Duke advanced a great deal of his own money to keep naval and military preparations going when the royal exchequer was empty, and it cannot be assumed that he was always repaid. Indeed, his own finances and those of the state had become so intertwined that it is virtually impossible to decide whether certain items of expenditure were public or private – a case in point being the £10,000 spent for 'preparations for his lordship's voyage to Rees [Ré]'.[118]

A substantial recurring item in Buckingham's annual expenditure consisted of the maintenance payments which he made to various members of his family. In 1620, as already mentioned, he had agreed to give his mother £1,300 a year 'in consideration of the dutiful love and great affection he . . . had and did bear unto the said Countess', and five years later he increased this amount to £2,000. Buckingham was connected, through his mother's third marriage, with the Compton family, and £1,000 a year went to Willian, Lord Compton. Buckingham's wife, the Duchess, had an annual allowance of £2,300, and when other items are taken into account the total outlay on pensions and allowances comes to £6,000. Even so, it is not complete; Lady Purbeck, for instance, had a thousand marks a year [£666 6s. 8d.] out of the New Hall estate. There were other members of Buckingham's family who looked to him for money, though not on a regular basis. When he went to the Hague in 1625 he took with him his brother, Purbeck, and his nephew, Lord Feilding. He gave Purbeck £30 for his expenses, and Feilding £20, but he also spent well over £100 on buying clothes for them. By the time he returned to England he had given Purbeck a further £1,400, and Feilding £350.

Feilding was obviously something of a favourite of the Duke, who also took him to Ré, for Buckingham later recommended that he should succeed Compton as Master of the Robes to the King. Feilding fully returned his uncle's affection, as was shown in an incident which Wotton recounts. Buckingham, on his return from Ré, was warned of a plot to assassinate him as he rode to London. Feilding immediately pressed the Duke to 'honour him with his coat and blue ribbon . . . and undertaking so to gesture and muffle up himself in his hood, as the Duke's manner was to ride in cold weather, that none should discern him from him . . . . At which sweet proposition the Duke caught him in his arms and kissed him, yet would not, as he said, accept of such an offer in that case from a nephew whose life he tendered as much as himself.'[119]

Buckingham's care for his relatives extended even into the peripheries of kinship, for no matter how distant the connexion, the Duke accepted his obligation to pay for a wedding, act as godfather, or do whatever else might be necessary. One of his Beaumont cousins, for instance, had married into a Sussex family, the Ashburnhams, and an Ashburnham daughter married a Kentish gentlemen, Sir Edward Dering. When the Ashburnhams were staying with the Duke at Burley they asked him whether he would consent to act as godfather to Dering's son. The Duke, as Sir John Ashburnham told Dering, 'was wondrous willing, with a promise to do any other good for you that lay in his power'. This typical example of Buckingham's commitment to his kindred occured in 1625. Two years later, despite the dire financial straits in which he found himself, he agreed to find 'the sum of £5,000 as soon as conveniently I may' as a marriage portion for one of his nieces, who was to become the wife of the Earl of Morton's eldest son.[120]

Marriages were a recognised way of cementing and extending social and political influence, and it was no coincidence that when Morton agreed to marry into the Villiers family the Duke proposed that he should in due course succeed the Earl of Mar as Lord Treasurer of Scotland. But the Duke accepted the obligation to protect and advance the interests of his friends, even when they were not connected to him by marriage ties. His favour could take the form of major grants, like the appointment of the Earl of Salisbury as Knight of the Garter in 1625, or minor interventions, such as the attempt to hold up a property transaction which appeared to run counter to the interests of his old friend Lord Montagu. The obligations of kinship and friendship were, however, reciprocal. Buckingham did not spare himself in the King's service, nor did he expect those with whom he was connected to do so. In December 1627, for instance, he wrote to his brother-in-law, the Earl of Denbigh, giving him detailed instructions about repairing ships, keeping watch over the Scilly Isles, looking out for French prizes and a hundred and one other matters. He ended by reminding him that 'I rely on your lordship's care in all these businesses which concerns [*sic*] me, and do assure myself you will employ such industry and diligence in all things as shall be most for the service of His Majesty'. [121]

Denbigh admittedly was a close relative, but the same degree of commitment was expected from those further out in the family circle. Sir John Drake of Ash, in Devon, was one of these. When Buckingham was in the west country in early 1626 he stayed at Ash and, at Lady Drake's request, agreed to secure promotion for her chaplain. In the following year it was Buckingham's turn to ask for assistance, and he called on Sir John Drake to provide supplies for the ships at Plymouth. Sir John did as he was asked, and the Duke was not slow to acknowledge his help: 'Good coz,' he wrote to him, 'I thank you for your care and forwardness in His Majesty's service.' This was the other face of the system of kinship and patronage connexions that Buckingham so carefully constructed. It gave him power and to some extent security, which worked to his advantage; but it also enabled him to cut through the tangles of bureaucracy and make the administrative machine work faster and more efficiently than it would otherwise have done. The advantage here was to the King and state. [122]

NOTES

(Abbreviations are explained in the Bibliography, pp. 477–86).
1. *C.S.P.V.* XX, 82; *Fr.MSS.* 81.12v.–13.
2. *C.S.P.V.* XX, 110, 116.
3. *Rub.* p. 162.
4. *Rus.* 804–5; *Rich.* VII, 42; *C.S.P.V.* XX, 134; *Harl.MSS.* 6988.19, 30.
5. *Harl.MSS.* 6988.19; *Dk.MSS.* 8.39, 33.
6. *C.S.P.V.* XX, 106, 146; *Chas.* 191, 187; *A.P.C. 1627.* 19.
7. *C.S.P.V.* XX, 117; *Merc.* XIII, 359; *Aven.* II, 385–6; *Fr.MSS.* 81.13v.
8. *Dom.MSS 16.* 49.28; 51.44.
9. *Dom.MSS 16.* 47.66; 49.68; 50.35, 45; 51.4; 53.29; *A.P.C. 1627.* 17.
10. *Dom.MSS 16.* 49.8; 53.3; *C.S.P.V.* XX, 126.
11. *Chas.* 188, 191, 194; *Dom.MSS 16.* 53.9; *C.S.P.V.* XX, 119.
12. *Lon.* 982.1003, 1024; *Aven.* II, 367–8, 374, n.1; *Rich.* VII, 56; *Rub.* p. 162.
13. *Sal.* 109; *Dom.MSS 16.* 53.67; 61.78; *Chas.* 208; *A.P.C. 1627.* 99–100, 158, 257; *P.S.* 695.
14. *A.P.C. 1627,* 201–2; *Dom.MSS 16.* 59.83; 60.53; *Add.MSS.* 37,817.58v.; *C.S.P.D.* 20 Mar. 1627.
15. *Dom.MSS 16.* 50.57; 51.13; 53.62; *A.P.C. 1627.* 222–3.
16. *Dom.MSS 16.* 54.46, 13, 33.
17. *A.P.C. 1627.* 191, 246, 282; *Dom.MSS 16.* 58.66, 97.
18. *Dom.MSS 16.* 54.52, 56; 55.25; 58.15.
19. *Dom.MSS 16.* 59.78, 79; *Add.MSS.* 37,817.76v.–77.

20. *Add.MSS.* 37,817.80, 56v.; *Dom.MSS 16.* 66.55.
21. *Add.MSS.* 37,819.50v.
22. *Dom.MSS 16.* 33.98; *Misc.MSS.* C.208.171; *Add.MSS.* 12,528.34v., 35.
23. *Add.MSS.* 37,819.39v.; 37,817.31v., 34; *A.P.C. 1627.* 162.
24. *Dom.MSS 16.* 61.9; *Add.MSS.* 26,051.3; *A.P.C. 1627.* 317.
25. *Dom.MSS 16.* 64.4; 66.43.
26. *A.P.C. 1627.* 411, 210, 246; *Rub.* No. 106.
27. *Sav.MSS.* 13.30; *Rub.* No. 100; *Lon.* 1022, 1055, 1030, 1053.
28. *Rich.* VII, 89–92; *Roh.* 199–200; *Sav.MSS.* 13.64 *et seq.*, 73, 75.
29. *C.S.P.V.* XX, 231; *Sal.* 117; *Sav.MSS.* 13.75; *Bass.* 290.
30. *C.S.P.V.* XX, 159; *Dom.MSS 16.* 59.1.
31. *C.S.P.V.* XX, 198; *Bas.MSS.* 65.24; *Chas.* 217; *Fr.MSS.* 81.137v.
32. *C.S.P.V.* XX, 247; *Sal.* 117; *Laud.* 198, 202, 76–7; *Heyl.* 160.
33. *Dom.MSS 16.* 73.102.
34. *Add.MSS.* 37,817.53v., 106v., 112v.; *Sal.* 116.
35. *Add.MSS.* 37,817.114–114v.
36. *Add.MSS.* 12,528.36–38v.; *Chas.* 223; Richard Graham's accounts, *Grah.MSS.; Dom.MSS 16.* 65.35; *McGowan.* 185–94; *Herrick.* 55-6.
37. *Chas.* 226; *Dom.MSS 16.* 61.68 I; *H.M.C.Sal.* 228; Henry IV, Part I,IV.ii.
38. *C.S.P.V.* XX, 248–51; *Sal.* 117–18; *Chas.* 233–7; *Dom.MSS 16.* 66.10.
39. *Chas.* 237, 240; *Dom.MSS 16.* 66.67; *Harl.MSS.* 6988.20.
40. *Harl.MSS.* 1580.336; *Holl.MSS.* 120.195; 127.19; *Snow.* 164; *P.S.* 368.
41. *Holl.MSS.* 134.18; *Dom.MSS 16.* 63.33; *Chas.* 247; *Slo.MSS.* 1792.5.
42. *Dom.MSS 16.* 68.18; *Den.MSS.* TD 70/9.33. A slightly inaccurate version is given in *H.M.C.(4).* 256.
43. *Dom.MSS 16.* 68.3.
44. *Dom.MSS 16.* 67.57.
45. *Roh.* 199.
46. *Mareuil.* 186.
47. *Holl.MSS.* 134.18v.; *Dom.MSS 16.* 70.26; 71.65; *Kent.MSS.* U.269.T 83/6.
48. *Add.MSS.* 9298.166; 26,051.2; *Fr.MSS.* 82.15–15v.; *Dod.MSS.* 79.174.
49. *Add.MSS.* 9298.166; 28,927.8–10; *Merv.* 1–6; *Roh.* 201–2.
50. *Roh.* 203; *Fr.MSS.* 82.15v.
51. *Fr.MSS.* 82.16.
52. *Fr.MSS.* 82.16–17.
53. *Add.MSS.* 26,051.2v.; *Fr.MSS.* 82.17–17v.; *Mylne MSS.* 3; *Rawl.MSS.* D.117; *Sal.* 127.
54. *Dod.MSS.* 79.174; *Merc.* XIII, 843.
55. *Add.MSS.* 4106.162; *Roh.* 201.
56. *Tann.MSS.* 303.89; *Add.MSS.* 4106.162; *Herb.* 50.
57. *Fr.MSS.* 82.17v.–18; *Jnl.* 4; *H.M.C.Var.* II, 250.
58. *Jnl.* 5–6; *Fr.MSS.* 78.18.
59. *Herb.* 53; *Merc.* XIII, 844; *Rich.* VII, 103; *Fol.* 107; *Tann.MSS.* 303.89; *Roh.* 207–8; *H.M.C.Bucc.* I, 266; *C.S.P.V.* XX, 304; *Aven.* II, 521–2.
60. *Holl.MSS.* 134.18v.–19, 53v.; *C.S.P.V.* XX, 279,292; *Dom.MSS 14.* 214, 271; *Dom.MSS 16.* 70.97; *Chas.* 253.
61. *Dom.MSS 16.* 72.15; *Harl.MSS.* 6988.27.
62. *Holl.MSS.* 134.18; *Tann.MSS.* 303.96v.; *Dom.MSS 16.* 72.22, 31; *A.P.C. 1627.* 455–6; *Fr.MSS.* 82.24.

63. *Fr.MSS.* 82.19; *Merc.* XIII, 845; *Add.MSS.* 26,051.13v., 16, 17; *A.P.C. 1627.* 313–14; *H.M.C.Coke.* 310; *Dom.MSS 16.* 72.31.

64. *Dom.MSS 16.* 73.1; *A.P.C. 1627.* 471–3.

65. *Herb.* 94; *Add.MSS.* 26,051.3v.

66. *Herb.* 108–9; *Rich.* VII, 132–3.

67. *Dom.MSS 16.* 75.53 I; *Rawl.MSS.* D.404.4.

68. *Dom.MSS 16.* 74.62; Middlesex, n.d. *Sack.MSS.* uncat.; *H.M.C.(4).* 256; *Den.MSS. 23.*

69. Duchess of Buckingham, 4 Sept. 1627, *Fair.MSS.; Den.MSS.* 23; *Dom.MSS 16.* 74.5, 40, 46, *A.P.C. 1627.* 492–3.

70. *Dom.MSS 16.* 74.4, 81, 98; 75.7

71. *Dom.MSS 16.* 75.9, 40; *A.P.C. 1627.* 499.

72. *Wot.* 227; *Harl.MSS.* 6988.37.

73. *Tann.MSS.* 303.97v.; *Rawl.MSS.* D.117; *Harl.MSS.* 6988.38; *Add.MSS.* 4106.163; 26,051.4v.; *Herb.* 107; *Dom.MSS 16.* 81.5.

74. *Tann.MSS.* 303.100; *Rawl.MSS.* D.117; *Add.MSS.* 26,051.3v; *Merc.* XIII, 853–5; *Mareuil.* 190.

75. *Add.MSS.* 26,051.4v.; 4106.163v.; *Dom.MSS 16.* 76.26; *H.M.C.Coke.* 319–20.

76. *Merc.* XIII, 855–7; *Rich.* VII, 153–4.

77. *Rich.* VII, 142–4; *Aven.* II, 611.

78. *Aven.* II, 620, 634.

79. *C.S.P.V.* XX, 404; *Sav.MSS.* 13.99; *Holl.MSS.* 134.229; 135.2v.; *H.M.C.Coke.* 322; *Rub.* Nos 124, 126, 127.

80. *M.D.MSS. France.* 42.117, 120; *Roh.* 217; *Clarke.* 157–8; *Reade MSS.* 4/5.

81. *M.D.MSS France.* 42.118; *Dom.MSS 16.* 78.16, 17,2; *A.P.C. 1627–8.* 16, 18.

82. *Dom.MSS 14.* 215.43, 44.

83. *Dom.MSS 16.* 78.65; 72.18; *Tann.MSS.* 303.101.

84. *Fr.MSS.* 81.178, 180.

85. *Harl.MSS.* 6988.40; *Dom.MSS 16.* 80.43; *Herb.* 139–41; *Rich.* VII, 164–5.

86. *Merc.* XIII, 882, 873; *Rich.* VII, 167–8.

87. *Fr.MSS.* 82.148–148v.; *Rich.* VII, 173.

88. *Dom.MSS 16.* 81.28; *Fr.MSS.* 82.148v.–149.

89. *H.M.C.Coke.* 324; *Harl.MSS.* 6988.42.

90. *Dom.MSS 16.* 80.60; *Add.MSS.* 22,548.14; *Harl.MSS.* 6988.42.

91. *Merv.* 47–8; *Dom.MSS 16.* 80.55; 81.28.

92. *Herb.* 200–4; *Merc.* XIII, 885; *Rawl.MSS.* D.117.27.

93. *Herb.* 167–8; *Add.MSS.* 26,051.18; *Mareuil.* 193.

94. *Herb.* 240–50; *Add.MSS.* 9298.185–186v.; *Aven.* II, 739; *Dom.MSS 16.* 85.94, 97.

95. *Merv.* 66; *Herb.* 275–8; *Dom.MSS 16.* 84.1.

96. *Dom.MSS 16.* 82.58; 84.26, 41, 56; *Add.MSS.* 9298.186v.

97. *Harl.MSS.* 6988.53, 76, 78; *Man.* I, 329; *Ball.MSS.* 11.19.

98. *Dom.MSS 16.* 82.42; *Knowler.* 41; *D'Ewes.* 367–8; *Rous.* 13, 14; *Fairholt.* 19–24.

99. *Add.MSS.* 37,817. 138, 144v.; *Chas.* 291; *A.P.C. 1627–8.* 162; *Dom.MSS 16.* 87.12.

100. *C.S.P.V.* XX, 518–19.

101. *Lon.* 1108.
102. *Rich.* VII, 270–75; *Lon.* 1112, 1143; *Dom.MSS 16.*'87.73.
103. *Sal.* 135, 136.
104. *Holl.MSS.* 135.138–138v.; *A.P.C. 1627–8.* 202.
105. *Dom.MSS 16.* 86.42, 63, 83; 87.2.
106. *Add.MSS.* 37,817.153.
107. *A.P.C. 1627–8.* 185–6; *Dom.MSS 16.* 84.20; *H.M.C. (12).* 483; *Chas.* 305.
108. *P.S.* 407.
109. *Chas.* 296; *Sal.* 137; *Fin.* 239–40.
110. *Prestwich.* 475; More, 27 April 1625, *Sack.MSS.* uncat; *Chas.* 124, 127–8; *Survey.* 59–60; *Summ.* 85; *Whinney.* 52.
111. *Goodman.* II, 369–76; *Bet. passim; Bass.* 276.
112. *Wal.* I, 305–6, 297–8; *Bet.* 255–6; Richard Graham's accounts, *Grah.MSS*; *Ty.MSS.* 10.204; 12.13.
113. *Ty.MSS.* 10.200; 11.168; 12.13; 10.265; 12.224.
114. *Fort.* 173; *Smith.* 257; *Bet.* 257.
115. *Caud. passim.* I am grateful to Michael Hunter for calling this thesis to my attention; *Hunter.* 160; *Dom.MSS 16.* 4.155; for Tradescant, see Mea Allan, *The Tradescants: their Plants, Gardens and Museum 1570–1622* (1964).
116. *Wot.* 223; *Add.MSS.* 12,528.28, 26v.; *Chas.* 208, 204; *Mul.* 72–6.
117. *Add.MSS.* 12,528.33, 30; Richard Graham's accounts, *Grah.MSS.*
118. *Dom.MSS 16.* 4.140; More, 27 April 1625, *Sack.MSS.* uncat.:*Misc. MSS.* C.208.171v.,172v.; *Clo.MSS.*C.54.2728,2729; *Crisis.*94;*Add.MSS.* 12,528.38v.
119. *Clo.MSS.*C.54.2616; *Misc.MSS.*C.208.172v.; *H.M.C.*(4).256; *Add.MSS.* 12,528.26, 28; *H.M.C.*(7). 223; *Wot.* 229.
120. *Kent MSS.* U.350.C/2/5; *H.M.C.Var.* V.125.
121. *H.M.C.Supp.* 243; *Ch.* II, 595; *H.M.C.Bucc.* III, 319; *Add.MSS.* 37,817.152v.
122. *Dom.MSS 16.* 30.47; *Add.MSS.* 37,817.36.

CHAPTER TEN

1628: 'The Duke shall die'

I

The new year, 1628, opened auspiciously for Buckingham, for on 30 January Kate gave birth to a boy. The bells of Westminster – of which the Duke was Steward – rang out to welcome the infant Earl of Coventry, who automatically became heir to his father's dignities, and from Dover Jack Hippesley wrote to give his patron 'good joy of your young son' and to express the hope that the Duke would 'long enjoy him to your great comfort'. Laud recorded the birth in his diary, and two weeks later he made his way to Wallingford House to officiate at the christening ceremony. The baby was named George, after his father, and the King and Theophilus Howard, Earl of Suffolk, were present as godparents. The Queen had also agreed to act in this capacity, but since she could not take part in a protestant function she was represented by the Duchess of Richmond.[1]

It was as well that Buckingham had this happiness in his private life, for in public affairs there was little or nothing to comfort him. La Rochelle was under siege from the French king, and unless it received prompt English assistance was unlikely to hold out. In early January a number of delegates from the town appeared at Court and urged the King to press ahead with preparations for a relief expedition. The supplies intended for La Rochelle were in fact almost ready, and Buckingham offered Soubise the command of the fleet. Soubise, however, was not willing to risk his reputation with a squadron that consisted of only seven merchant vessels and half a dozen warships, so Buckingham appointed his brother-in-law, Denbigh, to command it. Denbigh was about to sail when news was received that Spanish ships had at long last arrived to help their French allies, and that the combined fleet before La Rochelle numbered more than seventy vessels. To send Denbigh against a force of this strength would be no more than a futile and costly gesture, so the decision was taken to delay Denbigh's departure until such time as more ships could be provided for him.[2]

Buckingham, as Lord Admiral, took charge of the difficult task of increasing Denbigh's fleet. Much of the work of contracting for victuals and ordering the

419

pressing of ships and men had to be done in London, but the Duke also made frequent visits to Plymouth, to spur things on at that end. His presence there, in the words of one captain, 'hath given much life and quickening to the furthering of our business . . . which now goeth on day and night', and it was hoped that Denbigh would be able to sail by the third week of March, with roughly twice as many ships as originally intended. There was good reason to believe that if the Rochellois could be speedily supplied they would have sufficient strength, in both provisions and morale, to hold out until such time as Louis and his ministers gave up in despair and turned their attention elsewhere. Everything depended upon speed, but the English government was crippled by an acute shortage of money. Goods could not be obtained without ready cash, and the sailors deserted in droves rather than serve without pay. On 15 March, shortly before his anticipated departure date, Denbigh wrote to inform the Lord Admiral that 'here are so many wants and defects as, notwithstanding all the care and diligence that can be used, [the fleet] will not be ready by the time Your Grace expecteth'. A week later Denbigh sent another letter in which he emphasised that the major shortage was of sailors, and added his opinon that since these simply were not available in sufficient quantity, it would be better to reduce the fleet in size rather than send it out ill-manned. Buckingham, with the consent of the Privy Council, authorised him to take this course, and also to use men who had been pressed for service as soldiers to make up his numbers. They were to be 'distributed and disposed of in the fleet . . . to be employed as seamen and to have seamen's pay'. The soldiers did not relish this enforced change of status and occupation, and gave vent to what Denbigh described as 'much murmuring and grudging'. But their presence on board meant that he now had sufficient men to handle the ships, and on 17 April he wrote to inform his brother-in-law that he would leave with the first favourable wind.[3]

It was hardly surprising that sailors were in short supply, for those who were already in the King's service complained that they were treated like dogs. They had no clothes for themselves and no pay with which to relieve the suffering of their wives and children. There were no fresh victuals aboard their ships at Plymouth, nor any medicines for use when they fell sick. The seriously ill were put ashore in houses specially built for them, but there, according to one observer, they were 'suffered to perish for want of being looked unto, their toes and feet rotting from their bodies, and so smelling that none are able to come into the rooms where they are'. Complaints of lack of clothing were widespread. Sir Henry Mervyn reported from Portsmouth that his men needed a thousand suits of clothes and twice that number of shirts. Hammocks also were required, as most of the men had nowhere to sleep except on the bare decks. Sir John Watts, who was also at Portsmouth, told Nicholas that his men were so desperate that they had deserted their ships and gone ashore 'in a mutinous manner', intending to march up to London and make their condition known to the King and Lord Admiral. Watts had managed to get them back on board, though only with the use of 'much violence' and the promise that if they had received no pay within a week he would discharge them.[4]

If Watts's men had in fact reached London they would have found that Buckingham already knew about their grievances. The capital was itself plagued by bands of mutinous sailors, and in February one of these attacked Buckingham House and threw down the gates, 'so that the Duke was compelled, at first by promises and then sword in hand, to repel their audacity'. In early March, when Buckingham went to a banquet at the Lord Mayor's, he had to be guarded by a strong company of musketeers for fear that the sailors would attack him, and the Privy Council was so alarmed by the news of mutinies and disturbances all over southern England that it decided to take stern action. The commissioners for martial law at Plymouth had arrested one of the ringleaders of the mutineers from Denbigh's fleet and put him in prison. The Council now informed them of the King's 'express pleasure and command' that the sailor in question should 'receive exemplary punishment, according to martial law, to the end that by that example of justice executed upon him, others may be deterred from the like attempts'. But it could not be taken for granted that the mutineers would yield even to such harsh measures, for when the authorities at Plymouth erected a gallows to carry out the execution, the sailors promptly tore it down and threw it into the sea. They then advanced on the town jail, to free their imprisoned mess-mates, and were only driven off when a guard of soldiers, specially stationed there, opened fire. Two of the mutineers were killed, many others were wounded, and the rest withdrew in disorder. Incidents like these, which occurred in many places all over England, confirmed the law-abiding element of the population in its distaste for everything to do with war.[5]

The shortage of sailors for the King's service was critical, since it affected not only Denbigh's expedition but also plans to prepare a large new fleet for the spring. These plans were dictated by the need to counter the threat from France and Spain, whose forces were highly likely to join in an invasion attempt upon England or Ireland later in the year unless there was some unexpected change in the international situation. Richelieu hoped to have eighty ships ready by the end of April, and had instructed the French commander to take them to Portugal, where they would link up with a Spanish squadron. The combined fleet would number about a hundred ships and Charles would need at least as many if he was to ensure the safety of his own dominions. It had been decided as early as January 1628 to set out a fleet of this size, and estimates had been called for. However, the cost was put at well over £200,000 and this may have persuaded Charles to set his sights somewhat lower – for the time being, at any rate. He therefore informed Carleton, at the Hague, that he would have sixty ships ready by early March, and instructed him to ask for a Dutch contingent to join them. The Dutch were anxious not to be drawn into war against France since they valued the French subsidies which they received, but Carleton assured them that the purpose of the fleet was only to chase the Spaniards from La Rochelle.[6]

Even if these plans were put into effect there was always the possibility that enemy vessels might slip through the English fleet and land troops somewhere in Charles's dominions. It was with this eventuality in mind that the King, in January 1628, gave orders for a general muster of the county militias on Hounslow Heath in the following May. He was particularly concerned that the cavalry element of the trained bands should be brought to a higher level of efficiency, since only mounted troops had sufficient mobility to deal with a hostile invader before he could establish himself. The cavalry were therefore instructed to muster separately in April, and Charles also ordered the Gentlemen of his Privy Chamber to 'prepare and exercise themselves in such manner on horseback as may both give good example to the rest of the gentry of the kingdom and the rather invite His Majesty to bestow upon such of them as may be capable thereof places of charge and command in horse troops, as there may be occasion offered'. Despite these measures there was reason to suspect that cavalry forces composed of enthusiastic but essentially amateur English gentlemen would not be able to withstand an attack by professional soldiers, and it may have been for this reason that at the end of January 1628 the King despatched Sir William Balfour and John Dalbier to Germany with letters of credit for £30,000 and instructions to hire a thousand armed horsemen and to purchase muskets, pikes and armour.[7]

Infantry were not such a problem, since the regiments which returned from Ré had not been disbanded, nor had those which were waiting to go with the Earl of Holland. There was obviously much to be said from the point of view of military efficiency for maintaining a standing army – despite the fact that no declaration of war had ever been made by Charles and that his kingdoms were therefore in theory enjoying the blessings, and the liberties, of peacetime existence. The council of war which Charles had set up in 1626, at a time when a similar invasion scare made defence measures essential, now met three times a week, and its numbers were increased by the addition of men of experience, such as Edward Cecil, Viscount Wimbledon. The council dealt with naval as well as military matters, and it took into consideration the perennial problem of providing an effective guard for the Narrow Seas. In February 1628 Lord Harvey proposed that a fleet of twenty-four ships should be created for this important task. Six of the ships should be the King's, and the rest commandeered merchantmen. The fleet should be divided into three squadrons, each with a definite area for which it was responsible, and a further six ships should be added to those which were charged with guarding the North Sea coasts. The Council approved of Harvey's proposal and sent a delegation to Buckingham to ask him for permission to 'solicit the officers of the Navy for a speedy despatch of this fleet'. But the Duke was more concerned, at this stage, with procuring money for the ships already in service. The Privy Council had ordered that £40,000 should be provided for the Ordinary of the Navy, but not all of this had been made available. Buckingham therefore called the attention of the Council to this deficiency and reminded members 'how highly it imported the state of the Navy and defence of the realm to have a constant and certain assignation of the said £40,000 *per annum* for the

Ordinary of the Navy *de futuro*'. At this Council meeting, in early February, the Duke also proposed that in view of the need to conserve supplies of powder, none should be wasted in salutes, and that captains of ships and commanders of forts should be instructed not to 'use any shot except in action against the enemy' – a suggestion of which the board wholeheartedly approved.[8]

Buckingham was aware that more ships, even if they were to be made available, would not necessarily solve the problem of coastal defence. English ships had some virtues, but speed of sailing was not among them, and they were easily outstripped by the Dunkirkers. In February 1628, therefore, Buckingham ordered Pennington and Phineas Pett, the leading naval shipwright, to set in hand the building of ten pinnaces 'of extraordinary good sail, whereby to meet with the Dunkirkers . . . and with the most advantage as may be for sailing and rowing'. But even faster ships would not, by themselves, be sufficient. What was also needed was captains of spirit and ability, and such men were hard to come by. Buckingham therefore cherished those already in the King's service, and encouraged them to redouble their efforts. In January 1628, for example, he wrote to one of his captains who had shown 'extraordinary industry and diligence in recovery and preservation of His Majesty's ships which were distressed at Plymouth', to assure him that he had thereby 'not only confirmed my opinion and esteem of you, but added much to the reputation of your worth and sufficiency'. The captain was due to come to London, and Buckingham asked to be among the first to meet him, 'for I think it long till I present you to His Majesty, who hath not many so able and diligent servants as yourself'.[9]

Although the far-reaching enquiry into the administration of the Navy which Buckingham had set on foot in late 1626 had been aborted by the overriding need to get the Ré expedition to sea, it was only a short while after his return that the Duke decided to put an end to the rule of the Commissioners. On 16 February the King, 'taking into consideration that the . . . said government by Commissioners was established in times of peace, when the despatch of business might go a slower pace than the activeness of these times of war and danger (which require quicker motions and expedition) will safely permit', gave order that the 'governing of the Navy shall be reduced to the ancient manner and institution, as aforesaid, by the Lord Admiral and his subordinate ministers and officers'. At the same time as this decision was recorded the King also made known his pleasure that £1,000 should be permanently assigned to the Lord Admiral from the Exchequer 'to be by him disposed of for rewarding of persons of merit'. The Duke clearly intended that in future the major qualifications for advancement in the Royal Navy should be skill, determination, and an unswerving commitment to the King's service.[10]

No amount of skill or determination, however, could compensate for lack of money, and at the opening of 1628 the royal finances were in a worse state than ever. The City of London had agreed, in principle, to advance a further £120,000 on the security of crown lands, though not all of this was to be handed over at once. By the end of January, however, £60,000 had been paid into the Exchequer, and Dudley Carleton reported with delight that 'the stream begins to run again which hath been too long frozen up'. There was a slowing-down in February, when only a further £15,000 was paid in, but even so the Council was able to make some provision for necessary services. £2,000 was set aside for the purchase of gunpowder; £12,000 was sent to Captain Mason to pay the soldiers and billeters in the west country; £5,000 was remitted to the Victualler of the Navy (who, as it happened, was owed more than £40,000), and another £17,000 to the Treasurer of the Navy, of which £5,000 was to be used for the purchase of clothes and for sailors' pay.[11]

While these and similar disbursements went some way towards meeting immediate needs, there was no possibility of providing the great sums that were needed for major defensive and offensive preparations. There were not even sufficient funds to pay for small-scale operations. Four merchant vessels were needed to guard the fishing fleets off Iceland, at a cost, it was reckoned, of £4,400, but in early May Buckingham was informed that while the ships themselves had been duly commandeered, no work could be done on them because of lack of money. If the government could not find £4,000 with which to guard the east coast fishermen, how could it possibly raise the much larger sum of £200,000 which would be needed to set out a fleet of one hundred ships for the spring? One possible way was by self-help, and the Privy Council had already told Buckingham that if he received any more requests for fishery protection he must make it clear that the ports concerned would have to provide the necessary money. As far as national defence was concerned, it had long been accepted that the King could call on the port towns of England to provide him with ships, at their own cost, in time of emergency. However, the ports had suffered a great deal from piracy, trade depression and the royal press-gangs, and there had already been attempts to spread the burden more evenly by calling for financial assistance from adjacent counties. Now, in early February 1628, the decision was taken to extend the demand for ships – or rather for ship money – to the whole country. The King, in his letters to the shires, emphasised that speed was essential, for 'there is a necessity come upon us not so much of debating as acting our defence'. He justified the breach with precedent by adding that 'this great business of setting out ships [which] used to be charged upon the port towns and neighbouring shires is too heavy for them alone in this great proportion . . . . We have thought fit . . . to cause the whole charge of this fleet to be cast up and to be distributed amongst all the counties at a proportionable rate.' In fact individual towns as well as counties were called on to contribute to the ship money levy, according to a tariff drawn up by the Council, and it was estimated that the total proceeds would amount to well over £170,000.[12]

Ship money was only one of many expedients that the Council considered in its anxious deliberations about ways to raise money in the opening weeks of 1628. At one of these meetings members had discussed, with the King present, the proposal to lay a special temporary tax, or imposition, upon beer and wine. This would have been, in effect, an excise, and it was recognised that the very idea of such a tax would be abhorrent to the great mass of Englishmen, not simply because of its effect upon the cost of living but also because in contemporary Europe the levying of an excise was associated with absolutist regimes. It was in order to avoid 'the name that is not pleasing' that the Chancellor of the Exchequer proposed to put the imposition upon ale-houses rather than the drink consumed there. Buckingham, however, opposed this. A tax on ale-houses would be too limited in its scope: 'all men must drink', he added, 'so all men must pay'. The Duke accepted the King's arguments that there was no alternative to extraordinary measures. 'Had you not spent all your own means, and yet your friends lost, I would not have advised this way,' he said. 'But being raised to defend religion, your kingdoms and your friends, I see no other way but this.'[13]

There was, however, another way – that of Parliament. Buckingham had already proposed this, but the King was reluctant to give his consent and declared that 'the occasion will not let me tarry so long'. Other Councillors, however, argued that prerogative taxation – as the forced loans had shown – provoked such resistance that in the end it was no more productive than Parliamentary subsidies. They turned for advice to the learned antiquarian Sir Robert Cotton, who reinforced their opinion that 'the heedless multitude . . . are full of jealousy and distrust, and so unlike to comply to any unusual course of levy but by force, which if used, the effect is fearful, and hath been fatal to the state'. Cotton's advice was that the King should proceed by way of Parliament, and that he should ensure a generous response from that body 'by a gracious yielding to their just desires and petitions'. Cotton recognised that one of the stumbling-blocks in the way of a harmonious Parliament was 'a personal distaste of my Lord Duke of Buckingham amongst the people', but he thought this might well be lessened if 'he might be pleased, if there be a necessity of a Parliament, to appear first adviser thereunto'. Whether Buckingham merely followed this recommendation, or had called on Cotton's services in order to give further weight to a view he already held, is uncertain. But Sir John Coke had no doubt where the initiative came from. 'All of us at the Council', he said, 'can tell he [Buckingham] was the first mover and persuader of this assembly of Parliament to the King.'[14]

The Privy Council was obviously divided about the appropriate measures to take, and pursued a wavering course. In early January the King ordered the release of all those who were still in prison for refusing to contribute to the forced loans, which seemed to be a tacit abandonment of prerogative taxation and a preparatory step towards a Parliament. By the end of the month the decision had been taken to summon Parliament for 17 March; but a week later, when the King sent out his letters demanding ship money, he announced that the opening of Parliament would be postponed, and that it would not meet at all unless there was a swift and full payment of the sums demanded. These letters were subsequently withdrawn, the ship money project was dropped, and the original date for the assembly of Parliament was reinstated. But the King did not annul the commission which he had issued to a number of Councillors (including Buckingham) at the end of January, instructing them to 'enter into consideration of all the best and speediest ways and means ye can for raising of monies . . . the same to be done by impositions or otherwise as in your wisdoms and best judgements ye shall find to be most convenient in a case of this inevitable necessity'.[15]

II

The King had been torn between the desire to win the cooperation of Parliament and the need to make alternative arrangements in case this cooperation was not forthcoming, or if there was a sudden deterioration in the international situation. He feared that any new Parliament would be likely to start off where the previous one had ended, with the impeachment of his chief adviser, but in January 1628 the Venetian ambassador reported that a bargain had been struck between the King and the parliamentary leaders 'that nothing shall be said about Buckingham'. There may also have been a meeting at Sir Robert Cotton's house, at which the Duke's critics – among them Sir John Eliot, Sir Edward Coke, Sir Thomas Wentworth and Sir Robert Phelips – agreed to concentrate on the vital question of restoring and preserving the liberties of the subject and not revive the impeachment proceedings. There were increasing signs on all sides of a desire for reconciliation, and the King made it known that Archbishop Abbot, Bishop Williams and the Earls of Bristol and Arundel, who had earlier fallen under his displeasure and been ordered to retire into the country, would be allowed to come to London and resume their seats in the House of Lords.[16]

Buckingham took far more interest in the elections than he had done on earlier occasions, and the Venetian ambassador reported that while the King had gone off to Newmarket the Duke had stayed on in town, 'negotiating and working with all his might, so that the members returned for the Lower House may be on his side'. Further evidence comes from Sir Henry Wotton, who describes how Buckingham 'was not unmindful, in his civil course, to cast an eye upon the ways to win unto him such as have been of principal credit in the Lower House of Parliament; applying lenitives or subducting from that part where he knew the humours were sharpest'. At the end of January Sir John Hippesley wrote to Nicholas, asking for Buckingham's letters of recommendation for members for the Cinque Ports to be sent down as early as possible, and this time there was no delay. Buckingham also wrote to Portsmouth and presumably to other ports that came within his purview as Lord Admiral, requesting them to return his nominees. In addition to this direct intervention, Buckingham took advantage of the electoral patronage of friends and clients such as Sir James Bagg. His efforts were not always successful. At Westminster Buckingham had counted on securing the election of his friend and servant, Sir Robert Pye, but here, as elsewhere, the 'courtiers' were routed and 'patriots' were chosen instead. Nevertheless when the House of Commons at last assembled it contained a significant number of Buckingham's clients and supporters. If they failed to make much of an impact, this was because they were not frequent or forceful speakers, were apparently not directed or organised, and were defending an unpopular and discredited cause.[17]

The formal opening of Parliament took place on 17 March, and Buckingham, as Master of the Horse, came immediately after the King, while his father-in-law, the Earl of Rutland, carried the sword of state. Proceedings began with a brief speech from the King, in which he reminded his hearers that 'these times are for action . . . I think there is none here but knows what common danger is the cause of this Parliament, and that supply at this time is the chief end of it'. If members did not do their duty by 'contributing what this state at this time needs' he would be compelled to 'use those other means which God hath put into my hands'. But he hoped that this would not be necessary; he was, he assured them, ready to 'forget and forgive what's past', as long as they would leave their 'former ways of distractions'.[18]

The King was followed by the Lord Keeper, Sir Thomas Coventry, who developed these themes at greater length, and reminded members – though only in passing – that 'a war was advised here; assistance professed, yea and protested here'. His major argument in favour of supply was the danger arising out of the international situation, and his interpretaion of this was couched in terms that Buckingham would wholeheartedly have agreed with. 'The Pope and the House of Austria,' declared Coventry, 'have affected, the one a spiritual, the other a temporal, monarchy, and to effect all their ends they are joined together and they are become masters of Spain and Italy and the great country of Germany.' Only France, among the major powers, remained free of the Habsburgs' embrace, but even there 'they have got such an interest in that government that under pretence of rooting out the protestants of our religion, they have drawn that king to their adherence'. Louis, continued Coventry, had broken his engagements both to his own subjects and to England, and had been 'not only diverted from assisting the common cause but is enforced to engage himself in hostile acts against His Majesty and other princes; making way thereby for the House of Austria, to the ruin of his own and other kingdoms'.[19]

The Lord Keeper repeated the King's call for speedy action, and reminded the Houses, in a striking metaphor, that 'we may dandle and play as we will with the hour-glass that is in our power, but the hours will not stay for us'. But when debates subsequently got under way in the Commons it soon became clear that members were far more concerned with the threat to their liberties as free-born Englishmen than with the hypothetical dangers that the King had warned them about. 'I more fear the violation of public rights at home than a foreign enemy,' announced Sir Robert Phelips, and his words were echoed by the septuagenarian Sir Edward Coke, who declared that 'I fear not foreign enemies. God send us peace at home.' Edward Kirton, another of those who had taken a leading part in the attack on Buckingham in the 1626 Parliament, expressed similar sentiments: 'We are told of dangers abroad,' he said. 'We have as great at home.' There was nothing surprising about the Commons' concern with domestic matters. Members were the elected representatives of the local communities, and one of their major functions, as they conceived it, was to inform the King about the grievances of the country – grievances of which he was, they believed, insufficiently aware – and to obtain remedies. Among the topics they took up in the opening days of their debates were the forcible billeting of soldiers, which violated property rights, and the issuing of commissions of martial law, which apparently brushed aside traditional legal restraints upon the abuse of executive power.[20]

Sir John Coke, on behalf of the King, kept up the pressure on the Commons to make an early vote of supply, and on 26 March he presented a list of fourteen propositions which he asked the House to take into account. Foremost among these were the provision of thirty ships to guard the English coasts, ten more to succour La Rochelle, and another ten to block the mouth of the Elbe and control trade into and out of the Sound. He also invited the Commons to consider the costs of raising an army of ten thousand infantry and a thousand calvary for service overseas; of supplying six thousand men for the assistance of Denmark; and of making long-term provision for the strengthening of the Navy. 'You see the weight of this business,' said Coke, when he laid these propositions before the House. 'It is not the King's interest or pleasure, but the defence of us all. Every day we run into more danger. Consider of some time when you will debate of them.' The Commons, however, were not to be diverted from their main purpose, and went ahead with the discussion of grievances. Coke therefore made another intervention, on 1 April, and reminded his fellow members that 'February and March are the times for provision, and they are already spent'. He was supported by Sir Benjamin Rudyerd – whose patron, the Earl of Pembroke (now Lord Steward), had abandoned his earlier anti-Buckingham stance and was working for harmony between the King's ministers and Parliament. 'The hinges of the business of Christendom moves [sic] in Germany', said Rudyerd, and he called on the House to 'bring His Majesty out of necessity'. Earlier in the debate there had been implicit criticism of Buckingham in references to lack of good counsel, but Rudyerd deliberately played this down. Of all counsellors, he declared, necessity was the worst, and if the Commons did not relieve the King they would themselves be guilty of 'placing ill counsellors about' him.[21]

The Commons apparently found this argument convincing, for they decided that on the following day they would consider the question of supply. However, the House was still far from united on what course it should follow, as was shown in the debate on 2 April. One member gave his opinion that the country was too poor to supply the King's needs and that 'wars belong to sovereigns, and not to subjects'. He was challenged by Sir Robert Mansell (no longer to be numbered among Buckingham's opponents) who declared that 'now it is no time to plead disability'. Members should not be so obsessed with the 'sufferings of the commonwealth that we forget all tenderness towards His Majesty's necessity, which may justly challenge at least an equal regard', added Sir Robert, and he called on them to direct their attention to the propositions which Sir John Coke had earlier laid before the House. Some of the Commons' leaders were now pressing for a vote of supply, on the grounds that the House would thereby demonstrate its desire for unity with the King and so win his goodwill. Sir Edward Coke was one of these, and argued that where there was a common danger the community must come to the crown's assistance – though he was in favour only of defensive preparations and ruled out all consideration of an offensive war. Other members, however, were reluctant to provide the King with money while he was still subject to Buckingham's influence. Sir Francis Seymour claimed that 'unless His Majesty employ men of integrity and experience . . . all that we give will be as cast into a bottomless bag', and Sir John Eliot forecast that future expeditions would meet with no better success than past ones if 'the like instruments' were still responsible for the direction of them.[22]

The House of Commons, like the country as a whole, was full of rumours about Buckingham's malicious conduct and his attempts to prevent King and Parliament from reaching a good understanding. Charles was so worried about the effect of these rumours – regarding them as part of an orchestrated propaganda campaign which needed countering – that he sent Sir John Coke to tell the Commons that reports of 'some malicious words spoken at Council Board by the Duke against this House' were without foundation. Whether or not as a result of this message, the House, sitting as a committee, resolved on 4 April that five subsidies should in due course be voted to the King. Charles was delighted at this news, and told Sir John, who brought it to him, that 'although five subsidies be inferior to my wants, yet it is the greatest that ever was;' and now I see with this I shall have the affections of my people, and this will be greater with me than the value of many subsidies'. He added that while he had at first been a liker of Parliaments, he had later, 'I know not how', come to dislike them. But now 'I am . . . where I was. I love Parliaments. I shall rejoice to meet with my people often.'[23]

The King's delight was shared by Buckingham, for the proffer of supply was apparent proof of his contention that Parliament was the best way in which to raise money. The five subsidies – which eventually brought in £275,000 – would not go very far towards meeting the government's needs, which amounted to £1,300,000, but the Commons' gift, said Buckingham – speaking at a Council meeting in the King's presence – was 'the opening of a mine of subsidies that lieth in their hearts'. As for himself, he had long lived in pain and passed sleepless nights because he was accused of being 'the man of separation . . . that divided the King from his people, and them from him'. Now he hoped it would be clear that 'they were some mistaken minds that would have made me the evil spirit that walketh between a good master and loyal people, by ill offices'. He welcomed this reconciliation between the King and his people, and told Charles how happy he was 'to see myself able to serve them; to see you brought in love with Parliaments; to see a Parliament express such love to you'.[24]

The King's pleasure at the Commons' decision to vote supply did not last long, for the decision was one of principle only, and no time was fixed for the passing of the bill. Charles hoped that this next step would follow shortly, but it soon became apparent that the Commons were in no hurry. They were engaged in discussions with the House of Lords on how best to preserve the subjects' liberties, and until such time as agreement had been reached on this vital issue they were not prepared to commit themselves irrevocably to the subsidy grant. Once again Sir John Coke, at the King's command, intervened to remind the Lower House that speed was essential, and the very fact that he spoke on Good Friday was an indication of Charles's attitude, since he had rejected the Commons' request to adjourn over Easter on the grounds that the urgent affairs of state on which they were (or were supposed to be) engaged demanded prompt action. On the next day, Easter Saturday, the King sent a further message, commanding members 'without any further or unnecessary delay' to proceed in the business of supply, and bidding them take heed 'that we force not him to make an unpleasing end of that which was so well begun'. The Commons' reaction was to ask for an audience with their sovereign in order to assure Charles of their devotion and remind him that the redress of grievances was of no less advantage to him than the voting of supply. The King received them on 14 April, at which time they also delivered a petition against the billeting of soldiers on householders. In his reply Charles assured them that he approved of their desire to preserve their liberties, 'but for God's sake do not spend so much time in that, as a foreign enemy may hazard your liberties and my prerogative . . . . I must tell you, and it is for you to believe me as one that sits at the helm, that time calls fast on you, which will not stay, neither for me nor you.'[25]

Up to this point Buckingham had not taken a major part in the affairs of Parliament. His attendance at the House of Lords had been interrupted by frequent visits to Plymouth to try to overcome the problems that were still holding up Denbigh's departure. Because of the shortage of seamen, only fifteen ships could be adequately manned, instead of the thirty originally intended, and these were in no fit condition for a long voyage. Buckingham had sent his servant, Edward Clerke, to accompany Denbigh, because Clerke had experience of negotiating with the Huguenots which might be very useful. But when Clerke reached Plymouth he despaired of any success for Denbigh's expedition. 'The King's ships', he told Buckingham, 'are here in equipage scarce fit for a merchant's voyage.' The crews were so disaffected that they were 'more apt to run into a mutiny at sea than perform their duties'. As for the supplies destined for La Rochelle, these were 'so poor as will hardly prove one month's provision for the town'. Clerke left it to Buckingham to decide whether it was worth going ahead with the expedition, but his own opinion was all too apparent. Buckingham, however, was not convinced. La Rochelle was in desperate need, and even inadequate provisions were better than none at all. It was presumably at his suggestion that on 12 April the Privy Council instructed Denbigh not to wait for the men and supplies which were still lacking, but 'to put to sea and . . . proceed on your voyage with such forces and provisions as are ready'. Even so it was not until nearly the end of April that Denbigh was at last able to sail.[26]

When Buckingham did appear in the Lords, he intervened in a debate about incidents at Banbury and Witham in which soldiers had been involved.

Buckingham, as commander of the King's forces, was anxious to calm down passions and blunt the edge of prejudice. He therefore urged his fellow peers not to waste time over details of who did what and when: 'if the soldiers or Justice or Constable be punished, it may breed ill blood at their return. Therefore to call them in and reconcile them.' On the following day the Duke reverted to a proposal he had put forward seven years earlier, in his first Parliament. He 'moved the House to take care of the breeding and education of the children of the nobility and gentry of worth of this kingdom . . . and that an academy might be erected for that purpose'. He returned to this theme nearly two months later, when Parliament was near dissolution, for it seems to have been something that he really cared about. As a young man he had travelled in France and enjoyed the advantages of what was in effect a little academy at Angers. He did not see why well-born Englishmen should be unable to obtain the benefits of such an institution at home, without being put to the expense and dangers of overseas travel. In such an academy they could be trained in military exercises, riding the great horse, dancing and fencing, as well as the classical and modern languages, and these were essential attributes for any aspiring gentleman. They might also acquire an *esprit de corps* which would go far to counteract the prevailing spirit of factionalism.[27]

III

The main business before the Lords was the liberty of the subject, and they were considering proposals from the Commons which in effect denied the King's right to imprison without showing cause. Buckingham wanted a quick vote on this issue, on the grounds that the matter had already been discussed at length and that further delay would be against the national interest. It was essential, he reminded his fellow peers, 'to husband time, for if provision be not made now in April we can make none this year, neither for Rochelle nor the Baltic Sea'. Buckingham took it for granted that if there was an immediate vote the Commons' propositions would be rejected, for the Lords were more sensitive to the needs of government and they also realised that they must keep the goodwill of the King, since no settlement of the disputed issues would have a chance of working unless he consented to it. Buckingham's assumption was that once the Lords had made it clear that they would not go to the extreme lengths advocated by the Commons, the way would be open to an accommodation between the two Houses and a speedy passage of the supply bill. 'My heart is to do good offices betwixt the King and his subjects,' he assured the peers. 'Our vote would have laid by all disputes, and so the readier for an accommodation.'[28]

Buckingham's opponents, however – of whom the most skilful and pertinacious was Lord Saye and Sele – insisted that nothing should be done without the cooperation of the Lower House. Saye was supported by Archbishop Abbot, who gave his opinion that 'we are not ready to put this question to vote', and by Bristol, who expressed apprehension about the consequences of any breach with the Commons. These views swayed the House, and Buckingham therefore abandoned his call for an immediate vote. But he kept up his pressure on the Lords to prepare for a further conference with the Commons by defining their own position, and in this he was successful. A committee was appointed — of which Buckingham was himself a member — to draw up proposals, and it recommended that when the conference took place the Archbishop should inform the Commons' representatives 'that the Lords do concur with them in their desire of the just liberties of the subject', but that 'they do find it fit and necessary to preserve the just prerogative of the King also'. The Lords then approved five propositions, which were presented to the Commons on 25 April. These were more moderate than the Commons' own proposals, and while they limited the King's right to commit without immediately showing cause, they did not remove it altogether. Buckingham had, in fact, scored a considerable success, for he had persuaded the Upper House to play the mediating role he envisaged for it. If the Commons accepted these propositions then there would be good hope of a satisfactory settlement; if not, it seemed likely that the Lords would decide to go ahead by themselves, which would perhaps bring about a change of heart and direction in the Lower House. Buckingham was clearly working in close cooperation with the King, for it was no mere coincidence that on 28 April Charles appeared in the Upper House and announced, through the Lord Keeper, that in order to cut down the length of time needed in debate — 'more time than the affairs of Christendom can well permit' — he would give his solemn promise to 'maintain all his subjects in the just freedom of their persons and safety of their estates'. In other words Charles had committed himself to accepting the sort of settlement that the Lords had outlined in their proposals.[29]

When these were taken into consideration by the Commons it became apparent that the House was split between those who wished to work in harmony with the Lords, even if this meant modifying their own attitude, and those who were determined to stand firm. Sir Edward Coke belonged to the latter group, and rejected the Lords' proposals on the grounds that they were too general and unclear. He was supported by John Selden, who commented that 'there is not one of the five fit to be desired or asked'. Sir Nathaniel Rich, on the other hand, argued that at least three of the proposals were worthy of consideration, and William Noy was of much the same opinion. 'I conceive', he said, 'that many of those propositions may be so drawn that they may be without any hurt to us', and his views were echoed by John Pym and Sir Dudley Digges. Sir Robert Phelips came down on the other side, but Sir Thomas Wentworth was for an agreement if at all possible: 'as for those propositions,' he said, 'let us comply and go with them so far as we may stand on our own ground'. The House had still not arrived at a consensus when the King's message was reported to it on 28 April. Sir Benjamin Rudyerd took advantage of this to make a powerful plea for compromise. 'I doubt not but by a debating conference with the Lords we may happily fall upon a fair [and] fit accommodation concerning the liberties of our persons and propriety of our goods', he argued. But he could not carry the House with him. Sir John Eliot declared that the Lords' proposals were of no use to the Commons, and he was supported by John Glanville, who was of the clear opinion that he and his fellow members had 'no cause to recede from our resolutions'. In a last effort to swing the House behind the Lords' propositions Charles sent another message on 1 May, asking members if they were prepared to accept the promises he had given through the Lord Keeper, and assuring them that if they did so they would never have occasion to regret their action. But the Commons, in the last resort, were not prepared to trust the King – certainly not as long as he kept Buckingham by his side. On 2 May, therefore, they resolved that a public violation of the subjects' liberties – such as had occurred in the case of those imprisoned, without cause shown, for refusing to contribute to the forced loans – demanded public redress: 'less will not satisfy his subjects than a bill, and . . . nothing else will enable them cheerfully to serve His Majesty'. The King's response to this resolution showed a marked hardening of his attitude. While he was prepared to accept a statement of the subjects' liberties as they already existed, he would allow no 'new explanations, interpretations, expositions, or additions in any sort'. Not only this. Time was fast running out, and 'the weight of the affairs of the kingdom and Christendom do press him more and more'. He therefore gave notice that he intended to bring the session of Parliament to an end on 13 May.[30]

It was now clear to the Commons that if they went ahead with a bill, couched in general terms, to define and preserve the liberty of the subject, they would get nowhere. It was Sir Edward Coke who suggested, as a way out of the impasse, that they should proceed by a Petition of Right, in which they could list specific grievances and ask for confirmation that these were against the law. The House approved of this course of action, and on 9 May Sir Edward presented the draft Petition to the Lords. Its kernel consisted of a formal request to the King that he would not, in future, resort to forced loans, arbitrary arrest, the billeting of soldiers or the issuing of commissions of martial law. No doubt it was to sweeten the King's attitude – and also because they had time to spare, having finished their major work on the liberty of the subject – that the Commons returned to the question of supply and fixed a time for payment of the five subsidies.[31]

The centre of attention now shifted to the Lords, for it was up to them to decide whether or not to accept the draft Petition. The Commons could, of course, have presented their petition direct to the King, but this would have deprived it of the force which Coke assured them it would have if it came from both Houses. A Petition of Right of this sort was a highly unusual form of procedure, and the Commons had only accepted it, as second best, because of Coke's insistence that if it passed both Houses, was formally accepted by the King and inscribed on the Parliament Roll, it would have the force of law. This gave the Lords a strong hand, for by threatening to withhold their consent they could bring pressure to bear upon the Commons to modify the Petition.

The clause which gave rise to greatest dispute was that restricting the King's right to arrest without showing cause, and on 12 May Buckingham delivered a letter from Charles to the Lords in which the crown's case was clearly stated. The Commons, said Charles, were still insisting 'that in no case whatsoever, should it never so nearly concern matters of state and government, we or our Privy Council have power to commit any man without the cause showed'. Such a restriction was unacceptable, for it would 'soon dissolve the very frame and foundation of our monarchy'. Charles gave his solemn promise that he would never again imprison any of his subjects for refusing to lend money 'or for any other cause which, in our conscience, doth not concern the state, the public good and safety of us and our people', but he would not abandon his right altogether. Pembroke proposed that the Commons should be asked to modify their petition in order to bring it within the compass of the King's letter, and Buckingham seconded him. Later that day, after a number of peers had left the House, there was a snap vote confirming this course of action. When the Lords assembled the next morning there was considerable dispute over whether or not the vote was valid, but in the end it was confirmed. This was a victory for what one observer had already termed the 'ducal party', and it was driven home by further pressure from the King on the Commons to complete the outstanding stages of the subsidy bill. Speaking in the Lower House on 13 May, Sir John Coke reminded members that 'this day was the day appointed for the conclusion of this session'. The King had therefore commanded him to 'acquaint you that if you do not speedily proceed in the bill of subsidy you shall shortly hear from him. He expects no answer but actions.'[32]

On 14 May Buckingham proposed that the Lords should draw up a list of arguments, based on suggestions by Pembroke, designed to persuade the Commons to modify their petition. He was duly appointed to a committee to undertake this task, and later that day was present at a conference between the two Houses, at which Lord Keeper Coventry summarised the Lords' attitude. 'Our coast is infested by enemies,' said Coventry, 'and likely to be more if there be not present preparations against them . . . . The state of the reformed religion abroad is miserable and distressed, and expects and depends on the success of this Parliament.' The Lords, he explained, wished 'such a course to be taken as may best beget a right understanding between the King and his people'. It was for this reason that they were asking the Commons that the section of their petition which concerned the crown's right to imprison 'be reduced into such a form as may be most agreeable to that which, by this letter, we may expect to have from the King'.[33]

The Commons, however, rejected any suggestion of compromise, and when debate resumed in the Upper House, Buckingham did not conceal his disappointment. 'They said they have voted the Petition of Right and will not recede from it,' he commented despairingly. 'Then why should we confer about it any more, considering in what manner our offer was?' He suggested that the Lords should now take it upon themselves to alter the wording of the offending section, without changing its substance, and then ask the Commons for a decision on whether or not they would accept the new version. He wanted it to be in line with the King's letter, and was supported in this by

Dorset and by Pembroke, who argued that since 'we had a light from the King in the point of imprisonment, I think it is our work to draw the Petition in that point to the effect of that light we have received from the King'. But other peers, including John Williams, the Bishop of Lincoln, and Lord Saye, insisted that they should not be bound by the exact terms of the King's letter. The letter, said Saye, was 'very gracious' but 'in some points it secures not the subjects in their liberties. It may be prejudicial to posterity, howsoever it is satisfactory to the present.'[34]

The Lords eventually followed the lead given by Pembroke and Buckingham, and on 16 May the Lord Keeper informed the House of a proposed amendment drawn up in committee. This was debated on the 17th, but it soon became clear that the amendment would not command the support of the House as a whole. Buckingham therefore called the attention of the peers to a suggestion from Arundel that in the opening or narrative part of the Petition there should be 'some addition or explanation not to prejudice the King's just prerogative'. Arundel had pointed out that the Commons had themselves declared that they had no intention 'to weaken the sovereignty or just prerogative', and Buckingham now suggested that those words should be taken as the basis of an explanatory clause. He was supported by Richard Weston, the recently ennobled Chancellor of the Exchequer and an old ally of Buckingham, who formally proposed that 'upon the offering of the Petition a protestation [should] be made that as they desire the subjects' liberty, so they likewise desire the preservation of the prerogative'. The House accepted this proposal and decided to communicate it to the Commons. But there was general agreement that it should be put forward only as a suggestion and not as a *sine qua non*. A conference duly took place, but the Commons were firm in their insistence that the Petition should be accepted without any alteration except on minor points of wording. Buckingham now urged the Lords to evince an equal firmness. The King's letter had indicated the limits beyond which he would not go, and it would be unwise to press him further. Let them therefore resolve in principle to have a clause in the Petition 'saving' the prerogative, and then decide upon the wording.[35]

Buckingham urged the Lords to make a speedy conclusion to the whole business, and his arguments were reinforced by a message from the King informing them, on 21 May, that his affairs were very pressing and that he was shortly to leave for Portsmouth: he therefore expected them to 'grow to a resolution this day whether you will join with the House of Commons in the Petition or not'. The Lords appointed a committee to set out the reasons why they considered a 'saving clause' necessary, and later that day they presented these arguments to the Commons with a request that they should be given immediate consideration. The Commons, however, declined to give an answer straight away, and Buckingham therefore urged the Lords to hesitate no longer but to resolve among themselves whether or not they would join in the Petition as it stood. He could not carry the House with him, though, and so he developed a proposal from John Williams that they should inform the King that they had done their best but were now waiting for a reply from the

435

Commons. When no reply came on the next day, the Lords, at Buckingham's suggestion, sent to know whether one would be forthcoming, but they were told that the Commons were still debating the matter. Not until 23 May were the Commons ready for a conference, and then it was only to announce that they were unwilling to accept the proposed addition to the Petition of Right. In other words, the Lords were left with no alternative but to accept the Petition as it stood or to reject it. Arundel suggested that they should accept it and add a declaration of their own 'for the preserving of His Majesty's prerogative'. He was supported by Bristol, but Buckingham was of another opinion. He argued that the Lords should stand their ground, for 'if we now depart from our addition, we do in a manner depart from ourselves'. He did not mind whether the addition came in the preamble to the Petition, or in the main body, or at the end, but 'if it be nowhere, I cannot give my vote to it'. If they could not agree with the Lower House, he added, let them petition separately. Saye would not accept this. 'If we go apart,' he said, 'it will be a division betwixt us. The refusing to join with them in petition to enjoy this right will seem strange to posterity.' But there was, as both Saye and Buckingham well knew, a much more fundamental objection to the two Houses acting separately. In Saye's words, 'If we petition by ourselves and they by themselves, the Petition will be of no strength.' It was this consideration that weighed most heavily with the Lords, and in the last resort they preferred to accept the Petition as it stood rather than weaken it by acting unilaterally. On 26 May, therefore, the Lords gave their approval to a declaration designed to reassure the King, in which they affirmed their intention 'not to lessen or impeach anything which, by the oath of supremacy, we have sworn to assist and defend'. They subsequently voted, without a dissentient voice, to join with the Commons in the Petition of Right. The Earl of Essex then proposed that if any words uttered in the heat of debate had given offence, they should be overlooked, and he was seconded by Bristol, who asked to be either censured or acquitted for the 'earnest speeches' he had uttered. Buckingham accepted Essex's suggestion but would not accede to Bristol's request, for fear that this would reopen old wounds. 'All to be forgotten,' he said. 'All to be forgotten. This to be entered in every man's heart, not in the book.'[36]

Buckingham had fought a long, skilful and honourable campaign on the King's behalf, and he accepted defeat gracefully. His principal concern had always been to stop the Commons provoking Charles into a sudden dissolution, so that the much-needed subsidies could in due course be made available and the crown's credit restored. The need for money was by now even more urgent, for Denbigh's expedition, which had been designed to give a temporary respite to the Rochellois and enable them to hold out until a really powerful relief operation could be mounted, had failed miserably. On 9 May Denbigh wrote to his brother-in-law to explain the reasons for his failure. He had been led to believe that when he arrived off La Rochelle he would be given powerful assistance from within the town, but in fact the French blockade was so effective that he was unable to break through it. During a stay which lasted eight days he could establish no contact with the citizens and had therefore been compelled to send back the provisions. Denbigh's account, however, was not confirmed from other sources. Sir Ferdinando Gorges, writing from Plymouth, informed the Duke that there was 'no such difficulty in the relief of that place as it seems was pretended'. He added a comment that must surely have struck home: 'He that shall enterprise businesses of this nature must be a captain capable of the affairs, both by sea and land, and one whose spirit and judgement must sway without fear in the greatest distress.'

Charles was bitterly angry when he heard of Denbigh's failure. One observer reported that 'the King was never seen to be so moved, saying if ships had been lost he hath timber enough to build more'. Charles ordered Sir John Coke to leave immediately for Portsmouth, find out why the fleet had come back without completing the task assigned to it, and instruct Denbigh to return to La Rochelle immediately. The Duke was deeply sensible of the blow to his own honour which Denbigh's lack of resolution had given. Not only this. The principal defeatist on board the fleet, and one who had apparently persuaded Denbigh not to attempt anything, was Edward Clerke, who was Buckingham's servant and representative.[37]

The news of Denbigh's failure reached town in the third week of May, and lessened Buckingham's prestige and influence at the very moment when he needed all his strength to persuade the Lords to take a firm line over the Petition of Right. Indeed it may be said that Denbigh contributed, however unintentionally, to the collapse of the 'ducal party' and to the relatively smooth progress of the Petition through its final stages. He also affected the King's attitude, for Charles now realised that if La Rochelle was to be saved – and this was something on which he had set his heart – he would have to accept the Petition, for only by doing so would he obtain supply.[38]

IV

On 27 May the Petition of Right completed its passage through both Houses, being given three readings, just like a bill. On the following day Buckingham informed Sir John Coke, who was now at Portsmouth, that he had despatched a number of messengers overland to La Rochelle to assure the town of 'His Majesty's resolution presently to send a greater force to open the passage for relief thereof'. Coke was to stay on at Portsmouth and supervise the preparations for the new expedition. The sum of £1,500 was being despatched to him forthwith, and, added the Duke, 'I doubt not in a few days the bill of subsidies will be passed; for there is now likely to be a happy agreement between the King and his people.' The Petition was due to be presented on 2 June, and on that day the Lord Keeper declared that the King had come 'to strike a league with his people . . . which cannot be in a more happy estate than when their liberties are an ornament and strengthening of His Majesty's prerogative, and his prerogative the defence of their liberties'. He was followed by the King himself, who gave his formal answer to the Petition: 'The King willeth that right be done according to the laws and customs of the realm; and that the statutes be put in due execution, that his subjects may have no cause to complain of any wrongs or oppressions contrary to their just rights and liberties; to the preservation whereof he holds himself in conscience as well obliged as of his prerogative.'[39]

On another occasion and under different circumstances such an answer might well have pleased the Commons, but it was not what they were expecting to hear, nor did it fulfil their hopes. They had regarded the Petition as a surrogate bill and given it the formal treatment that bills received. To complete the process they wished the King to make the traditional response to a petition, '*Soit droit fait comme est désiré.*' Following this the Petition would be incorporated into the Parliament Roll and would be binding on the judges. Charles's answer had given them the substance of what they wanted without the form, and at this stage it was the form that mattered most. He had also tempered his reply by the reference to the prerogative, and although he had said little or nothing with which members of the Commons would disagree, the very mention of prerogative on such an occasion seemed to be a breach of faith. The Commons therefore returned to their chamber in a discontented frame of mind. They were unsure what to do or how to proceed, and it may safely be assumed that many of them believed that the unsatisfactory answer to the Petition was yet another example of Buckingham's pernicious influence. They were therefore only too ready to listen to Sir John Eliot, who now renewed the attack on the Duke that had hung fire since the beginning of the session. 'I have had many a sad thought, in respect of disasters abroad and disorders at home,' said Eliot. What was the cause of these disasters, and of the 'waste of our men and ships and Navy?' He did not specify a cause himself, but since his words echoed the impeachment proceedings against Buckingham in 1626 his listeners can have been in no doubt about his opinion. The House of Commons, declared Eliot, was 'the great council of the kingdom'. It was the duty of members to inform the King accurately of what was happening in his dominions, and he therefore proposed that the Commons should draw up a remonstrance. A number of members objected, on the grounds that such an action would stir up discontent at a time when harmony was the watchword. However, Eliot's proposal received powerful support from Sir Edward Coke, who protested that if he thought the King 'were truly informed of the true cause of our dishonours and disasters, I would leave this remonstrance. But he knows not the true cause, which we know, and some of us feel'. Therefore the House should draw up a remonstrance to inform him.[40]

Eliot was an impulsive speaker, but there was nothing unpremeditated about his attack on Buckingham, except perhaps the timing. He confessed that he had discussed the matter with other members and was only waiting for an appropriate moment to raise it. What better time than now, when the major work of preserving the subjects' liberties had been accomplished? This was not Charles's view, however. Having accepted the Petition of Right he expected the Lower House to pass the subsidy bill as quickly as possible, and he was afraid that if members took up the attack on Buckingham once again there would be no stopping them. He sent a message to the House, on 5 June, pointing out that the date for the end of the session was rapidly approaching and that it could not be adhered to 'if you enter into any new matter, which may exceed the time'. He therefore ordered them not to embark upon fresh topics or to consider anything that might 'lay scandal or aspersion of the state or the ministers thereof'.[41] This message led, in the words of one reporter, to

such a spectacle of passions as the like had seldom been seen in such an assembly; some weeping, some expostulating, some prophesying of the fatal ruin of our kingdom, some playing the divines in confessing their own and country's sins which drew those judgements upon us; some finding as it were fault with those that wept and expressing their bold and courageous resolutions against the enemies of the King and kingdom.

It was as if the long strain of fighting for the Petition of Right, culminating in the anti-climax of the King's unsatisfactory answer, had unstrung members' nerves. They were now in a state bordering on paranoia, and saw enemies all around them. Sir Edward Coke rose from his seat to declare that 'God has laid this upon us because we have hoodwinked ourselves and have not spoken plainly.' There was only one way in which to remedy this, and he took it. 'The Duke of Buckingham is the man,' he declared. 'As long as he sits in Parliament, we shall never sit here or go hence with honour. Let us present this as our grievance of grievances. Present him to the King. Set down the causes of all our disasters, and all will reflect upon him.' Where Coke had led, others were only too eager to follow, for as one member observed, 'when one good hound recovers the scent, the rest come in with a full cry'. William Coryton affirmed that 'this Duke is the great enemy of the kingdom'. Edward Kirton expressed the widely-held view that Buckingham was involved in a plot to take over the country and drive out the King. 'He has gotten all our ships, forts, into his hands . . . [He] makes us all slaves.' Christopher Sherland declared that Buckingham was a Spanish agent, and Benjamin Valentine revealed that 'this great man has soldiers every place to cut our throats'. He moved that the House should vote him to be 'the common enemy of the kingdom'. 'This must be so,' he added. 'This is so.'[42]

Buckingham was not without his defenders. John Ashburnham, carried away with indignation, accused the House of being so obsessed by its search for grievances that it was rapidly becoming itself 'the greatest grievance of Christendom'. This attack upon the House's dignity was not allowed to pass unchallenged, and Ashburnham was ordered to keep silent. Edward Nicholas was more cautious in his remarks, and concentrated on defending Buckingham against the charge that the King's ships were captained by papists. But the House was not interested in questions of proof. As Selden said, there was no need to appoint a subcommittee to enquire into the causes of their griefs, since they knew who the principal cause was. All that was necessary was 'to express the cause: the Duke'.[43]

On 6 June the King sent another message to the House, making it clear that he had not intended to limit their rights in any way, but to stop them

439

raking up the past at this stage 'that so for this time Christendom might take notice of a sweet parting'. The King's explanation calmed passions to some extent, but it did not deter members from pressing ahead with their remonstrance. All their fears found expression in this document. Religion was being subverted by failure to enforce the penal laws against the Roman Catholics and by encouragement of Arminians. The billeting of Irish catholic troops along the Kent coast was designed to open the way to popish invading armies. The thousand horsemen hired in Germany were to be brought over to enforce an excise at the sword's point. The captains of the King's ships were all papists, and this was why they refused to take effective action against the Dunkirkers.[44]

While the Commons were engrossed in recording the grievances of the kingdom, the King himself was busy restoring good relations with the peers, on whom he might have to rely to hold the turbulent Lower House in check. The dissident lords, including the Archbishop of Canterbury, the Bishop of Lincoln and the Earls of Essex, Lincoln, Warwick and Bristol, as well as Lord Saye, had all been welcomed to the royal presence and given the King's hand to kiss as a symbol of reconciliation. Now, on 6 June, Charles sent a message to the Upper House, by the Lord Keeper, informing members that nothing had been more acceptable to him 'all the time of this Parliament, than this dutiful and discreet proceeding of your lordships'. It was formerly-dissident peers who took the initiative on 7 June in proposing that since the King's answer to the Petition of Right had apparently not satisfied the Commons, he should be asked to give another. Buckingham – who must surely have been involved in this initiative – gave it his blessing. 'Since you think these distractions have risen from this answer,' he told the Lords, 'I am glad you are fallen upon this way.' He was thereupon appointed a member of a small delegation which was sent to the King to know whether he would be willing to follow the proposed course. The length of their audience suggests that Charles still needed some persuading, but eventually they won his assent and returned to the House with the assurance that the King would come later that day to give his second answer. When Charles did so, he began by rebutting the widely-held assumption that his first answer had been the work of Buckingham. It had, on the contrary, been made 'with so good deliberation and approved by the judgement of so many wise men that I could not have imagined but that it should have given you full satisfaction'. Nevertheless, to show the assembled members that there was no element of double-dealing in his attitude, he was prepared to 'please you in words as well as in substance'. He thereupon instructed the clerk to read his formal answer to the Petition of Right, '*Soit droit fait comme est désiré.*'[45]

When the members heard the traditional formula used, they gave a great roar of applause. The news rapidly spread to the City, where bells were set ringing and bonfires were lit – 'the number whereof', according to one report, 'at length equalled those at His Majesty's coming from Spain'. But it was noted that these spontaneous outbreaks of joy were not prompted solely by the news that the Petition of Right had finally completed its course. Buckingham had become so identified in popular imagination with opposition to this measure that it was assumed that its acceptance by the King must inevitably entail his downfall. A band of City boys was said to have pulled down the scaffold on Tower Hill, declaring that they must have a new one built for Buckingham, and this mood infected members of the Commons, for there was no slackening of their campaign against the Duke. They were determined that the King should be truly informed of the grievances from which his kingdoms were suffering, and therefore pressed ahead with the remonstrance. 'The debate', in the words of one account, 'was as hot as ever, and the crimes so frequently objected against the Duke were brought in afresh, as if they had never been proposed in the House.' Sir Edward Coke declared it to be the duty of members to 'free the King, who hears and sees by other men's ears and eyes', and on 11 June the Commons passed a resolution that 'the excessive power of the Duke of Buckingham, and the abuse of that power, are the chief cause of these evils and dangers to the King and kingdom'.[46]

There was little that Buckingham could do to hold back the flood tide of charges, rumours and innuendoes. He protested to the Lords that one member of the Commons had accused him of saying 'Tush! I care not a pin what the Lower House can do against me, for without my leave and authority they shall not be able to touch the hair of a dog.' This charge, he assured the Lords, was completely unfounded. 'I profess, upon the faith of a Christian and as I hope to have part in heaven, I never spake any such words or words to that effect.' The Lords gave him leave to justify himself before the Commons, but even had he done so it would have made no difference. On 12 June the Commons spent four hours debating whether or not to name the Duke in their remonstrance, and decided by a majority of more than a hundred that they would do so. On that day they also gave the final reading to the bill for the grant of five subsidies to the King.[47]

On 17 June the Commons assembled in the Banqueting House at Whitehall to present their remonstrance to the King. This began with the statement that it was their duty 'faithfully and dutifully to inform Your Majesty', and the assurance that 'it is far from our thoughts to lay the least aspersion upon your sacred person, or the least scandal upon your government'. The remonstrance then went on to inform Charles of a general fear among his subjects that there was a 'secret working and combination to introduce into their kingdom innovation and change of our holy religion'. The catholics, despite the good and wholesome laws against them, were openly tolerated and found 'extraordinary favours and respect in Court from persons of great quality and power, whom they continually resort unto, and in particular to the Countess of Buckingham'. Not only this. The Arminians were daily increasing in strength, and this was 'but a cunning way to bring in popery' since, as was well known, Arminians were 'protestants in show, but Jesuits in opinion'.[48]

The remonstrance called on the King to consider whether there were not good grounds for thinking that 'there is some secret and strong cooperating here with the enemies of our religion abroad, for the utter extirpation thereof', and then turned to the fears of a change of government. It instanced the billeting of troops and in particular the stationing of popish soldiers in coastal regions 'where, making head amongst themselves, they may unite with the popish party at home, if occasion serve, and join with an invading enemy to do extreme mischief'. It referred to the 'strange and dangerous purpose of bringing in German horse and riders', and the possible connexion between this and the King's instructions to his Councillors to consider raising money by an excise. It objectd to the 'standing commission granted to the Duke of Buckingham to be General of an army in the land in the time of peace', and called the King's attention to the fact that the recent disasters to English arms had 'extremely wasted that stock of honour that was left unto this kingdom, sometimes terrible to all other nations and now declining to contempt beneath the meanest'. It complained of the decay of forts, the insufficient supply of gun-powder, the contraction of trade and loss of ships, and the inadequate guard kept in the Narrow Seas. And it reached its climax in the categorical assertion that the principal cause of all these evils and dangers was 'the excessive power of the Duke of Buckingham, and the abuse of that power'. The King, it suggested, should consider whether it was in the interests of his own and his kingdom's safety that 'so great power as rests in him [Buckingham] by the sea and land should be in the hands of any one subject whatsoever', and whether it was possible for one man to manage 'so many and weighty affairs of the kingdom' as the Duke had undertaken. Finally it called upon Charles to take into his most princely consideration 'whether, in respect the said Duke hath so abused his power, it be safe for Your Majesty and your kingdom to continue him either in his great offices or in his place of nearness and counsel about your sacred person'.[49]

Charles had already implicitly given his answer to the remonstrance, for on the previous day he had ordered that all charges pending against Buckingham in the Star Chamber should be removed from the file, since 'His Majesty is fully satisfied of the innocency of that Duke in all those things mentioned in the said information, as well by his own certain knowledge as by the proofs in the cause.' Now, when the remonstrance was presented, Charles made no attempt to hide his feelings. He expressed his astonishment that the Commons should be so presumptuous as to assume that they knew more about state affairs than he did, and when Buckingham knelt before him and asked leave to reply to the Commons' complaints, he lifted him to his feet again and gave him his hand to kiss. 'It is certain that His Majesty's favour to the Duke is no way diminished,' commented one member. But he added that 'the ill will of the people is like to be thereby much increased'.[50]

The Parliamentary session was still not over, even though the Lords gave the third reading to the subsidy bill on 17 June. Perhaps Charles hoped, now that he had satisfied the Commons over the Petition of Right and received the remonstrance, that there would be a change of heart among members and some practical demonstration of the goodwill and devotion which they constantly professed towards him. If so, he was disappointed. With major business out of the way the Commons turned their attention to the case of Roger

Mainwaring, one of the King's chaplains, who had preached sermons defending the King's right to levy money without consent. The Commons decided
that such sentiments tended to the subversion of the constitution and law of
England, and therefore drew up articles of impeachment against Mainwaring.
At the same time they took up the question of the Customs duties, Tunnage
and Poundage, which had still not been voted to the King. It had been traditional, since the late fifteenth century, for these duties to be voted to every
monarch, for life, by his first Parliament, but in 1625 the Commons had been
unwilling to follow precedent. Ever since the early years of James I's reign
they had been alarmed by the exercise of the crown's prerogative right to levy
Impositions, or additional duties, upon trade, and the opening of a new
reign seemed to offer an appropriate opportunity for clarifying the situation.
They were prepared to vote Tunnage and Poundage for one year, in the first
instance, but the Lords would not accept such an unprecedented step, and the
grant remained in limbo.[51] Charles regarded this as an unfriendly gesture,
particularly since he was involved in a war which the Commons had pressed
him to undertake. Tunnage and Poundage was far too important a part of his
already insufficient revenue for him to be able to do without it, and he therefore collected it on grounds of necessity until such time as the Commons
should be prepared to make the traditional grant. This extension of the prerogative became a further cause of complaint, and now, in the closing weeks
of the 1628 Parliament, the Commons began drawing up a remonstrance on
the subject. Charles did not wait for this to be presented. On 26 June he
arrived unexpectedly in the House of Lords, took his seat on the throne, and
sent for the Commons to attend him. 'It may seem strange', he told his
audience,

that I come so suddenly to end this session. Therefore, before I give my assent to the
bills, I will tell you the cause . . . It is known to everyone that a while ago the
House of Commons gave me a remonstrance – how acceptable every man may judge,
and for the merit of it I will not call that in question, for I am sure no wise man can
justify it. Now since I am certainly informed that a second remonstrance is preparing
for me, to take away my profit of Tunnage and Poundage (one of the chief mainte-
nances of the crown) . . . this is so prejudicial unto me that I am forced to end this
session some few hours before I meant it, being not willing to receive any more
remonstrances to which I must give a harsh answer.

All that remained for him to do before bringing the session to a close was to
give his assent to those bills which had completed their passage through both
Houses. Among them was that which granted him five subsidies. After a
meeting which, in spite of the King's repeated appeals for speedy action, had
dragged on for more than fourteen weeks, Parliament had provided the King
with some at least of the sinews of war. The frost had been broken and public
business could begin to move forward again, for an accord between the King
on the one hand and his Parliament and people on the other was, as Carlisle
correctly observed, 'the centre and stable point upon which all Your Majesty's
motions abroad must subsist and enlarge themselves'.[52]

V

The most urgent business was, of course, the relief of La Rochelle, and already, on 27 May, Buckingham had moved the Privy Council, 'out of his great zeal to religion and the commiseration he hath of the distressed and lamentable estate of the town of Rochelle', that all possible steps should be taken to speed up the flow of provisions to the fleet. The Privy Council had managed to scrape together £1,500, of which one third was to be used for the preparation of fireships, and on 1 June it ordered Buckingham to provide for the maintenance of an army of three thousand men that was to go with the expedition. Yet such was the disheartening effect of Denbigh's failure and of the continuing shortage of money that many people had come to the conclusion that the Huguenot stronghold was past salvation. There were some, of course, who suspected that this was not by mischance but by calculation on Buckingham's part, and that he was in the pay of Louis XIII. These rumours reached the Hague, where they made an impression on Elizabeth of Bohemia, who told the Venetian ambassador that 'she believed the worst, and it was always best in such cases'.[53]

There were no indications, however, that either Buckingham or the King had lost heart. On 6 June Charles sent the Duke a formal command 'to draw my army together to Portsmouth, to the end I may send them speedily to Rochelle', and he announced his intention of going to Portsmouth in person just as soon as he was free from Parliamentary business. Buckingham, like the King, was held in town by the need to attend to what was going on in the two Houses, but he kept in constant touch with his agent at Portsmouth, Sir John Coke. He had ordered Coke to provide fireships for forcing a passage into the harbour of La Rochelle, and had promised that money would be made available for this purpose. But Coke pointed out that promises of money were no longer sufficient. Fireships could only be had in return for cash, 'and if the fleet stay for fireships, and the fireships for money, and monies be sent in paper only, I assure Your Grace that the time which is given to send the fleet together will consume the provisions and disable it to proceed'. Buckingham, in his reply, assured Coke that the £500 provided by the Council for fireships would be sent down to him within a few days, and that there could be no question of the fleet going without them. Denbigh's expedition had suffered from being forced to sail before it was ready, and the Duke was determined that the same thing should not happen again. The ships must leave together, not in dribs and drabs as men, money and supplies became available, 'for if they go broken [up], the service may suffer a second and worse foil than it hath'.[54]

Coke seems to have been infected by the general gloom at Portsmouth, for his letters were full of complaints about the defects which daily appeared and augmented. In one despairing outburst he informed Conway that 'the longer I stay here, I shall every day see the fleet and voyage go further backward, and all my travails and endeavours spent in vain and worn out'. He had earlier complained to Conway about the fact that although he had sent the Lord

Admiral many 'tedious letters' full of detailed questions, Buckingham's replies were often lacking in precision. One reason for this was that Buckingham had to make frequent attendances at meetings of the Privy Council, where the whole business of the fleet was under constant discussion, and Conway describes him on one of these occasions reading Coke's letters 'by pieces, as the debate gave him leave, which was then in agitation, about that fleet which you now have in care and to which all other necessities gave place'. Among the detailed instructions which Coke was waiting for were those about the fireships, but as one of his messengers pointed out, the Lord Admiral's 'distractions in Parliament have been so great that he hath had little time to think of fireships'. It was typical of Buckingham that despite such distractions, and at the very moment when the Commons were accusing him of being the cause of all ills, he found time to write to Coke to thank him for all the trouble he had taken. 'Had it not been for your extraordinary diligence,' said the Duke, 'it would have been a work almost impossible to have fitted the fleet and provisions to return to Rochelle.'[55]

The concern about fireships was one indication that Buckingham's expedition, unlike Denbigh's, was going to be fully prepared for the hazards that would confront it at La Rochelle. The big problem was how to break through the floating palisade that the French had constructed. Buckingham gathered as much information as he could about this from Soubise and the delegates from La Rochelle, and worked out his plans in close cooperation with them. He also turned for advice to professional soldiers, and once again showed the partiality he had for Mansfeld's former officers by inviting two of them over to England to assist him. He had conceived the idea of constructing a number of floating mines, which could be sailed up against the palisade and then exploded. In mid-July the Privy Council authorised the construction of three of these 'extraordinary fireships . . . and likewise six engines for fireworks'. The three ships had brick-lined chambers built inside them, which were then filled with huge stones and several thousand pounds' weight of gunpowder. It was because they were so central to the whole operation that Buckingham insisted there could be no question of going without them – even though there were delays, as usual, in getting them ready.[56]

Buckingham knew that the time available to him was limited, for at the beginning of July letters arrived from La Rochelle warning that the inhabitants were in great extremity and could not hold out much longer. A few days later the King, sitting in Council, gave orders that 'no monies be issued from after this day to any person upon any occasion whatsoever, . . . until the present expedition for Rochelle be satisfied'. A third of the £18,000 which was still needed to supply the expedition was to be provided immediately and the remainder was to be assigned upon the first Parliamentary subsidy. In mid-July the Council ordered the three thousand troops who were billeted along the south coast to be marched to Portsmouth, and on the 21st the King left town on the first stage of his journey towards them. All that was needed now was Buckingham's presence to hasten along the final preparations. Coke was doing his best, but warned the Lord Admiral that affairs were at a standstill;

or going backwards, mainly because of shortage of funds. There was also 'a general distaste (or rather despair) in the action', which could only be overcome if Buckingham were to appear in person, bringing with him 'some mastering spirits and store of money'.[57]

Buckingham, however, would not quit London until he was sure that the supply ships had left the Thames. 'All the ships and provisions prepared here are now for the most part in the Downs,' he told Coke on 25 July. 'I stay here only to see the remainder, which is not much, to follow after, and to hasten away monies for the mariners, which will be all done before Monday next, when I hope at the furthest to be with you.' There were still many details to be attended to, and Buckingham made sure they were not overlooked. He instructed the long-suffering Coke to 'cause four barrels of powder to be delivered to the . . . Earl of Morton's regiment in the Isle of Wight', and to 'cause watch to be kept in the Isle of Wight and all parts about Portsmouth, that no seamen or mariners be suffered to land'. And when the vessels from London arrived, Coke was to 'cause the provisions to be issued and disposed of amongst the ships there [at Portsmouth] which are to have supply for two months for their complements of seamen and three months for such landmen as shall be appointed to them'. Whatever his critics might say of him, the Lord Admiral had an infinite capacity for taking pains.[58]

VI

Although Buckingham's principal concern in the spring and summer of 1628 was the relief of La Rochelle, it was not his only one. As Lord Admiral he was responsible for all aspects of naval administration and no matter was too small for his attention: in March, for instance, he persuaded the Privy Council to agree that chaplains' pay of fourpence a month taken out of seamen's wages should be calculated according to the nominal complement of the ships they served in and not be subject to deductions for deaths or desertions. On a different level he was pursuing his aim of making the King's ships faster and more manoeuvrable. He had an eye for a well-designed boat, and when he noticed that a pinnace which Lord Mountjoy had bought in the Ile de Ré had exceptionally good sailing qualities he ordered the Navy officers to buy it and use it as a pattern for those which were to be built for the King's service. Mountjoy's pinnace may have contributed to the design of the *Lion's Whelps*, which were ready for launching by the end of May 1628. In June Buckingham accompanied the King to Deptford to see the new ships, and two months later he received the first reports about their success in action. One of his captains described with delight how four of the *Whelps* had given chase to five French and Dunkirk ships, and captured three of them. 'Here is very good sport,' he said, and added that 'the country is wondrous well pleased with the *Whelps*, for they have given them great ease'. A few days later Hippesley wrote to Buckingham from Dover to tell him that 'your *Whelps* doth wonders here'

He also made the pertinent comment that 'I would to God this had been done before the Parliament. Then had Your Grace never been spoken on there'.[59]

Buckingham had hoped that by taking naval administration out of the hands of the Commissioners and restoring it to the principal officers, he would improve its quality. But the apparently endless delays in preparing the relief expeditions for La Rochelle soon disillusioned him and made him regret his action. In fact there was little that either Commissioners or officers could do to overcome the crippling effects of shortage of money. At the end of May the Privy Council was informed that 'His Majesty's revenues are so straitened, by reason of anticipations the last year, that the Ordinary of the Navy cannot this year be fully assigned', and it asked the Lord Treasurer to anticipate revenues still further in order to provide cordage, without which the Navy would not be able to function. The sailors continued to suffer great privation, and hunger and despair drove them to mutiny or desertion. Exemplary punishment might terrify them into submission for a time, but it was not, as Coke realised, the final answer. When Coke wrote to Buckingham from Portsmouth at the end of June he told him that there had been two mutinies so far, but that he had dealt with them in 'a patient and moderate way'. Many of the sailors had been in the King's service for years on end without ever being discharged, 'and to most of them nine or ten months' pay is now due. They have no shift of clothes. Some have no shirts, and others but one for the whole year.' Buckingham recognised the justice of the sailors' cause, but resented the fact that they blamed him for their plight. He caused a declaration to be set up on the pillars of the Royal Exchange in London, in which he protested that

I have done more for you than ever my predecessors did. I procured the increase of your pay to a third part more than it was. I have parted with mine own money to pay you, and engaged all mine own estate for your satisfaction, albeit it belong not to my place to provide your payment, nor was it ever expected from any my predecessors.

He reminded them that before leaving for Ré he had arranged for monies to be set aside to cover their arrears, but that by the time he returned those funds had been diverted to different purposes, 'and how myself and you suffered by forgetfulness and neglect when I was absent in that service, yourselves well know'. He also pointed out that they were wasting their time demanding money from the King, for 'the King hath no means to pay you till the Parliament give it, or that, by the breach of it, His Majesty may raise money otherwise'. As for the threat that they would pull down his house about his ears, 'I will let you know that I can and will correct you as sharply for your insolencies and disorders as I have been forward to give you satisfaction and have been sensible of your sufferings.'[60]

The mood of the sailors might have become even uglier had it not been for the hope that Parliamentary subsidies would soon be flowing into the Exchequer. On 2 July the Privy Council wrote to Denbigh to acknowledge a report it had received from him about the 'refractory and disobedient manner' in which the sailors were behaving. It instructed him to continue his efforts to reduce them to obedience and to assure them that when the King left for

Portsmouth in a few days he would take sufficient money with him to pay their arrears. This assurance seems to have had the required effect, for Denbigh subsequently informed Buckingham that the seamen were behaving in an orderly fashion; but he repeated his warning that unless the money arrived shortly they would break out into worse mutinies than before. The sum of £20,000 would have sufficed to pay Denbigh's sailors all that was owing to them, and once the subsidies were assured this amount could have been raised without too much trouble. But here the government's order of priorities intervened. Charles had decided to make a number of major changes in his administration, including the removal of the Lord Treasurer, and in order to facilitate this he had promised to give Marlborough £10,000 by way of compensation and his wife £5,000. The sailors therefore had to be satisfied with a payment on account. But even the money for this could not be found at short notice, and as late as the third week of July the King was still in London – waiting, in Sackville Crowe's phrase, for the Lord Treasurer to 'lift him out of town'.[61]

Marlborough had been removed from the Treasury because Buckingham held him to blame for the failure to provide money on an adequate scale and with sufficient regularity for English military and naval operations. He was replaced by Sir Richard, now Baron, Weston, the former Chancellor of the Exchequer, who was an old friend and client of Buckingham. The Duke himself gave up one of his offices, the Lord Wardenship of the Cinque Ports, in favour of another friend and ally, Theophilus Howard, second Earl of Suffolk. There were further changes, this time in the Queen's household, which also benefited the Duke's allies. The Earl of Dorset was appointed the Queen's chamberlain and Sir Thomas Jermyn her vice-chamberlain, while Sir George Goring became her master of the horse. These new appointments show how Buckingham was strengthening his position and rewarding those who had remained firmly committed to him during the recent storms. But at the same time he was pursuing a policy of reconciliation with his former critics and enemies. John Williams, Bishop of Lincoln, 'had a very courteous interview with the Lord Duke', and agreed that 'he would be His Grace's faithful servant in the next session of Parliament'. The Earl of Arundel was invited to Buckingham House and, on arriving there, was presented by the Duke to the King, who received him most graciously and twice gave him his hand to kiss'. Buckingham was also searching for some way in which to curb the antagonism of the leaders of the Commons, and Eliot and Wentworth – both of whom were men of great ambition who chafed under the sense that their talents were being wasted – were considered as possible recipients of his favour. In the end the Duke chose Wentworth, largely because he was a friend of Weston, who determined to 'make him the King's creature'. In July 1628 Wentworth was created a baron, and thereby took 'the first step of his rising'.[62]

Buckingham was clearly making preparations, well in advance, for the session of Parliament that was likely to take place later in the year, and this alone indicated his preference for 'the Parliamentary way'. But he must by now have realised that doubts about his religious attitude were a major barrier to a good understanding between him and Parliament. There is no evidence that Buckingham, despite his friendship for Laud, was an Arminian, or that he had any marked inclinations in religion. While he believed in God, and hoped in due course 'to have part in heaven', his interests were essentially secular. When confronted by a gentleman who claimed to have been visited by the ghost of Buckingham's father, Sir George Villiers, who had given him messages for the Duke from the other world, Buckingham's only reaction was to offer the man a seat in the forthcoming Parliament. There is little doubt that the Duke was planning to renew his political alliance with the anti-Arminians, which had only been broken because of their failure to ward off the attack upon him in the Parliament of 1626. One indication of a change of course came in August 1628, when a royal proclamation ordered the enforcement of the penal laws against the catholics. There may also be some significance in the fact that whereas Laud had been asked to draw up the form of prayer for the blessing of God upon the expedition of 1627, this task was entrusted in 1628 to Archbishop Abbot, newly restored to favour. Buckingham had learnt the lesson that a nation at war could not afford to be disunited. Hence his 'firm resolution', as he told Carleton, 'to walk new ways, but upon old grounds and maxims, both of religion and policy'.[63]

VII

There had already been indications of new directions in foreign policy. In January 1628 Weston informed the Archduchess Isabella that Charles was inclined towards peace with Spain, and that Carlisle and Endymion Porter would shortly be sent on missions designed to bring this about. Charles's overture was no doubt prompted to some extent by necessity, since it was becoming clear that even with Parliamentary assistance he could not maintain war against two great powers simultaneously. There was also, as before, an element of deception in the design, since rumours of an Anglo-Spanish peace were calculated to alarm the French and soften their attitude towards England. But these were not the only considerations. By 1628 there was considerable war-weariness among the states of western Europe. The Danes were actively searching for peace, and the Dutch would have welcomed a settlement if only Spain would have agreed to acknowledge their independence. On the Habsburg side, the Netherlands were exhausted, and Spinola had thrown up his command of the army there and returned to Spain to try to persuade Philip IV to set negotiations on foot for a peaceful resolution of all outstanding problems. This was what Buckingham had long been hoping for, and if Philip was now willing to negotiate it was essential, and consistent with Buckingham's policy, that Charles should make a positive response.[64]

There was one further, and major, reason for the revival of negotiations with Spain. A small cloud, no bigger than a man's hand, had made its appearance over Italy in the closing weeks of 1627, and to those who could read such signs, it portended great changes. In December of that year the Gonzaga ruler of the Duchy of Mantua died without a direct heir. His rule extended to the tiny Alpine state of Montferrat which included the fortress of Casale, one of the principal gateways to northern Italy. France could not afford to let this inheritance pass to a Spanish puppet, since that would draw the Habsburg noose even more tightly around her. Nor, on the other hand, could Spain remain aloof while a French-supported candidate took control of the duchy. In short, there was an increasing likelihood that the Franco-Spanish agreement to maintain peace in Italy would be broken. It was the conclusion of this agreement that had shocked Buckingham and confirmed him in his belief that France would have to be forced back on to her original course, if necessary by sacrificing Richelieu. Now it looked as though the change of direction would come about anyway.

From Buckingham's point of view, war between Spain and France over Italy was highly desirable, since France would thereby be committed once again to the common cause, while Spain, fearful of being attacked on more than one front simultaneously, might well be prepared to restore the Palatinate as the price of English neutrality. The worsening of relations between Spain and France would also remove the threat of combined operations against England which was all too real at the beginning of 1628. These and similar consideraations explain why Buckingham told one of his confidants in July 1628 that 'he hoped very soon to kindle a fierce war between the Spaniards and the French'. The development of the Mantuan crisis also confirmed Buckingham in his determination to sustain La Rochelle. It had long been a maxim of French governments that they would not engage in foreign wars while they had insurrection at home. But the reverse was also true, and as the need to intervene in Italy became more and more compelling, so Louis and his ministers would be tempted to cut their losses and offer terms to the Huguenots – but only if La Rochelle could demonstrate its capacity, with English help, to hold out indefinitely. From the English point of view, therefore, and for the good of the common cause, it was essential to mount a relief operation without delay.[65]

Buckingham would have been happy to make peace with France on condition that La Rochelle and the Huguenots were included in it. The Venetian ambassador at the court of Louis XIII proposed mediation to effect this, and when it was suggested that the best way to resolve differences was by a personal interview between the two favourites, Buckingham expressed his approval. This, he said, 'will settle everything in two days, and the French will not be able any longer to excuse themselves for not assisting Italy, on the plea of war with England and civil strife at home'. Buckingham gave his word that if the French would agree to an honourable settlement he would immediately withdraw his fleet and sail to the help of the King of Denmark. The Venetian ambassador in London, however, warned his colleague 'that the peace with the Huguenots and between the two kingdoms must go together, as here they do not mean them to be separated, and they also want to add the assistance for the common cause'. Richelieu, on his part, declared his readiness to work towards a negotiated settlement and professed his continuing esteem for Buckingham. But he insisted that there could be no question of including the Huguenots in the negotiations, for they were subjects of Louis XIII, and no king would ever admit the interposition of another in his own affairs. Richelieu had some doubts about the genuineness of English intentions, and feared that Buckingham's main aim was to use the prospect of a settlement with France to extract better terms from Spain. Buckingham, on the other hand, was afraid that Richelieu would pass on the details of any peace proposals to the Huguenots as 'proof' that they were being betrayed and could no longer count on English aid. He also suspected that Richelieu hoped to delay the despatch of the English relief expedition until it was too late for it to accomplish anything. He therefore informed the Venetian ambassador that negotiations must wait until he had actually arrived off La Rochelle and completed his mission. He would then be only too glad to have an interview with Richelieu and settle the outstanding problems between the two countries.[66]

VIII

Buckingham's commitment to the Huguenot cause did not make him any more popular in England. Indeed, anger against him had been intensified by the Parliamentary remonstrance, and was now erupting into open violence. In mid-June an astrologer named John Lambe was hacked to death by a London mob as he made his way home from a playhouse. Lambe had been frequently consulted by Buckingham — who wanted his advice, among other things, on the suggestion that Purbeck's attacks of insanity were the result of sorcery — and was popularly known as 'the Duke's wizard'. It was the Buckingham connexion that proved fatal to Lambe, and the jingle which celebrated this event contained the threat of violence against the Duke's own person:

> Let Charles and George do what they can,
> The Duke shall die like Dr Lambe.

Shortly after this incident, when Buckingham was playing at bowls with the King, a soldier who was among the throng of onlookers suddenly stepped forward, plucked the Duke's hat off his head and threw it to the ground, declaring as he did so that 'there were as good and as loyal men as himself stood bare [-headed]'. Buckingham threatened to strike the man, and would have done so had not the King restrained him. 'George', he said, 'let him alone. He is mad'; to which the soldier replied 'I have done this for Your Majesty's service, and will do more.' Reports of this incident rapidly spread into the country, and John Rous, writing in his Suffolk parsonage, included an account of it in his diary. He also noted some of the tales about Buckingham that were current in these fevered summer months of 1628. There was a rumour, for instance, that 'the Duke was gone to the Tower, and the King accompanied him for fear he should be thrown over the bridge or knocked on the head'. Indeed a popular indoor sport in England at this time consisted in adding up the letters of the Duke's name, or making anagrams out of it, in order to see what the fates held in store for him. Some people turned for enlightenment to the self-styled prophetess, Lady Eleanor Davis, who repeated what she had said for many months past, that the Duke would not outlive August.[67]

Buckingham professed his contempt for all these rumours and prophecies, and in any case was far too busy to bother about them. He had frequent Council meetings to attend, and he also spent many hours writing letters and issuing instructions, so as to ensure, among other things, that the victualling ships now in the Thames should leave on time. On 6 August he told Conway – who was with the King at Portsmouth – that 'I find nothing of more difficulty and uncertainty than the preparations here for this service of Rochelle. Every man saith he hath all things ready, and yet all remains as it were at a stand.' He added that while he had no wish to linger in town a moment longer than necessary, he had to make sure that work on the victualling ships was carried through to completion. 'I dare not come from hence till I see that despatched, being of such importance.' In the event he was not able to get away until 12 August, but he rode hard to Portsmouth and by the afternoon of the 14th was at Southwick House, just outside the town, where the King was now resident.[68]

Buckingham did not stay long at Court, for the centre of activity was the dockyard and harbour at Portsmouth, and it was there that his presence was needed. He took up his quarters at the Greyhound Inn, which had recently been purchased by Captain John Mason, cousin to Robert Mason, one of Buckingham's secretaries and paymaster of the forces under his command. At the Greyhound Buckingham lived in the midst of a swirling throng of courtiers, army officers, naval officers, clients and potential clients, place-seekers, and all those who had nothing better to do. Soubise was there, as were the delegates from La Rochelle. Kate was also in the house, to enjoy the brief time that she had until her husband was due to embark. She was accompanied by her sister-in-law, Lady Anglesey, the wife of Kit Villiers.

Buckingham's 'mastering spirits' had their customary effect, and the last-minute preparations were pushed ahead at breakneck speed. There were endless details to be settled – including the provision of ten pieces of tapestry for the Lord Admiral's cabin, as well as a tent for his personal use. Buckingham also had to restore discipline among the sailors, who were increasingly restive as the day of departure drew near. On the 17th, as he was leaving the Greyhound to go and report to the King at Southwick, a crowd of several hundred sailors surrounded his coach, shouting for pay. One man, bolder than the rest, tried to drag the Duke out of his seat, but Buckingham, who was never lacking in personal courage, leapt out himself, grabbed the man by the scruff of the neck, and carried him back into the inn, where he told Mason to keep him prisoner. He then drove off to Southwick, where his reception was in marked contrast. An eye-witness described how 'the King looked out of a window towards the down a whole hour, expecting his coming, before he

452

came; and when they found him coming, they all, lords and all, left the King and went down into the base court to meet him, as if he had been the greatest prince in the world'.[69]

When Buckingham returned to the Greyhound he found that Mason had handed his prisoner back to the sailors for fear that if he held on to him they would pull his house down. But the Duke summoned a council of war which condemned the mutineer in his absence and sentenced him to death. He was recaptured a few days later and was being conducted to prison when once again the sailors surged round his escort and threatened to carry him off by brute force. But the Duke, determined that the contagion of disobedience and insurrection should not be allowed to spread, was ready for them. He and

divers of his followers, colonels, captain[s] and others, went on horseback and, having their swords drawn, rode down the street and drove all the mariners before them . . . in a most furious manner, killing some two of them and wounding divers. After they were aboard, the Duke, with the Marshal and others, rode with the condemned mariner to the execution, which presently was performed on the gibbet between Portsmouth and Southsea Castle.[70]

On 22 August Buckingham wrote to Pennington to tell him that 'there can be no happy success expected in any enterprise . . . without an especial blessing from God', and to order him therefore 'to begin this great expedition for relief of Rochelle with a solemn worship of His almighty power'. Buckingham himself was indisposed and took to his bed, where he was visited by the King and the Earl of Holland. It was noted that when the Duke said goodbye he embraced the King 'in a very unusual and passionate manner, and in like sort his friend'. By the following morning, however, Buckingham had fully recovered, and when he went down into Mason's parlour he was greeted by Soubise with the (false) news that La Rochelle had been relieved. He was so delighted that he literally danced for joy, and then took a hasty breakfast before calling for his coach so that he could carry the good tidings to Southwick. By this time the parlour, like the hall beyond it, was crowded with people, and as the Duke moved towards the doorway that separated the two rooms he was stopped by Sir Thomas Fryer, one of his colonels, who had some business to discuss with him. After a brief consultation Sir Thomas bowed in salutation, and Buckingham, ever courteous, responded with an equally deep reverence. As he straightened up, a man leaned forward over the shoulder of Fryer, who was still bowing, and stabbed him through the left breast. Buckingham reeled back, with a cry of 'Villain!', plucked the knife from his wound, and reaching for his sword, which he half drew from its scabbard, staggered after his assassin. But he had stumbled only a few steps into the hall when he collapsed and would have fallen on the ground but for the press of people around him. He was laid on a table, while the astonished spectators, unable to credit the evidence of their own eyes, rushed from one room to another in search of the murderer. Kate Buckingham, who was with child again, had not come down with the Duke but stayed in bed. When she heard the noise below, she called out to Lady Anglesey and made her way on to an open gallery that overlooked the hall. She gazed down on a scene of indescribable confusion with one still point at its centre – the body of her husband, with blood gushing from its mouth.

So sudden and unexpected was the murder of the Duke that John Felton, the assassin, fled into the kitchens of the house before anyone was aware that he had committed the deed. He might have escaped altogether, but for the fact that many of those in the hall thought that the assassination must be the work of some agent of Louis XIII and rampaged through the lower floors of the house shouting that they were searching for 'A Frenchman! A Frenchman!' Felton, mishearing their shouts, assumed that it was his name they were calling, and came forward with his sword drawn, saying 'I am the man'. His pursuers would have killed him on the spot, but were restrained by some officers, who took charge of him and ordered him to be kept under guard until such time as he could be examined.[71]

The King was at Southwick, attending divine service in one of the rooms of the house, when a messenger from Portsmouth came in and whispered in his ear. According to Clarendon, Charles

continued umoved, and without the least change in his countenance, till prayers were ended; when he suddenly departed to his chamber, and threw himself upon his bed, lamenting with much passion and with abundance of tears the loss he had of an excellent servant and the horrid manner in which he had been deprived of him; and he continued in this melancholic . . . discomposure of mind many days.[72]

NOTES

(Abbreviations are explained in the Bibliography, pp. 477–86.)
1. *Chas.* 316, 324; *Dom.MSS* 16. 92.12; *Laud.* 207.
2. *A.P.C. 1627–8.* 221–4; *Roh.* 267; *Dom.MSS* 16. 90.49; 91.29, 35; *Fr.MSS.* 83.9; *Chas.* 317.
3. *Chas.* 325; *Dom.MSS* 16. 95.65, 79; 96.3; 98.27, 76; 100.84; 101.24; *C.S.P.V.* XX, 570; *A.P.C. 1627–8.* 363.
4. *Dom.MSS* 16. 98.29; 90.5, 38, 91.
5. *C.S.P.V.* XX, 607; *A.P.C. 1627–8.* 363; *H.M.C. (15).* 44; *Dom.MSS* 16. 98.26.
6. *C.S.P.V.* XX, 596; *Holl.MSS.* 136.37, 50, 103.
7. *Chas.* 313; *A.P.C. 1627–8.* 240; *Cab.* 330–31.
8. *Dom.MSS* 16. 28.56, 62v.–63; *A.P.C. 1627–8.* 266–7.
9. *Dom.MSS* 16. 94.37; 91.68.
10. *A.P.C. 1627–8.* 307–8.
11. *Crown.* 132–41; *A.P.C. 1627–8.* 231–2; *Holl.MSS.* 136.75.
12. *Dom.MSS* 16. 91.30; 103.19; 92.90, 93; *A.P.C. 1627–8.*251.
13. *Harg.MSS.* 321.140v.
14. *Harg.MSS.* 321.140; *C.S.P.V.* XX, 558–9; *Rush.* 470, 472; *Yale.* II, 277.
15. *Chas.* 309; *Dom.MSS* 16. 91.91, 93; 92.55, 90; *Swales; Rush.* 614–15.
16. *C.S.P.V.* XX, 584; *Hulme (2).* 184–5; *Sal.* 143.

17. *C.S.P.V.* XX, 605; *Wot.* 230–31; *Dom.MSS 16.* 91.91; 92.53; 96.36; *Chas.* 326.
18. *Chas.* 331; *L.J.* 687.
19. *L.J.* 688; *Yale.* II, 4.
20. *L.J.* 688; *Yale.* II, 61, 65, 122.
21. *Yale.* II, 121, 228, 56.
22. *Yale.* II, 244–5, 250, 246, 248; G.L. Harriss, 'Medieval Doctrines in the Debates on Supply, 1610–29', in *Sharpe. passim.*
23. *Yale.* II, 275, 302, 325.
24. *Dietz.* 246; *Rush.* 526.
25. *Yale.* II, 418–19, 430, 453.
26. *Dom. MSS 16.* 100.51, 64; 102.35; *A.P.C. 1627–8.* 375.
27. *Relf.* 75; *L.J.* 710, 851.
28. *Relf.* 132, 133.
29. *Relf.* 132; *L.J.* 767, 769, 772.
30. *Yale.* III, 94–8, 128–9, 189, 212–13.
31. *Yale.* III, 272, 338–41, 325.
32. *L.J.* 789–90; *Relf.* 152–5; *Chas.* 349; *Yale.* III, 391.
33. *Relf.* 155; *L.J.* 794–5.
34. *Relf.* 158, 163.
35. *Relf.* 169, 172, 166, 170, 173, 182, 186.
36. *L.J.* 808, 824; *Relf.* 192, 293, 200–1, 203, 205.
37. *Dom. MSS 16.* 103.57; 104.25.
38. *Dom. MSS 16.* 104.47, 21, 60.
39. *H.M.C. Coke.* 345; *L.J.* 835.
40. *Yale.* IV, 72–3, 75.
41. *Yale.* IV, 131.
42. *Chas.* 359–60; *Rush.* 610; *Yale.* IV, 124–5.
43. *Yale.* IV, 125–6, 128.
44. *Yale.* IV, 152.
45. *Chas.* 358; *L.J.* 840–44; *Relf.* 217.
46. *L.J.* 844; *Chas.* 362–3; *Rush.* 616; *Yale. IV, 260; C.J.* 911.
47. *Relf.* 225; *Chas.* 363.
48. *Rush.* 619–21.
49. *Rush.* 622–6.
50. *Rush.* 626; *Dom.MSS 16.* 107.78.
51. *Russell.* 227–9.
52. *L.J.* 860; *C.J.* 919; *Ven.MSS.* 30.58.
53. *A.P.C. 1627–8.* 447, 453; *Dom.MSS 16.* 106.4; *C.S.P.V.* XXI, 119.
54. *Harl.MSS.* 6988.87; *H.M.C.Coke.* 346–7.
55. *Dom.MSS 16.* 108.22; 106.31, 71; *H.M.C. Coke.* 348.
56. *Fr.MSS.* 83.127; *C.S.P.V.* XXI, 158, 213; *A.P.C. 1628–9.* 28; *Rob.* 293.
57. *H.M.C. Coke.* 357; *A.P.C. 1628–9.* 27, 23–4; *Dom.MSS 16.* 110.23, 10; *Chas.* 381.
58. *H.M.C. Coke.* 360.
59. *A.P.C. 1627–8.* 355, 451; *Dom.MSS 16.* 131.21; 112.55, 66; *Chas.* 371.
60. *H.M.C. Coke.* 357; *A.P.C. 1627–8.* 473; *Dom.MSS 16.* 108. 18; *Tann. MSS.* 276.114.
61. *A.P.C. 1628–9.* 5; *Dom.MSS 16.* 110.3; 109.20; *H.M.C.Coke.* 359.

62. *H.M.C.Coke* 359; *Dom.MSS 16.* 110.31; *Chas.* 378−9; *Hack.* II, 80, 82−3; *Sal.* 159.
63. *Notes and Queries*, Series II, Vol. 8 (1859), 222−3; *Sal.* 160; *A.P.C. 1628−9.* 103; *Dom.MSS 16.* 114.17.
64. *Lon.* 1170; *Rub.* Nos. 144, 146; p. 221.
65. *C.S.P.V.* XXI, 208; XX, 570.
66. *C.S.P.V.* XXI, 232, 234, 275−6, 260, 288; *H.M.C. Coke.* 364.
67. *Rous.* 16−18; *Rush.* 618; *D.N.B. sub* Lambe; *Dom.MSS 16. Addenda.* 528.78; *Kent MSS.* U.350.C/2/19.
68. *Dom.MSS 16.* 112.32; *Sal.*161; *Ogl.* 31.
69. *Dymond.* 3, 15; *Dom.MSS 16.* 133.139; *Ogl.* 33, 39.
70. *Ogl.* 33−4.
71. *Dom.MSS 16.* 113.49; 114.21; *Addenda.* 529.15; *Wot.* 235; *Ogl.* 34−5; *Eg.MSS.* 2533.62; *Rawl. MSS.* B. 183.191; *H.M.C. Sal.* 244−5; *H.M.C. Supp.* 244−5; *Kent MSS.* U.350.C/2/19; *Howell.* 253.
72. *Clar.* I, 37.

CHAPTER ELEVEN

Epilogue

I

The King ordered that nothing should be omitted which might in any way do honour to his dead friend, and when the embalmed body of Buckingham left Portsmouth, after a coroner's inquest, it was borne on the shoulders of the colonels of the army and escorted by all the lords who were in the town. As the cortège made its slow way to the point where a convoy of coaches was waiting to carry it to London, the town shot off its ordnance in salute and was followed by all the ships of the King's fleet, one after another. 'I never heard a braver peal of ordnance in my life,' declared one observer, 'or greater.' The coaches reached the outskirts of London late on 30 August, and the heralds, the chief officers of the Court and many of the nobility were waiting to escort the body, by torchlight, to Wallingford House. Among them was Laud, who, as he set out, was handed a letter which the Duke had written to him shortly before his death. Buckingham's corpse lay in state at Wallingford House for more than two weeks, while preparations were made for the funeral. The King had ordered that no expense should be spared and that a magnificent memorial should be erected to this greatest of his servants. But Weston, the Lord Treasurer, was said to have reminded Charles that the world would take notice if he built a rich sepulchre for the Duke before he had provided a suitable monument for his father, James I. And Buckingham's executors, appalled by the evidence of his heavy indebtedness, suggested that the money spared from his funeral would be better applied to the payment of his creditors.[1]

In the end, Buckingham was buried, without elaborate ceremony, on the night of 18 September. Torchlight burials were not uncommon at this time, but no doubt the organisers took into consideration the possibility that a daylight procession might give an opportunity for the rowdier elements among the onlookers to demonstrate their continuing hatred of the Duke. Even as it was, the London trained bands were stationed all along the route from Wallingford House, through Whitehall to Westminster Abbey, and according to one report the coffin which was carried in the procession was

457

empty, the corpse having been interred privately on the previous day. A great crowd lined the streets but there was no disturbance except 'some little noise', which, according to the Venetian ambassador, sounded 'more like joy than commiseration'. The soldiers of the trained bands, it was noted, kept up a loud tattoo on their drums, and carried their arms on their shoulders instead of trailing them as was customary at a funeral.[2]

Buckingham's last resting-place was on the north side of King Henry VII's chapel. Here he lay surrounded by monarchs and princes of the blood royal, the first commoner to be honoured in this way, although his baby son Charles and his nephew had already been interred there. In 1634 his widow, Kate, set up a magnificent tomb with an inscription that records her love for him and her belief that the world had misjudged him. On the black marble sarcophagus with weeping figures at each corner – among them Neptune and Mars – lie the bronze-gilt effigies of Buckingham and the Duchess, cast by Hubert Le Sueur. Buckingham is clad in armour, enriched with crossed anchors, and has his ermine robe about him. He wears on his breast the chain and George of the Garter, and on his head a ducal coronet. Looking down on their parents from the wall of the little side-chapel are the carved figures of their four children: Charles, who died as an infant and is shown recumbent, resting on a death's head; Mary ('Mall'); George, who was now the second Duke; and Francis, who was born in April 1629. The tomb was damaged, probably in the turbulent years of the mid-century, for the hatred which Buckingham inspired pursued him beyond the grave. But it is not the only memorial to him, for Susan Denbigh had a cenotaph erected in the parish church at Portsmouth to commemorate the brother whom she loved and whose affection for her had been demonstrated by the gift of an engraved crystal cross in the last year of his life.[3]

II

John Felton, the Duke's assassin, was interrogated at Portsmouth before being sent to trial. It was at first thought that he might be only one of a number of conspirators, but it soon became evident that he had acted alone and of his own volition. He was the younger son of a family of minor gentry in Suffolk, and had earned his living as a professional soldier, serving as a lieutenant in the Ré campaign. Anger at not being promoted to a captaincy, and bitterness at the indebtedness into which he had been plunged by endless delays in receiving his pay, prompted him to some desperate action, but it was, in his own words, through 'reading the remonstrance of the House of Parliament [that] it came into his mind [that] by . . . killing the Duke he should do his country great service'. He assumed that he would himself be cut down without having time to explain his motives, so he stitched a paper into the lining of his hat which recorded his belief that 'that man is cowardly, base, and deserveth not the name of a gentleman or soldier, that is not willing to sacrifice his life for the honour of his God, his King and his country. Let no man commend me for doing of it, but rather discommend themselves as the cause of it. For if God had not taken away our hearts for our sins, he [Buckingham] would not have gone so long unpunished.'[4]

Felton was a melancholy man, much given to reading, and of few words. He was the prototype of the puritan 'fanatics' who were to appear in extraordinary numbers when the great rebellion broke out in the 1640s. As far as the King and the law were concerned he was no more than a common murderer, but to the majority of his compatriots he was a hero and saviour. As he passed through Kingston on his way to London, one old woman cried out 'God bless thee, little David', for in her eyes Felton was the protestant champion who had slain Goliath. He was brought to the Tower and taken through Traitors' Gate to the lodgings previously occupied by Sir John Eliot. The crowds flocked to gaze on the place of his imprisonment and to pray that he would remain firm and unbowed. But in fact, as Felton brooded on what he had done, he came to believe that he had been guided not by God but by the devil. It cannot have been fear — other than fear of divine judgement — that prompted him to this change of heart, for he was well treated and never subjected to torture. Yet in his last speech he called on all those who were present not to think that the deed had been well done. 'It was abhorrent. I have much dishonoured God in it.' On 27 November Felton was brought to trial before the judges of the King's Bench in Westminster Hall, where the knife he had used, 'all defiled and besmeared with blood, as it came out of the Duke's breast', lay before him. Since he pleaded guilty the proceedings were purely formal, and he was sentenced to death. On the following day he received the sacrament, 'with great desire and devotion', and on the day after that, Saturday 29 November, he was carried to Tyburn, where he was hanged. His body was subsequently dumped in a cart and taken to Portsmouth — traversing the same route as that along which his victim's corpse had earlier been carried with so much honour — and was hung up in chains just outside the town. Felton, unlike Buckingham, had no marble tomb or engraved epitaph, but poems in praise of him circulated all over England. Their sentiment was unmistakable:

> Awake sad Britain and advance at last
> Thy drooping head: let all thy sorrows past
> Be drowned and sunk with their own tears; and now
> O'erlook thy foes with a triumphant brow.
> Thy foe, Spain's agent, Holland's bane, Rome's friend,
> By one victorious hand received his end.
> Live ever, Felton: thou hast turned to dust
> Treason, ambition, murder, pride and lust.[5]

III

By the time Felton was executed, news had reached London of the fall of La Rochelle. The King had not allowed Buckingham's death to delay the sailing of the relief expedition, and he had given command of it to the Earl of Lindsey. But Lindsey was unable to break through the palisade. He was not without courage, but he was poorly supported by timid commanders and their defeatist men, and he did not have the panache that Buckingham would have shown nor the determination to succeed or die in the attempt. The only result of his efforts was to demonstrate beyond any possibility of doubt that the King of England was unable to keep his promise to aid La Rochelle, and on 18 October the Huguenot stronghold capitulated. Charles was reluctant to acknowledge defeat, but without Buckingham to spur him on and guide him he had no heart for a continuation of the war. In any case he could not afford it, for the five subsidies voted by Parliament would not meet his current needs, let alone provide for new ones. The Venetian offer to try to produce a settlement of the differences between the two crowns was now accepted, and eventually, in April 1629, peace was signed between England and France. Nothing was said about any of the major issues involved, but there was a tacit agreement to bury the past. By the end of the following year, 1630, England was also at peace with Spain. The terms of the treaty were in the main a repetition of those of 1604, but Philip IV gave a written promise to do all that he could to ensure the restoration of the Palatinate. England now withdrew into inglorious isolation, and the responsibility, as well as the credit, for checking the advance of Habsburg power, was left to the Dutch (as always), Gustavus Adolphus of Sweden, and, at long last, Richelieu.

IV

Buckingham's will, which he had drawn up in June 1627 before setting off on the expedition to Ré, made his wife and his son his principal heirs. There were a number of bequests to relatives and to members of his household. Susan Denbigh was left £5,000 and the Earl of Northampton (the brother of Buckingham's step-father) £7,000. Richard Oliver, who had been responsible, as receiver-general, for handling Buckingham's revenues, was bequeathed £1,000; Thomas Fotherly, his solicitor, was left £500, as were Edward Nicholas and Robert Mason, two of the Duke's secretaries. Nicholas's father wrote to his son to say how glad he was to hear of this testimony of his master's love, and to hope that he received it. His paternal caution was justified, for Buckingham was in debt to the tune of £70,000 and many of his lands were mortgaged. Charles appointed a special commission to enquire into the Duke's finances, but it proved impossible, in practice, to draw a clear line between Buckingham's public and private expenditure. Many of his financial obligations had been contracted in the King's service, but as Clarendon noted, this had been done 'in such a manner that there remained no evidence of it, nor was any of the Duke's officers entrusted with the knowledge of it, nor was there any record of it but in His Majesty's own generous memory'. The King, soon after he heard of Buckingham's assassination, had promised to be 'a husband to his Duchess, a father to his children, a master to his servants, and an executor to pay his debts', and he kept his word. Most of the debts had apparently been paid off within two years of the Duke's death, but the complicated issue of his mortgaged properties held up the probate of his will until March 1635.[6]

Charles continued to cherish Buckingham's memory, and it was noted in 1633 that 'not only his posterity, but the connexions of his house as well, are constantly experiencing the favour of the royal support and protection of their interests'. Charles was not alone in his devotion to the Duke. Some indication of the degree of loyalty and affection which Buckingham inspired in those who were close to him is given by the fact that Laud, in his will, remembered all the surviving members of the Duke's family, while Endymion Porter charged all his sons 'that they, leaving the like charges to their posterity, do all of them observe and respect the children and family of my Lord Duke of Buckingham, deceased, to whom I owe all the happiness I had in the world'.[7] When Kate – who also never wavered in her love for her dead husband, but could not endure the strain of widowhood – decided to remarry, she did so without informing the King, since she feared, rightly, that he would not approve of her action. And when she subsequently reverted to the Roman Catholic faith which she had only abandoned in order to wed Buckingham, Charles took her children away from her and had them brought up with his own.[8]

Until she remarried, Kate lived on in York House and kept the magnificent art collection largely intact. In law, however, both the house and its treasures belonged to her eldest son, the second Duke, and when, as a consequence of his support of the King in the civil war, his estates were confiscated by order of Parliament, York House was granted to Sir Thomas Fairfax, commander of the Parliamentary armies. In 1655 Evelyn described the house and its gardens as 'much ruined through neglect', but two years later the second Duke married Fairfax's daughter and went back to live in his old home.[9] Formal ownership was restored to him in 1660, at the return of Charles II, but from then on York House was usually let, and in the early 1670s he sold it. Apart from the water-gate, now marooned in Embankment Gardens, only the names of Villiers Street, Buckingham Street and Duke's Alley bear silent testimony to a glory long since departed.

Wallingford House passed to the second Duke after his father's assassination, but he did not live there until 1660. From then on, however, Wallingford House was his principal London residence. It was pulled down a few years after his death in 1687, and the site is now occupied by the Admiralty buildings in Whitehall.

Chelsea House, which Evelyn described as 'a spacious and excellent place for the extent of ground and situation, in a most sweet air', served as a place of retreat for Kate Buckingham when she tired of York House.[10] It was sequestrated, along with the second Duke's other properties, in the civil war, but handed back at the Restoration. In 1674 it was sold to the second Earl of Bristol, the son of Buckingham's old enemy, and later passed into the possession of the Duke of Beaufort. It was pulled down in the early eighteenth century, and Beaufort Street now runs through the site.

Burley-on-the-Hill, which was, according to Evelyn 'worthily reckoned among the noblest seats in England, situate·on the brow of an hill, built *à la modern* near a park walled-in, and a fine wood at the descent', was burnt down by Parliamentary soldiers during the civil war.[11] Only the stables survived until, in 1705, they too were burnt, this time by accident. The property was bought from the second Duke's executors by Daniel Finch, Earl of Nottingham, who built the present mansion.

Of all the houses which Buckingham inhabited, only New Hall remains. After its sequestration during the civil war it became for a time the property of Oliver Cromwell, but in 1660 it returned to the ownership of the second Duke. He sold it, however, to George Monck, Duke of Albemarle, from whom it passed through many hands. A large part of the house was pulled down in the eighteenth century, but enough remains for the ghost of Buckingham to recognise if ever he revisits it.

The great collection of paintings at York House was dispersed during the civil war. The second Duke, who went into exile in Holland after the collapse of the royalist. cause, and was desperately short of money, sold some two hundred pictures at Antwerp in 1648, among them many of the finest, and they thereby passed into public and private collections throughout Europe. Other items were bought by English purchasers to adorn their country houses, while some remained in possession of various members of the Villiers family.[12]

The dynasty which Buckingham had hoped to found did not last long. The second Duke, who was a politician, playwright, spendthrift and debauchee (not necessarily in that order) died at the age of fifty-nine, in April 1687. He left no legitimate heirs, and all the titles that he had inherited from his father died with him. They could not pass to his younger brother, Francis Villiers, for Francis – whom Clarendon described as 'a youth of rare beauty and comeliness of person' – had been killed in a skirmish with roundhead troops in 1648, when he was only nineteen.[13]

Buckingham's brothers were hardly more fortunate than the Duke in their efforts to establish their dynasties. The younger brother, Christopher, passed on his Earldom of Anglesey to a son, but the line stopped there. The elder brother, John, Viscount Purbeck, had no legitimate issue. His wife, Frances, gave birth to a son whom she called Robert Villiers, but it seems likely that his father was her lover, Sir Robert Howard. Under the terms of the patent which granted Buckingham his earldom, the title was to pass, in default of heirs of his own body, to Purbeck's children, and in due course a claimant appeared in the shape of Robert Villiers's grandson, who assumed the style of Earl of Buckingham and was buried under that name in 1723. But neither the crown nor the House of Lords ever acknowledged his right to this or any other dignity.

The senior branch of the Villiers family was represented by Buckingham's half-brother, Sir William Villiers, but his descendants did not survive beyond the early eighteenth century. Indeed the Villiers name might have died out altogether had it not been for the children of Buckingham's other half-brother, Sir Edward Villiers. Sir Edward's eldest son had no male heirs, though he achieved the unlooked-for distinction of fathering Barbara Villiers, who became one of the most notorious of Charles II's mistresses. It was through Sir Edward's fourth son that the line was continued into the present day, in the persons of the Villiers Earls of Jersey.

V

At the time of his assassination Buckingham was without doubt the most unpopular man in England. As a person he was renowned for his courtesy, his charm of manner, and his readiness to oblige all those who were in any way linked to him. Yet despite these qualities he aroused a hatred among the public at large that was without precedent. Part of the reason for this was his position as favourite. As Sir Henry Wotton commented, drawing on his long experience both at home and abroad, 'everywhere all greatness of power and favour is circumvested with much prejudice'. Previous favourites had been targets for criticism and abuse from those who were envious of their good fortune or had suffered under their displeasure. Elizabeth's favourite, Robert Dudley, Earl of Leicester, for instance, earned the tribute of a bitter epitaph from Sir Walter Raleigh that could, with a few changes, be equally applied to Buckingham:

> Here lies the noble warrior that never blunted sword;
> Here lies the noble courtier that never kept his word;
> Here lies His Excellency that governed all the state;
> Here lies the Lord of Leicester that all the world did hate.[14]

Yet although Leicester aroused intense dislike in certain quarters, he was never singled out as the sole cause of all evils. The explanation for this lies in the character of Queen Elizabeth. She was a capable and determined ruler, who enjoyed the exercise of power and appreciated the need to balance one faction against another if she was to retain her freedom of action. She was also mistress of her own emotions, and seldom allowed her personal inclinations to dominate her attitude towards public business. While Leicester, and subsequently Essex, enjoyed the benefits of her favour they never acquired a monopoly of influence over her; indeed, when Essex tried to break out of the restraints imposed upon him, he ended up on the scaffold. In short, there could be no doubt that in Elizabethan England it was the Queen who ruled, and just as she accepted the credit for the glories of her reign, so she acknowledged her responsibility for whatever went wrong.

Elizabeth was not alone in this respect, for her contemporaries, Philip II of Spain and Henri IV of France, were equally dedicated and effective sovereigns. But the early seventeenth century saw the emergence of *Rois fainéants*, monarchs who made a pretence of ruling but found the business of government uncongenial and often beyond their capabilities and preferred to leave it to others. This was, on the face of it, a sensible attitude, since sovereigns only attained their high position through the accident of birth and there was no logical reason why they should thereby be fitted for the complex task of ruling a state. Yet the *Rois fainéants* came at a stage in the development of the political communities of Europe when the authority of the sovereign had expanded enormously and was continuing to expand. The threat to stability arising from the struggles of ambitious magnates in the late Middle Ages had been overcome by concentrating power in the monarch, and this development had been intensified as a result of the disorder that accompanied the Reformation of the sixteenth century. Only by dictating the nature of the religious settlement which his dominions should adopt, and forcing his subjects to accept it, could a ruler hope to hold in check the centrifugal forces of religious change. Whether a state broke with Rome or remained within the papal fold made little difference to the process whereby the temporal ruler became, to a greater or lesser extent, a spiritual head as well. The sovereigns of Europe by the seventeenth century were therefore entrusted with the guardianship not simply of their subjects' bodies but also of their souls.

The duty of controlling the spiritual as well as the temporal destinies of their people devolved on kings because they were appointed directly by God for this purpose. What later centuries might regard as the random operation of chance was generally accepted as an indication of providence at work. Christ had declared that even a humble sparrow could not fall to the ground except through an act of God, and if the divine ordering of the universe extended to such apparently trivial occurrences, it could be taken for granted that it operated with equal force in major matters such as the choice of monarchs to rule God's people. 'The state of monarchy', as James I informed the House of Commons, 'is the supremest thing upon earth. For kings are not only God's lieutenants upon earth and sit upon God's throne, but even by God himself they are called gods.'[15] If kings were unwilling or unable to exercise their sacred functions in person, they could do so by deputy. But the man singled out for this task was much more than a minister. He was, in effect, an aspect of the sovereign's person, a surrogate monarch – not exactly a king, since he had not been born to the throne; but not exactly a subject either, so long as he had the halo of regal authority around him.

The status of a favourite, and the range of his power, depended upon the extent to which the king was or was not prepared to exercise in person those functions with which he alone had been entrusted. James I, despite appearances, was not a *roi fainéant*. He loved power – even though he used it in a way that was markedly different from that of Elizabeth – and in the face of considerable opposition he kept control over English foreign policy firmly in his own hands until the last year of his life. James's favourites, therefore, were literally playthings – young men whose company relieved the tedium of both work and leisure, as well as satisfying his emotional needs. Buckingham was typical in this respect, since he enjoyed all the rewards of favour in James's reign but was in no sense a maker of policy – not, that is, until after his return from Spain in the autumn of 1623. In Spain, however, he saw at first hand how a favourite (*privado*) could establish his political supremacy (*privanza*) and become a virtual ruler. Philip IV was not much more than a puppet, and although he saw the minutes of council meetings and scrawled his approval – *Yo, el Rey* (I, the King) – at the bottom of them, he was usually content to follow the lead of Olivares. Unlike Buckingham, Olivares was not his King's plaything; indeed he had little time for anything except work. He was Philip's political *alter ego*, the executor of those powers of decision-making which belonged to Philip by birth but which Philip preferred to exercise by deputy.

It cannot be taken for granted that Buckingham returned from Spain determined to arrogate to himself the functions of a chief minister, and thereby create an English *privanza*, but the pressure of events drove him inexorably in this direction. The long months of negotiations in Madrid had brought him up against the harsh realities of the European power struggle and forced him to the conclusion that James's policy was not only unsound but positively dangerous to the state over which he ruled. Yet James remained king and could not simply be dispensed with. He had to be persuaded to change his mind, and this could only be done through an alliance between Buckingham and those elements within the political nation that wanted England to play a far more positive and committed part in the European power struggle. This combination was successful, for James was eventually manoeuvred into war; and in the process Buckingham completed his political education at breakneck speed by extending his skills in management from the sphere of patronage – in which he was already well versed – to that of public affairs.

It was with the accession of Charles I that Buckingham became an English *privado*, for Charles was much more of a *roi fainéant* than his father had been. He was not without ideas of his own, of course – though they were conceived in personal rather than political terms – and during the period of Buckingham's illness in 1624 he had shown himself to be quite capable of directing the campaign which the Duke had set in motion. Charles could never simply be taken for granted, and on matters that interested him – religion, for instance, and the royal prerogative – he would make his will known. But he was not a natural politician, and the details of administration bored him. Part of the reason for his involvement in 1624 was that he had little else to occupy him, but this state of affairs gradually changed after his marriage to Henrietta Maria. Relations between the young couple were at first very strained, but after the expulsion of the French household they rapidly improved, and by August 1627 Charles was able to inform Buckingham that 'my wife and I were never better together; she . . . showing herself so loving to me . . . upon all occasions that it makes us all wonder and esteem her'. The Queen took little or no interest in political matters. She had not been brought up to do so; she had little understanding of the workings of English government; and, above all, she was a young and attractive woman, determined to enjoy life to the full. One of the Duke's correspondents when he was in Ré commented on the fact that the Queen did not seem unduly troubled by the war between her husband and her brother: 'only at the first she was a little sad, but now she is very merry'. Her irresponsible high spirits infected the whole Court, and although Charles was full of good intentions towards his absent friend, most of his time was passed in hunting and other agreeable diversions. When, on Buckingham's return, Charles sent letters and envoys to welcome him home and assure him that he was not held responsible in any way for the failure of English arms, the King was expressing his awareness of his own limitations as a ruler.[16]

Charles was by nature a reserved man, with an exalted view of the kingly office to which God had summoned him. As a boy he had been jealous of Buckingham, but as he grew up the friendship between the two men ripened and was confirmed by their journey together to Spain. As far as Charles was concerned, Buckingham was a *de facto* member of the royal family, on whose devotion and loyalty to the interests of his crown and state he could unquestioningly rely. It must have been a great relief to him to know that the political aspect of kingship which he was unsuited to exercise in person was in the hands of someone who stood so close to him that he was, to all intents and purposes, part of himself. Buckingham, then, in Charles's eyes, was not simply a minister, to be dismissed if necessary in response to public pressure. Power and authority derived from God, not from the people, and they were transmitted through the King and not through any representative assembly. Charles's model of the relationship between him and his favourite derived from the Bible, as he had shown in 1626 when he reminded Parliament that 'the old question was "What shall be done to the man whom the King will honour?"' This was the question that King Ahasuerus asked the prophet Haman, and Haman's reply was immediate and unequivocal. 'Let the royal apparel be brought which the King useth to wear,' he answered, 'and the horse that the King rideth upon, and the crown royal which is set upon his head . . . that they may array the man withal whom the King delighteth to honour.'[17]

The creation of a *privanza* in England had constitutional implications which the leaders of the Commons instinctively recognised, even if they could not define them. These men were not in any sense republican. In April 1628 the Commons assured Charles that he was 'the breath of our nostrils and the light of our eyes', and begged him to believe 'that nothing is or can be more dear to us than the sacred rights and prerogatives of your crown'. Yet it was clear to them that something had gone wrong with the running of the state, and since it was axiomatic that the King could not be responsible, the blame must rest on his favourite. There was nothing consciously hypocritical about their attitude. Sir John Eliot, a devout monarchist, was convinced that with Buckingham out of the way the goodness of the King — which he compared to 'the glory of the sun, not capable in itself of any obscurity or eclipse' — would once again shine upon them. After all, the political assumptions of the day provided no alternative to royal rule. If the Commons had accepted that it was the King and not his counsellors who was responsible for the mistakes in judgement that had been made, they would have been forced to acknowledge that the constitutional foundations upon which the state and society rested had collapsed. This was a truth too dreadful to contemplate, and it explains why even as late as 1642, when civil war had actually broken out, Parliament still insisted that it was fighting for the King against his evil advisers.[18]

The King was entrusted by law with a large and ill-defined prerogative, and a basic constitutional assumption – without which the system could not work satisfactorily, if at all – was that he would not abuse this trust. If he did so, God would call him to account. There was no such restriction on a favourite, however, since favourites were appointed by Kings and not directly by the Almighty. Yet the very fact that a favourite derived his authority from the King meant that there was no way of removing him other than by persuading the King to change his mind and withdraw his confidence. This is what the Commons were pressing Charles to do throughout the opening years of his reign, and this is why they would never accept what the King took for granted, that Buckingham's policies and actions had his full assent. It was this desperate need to separate the King in his public capacity from his *alter ego*, the favourite, that accounts for Eliot's hostile reaction, in the 1628 Parliament, to Sir John Coke's report that Buckingham, as well as the King, had been delighted at the Commons' offer of five subsidies. 'It is our King we serve,' said Eliot. 'We wholly rely on his goodness, and on none else.'[19]

The debates in the Commons in 1628 show that what members dreaded more than anything else was a change in the established form of government and an alteration of the religious settlement. Their fear of innovation in the state was derived in large part from their instinctive awareness of the arbitrariness of Buckingham's authority, of the great power that he wielded without being formally accountable to either man or God. Yet there are few signs that Buckingham himself felt that radical changes in the English system of government were needed. As one who had made his way in the Court and was dependent upon royal favour, he had a natural veneration for the prerogatives of the crown. But as a country gentleman, and an Englishman to boot, he took it for granted that traditional ways were best. He was as incapable as were his opponents of accepting that the English constitution, that great work of time, was unable to resolve the problems of government in a peaceful and acceptable manner. He always looked back to what in retrospect seemed to be the golden days of 1624, when he and Parliament seemed to be as one in pursuit of the common cause, and he never gave up hope of restoring that harmony.

Yet Buckingham was also responsible, by the King's appointment, for conducting the course of a major war. One of the basic tenets of the English constitution was that the King's subjects should come to his aid in times of emergency, and what emergency could be greater than war? It was the (to him inexplicable) failure of the House of Commons to play its traditional role in this respect that led Buckingham to approve of the extension of the prerogative, through such actions as the forced loans of 1626. In the last resort the King was responsible for the safety of his subjects, and if the subjects refused to save themselves then the King was obliged to act for them. It was a question of priorities. Constitutional liberties were a valuable, indeed an essential, part of the relationship between the King and his people, but they were not an end in themselves. The supreme consideration must always be the safety of the state. After all, if Spanish or French troops had ever actually landed in England and marched on London, it is unlikely that they would have been deterred by the sight of old Sir Edward Coke brandishing the Petition of Right in their faces.

Was Buckingham correct in believing that England was in danger? The brief answer must be yes, because in 1626 and 1628 there were very real possibilities of foreign invasion. But a more considered and long-term response to this question must depend upon the acceptance or otherwise of Buckingham's evaluation of the international situation as it developed after his return from Spain in 1623. He believed that the House of Austria, in the persons of the King of Spain and the Holy Roman Emperor, was aiming at domination of the entire western world, and that unless England joined with other threatened states to prevent the achievement of this ambition she would lose her capacity to determine her own future. This view may have been unsound, but it accorded remarkably well with the facts of the European situation. The Emperor Ferdinand II was actively extending his authority in Germany, with the help of Spanish money and (in the case of the Palatinate) Spanish arms, while Spain herself was engaged in the struggle against the Dutch which, if only she could bring it to a successful conclusion, would leave her firmly established in one of the most strategically important parts of the European continent, well placed to expand in all directions.

If, as seems credible, Buckingham's reading of the international situation was correct, why did not his fellow-Englishmen rally round him in their own defence? One reason was that they distrusted him. As James I's favourite he had been identified with the pro-Spanish policy and had been held to a considerable extent responsible for it. Why should the poacher be trusted simply because he now declared himself to be a gamekeeper? But this was not the only, or indeed the major, reason. Buckingham realised that no anti-Habsburg league would be effective in the long run unless it included France – an assumption which, as events were to show, was justified – and that France would not join any alliance which was specifically protestant. In other words, the best interests of England demanded a marriage link and military cooperation with a major catholic power. If part of the price for this had to be a relaxation of the laws against the English catholics, so be it. No single issue aroused more distrust of Buckingham than this. Whereas his cast of mind, like his strategy, was essentially secular, that of the leaders of the Commons, and indeed of the people of England as a whole, was essentially religious. They wanted a holy war against the catholics, particularly the Most Catholic King of Spain, and they regarded it as an integral part of this crusade to suppress the enemy within their own gates. This was a duty imposed upon them by God, for only if they demonstrated their commitment to true religion by actively persecuting the catholics at home could they be sure that He would bless and prosper their endeavours abroad. They looked for evidence that Buckingham shared this assumption, and found none. Far from abhorring Roman Catholics and keeping his distance from them, Buckingham was closely linked to the catholic community in England. His mother and father-in-law were professed adherents of the old faith; his wife had abandoned her religion only out of love for him, and might well relapse; and among his friends were many practising catholics. Was it any wonder therefore that God did not bless his endeavours? The failure of English arms under Buckingham's leadership was, in the general opinion, directly attributable to his ambivalent attitude towards the English catholics.

Buckingham's critics might have felt less apprehensive if they had been convinced that the King was firmly on their side. Charles was, after all, supreme governor of the Church of England and defender of the protestant faith established in his kingdom. But there were grounds, or so it seemed, for doubting the depth of his commitment. When Charles was in Spain he wrote to Gregory XV using terms of respect and friendship that shocked all those who believed that the Pope was anti-Christ and should be treated as such.[20] Then, after his accession to the throne, he showed favour to the Arminian wing of the anglican church, and Arminians, as the Commons informed him, were nothing less than papists in disguise. Yet in religious as in constitutional matters, the King's potential critics could not face up to the awful possibility that the cornerstone of the entire structure might be unsound. They therefore laid the blame upon Buckingham, whose catholic connexions and friendship with Laud, a noted Arminian, seemed to demonstrate his own perverse religious inclinations. This made their dislike and hatred of the favourite even more intense.

Had Buckingham simply been a playboy-favourite he would probably have been tolerated. It was his political and, above all, his military power, that made him so feared. Wars cannot be fought without armies, and although troops may be raised in the first instance to fight a foreign enemy they can easily be turned against opponents nearer home. This was particularly the case when, as with the Irish troops in 1628, the soldiers included catholics among their ranks. The English had only to lift their eyes across the Channel to see that standing armies were not compatible with political liberties. Had the royal army been commanded by the King in person there might have been less apprehension, since the King's authority, while potentially very great, had the sanction of legitimacy, and in practice operated within limits that were thought to be known and capable of definition. But for the army to be under the control of an irresponsible subject, whose catholic connexions seemed likely to incline him towards support of despotism on the Spanish or French model, was too much for the country gentlemen who set the tone of English life. Hence their refusal in Parliament to finance war on anything like the scale that was needed. Why should they provide money for armies that might be turned against them? Yet by starving the executive they laid the kingdom open to the peril of invasion and forced Charles to take those self-same prerogative measures which they were so anxious to avert. In other words it was their own actions which, however well intentioned, brought down upon themselves the evils that they feared.

There was one further reason for the distrust which Buckingham aroused. Despite the sneers about frivolous courtiers who were fit only for dancing, gambling and whoring, Buckingham's enemies recognised that he was a man who got things done. Through the networks of patronage and family connexions which he had so carefully and laboriously established he wielded considerable influence – though nothing like as great or as coordinated as many people assumed. And through his good choice of subordinates, his capacity for hard work, and his 'mastering spirits', he achieved what were, in the prevailing circumstances, miracles of organisation. If Buckingham really had been nothing more than an empty-headed courtier, committed to the pursuit of endless fripperies, his enemies would not have feared him so much. Their hatred of him was the involuntary tribute they paid to a man who had power and knew how to use it.

The Commons professed to believe that the financial wounds from which the crown was suffering were largely self-inflicted, and that any reconstruction of the royal revenue system must be preceded by a resumption of all those lands and other sources of income which had been given away, particularly to Buckingham and his kindred. This belief was to some extent justified, for James's reckless generosity had clearly weakened the financial position of the crown, and Buckingham had been a major beneficiary of royal favour. But his rewards, however unjustified they may have been in the eyes of most men, were not out of proportion to those which others received for service to the crown. Appointment to high office was sought after because it provided an opening to wealth as well as power. Even under the parsimonious Elizabeth, William Cecil, Lord Burghley, had built up a great fortune, and left his descendants, the Earls of Exeter and Salisbury, firmly established among the leading English families. Salisbury himself was an office holder on a far larger scale than Buckingham, and his income, in the closing years of his life, was at least £25,000 a year. Buckingham, even when full allowance is made for underhand payments, is unlikely to have received more, and probably got a good deal less. It could be argued that Salisbury was untypical in this respect, yet even in the years of relative stringency which followed Buckingham's death, royal service still offered much the same rewards. This was shown in the career of Sir Thomas Wentworth, later Earl of Strafford, who by 1639 had increased his income, mainly as a result of holding high office, to £23,000 a year. The figure for Buckingham does not, of course, take into account the gifts which his kindred received, but Salisbury and Wentworth likewise were not without dependants who benefited from their success. In short, Buckingham's rewards in the King's service – and it was a service to which he committed himself wholeheartedly – were not exceptional by the standards of his day. Nor would the crown's financial problems have been solved if his entire estate had been handed over to the royal treasury. It was the great inflation of the years after 1540 and the increasing costs of government which had under-

470

mined the financial position of the crown; and James – a spendthrift on a truly regal scale – had pushed matters beyond hope of recovery. By the time Charles I came to the throne, the royal revenues were insufficient to cover day-to-day expenditure; they certainly could not satisfy the demands of war. Hence the King's repeated appeals to Parliament, for as Charles frequently reminded members, it was only after their promise to assist the crown in the event of war, 'both with our persons and abilities', that his father had broken off the negotiations with Spain.[21]

The Commons were not unresponsive, but they were never prepared to provide anything like the sums required to meet the various commitments entered into by James and Charles – Mansfeld's expedition, the setting-out of the fleet, and subsidies to the Danes and the Dutch. There was nothing surprising about this. Members of the Commons were, after all, representatives of the local communities, and these consisted of ordinary men and women whose main concern was with local issues, in particular the trade recession, shortage of coin, continuing inflation and the problem of poor relief. They approved of war in principle, but only on condition that it was in support of the protestant cause, was directed against Spain, was successful, and cost virtually nothing. They dreaded the idea of being required to contribute more and more by way of subsidies to the crown, and they were also deeply resentful of the disturbance of their traditional pattern of life which war produced. They had to pay for the better arming and training of the local militia; they had to provide soldiers for the King's service, billet them, and issue them with clothes, all at their own expense. If they lived in coastal regions they were called on to provide ships or ship money at a time when their trade was suffering from enemy action, and their lives, as well as their livelihoods, were threatened by the dreaded Dunkirkers and Barbary corsairs. Even the inhabitants of inland regions were affected by war. They were liable to be disturbed by bands of mutinous sailors and soldiers; they were required to pay pensions to local men maimed or wounded in the King's service; and they were increasingly subject to the prerogative authority of the Lord Lieutenants and their deputies – which Sir Robert Phelips described as 'the strangest engine to rend the liberty of the subject that ever was'.[22]

The attitude of the local communities was not heroic, but in this they were no different from ordinary men and women throughout western Europe. The big difference between England and continental states such as France and Spain consisted in the relative lightness of the English tax burden and the limited powers which the King had to compel his subjects to pay for their defence. In Spain the government could rely on the silver bullion flowing from the New World, but even so the burden of taxation, particularly on Castile, was immense, and when Olivares tried to spread it more evenly among the constituent kingdoms he provoked a revolt which led to the partial break-up of the Spanish state. In France there was no bullion supply to depend upon. Louis's subjects had to provide the money which kept his armies in the field, and they were taxed to such an extent that the life of the poor was hardly worth living. Taxation revolts became so frequent that by the second half of the seventeenth century the French king had to keep an army permanently stationed within his own territories to suppress rebellions and enable the task of tax collection to go ahead. In comparison with such actions Charles I's force loans were a measure of extreme conservatism and gentleness, and while he no doubt would have liked to command not only the resources but also the unquestioning obedience accorded to his fellow monarchs, he never made any pronounced move in the direction of absolutism while Buckingham was alive. Even if – which seems unlikely – the 'German horse' were designed to facilitate the collection of an excise, one thousand foreign cavalrymen would hardly have been able to subdue the entire English nation.

It has been argued that Buckingham, in view of the obvious impossibility of finding the sums needed to finance the policies of which he was the executor, should have scaled them down. But there were a number of objections to such a course. For one thing, his designs were not all that grandiose. A naval and military expedition against Spain and the despatch of twelve thousand men to Germany, as part of a combined operation with France, were hardly extravagant gestures for a state committed to war against a powerful enemy. As for subsidies to foreign allies, these have at all times been unpopular, but unless England were to fight in isolation – in which case she would probably fight to no purpose – she would have to contribute to the costs of keeping her allies in the field. There was the further consideration that after the long period of non-involvement of James's reign, potentially friendly foreign powers needed convincing that a change of heart really had taken place. Buckingham's strategy was intended to provide just such an assurance. And while the commitments which the King undertook were in one sense open-ended, they were not meant to go on for ever. The aim of Buckingham's policy was to bring Spain – and through her the Emperor – to the negotiating table. Commerce-raiding and attacks on the Spanish coast would not, of themselves, do this; only if Spain were confronted by a coalition of states which clearly meant business would she be forced to think again. There was an element of bluff in Buckingham's policy – as there was in that of all other states – but there were good grounds for hoping that it would yield results before the bluff was called. As for the argument that Buckingham's strategy, even if it was not grandiose, was more than the country could afford, it has to be borne in mind that there was virtually no limit on the amount that England, France, Spain or any other state could afford. What proportion of the nation's wealth was to be spent on fighting was a political question, not an economic one. The civil war was to show that English local communities were capable of providing, under pressure, sums of money on a scale that would have financed all Buckingham's objectives and a good deal more besides. That they did not choose to do so in the 1620s was a factor that the Duke had to take increasingly into account, but it was the will that was lacking, and not, in the last resort, the wealth.

Buckingham's identification with a policy of war, and his commitment to a secular rather than a religious strategy, are the fundamental reasons for the intense fear and therefore hatred that he aroused in Charles I's reign. War meant soldiers, and soldiers were a threat to the liberties of free-born Englishmen, for as a member of Parliament in Charles II's reign later observed, 'in peace there is nothing for an army to subdue but Magna Carta'. As for a secular strategy, this was bound to involve concessions to English catholics, and once the rot had set in there would be no stopping it. John Pym, speaking in the 1621 Parliament, declared that the papists, 'having gotten favour . . . will expect a toleration. After toleration they will look for equality. After equality, for superiority. And having superiority, they will seek the subversion of that religion which is contrary to theirs.'[23]

Since Buckingham was blamed for those aspects of Charles's policy which his subjects found unacceptable and alarming, there was a general assumption that the Duke's removal from the scene would mean the end of disharmony. Pembroke gave voice to this when he wrote to Carlisle, shortly after the assassination had taken place, and told him that 'the King our master begins to shine already, and I hope this next session to see a happy agreement between him and his people'. But Pembroke and those who thought like him were mistaken, for the next session ended with the Speaker being held down in the chair – the first open act of violence in a Stuart Parliament – and the beginning of eleven years of non-Parliamentary, prerogative rule. Buckingham's death did not solve the problem of the crown's lack of money, nor did it lessen the King's favour towards Arminian clergy or his tolerance of Roman Catholics. As Sir Philip Percival commented years later, in 1641, 'I remember I was in England when the Duke of Buckingham fell, whom many men thought the only cause of all the evils; but those that were of that opinion did not find it so afterwards.'[24]

While Buckingham was alive he fulfilled what James, according to one of the earliest historians of his reign, regarded as an essential function of his favourites. They were to be 'like burning-glasses [which] were daily interposed between him and the subject, multiplying the heat of oppressions in the general opinion, though in his own he thought they screened them from reflecting upon the crown'. With the screening mirror removed, the King was exposed to public criticism, for as Wentworth noted, following Buckingham's assassination, 'it is said at Court there is none now to impute our faults unto'. Charles himself was apparently unaware of the danger, for he had never understood how people could possibly believe that there was any distinction between Buckingham's policy and his own. According to one observer, writing in September 1628, 'the King is resolved to employ himself more, and by that to satisfy the people that the Duke was but his instrument to execute his commands; by which he will show how wrongfully he [Buckingham] was taxed'. Fortunately for Charles he did not carry out his resolution for long, and although he never had another favourite, never committed his government totally into the hands of any one person to the extent that he had done with Buckingham, he made use of ministers who in due course became objects of criticism and even hatred. As early as 1629, Sir John Eliot, always searching for scapegoats, accused Lord Treasurer Weston of following in the Duke's footsteps. Twelve years later, in 1641, the House of Commons attacked and destroyed one of its former heroes, Sir Thomas Wentworth, Earl of Strafford, for undermining the constitution by his too ardent championship of the royal prerogative. Ultimately, however, there was no one left to bear the blame for the King's actions except the King himself, but by that stage the framework of the constitution had collapsed and civil war was inevitable.[25]

Buckingham, then, was not the cause of all the evils from which England suffered in the 1620s. As long as he lived there was always an element of flexibility in the King's reaction to events – a flexibility which was lacking after he was no longer there to advise Charles. He was not a proponent of innovations in government, despite the general assumption to the contrary, and he constantly worked towards the objective of reconciliation between King and people – as was shown most clearly in the 1628 Parliament, when Sir John Coke, who was speaking for Buckingham as well as the King, went out of his way to acknowledge that the government had committed faults and to plead that the past should be consigned to oblivion by a gesture of trust and goodwill. The Commons were unable to make such a gesture. As befitted a body which was concerned with the drawing up of laws, they preferred formal, written guarantees to reliance on the mere word of a King. Perhaps they were right. Yet if only, during those early years of Charles's reign, they had been able to make a positive response to the King's repeated pleas for harmony and cooperation, the future course of events might have been very different. The Commons would not do so, however, as long as Buckingham kept his place at the King's side, for they distrusted everything he seemed to represent. It may be that they also hated him because he had called England, through them, to a greatness which they longed for but were – like those they represented – incapable of achieving. It was much easier to blame Buckingham for everything that had gone wrong than to consider the possibility that the causes went far deeper than personalities and might have to be located in fundamental weaknesses in the system of government and the structure of society that they had inherited. They clung to this inheritance with all the tenacity of drowning men, for they could not conceive of any acceptable alternative. They believed they had a duty, no less God-given than the King's, to maintain those rights which their ancestors had won for them and to pass them on, essentially unaltered, to future generations. What they abhorred above all was the idea of change, for in the context of early seventeenth-century Europe change meant movement towards despotism, and catholic despotism at that. Buckingham's catholic connexions and his constant involvement in diplomacy with foreign powers made him suspect in their eyes; his horizons, they feared, were not bounded by the sea that mercifully insulated England from a troubled continent. Who knew what ambitions he might have for establishing his own power and authority upon the ruins of the English church and state? They hated him not so much for what he was, as for what they feared he might become. He was, in short, the personification of their own neuroses, and they succeeded in convincing not only themselves but subsequent generations that Buckingham was an enemy to everything that the name and history of England symbolised. Yet now that the dust of more than three centuries has settled on the embers of those bitter passions, the Duke may be given a chance to speak for himself, in the words he used to Parliament in 1625.

I have not had a thought, nor entered into an action [he told the assembled members] but what might tend to the advancement of the business [the common cause] and please your desires. . . When I consider the integrity of mine own soul and heart to the King and state, I receive courage and confidence . . . being so well assured of your justice that without cause you will not fall on him that was so lately approved by you, and who will never do anything to irritate any man to have other opinion of me than of a faithful, true-hearted Englishman.[26]

NOTES

(Abbreviations are explained in the Bibliography, pp. 477–86.)
1. *Eg.MSS.* 2533.62v.; *Dom.MSS 16.* 114.27; *Ogl.* 40–1; *Sal.* 163; *Laud.* 209; *Chas.* 391, 400.
2. *C.S.P.V.* XXI, 337; *Chas.* 399.
3. *Add.MSS.* 12,528.36v.
4. *Wot.* 231; *Dom.MSS 16.* 114.52; 116.101; *Rawl.MSS.* B.183.191. A facsimile engraving of Felton's paper is printed in C.J.Smith, *Historical and Literary Curiosities* (1840).
5. *Chas.* 396; *C.S.P.V.* XXI, 337; *Rawl.MSS.* B. 183.191v–192; *D'Ewes.* 387; *Fairholt.* 66–7.
6. P.R.O. PCC 31 Sadler; *Dom.MSS 16.* 117.54; 116.14; *Clar.* I, 38; *Kent MSS.* U.350.C/2/19; *Eg.MSS.* 1533.62v.
7. *Trevor.* 89; *Endym.* 303–4.
8. *C.S.P.V.* XXIII, 63, 377; XXIV, 150.
9. *Evelyn.* III, 162.
10. *Evelyn.* IV, 161–2.
11. *Evelyn.* III, 124.
12. *Bet.* 259.
13. *Clar.* IV, 385.
14. *Wot.* 207; Sir Walter Raleigh: 'Epitaph on the Earl of Leicester'.
15. *Jas.* 243.
16. *Rawl.MSS.* D.404.4; *Dom.MSS 16.* 75.83.
17. *Esther.* vi, 6–9.
18. *Yale.* II, 450; III, 173.
19. *Yale.* II, 327.
20. *Rush.* 82–3; *Ch.* II, 513.
21. *Family.* 27; *Went.*; *C.J.* 733.
22. *Yale.* II, 62.
23. *Grey.* VI, 280; *C.D.* II, 463.
24. *Dom.MSS 16 Addenda.* 529.9; *H.M.C. Egmont.* 131.
25. *Osborne.* 274; *Knowler.* 47; *Dom.MSS 16 Addenda.* 529.15.
26. *Debs.* 96.

Bibliography

BIBLIOGRAPHICAL NOTE
(The place of publication is London, unless otherwise stated)

While the Bibliography lists many of the works I have consulted, it is not, of course, exhaustive; nor does the number of references to any particular work necessarily indicate its usefulness. S.R. Gardiner's majestic *History of England from the Accession of James I to the Outbreak of the Civil War* is a case in point. Although the second edition was published as long ago as 1883 it is still central to any study of the period and I gratefully acknowledge my dependence upon it.

Among somewhat later works I would like to make special mention of four biographies: Harold Hulme, *The Life of Sir John Eliot* (1957); Menna Prestwich, *Cranfield: Politics and Profits under the Early Stuarts* (Oxford, 1966); H.R. Trevor-Roper, *Archbishop Laud* (2nd edition, 1962); and C.V. Wedgwood, *Thomas Wentworth, First Earl of Strafford: A Revaluation* (1961).

The Whig interpretation of early seventeenth-century English history, to which Gardiner gave classic exposition, has shown a remarkable capacity for survival, but is now under strong attack on many fronts. This is shown by the number of books published on the period in recent years. Among those which have appeared during the last decade are: Michael Van Cleave Alexander, *Charles I's Lord Treasurer: Sir Richard Weston, Earl of Portland* (1975); Martin J. Havran, *Caroline Courtier: The Life of Lord Cottington* (1973); Derek Hirst, *The Representative of the People? Voters and Voting in England under the Early Stuarts* (Cambridge, 1975); Robert W. Kenny, *Elizabeth's Admiral: The Political Career of Charles Howard, Earl of Nottingham* (Baltimore, 1970); Kevin Sharpe (ed.), *Faction and Parliament: Essays on Early Stuart History* (Oxford, 1978); Kevin Sharpe, *Sir Robert Cotton 1586–1631: History and Politics in Early Modern England* (Oxford, 1979); and Stephen D. White, *Sir Edward Coke and the Grievances of the Commonwealth* (Manchester, 1979).

Conrad Russell's *Parliaments and English Politics 1621–1629* (Oxford) was also published in 1979. This is not only a major work in its own right but is also full of insights and fruitful hypotheses about Buckingham's relations with the members of both Commons and Lords. Readers should not omit the Appendix, which lists some supporters and opponents of Buckingham in 1626 and gives their allegiances in the Civil War. While I cannot accept Mr Russel's conclusions on every point I should like to express my admiration for his work and my general agreement – which I hope will be obvious to readers of this biography – with his argument that many, if not most, of the 'constitutional' difficulties of the 1620s derive from the impact of war upon a society that was unprepared for it economically, psychologically, or in any other way.

I. PRINTED SOURCES AND SECONDARY WORKS

A.P.C. Acts of the Privy Council of England.

Absolutism. D. Parker, 'The Social Foundation of French Absolutism 1610–30', *Past & Present*, 53 (1971).

Albion. G. Albion, *Charles I and the Court of Rome* (1935)

Allison. A.F. Allison, 'Richard Smith, Richelieu and the French Marriage', *Recusant History*, Vol. 7 (1964).

Andrews. K.R. Andrews, *Drake's Voyages: a Reassessment of their Place in Elizabethan History* (1967).

Arch. Archaeologia.

Arch.Cam. Archaeologia Cambrensis, 1st series, Vol. 2 (1847).

Arun. M.F.S. Hervey, *The Life, Correspondence and Collections of Thomas Howard, Earl of Arundel* (Cambridge, 1921).

Ashton. R. Ashton. 'The Disbursing Official under the Early Stuarts: the Cases of Sir William Russell and Philip Burlamachi', *Bulletin of Institute of Historical Research*, Vol. 30 (1957).

Aulus. Aulicus Coquinariae, in *Secret History of the Court of James I*, Vol. II (Edinburgh, 1811).

Aven. M. Avenel (ed), *Lettres, Instructions Diplomatiques, et Papiers d'Etat du Cardinal de Richelieu.* Vol. II, 1624–27; Vol. III, 1628–30 (Paris, 1856).

Aylmer. G.E. Aylmer, *The King's Servants: the Civil Service of Charles I* (1961).

Bac. The Works of Francis Bacon, ed. J. Spedding, (1857–74).

Ball. J.N. Ball, *The Parliamentary Career of Sir John Eliot, 1624–29*, Cambridge University Ph.D thesis (1953).

Bass. Journal de ma Vie: Mémoires du Maréchal de Bassompierre, Vol. III (Paris, 1875).

Bat. L. Batiffol, *La Duchesse de Chevreuse* (Paris, 1913).

Ber. M. Houssaye, *Le Cardinal de Bérulle et le Cardinal de Richelieu 1625–1629* (Paris, 1875).

Bet. L.-R. Betcherman, 'The York House Collection and its Keeper', *Apollo*, Vol. 92 (Oct. 1970).

Birch. Thomas Birch, *Court and Times of James I* (ed. R.F. Williams), 2 vols (1848).

Blain. M. Houssaye, 'L'ambassade de M. de Blainville à la Cour de Charles Ier, Roi d'Angleterre', *Revue des Questions Historiques*, Vol. 23 (Paris, 1878).

Bowen. C.D. Bowen, *The Lion and the Throne: the Life and Times of Sir Edward Coke* (1957).

Briley. J.R. Briley, *A Biography of William Herbert, 3rd Earl of Pembroke, 1580–1630*, University of Birmingham Ph.D. thesis (1961).

Brist. 'The Earl of Bristol's Answer, unto a Paper of Propositions sent unto him by the Duke of Buckingham', ed. S.R. Gardiner, *Camden Miscellany*, Vol. VI (Camden Society, 1871).

Burck. C.J. Burckhardt, *Richelieu: his Rise to Power* (1940).

C.D. Commons Debates 1621, ed. W. Notestein, F.H. Relf and H. Simpson (1935).

C.J. Journals of the House of Commons, Vol. I.

C.S.P.C. Calendar of State Papers Colonial, Vol. IV, East Indies, China and Japan 1622–24 (1878).

C.S.P.D. Calendar of State Papers Domestic.

C.S.P.I. Calendar of State Papers Ireland 1625–32.

C.S.P.V. Calendar of State Papers Venetian.

Cab. Cabala, Sive Scrinia Sacra (1691).

Cam. 'The Annals of Mr William Camden in the Reign of King James I', in *A Complete History of England, with the Lives of all the Kings and Queens thereof*, Vol. II (1719).

Carr. P.R. Seddon, 'Robert Carr, Earl of Somerset', *Renaissance and Modern Studies*, Vol. 14 (1970).

Carte. Thomas Carte, *A General History of England* (1747–55).

Case. V.F. Snow, 'The Arundel Case', *The Historian*, Vol. 26 (1964).

Caud. Randall L.-W. Caudill, *Some Literary Evidence of the Development of English Virtuoso Interests in the Seventeenth Century*, Oxford University D. Phil. thesis (1975).

Ch. The Letters of John Chamberlain, ed. N.E. McClure (Philadelphia, 1939).

Chas. Thomas Birch, *Court and Times of Charles I*; ed. R.F. Williams, Vol. I (1848).

Chev. Pierre Chevalier, *Louis XIII* (Paris, 1979).

Clar. Edward, Earl of Clarendon, *The History of the Rebellion and Civil Wars in England*, ed. W.D. Macray (Oxford, 1888).

Clarke. J.A. Clarke, *Huguenot Warrior: the Life and Times of Henri de Rohan, 1579–1638* (The Hague, 1966).

Cooper. J.P. Cooper (ed.), *Wentworth Papers 1597–1628*, Camden, 4th series, Vol. 12 (Royal Historical Society, 1973).

Corbett. J.S. Corbett, *England in the Mediterranean*, Vol. I (1904)

Corn. The Private Correspondence of Jane, Lady Cornwallis, 1613–44 (1842). [Ed. by Lord Braybrooke]

Cos. The Correspondence of John Cosin, D.D. Part I, Surtees Society, Vol. LII (1868). [Ed. by J. Sansom]

Crisis. L. Stone, *The Crisis of the Aristocracy 1558–1641* (Oxford, 1965).

Crown. R. Ashton, *The Crown and the Money Market 1603–40* (Oxford, 1960).

Cum. G.J. Cuming, 'The Life and Works of Anthony Cade, B.D., Vicar of Billesdon, 1599–1639', *Transactions of the the Leicestershire Archaeological and Historical Society*, Vol. 45 (1969–70).

D.N.B. Dictionary of National Biography.

D.L. S.R. Gardiner (ed.), *Notes of the Debates in the House of Lords . . . A.D. 1624 and 1626* (Camden Society, 1879).

Dalton. Charles Dalton, *The Life and Times of General Sir Edward Cecil, Viscount Wimbledon* (1885).

Debs. S.R. Gardiner, (ed.), *Debates in the House of Commons in 1625* (Camden Society, 1873).

Detection. Roger Coke, *A Detection of the Court and State of England* (1719).

Devon. F. Devon, *Issues of the Exchequer* (1836).

D'Ewes. *The Autobiography and Correspondence of Sir Simonds D'Ewes, Bart.*, ed. J.O. Halliwell, Vol. I (1845).

Dietz. F.C. Dietz, *English Public Finance 1558–1641* (reprinted 1964).

Dissolving. D.H. Willson, 'Summoning and Dissolving Parliament 1603–25', *American Historical Review*, Vol. 45. (1939).

Docs. Documentos Inéditos para la Historia de España (Madrid, 1936–45).

Dumont. J. Dumont, *Corps Universel Diplomatique du Droit des Gens*, Vol. V, Part ii (Amsterdam, 1728).

Dymond. D. Dymond, *Captain John Mason and the Duke of Buckingham*, The Portsmouth Papers No. 17 (Portsmouth, 1972).

Eglish. George Eglisham, 'The Forerunner of Revenge', *Harleian Miscellany*, Vol. II (1744).

Eliot. Sir John Eliot, *Negotium Posterorum*, ed. A.B. Grosart (1881).

Endym. G. Huxley, *Endymion Porter, the Life of a Courtier 1587–1649* (1959).

Essays. Francis Bacon, *The Essays, or Counsels Civil and Moral* (1625).

Evelyn. *The Diary of John Evelyn*, ed. E.S. De Beer (Oxford, 1955).

Fairholt. F.W. Fairholt (ed.), *Poems and Songs relating to George Villiers, Duke of Buckingham* (Percy Society, 1850).

Family. L. Stone, *Family and Fortune: Studies in Aristocratic Finance in the Sixteenth and Seventeenth Centuries* (Oxford, 1973).

Farnham. G.F. Farnham, *Leicestershire Village Notes* (Leicester, 1933).

Field. Theophilus Field, *Parasceve Paschae* (1624).

Fiennes. D. Fiennes, 'William Fiennes, first Viscount Saye and Sele (1582–1662) and George Villiers, first Duke of Buckingham (1592–1628)', *Genealogists' Magazine*, Vol. 16, No. 7 (1970).

Fin. Sir John Finett, *Finetti Philoxenis* (1856).

Fol. F. de Vaux de Foletier, *Le Siège de La Rochelle* (La Rochelle, reprinted 1978).

Fort. *The Fortescue Papers*, ed. S.R. Gardiner (Camden Society, 1871).

Frank. T. Frankland, *Annals of King James and King Charles the First* (1681).

Fuller. Thomas Fuller, *The Church History of Britain*, ed. J. Nichols, Vol. III (1868).

Gard. S.R. Gardiner, *History of England from the Accession of James 1 to the Outbreak of the Civil War 1603–42* (1883).

Gerb. Sir Balthazar Gerbier, *A Brief Discourse concerning the Three Chief Principles of Magnificent Building* (1662).

Glan. J. Glanville, *The Voyage to Cadiz in 1625* (Camden Society, 1883).

Goitein. E.S. Goitein, *Buckingham's Influence on England with regard to France*, London University M.A. Thesis (1926).

Gond. C.H. Carter,. 'Gondomar: Ambassador to James I', *Historical Journal*, Vol. VII (1964).

Goodman. Godfrey Goodman, *The Court of King James the First* (1839).

Grey. Anchitel Grey, *Debates in the House of Commons 1667–99* (1763).

Gruen. J.K. Gruenfelder, 'The Lord Wardens and Elections 1604–28', *Journal of British Studies*, Vol. 16 (1976).

Gutch. J. Gutch, *Collectanea Curiosa* (1781).

Hack. J. Hacket, *Scrinia Reserata: a Memorial offered to the great Deservings of John Williams D.D.* (1693).

Hall. J.O. Halliwell, *Letters of the Kings of England* (1846).

Hard. Hardwicke State Papers 1501–1726 (1778).

Hast. *The Hastings Journal of the Parliament of 1621*, ed. Lady de Villiers, *Camden Miscellany*, Vol. XX (Camden Society, 1953).

Havran. M.J. Havran, *Caroline Courtier: The Life of Lord Cottington* (1973).

Hawkins. J.A. Williamson, *Sir John Hawkins: the Time and the Man* (Oxford, 1927).

Hecho. Francisco de Jesus, *El Hecho de los Tratados del Matrimonio Pretendido por El Principe de Gales con La Serenissima Infanta de España Maria'*, ed. S.R. Gardiner (Camden Society, 1869).

Herb. Lord Herbert of Cherbury, *The Expedition to the Isle of Rhé*, ed. Lord Powis (Philobiblon Society, 1860).

Herrick. G.W. Scott, *Robert Herrick* (1974).

Heyl. P. Heylyn, *Cyprianus Anglicus, or the History of the Life and Death of . . . William {Laud}, by divine providence Lord Archbishop of Canterbury* (1671).

Holl. *Letters of John Holles, 1587–1637*, ed. P.R. Seddon, Thoroton Society Record Series, Vol. 31 (Nottingham, 1975).

Howard. Michael Howard, *The British Way in Warfare*, Neale Lecture in History (1974).

Howell. James Howell, *Epistolae Ho-Elianae* (1892).

Hulme. *Sir John Eliot and the Vice-Admiralty of Devon*, ed. H. Hulme, *Camden Miscellany*, Vol. XVII (Camden Society, 1940).

Hulme (2). H. Hulme, *The Life of Sir John Eliot 1592 to 1632* (1957).

Hunter. M. Hunter, *John Aubrey and the Realm of Learning* (1975).

Imp. *Documents illustrating the Impeachment of the Duke of Buckingham in 1626*, ed. S.R. Gardiner (Camden Society, 1889).

Jas. D.H. Willson, *King James VI and I* (1956).

Jnl. *A Journal of all the Proceedings of the Duke of Buckingham, His Grace, in the Isle of Ree* (1627).

Jonson. *Ben Jonson*, ed. C.H. Herford and P. and E. Simpson, Vol. VII (Oxford, 1941).

Joubert. A. Joubert, 'Les Gentilshommes étrangers . . . à l'Académie d'Equitation d'Angers au XVIIe Siècle', *Revue d'Anjou*, Vol. I (1893).

Kepler. J.S. Kepler, 'The Value of Ships gained and lost by the English Shipping Industry during the Wars with Spain and France 1624–30', *Mariner's Mirror*, Vol. 59 (1973).

Knowler. W. Knowler (ed.), *The Earl of Strafford's Letters and Dispatches (1739)*.

Knyvett. *The Knyvett Letters 1620–44*, ed. B. Schofield (1949).

L.D. S.R. Gardiner (ed.), *Notes of Debates in the House of Lords . . . A.D. 1621* (Camden Society, 1870).

L.J. Journals of the House of Lords, Vol. III.

Laud. *The Works of the Most Reverend Father in God, William Laud*, ed. J. Bliss, Vol. III, Devotions, Diary and History (Oxford, 1853).

Leics. J. Nichols, *The History and Antiquites of the County of Leicester* (1795– 1800).

Leland. *The Itinerary of John Leland*, ed. L. Toulmin Smith (1909).

Lib. Sir James Whitelocke, *Liber Famelicus*, ed. J. Bruce (Camden Society, 1858).

Lon. H. Lonchay and J. Cuvelier, *Correspondance de la Cour d'Espagne sur Les Affaires des Pays Bas au XVIIe Siècle*, Vol. II, Précis de la Correspondance de Philippe IV avec l'Infante Isabelle, 1621–33 (Brussels, 1927).

McGowan. A.P. McGowan, *The Royal Navy under the first Duke of Buckingham*, London University Ph.D. thesis (1967).

Man. Duke of Manchester, *Court and Society from Elizabeth to Anne* (1864).

Mareuil. 'Mémoires de Messire François Duval, Marquis de Fontenay-Mareuil', in J.F. Michaud and J.J.F. Poujoulat, *Nouvelle Collection des Mémoires pour Servir à l'Histoire de France*, Vol. V (Paris, 1850).

Marsden. R.G. Marsden, 'Early Prize Jurisdiction and Prize Law in England, II', *English Historical Review*, Vol. 25 (1910).

Mayes. C.R. Mayes, 'The Early Stuarts and the Irish Peerage', *English Historical Review*, Vol. 73 (1958).

Meditation. James I, *Meditation upon the Lord's Prayer* (1619).

Memorials. Bulstrode Whitelocke, *Memorials of the English Affairs* (1732).

Merc. Le Mercure françois, Vols IX–XIII (Paris, 1624–27).

Merv. P. Mervault, *Journal des Choses Plus Memorables qui ce sont passées au Dernier Siège de La Rochelle* (La Rochelle, 1648).

Moore. N. Moore, *History of the Study of Medicine in the British Isles* (Oxford, 1908).

Motte. *Mémoires de Madame de Motteville*, ed. M.F. Riaux, Vol. I (Paris, 1886).

Mul. J.B. Mullinger, *The University of Cambridge*, Vol. II (Cambridge, 1911).

Notes. S.R. Gardiner, 'Notes on Buckingham's Mother', *Notes and Queries*, 4th series, Vol. VII (1871).

Ogl. *The Commonplace Book of Sir John Oglander, Knight, of Nunwell*, ed. F. Bamford (1936).

Osborne. F. Osborne, 'Traditional Memoirs of the Reign of King James the First', in *Secret History of the Court of James the First*, Vol. I (Edinburgh, 1811).

Oxford. J.N. Ball, 'Sir John Eliot at the Oxford Parliament, 1625', *Bulletin of*

Institute of Historical Research, Vol. 28 (1955).

P.D. Proceedings and Debates in 1621 by [Edward Nicholas], ed. by T. Tyrwhitt. Oxford 1766.

P.S. Privy Seals of Charles I, 43rd Report of the Deputy Keeper of Public Records, Appendix I (1881).

Parker. L.A. Parker, 'Depopulation Returns for Leicestershire in 1607', *Transactions of the Leicestershire Archaeological Society*, Vol. 23 (1947).

Peck. F. Peck, *Desiderata Curiosa* (1779).

Pett. *The Autobiography of Phineas Pett*, ed. W.G. Perrin (Navy Records Society, 1918).

Peyton. Sir Edward Peyton, *The Divine Catastrophe of the Kingly Family of the House of Stuarts* (1652).

Piper. David Piper, *Catalogue of Seventeenth-Century Portraits in the National Portrait Gallery, 1625–1714* (Cambridge, 1963).

Plaja. F. Diaz-Plaja, *La Historia de España en sus Documentos*, Vol. III, El Siglo XVII (Madrid, 1957).

Porte. 'Mémoires de P. de La Porte, Premier Valet de Chambre de Louis XIV', in J.F. Michaud and J.J.F. Poujoulat, *Nouvelle Collection des Mémoires pour Servir à l'Histoire de France*, Vol. VIII (Paris, 1850).

Preston. *The Life of the Renowned Doctor Preston, writ by his pupil, Master Thomas Ball, D.D., Minister of Northampton, in the Year 1628*, ed. E. W. Harcourt (1885).

Prestwich. M. Prestwich, *Cranfield: Politics and Profits under the Early Stuarts* (Oxford, 1966).

Prior. C.M. Prior, *The Royal Studs of the Sixteenth and Seventeenth Centuries* (1935).

Progresses. J. Nichols, *The Progresses of King James I* (1828).

Rebholz. R.A. Rebholz, *The Life of Fulke Greville, first Lord Brooke* (Oxford, 1971).

Relf. F.H. Relf (ed.), *Notes of Debates in the House of Lords, 1621, 1625 and 1628* (Camden Society, 1929).

Retz. 'Mémoires du Cardinal de Retz', in J.F. Michaud and J.J.F. Poujoulat, *Nouvelle Collection des Mémoires pour Servir à l'Histoire de France*, Vol. I (Paris, 1850).

Rich. *Mémoires du Cardinal de Richelieu*, Vols. III–VIII (Paris, 1912–27).

Ritchie. J. Ritchie, *Reports of Cases decided by Francis Bacon in the High Court of Chancery* (1932).

Roche. 'Mémoires de La Rochefoucauld', in J.F. Michaud and J.J.F. Poujoulat, *Nouvelle Collection des Mémoires pour Servir à l'Histoire de France*, Vol. V (Paris, 1850).

Roh. *Mémoires du Duc de Rohan* (Paris, 1675).

Rous. *The Diary of John Rous*, ed. M.A. Green (Camden Society, 1856).

Rowe. V.A. Rowe, 'The Influence of the Earls of Pembroke on Parliamentary Elections 1625–41', *English Historical Review*, Vol. 50 (1935).

Rub. *The Letters of Peter Paul Rubens*, ed. R.S. Magum (Cambridge, Mass., 1955).

Ruigh. R.E. Ruigh, *The Parliament of 1624* (Cambridge, Mass., 1971)

Rus. *Mémoires et Négociations Secrètes de M. de Rusdorf*, Vol. I (Leipzig, 1789).

Rush. John Rushworth, *Historical Collections*, Vol. I. (1721).

Russ. Constance Russell, 'Notes on Buckingham's Mother', *Notes and Queries*, 6th series, Vol. XI (1885).

Russell. Conrad Russell, *Parliaments and English Politics 1621–1629* (Oxford, 1979).

Sainty. J.C. Sainty, 'Lieutenants of Counties, 1585–1642', *Bulletin of Institute of Historical Research*, Special Supplement No. 8 (May 1970).

Sal. Salvetti Correspondence, in *H.M.C. 11th Report, Appendix, Part I*, The MSS of Henry Duncan Skrine (1887).

Sharpe. K. Sharpe (ed.), *Faction and Parliament* (Oxford, 1978).

Shaw. W.A. Shaw, *The Knights of England* (1906).

Side. H.G.R. Reade, *Sidelights on the Thirty Years War* (1924).

Simon. *Mémoirs Complets et Authentiques du Duc de Saint-Simon* (Paris, 1840).

Smith. Logan Pearsall Smith (ed.), *The Life and Letters of Sir Henry Wotton* (Oxford, 1907).

Snow. V.F. Snow, *Essex the Rebel* (Lincoln, Nebraska, 1970).

State. Thomas Wilson, *The State of England Anno Dom.1600*, ed. F.J. Fisher, *Camden Miscellany*, Vol. XVI (Camden Society, 1936).

Stearns. S.J. Stearns, 'Conscription and English Society in the 1620s', *Journal of British Studies*, Vol. 11 (1972).

Summ. J. Summerson, *Architecture in Britain 1530 to 1830* (Pelican History of Art, 1953).

Survey. *The survey of London*, ed. Sir G. Gater and E.P. Wheeler, Vol. XVIII, The Strand (1937).

Swales. R.J.W. Swales, 'The Ship Money Levy of 1628', *Bulletin of Institute of Historical Research*, Vol. 50 (1977).

Tanner. J.R. Tanner, *Constitutional Documents of the Reign of James I*, (Cambridge, 1930).

Thom. G.W. Thomas, 'James I, Equity and Lord Keeper John Williams', *English Historical Review*, Vol. 91 (1976).

Thomp. G. Thompson, 'The Origins of the Politics of the Parliamentary Middle Group 1625–29, *Transactions of Royal Historical Society* (1972).

Till. *Mémoires Inédits du Comte Leveneur de Tilliéres*, ed. M.C. Hippeau (Paris, 1863).

Tite. C.G.C. Tite, *Impeachment and Parliamentary Judicature in Early Stuart England* (1974).

Trevor. H.R. Trevor-Roper, *Archbishop Laud 1573–1645* (2nd edition, 1962).

Upton. A.F. Upton, *Sir Arthur Ingram* (Oxford, 1961).

Vautor. T. Vautor, *The First Set* (1621).

Ville. 'Mémoires de Messire Henri-Auguste de Loménie de la Villa-aux-Clercs, Comte de Brienne', in M. Petitot, *Collection des Mémoires relatifs à l'Histoire de France*, Vol. 35 (Paris, 1824).

Wal. Horace Walpole, *Anecdotes of Painting in England* (1888).

Wel. Sir A[nthony] W[eldon], *The Court and Character of King James* (1650).

Went. J.P. Cooper, 'The Fortune of Thomas Wentworth, Earl of Strafford', *Economic History Review*, Vol. XI (1958).

Whinney. M. Whinney and O. Millar, *English Art 1625–1714* (Oxford History of English Art, 1957).

Wil. Arthur Wilson, 'The Life and Reign of James I', in *A Complete History of England, with the Lives of all the Kings and Queens thereof*, Vol. II (1719).

Wot. Sir Henry Wotton, 'The Life and Death of George Villiers, Late Duke of Buckingham' and 'Of Robert Devereux, Earl of Essex, and George Villiers, Duke of Buckingham', in *Reliquiae Wottonianae* (1672).

Wright. L.B. Wright (ed.), *Advice to a Son* (Ithaca, 1962).

Wynn. Calendar of Wynn (of Gwydir) Papers, 1515–1690 (1926).

Yale. Commons Debates 1628, ed. R.C. Johnson and M.J. Cole (Yale Centre for Parliamentary History, 1977).

Young. M.B. Young, 'Illusions of Grandeur and Reform at the Jacobean Court: Cranfield and the Ordnance', *Historical Journal*, Vol. 22 (1979).

Zaller. R. Zaller, *The Parliament of 1621* (1971).

II. REPORTS OF THE ROYAL COMMISSION ON HISTORICAL MANUSCRIPTS (H.M.C.)

H.M.C. (4). Fourth Report (1874), Part I, Appendix, De La Warr and Denbigh MSS.

H.M.C. (5). Fifth Report (1876), Part I, Appendix, Conway Griffith MSS.

H.M.C. (7. Seventh Report (1879), Part I, Appendix, Denbigh MSS.

H.M.C. (8). Eight Report (1881), Part I, Appendix, Digby MSS.

H.M.C. (9). Ninth Report (1883), Part II, Appendix, Morrison MSS.

H.M.C. (10). Tenth Report (1885), Appendix I, Moray MSS.

H.M.C. (11). Eleventh Report (1887), Part IV, Townshend MSS.

H.M.C. (12). Twelfth Report (1888), Appendix, Part IV, Rutland MSS, Vol. I.

H.M.C. (13). Thirteenth Report (1893), Appendix, Part VII, Lonsdale MSS.

H.M.C. (14). Fourteenth Report (1894, 1901), Appendix, Part II, Portland MSS, Vols. III and VII.

H.M.C. (15). Fifteenth Report (1897), Appendix, Part II, Hodgkin MSS.

H.M.C. Bath. Bath. MSS, Harley Papers, Vol. II (1907).

H.M.C. Bucc. Buccleuch MSS, Vol. I (1899), Vol. III (1926).

H.M.C. Coke. Twelfth Report (1888), Appendix, Part I, MSS of the Coke Family belonging to Earl Cowper.

H.M.C. Egmont. Egmont MSS, Vol. I, Part I (1905).

H.M.C. Hast. Hastings MSS, Vol. IV (1947).

H.M.C. Mar. Mar and Kellie MSS (1904).

H.M.C. Sal. Calendar of Salisbury MSS, Part 22, 1612–68 (1971).

H.M.C. Sid. De l'Isle MSS, Vol. V, Sidney Papers 1611–26 (1962).

H.M.C. Supp. Mar and Kellie MSS, Supplementary Report (1930).

H.M.C. Var. MSS in Various Collections, Vol. II (1903); Vol. IV (1907); Vol. V (1909).

III. MANUSCRIPT COLLECTIONS

Add.MSS. British Library [B.L.], Additional MSS.

Ball.MSS. Bodleian Library, Oxford [Bod.], Ballard MSS.

Bas. MSS. Public Record Office, Chancery Lane [P.R.O.], Baschet Transcripts, PRO 31/3.

Bod.MSS. Bod. Additional MSS.

Cam.MSS. Cambridge University Library, MS Dd.12.20.

Carte MSS. Bod. Carte MSS.

Clo.MSS. P.R.O. Close Rolls.

Cod.MSS. All Souls College, Oxford, Codrington Library MSS.

Crisp MSS. P.R.O. Crisp Transcripts, PRO 31/4.

Den.MSS. Warwickshire Record Office, Warwick, Denbigh MSS (on microfilm).

Denimilne MSS. National Library of Scotland, Edinburgh [N.L.S.], Denmilne MSS.

Dig.MSS. P.R.O. Digby Transcripts, PRO 31/8, Vol. 198.

Dk.MSS. P.R.O. State Papers Denmark, SP 75.

Dod.MSS. Bod. Dodsworth MSS.

Dom.Add.MSS. P.R.O. State Papers Domestic Addenda, SP 15.

Dom.MSS 14. P.R.O. State Papers Domestic of the Reign of James I, SP 14.

Dom.MSS 16. P.R.O. State Papers Domestic of the Reign of Charles I, SP 16.

Eg.MSS. B.L. Egerton MSS.

Elm.MSS. Sheffield Central Library, Elmhirst MSS.

Est.MSS. Archivo General de Simancas, Sección Estado.

Fair.MSS. Uncatalogued MSS in the possession of Lady Fairfax of Cameron.

Flan.MSS. P.R.O. State Papers Flanders, SP 77.

Fr.MSS. P.R.O. State Papers France, SP 78.

Grah.MSS. Uncatalogued MSS in the possession of Sir Richard Graham.

Gros.MSS. Trinity College, Dublin, MS.612, The Diary of Sir Richard Grosvenor.

Gy.MSS. P.R.O. State Papers Germany, SP 81.

Harg.MSS. B.L. Hargrave MSS.

Harl.MSS. B.L. Harleian MSS.

Hearne MSS. Bod. Hearne's Diaries.

Holl.MSS. P.R.O. State Papers Holland, SP 84.

Kent MSS. MSS other than Sackville in the Kent Archive Office, Maidstone.

King's MSS. B.L. King's MSS.

M.D.MSS France. Ministère des Affaires Etrangères, Paris, Archives Diplomatiques, Ref.M.D.

Misc.MSS. Bod. English Miscellaneous MSS.

Mylne MSS. N.L.S. R.Mylne's Collections, 31.2.1.

Pal.MSS. MSS in the Biblioteca del Palacio Real, Madrid.

Pat.MSS. P.R.O. Patent Rolls.

Perr.MSS. Bod. Perrott MSS.

Ph.MSS. Somerset Record Office, Taunton, Phelips MSS.

Rawl.MSS. Bod. Rawlinson MSS.

Reade MSS. P.R.O. Reade Papers, PRO 30/18.

Sack.MSS. Kent Archive Office, Maidstone, Sackville MSS.

Sav.MSS P.R.O. State Papers Savoy, SP 92.

Slo.MSS. B.L. Sloane MSS.

Sp.MSS. P.R.O. State Papers Spain, SP 94.

Spring MSS. Harvard University, Houghton Library. MS English 980, Sir William Spring: Proceedings in the Commons, 19 Feb.–27 May 1624.

Sp.Tr.MSS. P.R.O. Spanish Transcripts, PRO 31/12.

Str.P.MSS. Sheffield Central Library, Wentworth Woodhouse Muniments, Papers of Thomas Wentworth, Earl of Strafford.

Tann.MSS. Bod. Tanner MSS.

Trum.MSS. Berkshire Record Office, Reading, Downshire Papers, Trumbull Alphabetical MSS.

Ty.MSS. P.R.O. State Papers Turkey, SP 97.

Ven.MSS. P.R.O. State Papers Venice, SP 99.

Index

00